Lecture Notes in Computer Science 507

Edited by G. Goos and J. Hartmanis

Advisory Board: W. Brauer   D. Gries   J. Stoer

N. A. Sherwani   E. de Doncker
J. A. Kapenga (Eds.)

Computing in the 90's

The First Great Lakes Computer Science Conference
Kalamazoo, Michigan, USA, October 18-20, 1989
Proceedings

Springer-Verlag

Berlin Heidelberg New York
London Paris Tokyo
Hong Kong Barcelona
Budapest

Series Editors

Gerhard Goos
GMD Forschungsstelle
Universität Karlsruhe
Vincenz-Priessnitz-Straße 1
W-7500 Karlsruhe, FRG

Juris Hartmanis
Department of Computer Science
Cornell University
Upson Hall
Ithaca, NY 14853, USA

Volume Editors

Naveed A. Sherwani
Elise de Doncker
John A. Kapenga
Department of Computer Science
Western Michigan University
Kalamazoo, MI 49008-5021, USA

CR Subject Classification (1991): A.0

ISBN 3-540-97628-0 Springer-Verlag Berlin Heidelberg New York
ISBN 0-387-97628-0 Springer-Verlag New York Berlin Heidelberg

Printing and binding: Druckhaus Beltz, Hemsbach/Bergstr.
2145/3140-543210 - Printed on acid-free paper

Technical Chair's Message

It was a great pleasure and honor for me to serve as the technical committee chairman for the First Great Lakes Computer Science Conference. The main goal of organization of this conference is to create a forum for presentation of new research results in the field of computer science. The Great Lakes area has several major universities and industries with strong computer science departments, but we lacked a major computer science conference to share and exchange ideas in our field. We hope that the Great Lakes Computer Science Conference can fill this gap and develop into a major conference in future.

Despite the fact that it was the First Great Lakes Computer Science Conference, attendance exceeded our expectation. Due to submission of many good papers, we are able to put together an excellent technical program. This year we had 195 attendees and 168 papers were presented in 31 sessions. From 114 papers submitted, 64 papers have been selected for publication. Sessions concerned all areas of computer science including graph algorithms, artificial intelligence, database, VLSI design among others.

The Conference was organized by a team of very dedicated people and I would like to thank them all. In particular, I would like to thank Kenneth Williams and Carolyn Oberlink for doing a great job for local arrangements. I would also like to thank James N. Lyness, Michael Fellows, Roy F. Keller, Elizabeth Jessup, Ahmed Sameh, Selim G. Akl, Paul Messina, Jack Dongerra and John R. Rice for giving excellent invited talks. The toughest part was the refereeing and publication and it would have been impossible without the expert and timely reviews of our referees. I have included the list of referees and I thank them for their dedication. Finally, I would like to acknowledge the help of graduate students (from van-driving to making up registration tags). Finally, I would like to thank graduate student Mariko Hirano for her expert preparation of the proceedings manuscripts.

I hope all attendees enjoyed the conference, our post-conference evaluation certainly indicated that. We are very encouraged by the support of the attendees and decided to make this conference biannual. Therefore, the Second Great Lakes Computer Science Conference is scheduled for **October 1991** at Western Michigan University.

I would like to thank the attendees, invited speakers, organization committee members and our sponsors, and I hope to spe you all at the Second Great Lakes Computer Science Conference.

Naveed Sherwani

Organization Committee:

Technical Program Chair:
Naveed Sherwani

Publication:
Elise de Doncker
John Kapenga

Local Arrangements:
Kenneth Williams
Carolyn Oberlink
Donna Kaminski

Finance:
Alfred Boals

Exhibits:
Ben Pinkowski

Tutorials:
Mark Kerstetter

Technical Program Committee:

Graph Algorithms:
Alfred Boals

Artificial Intelligence:
Ben Pinkowski

Parallel Processing:
Ajay Gupta

Algorithms:
Naveed Sherwani

Circuits and Systems:
Eltayeb Abuelyaman

Operating Systems:
Mark Kerstetter

Data Base:
Dalia Motzkin

Numerical Analysis:
Elise Kapenga

VLSI Design:
Majid Sarrafzadeh

Distributed Systems:
Ajay Gupta

Programming Languages:
Kenneth Williams

Software Engineering:
Mark Kerstetter

Biological Information and Neural Networks:
Robert Trenary

Computer Science Education:
Carolyn Oberlink

List of Referees

Alijnai, G. S.
Angelos, J.
Arendsen, C.
Batayeb, S.
Bhargava, B.
Bhatia, S. K.
Boals, A.
Carpenter, D.
Carpenter, R.
Coleman, W.
Crary, S. B.
Cripps, A.
Curliss, G. F.
Czerny, B. J.
Deogun, J.
Dershem, H.
Dewan, P.
Dilworth, J.
Donaldson, M. P.
Doss, D.
Dunning, L. A.
El-Ruby, M.
Evens, M.
Fotouhi, F.
Frank, C.
Genz, A.
Georgakis, D. C.
Gold, G.
Gordon, G. L.
Gunawardena, K. L. D.
Gupta, T.
Hambrusch, S. E.
Hartley, S. J.
Hartman, J.
Kaminski, D.
Kaur, H.

Kerstetter, M.
Makowski, G.
Malla, V. J.
Manning, J.
McGrew, J. M.
Mckean, J. W.
Mehidi, A. N.
Mili, F.
Nelson, D.
Oberlink, C.
Ongwisesphaiboon, V.
Perl, Y.
Pinkowski, B.
Ramakrishnan, S.
Rapp, C.
Rattan, I.
Rubin, S.
Sager, T. J.
Samal, A.
Sanders, D.
Severance, F.
Shah, A. A.
Shanthi, R.
Sherwani, N.
Swafford, B. E.
Tellep, A.
Trenary, R.
Tzeng, C.-H.
Underkoffler, M. M.
Vashishta, A.
Vishnubhotla, S. R.
Williams, K.
Xu, J.
Yim, R.
Zheng, S.-Q.

TABLE OF CONTENTS

Track1: Graph Algorithms
(Chair: Alfred Boals)

1.1   Computational Complexity of Geometric Symmetry Detection in Graphs 1
      Joseph Manning

1.2   Low Dimensional Middle Cubes Are Hamiltonian 8
      Kunwarjit S. Bagga and Frank W. Owens

1.3   Approximation Algorithms for the Chromatic Sum 15
      Ewa Kubicka, Grzegorz Kubicki and Dionisios Kountanis

1.4   A Color-Exchange Algorithm for Exact Graph Coloring 22
      Thomas J. Sager and Shi-Jen Lin

1.5   S-Distance in Trees 29
      Garry L. Johns and Tai-Chi Lee

1.6   Algorihtms on Block-Complete Graphs 34
      Zhugou Mo and Kenneth Williams

Track 2: Artificial Intelligence
(Chair: Ben Pinkowski)

2.1   Heuristic-Based Learning 41
      Stuart H. Rubin

2.2   A Template-based Approach for Recognition of Intermittent Sounds 5
      Ben Pinkowski

2.3   A Mathematical Model of Uncertain Information 58
      Chun-Hung Tzeng

2.4   A Word to Phoneme Translator 6
      Gary Gold

2.5   Performance Evaluation of Medical Expert Systems 7
      D. Christine Georgakis, Martha Evens,
      Frank Naeymi-Rad and David A. Trace

2.6   Spelling Correction for an Intelligent Tutoring System 77
      Yoon Hee Lee, Martha Evens,
      Joel A. Michael and Allen A. Rovick

2.7   An Informational Network for a Natural Talking System 8
      Paul Buchheit

2.8   Formation of Categories in Document Classification Systems 9
      Sanjiv K. Bhatia, Jitender S. Deogun and Vijay V. Raghavan

2.9   An Expert System for Creativity Management 9
      Vipa Ongwisesphaiboon, Ilene Burnstein, Martha Evens,
      Anjali Puri and Martin E. Ginn

2.91   A More Flexible Method for Recognizing Signals Using
      Back Propagation: Piecewise Linear Regression Vectors 10
      Greg Makowski

2.92   A Cooperative Algorithm for the Dynamic Stereo Problem 111
      Gerald Leonard Gordon

.93 Design of Hierarchical Classifiers 118
Richard E. Haskell and Ali Noui-Mehidi

Track 3: Parallel Processing
(Chair: Ajay Gupta)

.1 Designing and Implementing Parallel Constructs 125
Roy F. Keller, R. Mark Meyer and Thomas L. Seevers
.2 Performance of Parallel Consistency Algorithms 132
Ashok Samal
.3 Delay Analysis of the N-Cube Network 139
Mokhtar A. Aboelaze and Catherine E. Houstis
.4 A Note on Conway's Parallel Sorting Algorithm 147
Kazem U. Ahmed and Der-Yun Yeh
.5 Visualization of Program Performance on Concurrent Computers 154
Diane T. Rover, G. M. Prabhu and Charles T. Wright

Track 4: Algorithms
(Chair: Naveed Sherwani)

.1 Minimum Odd Neighbourhood Covers for Trees 161
Robin W. Dawes
.2 Cascading LZW Algorithm with Huffman Coding:
A Variable to Variable Length Compression Algorithm 170
Yehoshua Perl and Ashish Mehta
.3 Dendrograms and Irreducible Prefix Codes 179
John McAlpin and Christos Nikolopoulos
.4 Massively Parallel Implementations of Adaptively Subdividing
Fractal Generating Algorithms with Parameter Extensions 185
Michael S. Wainer
.5 A Simple and Powerful Representation of Binary Search Trees 192
Si-Qing Zheng
.6 Random Permutations from Logarithmic Signatures 199
Spyros S. Magliveras and Nasir D. Memon

Track 5: Circuits and Systems
(Chair: Eltayeb Abuelyaman)

.1 Novel Design Techniques for RNS Systolic VLSI Arrays 206
Paruvachi V. R. Raja
.2 A Compound Decision Theory Approach to
Digital Signal Reconstruction 213
K. L. D. Gunawardena
.3 Real-time Parameter Control in Space Vehicles:
A Parallel Architecture and the Protocols 220
Sarma R. Vishnubhotla

5.4　A Microinstruction Based Procedure to Diagnose
Hardware Failures in Industrial Robots 227
Sarma R. Vishnubhotla

Track 6: Operating Systems
(Chair: Mark Kerstetter)

6.1　A Specification and Verification Tool for
Communication Protocols 23
Harbans Kaur, James Brown Grier and Graham Campbell
6.2　Structured On-Line Directory and File Organization 24
Phil G. Richards and Meng-Chun Chao

Track 7: Data Base
(Chair: Dalia Motzkin)

7.1　Genetic Algorithms and the Search for
Optimal Database Index Selection 249
Farshad Fotouhi and Carlos E. Galarce
7.2　An Object-Based Approach to the Specification
of Office Entities 25
Hossein Saiedian
7.3　Lexical Acquisition for Lexical Databases...................................264
Sumali Pin-Ngern, Robert Strutz and Martha Evens

Track 8: Numerical Analysis
(Chair: Elise Kapenga)

8.1　A Search for Good Lattice Rules Based on the Reciprocal Lattice
Generator Matrix 271
James N. Lyness and W. Newman
8.2　An Adaptive Numerical Integration Algorithm for Simplices 279
Alan Genz
8.3　The HK Singular Value Decomposition of
Rank Deficient Matrix Triplets 286
L. Magnus Ewerbring and Franklin T. Luk
8.4　Approximate Integration Using Iterated Levin Transformations 293
Ricolindo Carino, Elise de Doncker and Ian Robinson
8.5　Recent Advances in Shape Preserving Piecewise Cubic Interpolation 300
Thomas Sprague

Track 9: VLSI Design
(Chair: Majid Sarrafzadeh)

9.1　Structured Graph Models: An Efficient Tool for VLSI Design 307
M. Ancona, K. S. Bagga, E. Bruzzone,
L. De Floriani and J.S. Deogun

.2   A Stochastic Algorithm for Circuit Bi-Partitioning 313
      Youssef Saab and Vasant Rao
.3   An Optimal Channel-Routing Algorithm for a Restricted Class of
      Multi-Terminal Nets 322
      Dee Parks
.4   Correct and Provably Efficient Methods for
      Rectilinear Steiner Spanning Tree Generation 329
      F. D. Lewis and N. Van Cleave

Track 10: Distributed Systems
(Chair: Ajay Gupta)

0.1   A Three-Phase Task Scheduling Scheme in
      A Hard Real-Time Distributed Environment 336
      Ghasem S. Alijnai and Horst F. Wedde
0.2   A Broadcast Protocol: Functional Properties and Specification 343
      Sub Ramakrishnan
0.3   Leader Election in Distributed Computing Systems 350
      Mohamed El-Ruby, James Kenevan,
      Robert Carlson and Khalid Khalil
0.4   A New Approach to System-Level Fault-Tolerance in Message-Passing
      MultiComputers 357
      Guy W. Zimmerman and Abdol-Hossein Esfahanian

Track 11: Programming Languages
(Chair: Kenneth Williams)

1.1   A Functional Language with Classes 364
      Mike Beaven, Ryan Stansifer and Dan Wetklow
1.2   Using ML as a Command Language 371
      Steve J. Chapin and Ryan Stansifer

Track 12: Software Engineering
(Chair: Mark Kerstetter)

2.1   An Interactive System for Generating Hospital Progress Notes 378
      Huei-Ning Natasha Ma, Martha Evens,
      David A. Trace and Frank Naeymi-Rad

Track 13: Biological Information and Neural Network
(Chair: Robert G. Trenary)

3.1   Biological Evolution as A Paradigm for Performance Driven Design
      Processes 385
      Mateen M. Rizki, Louis A. Tamburino and Michael A. Zmuda
3.2   Predicting Chemical Reactions with a Neural Network 392
      David W. Elrod, Gerry M. Maggiora and Robert G. Trenary

13.3   Mutation and Recombination Effects on the
       Adaptability of Sexual and Asexual Organisms ....39?
       Mateen M. Rizki and Jong Chen
13.4   Logical Structure of Neurobiological Information Processing 406
       William P. Coleman, David P. Sanford,
       Andrea De Gaetano and Fred Geisler

Track 14: Computer Science Education
(Chair: Carolyn Oberlink)

14.1   Development of an Experimental Setup for
       Studying Parallel Processing ....41?
       Gretchen Vogel, Diane Rover,
       Charles Wright and Gurpur Prabhu
14.2   Compiler Course with a Semi-Challenging Project ....41?
       Roger Yim and Gongzhu Hu
14.3   Report on a PC Based System Designed to Enhance the Teaching of
       IBM 370 Assembly Language ....42?
       Bill E. Swafford
14.4   Teaching the Spirit of Computational Science ....43?
       Dean Sanders

Author Index 441

Computational Complexity
of
Geometric Symmetry Detection in Graphs

Joseph Manning
Department of Computer Science
University of Missouri – Rolla
Rolla, MO 65401, U.S.A.

joseph@shamrock.cs.umr.edu

Abstract

Constructing a visually informative drawing of an abstract graph is a problem of considerable practical importance, and has recently been the focus of much investigation. Displaying symmetry has emerged as one of the foremost criteria for achieving good drawings. Linear-time algorithms are already known for the detection and display of symmetry in trees, outerplanar graphs, and embedded planar graphs. The central results of this paper show that for general graphs, however, detecting the presence of even a single axial or rotational symmetry is NP-complete. A number of related results are also established, including the #P-completeness of counting the axial or rotational symmetries of a graph.

1. Introduction

Mathematically, an abstract graph simply consists of two sets, V and $E \subseteq V \times V$, and as such is completely specified by an enumeration of these sets or by adjacency lists or an adjacency matrix [1]. Such textual representations, however, convey very little structural information, and so graphs are instead often presented using drawings. Every given abstract graph has several different drawings, all equally "correct" but some certainly "better" than others in the sense that they clearly display important structural properties of the graph. For example, both drawings in Figure 1 represent the same graph, but properties such as planarity, biconnectivity, symmetry, diameter, and even bipartition are revealed by the second drawing but not by the first.

As discussed in [9], there are many different and sometimes mutually incompatible criteria for guiding the construction of good drawings of a graph. Amongst these, the best overall *general* criteria appear to be the display of axial symmetry and, to a somewhat lesser extent, the display of rotational symmetry. This stems primarily from the fact that by means of a symmetric drawing, an understanding of the entire graph may be built up from that of a smaller subgraph, replicated a number of times.

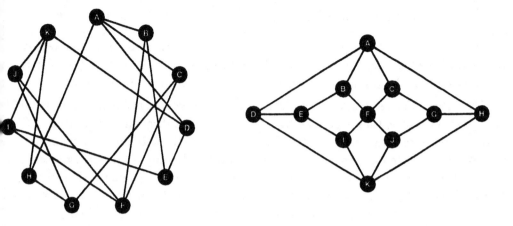

Figure 1: *Two drawings of the same graph*

Note that axial and rotational symmetry are considered inherent properties of the *abstract graph*, independent of any particular *drawing*. In fact these properties can be defined in a purely algebraic manner in terms of automorphisms of the graph [6]. However, it is more convenient here to work with the equivalent geometric concepts: an abstract graph is defined to have an axial (rotational) symmetry if there is *some* drawing of the graph having that axial (rotational) symmetry in the geometric sense. Here, a *drawing* of a graph consists of a set of distinct disks in the plane, one disk for each vertex, with continuous curves joining disks which represent adjacent vertices. For directed graphs, these curves carry arrowheads indicating edge direction. A curve and a disk must not intersect unless the corresponding edge and vertex are incident. For simplicity, all edge curves may be restricted to straight line segments; this ensures that every drawing of a graph is specified merely by the positions of its vertex disks, yet does not conflict with the display of either symmetry [6] or planarity [2].

In light of its relevance to the practical problem of graph drawing, it is important to develop computationally efficient algorithms for finding symmetry in abstract graphs. Linear-time algorithms (optimal) have been obtained for the detection and display of both axial and rotational symmetry in trees [7], outerplanar graphs [8], and embedded planar graphs [6]. Algorithms for the restricted class of *perfectly drawable* graphs are outlined in [4], although these appear to be inefficient as they involve the seemingly intractable problem of determining the automorphism group of the graph.

For general graphs, it was shown in [7] that symmetry detection is computationally at least as hard as graph isomorphism. This result is of fairly limited power, however, since the exact complexity status of graph isomorphism remains unknown.

The results below essentially resolve the complexity status of symmetry detection. The theorems which follow reveal that the basic problems of detecting if a general graph has even a single axial or rotational symmetry, as well as several refinements, are all NP-Complete. Under the widely-held assumption that $P \neq NP$, these results then preclude the existence of efficient general symmetry-detection algorithms.

2. NP-Completeness of Geometric Symmetry Detection

Let G be an arbitrary graph. For simplicity, G is assumed to be undirected; however, all the following results are readily extended to directed graphs by uniformly replacing each arc by a small undirected graph which encodes its orientation.

Throughout this section, the term *rotational symmetry* always refers to *non-trivial* rotational symmetry, thus excluding the identity rotation through $0°$. A vertex of G is said to be *fixed* under a symmetry if it is mapped onto itself by that symmetry. Clearly, G can have only zero or one vertices fixed under any rotational symmetry, whereas there are no such restrictions in the case of an axial symmetry. Recall that a *central symmetry* is a rotational symmetry through $180°$. An axial, rotational, or central symmetry of a graph is called a *geometric* symmetry, to help distinguish it from a general *symmetry*, which usually denotes any automorphism of the graph.

Several problems in the area of geometric symmetry detection are considered:

DAS : does G have any axial symmetry?

DAS-0 : does G have any axial symmetry with no fixed vertex?

DRS : does G have any rotational symmetry?

DRS-0 : does G have any rotational symmetry with no fixed vertex?

DRS-1 : does G have any rotational symmetry with one fixed vertex?

DCS : does G have any central symmetry?

DCS-0 : does G have any central symmetry with no fixed vertex?

DCS-1 : does G have any central symmetry with one fixed vertex?

The remainder of this section shows that each of these problems is NP-complete. Note, at the outset, that each of the problems lies in NP, since a polynomial-time algorithm can non-deterministically select a permutation of the vertices and then deterministically check that it yields a symmetry of the desired type.

Theorem 1: *DAS is NP-Complete.*

Proof: A polynomial-time reduction from *3-SAT* [1] is presented: given a Boolean expression C in 3-CNF, a graph G is constructed in polynomial time such that:

$$C \text{ is SATISFIABLE} \iff G \text{ has an AXIAL SYMMETRY.}$$

Let $C = c_1 \wedge c_2 \wedge \ldots \wedge c_m$, where, without loss of generality, each c_j is a *distinct* disjunct of *exactly* three *distinct* literals; for $1 \leq j \leq m$, let $c_j = (x_{j,1} \vee x_{j,2} \vee x_{j,3})$. Let $a_1, a_2, \ldots, a_n$ be the variables appearing in C; thus each $x_{j,r}$ is some a_i or $\bar{a}_i$.

The corresponding graph G is constructed from the n subgraphs H_i $(1 \leq i \leq n)$ and the $8m$ vertices $z_{j,k}$ $(1 \leq j \leq m, 0 \leq k \leq 7)$. H_i is shown (twice) in Figure 2, where the broken line between v_i and w_i denotes a path of $i+1$ vertices, and the dotted vertical lines indicate axes of symmetry. Each vertex $z_{j,k}$ is joined to one vertex in each of three distinct H_i as follows: if $k = b_1 b_2 b_3$ in binary (so $k = 4b_1 + 2b_2 + b_3$) then $z_{j,k}$ is joined to $x_{j,1:b_1}$, $x_{j,2:b_2}$, and $x_{j,3:b_3}$. Thus, for example, if $c_4 = a_2 \vee \bar{a}_7 \vee a_9$ then $z_{4,6}$ is joined to $a_{2:1}$, $\bar{a}_{7:1}$, and $a_{9:0}$, since $6 = 110_2$.

Clearly, for each C the corresponding G may be constructed in polynomial time.

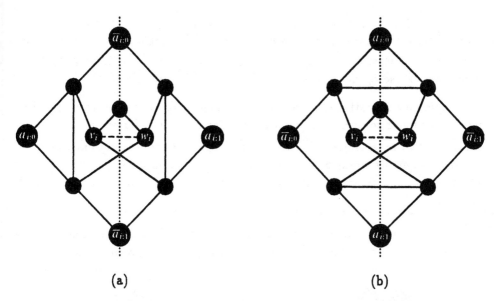

(a)   (b)

Figure 2: *The two axially-symmetric drawings of the subgraph H_i*

C is SATISFIABLE $\implies$ G has an AXIAL SYMMETRY:

Let $\varphi : \{a_1, \ldots, a_n\} \longrightarrow \{T, F\}$ be a satisfying truth-assignment for C, and extend φ by setting $\varphi(\bar{a}_i) = \overline{\varphi(a_i)}$, for each i. Construct a drawing of G as follows:

(a) Pick an arbitrary straight line L in the plane.

(b) For each $1 \leq i \leq n$, draw H_i as in Figure 2(a) or Figure 2(b), according as $\varphi(a_i) = T$ or $\varphi(a_i) = F$, and place it symmetrically astride of L.

(c) For each $1 \leq j \leq m$, the clause $c_j = (x_{j,1} \vee x_{j,2} \vee x_{j,3})$ is satisfied; thus $\varphi(x_{j,r}) = T$ for some least $1 \leq r \leq 3$, so vertices $x_{j,r:0}$ and $x_{j,r:1}$ are placed *off* L in step (b). Vertices z_{j,k_1} and z_{j,k_2} are termed *partners* if the 3-bit binary representations of k_1 and k_2 differ only in the rth bit. For each $0 \leq k \leq 7$ ($k = b_1 b_2 b_3$ in binary) place vertex $z_{j,k}$ on the same side of L as vertex $x_{j,r:b_r}$, partners being placed symmetrically opposite one another, relative to L. Complete the drawing by now joining all vertices $z_{j,k}$ to their neighbors in G by means of straight line segments.

It is readily verified that L is an axis of symmetry in this drawing of G.

G has an AXIAL SYMMETRY $\implies$ C is SATISFIABLE:

Let L be an axis of symmetry in a drawing of G. For each $1 \leq i \leq n$, the subgraph H_i must be mapped onto itself by the symmetry, since the path of $i+1$ degree-2 vertices between v_i and w_i is unique in G. A detailed but straightforward inspection reveals that the *only* axial symmetries of H_i are those displayed in Figure 2. Construct a truth-assignment $\varphi : \{a_1, \ldots, a_n\} \longrightarrow \{T, F\}$ by setting $\varphi(a_i) = T$ or $\varphi(a_i) = F$, according as L induces the symmetry of Figure 2(a) or Figure 2(b) in H_i, and extend φ to $\{\bar{a}_1, \ldots, \bar{a}_n\}$ as before. Note that $\varphi(a_i) = T$ iff vertices $a_{i:0}$ and $a_{i:1}$ lie off L, while $\varphi(\bar{a}_i) = T$ iff vertices $\bar{a}_{i:0}$ and $\bar{a}_{i:1}$ lie off L.

For each $1 \leq j \leq m$, consider now any vertex $z_{j,k}$ ($0 \leq k \leq 7$). Since the entire drawing of G is symmetric about L and all clauses of C are distinct, it follows that $z_{j,k}$ must have at least one neighbor, say $x_{j,r:b}$, which lies off L. Then $\varphi(x_{j,r}) = T$, so φ satisfies clause c_j, and since j is arbitrary, φ thus satisfies C. $\square$

Inspiration for the rather esoteric definition of the graph G above was drawn from a somewhat similar construction found in an elegant proof of Lubiw [5].

Throughout the remainder of the current section, the term *fixed-point-free* (FPF) refers to a symmetry which fixes no vertex of the graph in question. Furthermore, axial, rotational, and central symmetry are abbreviated AS, RS, and CS, respectively.

Theorem 2: *DAS-0 is NP-Complete.*

Proof: In the proof of Theorem 1, replace each subgraph H_i by the corresponding $\widehat{H}_i$ shown (twice) in Figure 3, where the path between v_i and w_i now contains $2i$ vertices:

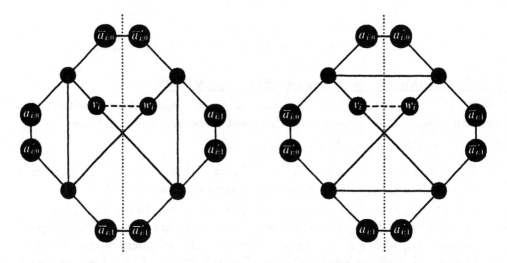

Figure 3: *The two fixed-point-free axially-symmetric drawings of the subgraph $\widehat{H}_i$*

In addition, replace each edge between a vertex $z_{j,k}$ and a vertex u_i in H_i by edges between $z_{j,k}$ and both u_i and u'_i in $\widehat{H}_i$. Any axial symmetry of the modified graph must clearly be FPF. The proof of Theorem 2 otherwise parallels that of Theorem 1. $\square$

Theorem 2 also follows from the result of Lubiw [5] that the detection of order-2 FPF graph automorphisms is NP-Complete; using algebraic definitions of symmetry, it is shown in [6] that automorphisms of this type are precisely FPF axial symmetries. However, the present proof has the advantage of being easily adapted, as shown below, to produce corresponding results regarding rotational and central symmetries.

Recall that AS, RS, and CS are essentially graph automorphisms, and as such are inherent properties of *abstract* graphs. The following technical Lemma establishes a simple but useful equality by showing that the concepts of FPF AS and FPF CS, although distinct geometrically, are in fact identical from a graph-theoretic viewpoint.

Lemma 1: *A graph automorphism is a FPF AS iff it is a FPF CS.*

Proof: Any drawing which displays a FPF AS can be transformed to display the same abstract symmetry as a FPF CS, simply by taking that portion of the graph lying on one side of the axis of symmetry and reflecting it in any line perpendicular to the axis (Figure 4 (a) → (b)). Conversely, any straight line passing through the center point of a FPF CS drawing, but avoiding all vertex disks, becomes the axis for a FPF AS upon a similar reflection (Figure 4 (b) → (c)). (A more rigorous proof of this Lemma, based on the formal algebraic definitions of symmetry, is presented in [6].) □

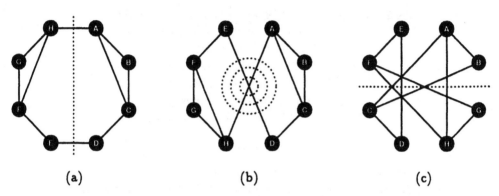

$$(a) \qquad\qquad (b) \qquad\qquad (c)$$

Figure 4: *Example of the equality of FPF AS and FPF CS*

Lemma 2: *Let $\widehat{G}$ denote the modified graph constructed in the proof of Theorem 2. Then any (non-trivial) RS of $\widehat{G}$ is a FPF CS (and, by definition of CS, conversely).*

Proof: A non-trivial RS can fix at most one vertex. Now for each i, vertices v_i and w_i are distinguished in $\widehat{G}$, so such a RS must clearly interchange them. By the nature of rotational symmetry, it must then interchange *all* other vertices in pairs, except for possibly one fixed vertex, so the RS is a CS. But $\widehat{G}$ has an *even* number of vertices of any degree, so there can be no such fixed vertex; hence the CS is FPF. □

Lemmas 1 and 2 thus show that any FPF AS of $\widehat{G}$ is also a RS, a FPF RS, a CS, and a FPF CS, and conversely. Combining this with Theorem 2 yields the following:

Theorem 3: *DRS is NP-Complete.* □

Theorem 4: *DRS-0 is NP-Complete.* □

Theorem 5: *DCS is NP-Complete.* □

Theorem 6: *DCS-0 is NP-Complete.* □

Construct a graph $\widetilde{G}$ from $\widehat{G}$ by adding a new vertex y, and joining it to every vertex in $\widehat{G}$. Clearly, y is distinguished in $\widetilde{G}$ and so must be fixed under any symmetry. In particular, note that $\widetilde{G}$ has a RS or CS (fixing y) iff $\widehat{G}$ has a FPF RS or FPF CS, respectively. Combining this with Theorems 4 and 6 produces the further results:

Theorem 7: *DRS-1 is NP-Complete.* □

Theorem 8: *DCS-1 is NP-Complete.* □

Low Dimensional Middle Cubes Are Hamiltonian

Kunwarjit S. Bagga   Frank W. Owens

Department of Computer Science
Ball State University
Muncie, Indiana 47306
ARPANET: fwo@bsu-cs.bsu.edu
BITNET: 00fwowens@bsuvax1
UUCP: ...!{iuvax|pur-ee}!bsu-cs!fwo

Abstract

Let Q_n be the n-dimensional hypercube. If $n = 2k + 1$, then the subgraph M_n of Q_n induced by the nodes having exactly k or $k + 1$ ones is called the middle cube of dimension n. A famous conjecture is that M_n is hamiltonian if $n > 1$.

Clearly, M_3 has two oriented hamiltonian cycles. This paper includes the following new results:

1. The number of oriented hamiltonian cyles of M_n is divisible by $k!(k+1)!$.

2. M_5 has exactly 48 oriented hamiltonian cycles.

3. M_7 is hamiltonian.

4. Some interesting new combinatorial identities which are relevant to the structure of M_n.

1   Introduction

Q_n denotes the n-dimensional hypercube graph. The nodes of Q_n consist of all bit strings of length n. Two nodes are adjacent if and only if the Hamming distance between them equals one. Thus, Q_n has 2^n nodes and is regular of degree n. By the Handshaking Lemma Q_n has $n2^{n-1}$ edges. Q_n may also be defined recursively as follows. $Q_0 \cong K_1$ and $Q_n \cong Q_{n-1} \times K_2$ if $n > 0$.

Let $n = 2k + 1$. M_n denotes the n-dimensional middle cube graph. The nodes of M_n consist of all bit strings of length n containing exactly k or $k + 1$ ones. M_n is an induced subgraph of Q_n. Thus, M_n has $\binom{n}{k} + \binom{n}{k+1} = 2\binom{n}{k}$ nodes and is regular of degree $k + 1$. By the Handshaking Lemma M_n has $(k + 1)\binom{n}{k}$ edges. In particular, $M_1 \cong K_2$ and $M_3 \cong C_6$. M_n is also a bipartite graph.

3. #P-Completeness of Geometric Symmetry Counting

For a given problem Π, the associated *decision problem* asks whether there exists any solution for Π, while the *counting problem* asks how many such solutions exist. The class of *#P-Complete* problems can be characterized informally as consisting of all counting problems whose time complexities are polynomially equivalent to that of counting the number of satisfying truth-assignments for a general 3-CNF formula. For further details regarding #P-Completeness, consult Garey and Johnson [3].

Each of the counting problems corresponding to the decision problems of Section 2 is #P-Complete, since the reductions from 3-SAT are all *parsimonious* (see [3]):

Theorem 9: *The problems of counting the number of axial symmetries, axial symmetries fixing no vertex, rotational symmetries, rotational symmetries fixing no vertex, rotational symmetries fixing one vertex, central symmetries, central symmetries fixing no vertex, and central symmetries fixing one vertex of a given graph, are all #P-Complete.* □

References

[1] A. AHO, J. HOPCROFT, J. ULLMAN. *The Design and Analysis of Computer Algorithms*, Addison-Wesley, 1974.

[2] I. FÁRY. "On Straight Line Representation of Planar Graphs", *Acta Scientiarum Mathematicarum Szeged 11*, 4, pp 229–233, 1948.

[3] M. GAREY, D. JOHNSON. *Computers and Intractability*, W. H. Freeman, 1979.

[4] R. LIPTON, S. NORTH, J. SANDBERG. "A Method for Drawing Graphs", *Proc. of the First ACM Symposium on Computational Geometry*, pp 153–160, Jun 1985.

[5] A. LUBIW. "Some NP-Complete Problems Similar to Graph Isomorphism", *SIAM Journal on Computing 10*, 1, pp 11–21, Feb 1981.

[6] J. MANNING. "Geometric Symmetry in Graphs", Ph.D. Thesis, Department of Computer Sciences, Purdue University, Aug 1990 (forthcoming).

[7] J. MANNING, M. J. ATALLAH. "Fast Detection and Display of Symmetry in Trees", *Congressus Numerantium 64*, pp 159–168, Nov 1988.

[8] J. MANNING, M. J. ATALLAH. "Fast Detection and Display of Symmetry in Outerplanar Graphs", Technical Report CSD-TR-606, Department of Computer Sciences, Purdue University, Jun 1986. (Submitted for publication to *Discrete Applied Mathematics*.)

[9] E. MESSINGER. "Automatic Layout of Large Directed Graphs", Technical Report 88-07-08, Department of Computer Science, University of Washington, Jul 1988.

A famous conjecture is that M_n is hamiltonian if $n = 2k + 1 > 1$. Clearly, $M_1 \cong K_2$ is not hamiltonian, but the conjecture is obvious for $n = 3$. The nodes of Q_3 are $000 = 0$, $001 = 1$, $010 = 2$, $011 = 3$, $100 = 4$, $101 = 5$, $110 = 6$ and $111 = 7$. The nodes of M_3 are therefore 1, 2, 3, 4, 5 and 6. M_3 has exactly two oriented hamiltonian cycles: 132645 and 154623.

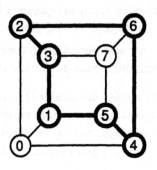

M_3 as an induced subgraph of Q_3

FIGURE 1

We shall prove the following results in this paper:

1. The number of oriented hamiltonian cycles of M_n is divisible by $k!(k+1)!$.

2. M_5 has exactly 48 oriented hamiltonian cycles.

3. M_7 is hamiltonian.

4. Some interesting new combinatorial identities which are relevant to the structure of M_n.

Duffus, Sands and Woodrow [1] have shown that for odd $n > 3$ the union of two lexicographic matchings in M_n considered as a bipartite graph is never a hamiltonian cycle. Graham [2] and Pippert [3] have both independently discovered hamiltonian cycles of M_5.

We shall begin with

Theorem 1 *If $n = 2k + 1$, then the number of oriented hamiltonian cycles of M_n is divisible by $k!(k+1)!$.*

Proof The theorem is obvious if M_n is not hamiltonian. Assume that M_n is hamiltonian. Let $0^{(k)}$ and $1^{(k)}$ denote bit strings consisting of k consecutive zeros and ones, respectively. Each oriented hamiltonian cycle of M_n has a canonical representation as a list of its $2\binom{n}{k}$ nodes beginning with $0^{(k+1)}1^{(k)}$. Any permutation of the bits of the nodes preserves all Hamming distances between nodes. The first $k + 1$ bits and the last k bits of the nodes can be independently permuted in $k!(k+1)!$ ways. Each of these permutations leaves $0^{(k+1)}1^{(k)}$ fixed. Define two oriented hamiltonian cycles of M_n to be related if and only if the canonical representation of one may be obtained from the canonical representation of the other by independently permuting the first $k+1$ bits and the last k bits of the nodes. This defines an equivalence relation on the set of all oriented hamiltonian cycles of M_n. By considering those nodes having exactly one 1 in either the first $k+1$ bits or the last k bits it follows that an oriented hamiltonian cycle is related to itself only under the identity permutation. Thus each equivalence class contains $k!(k+1)!$ oriented hamiltonian cycles. •

Corollary *M_7 has at least 144 oriented hamiltonian cycles.*

Proof If $n = 2k + 1 = 7$, then $k = 3$ and $k!(k+1)! = 144$. We will present an oriented hamiltonian cycle of M_7 later in this paper. •

2 M_5 Has 48 Oriented Hamiltonian Cycles

Theorem 2 *M_5 has exactly 48 oriented hamiltonian cycles.*

Proof M_5 has 20 nodes and 30 edges. We have implemented a depth first search with a Turbo Prolog® 2.0 program to determine the canonical representation of all oriented hamiltonian cycles of M_5. The program listing (minus a few predicates and clauses to format the output) is given below followed by a listing of the output containing the 48 oriented hamiltonian cycles of M_5. These are obtained in response to the goal *hamilton(3,OHC)*. The canonical representation of each oriented hamiltonian cycle begins with $00011 = 3$ and is a list of all 20 nodes in decimal format. •

```
domains
    node = integer
    path = node*
predicates
    depthfirst(path,path)
    adjacent(node,node)
    ok(node,node)
    hamilton(node,path)
    count(path,integer)
    member(node,path)
clauses
    depthfirst(Candidate,Candidate) :- count(Candidate,20).
    depthfirst(Path,Candidate) :-
        Path = [Node|_],
        adjacent(Node,NextNode),
        not(member(NextNode,Path)),
        depthfirst([NextNode|Path],Candidate).
    adjacent(X,Y) :- ok(X,Y).
    adjacent(X,Y) :- ok(Y,X).
    ok(3,7).
```

```
ok(3,11).
ok(3,19).
ok(5,7).
ok(5,13).
ok(5,21).
ok(6,7).
ok(6,14).
ok(6,22).
ok(9,11).
ok(9,13).
ok(9,25).
ok(10,11).
ok(10,14).
ok(10,26).
ok(12,13).
ok(12,14).
ok(12,28).
ok(17,19).
ok(17,21).
ok(17,25).
ok(18,19).
ok(18,22).
ok(18,26).
ok(20,21).
ok(20,22).
ok(20,28).
ok(24,25).
ok(24,26).
ok(24,28).
hamilton(StartNode,OHC) :-
    depthfirst([StartNode],OHC),
    OHC = [LastNode|_],
    adjacent(LastNode,StartNode).
count([],0).
count(L,N) :-
    L = [_|Tail],
    count(Tail,NumTail),
    N = NumTail + 1.
member(X,[X|_]).
member(X,[_|Y]) :- member(X,Y).
```

```
3   7   5  13   9  11  10  26  24  25  17  21  20  28  12  14   6  22  18  19
3   7   5  13   9  25  24  28  12  14   6  22  20  21  17  19  18  26  10  11
3   7   5  13  12  14   6  22  18  26  10  11   9  25  24  28  20  21  17  19
3   7   5  13  12  28  20  21  17  19  18  22   6  14  10  26  24  25   9  11
```

```
3  7  5 21 17 19 18 26 24 25  9 13 12 28 20 22  6 14 10 11
3  7  5 21 17 25 24 28 20 22  6 14 12 13  9 11 10 26 18 19
3  7  5 21 20 22  6 14 10 26 18 19 17 25 24 28 12 13  9 11
3  7  5 21 20 28 12 13  9 11 10 14  6 22 18 26 24 25 17 19
3  7  6 14 10 11  9 25 24 26 18 22 20 28 12 13  5 21 17 19
3  7  6 14 10 26 24 28 12 13  5 21 20 22 18 19 17 25  9 11
3  7  6 14 12 13  5 21 17 25  9 11 10 26 24 28 20 22 18 19
3  7  6 14 12 28 20 22 18 19 17 21  5 13  9 25 24 26 10 11
3  7  6 22 18 19 17 25 24 26 10 14 12 28 20 21  5 13  9 11
3  7  6 22 18 26 24 28 20 21  5 13 12 14 10 11  9 25 17 19
3  7  6 22 20 21  5 13  9 25 17 19 18 26 24 28 12 14 10 11
3  7  6 22 20 28 12 14 10 11  9 13  5 21 17 25 24 26 18 19
3 11  9 13  5  7  6 22 20 21 17 25 24 28 12 14 10 26 18 19
3 11  9 13  5 21 20 28 12 14 10 26 24 25 17 19 18 22  6  7
3 11  9 13 12 14 10 26 18 22  6  7  5 21 20 28 24 25 17 19
3 11  9 13 12 28 24 25 17 19 18 26 10 14  6 22 20 21  5  7
3 11  9 25 17 19 18 22 20 21  5 13 12 28 24 26 10 14  6  7
3 11  9 25 17 21 20 28 24 26 10 14 12 13  5  7  6 22 18 19
3 11  9 25 24 26 10 14  6 22 18 19 17 21 20 28 12 13  5  7
3 11  9 25 24 28 12 13  5  7  6 14 10 26 18 22 20 21 17 19
3 11 10 14  6  7  5 21 20 22 18 26 24 28 12 13  9 25 17 19
3 11 10 14  6 22 20 28 12 13  9 25 24 26 18 19 17 21  5  7
3 11 10 14 12 13  9 25 17 21  5  7  6 22 20 28 24 26 18 19
3 11 10 14 12 28 24 26 18 19 17 25  9 13  5 21 20 22  6  7
3 11 10 26 18 19 17 21 20 22  6 14 12 28 24 25  9 13  5  7
3 11 10 26 18 22 20 28 24 25  9 13 12 14  6  7  5 21 17 19
3 11 10 26 24 25  9 13  5 21 17 19 18 22 20 28 12 14  6  7
3 11 10 26 24 28 12 14  6  7  5 13  9 25 17 21 20 22 18 19
3 19 17 21  5  7  6 14 12 13  9 25 24 28 20 22 18 26 10 11
3 19 17 21  5 13 12 28 20 22 18 26 24 25  9 11 10 14  6  7
3 19 17 21 20 22 18 26 10 14  6  7  5 13 12 28 24 25  9 11
3 19 17 21 20 28 24 25  9 11 10 26 18 22  6 14 12 13  5  7
3 19 17 25  9 11 10 14 12 13  5 21 20 28 24 26 18 22  6  7
3 19 17 25  9 13 12 28 24 26 18 22 20 21  5  7  6 14 10 11
3 19 17 25 24 26 18 22  6 14 10 11  9 13 12 28 20 21  5  7
3 19 17 25 24 28 20 21  5  7  6 22 18 26 10 14 12 13  9 11
3 19 18 22  6  7  5 13 12 14 10 26 24 28 20 21 17 25  9 11
3 19 18 22  6 14 12 28 20 21 17 25 24 26 10 11  9 13  5  7
3 19 18 22 20 21 17 25  9 13  5  7  6 14 12 28 24 26 10 11
3 19 18 22 20 28 24 26 10 11  9 25 17 21  5 13 12 14  6  7
3 19 18 26 10 11  9 13 12 14  6 22 20 28 24 25 17 21  5  7
3 19 18 26 10 14 12 28 24 25 17 21 20 22  6  7  5 13  9 11
3 19 18 26 24 25 17 21  5 13  9 11 10 14 12 28 20 22  6  7
3 19 18 26 24 28 20 22  6  7  5 21 17 25  9 13 12 14 10 11
```

3 M_7 Is Hamiltonian

Theorem 3 *M_7 is hamiltonian.*

Proof M_7 has 70 nodes and 140 edges. We implemented a similar depth first search with a Turbo Prolog® 2.0 program to determine the canonical representation of all oriented hamiltonian cycles of M_7. This program was too slow to be of value. We modified the program to incorporate the following interesting heuristic. Let v be any node of M_n. Let v^* denote the node obtained by reversing and taking the ones complement of v. Clearly, $v \neq v^*$ and $v = v^{**}$. The *-operation also preserves all Hamming distances between nodes. We then searched for a partial path $v_1, \cdots, v_{34}, v_{35}$ of distinct nodes of M_7, where $v_1 = 0000111 = 7$, which did not contain both v and v^* for any node v and which had the property that v_{35} was Hamming distance one from v_{35}^*. There are eight pairs of nodes with this latter property:

$$0000111^* = 0001111$$
$$0010011^* = 0011011$$
$$0100101^* = 0101101$$
$$0110001^* = 0111001$$
$$1000110^* = 1001110$$
$$1010010^* = 1011010$$
$$1100100^* = 1101100$$
$$1110000^* = 1111000$$

If $v_1, \cdots, v_{35}$ is such a partial path, then $v_1, \cdots, v_{35}, v_{35}^*, v_{34}^*, \cdots, v_1^* = 0001111 = 15$ is the canonical representation of an oriented hamiltonian cycle of M_7. The modified program is much faster and has discovered thousands of oriented hamiltonian cycles of M_7. Two of these cycles in decimal format are 7, 23, 19, 51, 35, 39, 37, 53, 21, 85, 69, 71, 70, 86, 22, 30, 28, 92, 84, 116, 52, 60, 44, 108, 76, 77, 73, 89, 81, 83, 82, 114, 112, 113, 49, 57, 56, 120, 88, 90, 26, 58, 50, 54, 38, 102, 100, 101, 97, 105, 104, 106, 98, 99, 67, 75, 74, 78, 14, 46, 42, 43, 41, 45, 13, 29, 25, 27, 11, 15 and 7, 23, 19, 51, 49, 53, 21, 29, 13, 45, 44, 46, 14, 78, 74, 75, 67, 83, 82, 114, 50, 54, 38, 102, 100, 116, 52, 60, 28, 92, 84, 85, 81, 113, 112, 120, 56, 58, 42, 106, 98, 99, 97, 105, 104, 108, 76, 77, 73, 89, 88, 90, 26, 30, 22, 86, 70, 71, 69, 101, 37, 39, 35, 43, 41, 57, 25, 27, 11, 15. •

However, there are many oriented hamiltonian cycles of M_7 whose canonical representations do not satisfy the above heuristic, e.g., if $v_1, \cdots, v_{35}, v_{35}^*, v_{34}^*, \cdots, v_1^*$ is the canonical representation of an oriented hamiltonian cycle of M_7 which does satisfy the above heuristic, then $v_1, v_1^*, v_2^*, \cdots, v_{35}^*, v_{35}, \cdots, v_2$ is the canonical representation of an oriented hamiltonian cycle of M_7 which does not satisfy the above heuristic.

4 Middle Cube Identities

Theorem 4 *If $n = 2k + 1$, then*

(1)
$$\sum_{d=0}^{2k+1} \binom{k}{\lfloor d/2 \rfloor}\binom{k+1}{\lceil d/2 \rceil} = 2\binom{n}{k}$$

(2)
$$\sum_{d=0}^{k} \binom{k}{\lfloor d/2 \rfloor}\binom{k+1}{\lceil d/2 \rceil} = \binom{n}{k}$$

(3)
$$\sum_{d=0}^{2k+1} d\binom{k}{\lfloor d/2 \rfloor}\binom{k+1}{\lceil d/2 \rceil} = n\binom{n}{k}$$

Proof $\binom{k}{\lfloor d/2 \rfloor}\binom{k+1}{\lceil d/2 \rceil}$ is the number of nodes of M_n which are Hamming distance d from $0^{(k+1)}1^{(k)}$. Identity (1) states that the sum from $d = 0$ to n of these numbers equals the total number $2\binom{n}{k}$ of nodes of M_n. Let v be any node of M_n. Let $\bar{v}$ denote the ones complement of v. Let $H(v_1, v_2)$ denote the Hamming distance between v_1 and v_2. Clearly, $H(v, 0^{(k+1)}1^{(k)}) + H(\bar{v}, 0^{(k+1)}1^{(k)}) = n = 2k+1$. Hence, exactly one of v or $\bar{v}$ is Hamming distance at most k from $0^{(k+1)}1^{(k)}$. Identity (2) states that exactly half of the nodes of M_n are Hamming distance at most k from $0^{(k+1)}1^{(k)}$. To prove identity (3) we observe that the number of nodes of M_n which are Hamming distance d from $0^{(k+1)}1^{(k)}$ equals the number of nodes of M_n which are Hamming distance $n-d$ from $0^{(k+1)}1^{(k)}$, i.e., $\binom{k}{\lfloor d/2 \rfloor}\binom{k+1}{\lceil d/2 \rceil} = \binom{k}{\lfloor (n-d)/2 \rfloor}\binom{k+1}{\lceil (n-d)/2 \rceil}$ for all d, $0 \le d \le n$. Thus, $d\binom{k}{\lfloor d/2 \rfloor}\binom{k+1}{\lceil d/2 \rceil} + (n-d)\binom{k}{\lfloor (n-d)/2 \rfloor}\binom{k+1}{\lceil (n-d)/2 \rceil} = n\binom{k}{\lfloor d/2 \rfloor}\binom{k+1}{\lceil d/2 \rceil}$ and

$$\sum_{d=0}^{2k+1} d\binom{k}{\lfloor d/2 \rfloor}\binom{k+1}{\lceil d/2 \rceil} = \sum_{d=0}^{k} n\binom{k}{\lfloor d/2 \rfloor}\binom{k+1}{\lceil d/2 \rceil} = n\binom{n}{k}. \quad \bullet$$

References

[1] Dwight Duffus, Bill Sands and Robert E. Woodrow. Lexicographic Matchings Cannot Form Hamiltonian Cycles. *Abstracts of Contributed Talks*, Eleventh British Combinatorial Conference, University of London, Goldsmiths' College, 13–17 July 1987.

[2] Niall Graham. *center of Q hamiltonian?*. E-mail message from niall@nmsu.edu to 00ksbagga@bsuvax1.bitnet sent Friday, 1 December 1989, 13:22:05 MST.

[3] Raymond E. Pippert. Personal communication, May 1989.

Approximation Algorithms for the Chromatic Sum

Ewa Kubicka   Grzegorz Kubicki

Department of Mathematics and Computer Science
Emory University
Atlanta, GA 30322

Dionisios Kountanis

Department of Computer Science
Western Michigan University
Kalamazoo, MI 49008

Abstract

The chromatic sum of a graph G is the smallest total among all proper colorings of G using natural numbers. It was shown that computing the chromatic sum is NP–hard. In this article we prove that a simple greedy algorithm applied to sparse graphs gives a "good" approximation of the chromatic sum. For all graphs the existence of a polynomial time algorithm that approximates the chromatic sum with a linear function error implies $P = NP$.

1   Introduction

We begin by presenting some of the basic definitions and notation which are fundamental to this paper. All other graph–theoretical terms will be defined as in Chartrand and Lesniak [1]. Algorithmic complexity terminology is fairly standard and follows that used by Garey and Johnson [3].

As usual, $|S|$ denotes the cardinality of a set S. We will use V(G) and E(G) to denote the vertex set and edge set of a graph G, respectively. The number $|V(G)|$, sometimes denoted p(G), or simply p, is called the *order* of G and $|E(G)|$, denoted by q(G) or q, is called the *size* of G. By the *degree* of a vertex u, denoted *deg(u)*, we understand the number of edges incident with that vertex.

In this paper we deal with proper colorings of graphs. A *proper coloring* of a graph G is such an assignment of colors to its vertices (colors are usually represented by natural numbers) so that two adjacent vertices receive different colors. The minimum number of colors needed for a proper coloring of a graph G is called the *chromatic number* of G and is denoted by $\chi(G)$. Graph coloring has considerable application to a large variety of optimization problems. It would be very useful to be able to determine quickly the chromatic number of a graph. However, it is well known that this problem is NP – hard ([3], [8]), and therefore we do not expect to find a polynomial algorithm for it. Many polynomial time approximation algorithms are known for finding good colorings ([9], [7], [4], [5],[10], [11]). Almost all of these algorithms have extremely bad worst case behavior. More formally, let A(G) be the number of colors in a proper coloring found for G by the approximation algorithm A and let

$$R_A(n) = \max\{ \frac{A(G)}{\chi(G)} : \text{ G has no more than } n \text{ vertices } \}.$$

($R_A(n)$ is called the worst case performance ratio). The value $R_A(n)$ is of order $O(n)$ for most of the known heuristics. The approximation algorithm with the best known worst case was given by D.S. Johnson in [5] and here $R_A(n) = O(\frac{n}{\log n})$.

In this paper we discuss the performance of approximation algorithms for the chromatic sum. Throughout this paper we will consider only polynomial time approximation algorithms but the phrase "polynomial time" will be omitted.

2 Chromatic Sum - Preliminary Definitions and Facts

The *chromatic sum* of a graph G, $\Sigma(G)$, is a new variation of the chromatic number and has been recently introduced in E. Kubicka and A. Schwenk [6]. It is defined as the smallest possible sum of the colors taken over all possible proper colorings using natural numbers. It is shown in [6] that determining the chromatic sum for arbitrary graphs is an NP–hard problem. One might suspect that we will attain the minimum sum by first selecting a coloring that achieves the chromatic number and then arranging the color classes so that the largest is colored with 1, the second largest is colored with 2 and so on. But it is shown in [6] that even for trees (whose chromatic number is of course 2) we might be forced to use more than the chromatic number of colors to attain the chromatic sum. The tree T on Figure 1 illustrates this property.

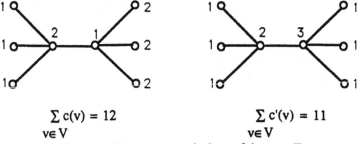

$$\sum_{v \in V} c(v) = 12 \qquad \sum_{v \in V} c'(v) = 11$$

Figure 1: Two proper colorings of the tree T

Moreover, in the paper by P. Erdös, E. Kubicka and A. Schwenk [2] it is shown that for arbitrary natural numbers k and t there exists a k–chromatic graph that requires as many as k + t colors to achieve its chromatic sum.

A proper coloring c of a graph G is called a *best coloring* of G whenever

$$\sum_{v\in V} c(v) = \Sigma(G)$$ and the *k–chromatic sum* of G, $\Sigma_k(G)$, is the minimum sum $$\sum_{v\in V} c(v)$$

taken over all proper colorings c of graph G using exactly k colors.

3   Approximation Algorithms for Sparse Graphs

In this section we consider a family of sparse graphs, i.e. such graphs for which the number of edges is linear with respect to the number of vertices. More precisely, for any positive integer k, define family F_k of graphs as follows:

$$G \in F_k \iff q(G) \le k\, p(G).$$

We consider now the following greedy algorithm A:
1. Determine an ordering of all vertices of a given graph G:
   $$v_1, v_2, v_3, \dots , v_p.$$
2. Color v_1 using color 1. Then, for each consecutive i, $2 \le i \le p$, color the vertex v_i with the smallest available color.

Theorem 1.   For every k and for each $G \in F_k$ the performance of the algorithm A is given by the following inequalities

$$\Sigma(G) \le A(G) \le (k+1)\Sigma(G).$$

Proof.   The method used here is similar to the one presented in Thomassen, Erdös, Alavi, Malde, Schwenk [12]. It was shown there, that $\Sigma(G) \le n + q$, where n and q denote order and size of G, respectively.

Let $v_1, v_2, v_3, \dots , v_n$ be the vertices of $G \in F_k$ listed in the order given by Algorithm A. For any i, let t_i denote the number of vertices among $v_1, v_2, \dots , v_{i-1}$ adjacent to the vertex v_i. If c is a coloring given by Algorithm A, then obviously

$$c(v_i) \le 1 + t_i.$$

Hence, $$A(G) = \sum_{i=1}^{n} c(v_i) \le \sum_{i=1}^{n}(1+t_i) = n+q.$$

Since $q \le kn$ and $n \le \Sigma(G)$, the inequalities follow.   ◆

Theorem 1 shows that the performance ratio of any greedy approximation algorithm for the chromatic sum applied to the family F_k of sparse graphs is bounded by a constant $k + 1$. Since planar graphs are sparse ($q \leq 3p - 6$), any greedy algorithm for the chromatic sum applied to planar graphs has the performance ratio bounded by 4.

4   General Case

In this section we deal with some restrictions on approximation algorithms for the chromatic sum in general case. We will use the similarities between the chromatic number problem and the chromatic sum problem.

It is known [3] that under the assumption $P \neq NP$ there is no polynomial time approximation algorithm for the chromatic number with the performance ratio less than 2. Using this fact it is very easy to show (assuming $P \neq NP$), that for any constant k there is no approximation algorithm A for the chromatic number such that

$$\chi(G) \leq A(G) \leq \chi(G) + k.$$

For the chromatic sum we have the following result.

Theorem 2. Let $f(n)$ be a linear function on n, the order of a graph. Then the existence of an approximation algorithm A for the chromatic sum that for all graphs G_n of order no more than n fulfils
$$\Sigma(G_n) \leq A(G_n) \leq \Sigma(G_n) + f(n)$$
would imply $P = NP$.

Proof. Assume that such an algorithm A exists. We will construct an approximation algorithm B for the chromatic number.

Let G_p be any graph of order p. Define a new graph $H_n = G_p + K_{p^2}$ of order $n = p + p^2$, i.e. H_n consists of a copy of G_p and a copy of the complete graph on p^2 vertices together with all possible edges between these two copies (see Figure 2).

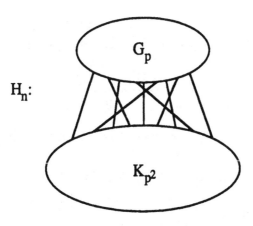

Figure 2: Description of the graph H_n

First we will show that

$$\Sigma(H_n) = \Sigma_{\chi(G)}(G_n) + p^2\chi(G_n) + \frac{p^2(p^2+1)}{2}$$

In fact, we can achieve this value by coloring a copy of G_n in H_n using $\chi(G_n)$ colors and using colors $\chi(G_n)+1$ through $\chi(G_n)+p^2$ to color K_{p^2}.

To show that we can not do better, observe first that the sets of colors used on G_n and K_{p^2} have to be disjoined. Furthermore, the colors used on K_{p^2} cannot be repeated so one can assume that the highest colors are used on K_{p^2}. Using more than $\chi(G_n)$ colors on G_n can possibly decrease the sum of colors on G_n but the difference is smaller than p^2 since even using different colors for different vertices the maximum sum is $\frac{p(p+1)}{2}$. Then, however, the colors available for K_{p^2} increase the sum by at least p^2.

Since $f(n)$ is a linear function, there exist positive numbers r and n_0 such that $\frac{f(n)}{n} \le r$ for all $n > n_0$. From the assumption, we have

$$\Sigma(H_n) \le A(H_n) \le \Sigma(H_n) + f(n).$$

Therefore

$$\Sigma_{\chi(G)}(G_p) + p^2\chi(G_p) + \frac{p^2(p^2+1)}{2} \le$$
$$\le A(H_n) \le$$
$$\le \Sigma_{\chi(G)}(G_p) + p^2\chi(G_p) + \frac{p^2(p^2+1)}{2} + f(n).$$

A new algorithm B for the chromatic number operates in the following way. For a given graph G_p, a corresponding graph H_n ($n = p + p^2$) is constructed (can be done in polynomial time), the algorithm A is applied to the graph H_n and the resulting approximation for $\chi(G_p)$ is computed according to the following formula

$$B(G_p) = \frac{A(H_n) - \frac{p^2(p^2+1)}{2}}{p^2}.$$

The algorithm B is obviously a polynomial time algorithm and its performance is as follows

$$\chi(G_p) \le B(G_p) \le \chi(G_p) + r + 1.$$

This implies however that $P = NP$. ◆

Notice that any approximation algorithm for the chromatic number can be viewed as an approximation algorithm for the chromatic sum. As it was mentioned in the introduction, most of the known approximation algorithms for the chromatic number have the worst case performance ratio of order $O(n)$. The same occurs when these algorithms are used to approximate the chromatic sum. The Johnson's Algorithm [5] for the chromatic number of the best known performance ratio $O(\frac{n}{\log n})$ when used for the chromatic sum gives the same performance ratio for any sequence of graphs of bounded chromatic numbers.

It should be pointed out that the worst possible performance ratio for any approximation algorithm for chromatic sum is of order $O(n)$, since

$$n \leq \Sigma(G_n) \leq \frac{n(n+1)}{2}.$$

All the above observations suggest that approximating the chromatic number or approximating the chromatic sum are of similar level of difficulty.

It has been shown [3] that the existence of an approximation algorithm for the chromatic number with the performance ratio $R(n) < 2$ would imply $P = NP$. We suspect the similar situation for the chromatic sum. More precisely, we have the following conjecture.

Conjecture. For any constant $c > 1$, the existence of an approximation algorithm A for the chromatic sum with performance ratio $R_A(n) < c$ would imply the existence of a constant $k > 1$ and an approximation algorithm B for the chromatic number with the performance ratio $R_B(n) < k$.

References

[1] G. Chartrand and L. Lesniak, *Graphs & Digraphs*, 2nd Edition. Wadsworth and Brooks/Cole (1986).

[2] P. Erdös, E. Kubicka and A. Schwenk, *Graphs that require extra colors to attain the chromatic sum*, submitted to Congr. Numerantium.

[3] M. R. Garey, D. S. Johnson, *Computers and Intractability*, W. H. Freeman (San Francisco) (1979).

[4] D. S. Johnson, *Approximation algorithms for combinatorial problems*, Journal of Computer and System Sciences **9** (1974) 256–278.

[5] D. S. Johnson, *Worst Case Behavior of Graph Coloring Algorithms*, Proc. of 5th Southeastern Conference on Combinatorics, Graph Theory and Computing (1974) 513–524.

[6] E. Kubicka and A. J. Schwenk, *Introduction to Chromatic Sums*, Proceedings of ACM 1989 Computer Science Conference (1989) 39–45.

[7]   F. T. Leighton, *A Graph Coloring Algorithm for Large Scheduling Problems*, Journal of Research on the NBS **84** (1979) 489–506.

[8]   A. J. Mansfield and D. J. A. Welsh, Some colouring problems and their complexity, Annals of Discrete Mathematics **13** (1982) 159–170.

[9]   B. Manvel, *Coloring Large Graphs*, Congressus Numerantium **33** (1981) 197–204.

[10]   D. W. Matula, G. Marble, and J. D. Isaacson, *Graph coloring algorithms*, in R. C. Read (ed), Graph Theory and Computing, Academic Press, New York (1972).

[11]   D. W. Matula, *Bounded color functions on graphs*, Networks **2** (1972) 129-44.

[12]   C. Thomassen, P. Erdös, Y. Alavi, P. J. Malde, and A. J. Schwenk, *Tight Bounds on the Chromatic Sum of a Connected Graph*, J. Graph Theory **13** (1989) 353-357

A Color-Exchange Algorithm For Exact Graph Coloring

Thomas J. Sager
Department of Computer Science
University of Missouri-Rolla
Rolla, Missouri 65401 USA
email: tomsager@cs.umr.edu

Shi-Jen Lin
Department of Computer Science
Chung-Yung University
Chung-Li, Taiwan

Keywords: algorithms, branch-and-bound, chromatic number, graph-coloring, $\mathcal{NP}$-Complete, scheduling.

Abstract

DEXCH, a color-exchange exact graph coloring algorithm is presented. On many classes of graphs, *DEXCH* can, in the mean, find the chromatic number of a graph considerably faster than the *DSATUR* algorithm. The improvement over *DSATUR* stems from the ability to reorganize the subset of colored vertices and to detect in certain instances the existence of a complete subgraph of cardinality equal to the number of colors used in the best coloring found so far. The mean improvement over *DSATUR* is greatest on high edge-density graphs attaining the value of 42% on random graphs of edge-density 0.7 on 64 vertices.

1 Introduction

The graph coloring problem can be stated as: *Given an undirected graph, $G = (V, E)$, with no loops or multiedges, find a function $f : V \to 1..k$, for some positive integer k, such that if $(v, w) \in E$ then $f(v) \neq f(w)$.* Such a function f is called a *coloring function*. If k is minimal over all of G's coloring functions, then f is called an *exact coloring function* and k is called the *chromatic number*. An algorithm which, given a graph G, guarantees an output which is an exact coloring function is called an *exact graph coloring algorithm*. An algorithm whose output is a coloring function which is not necessarily exact is called a *heuristic graph coloring algorithm*.

Exact graph coloring is known to be $\mathcal{NP}$-Complete. In fact, heuristic graph coloring within a factor of 2 of the chromatic number is also $\mathcal{NP}$-Complete [2]. Generally, because it can be quite time-consuming to find the chromatic number of large graphs, graphs of more than 60 or 70 vertices are colored with heuristic algorithms.

Graph coloring can be applied to solve scheduling problems with constraints of the form: events e and e' can not be scheduled together. One such problem is the examination scheduling problem: *"Find the minimum number of periods in which a set of examinations can be scheduled under the constraint that examinations v and* *w can not be scheduled in the same period if at least one person must sit for both exams."* Here V is the set of examinations and $(v, w) \in E$ iff $h(v) \bigcap h(w) \neq \emptyset$, where $h(v)$ is the set of people who will take examination v.

Exact graph coloring algorithms have been studied by Korman [5] and Kubale and Jackowsky [6]. Both studies found that vertex sequential exact algorithms which use dynamic reordering of vertices usually give the best performance in practice.

Exact graph coloring algorithms can be used by themselves to color small graphs or as components of certain heuristic algorithms which can color large graphs. One such heuristic algorithm, *XRLF* [3], was found to outperform other known heuristic graph coloring algorithms on some classes of graphs. Thus, an improved exact graph coloring algorithm can yield improved heuristic graph coloring as well.

XRLF uses a color sequential algorithm based on the work of Leighton [7] and Johri and Matula [4] to reduce a graph to manageable size and then uses the *DSATUR* algorithm to finish the coloring. Although originally presented by Brelaz [1] as a heuristic algorithm, a branch-and-bound version of *DSATUR* has come to represent a *de facto* standard among exact graph coloring algorithms. The branch-and-bound version, which we will refer to simply as *DSATUR*, is a vertex sequential algorithm with dynamic reordering of vertices.

In [9] we presented an exact graph coloring algorithm *DSWAP* which improved on the *DSATUR* algorithm by reorganizing the colored vertex subset according to a procedure which we called *swap*. In [10] we showed that most of the gain from *swap* comes from the portion of the algorithm which prunes the search tree and that furthermore as the size of a graph grows, the *swap* algorithm becomes more and more erratic with respect to *DSATUR*. We hypothesized the existence of a procedure for reorganizing the colored vertex set which would represent a significant improvement over *DSATUR*, but would not behave erratically as the size of the vertex set increased.

In this paper we present the *DEXCH (DSATUR COLOR-EXCHANGE)* algorithm. Unlike DSWAP, its behavior does not become erratic as the size of the vertex set increases. Also unlike *DSWAP*, on graphs of high edge-density and large vertex size, the colored vertex set reorganization component of the algorithm represents a significant part of the total improvement over *DSATUR*.

In section 2, we describe the *DEXCH* algorithm. Section 3 describes the methodology employed to compare the algorithms and the results of our comparisons.

2   The DEXCH Algorithm

In the folowing discussion, the vertices of a graph are named originally $1, 2, 3, \ldots$. As colors are created, the colored vertices are named $-1, -2, -3, \ldots$. A *completely colored graph* contains only colored vertices. A *partially colored graph* may contain both colored and uncolored vertices. We let C be the set of colored vertices and W (white) be the set of uncolored vertices. $cadj(v)$ is the set of colored vertices adjacent to v and $cdegree(v)$ is the cardinality of $cadj(v)$. Similarly, $wadj(v)$ is the set of uncolored vertices adjacent to v and $wdegree(v)$ is the cardinality of $wadj(v)$.

A *partially colored graph* always has the following properties: first, there is never more than one vertex of a particular color and second, the set of colored vertices, $C = -k.. - 1$, always forms a complete subgraph.

As we color a graph, we *merge* pairs of non-adjacent vertices together until we arrive at a complete graph. In order to keep track of the vertices that have been *merged* together, we introduce the function *vertices* from V' to $\mathcal{P}(V)$ where V' is the vertex set of a partially colored graph and $\mathcal{P}(V)$ is the power set of the vertex set of the original graph before beginning the coloring process.

In the following discussion, let $G = (V, E)$ be a partially colored graph with the set of colored vertices $C = -k.. - 1$. Also let v and w be uncolored vertices of G, c be a colored vertex of G and x, y and z be vertices of G. Four procedures for transforming partially colored graphs are shown in Figure 1.

The *DEXCH* algorithm is based on the *DSATUR* algorithm but contains two additional components: a tree-pruning component and a colored vertex subset reorganization component. Pseudo-code for *DEXCH* is given in Figure 2. *DEXCH* with the colored vertex reorganization component removed will be referred to as algorithm *DPRUNE*. *DEXCH* with both the tree-pruning and colored vertex reorganization components removed is equivalent to *DSATUR*. The differences in behavior among the three algorithms are depicted in Figure 3.

The tree pruning component is based on the observation that if there exists v, w and c with $(v, w) \in E$ and $cadj(v) = cadj(w) = C \setminus \{c\}$ then G contains a complete subgraph of cardinality $| C | +1$, namely $C \setminus \{c\} \cup \{v, w\}$. Therefore, G is not colorable with fewer than $| C | +1$ colors. The tree-pruning component is invoked whenever the current partially colored graph contains exactly one color fewer then the best coloring found so far. If three vertices with the above attributes are found, then the subtree rooted at the current partially colored graph is pruned since it cannot contain a completely colored graph using fewer colors than the best coloring found so far.

procedure $rename(G, vertices, y, z)$;
  $vertices(z) \leftarrow vertices(y)$; $vertices(y) \leftarrow undefined$;
  $E \leftarrow E \cup \{(z, x) \mid (y, x) \in E\} \setminus \{(y, x) \mid x \in V\}$; $V \leftarrow V \cup \{z\} \setminus \{y\}$;

procedure $newcolor(G, vertices, v)$;
  $rename(G, vertices, v, -(k + 1))$;   {Create a new colored vertex.}
  $E \leftarrow E \cup \{(c, -(k + 1) \mid c \in -k.. - 1\}$;   {Ensure C is still a complete subgraph.}

procedure $merge(G, vertices, v, c)$;
  $vertices(c) \leftarrow vertices(c) \cup vertices(v)$; $vertices(v) \leftarrow undefined$;
  $E \leftarrow E \cup \{(c, w) \mid (v, w) \in E\} \setminus \{(v, x) \mid x \in V\}$; $V \leftarrow V - \{v\}$;

procedure $exch(G, vertices, v, c)$;
  Let $x \notin V$; $rename(G, vertices, v, x)$;
  $rename(G, vertices, c, v)$; $rename(G, vertices, x, c)$;

Figure 1: Four operations on partially colored graphs.

algorithm *DEXCH*;

   input: $G = (V,E)$: graph;

   output: $\chi(G)$: positive integer;   {Chromatic number}

                    exactcf: function: $V \to 1..\chi(G)$;   {Exact coloring function}

  procedure *color(* $G = (V, E)$: a partially colored graph;

                vertices: function: $V \to \mathcal{P}(1..\infty))$;

    if G is completely colored **then**   {In which case $V = C$}

      if $\mid V \mid <$ *ncolors* **then**

        ncolors $\leftarrow \mid V \mid$;

        $\forall j \in V, \forall i \in vertices(j), exactcf(i) \leftarrow -j$;

    else

      if $\exists v \in V \mid cadj(v) = C$ **then**

        if $\mid C \mid <$ *ncolors* $- 1$ **then**

            choose $v \in V \mid cadj(v) = C$ and *wdegree(v)* is maximal among all

                $v' \in V \mid cadj(v') = C$

            newcolor(G, vertices, v);   *color(G, vertices)*;

        else if $\mid C \mid =$ *ncolors* $- 1$ and $\exists$ distinct v, w and $c \in V \mid (v, w) \in E$ and

           $cadj(v) = cadj(w) = C \setminus \{c\}$ **then return**   **{Pruning Component}**

        else if $\exists v \in W$ and $c \in C \mid cadj(v) = C \setminus \{c\}$ and *wdegree(v) > wdegree(c)*

        then   **{Reorganization Component}**

          choose $v \in V$ and $c \in C \mid cadj(v) = C \setminus \{c\}$ and *wdegree(v) − wdegree(c)*

             is maximal among all $v' \in V$ and $c' \in C \mid cadj(v') = C \setminus \{c'\}$;

          exch(G, vertices, v, c);   *color(G, vertices)*;

      else

        choose $v \in V \mid cdegree(v)$ is maximal and *wdegree(v)* is maximal

           among all $v' \in V \mid cdegree(v')$ is maximal;

        $\forall c \in C \mid c \notin cadj(v)$,

          if $\mid C \mid <$ *ncolors* **then**

            $G' \leftarrow G$;   *vertices'* $\leftarrow$ *vertices*;

            merge(G', vertices', v, c);   *color(G', vertices')*;

          if $\mid C \mid <$ *ncolors* $- 1$ **then**

            newcolor(G, vertices, v);   *color(G, vertices)*;

ncolors $\leftarrow \infty$; $\forall v \in V, vertices(v) \leftarrow \{v\}$;

color(G, vertices); $\chi(G) \leftarrow$ *ncolors*;

Figure 2: The *DEXCH* algorithm.

The colored vertex reorganization component is based on the desireability of having as many edges as possible incident to the colored vertex subset. *DSATUR* attempts to maximize this attribute by choosing at each step an uncolored vertex with maximal *wdegree* among those uncolored vertices with maximal *cdegree*. *DEXCH*, in addition, will attempt to maximize this attribute by searching for two vertices, v and c such that $cadj(v) = C \setminus \{c\}$ and $wdegree(v) > wdegree(c)$. If such a pair is found, *DEXCH* replaces c by v in the colored vertex subset.

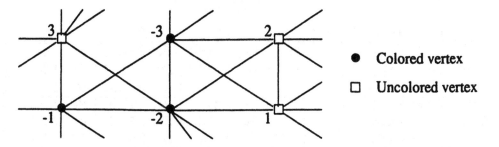

Since $wdegree(3) > max(wdegree(1), wdegree(2))$, *DSATUR* merges vertex 3 into vertex -3.

If the best coloring so far uses 4 colors, *DPRUNE* detects the complete subgraph $\{-3, -2, 1, 2\}$ and prunes the search tree; otherwise *DPRUNE* merges vertex 3 into vertex -3.

If the best coloring so far uses more than 4 colors, *DEXCH* reorganizes the colored vertex set as $\{-2, -1, 3\}$; otherwise *DEXCH* prunes the search tree.

Figure 3: Behavior of three algorithms.

We note that all three algorithms indeed find an exact coloring function through exhaustive search. Each instantiation of the procedure *color* either increases the number of colored vertices (*newcolor*), increases the number of edges incident to the set of colored vertices (*exch*) or decreases the number of uncolored vertices (*merge*). *color* calls itself recursively until its argument is either completely colored or contains no fewer colored vertices than the best coloring found so far.

3 Methodology and Results

All three algorithms, *DSATUR, DPRUNE* and *DEXCH*, were programmed in Turbo Pascal using a similar programming style and degree of optimization. For each of the vertex sizes: 32, 40, 48, 54 and 64; and for each of the edge densities: 0.1, 0.3, 0.5, 0.7 and 0.9; 100 random graphs were generated using Park and Miller's minimal standard random number generator [8]. Each algorithm was executed on a PC AT computer to produce an exact coloring function for all 100 random graphs except for densities of 0.5 and 0.7 on 64 vertices where, because of the time involved, an exact coloring for only the first 30 random graphs generated and the first 10 random graphs generated respectively was produced. Execution times of the three algorithms were compared with the *paired t test*. Mean execution times and the results of the *paired t test* at the 95% confidence level are shown in Table 1.

We found that both *DEXCH* and *DPRUNE* are consistently faster than *DSATUR* at the 95% confidence level for all graphs of between 40 and 64 vertices and all densities between 0.3 and 0.9. In addition, we found that *DEXCH* performs significantly faster than *DPRUNE* on most classes of graphs of high density (0.7 and 0.9) on 40 through 64 vertices. The relative improvement of *DEXCH* over *DSATUR* reaches its maximum

		VERTICES								
		32		40		48		56		64
	0.1	D† 1.86E-1	D† 3.47E-1	P•† 5.11E-1	D⋆† 5.88E-1	E 1.02
		P† 1.87E-1	P† 3.48E-1	D† 5.22E-1	P† 6.04E-1	P 1.06
		E 2.07E-1	E 3.74E-1	E 5.42E-1	E 6.33E-1	D 1.14
	0.3	P•† 4.19E-1	P• 1.56	E• 9.89	P•† 3.22E1	P• 7.14E2
D		D 4.42E-1	E• 1.57	P• 1.03E1	E• 3.38E1	E• 7.37E2
E		E 4.44E-1	D 1.77	D 1.20E1	D 3.91E1	D 8.54E2
N	0.5	P• 1.40	E•⋆ 9.89	E• 9.93E1	P• 7.09E2	E• 3.91E3
S		E• 1.46	P• 1.08E1	P• 1.01E2	E• 7.25E2	P• 4.58E3
I		D 1.60	D 1.31E1	D 1.24E2	D 8.81E2	D 5.81E3
T	0.7	E•⋆ 1.70	E•⋆ 7.90	E•⋆ 1.21E2	E• 1.54E3	E•⋆ 1.29E4
Y		P• 1.88	P• 1.01E1	P• 1.46E2	P• 1.63E3	P• 1.72E4
		D 2.23	D 1.24E1	D 1.84E2	D 2.09E3	D 2.21E4
	0.9	P•† 3.89E-1	E• 9.82E-1	E•⋆ 5.68	E•⋆ 5.34E1	E•⋆ 3.76E2
		D 4.12E-1	P• 1.01	P• 6.39	P• 7.24E1	P• 4.91E2
		E 4.21E-1	D 1.15	D 7.59	D 8.65E1	D 5.88E2

D	DSATUR algorithm.	P	DPRUNE algorithm.
E	DEXCH algorithm.	yEx	means $y * 10^x$.

•	faster than *DSATUR* algorithm at 95% confidence level.
⋆	faster than *DPRUNE* algorithm at 95% confidence level.
†	faster than *DEXCH* algorithm at 95% confidence level.

Table 1: Mean execution time in seconds.

value of 42% on graphs of density 0.7 on 64 vertices, the most time-consuming class of graphs to color. On graphs of moderate density (0.3 and 0.5) on 40 through 64 vertices, both *DEXCH* and *DPRUNE* appear equally good. On most classes of low density (0.1) or small (32 vertices) graphs, *DEXCH* is outperformed by at least one of the other two algorithms. The relative performance of the three algorithms with *DSATUR* normalized at 1.0 is depicted graphically in Figure 4.

References

[1] Brelaz, D.: New methods to color vertices of a graph. *Comm. ACM*, **22**, 4, Apr. 1979, pp251-256.

[2] Garey, M.R. and D.S. Johnson: The complexity of near-optimal graph coloring. *J. ACM*, **23**, 1, Jan. 1976, pp43-49.

[3] Johnson, D.S., C.R. Aragon, L.A. McGeoch and C. Schevon: Optimization by simulated annealing: an experimental evaluation, Part II (graph coloring and number partitioning). *Manuscript*, 1989.

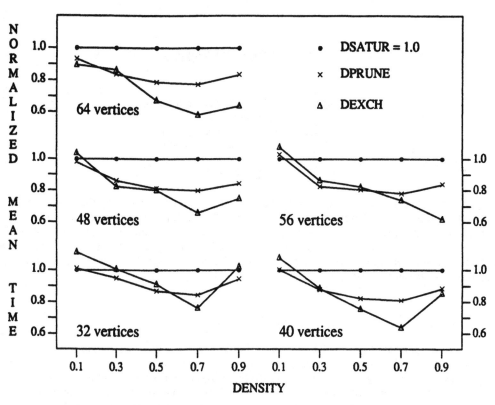

Figure 4: Normalized mean time to find chromatic number.

[4] Johri, A. and D.W. Matula: Probabilistic bounds and heuristic algorithms for coloring large random graphs. *Tech. Rep. 82-CSE-6*, Southern Methodist University, Dallas, Tex., June 1982.

[5] Korman, S.M.: The graph coloring problem. In *Combinatorial Optimization*, Eds. N. Christofides et al., Wiley, New York, 1979, pp211-235.

[6] Kubale, M. and B. Jackowski: A general implicit enumeration algorithm for graph coloring. *Comm. ACM*, **28**, 4, April 1985, pp412-418.

[7] Leighton, F.T.: A graph coloring algorithm for large scheduling problems. *J. Res. Nat. Bur. Standards*, **84**, 6, Nov. 1979, pp489-506.

[8] Park, S.K. and K.W. Miller: Random number generators: good ones are hard to find. *Comm. ACM*, **31**, 10, Oct. 1988, pp1192-1201.

[9] Sager, T.J. and S.J. Lin: An improved exact graph coloring algorithm. *Tech. Rep. CSc-89-1*, University of Missouri-Rolla, Rolla, Missouri, April 1989.

[10] Sager, T.J. and S.J. Lin: A pruning procedure for exact graph coloring. *Tech. Rep. CSc-89-3*, University of Missouri-Rolla, Rolla, Missouri, October 1989.

S-DISTANCE IN TREES

Garry L. Johns*
Department of Mathematical Sciences
Tai-Chi Lee
Department of Computer Science
Saginaw Valley State University

ABSTRACT

For a connected graph G, a subset S of V(G) and vertices u, v of G, the S-distance $d_s(u,v)$ from u to v is the length of a shortest u - v walk in G that contains every vertex of S. The S-eccentricity $e_s(v)$ of a vertex v is the maximum S-distance from v to each vertex of G and the S-diameter $diam_s G$ is the maximum S-eccentricity among the vertices of G. For a tree T, a formula is given for $d_s(u,v)$ and for $S \neq \emptyset$, it is shown that $diam_s T$ is even. Finally, the complexity of finding $d_s(u,v)$ is discussed.

INTRODUCTION

For a connected graph G, a subset S of V(G) and $u,v \in V(G)$, we define a u - v S-walk as a u - v walk in G that contains every vertex of S. The S-distance $d_s(u,v)$ from u to v, is the length of a shortest u - v S-walk. For other graph theory terminology, we follow [1].

These ideas are illustrated in the tree T in Figure 1. We will indicate the vertices of S, here and in the sequel, by shading them. Hence, $S = \{v,x\}$ and a shortest u - v S-walk is W : u, w, x, w, v. The length of W is 4, so $d_s(u,v) = 4$. Similarly, $d_s(u,x) = 4$, $d_s(u,w) = 5$ and $d_s(u,u) = 6$. It is interesting to note that the S-distance from u to itself is greater than the S-distance from u to any other vertex of T. This is not coincidental as we will show later.

Note that the S-distance in a connected graph G is a generalization of distance because $d_s(u,v) = d(u,v)$ for all $u,v \in V(G)$; however, it is not a metric (not even a pseudo-metric) because for the tree in Figure 1, we showed that $d_s(u,u) \neq 0$.

T:

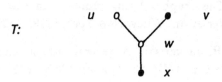

FIGURE 1

The following observations will be used throughout this paper. For $u,v,w \in V(G)$ and $S \subseteq V(G)$:

(a) $d_s(u,v) \geq max\{|S| - 1, 0\}$;

(b) $d_s(u,v) = d_s(v,u)$;   [Symmetry]

(c) if $S \subseteq T \subseteq V(G)$, then $d_s(u,v) \leq d_T(u,v)$;

(d) $d_s(u,v) \leq \begin{cases} d(u,w) + d_s(w,v) \\ d_s(u,w) + d(w,v); \end{cases}$

(e) $d_s(u,v) \leq d_s(u,w) + d_s(w,v)$; and   [Triangle Inequality]

(f) $d_s(u,v) = 0$ if and only if $u = v$ and $S \subseteq \{u\}$.

For each vertex v of a connected graph G with $S \subset V(G)$, we define the S-eccentricity of v as $e_s(v) = max\{d_s(v,u) \,|\, u \in V(G)\}$. Recall that $d(v,v) = 0$; however, as we showed for the tree in Figure 1, $e_s(u) = d_s(u,u) > 0$. For a connected graph G and $S \subset V(G)$, the S-radius of G is $rad_s(G) = min\{e_s(v) \,|\, v \in V(G)\}$ and the S-diameter of G is $diam_s(G) = max\{e_s(v) \,|\, v \in V(G)\}$. Note that if $S = \varnothing$, these definitions give the conventional radius and diameter of G.

It is also natural to define extensions of the center $C(G) = \langle \{v \in V(G) \,|\, e(v) = radG\} \rangle$ and the periphery $Per(G) = \langle \{v \in V(G) \,|\, e(v) = diamG\} \rangle$. For a connected graph G with $S \subset V(G)$, the S-center of G is $C_s(G) = \langle \{v \in V(G) \,|\, e_s(v) = rad_s(G)\} \rangle$ and the S-periphery of G is $Per_s(G) = \langle \{v \in V(G) \,|\, e_s(v) = diam_s(G)\} \rangle$.

S-DISTANCE IN TREES

By focusing our attention on trees, even more can be said about S-distance. The next result was proved in [3]; however, we include it here for completeness.

THEOREM 1. *Let T be a tree with nonempty subset S of V(T) such that every end-vertex of T is in S. Then for every pair u,v of vertices, $d_s(u,v) = 2q(T) - d(u,v)$.*

PROOF: We first show that $d_s(u,v) \geq 2q(T) - d(u,v)$. Let W be a shortest u - v S-walk and let P be the unique u - v path in T. Suppose that e is an edge of P. Since W is a u - v walk, it contains every edge in P; so e appears at least once in W.

Now suppose f is an edge of T that is not in P. Then there exists an end-vertex w of T such that f is on the u-w path P_u in T. Since $w \in S$ and every edge in P_u appears in W, it follows that f occurs at least once in W. If f is also on the v - w path P_v in T, then f occurs at least twice in W. If f is not on P_v then P_u is a u - w path containing f and P followed by P_v is a u - w walk (containing a u - w path) not including f. Hence, T would contain a cycle, which is impossible. Therefore $d_s(u,v) \geq d(u,v) + 2[q(T) - d(u,v)] = 2q(T) - d(u,v)$.

To show that $d_s(u,v) \leq 2q(T) - d(u,v)$, let M be the multigraph formed by duplicating each edge of T that is not on the u - v path P. Now the degree of every vertex is even except for u and v. Hence M contains an eulerian u - v trail of length $2q(T) - d(u,v)$ and the associated u - v walk W in T is an S-walk of length $2q(T) - d(u,v)$. Since $d_s(u,v) \leq 2q(T) - d(u,v)$, we have the desired result. •

An important corollary follows immediately.

COROLLARY 1A. *Let T be a tree with a nonempty subset S of V(T) such that every end-vertex of T is in S. Then for every vertex v, the S-eccentricity $e_s(v) = d_s(v,v) = 2q(T)$.*

Theorem 1 can be extended to all trees with the help of the next lemma. To do this we first define for a tree T and a nonempty subset S of V(T), the tree T_s generated by S as the smallest subtree of T containing every vertex of S. It is useful to note that every end-vertex of T_s is a vertex of S and for each vertex u in T there exists a unique vertex u' of T_s satisfying $d(u,u') = min\{d(u,w) \,|\, w \in V(T_s)\}$.

LEMMA 2. *Let T be a tree with a nonempty subset S of V(T). For every pair u,v of vertices in T_s, the S-distance $d_s(u,v) = 2q(T_s) - d(u,v)$.*

PROOF: Let W be a shortest u - v S-walk in T. Suppose that e is an edge in W that is not in $E(T_s)$. Then at least one of the vertices, say w, incident with e is not in $V(T_s)$; otherwise, T would contain a cycle. Let x be the last vertex in T_s that precedes w on W and let y be the first vertex in T_s that follows w on W. Now $x = y$. For if not, then T contains an x - y path in T_s and an x - y path passing through w that is not in T_s. Hence T contains a cycle. Now a shorter u - v S-walk W' can be formed from W by removing the edges between x and w and those between w and y. However, this contradicts the minimality of W. Therefore, every edge of W is in $E(T_s)$. Since Theorem 11 applies to T_s, it follows that $d_s(u,v) = 2q(T_s) - d(u,v)$. •

We are now ready to give a formula for $d_s(u,v)$ for every pair u,v of vertices in a tree T with a nonempty subset of S of $V(T)$.

THEOREM 3. *Let T be a tree with a nonempty subset S of $V(T)$. For every pair u,v of vertices, define vertices u', v' of T_s such that $d(u,u') = min\{d(u,w)\,|w \in V(T_s)\}$ and $d(v,v') = min$ $\{d(v,w)\,|w \in V(T_s)\}$. Then $d_s(u,v) = d_s(u,u') + d(v,v') + 2q(T_s) - d(u',v')$.*

PROOF: Let W be a shortest u - v S-walk in T. Let w be the first vertex of T_s on W and let x be the last vertex of T_s on W. Then
$$d_s(u,v) = d(u,w) + d_s(w,x) + d(x,v).$$
If $u \in V(T_s)$ then $u = w = u'$. For $u \notin V(T_s)$ suppose $w \neq u'$. Then there exists a w - u' path in T_s and a w - u' path passing through u that is not in T_s. Thus, T would have a cycle; a contradiction. Therefore, $w = u'$ and by a similar argument, $x = v'$. Finally, by Lemma 2 we have $d_s(w,x) = 2q(T_s) - d(w,x)$, so $d_s(u,v) = d(u,u') + d(v,v') + 2q(T_s) - d(u',v')$. •

We can now give two results on the S-diameter for trees.

THEOREM 4. *Let T be a tree with a nonempty subset S of $V(T)$. If vertices u,v satisfy $d_s(u,v) = diam_s(T)$, where possibly $u = v$, then $e_s(u) = d_s(u,u) = diam_s(T)$ and $e_s(v) = d_s(v,v) = diam_s(T)$.*

PROOF: By Theorem 3, there exist vertices u' and v' in T_s such that $d(u,u') = min\{d(u,w)\,|w \in T_s\}$ and $d(v,v') = min\{d(v,w)\,|w \in T_s\}$ and such that
$$d_s(u,u) = 2d(u,u') + 2q(T_s) \text{ and}$$
$$d_s(v,v) = 2d(v,v') + 2q(T_s).$$
Suppose that $d_s(u,u) < d_s(u,v)$. Then, because $d_s(u,v) = d(u,u') + 2q(T_s) - d(u',v') + d(v',v)$, we have $d(u,u') < d(v,v') - d(u',v')$. This implies that $d(u,u') + d(u',v') < d(v,v')$, and by the triangle inequality, $d(u,v') < d(v,v')$.

Similarly, if $d_s(v,v) < d_s(u,v)$ then $d(v,u') < d(u,u')$. Thus, suppose that $d_s(u,u) < d_s(u,v)$ and $d_s(v,v) < d_s(u,v)$. Since $d(u,u') < d(u,v')$ and $d(v,v') < d(v,u')$, we have
$$d(u,v') < d(v,v') < d(v,u') < d(u,u') < d(u,v'),$$
which is a contradiction. Therefore, either $e_s(u) = d_s(u,u) = diam_s(T)$ or $e_s(v) = d_s(v,v) = diam_s(T)$.

Without loss of generality, suppose that $d_s(u,v) = e_s(u) = diam_s(T)$. We show next that $e_s(v) = diam_s(T)$ also. Assume, to the contrary, that $d_s(v,v) < d_s(u,u) = diam_s(T)$. Then since $d_s(v,v) = 2d(v,v') + 2q(T_s) < d_s(u,u) = 2d(u,u') + 2q(T_s)$, we have $d(v,v') < d(u,u')$. However, since $d_s(u,u) = diam_s(T) = d_s(u,v)$ we have, by Theorem 3 and the above remark, $2d(u,u') + 2q(T_s) = d(u,u') + 2q(T_s) - d(u',v') + d(v',v)$. This implies that $d(u,u') = d(v,v') - d(v',u') \leq d(v,v')$, giving a contradition. Therefore, $e_s(u) = d_s(u,u) = diam_s(T)$ and $e_s(T) = d_s(v,v) = diam_s(T)$. •

We can now state an immediate corollary.

COROLLARY 4A. *For a tree T and a nonempty subset S of V(T), there exists a vertex v of T such that $e_s(v) = d_s(v,v) = diam_s(T)$.*

The next result follows easily.

COROLLARY 4B. *For a tree T and a nonempty subset S of V(T), the S-diameter of T is always even.*

PROOF: Let u be a vertex of T such that $d_s(u,u) = diam_s(T)$ and let u' be the vertex in T_s such that $d(u,u') = min\{d(u,w) \,|\, w \in T_s\}$. Then
$$d_s(u,u) = 2d(u,u') + 2q(T_s)$$
and $diam_s(T)$ is even. •

We conclude this section with two results that relate $C_s(T)$ and $Per_s(T)$ to T_s. In Corollary 1A, we saw that it is possible for $T_{V(C_s(T))}$ and T_s to be the same; however, this is not always the case. For example, in the tree T in Figure 2, if $S = \{v,w,z\}$, then $T_s = \langle\{v,w,x,z\}\rangle$ and $T_{V(C_s(T))} = \langle\{v,x,z\}\rangle$. This leads to our next result.

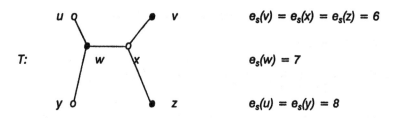

$$e_s(v) = e_s(x) = e_s(z) = 6$$
$$e_s(w) = 7$$
$$e_s(u) = e_s(y) = 8$$

Figure 2

THEOREM 5. *Let T be a tree and let S be a nonempty subset of V(T). If $V = V(C_s(T))$, then $T_V \subset T_s$.*

PROOF: Since every subtree of a given tree T' is an induced subgraph of T', it follows that $T_V \subset T_s$ only if there exists an end-vertex v of T_V that is not in $V(T_s)$. Since every end-vertex of T_V is in $V = V(C_s(T))$, suppose that $v \in V$ and $v \notin V(T_s)$. Let v' be the vertex of T_s such that $d(v,v') = min\{d(v,w) \,|\, w \in V(T_s)\}$. For every vertex v of T, the S-distance $d_s(v,u) = d(v,v') + d_s(v',u)$. Thus, $e_s(v) > e_s(v') \geq rad_s(T)$ and so, $v \notin V(C_s(T))$ which is a contradiction. Thus, $T_V \subset T_s$. •

Finally, for a tree T and a nonempty subset S of $V(T)$, we can use T_s to classify those vertices of T that are in $Per_s(T)$.

THEOREM 6. *Let T be a tree and let S be a nonempty subset of V(T) that does not include every end-vertex of T. A vertex v of T is in $Per_s(T)$ if and only if v is an end-vertex of T such that $d(v,T_s) = max\{d(w,T_s) \,|\, w \in V(T)\}$.*

PROOF: First, let v be a vertex of $Per_s(T)$. Then there exists a vertex v' in $V(T_s)$ such that $d(v,v') = min\{d(v,w) \,|\, w \in V(T_s)\}$ and by Theorem 4, the S-distance $d_s(v,v) = 2d(v,v') + 2q(T_s) = diam_s(T)$. Suppose that v is not an end-vertex of T. Then there exists a vertex u adjacent to v with $d(u,v') = d(v,v') + 1$. However, then $d_s(u,u) = 2d(u,v') + 2q(T_s) = 2 + 2d(v,v') + 2q(T_s) > diam_s(T)$, which is impossible. Now, suppose that $d(v,T_s) < d(w,T_s)$ for some vertex

w of G. Then $diam_s(T) = d_s(v,v) = 2d(v,T_s) + 2q(T_s) < 2d(w,T_s) + 2q(T_s) = d_s(w,w) \leq diam_s(T)$, but this is a contradiction. Therefore, if $v \in V(Per_s(T))$ then v is an end-vertex of T such that $d(v,T_s) = max\{d(w,T_s) | w \in V(T)\}$.

For the converse, let v be an end-vertex of T such that $d(v,T_s) = max\{d(w,T_s) | w \in V(T)\}$ and let u be a vertex in $Per_s(T)$. We know that $diam_s(T) = 2d(u,T_s) + 2q(T_s) \leq 2d(v,T_s) + 2q(T_s) = d_s(v,v) \leq diam_s(T)$. Therefore, $v \in V(Per_s(T))$.   •

COMPLEXITY OF COMPUTING S-DISTANCE

Although the problem of finding $d_s(u,v)$ for vertices u and v and nonempty set S in an arbitrary graph is difficult, the complexity for computing $d_s(u,v)$ in a tree with p vertices is $O(p^2)$. This follows from the algorithm below which uses the breadth-first search (BFS) algorithm to find the shortest paths [2].

Algorithm

Input   The tree T (as an adjacency matrix, edge list or adjacency listing).
             The nonempty set S of specified vertices. Vertices u and v.

Output $d_s(u,v)$ (i.e. a number for the S-distance from u and v).

Step 1.   Let $T_o = T$ and $i=0$.

Step 2.   Remove one end-vertex w from T_i that is not in S (deg $w = 1$). Let $i=i+1$ and $T_i = T_{i-1} - w$. Go to Step 2.

Step 3.   If every end-vertex of T_i is in S let V be the set of remaining vertices and let $q(T_s) = |V| - 1$.

Step 4.   Use BFS to find $d(u,w)$ for every w in V. Label the vertex w closest to u by u'.

Step 5.   Use BFS to find $d(v,w)$ for every $w \in V$. Label the vertex w closest to v by v'.

Step 6.   Use BFS to find $d(u',v')$.

Step 7.   Let $d_s(u,v) = d(u,u') + d(v,v') - d(u',v') + 2q(T_s)$.

Steps 1-3 find T_s in at most $O(p^2)$ time where Step 2 dominates while searching for the end-vertices. This search is bounded above by checking the p vertices p times. Steps 4-6 compute the distances using BFS which is known to be $O(p^2)$. Hence the entire algorithm can be completed in $O(p^2)$ time.

REFERENCES

1.   G. Chartrand and L. Lesniak, *Graphs and Digraphs, 2nd Edition*. Wadsworth and Brooks/Cole, Monterey, CA (1986).
2.   J. Dossey, A. Otto, L. Spence, C. VanderEynder, *Discrete Mathematics*. Scott, Foresman and Co., Glenview, IL (1987).
3.   G. Johns, *S-distance in graphs*. Submitted for publication.

Algorithms on Block-Complete Graphs

Zhuguo Mo
Computer & Engineering Services, Inc.
Kenneth Williams
Western Michigan University

Abstract. *Graphs whose blocks are complete subgraphs are said to be block-complete graphs. Polynomial time algorithms to solve several problems, problems which are not believed to be polynomial for general graphs, are presented for connected block-complete graphs. These include: finding a minimum vertex cover, finding a minimum dominating set of radius r, and finding a minimum m-centrix radius r augmentation.*

1. Introduction

Definitions follow [1]. A nontrivial connected graph with no cut-vertices is said to be a *block*. A *block of a graph* G is a subgraph of G which is maximal with respect to the block property. The class of graphs whose blocks are complete subgraphs is denoted by β_c. Graphs in β_c are called *block-complete graphs*.

A graph H of order n is complete if and only if H has $n(n-1)/2$ edges. Thus the completeness of a graph can be determined in linear time. Therefore, given a graph G and a block B of G, the completeness of the block B can be determined in linear time. Hopcroft and Tarjan [3] have proved that the components of a graph and the blocks of a connected graph $G = (V, E)$ can be found in linear time $O(|E| + |V|)$. Thus we have:

Theorem 1.1 There is a linear time algorithm which recognizes the class β_c of graphs. $\qquad\qquad\qquad\Box$

Since each block in a forest is either K_1 or K_2, the class of forests is a proper subclass of β_c. A *triangulated graph* is a graph which does not contain a cycle of length at least four as an induced subgraph. It is clear that β_c is also a proper subclass of the class of triangulated graphs.

We will consider the following decision problems:

Vertex Cover

Instance: Graph $G=(V,E)$, positive integer $k \leq |V|$.
Question: Is there a vertex cover of size k or less for G, i.e. a subset V' of V with $|V'| \leq k$ such that for each edge uv in E at least one of u and v belongs to V'?

Dominating Set of Radius r

Instance: Graph $G=(V,E)$, positive integers r, $k \leq |V|$.
Question: Is there a dominating set of radius r with size k or less for G, i.e. a subset V' of V with $|V'| \leq k$ such that for all u in $V-V'$ there is a v in V' for which $d(v,u) \leq r$?

m-Centrix Radius r Augmentation

Instance: Graph $G=(V,E)$, non-empty subset C of V called an m-centrix with $|C|=m$, positive integers k and r.
Question: Is there a set E' of unordered pairs of vertices from V such that $|E'| \leq k$ and for the graph $G'=(V, E \cup E')$, $d_{G'}(C,v) \leq r$ for all v in V?

It is shown in Garey and Johnson [2] that the vertex cover problem is NP-complete. It is shown in Mo [5] that the dominating set of radius r problem and the m-centrix problem are NP-complete. In each case the corresponding computational problem (i.e. finding, respectively, a minimum vertex cover, a minimum dominating set of radius r and a minimum m-centrix radius r augmentation) is NP-hard.

2. Vertex cover

We know that the vertex cover number for the complete graph K_n is $\alpha(K_n) = n-1$. Algorithm 2.1 finds a minimum vertex cover U in an arbitrary connected block-complete graph G using a technique developed in Kariv and Hakimi [4]. The algorithm is carried out through a search on the blocks of G, starting from the end-blocks and moving toward the "middle." During this search, we locate the vertices of the desired vertex cover set in an "optimal fashion" until all edges in the graph are covered by some minimum set of vertices.

Algorithm 2.1 Finds a minimum vertex cover U in a connected block-complete graph G.

1) $G' \leftarrow G$; $U \leftarrow \emptyset$
2) while G' is not complete loop
3)   Find an end-block B of G'.
4)   Let v be the cut-vertex of B in G'.
5)   if $(|V(B) \cap U| < |V(B)| - 1)$ then
6)   Select a vertex, say u, in $V(B) - \{U \cup \{v\}\}$.
7) $U \leftarrow U \cup \{V(B) - \{u\}\}$
8)   end if
9) $G' \leftarrow G' - \{V(B) - \{v\}\}$
10) end loop
    /* At this point, G' is a complete graph */
11) if $(|U \cap V(G')| < |V(G')| - 1)$ then
12)   Find a set, say W, consisting of $|V(G')| - 1 - |U \cap V(G')|$ vertices in $V(G') - U$.
13) $U \leftarrow U \cup W$
14) end if
end Algorithm 2.1

Theorem 2.1 Algorithm 2.1 finds a minimum vertex cover U in a connected block-complete graph G.

Proof: If G is a complete graph of order n, then $|U| = |V(G)| - 1$ by steps 11 to 13. So we assume that G is not complete. An end-block B is found with cut vertex v.

If $|V(B) \cap U| \geq |V(B)| - 1$, then all edges in the block B are already covered by vertices in the vertex cover which have been located so far, so there is no need to select vertices of B into U. Otherwise, $|V(B)| - 1 - |V(B) \cap U|$ additional vertices of B must be added to U. By steps 11 to 13, the vertex that is not selected into U is not the cut-vertex v of B. This implies that the number of new vertices selected into U is required and the set of vertices selected is "optimal". □

3. Minimum dominating set of radius r

The following linear time algorithm finds a minimum dominating set of radius r, U, in an arbitrary connected block-complete graph G. The process is carried out through a search on the blocks of G, starting from the end-blocks and moving toward the "middle." During this search, we locate the vertices of the desired dominating set of radius r in an "optimal fashion" until all vertices in the graph are dominated by vertices in U within distance r. To do this, we use a copy G' of the original graph as an auxiliary graph on which the algorithm is carried out, and we attach two variables $C(v)$ and $R(v)$ to each vertex v of G'. $C(v)$ is a boolean variable which has value TRUE if v is already dominated (within distance r) by some vertex in U has value FALSE otherwise. (The interpretation of $R(v)$ will be given later.) If B is an end-block of the auxiliary graph G' and v_c is the cut-vertex of B in G', then we update the variables $C(v_c)$ and $R(v_c)$ and remove all vertices in $V(B) - v_c$ (and incident edges) from G'. As a result, a new block may become an end-block of G', and the process is repeated until the graph G' becomes a complete graph. Then an appropriate set of vertices is added to U if necessary.

The variable $R(v)$ has the following interpretation (based on $C(v)$):

Case 1: If the vertex v is already dominated by one of the vertices in U which have been located so far, then $R(v)$ is the distance between v and the nearest located vertex in U.

Case 2: If the vertex is not yet dominated, then let $S(v)$ be the set of all the vertices of the original graph G which are not yet dominated, and for which v is the nearest vertex in the auxiliary graph G'. Notice that v is the only vertex in $S(v)$ which belongs to G'; in fact, $S(v)$ is the set consisting of the vertex v and all those vertices which have already been removed from G' and are to be dominated by the same vertex of the dominating set of radius r as v. $R(v) = \max \{d_G(u, v) \mid u \in S(v)\}$.

Algorithm 3.1 Finds a minimum dominating set of radius r for a connected block-complete graph G.

1) $G' \leftarrow G$; $U \leftarrow \emptyset$
   for each vertex v in G' loop
2) $C(v) \leftarrow$ FALSE; $R(v) \leftarrow 0$
   end loop
3) while (G' is not complete) loop
4)   Find an end-block B in G'.

5)   Let v_c be the cut-vertex of B in G'.

/* For convenience, define min $\{R(v) \mid v \in \emptyset\} = r + 1$ and max $\{R(v) \mid v \in \emptyset\} = 0$ */

$R_t \leftarrow$ min $\{R(v) \mid v \in V(B)$ and $C(v) =$ TRUE$\}$

$R_f \leftarrow$ max $\{R(v) \mid v \in V(B)$ and $C(v) =$ FALSE$\}$

$R' \leftarrow$ min $\{R(v) \mid v(\neq v_c) \in V(B)$ and $C(v) =$ TRUE$\}$

$R'' \leftarrow$ max $\{R(v) \mid v(\neq v_c) \in V(B)$ and $C(v) =$ FALSE$\}$

/* Update $C(v_c)$ and $R(v_c)$ */

6)   if $C(v_c)$ then

            if $(R_t + R_f + 1 \le r$) then

                $R(v_c) \leftarrow$ min $\{R' + 1, R(v_c)\}$

           else $C(v_c) \leftarrow$ FALSE; $R(v_c) \leftarrow R'' + 1$

          end if

       else   if $(R_t + R_f + 1 \le r$) then

                $C(v_c) \leftarrow$ TRUE; $R(v_c) \leftarrow R' + 1$

              else $R(v_c) \leftarrow$ max $\{R'' + 1, R(v_c)\}$

           end if

7)   end if

/* Select vertex into U in an optimal way */

8)   if $(C(v_c) =$ FALSE) and $(R(v_c) = r)$ then

             $U \leftarrow U \cup \{v_c\}$; $C(v_c) \leftarrow$ TRUE; $R(v_c) \leftarrow 0$

9)   end if

/* $R(v_c) = r + 1$ only if $C(v_c) =$ TRUE */

10)   if $(R(v_c) = r + 1)$ then

             $C(v_c) \leftarrow$ FALSE; $R(v_c) \leftarrow 0$

11)   end if

         $G' \leftarrow G' - \{V(B) - \{v_c\}\}$

end loop

12) $R_t \leftarrow$ min $\{R(v) \mid v \in V(G')$ and $C(v) =$ TRUE$\}$

      $R_f \leftarrow$ max $\{R(v) \mid v \in V(G')$ and $C(v) =$ FALSE$\}$

      if $(R_t + R_f \ge r$) then

           Select a vertex u in G'; $U \leftarrow U \cup \{u\}$

13) end if

end Algorithm 3.1

Theorem 3.1 Algorithm 3.1 finds a minimum dominating set of radius r in an (unweighted) connected block-complete graph G in linear time $O(|E| + |V|)$.

Proof: Steps 1 and 2 initialize G', U, C(v), and R(v) for v ∈ V(G'). The interpretations for these symbols have already been given. If G is a complete graph, then steps 12 to 13 find a desired set U. Suppose that G is not complete. Steps 4 and 5 find a block in G' with cut-vertex v_c. In is easy to verify that the if statement from steps 6 to 7 updates the two variables $C(v_c)$ and $R(v_c)$ correctly. Steps 8 to 9 select vertex into U in an "optimal fashion". The if statement from steps 10 to step 11 resets $C(v_c)$ and $R(v_c)$ since the vertex v_c is not yet dominated. Finally, steps 12 to 13 handle the resulting complete graph. □

It can be seen that the time complexity of Algorithm 3. 1 is $O(|E|+|V|)$.

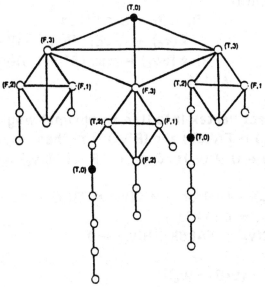

Figure 3. 1 - Example for Algorithm 3. 1 (r = 4)

4. m-Centrix radius r augmentation

Algorithm 4. 1

Given a block-complete graph G = (V, E) with m-centrix C = {$c_1, c_2, \ldots, c_m$} ⊆ V, and positive integer r. This algorithm finds a minimum m-centrix radius r augmentation of G.

(1)   Find the set V_1 = {v ∈ V | $d_G(C, v)$ ≤ r} , $V_2 = V - V_1$
        and H = the subgraph of G induced by V_2

(2)   If $r = 1$, $E' = \{c_1v \mid v \in V_2\}$ is a desired set of edges then go
            to step 5
(3)   /* Let the components of H be C_1, C_2, ..., C_k. The
            blocks of C_i are complete, $1 \leq i \leq k$.   */
            For each component C_i of H , use Algorithm 3.1 to find
                    a minimum dominating set, U_i, of radius r in H
(4) $U \leftarrow \cup \{U_i \mid 1 \leq i \leq k\}$
            $E' = \{c_1v \mid v \in U\}$ is a desired set of edges
(5)   Stop
end Algorithm 4.1

It is easy to see that algorithm 4.1 finds a minimum m-
centrix radius r augmentation of block-complete graph G in
polynomial time.

5. Summary
It is known that for arbitrary graphs, finding a minimum
vertex cover, finding a minimum dominating set of radius r and
finding a minimum m-centrix radius r augmentation are all NP-hard
problems and the corresponding decision problems are NP-
complete. For block-complete graphs, algorithms have been
presented here to solve each of these problems in polynomial time.

Bibliography

[1]   G. Chartrand and L. Lesniak, Graphs and Digraphs, Second
      Edition, Wadsworth & Brooks/Cole, 1986.

[2]   M. R. Garey and D. S. Johnson, Computers and
      Intractability: A Guide to the Theory of NP-Completeness,
      W. H. Freeman, San Francisco (1979).

[3]   J. E. Hopcroft and R. E. Tarjan, Efficient algorithms for
      graph manipulation, Comm. ACM, 16 (1973) 372-378.

[4]   O. Kariv and S. L. Hakimi, An algorithmic approach to
      network location problems. I: The p-centers. SIAM J.
      Appl. Math. 37 (1979) 513-538.

[5]   Z. Mo, Graph and Directed Graph Augmentation Problems,
      Doctoral Dissertation, Western Michigan University, 1988.

HEURISTIC-BASED LEARNING

Stuart H. Rubin
Central Michigan University

Abstract. *Knowledge-based systems are becoming increasingly model oriented. Models enable the system a deeper understanding - something which is impractical to attain when all the system has are rules. Furthermore, it has become apparent that knowledge representations must become increasingly domain-specific in order to facilitate more sophisticated problem solving. The task of automating the solution of sophisticated problems in turn implies the use of analogic reasoning towards the goal of automatic knowledge acquisition.*

The approach taken here is to investigate new machine learning algorithms focusing on lateral model-based transformative induction methods similar to Quinlan's ID3 and Michalski's AQ algorithms - except that models are the generalized object(s) rather than simply decision trees or rules.

Keywords: Case-based reasoning, distributed computation, machine learning, transformation

1. Introduction - The Knowledge Acquisition Bottleneck

The problem concerning us here stems from the basic need to increase engineering productivity; more precisely, the central issue concerns providing for the further automation of the knowledge acquisition task in intelligent systems. Previous attempts along these lines all shared limited results. It is now known that the early machine learning algorithms incurred the deficiency of not including an operational model of the target domain. (Note: Prior algorithms such as GPS failed for the most part because they did not incorporate domain-specific problem-solving heuristics as well.)

Classical AI techniques for problem solving and planning often require extraordinary amounts of search in order to produce solutions for even moderately complex problems. The difficulty seems to lie in that the techniqes do not get smarter with exercise. This is in contradiction with our day-to-day experience.

Funding for this project was provided by the Office of Naval Technology (ONT) Postdoctoral Fellowship Program, Projects Office, ASEE, 11 Dupont Circle, Suite 200, Washington, DC 20036

Carbonell [4] has identified four major machine learning paradigms. They are:

1) Inductive learning (e.g., the data-intensive acquisition of concepts from sets of positive and negative examples)

2) Analytic learning (e.g., explanation-based learning and certain forms of analogical and case-based learning methods which are knowledge-intensive)

3) Genetic algorithms (e.g., classifier systems) and

4) Connectionist learning methods (e.g., nonrecurrent "backprop" hidden layer neural networks)

2.   Analogical Induction

Analogical induction can make inroads towards solving the knowledge acquisition bottleneck. Some more details pertaining to it are given below. Moreover, the improvement in learning efficiency is expected to be competitive with Explanation-Based Learning (EBL) - an analytic knowledge-intensive domain-general approach for the optimization of control rule sets through adaptive heuristic search [15, 18] where there is a rich underlying domain theory.

Briefly, EBL produces a learned description which is a domain independent disjunctive generalization of a given training example. The learned description is incrementally refined until it just covers each ordered training example [13]. In EBL, a pre-existing target concept is used to generate a complete generalization as soon as an example is encountered. These systems typically learn a knowledge structure that is used to improve the efficiency of a problem solver. For example, Bruynooghe [2] has developed an EBL method for explanation-based program transformation which can introduce new predicates and consequently can modify the structure of the prooftree.

Systems which perform analogical reasoning can be divided into two general categories - those for which the domain theory is incomplete and those which use analogy to speed up the derivation of a solution [7, 9, 10, 15]. If the domain theory is incomplete, then it is because deductive reasoning is incomplete - leaving open the possibility of augmenting the domain using transformative operations acting upon a similar domain. If such augmentation can be shown to render the domain theory complete, then the operating model - which includes the target domain - is said to be closed; otherwise it is said to be open. Closed models can utilize a theorem prover in order to deduce new facts [6, 11].

It should be noted that while an explanation may exist in principle in a closed model, finding it may take too long in practice; that is, the domain theory may be intractable. For example, the rules of chess form a complete theory of the game, but trying to prove that P-K4 belongs to the class of winning moves might take longer than the lifetime of the universe [16].

Veloso and Carbonell [22] have recently introduced a method in which the system evolves through experience from an initial random perception of its knowledge to an increasingly more adequate distribution. The method employs self-adjusting data structures for storing the acquired experience (including two simple heuristics) and is currently being implemented as an extension to the PRODIGY problem solving system.

3. Selecting A Transformative Method

Analogical reasoning is justifiable if the time required to solve a problem using a transformative method is much less than the time required to solve the same problem using a direct problem-solving method such as logical deduction (i.e., as in the predicate calculus) [10]. The time taken to solve a problem using analogy depends upon the time required to find the relevant analogous cases and the time required to derive the transformational maps. Solving a problem using direct problem-solving techniques such as resolution theorem-proving requires search through a knowledge base of rules (including facts).

It can hence be concluded that transformative methods constitute a useful supplemental problem-solving methodology where the problem to be solved is complex - requiring search through many rules for its solution and highly similar problems have been previously encountered and saved in a case-based memory. The ardent reader may wish to refer to Harandi and Bhansali [10] for some equations which suggest these results. Note that direct problem-solving techniques may be combined with analogical reasoning in order to find the solution of a problem as efficiently as possible.

A connection machine is ideal for the storage and retrieval of cases in as much as matching operations and the search for transformative maps can proceed with fine-grained parallelism. Cases for which the solutions were computationally costly (i.e., in space-time) to discover and for which the similarity (under transformation) with all previous problems is low (reducing the redundancy in the knowledge base) should be stored in the knowledge base.

4. Model-Based Transformation

Most analogy systems are based on a solution transformation method [6, 11]. These systems blindly transform the solution of a problem, guided by some heuristics, until it satisfies the requirements of the new problem [10]. Although this method works in some domains, the result is often inefficient and hence unacceptable in complex domains.

Carbonell [3] describes a derivational transformational method which saves and later replays the derivational traces of similar past problems and where necessary the operator sequences (and their subgoal structure) are modified to construct a solution to a similar new problem. The key notion is to reconstruct the relevant aspects of past problem-solving situations and thereby transfer knowledge to the new scenario, where that knowledge consists of decision sequences and their justifications rather than individual declarative assertions [14]. Unlike EBL methods, the operator sequences are not generalized before they are stored. Rather, a similarity metric is used to match explanations (or partial explanations) that are generated for each example. The increased efficiency of the result is dependent upon the transformation of similar cases which are stored in a knowledge base. That is, increases in efficiency positively correlate with increases in the magnitude of the domain-specific knowledge base.

Porter [20] argues that for many domains of interest (e.g., law, medicine), domain theory is too weak to compute similarity metrics. Hence, extensive domain-specific knowledge, including past cases of similarity assessment, is required. He further concludes that the knowledge base requirements for many domains have been grossly underestimated.

As a simplistic example, consider a rule for the game of chess which computes some aspect of the game tree to n-ply for a relatively large value of n. Further suppose that this rule is appropriate to apply to an end-game decision.

Now, suppose that the above rule is to be modified using a solution transformation method so as to apply to a mid-game decision. Unless this method gets lucky and reduces the magnitude of n by chance, the result will certainly prove to be inefficient and perhaps even intractable! A derivational transformational method avoids this difficulty by recording the relation between n and the rule for which it is slotted. Case-based reasoning can then lead to a reduction in the magnitude of n as desired.

5. The Derivational Transformation Method

The derivational transformation method [3] starts with the system making a heuristic selection of the most similar problem to the current problem - initially the root of a tree (which will be recursively traversed depth-first until it comes to a node for which the stored case is not a solution under the operation of simple transformation). If the stored case is in fact synonomous with the current sub-problem, then the solution has been found.

Otherwise, the system tries to generate a solution by transformation of another previous solution. This is termed reasoning from first principles in model-based reasoning.

If a previous solution cannot be found, then using the rules in the knowledge-base, the system reduces the current problem into a hierarchy of sub-problems and proceeds to solve them recursively. There may be several ways to decompose a problem, and the alternative versions are tested for solution in turn. Moreover, the method checks that the sub-problem solutions do not interact destructively. The solutions are re-ordered if necessary. If a problem solution is not thus attained, then the algorithm attempts another decomposition and/or backtracks. If this in turn fails, then user assistance is requested.

6. The Genetic Transformation Method

The genetic transformation method [21] extends a given rule-set(s) through the use of crossover operators and selection functions. This method is under the control of meta-rules - also subject to symmetric genetic transformations - and their collective actions are termed *pumping*. It is similar in principle to the mechanism for effecting parametric substitution in any function, procedure, or subroutine invocation as appropriate. In fact, parametric substitution is a special case of pumping.

One advantage of using meta-rules is that each transformation is understandable in isolation. If the results of the transformation are successful, then the rule is saved in the knowledge base and the antecedent of the applied meta-rule(s) are made more general (if possible) in an attempt to increase the extent of future successes. Otherwise, the antecedent of the applied meta-rule(s) are made more specific (if possible) in an attempt to avoid future errors. That is, the meta-rule base evolves meta-knowledge for constraining the search for a solution through the use of *version spaces* [17].

Moreover, it is anticipated that version spaces will find use in the automatic refinement of a heuristic-based control mechanism. The evidence strongly suggests that sets of domain-specific rules should be decomposed into a hierarchy of sub-domains - each of which shares a common characterization. Hence, heuristic search is to be partitioned.

A similar knowledge intensive system called KATE^{TM} is described by Manago [12]. It applies a slightly modified version space theory to the ID3 architecture. The resulting system uses slots in frames in lieu of ID3 attributes.

7.   Discovering Analogies

Transformations can be automatically searched out and effected without guidance from the user. This is where heuristic knowledge comes into play. Heuristics serve to guide the model to transform a 'closest' model based upon some similarity metric. Note that the similarity metric may itself be a sub-model. More formally, the definition of the heuristic model is such that it minimize the s-norm of the map π applied to model M defined by:

minimize $\| \pi \|_s$, where $\pi(M_i) \rightarrow M_j$ for all models i,j in the search space such that i≠j.

It is noted that the validity of the map π can be verified if the system is deductively closed under the rules in the knowledge base (i.e., even without analogy, it would have been possible to arrive at the solution). In this case the soundness of the system is assured, although many novel and elegant solutions will have necessarily been eliminated in view of the essential incompleteness of any formal deductive method. It is mentioned here because using this transformational method to speedup a deductive method provides fertile ground for some new approaches to EBL [5, 6, 11].

8.   The Functional Compression Heuristic

Consider the case of two defined similar rules having respective slots s_{1i} and s_{2i} in common or as instantiations of more general abstract slots. If these occurrences can be heuristically detected, then the corresponding slots s_{1i} and s_{2i} can be combined (i.e., through parametization and/or transformation) and represented as instantiations of more general slots in an object-oriented abstraction hierarchy or compression tree. Such a tree has the advantage that it may be instantiated in ways outside the scope of its derivation, leading to the induction of hypothetical rules based upon equivalence classes under the instantiation operation.

9.   The Systematicity Heuristic

The 'order' of a relation in a rule can be defined as follows: Constants are of order zero. The order of a predicate is one plus the maximum of the order of its arguments. Gentner [8] proposed a "systematicity principle" (i.e., heuristic) which can be interpreted to mean that if the input and output arguments of two rules are related by the same abstract relationship, then the two rules are more likely to be analogous.

According to Harandi and Bhansali [10], in order to detect analogous problems based on the systematicity heuristic, the system must determine and match the highest order relation from two presented problems (i.e., rules). If they belong to the same abstract relation, then the corresponding arguments of the relation have to be matched recursively until the zero-order relations are matched. An example using the following two rules (and pre-defined predicates / functions and objects adapted from the game of chess) should prove useful (note that users may define new predicates / functions and/or objects too):

R1: ... CONDITION: (And (Attack queen king) (> (value king) (value queen))) ...
R2: ... CONDITION: (And (Attack rook pawn) (< (value rook) (value pawn))) ...

Here, > and < are instantiations of the abstract relation 'comparison'. Hence, it follows that the above two rule antecedents can be viewed as instances of the following third-order relation:

(Rel3 (Rel1B (Rel0 Rel0)) (Rel2 (Rel1A (Rel0)) (Rel1A (Rel0))))

Thus, according to the systematicity heuristic, the two rules may be analogous.

10. The Genetic Heuristic

Genetic or syntactic similarity can be used to suggest that two rules are equivalent under the operation of transformation (i.e., analogous). For example, borrowing some of the terminology of molecular genetics, suppose that corresponding rule slots exhibit the complementary strands: ACTGTAGA and TGACATCT where the bases A,C,G,T denote appropriate elemental attributes. Note that two consecutive bases (or nucleotides) here form a codon or higher-order attribute. Discovering the two complementary base pairings; namely, A-T and G-C, enables the domain theory for say the partial strand TG?CAT?T to be completed as shown.

11. Ranking the Heuristics

In general, each of the above heuristics (and more may be discovered) will suggest several and probably different rule analogies. Thus, the order of search becomes of paramount concern. Again, it is desirable to learn to improve search efficiency here.

According to the results of Harandi and Bhansali [10], the systematicity heuristic may very well be the most important. Hence, it will be tried first in any serial search paradigm. Next in line comes the functional compression heuristic. The power of this heuristic comes from its capability to compress common rules through their parametization and/or transformation. Of similar power is the genetic heuristic since it functions like an associative neural memory and thus renders the system far less brittle (i.e., similar to a neural network in at least this respect).

In all cases, the more domain-specific heuristics are given precedence over the more general heuristics in determining the order of search where applicable. This is because 'strong' methods are preferable to 'weak' methods where available.

12. Conclusion

This line of pursuit will likely expedite the construction of a robot which learns to improve its performance over time, advance the state of the art of learning to program by analogy in the LISP language, facilitate the diagnosis of multiple simultaneous faults in model-based systems, et. al. The research also impacts upon the ability of the Navy to develop more powerful heuristic methods for target identification, target motion analysis, and contact / track correlation [19].

The development of more powerful and robust methods for transformative induction could also facilitate the exploratory research process and thereby indirectly lead to the development of an intelligent assistant. Several researchers at MIT and Princeton University have published on the utility of such an engineering assistant [1].

Acknowledgements

The author would like to express his gratitude to the ASEE, John Hansen and Richard St.Andre, CMU, and Linwood Sutton, NOSC, Code 411, for their helpful criticism of this work. Finally, a note of appreciation is also accorded to my parents, my brother, my friends, and the plethora of my students here at CMU.

References

[1] H. Abelson, M. Eisenberg, M. Halfant, J. Katzenelson, E. Sacks, G.J. Sussman, J. Wisdom, and K. Yip. Intelligence in Scientific Computing. *CACM*, 32(5), May 1989, pp. 546-562.

[2] M. Bruynooghe, L. De Raedt, and D. De Schreye. Explanation Based Program Transformation. *IJCAI-89*, 1989, pp. 407-412.

[3] J.G. Carbonell. Derivational Analogy and its Role in Problem Solving. *AAAI-83*, 1983, pp. 64-69.

[4] J.G. Carbonell. Introduction: Paradigms for Machine Learning. *Artificial Intelligence*, Special Volume on Machine Learning, 40(1-3), September 1989, pp. 1-9.

[5] T.R. Davies and S.J. Russel. A Logical Approach to Reasoning by Analogy. *IJCAI-87*, 1987.

[6] N. Dershowitz. *The Evolution of Programs*. Birkhauser, Boston, MA, 1983.

[7] B. Falkenhainer, K. Forbus, and D. Gentner. The Structure Mapping Engine. *AAAI-86*, August 1986.

[8] D. Gentner. Structure-mapping: A Theoretical Framework for Analogy. *Cognitive Science*, 7(2), 1983, pp. 155-170.

[9] R. Greiner. Learning by Understanding Analogies. *Artificial Intelligence*, 35, 1988, pp. 81-125.

[10] M.T. Harandi and S. Bhansali. Program Derivation Using Analogy. *IJCAI-89*, August 1989, pp. 389-394.

[11] R.E. Kling. A Paradigm for Reasoning by Analogy. *Artificial Intelligence*, 2, 1971, pp. 147-178.

[12] M. Manago. Knowledge Intensive Induction. *Proceedings of the Sixth International Workshop on Machine Learning*, 1989, pp. 151-155.

[13] R.S. Michalski and R.L. Chilausky. Learning by being told and learning from examples. *International Journal of Policy Analysis and Information Systems*, 4(2), 1980, pp. 125-161.

[14] R.S. Michalski, J.G. Carbonell, and T.M. Mitchell. *Machine Learning*, Volume II. Morgan Kaufman Publishers, Los Altos, CA, 1986.

[15] S. Minton. *Learning Search Control Knowledge: An Explanation-Based Approach*, Kluwer Academic Publishers, Boston, MA, 1988.

[16] S. Minton, J.G. Carbonell, C.A. Knoblock, D.R. Kuokka, O. Etzioni, and Y. Gil. Explanation-Based Learning: A Problem Solving Perspective. *Artificial Intelligence*, Special Volume on Machine Learning, 40(1-3), September 1989, pp. 63-118.

[17] T.M. Mitchell. "Version Spaces: A Candidate Elimination Approach to Rule Learning", in *Proceedings Fifth International Joint Conference on Artificial Intelligence*, 1977, pp. 305-310.

[18] T.M. Mitchell, R. Keller, and S. Kedar-Cabelli. Explanation-Based Generalization: A Unifying View. *Machine Learning*, 1(1), 1986, pp. 47-80.

[19] Office of Naval Technology. *Post Doctoral Fellowship Program*, 1987-88, ASEE, Projects Office, 11 Dupont Circle, Suite 200, Washington, DC 20036.

[20] B.W. Porter. Similarity Assessment: Computation Vs. Representation. *Proceedings of a Workshop on Case-Based Reasoning*, Pensacola Beach, FL, June 1989, pp. 82-84.

[21] S.H. Rubin. Requirement-Driven Decision Support Systems. *IEEE International Conference on Systems, Man, and Cybernetics*, Cambridge, MA, November 1989.

[22] M.M. Veloso and J.G. Carbonell. Learning Analogies by Analogy - The Closed Loop of Memory Organization and Problem Solving. *Proceedings of a Workshop on Case-Based Reasoning*, Pensacola Beach, FL, June 1989, pp. 153-158.

A Template-based Approach for Recognition of Intermittent Sounds

Ben Pinkowski
Computer Science Department
Western Michigan University
Kalamazoo, MI 49008

Abstract

Automatic speech and sound recognition typically involves some measure of distance between training and (possibly time-warped) test samples. Special problems arise when the spectral samples of interest are intermittent and contain temporal patterns of alternating periods of sounds and pauses that are significant for recognition. In such cases a recognizer must be capable of distinguishing between the end-points and the pauses of digitized samples and economically searching the segmented sounds for the occurrence of significant spectral patterns. The usual distance metrics based on conventional dynamic time warping algorithms may be inappropriate because time-warping often corrupts the temporal structure of the sound. The problem can be solved by first searching a test sample for distinctive temporal patterns and, if more than one match is obtained, using a spectral distance measure to classify the sample with its nearest neighbor among these. Computational advantages can be obtained if both the temporal and spectral templates are maintained in a binary format reflecting the important sound components.

1 Introduction

Systems for automatic recognition of speech and other sounds are becoming increasingly common in a wide variety of applications. The typical approach to classifying sounds involves digitizing a representative set of training samples and extracting their important features to form reference templates. For speaker-dependent systems and isolated word recognition (IWR), 1 to 3 templates per word are required to obtain satisfactory classification; for speaker-independent systems, as many as 10 or 12 templates per word may be needed [10]. In IWR, single words are assumed to be uttered in advance for training [17]. As vocabulary size and speaker versatility increase in continuous speech recognition (CSR), the feasibility of exhaustive search with template-matching decreases and the need for concise representation of important sound characteristics becomes greater. One important feature of many sounds is frequency, and a common spectral approach is to divide the sound into a number of frames and obtain a frequency spectrum for each of these. For n frames, f frequency categories, and no filtering, the result is an n by f template. If the sounds are lengthy and are not comprised of pure tones, n and f may become unacceptably large. Even if n and f are not large, the use of templates may be prohibitive if the sounds to be searched are long, as in the non-trivial "word-spotting" problem, where error rates are often at least an order of magnitude greater than for simple CSR systems [6].

In addition to their spectral composition, many natural sounds are intermittent and contain a characteristic temporal structure of alternating sounds and pauses. The spectral and temporal structures are perceived as changes in pitch (frequency) and rhythm (tempo or cadence), respectively. Humans respond to these changes and may still recognize a melodic tune, for example, if it is played at a higher key or a more rapid tempo. Computer recognition systems should also be able to solve sound recognition tasks involving such changes, but conventional techniques that have been used for simple speech recognition [14] are often inappropriate for intermittent sounds because they discard silent intervals (pauses) during preprocessing or rely on some form of dynamic time warping. Time-warping algorithms are notorious for their heavy computational loads and, more importantly, for their failure to exploit temporal features that are important if the sound is intermittent.

Despite their limited usefulness for long or varied sounds, templates are an intuitively appealing medium for modeling many complex sounds because: 1) they present a pseudo-graphic representation of important sound features such as frequency variation over time; 2) template-matching can be a remarkably efficient process if all of the templates are the same size and represented in binary format, and 3) heuristics are employed to reduce the number of template comparisons that must be made. This paper describes a flexible template-based approach I have employed to recognize many natural and man-made sounds that contain significant temporal and spectral components. Examples of such sounds are various weather-related phenomena, geological events such as earthquakes, animal vocalizations including insect, frog, and bird calls, various man-made sounds such as a door knock or bell, sounds made by mechanical equipment (engines, alarms, etc.), and some musical tunes and speech idioms. A system capable of distinguishing these sounds may be useful for diagnosis, modeling, or monitoring the sounds, or it may assist a handicapped person that is unable to distinguish sounds.

2   General Approach

The overall approach involves constructing temporal templates to reflect alternating patterns of sound and silence, and frequency templates to capture the spectral properties of the sound segments (variously called pulses, syllables, or notes in the literature). Frequencies of sample sounds tested with this approach varied from less than 500 Hz to 8 kHz, which necessitated a sampling rate of 16,384 Hz and made both high-pass filtering and low-pass filtering somewhat impractical. Samples were obtained with an 8 bit A/D converter and the analyses were carried out on 128-byte (7.8 ms) hamming windows to reflect the gross structure of a sound, or smaller windows to examine its finer structure. Several adjacent windows together constitute a sound or silence frame, and alternating frames make up the tempo of the sound. A frequency template was then associated with one or more of the sound frames.

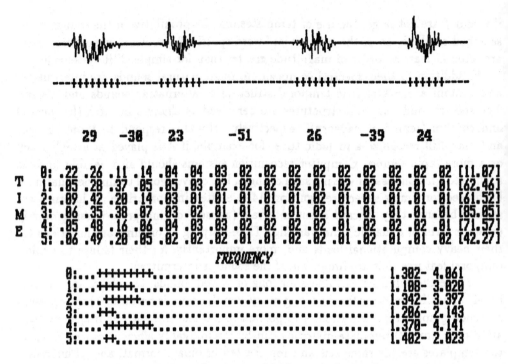

Figure 1: Sample temporal and spectral templates

Temporal and spectral templates showing the gross structure of a sample intermittent sound are depicted in Figure 1. In this case the rows of frequency template entries are calculated to express the relative contribution of each frequency category and thus sum to unity. The shortest syllable of a sound I tested required 6 evenly-spaced 128-byte windows. The minimum length of a sound frame determined the template size, but other spectral template sizes were required for different sound classes.

Examination of the temporal structure required classification of each window as sound or silence and thus is analogous to the end-point detection problem for isolated words [9, 2]. For relatively noiseless samples, a simple energy threshold proved sufficient for this classification, particularly if the signal energy was high. For noisy samples, analysis of the zero crossing rate appeared helpful, and a modification of a general end-point detection algorithm [15] was employed as follows. Based on digitized energy values obtained during known silent intervals, a lower energy threshold lth was specified. Digitizing began when lth was exceeded and continued for a time period longer than the longest sound likely to occur. A "tight" upper threshold uth was then used to isolate the endpoints, which were expanded outward as long as any one or more of three consecutive frames exceeded the ZCR observed prior to digitizing. The $\bar{x} + 2\,SD$ ZCR for the silent end periods then becomes the ZCR threshold used to classify internal windows as sound (window ZCR $> \bar{x} + 2SD$) or silence (window ZCR $\le \bar{x} + 2SD$).

3 Temporal Structure

Temporal patterns were expressed using regular expression notation in a set of if-then rules that were used to determine sound candidates for more detailed frequency analysis. An index associated with each rule indicated which sound frame was to be used for frequency comparisons in the event of a successful parse.

Sample temporal rules are shown in Figure 2. Stereotypic sounds of fixed patterns (e.g., Sounds 1 and 2) are easily represented, as are sequences that characterize the beginning of samples (Sounds 4 and 5) or the ends (Sounds 3 and 6). A few diagnostic temporal patterns may occur virtually anywhere in a sample (Sound 8). A sample can have more than one temporal pattern (Sound 5) and frequency templates may be associated with more than one sound frame (Sound 7); these provisions are analogous to using multiple templates for isolated words that have several pronunciations [1].

Since temporal training templates were of various sizes, a standard measure of similarity was needed to assess the similarity among templates. For binary features, many indices are available [4, 19]. I used the standard correlation coefficient, r or S_c here,

$$S_c^2 = \frac{[\sum_i (x_i - \bar{x})(y_i - \bar{y})]^2}{\sum_i (x_i - \bar{x})^2 \sum_i (y_i - \bar{x})^2},$$

with modfications to reduce computational load [8]. If means $\bar{x}$ and $\bar{y}$ are adjusted to 0 beforehand, the similarity reduces to:

$$S_c^2 = \frac{(\sum_i x_i y_i)^2}{\sum_i x_i^2 \sum_i y_i^2}.$$

If values are adjusted for the sum of squares beforehand so that,

$$\sum_i x_i^2 = 1, \sum_i y_i^2 = 1,$$

then the similarity can be computed by summing the products of corresponding terms:

$$S_c^2 = (\sum_i x_i y_i)^2.$$

Parsing of the temporal patterns alleviates an approach involving similarity thresholds [4], which I found difficult to implement in noisy environments. It is also amenable to a rule-based representation that allows for incorporation of unusual or erroneous samples [12].

4 Spectral Structure

Typically, the vast majority of points in a Fourier frequency spectra have very low values [5]. Because of this, and to make frequency template search feasible in real time, the templates were converted to a binary format somewhat arbitrarily by identifying the middle 50'th percentile of the spectral window. The included frequencies were

0.5/0.0	Sound1 :-		44		1
0.1/0.2	Sound2 :-		37 -22 12		1
0.5/0.5	Sound3 :-	*	12 -12 12		2
0.1/0.1	Sound4 :-		27 -85 88 +		1
0.3/0.3	Sound5 :-		23 -10 23 * 55		1
0.3/0.3	Sound5 :-		[97 -10 76]		2
0.0/0.0	Sound6 :-	+	[18 -01 18]		0
0.6/0.6	Sound7 :-	+	[20 -20 20]+		1,2

Figure 2: Sample temporal pattern rules

either contiguous in the case of pure sounds (Figure 2), or discontiguous if the sounds consisted of several harmonics. This approach incorporates features related to both the dominant frequencies as well as other aspects of the spectrum. The similarity, S_f, between a training template and a test sample was then computed by translating the training template in every position relative to the test sample and simply calculating the percentage of matches. The translation is necessary to accommodate noise or inaccurate end-point detection among test samples compared with training samples, and maintaining a constant template size (6 equal-spaced windows) allows for a limited amount of time-warping at the level of a sound frame.

Of several approaches used with a variety of sounds, I found it useful to simply classify a test sample with the nearest training template (the $NN1$ model [11]) for which a successful parse was obtained. Another approach involved calculating the overall similarity, S, between a test and training sample:

$$S = S_c + S_f - 1.$$

This metric incorporates the temporal similarity into the final classification, which I found desirable in some cases.

5 Conclusions

The recognition method proposed here for intermittent sounds is a 2-stage approach first involving temporal patterns and then assessing spectral similarity. The use of binary templates is suggested for both stages to reduce search time. However, for many classes of sounds that have been tested with the system, the temporal rules produced only a single candidate sound which represented a correct classification. For others, only a few candidates emerged. Clearly, temporal structure is more important in some sounds than others, and a flexible rule-based approach with tolerance limits allows for incorporation of any differences in the sounds under consideration at a given time.

The approach described here is not only useful for identifying many natural sounds, but its also models many aspects of natural sound recognition as well. For example, both temporal and spectral cues are important in the bioacoustic communication systems of animals that must be able to recognize conspecific sounds [16, 13]. Many higher animals are thought to judge auditory input against species-specific sound templates to determine behavioral response [3]. In some cases the templates are believed to share neural elements with the sound-pattern generator [3]. Such a template-based approach to recognition seems most likely in higher vertebrates (e.g., dolphins; some birds) that detect a broad range of signals and possess a sufficiently advanced brain to process these efficiently. For less advanced systems, only certain sound features are detected and sensory filters may be a more appropriate model.

Perhaps the simplest bioacoustic recognition scheme suggested to date is the so-called "30-Hz hypothesis" proposed for some crickets. This hypothesis states that the only feature required by the recognizer is a 30 Hz syllable rate [18] and corresponds to usage of a temporal template and no spectral template. In other cases rhythmic natural sounds vary linearly with temperature [7], which corresponds to constant tolerance limits on all temporal frames. Finally, in some cases the rhythm pattern may be a sufficient, but not necessary, prerequisite for accurate recognition, and both temporal and spectral properties of the sound contribute to its message[3]. A template-based approach to recognition such as that described in this paper models these behaviors by incorporating both temporal and spectral features in a flexible manner.

Acknowledgments

Equipment for this study was funded by a research grant from the College of Arts and Sciences, Western Michigan University.

References

[1] J. S. Bridle. An efficient elastic-template method for detecting given words in running speech. *Spring Meeting, British Acoust. Soc*, 1973.

[2] P. deSouza. A statistical approach to the design of an adaptive self-normalizing silence detection. *IEEE Trans. ASSP*, ASSP-31:678–684, 1983.

[3] J. Doherty and R. Hoy. Communication in insects. III. The auditory behavior of crickets: some views of genetic coupling, song recognition, and predator detection. *Quarterly Review of Biology*, 60:457–472, 1985.

[4] R. O. Duda and P. E. Hart. *Pattern Classification and Scene Analysis*. John Wiley and Sons, New York, New York, 1973.

[5] J. L. Elman and D. Zipser. Learning the hidden structure of speech. *Journal Accoust. Soc. Amer.*, 83:1615–1626, 1988.

[6] A. L. Higgins and R. Wohlford. Keyword recognition using template concatenation. *Proc. IEEE Int. Conf. ASSP*, pages 1233–1236, 1985.

[7] R. R. Hoy. Acoustic communication in crickets: a model system for the study of feature detection. *Federation Proc.*, 37:2316–2323, 1978.

[8] M. James. *Pattern Recognition*. John Wiley and Sons, New York, New York, 1988.

[9] L. R. Lamel, L. Rabiner, A. Rosenberg, and J. Wilpon. An improved endpoint detector for isolated word recognition. *IEEE Trans. ASSP*, ASSP-29:777–785, 1981.

[10] D. O'Shaughnessy. *Speech Communication Human and Machine*. Addison-Wesley Publishing Company, Reading, Massachusetts, 1987.

[11] B. Pinkowski. Discrete discriminant models: A performance simulation with reference to expert systems applications. In *20th Annual Simulation Symposium*, pages 103–119. IEEE, 1987.

[12] B. Pinkowski. A rule-based approach for simulating errors in discrete sequential processes. In *22nd Annual Simulation Symposium*, pages 145–152. IEEE, 1989.

[13] G. S. Pollack and R. R. Hoy. Temporal pattern as a cue for species-specific calling song recognition in crickets. *Science*, 204:429–432, 1979.

[14] L. R. Rabiner. On creating reference templates for speaker independent recognition of isolated words. *IEEE Trans. ASSP*, ASSP-26:34–42, 1978.

[15] L. R. Rabiner and M. R. Sambur. An algorithm for determining the endpoints of isolated utterances. *Bell Sys. Tech. Journal*, 54:297–315, 1975.

[16] J. J. Schwartz. The importance of spectral and temporal properties in species and call recognition in a neotropical treefrog with a complex vocal repertoire. *Animal Behavior*, 35:340–347, 1987.

[17] N. Sugamura, K. Shikano, and S. Furui. Isolated word recognition using phoneme-like templates. *ICASSP*, pages 732–726, 1983.

[18] J. Thorson, T. Weber, and F. Huber. Auditory behavior of the cricket. II. Simplicity of calling-song recognition in gryllus, and anomalous phonotaxis at abnormal carrier frequencies. *Journal Comp. Physiol.*, 146:361–378, 1982.

[19] J. D. Tubbs. A note on binary template-matching. *Pattern Recognition*, 22:359–365, 1989.

A Mathematical Model of Uncertain Information

Chun-Hung Tzeng
Computer Science Department
Ball State University
Muncie, IN 47306

Abstract

This paper introduces a mathematical evidence model for uncertain information in artificial intelligence. Each evidence model contains prior information as well as possible new evidence to appear later. Both Bayesian probability distribution and Dempster-Shafer's ignorance are special evidence models. A concept of independence is also introduced. Dempster-Shafer's combination rule becomes a formula to combine basic probabilities of independent models.

1   Introduction

In handling uncertainty in artificial intelligence (AI), a conventional Bayesian approach consider actual probability of the truth under consideration. Dempster-Shafer's evidence is introduced as an extension of probability (Dempster 1968; Shafer 1976). If t is a variable, let T represent the set of all possible values of t Then the propositions may be represented as "the value of t is in A," abbreviated as "$t \in A$," where A is a subset of T. The set T is called the frame of discernment for t. A given probability assignment m over 2^T is called a (Dempster) *basic probability assignment* and represents a body of evidence regarding the value of t.

Kyburg (1987) studied formal relations between the Bayesian theory and the Dempster-Shafer's belief functions. It is shown that every belief function can be represented by a closed convex set of probability distributions. Furthermore, the input of uncertain evidence can be represented in the framework of convex sets of probabilities by classical conditionalization. He argued that Dempster's rule yields more determinate belief states as outcomes, but the benefits afforded by this non-Bayesian updating are limited and questionable.

Ruspini (1987) introduced a logical foundation of Dempster-Shafer's evidence by use of an epistemic universe, a space of possible worlds or states of affairs. Dempster-Shafer combination rule is a special additive combination formula for combining independent knowledge.

From a statistical point of view, Hummel and Landy (1988) provided an interpretation of Dempster-Shafer's evidence by introducing probabilistic and Boolean opinion spaces of experts. Dempster-Shafer's combination rule is interpreted as an application of Bayesian formula to sets of Boolean opinions in updating on product sets of those opinions. This interpretation makes clear the implicit independence assumptions in Dempster-Shafer's combination rule.

This paper introduces a mathematical evidence model, in which the truth $t \in T$ is probabilistic, but its probability distribution is not necessarily known. Each piece of uncertain information about t is represented by a 4-tuple $(S, M, i, \mathbf{E})$, called an *evidence model*. M is a probability space, called a *message space*, in which each element represents a proposition about the truth t through an *information function* i, a function from M to 2^T. S is also a probability space, which is independent of the truth and is called a *code space*. $\mathbf{E}$, called an *evidence space*, is a set of functions from S to M representing possible encoded messages about the truth. An evidence model contains prior information about the truth (i.e., the message space M) as well as possible new evidence to appear later (i.e., the evidence space $\mathbf{E}$). Given new evidence (i.e., an element in $\mathbf{E}$), we use Bayes rule to update the evidence model.

Both conventional Bayesian approach and Dempster-Shafer's approach are special evidence models. Between evidence models, we define a concept of independence and introduce independent combination of models, where Dempster's combination rule is a formula to combine prior basic probabilities as well as posterior basic probabilities of any two independent evidence models. A detail formulation of this evidence model is in a reference (Tzeng 1989).

2 Definitions

Let T be the set of hypotheses of a truth t. We assume that the occurrence of the truth $t \in T$ is probabilistic. For convenience, we assume that all of probability spaces discussed in this paper are discrete, although our discussion could be extended to continuous cases.

Message Space and Code Space. Let M be a probability space with a function $i : M \to 2^T$. If $A \in M$ and $i(A) = X \in 2^T$, then we treat A as a proposition meaning "the truth t is in X" or "$t \in X$." We call an element $A \in M$ a *message* and $i(A)(\in 2^T)$ the corresponding *plaintext message* about t. We assume that the occurrence of message depends on the truth $t \in T$ in the sense that an occurring message A always implies "$t \in i(A)$." The probability distribution of message is previously given and represented by P_M. We call such a pair (M, i) a *message model* of T, in which M is the *message space* and i is the *information function*.

A *code space* S is a given probability space independent of both the truth t and the message space M. Let the probability distribution over S be denoted by P_S. Each element of S is called a *code*. Later a randomly chosen code will be used to encode an occurring message from the above message space.

Evidence Function and Evidence Model. Given the message model

(M, i) and the code space S, we call any partial function from S to M an *evidence function*. We consider a special space of evidence functions:

Definition 1. A nonempty set $\mathbf{E}$ of evidence functions is an *evidence space* if the following two conditions are true:

1. For any $E_1, E_2 \in \mathbf{E}$, if $E_1(s) = E_2(s)$ for an $s \in S$, then $E_1 = E_2$.

2. For any $A \in M$, if $P_M(A) > 0$, then there is at least an $E \in \mathbf{E}$ such that $E(s) = A$ for some $s \in S$ with $P_S(s) > 0$.

Given an evidence space $\mathbf{E}$, an encoder encodes an occurring message as follows. Suppose that a message $A \in M$ has occurred. After the encoder independently choses a code $s \in S$ according to P_S, he sends an evidence function $E \in \mathbf{E}$ such that $E(s) = A$. If such an evidence function does not exit, a code will be repeatedly and independently chosen until a suitable one is found.

The first condition of $\mathbf{E}$ guarantees that the evidence function sent is uniquely determined by the occurring message and the chosen code. The second condition guarantees that any possible message $A \in M$ (i.e., $P_M(A) > 0$) can be encoded to an evidence function. An evidence model for the truth $t \in T$ is defined as follows.

Definition 2. An *evidence model* of the truth $t \in T$ is a 4-tuple $(S, M, i, \mathbf{E})$ of a code space S, a message space M, a corresponding information function i, and a corresponding evidence space $\mathbf{E}$.

Prior Information. In an evidence model $(S, M, i, \mathbf{E})$, the current information about t is the probability distribution P_M of the message space M. Using this information, we define the basic probability and the belief function about the truth $t \in T$ as follows. Let $X \subseteq T$ be a subset of T. Then the *basic probability* m and the *belief function* Bel (of the evidence model) are defined as

$$m(X) = \sum_{A \in M; i(A) = X} P_M(A); \quad \mathrm{Bel}(X) = \sum_{Y \subseteq X} m(Y).$$

The value of $m(X)$ is the probability that the plaintext message is X. The value of $\mathrm{Bel}(X)$ is the probability that the plaintext message is contained in X.

Posterior Information. The evidence space $\mathbf{E}$ of the evidence model $(S, M, i, \mathbf{E})$ consists of evidence to appear later. Each occurring evidence function in $\mathbf{E}$ provides new evidence about the truth t. In the following, we update the evidence model based upon an occurring evidence function.

Given an evidence function E, consider the posterior probability of $A \in M$: $P(A|E) = P(E|A)P_M(A)/P(E)$. We incorporate this posterior probability $P(\cdot|E)$ into a new evidence model $(S, M, i, \{E\})$, where the probability over M is updated by the posterior probability $P(\cdot|E)$ and E becomes the only evidence function. This model with the posterior information is the *posterior evidence model* (given the evidence function E). The posterior basic probability and the posterior belief function of the posterior evidence model are

$$m(X|E) = \sum_{i(A) = X} P(A|E); \quad \mathrm{Bel}(X|E) = \sum_{Y \subseteq X} m(Y|E), \quad X \subseteq T.$$

3 Special Models

In the following, we list some familiar models as special cases in our formulation.

Probability Distribution over T. In a conventional Bayesian approach, we start with a probability distribution P over T as prior information. Let $M_P = T$ with the given probability distribution P. The information function $i_p : T \to 2^T$ is defined as $i_p(x) = \{x\}$ for $x \in T$. Let $S_0 = \{s_0\}$, consisting of only one element, and $\mathbf{E}_T = \{E_x : x \in T\}$, where $E_x(s_0) = x$ for each $x \in T$. Then the 4-tuple $(S_0, M_P, i_p, \mathbf{E}_T)$ is an evidence model of the truth t.

The evidence model $(S_0, M_P, i_p, \mathbf{E}_T)$ defined above represents the probability distribution P over T. The current information (about $t \in T$) of this evidence model is the probability distribution P. The basic probability m is the given probability assignment and the belief function Bel is the probability distribution P; that is, $m(x) = P(x)$ for $x \in T$ and $\mathrm{Bel}(X) = P(X)$ for $X \subseteq T$. Therefore, we have the following theorem:

Theorem 1. Each probability distribution P over T is the belief function of the evidence model $(S_0, M_P, i_p, \mathbf{E}_T)$.

The Information $t \in X$. Consider the information "$t \in X$" for a subset $X \subseteq T$. Let $M_0 = \{m_0\}$, consisting of only one element. Let the function i_X, defined as $i_X(m_0) = X$, be the information function. Let $\mathbf{E}_0$ consist of only one element E_0 such that $E_0(s_0) = m_0$. Then the evidence model $(S_0, M_0, i_X, \mathbf{E}_0)$ represents the information "$t \in X$."

In this model, the basic probability m satisfies $m(X) = 1$; $m(Y) = 0$ if $Y \neq X$. Since $\mathbf{E}_0$ consists of only one element, this model does not have any non-trivial new evidence. This model ignores the probability distribution of t. It has the complete ignorance if $X = T$, the whole space.

Dempster's Evidence. A piece of Dempster's evidence (Dempster 1967) is represented by a function E from a given probability space S to 2^T, the occurrence of E being based on both the truth $t \in T$ and the uncertainty of S. Suppose that $X \subseteq T$. Let $S_{X,E} = \{s : E(s) = X\}$ and $S_E = \{s : E(s) \text{ is defined}\}$. Then the Dempster's basic probability, m_D, and the Dempster's belief function of X, Bel_D, are defined as follows:

$$m_D(X) = P(S_{X,E}|S_E) = \frac{P(S_{X,E})}{P(S_E)}; \quad \mathrm{Bel}_D(X) = \sum_{Y \subseteq X} m_D(Y).$$

Let $M = 2^T$ and P_M be the probability distribution over M such that $P_M(X) = m_D(X)$ for each $X \in M$. Let id be the identity: $id(X) = X$ for $X \in 2^T$. Let $\mathbf{E}$ consist of the given E only. Then the 4-tuple $(S, M, id, \{E\})$ form an evidence model of t. It is true that $m(X) = m_D(X)$ and $\mathrm{Bel}(X) = \mathrm{Bel}_D(X)$ for each $X \subseteq T$. That is, we have the following theorem.

Theorem 2. Each body of Dempster's evidence is represented by an evidence model of which the basic probability distribution and the belief function are identical with the Dempster's basic probability distribution and the Dempster's belief function, respectively.

4 Evidence Combination

This section introduces the concept of independent models and their combinations.

Independent Model. Let $(S_1, M_1, i_1, \mathbf{E}_1)$ and $(S_2, M_2, i_2, \mathbf{E}_2)$ be two evidence models for a same truth $t \in T$. Let P_{M_1} and P_{M_2} be the respective probability distributions over M_1 and M_2. Let $M = M_1 \times M_2$ be the product space and $P = P_{M_1} \times P_{M_2}$ be the product probability measure. Let $S = S_1 \times S_2$ be the product space of the code spaces and $P_S = P_{S_1} \times P_{S_2}$.

Let a_1 and a_2 be the random variables representing the occurring messages from M_1 and M_2, respectively: $a_1 \in M_1$ and $a_2 \in M_2$. Consider the random vector $a = <a_1, a_2>$. If $a_1 = A_1$ and $a_2 = A_2$ (i.e., $a = <A_1, A_2>$), then we call the pair $<A_1, A_2>$ a *message pair*. Since the messages A_1 and A_2 mean that t is in both $i_1(A_1)$ and $i_2(A_2)$, it is necessary that $i_1(A_1) \cap i_2(A_2) \neq \emptyset$. Therefore, if both a_1 and a_2 are defined, then there is at least a pair $<A_1, A_2> \in M_1 \times M_2$ such that $P_{M_1}(A_1) > 0$, $P_{M_2}(A_2) > 0$, and $i_1(A_1) \cap i_2(A_2) \neq \emptyset$.

Let M_T be the subset of $M_1 \times M_2$ defined as follows

$$M_T = \{<A_1, A_2> : A_1 \in M_1, A_2 \in M_2, i_1(A_1) \cap i_2(A_2) \neq \emptyset\}.$$

Then M_T contains all possible message pairs.

Definition 3. The evidence models $(S_1, M_1, i_1, \mathbf{E}_1)$ and $(S_2, M_2, i_2, \mathbf{E}_2)$ are *independent* if the following conditions are true:

1. It is possible that both a_1 and a_2 are defined simultaneously.

2. The two codes of the two evidence models are to be chosen independently.

3. The condition of $<A_1, A_2>$ ($\in M_1 \times M_2$) being a possible message pair is that $<A_1, A_2> \in M_T$; that is, the probability that $a = <A_1, A_2>$ is identical with the conditional probability $P(a = <A_1, A_2> \mid a \in M_T)$, where $P = P_{M_1} \times P_{M_2}$.

Independent Combination. Suppose that $(S_1, M_1, i_1, \mathbf{E}_1)$ and $(S_2, M_2, i_2, \mathbf{E}_2)$ are independent. Let the product space $M_1 \times M_2$ be a new message space with the information function i defined by $i(<A_1, A_2>) = i_1(A_1) \cap i_2(A_2) \subseteq T$. Let the probability distribution P_{M_T} over $M_1 \times M_2$ be identical with the probability distribution of the random vector $a = <a_1, a_2>$. Then, the value $P_{M_T}(<A_1, A_2>)$ ($= P(<A_1, A_2> \mid <A_1, A_2> \in M_T)$) is

$$\frac{P_{M_1}(A_1)P_{M_2}(A_2)}{1 - \sum_{i_1(A_1) \cap i_2(A_2) = \emptyset} P_{M_1}(A_1)P_{M_2}(A_2)} \tag{1}$$

if $<A_1, A_2> \in M_T$. The space $(M_1 \times M_2, i)$ with the probability distribution P_{M_T} forms a message model of the truth t, which is called the *independent product* of (M_1, i_1) and (M_2, i_2).

Consider any two evidence functions E_1 and E_2, $E_1 \in \mathbf{E}_1$ and $E_2 \in \mathbf{E}_2$. Let $E_1 * E_2$ be a partial function from $S_1 \times S_2$ to $M_1 \times M_2$ defined as follows: $E_1 * E_2(<s, u>) = <E_1(s), E_2(u)>$ if both $E_1(s)$ and $E_2(u)$ are defined; $E_1 * E_2$ is not defined for other cases. $E_1 * E_2$ is called the *independently combined evidence function* (of E_1 and E_2) if it is defined for at least a pair $<s, u>$ ($\in S_1 \times S_2$). Let $\mathbf{E}_1 * \mathbf{E}_2$ be the set of all independently combined evidence functions. It can be shown that $\mathbf{E}_1 * \mathbf{E}_2$ is an evidence space with respect to the message model $(M_1 \times M_2, i)$ and the code space $S_1 \times S_2$ (i.e., $\mathbf{E}_1 * \mathbf{E}_2$ satisfies the two conditions of Definition 1). Then the 4-tuple $(S_1 \times S_2, M_1 \times M_2, i, \mathbf{E}_1 * \mathbf{E}_2)$ becomes an evidence model of the truth $t \in T$.

Definition 4. The *independent combination* of the two independent models $(S_1, M_1, i_1, \mathbf{E}_1)$ and $(S_2, M_2, i_2, \mathbf{E}_2)$ is the evidence model $(S_1 \times S_2, M_1 \times M_2, i, \mathbf{E}_1 * \mathbf{E}_2)$ defined above.

The basic probability of the above independent combination can be derived from Equation (2) as follows:

$$m(X) = \sum_{i(<A_1, A_2>)=X} P_{M_T}(<A_1, A_2>) = \frac{\sum_{X_1 \cap X_2 = X} m_1(X_1) m_2(X_2)}{1 - \sum_{X_1 \cap X_2 = \emptyset} m_1(X_1) m_2(X_2)}. \tag{2}$$

where m_1 and m_2 are the basic probabilities of $(S_1, M_1, i_1, \mathbf{E}_1)$ and $(S_2, M_2, i_2, \mathbf{E}_2)$, respectively. Equation (3) is an original form of Dempster's rule.

Given an independently combined evidence function $E_1 * E_2$, the posterior basic probability of the independent combination is a combination of $m_1(\cdot | E_1)$ and $m_2(\cdot | E_2)$, also by the rule (3). That is, we have the following theorem.

Theorem 4. If two evidence models of the truth $t \in T$ are independent, then Dempster's rule is a right method to combine their prior as well as posterior basic probabilities.

Bayesian Conditioning.

Consider a conventional Bayesian approach. Let P be the prior probability distribution over T. Given information $t \in X$, $X \subseteq T$, the posterior probability distribution is the conditional probability $P(\cdot | X)$.

Let the prior probability P be represented by the evidence model $(S_0, M_P, i_p, \mathbf{E}_T)$ and the information $t \in X$ represented by the evidence model $(S_0, M_0, i_X, \mathbf{E}_0)$. Consider their independent combination $(S_0 \times S_0, M_P \times M_0, i, \mathbf{E}_T * \mathbf{E}_0)$, assuming their independence. Let m and Bel be the basic probability and belief function, respectively. Then, it can be shown that $m(x) = P(x | X)$ for $x \in T$, and $\text{Bel}(Y) = P(Y | X)$ for $Y \subseteq T$. That is, we have the following theorem.

Theorem 5. The conventional Bayesian conditioning $P(\cdot | X)$ is the belief function of the independent combination of the prior probability and the information $t \in X$.

5 Conclusions

Our new evidence models are based upon probability theory and Bayes rule. Dempster's combination rule is derived mathematically. Each piece of Dempster's evidence is a special evidence model. Both conventional Bayesian approach and Dempster-Shafer's approach can be derived from this same mathematical theory.

References

[1] Dempster, A P (1967) Upper and lower probabilities induced by a multivalued mapping, *Annals of Mathematical Statistics* (**38**) 325-339

[2] Dempster, A P (1968) A generalization of Bayesian inference, *Journal of the Royal Statistical Society* (**38**) 205-247

[3] Folland, G B (1984) *Real Analysis*, A Wiley-interscience publication, John Wiley & Sons, New York, NY

[4] Hummel, R A and Landy, M S (1988) A Statistical Viewpoint on the Theory of Evidence, *IEEE Transactions on Pattern Analysis and Machine Intelligence* **10**, no. 2, 235-247

[5] Kyburg, H E Jr (1987) Bayesian and non-Bayesian evidential updating, *Artificial Intelligence* **31**, 271-293

[6] Laskey, K B (1987) Belief in belief functions: an examination of Shafer's canonical examples, in *Uncertainty in Artificial Intelligence, Third Workshop on Uncertainty in Artificial Intelligence,* Seattle, Washington, 39-46

[7] Ruspini, E H (1987) Epistemic logics, probability, and the calculus of evidence, in *Proceedings of IJCAI-87*, 924-931

[8] Shafer, G (1976) *A mathematical theory of evidence*, Princeton University Press, Princeton, New Jersey

[9] Shafer, G (1981) Constructive probability, *Synthese* **48**, 1–60

[10] Tzeng, CH (1988a) *A Theory of Heuristic Information in Game-Tree Search*, Springer-Verlag, Berlin, 1988.

[11] Tzeng, CH (1988b) A Study of Dempster-Shafer's Theory through Shafer's Canonical Examples, *Proceedings of International Computer Science Conference '88, Artificial Intelligence: Theory and Applications*, Hong Kong, December 19-21, 1988, 69-76

[12] Tzeng, CH (1989) Uncertain Information and Dempster Combination Rule, WP-15, Computer Science Department, Ball State University.

A Word to Phoneme Translator

Gary Gold
Department of Computer Science
Western Michigan University
Kalamazoo, Michigan 49008 U.S.A.

Abstract

The problem of translating text to speech is usually approached at the phoneme level using a rule-based system. A rule based system specifies how each letter, or group of letters, will be translated into a basic unit of sound, a phoneme. These rules are very context sensitive, depending on possibly lengthy left and right contexts. The rule based approach in Elovitz [1] and also in Yannakoudakis [5] is the system that was used as the basis for the program which I recently developed using the compiler writing utility lex. This rule-based system uses over 300 rules and a set of 42 phonemes to translate unrestricted text into a string of phonemes.

1 Introduction

Speech synthesis systems are of interest to several classes of people. Among these are

1) people who are visually impaired;

2) people whose work requires their visual attention and can not, or should not, look aside at printed text;

3) people that have not learned to read;

4) users and designers of voice response systems such as dial up information systems.

An overview of speech synthesis systems was written by Klatt in [2]. One of several methods used to translate text into speech is through the use of a rule based system that translates each letter based on the adjoining letters. Such systems do not rely on a dictionary or syntactic analysis of the sentence structure. One such system was described by Elovitz in [1].

The process of translating written text into speech using a rule based system involves several steps.

1) The input text is preprocessed to translate such things as numbers, abbreviations, acronyms, etc. into text and suitably handle punctuation.

2) The preprocessed text is then translated into a string of phonemes.

3) The string of phonemes is then used as input to a speech generator.

This paper is concerned with the second of these steps, the translation of the preprocessed text into a string of phonemes in a quick and efficient manner.

2 Background

The system described by Elovitz is a system that uses rules of

> "the form
> $$A[B]C = D,$$
>
> ... . The meaning is 'The character string B, occurring with left context A and right context C, gets the pronunciation D.'
>
> D consists of IPA symbols — or rather a latin-letter representation of IPA to cater to computer character sets ..."

When a given letter is to be translated the rules for that letter are searched from first to last until a match is found, and that rule is used to produce the phoneme output. Use of some rule precludes the use of a rule that appears subsequent to it. The last rule of each letter has A and C as empty strings to catch all possibilities that have not been translated by a prior rule.

Implementations such as [4] and [5] use an explicit table search for the translation. The table is searched in order until a match is found.

3 Lex Syntax and Capabilities

The compiler writing tool lex, described in [3], is used to generate programs that will recognize strings in context. A lex generated program has the ability to use start conditions that can be used to recognize left contexts. For example, the fragment

```
%start CONTEXT1, CONTEXT2, ...
    ⋮
<CONTEXT1>b { /* action for b with left context 1 */ }
<CONTEXT2>b { /* action for b with left context 2 */ }
```

would treat the letter b differently depending on whether the start condition CONTEXT1 were true or the start condition CONTEXT2 were true.

Due to the large number of different left contexts that would need to be followed in parallel it was decided not to use the start conditions that lex provides. Instead as each part of the word is translated the word is also accumulated in a storage location. If a left context needs to be checked the accumulated word can be scanned backward from its end to see if the particular left context is present. When the end of the word is reached the accumulated word is discarded in preparation for the next word.

Table 1: Special Symbols Appearing in Translation Rules

#	one or more vowels
ˆ	one consonant
:	zero or more consonants
%	one of the suffixes er, e, es, ed, ing, or ely
+	one of b, d, v, g, j, l, m, n, r, w, or z — voiced consonant
$	beginning or end of the word

Lex also has the ability to generate a program that will recognize a string with a specified right context. For example, the fragment

```
b/abc { /* action for b with right context abc */ }
b/def { /* action for b with right context def */ }
```

would treat the letter *b* differently depending on whether is was followed by *abc* or *def*.

The tool lex provides the basis for building a text to phoneme translator. Each of the rules in [1] can be translated in two parts. First, the letter(s) of interest and the right context are translated into the form

```
l/rightcontext { /* action for this rule */ }
```

If there is a left context that needs to be checked for a rule it can be checked as part of the action for the rule.

4   Translation of the rules for the letter L

The letter L provides a good example of translating the rules into a lex grammar. The rules for the letter L show all the combinations of with and without left and right context.

From [1] the translation rules for the letter L are

```
[LO]C#     =/L OW/
L[L]       =/ /
#ˆ:[L]%    =/AX L/
[LEAD]     =/L IY D/
[L]        =/L/
```

The meaning of special symbols in the translation rules is shown in table 1. It is convenient to use the definition part of lex to define shorthand equivalents to the special characters.

```
consonant   [bcdfghjklmnpqrstvwxz]
vconsonant  [bdvgjlmnrwz]
```

```
vowel       [aeiouy]
suffix      e|er|es|ed|ing|ely
```

The conversion of the rule system is then accomplished by first writing the letter of interest and its right context and then adding a function call to check for any necessary left context. When a rule is recognized a function is then called to output the appropriate phoneme string.

The translation rules for the letter L then become

```
lo/c{vowel}     emit("l ow",0);
l               { if (p_context("l")) emit(" ",0);
                  else                 emit("l",0); }
l/{suffix}      { if (p_context("#:"))emit("ax l",0);
                  else                 emit("l",0); }
lead            emit("l iy d",0);
```

The function p_context() checks the accumulated word against the specified left context and returns true or false if the left context is present or not. The function emit() emits the specified phoneme string and advances the input text the specified number of characters in addition to the characters recognized by the rule.

Notice that two of the translation rules for the letter L (the second and the last) have the same right context. These have been combined into the same lex rule and the left context check is used to distinguish which phoneme string to output.

5 A problem

The letter-to-sound rules are designed to use the first match found in the table of rules. A lex generated scanner uses the longest match. This is a problem for some of the rules where the first match and longest match would pick different rules. As an example, look at two of the rules for the letter A.

$ARO   =/ax r/

$\vdots$

AR#   =/eh r/

The straight forward translation of these rules would give the program fragment:

```
a/ro    { if p_context("$") emit("ax r",1);
          else REJECT; /* Not this rule */ }

        :

a/r{vowel}+  emit("eh r",0);
```

The pattern match part of both of these rules will match such words as around and arouse. In order to follow the first match, as the rule system expects, these will need to be altered so that the first one is matched instead of the longer match of the second one. A suitable modification is

```
a/ro    { if p_context("$") emit("ax r",1);
          else REJECT; /* Not this rule */ }
        ⋮
a/r[aeiuy]{vowel}*  emit("eh r",0);
```

All of the rules need to be examined in this manner. If a rule will match the same string that an earlier rule would plus more, the rules need to be suitably modified so that the longest match is the first match.

6   Conclusions

This program was implemented without major problem. The choice to accumulate each word as it is processed was a good choice. The code to implement this method is very straight forward and statistics show that a preceding context needs to be checked for approximately every other rule that is applied.

Translation problems relating to the first match versus longest match were noted for some letters, especially the letter A. This required modification of some of the rules as discussed above.

Performance tests show that this program will translate 620 words per second on a Sun 4/110 workstation. This includes time to run a front end that preprocesses the text. The front end used in this test was also written using lex.

Acknowledgement

The author is grateful to Dr. Ben Pinkowski for his encouragement.

References

[1] Honey S. Elovitz, Rodney Johnson, Astrid McHugh, and John E. Shore, *Letter-to-sound rules for Automatic Translation of English Text to Phonetics*. IEEE Transaction on Acoustics, Speech and Signal Processing, **ASSP-24** (1976), 446-459

[2] Dennis H. Klatt, *Review of text-to-speech conversion for English*, Journal of the Acoustical Society of America, **82** (1987), 737-793

[3] M. E. Lesk and E. Schmidt, *Lex — A Lexical Analyzer Generator*, in B. W. Kernighan and M. D. McIlroy, *UNIX Programmer's Manual*, Bell Laboratories, 1978.

[4] L. Robert Morris,*A Fast FORTRAN Implementation of the U. S. Naval Research Laboratory Algorithm for Automatic Translation of English Text to Votrax Parameters*,Proc. Int. Conf. Acoust. Speech Process. **ICASSP-79**,907-913

Performance Evaluation of Medical Expert Systems [1]

D. Christine Georgakis
Northeastern Illlinois University
Chicago, Illinois 60625

Martha Evens
Illinois Institute of Technology
Chicago, Illinois 60616

Frank Naeymi-Rad   David A. Trace
University of Health Sciences/The Chicago Medical School
North Chicago, Illinois 60064

Abstract

The major problem in the evaluation of expert systems is the selection of the appropriate statistical measures of performance consistent with the parameters of the system domain. The objective of this paper is to develop the statistical evaluation methodology needed to assess the performance of medical expert systems including MEDAS - the Medical Emergency Decision Assistance System. The measures of performance are selected so as to have an operational interpretation and also reflect the predictive diagnostic capacity of a medical expert system. Certain summary measures are used that represent the sensitivity, specificity, and system response of a medical expert system. Measures of agreement such as the kappa statistic and the measure of conditional agrement are used to measure the agreement between the medical expert system and the physician. Goodman and Kruskal's lambda and tau measures of predictive association are introduced to evaluate the predictive capacity of a medical expert system. This methodology has been partially implemented in the performance evaluation of MEDAS.

1   Introduction

Medical expert systems require comprehensive evaluation of their diagnostic accuracy at every stage of development. Without established evaluation methods, the

---

[1]We want to thank Dr. Daniel Woodard of Bionetics and Dr. Paul Buchanan of NASA for their advice and support.

usefulness of medical expert systems is limited. Acceptance in the clinical arena is contingent on the verification of diagnostic accuracy first and foremost.

This paper addresses the need for formal evaluation in the development of medical expert systems. We develop a statistical evaluation methodology that assesses the performance of medical expert systems. This methodology includes standard summary measures, measures of agreement such as the kappa statistic and the measure of conditional agreement, and Goodman and Kruskal's λ and τ measures of predictive association. The various statistical measures are developed using the medical expert system MEDAS as an example.

2   The MEDAS Diagnostic System

MEDAS (the Medical Emergency Decision Assistance System) is a multimembership Bayesian diagnostic expert system designed to assist the clinician in determining diagnoses, ordering tests, and prescribing treatment. It can handle patients with one or more disorders.

The input to the diagnostic system consists of the patient's features. A feature is any piece of clinical data, age, sex, race, complaints, signs, symptoms, findings from the physical examination, results of tests and diagnostic medical procedures. The system's output consists of an ordered list of the possible disorder patterns ranked by their probability. Detailed description of the system is given by Ben-Bassat et al. [1].

MEDAS is the outgrowth of fourteen years of research on pattern recognition and expert systems carried on originally at the University of Southern California and continued for the past seven years at the Chicago Medical School. The knowledge base of the system consists of disorder patterns, each of which is composed of a list of features which may be relevant for the diagnosis of the disorder, coupled with two probability estimates which represent the sensitivity and specificity of these features with respect to this disorder.

3   Summary Measures

In our methodology we broaden the use of the sensitivity, specificity, and system response measures used by Ben-Bassat [2]. We utilize these measures through stratified random sampling and devise confidence limits according to established statistical practice [3].

Sensitivity Measure. This measure is the probability p_{ij} that the ith test disorder diagnosed by the physician is included in the list of the top j disorders given by the MEDAS output, where $i = 1, 2, \ldots, 10$ and $j = 1, 2, 3$. Note that p_{i1} is the number of times that MEDAS correctly predicts that the ith test disorder is the primary disorder present in the patient over the total number of times the ith disorder occurs in the ith test population group. In the traditional error rate approach for measuring the accuracy of a medical expert system, this describes the *sensitivity* of the MEDAS system relative to the ith test disorder.

For each of the 10 test disorders, we analyze the available sample data and obtain 95% confidence limits for the probabilities p_{ij}, which are given by

$$\hat{p}_{ij} \pm (1.96) \left(\left(\frac{N_i - n_i}{N_i} \right) \frac{\hat{p}_{ij}(1 - \hat{p}_{ij})}{n_i - 1} \right)^{1/2}$$

where $\hat{p}_{ij}$ is the sample proportion of observed patient records in which the ith test disorder diagnosed by the physician is included in the list of the top j disorders given by the MEDAS output.

N_i is the group size of patient records for which the primary diagnosis given by the physician is the ith test disorder, and n_i is the sample size drawn from the corresponding group of size N_i.

Overall Sensitivity Measure. An overall sensitivity measure of performance of MEDAS is the probability π_j that the physician's primary diagnosis is listed among the top j disorders in the MEDAS output, where $j = 1, 2, 3$. Because the 10 test disorder groups of sizes $N_1, N_2, \ldots, N_{10}$ form the 10 strata in a stratified random sample of sizes $n_1, n_2, \ldots, n_{10}$, we can obtain 95% confidence limits for π_j given by

$$\frac{1}{N} \sum_{i=1}^{10} N_i \hat{p}_{ij} \pm (1.96) \left(\frac{1}{N^2} \sum_{i=1}^{10} N_i^2 \left(\frac{N_i - n_i}{N_i} \right) \frac{\hat{p}_{ij}(1 - \hat{p}_{ij})}{n_i - 1} \right)^{1/2}$$

where $N = \sum_{i=1}^{10} N_i$ is the total population size.

System Response Measure. A measure used for the performance evaluation of MEDAS is the probability q_k that k false disorders are ranked in the MEDAS output above the correct primary test disorder diagnosed by the physician for $k = 0, 1, 2, 3$, or > 3. The 95% confidence limits for q_k are given by

$$\frac{1}{N} \sum_{i=1}^{10} N_i \hat{q}_{ik} \pm (1.96) \left(\frac{1}{N^2} \sum_{i=1}^{10} N_i^2 \left(\frac{N_i - n_i}{N_i} \right) \frac{\hat{q}_{ik}(1 - \hat{q}_{ik})}{n_i - 1} \right)^{1/2}$$

where $\hat{q}_{ik}$ is the sample proportion of observed patient records for which the MEDAS output listed k false disorders above the correct ith test disorder diagnosed by the physician.

Specificity Measure. A measure r_i for the *specificity* of the MEDAS system relative to the ith disorder is defined as the number of times MEDAS correctly predicts a disorder i to be absent divided by the total number of patients who are free of that disorder in the test population.

The nine samples of sizes $n_1, n_2, \ldots, n_9$, with the sample drawn from the ith disorder group left out, form the nine strata in a stratified random sample from the population of size $N - N_i$. The 95% confidence limits for r_i are given by

$$\frac{1}{N - N_i} \sum_{\substack{k=1 \\ k \neq i}}^{10} N_k \hat{r}_{ik} \pm (1.96) \left(\frac{1}{(N - N_i)^2} \sum_{\substack{k=1 \\ k \neq i}}^{10} N_k^2 \left(\frac{N_k - n_k}{N_k} \right) \frac{\hat{r}_{ik}(1 - \hat{r}_{ik})}{n_k - 1} \right)^{1/2}$$

where $\hat{r}_{ik}$ is the number of times that MEDAS correctly predicts the ith disorder to be absent among the patients in the kth sample over the sample size n_k.

4 Measures of Agreement

We use the kappa statistic as a measure of agreement between the medical expert system and the physician following Reggia [4]. In addition, we introduce the measure of conditional agreement, which complements the kappa statistic when studying performance from the viewpoint of diagnostic agreement.

The Kappa Statistic. The Kappa Statistic provides a *measure of agreement* or reliability between two "judges," which subtracts out the percentage of agreements that could be accounted for by chance alone. It was introduced by J. Cohen [5], and was used by J.A. Reggia [4] as a method for measuring the performance of the TIA (Transient Ischemic Attack) expert system.

In our case the two "judges" are the attending physician and the MEDAS system. Each gives a diagnosis for every patient in the population of size N which consists of all the well documented cases. Their diagnoses are used to generate a 10x10 classification table, where 10 is the number of test disorder classes. Note that $D_1, D_2, \ldots, D_{10}$ are the ten test disorders.

P^o_{ij} is the *observed* population proportion of patients that have been diagnosed as having disorder D_i by the physician but as having disorder D_j by MEDAS. P^c_{ij} is the proportion of agreement which can be accounted for by chance in the cell (i,j):

$$P^c_{ij} = P^o_{i.} P^o_{.j} \quad \text{where} \quad P^o_{i.} = \sum_{j=1}^{10} P^o_{ij} \quad \text{and} \quad P^o_{.j} = \sum_{i=1}^{10} P^o_{ij}$$

The entries P^o_{ij} in the classification table along the diagonal $i = j$ indicate the proportion of agreement between the physician's diagnosis and the MEDAS diagnosis. On the other hand, the entries P^o_{ij} off the diagonal $(i \neq j)$ represent the proportion of disagreement.

The kappa statistic is defined by

$$\kappa = \frac{P^o - P^c}{1 - P^c}$$

where $P^o = \sum_{i=j=1}^{10} P^o_{ij}$ which is the observed proportion of agreement, and

$P^c = \sum_{i=j=1}^{10} P^c_{ij}$ the proportion of agreement that could be attributed to chance.

The kappa statistic has the following interpretation: $\kappa = 1$ indicates perfect agreement; $\kappa = 0$ indicates a level of agreement attributed only to chance; $\kappa < 0$ indicates less than chance agreement.

Measure of Conditional Agreement A variation of the kappa statistic can be used to measure the conditional agreement between the diagnosis of the MEDAS system and that of the attending physician for that class of patients to whom MEDAS assigns disorder D_i in its diagnosis. This measure is defined by

$$\kappa_i = \frac{P^o_{ij} - P^o_{i.}P^o_{.j}}{P^o_{i.} - P^o_{i.}P^o_{.j}}$$

Its sample estimate $\hat{\kappa}_i$ and its sample variance are given by formulas similar to those for κ [6, 7].

The kappa statistic is a good overall measure of the reliability of the two "judges" when all disorders are considered, whereas κ_i is a similar measure for a particular disorder D_i.

5 Measures of Predictive Association

A novel feature of this paper is the introduction of two measures of predictive association for the evaluation of a medical expert system. These are the λ and τ measures of Goodman and Kruskal. The λ measure was first used in the evaluation of medical expert systems by Georgakis et al. [8].

Goodman and Kruskal's Lambda Measure. Goodman and Kruskal's λ measure can be used to analyze the extent to which the MEDAS diagnosis can predict the one given by the physician. It is a good measure of predictive association because of its operational interpretation [6,9,10].

In predicting the physician's diagnosis from that of MEDAS we consider that (1) the physician's diagnosis is statistically independent of MEDAS, or (2) the physician's diagnosis is a function of the MEDAS diagnosis.

The λ measure is defined by

$$\lambda = \frac{\text{Probability of error in (1)} - \text{Probabiliy of error in (2)}}{\text{Probability of error in (1)}}$$

Thus the degree of association shown by λ is defined as the relative improvement in predicting the physician's diagnosis obtained when the MEDAS diagnosis is known, as opposed to when the MEDAS diagnosis is not known. λ ranges between 0 and 1, and remains unchanged by permutation of rows or columns.

$\lambda = 0$ if and only if the knowledge of the MEDAS diagnosis is of no help in predicting the physician's diagnosis.

$\lambda = 1$ if and only if the knowledge of the MEDAS diagnosis completely specifies the physician's diagnosis.

A more explicit formula for λ is

$$\lambda = \frac{\max_i \left(P^o_{ij}\right) - \max_i \left(P^o_{i.}\right)}{1 - \max_i \left(P^o_{i.}\right)}$$

where P_{ij}^o is the observed population proportion of patients that have been diagnosed as having disorder D_i by the physician but as having disorder D_j by MEDAS and

$$P_{i.}^o = \sum_j P_{ij}^o$$

Its sample estimate $\hat{\lambda}$ is given by a similar formula, where p_{ij}^o replaces P_{ij}^o, and has a known standard error. Moreover, $(\hat{\lambda} - \lambda)/(\text{S.E.}(\hat{\lambda}))$ has a standard normal distribution when the sample is large.

Goodman and Kruskal's Measure of Proportional Prediction. Goodman and Kruskal's λ measure does not provide a measure of association based on optimal prediction, instead it describes the relative decrease in the proportion of incorrect predictions as we make the transition of guessing without any information to guessing with some prior knowledge. The λ measure is defined as follows: for each individual patient selected at random we are asked to guess the attending physician's diagnosis either

(1) Given the marginal probabilities $P_{i.}^o$, or
(2) Given the conditional probabilities $P_{ij}^o/P_{.j}^o$.

Clearly we should guess the physician's diagnosis as being disorder D_i with probability $P_{i.}^o$ in (1) and with probability $P_{ij}^o/P_{.j}^o$ in (2). The long run proportion of *correct* predictions will be

$$\tau_1 = \sum_i P_{i.}^o \text{ in (1) and } \tau_2 = \sum_i \sum_j (P_{ij}^o/P_{.j}^o) \text{ in (2)}$$

The τ measure is defined as the relative decrease in the proportion of incorrect predictions as we go from (1) to (2) and is given by

$$\tau = \frac{\tau_2 - \tau_1}{1 - \tau_1}$$

The τ measure takes values between 0 and 1; $\tau = 0$ if and only if there is diagnostic independence between the physician and MEDAS, and $\tau = 1$ if and only if knowledge of MEDAS completely determines that of the physician [11].

6 Conclusion

The formal evaluation of a medical expert system plays an important role in its development and represents a deciding factor in the utilization of the system in clinical practice on a wide scale. In this paper we develop a statistical evaluation methodology to assess the diagnostic performance of medical expert systems. The measures of performance are selected so as to have an operational interpretation and also reflect the predicitive diagnostic capacity of a medical expert system. Our methodology was tested in a pilot study [8] that evaluated the performance of MEDAS using a knowledge base of 30 disorders. This pilot study showed that measures used by the social sciences to examine the performance of human experts in the decision making process can be used in medical artificial intelligence.

References

[1] M. Ben-Bassat, R.W. Carlson, U.K. Puri, M.D. Davenport, J.A. Shriver, M. Latif, R. Smith, L.R. Portigal, E.H. Lipnick, and M.H. Weil. Pattern-Based Interactive Diagnosis of Multiple Disorders: The MEDAS System. *IEEE Transactions on Pattern Analysis and Machine Intelligence*, PAMI-2, no. 2, March, 1980, pp. 148-160.

[2] M. Ben-Bassat, D. Campell, A. MacNeil, and M.H. Weil. Evaluating Multimembership Classifiers: A Methodology and Application to the MEDAS Diagnostic System. *IEEE Transactions on Pattern Analysis and Machine Intelligence*, PAMI-5, 2, March, 1983, pp. 225-229.

[3] W.G. Cochran. Sampling Techniques. John Wiley & Sons, New York, 1977.

[4] J.A. Reggia. Evaluation of Medical Expert Systems: A Case Study in Performance Analysis. *Proceedings of the Ninth Annual Symposium on Computer Applications in Medical Care*, Baltimore, MD, 1985. pp. 287-291.

[5] J. Cohen. A Coefficient of Agreement for Nominal Scales. *Educational and Psychological Measurement*, 20, 1960, pp. 37-46.

[6] Y. Bishop, S. Fienberg, and P. Holland. *Discrete Multivariate Analysis: Theory and Practice*. MIT Press, Cambridge, MA. 1984.

[7] R. Light. *Analysis of Variance for Categorical Data, with Applications to Agreement and Association*. Ph.D. Dissertation, Department of Statistics, Harvard University, 1969..

[8] D.C. Georgakis, R. Rosenthal, D.A. Trace, and M. Evens. Measures of Performance of the MEDAS System. *Proceedings of the Fourth Annual Artificial Intelligence and Advanced Computer Technology Conference*, Long Beach, CA, May, 1988, pp. 50-65.

[9] L. Goodman and W. Kruskal. Measures of Association for Cross-Classifications. Springer-Verlag, New York, 1979.

[10] B.S. Everitt. *The Analysis of Contingency Tables*. Halsted Press, John Wiley & Sons, New York, NY, 1977.

[11] L. Goodman and W. Kruskal. Measures of Association for Cross-Classifications, Part I. *Journal of the American Statistical Association*, 49, 1954, pp. 732-764.

Spelling Correction
for an Intelligent Tutoring System [1]

Yoon Hee Lee   Martha Evens

Illinois Institute of Technology
Chicago, Illinois 60616

Joel A. Michael   Allen A. Rovick

Rush Medical College
Chicago, Illinois 60612

Abstract

Our spelling correction program is part of a system for understanding ill-formed input in an intelligent tutoring system for medical students. Speed and user-friendliness were the most important considerations in the design. The system can correct most kinds of spelling errors including order reversal, missing characters, added characters, and character substitutions. It also handles novel abbreviations and word boundary errors. It is implemented on a Xerox 1108 AI machine in Interlisp-D. The lexicon is stored in a trie structure to speed up searching. We provide the students with a full-screen editor and an input tracer to simplify the input process as much as possible.

1   Introduction

This paper is concerned with the development of the spelling correction component of a program that tries to deal with ill-formed student input in a tutoring context. This implementation of our ideas was written in Interlisp-D on a Xerox 1108 Artificial Intelligence machine. This research forms part of a larger project – the design of a computer-aided instruction program to assist first-year medical students in solving problems in cardiovascular physiology. We are starting with an existing CAI program CIRCSIM [1] and attempting to build a succession of increasingly intelligent versions. The goals of our research project are add facilities to understand ill-formed student input, model student knowledge, and generate natural language explanations tailored to individual students [2].

---

[1]This work was supported by the Cognitive Science Program, Office of Naval Research under Grant No. N00014-89-J-1952, Grant Authority Identification Number NR4422554 to Illinois Institute of Technology. The content does not reflect the position or policy of the government and no official endorsement should be inferred.

The tutor provides users of the system with a full screen text editor for use in text input. This has advantages both for us and for the student. It makes the student comfortable and it makes it easy for the student to correct his/her own mistakes – leaving fewer problems for us to deal with. The programmable Interlisp-D text editor, TEdit, proved to be a very satisfactory tool for this purpose, making it easy to update and trace the student input. A trace facility is essential to a program supporting interactive input. We use a temporary buffer for input tracing. As a result, students can return to the latest updated version of their text input and make changes at any point.

2 Sublanguage

A sublanguage is a form of natural language used by a particular community of specialists to describe a particular subject matter [3,4]. In order to analyze natural language reliably, a computer system requires a great deal of information about the syntax of the language, about the structure of the discourse, and about the subject matter for the language. Because of the need for detailed knowledge of the subject matter, natural language input systems perform better within a very limited domain of discourse. For this project we needed to analyze the student cardiovascular sublanguage and formulate a sublanguage grammar and lexicon.

We collected and studied student language samples collected in face-to-face tutoring sessions. We are now collecting still more examples from keyboard-to-keyboard tutoring sessions. We made KWIC indexes and concordances of the student language samples using the VAX computer system. Then we used a phrase counting program to isolate common phrases and added them to the lexicon. In the process of sublanguage analysis, we found about 1650 words and phrases belonging to the student cardiovascular sublanguage. We are using a Lexical Functional Grammar parser built by Lee to discover sublanguage specific grammar rules as well.

3 Lexicon

The lexicon contains essential data entries for the spelling correction system and the parser/understander. Each lexical entry contains orthographic, syntactic, and semantic information so that the system can retrieve information for both spelling correction and the parser/understander at the same time.

The lexicon data structure is very important for the spelling correction and parsing system because the search algorithm depends on this structure. These, in turn, determine program run time. We decided to use the kind of tree structure call a trie [5]. The trie is an index structure that is particularly useful when key values are of varying size. A trie is a tree of degree $m > 1$ in which the branching at any level is determined not by the entire key value but only a portion of it.

The trie contains two type of nodes, branch nodes and information nodes. Our lexical database is a trie of degree m = 3. Each branch node contains 27 linked fields, 26 letters of the alphabet and a blank. At level 1 the branch node contains 26 alphabetic characters and one special character. At any level all key values are partitioned into 27 disjoint classes depending on their first character. This kind of data structure may be slow in other computer systems, but it works very well on a Xerox AI system.

4 Spelling Correction

4.1 Spelling Errors

In our studies of examples of student language we identified three classes of student spelling errors: general errors, abbreviations, and word boundary errors.

(1)General spelling errors
   A) Character case: caRDiac → cardiac
   B) Reversed order: hte → the
   C) Missing character(s): occuring → occurring
   D) Added character(s): endema → edema
   E) Character substitution(s): resistanse → resistance

These kinds of errors are very common. All but type (A) errors can seriously confuse a system. Types (A) – (E) demonstrate common typing mistakes, types (C) – (E) arise from typing errors or from technical or general mistakes. Also, we can respond to several types at once as in "dyfuncsion" → "dysfunction," repairing both missing character and character substitution problems. We handle homophone errors by making an extra lexical entry as in: (rails (HOMOPHONE rales) .....).
(2) Abbreviations.

We decided to add to the lexicon frequently used abbreviations that appeared in our study of student language samples such as DR for Direct Response, CO for Cardiac Output, MAP for Mean Arterial Pressure, fcn for function, ht for heart, etc. We also found unexpected abbreviated words such as: "conduc." for "conduction" and "incre" for "increase."
(3) Word boundary errors.

Generally, there exist two types of word boundary errors: *join* and *separation*, as in: "breathingrate" for "breathing rate" and "ortho pneic" for "orthopneic." These kinds of errors are also very common. They may stem from typing errors or from a technical misunderstanding of the prefix, e.g., milli, pico.

4.2 Basic Spelling Correction Algorithms

The basic idea underlying our spelling correction algorithms is to count the number of disagreements between two words, and use this number divided by the length of the longer of the two words as a measure of their relative disagreement. For example, "resistanse" and "resistance" differ by only one character, so that these two words are in 10% disagreement. Some spelling correction systems such as DWIM of Xerox Corp. only attempt to handle cases with a relative disagreement of no more than 30%. But, we decided to use a 40% disagreement threshold, so that an error can be corrected in words of only three characters. We then find the word that disagrees least with our input string and automatically correct it.

The basic spelling correction algorithm begins by comparing strings. The best match algorithm is based on the work of Hall and Dowling [6]. When the input string is compared with the possible lexical entry in lexicon data lists, each pair of characters in the two strings is compared in three ways. If the nth character of the input string is not same as the mth character of the word from the lexicon, there is probably a spelling error at this point. The system makes a further comparison to detect the type of error. If the nth character of the input string is same as the (m+1)st character of the word from the lexicon and the (n+1)st character is different from the mth character in the word from lexicon, we have found a type C missing character error. If the nth character of the input string matches the (m+1)st character of the word in the lexicon and the (n+1)st character matches the mth character, then we have a type B order reversal. Type D added character errors are the reverse of missing characters. Each type of error has a priority: the priority is from type A to E in order, but types C and D have the same priority. So, there exists a first come first serve relationship between types C and D.

An example of the best comparison between the two strings is as follows:

```
d y f n u c s i o n
| |  \  |  \   \ \ \
d y s f u n c t i o n
```

The best match occurs with a difference of three, and the manner of this best match can be deduced from the shortest path.

The comparison process may terminate in several ways. If the error count is bigger than the maximum error count, the word from the lexicon is discarded. We get the next appropriate lexical entry and compare again. If we reach the end of both strings with an error count of 0, the input string has been found in the lexicon. So, we get the next input string and continue. If the error count is not zero, we put the word from the lexicon and the error count in the possible word table and change the maximum error count to the current error count. Then we get the next possible lexical entry, and compare. If one of the input string or lexicon is nil, we check for a word boundary error or abbreviation.

4.3 Supplementary Spelling Correction Algorithms

Our system will also handle abbreviated words and word boundary errors. If an input string does not satisfy the 40% disagreement threshold but it is the same as the initial segment of another word, we assume it is an abbreviation of that word and expand it. We may also need to combine two input strings to make one word. Also, if an initial segment of the input string is same as a word in the lexicon, we consider the possibility that it may consist of two words.

If the input string is shorter than three characters, it is ordinarily impossible to correct it because of the 40% disagreement threshold. But the system will make just one reverse order correction if the input string is two characters long.

After all possible lexical entry comparisons are finished, there exist several table entries to consider. First, we check the possible word table. If no possible lexicon entry matches, we check the possible abbreviation table. And then we check the word boundary table, to find out whether we have a join or separation. If nothing is found, the system asks the user for a correction.

4.4   Searching the Lexicon Data Base

The lexicon data base is a trie structure of degree m = 3. It means the key is the initial three characters of the word. By the 40% disagreement threshold, one error is permitted in the key string. If we permit more than one error in three characters, the system will be required to search too many meaningless lists in the lexicon and take a long time for the search.

In this algorithm and the character comparison algorithm we have to search the following lists if the input string is "abcd..." ("*" stands for all alphabetic characters from "a" to "z").

Type of Comparison	Information Node Name
No Error	abc
Reverse Order	bac, acb
Added Character	bcd, acd, abd
Missing Character	*ab, a*b, ab*
Character Substitution	*bc, a*c, ab*

With this search method, we have to search (26 * (6 − 1 (duplicated node)) + 6 = 136) lists. This means 136 lists out of total 18955 lists (0.72%). And so, the number of actual words which are compared with the input string is 0.72% * 1650 words = 11.8 words. Therefore, this algorithm is very efficient and fast.

5   Test Results

The spelling correction algorithm is very fast; no word tried so far takes more than 1.4 seconds. Complex general errors, unexpected abbreviation errors, word boundary errors, and fatal errors (e.g., "dfghjk") take maximum correction time because in these cases the word is checked against every possible error type by the spelling correction algorithm. The elapsed time depends on how many words there are in the list the erroreous word is compared with. It also depends on the length of the words compared. Most of the lists have two to six words. But a few lists starting with common prefixes such as "re," "co," and "in" have more than ten words. Figure 1 shows actual comparison times for typical spelling errors using our spelling correction system.

Input String	Correct Word	Error		No. of Compared Words	Actual Correction Time (sec)
		Type	Count		
attempt	attempt	N	0	1	0.012
carDiac	cardiac	A	0	5	0.026
hte	the	B	1	10	0.063
nveer	never	B	1	2	0.053
sugest	suggest	C	1	1	0.048
sitroke	stroke	D	1	20	0.123
reiative	relative	E	1	104	1.160
dyfuncsion	dysfunction	M	2	15	0.589
acomplasheed	accomplished	M	3	52	0.785
rails	rales	H	-	5	0.050
conduc.	conduction	U	-	215	1.400
incre	increase	U	-	97	0.941
ortho pneic	orthopneic	S	-	48	0.703
dfghjk	-	F	-	12	1.250

Figure 1. Actual Comparison Times for Typical Spelling Errors

(Error Types: A – Character Case; B – Reverse Order; C – Missing Character; D – Added Character; E – Character Substitution; F – Fatal Error; H – Homophone Error; J – Join (Word Boundary Error); N – No Error; M – Complex Error; S – Separation (Word Boundary Error); U – Unexpected Abbreviation.)

6 Conclusion

In the commercial market, there exist many spelling checker programs in word processing systems for PC level computers (e.g., First Choice, Word Perfect). The DWIM (Do What I Mean) system is the utility provided by Xerox AI systems for spelling correction in the Interlisp-D Language. DWIM is called automatically whenever an error occurs in the evaluation of an Interlisp expression. But it only operates on unbound atoms and undefined function errors. It corrects spelling errors automatically with a 30% disagreement threshold. The New World of Computing System [7] was built by the Thompsons at California Institute of Technology. This excellent system written in C, Pascal, Fortran runs on VAX and PC computers. Spelling correction in the New World system consists of two parts, small corrections and large corrections. The small correction part handles general spelling errors and asks for confirmation. The large correction system handles word boundary errors while the parser is working. Figure 2 compares the capabilities of our system with some other systems.

System	General Spelling Checker	Xerox DWIM	New World of Computing	Our System
Programming Language	Depends on System	Lisp	C,PASCAL, FORTRAN	Lisp
Threshold	None	30%	Unknown	40%
Expected Abbrev.	Yes	Yes	Yes	Yes
Unexpected Abbrev.	No	No	No	Yes
Boundary Errors	No	No	Yes	Yes
Homophone Errors	No	Yes	Yes	Yes

Figure 2. Comparison with Other Systems

We are using Interlisp-D on a Xerox AI system, which makes this algorithm relatively easy to implement. It will cover most cases of spelling correction in DWIM and in the Thompsons' New World of Computing System. In addition, our system can correct unexpected abbreviations automatically.

References

[1] A.A. Rovick and J.A. Michael. CIRCSIM: An IBM PC Computer Teaching Exercise on Blood Pressure Regulation. *XXX IUPS Congress*, Vancouver. 1986.

[2] Y. Zhang, M. Evens, A.A. Rovick, and J.A. Michael. Knowledge Compiler for an Expert Physiology Tutor. *Proceedings of ESD/SMI Conference on Expert Systems* Dearborn. 1987: 245-259.

[3] R. Grishman and R. Kittredge. *Analyzing Language in Restricted Domains: Sublanguage Description and Processing*. Lawrence Erlbaum Associates, Hillsdale, NJ. 1986.

[4] N. Sager, Sublanguage: Linguistic Phenomenon, Computational Tool. In R. Grishman and R. Kittredge (eds.), 1986: 1–18.

[5] E. Horowitz and S. Sahni. *Fundamentals of Data Structures*. Computer Science Press, Rockville, MD. 1976.

[6] P. Hall and G. Dowling. Approximate String Matching. *Computing Surveys* 12(4): 381–402. 1980.

[7] B.H. Thompson and F. Thompson, *The New World of Computing*. Computer Science Department, California Institute of Technology. 1987.

An Informational Network for a Natural Talking System

Paul Buchheit

University of Illinois at Chicago
P.O. Box 4348
Chicago, Illinois 60680

Abstract

A Natural Language Processing System has been developed that communicates in the simple commonsense terms of a child. The system utilizes a knowledge representation scheme that facilitates the storage and retrieval of factual and inferential data through a massively-interlinked network of propositional information. Inferential analysis is handled by an organized matrix of predicate-based inferences that uses forward chaining to deduce new propositions. The potential for learning has been established through inductive generalization and the ongoing adjustment of uncertainty values on existing propositions.

1 Introduction

The Informational Network for a Natural Talking (INFANT) System is a fully automated Natural Language Processing (NLP) system that employs a semantic network of linguistic information to communicate in commonsense terms at a child's level of understanding. An actual conversation with the INFANT system follows.

How are you?	{Person speaking}	((HOW) YOU IS _)	{parser
I REAL GOOD.	{COMPUTER SPEAKING}		interpretation}
I was just at the park.		(I LOC PARK)	{Statement 1}
I SEE.			
I was playing with Joe.		(I PLAY JOE)	{Statement 2}
SO THEN YOU OFTEN PLAY WITH JOE?			
Yes. Do you know how Joe is?		((HOW) JOE IS _)	
JOE QUITE HAPPY.			
Why is he happy?		((WHY) JOE HAPPY _)	
BECAUSE YOU PLAY WITH JOE.			
Well, he is not very good to me.		(JOE -GOOD I)	{Statement 3}
BUT YOU ALMOST CERTAINLY GOOD TO JOE.			

Do you know why he is not good to me?   ((WHY) JOE -GOOD I)
    BECAUSE JOE POSSIBLY NOT LIKE YOU.
Well, I still like Joe.   (I HAPPY JOE)   {Statement 4}
    WHY?
He is at the bank right now.   (JOE LOC BANK)   {Statement 5}
    THEN YOU MAYBE LIKE MONEY.

The informational network of the INFANT system combines a complex linkage structure with a generalization method that provides the means for inductive learning. Propositions derived from an input statement by the "predictive wait-and-see" parser [1] are stored in original, indexed, inverted, and generalized form in the network, and as a result subsequent statements or questions have access to relevant knowledge through multiple entry points. For example, the information

JOE PLAYS WITH MARY

is accessible through the concepts JOE, PLAY, MARY, and ANIM (PERSON); thus the analysis of a subsequent input statement such as

MARY IS HAPPY

will involve consideration of JOE as a possible cause of MARY's emotional state. As another example, a question such as

WHO IS PLAYING?

will lead directly to the facts recorded about JOE. The storage techniques that permit such data retrieval flexibility will be examined in the next section of the paper.

Information presented to the INFANT system is also analyzed by an "inference engine" that uses forward chaining to deduce likely consequences from a given input statement. For example, acceptance of the assertion

JOE PLAYS WITH MARY

leads naturally to the proposition

MARY PLAYS WITH JOE ,

and thus later reaction to the input

MARY IS NOT HAPPY

will include consideration of the apparently conflicting information about MARY's playing with JOE. These newly derived inferences will themselves be stored in multiple forms in the knowledge base. Admittedly, such far-reaching forward chaining can lead to problems. The inferencing module in MARGIE [2] demonstrated that unrestricted inferencing results in a combinatorial explosion of new assertions. However, the declarative structure of the inference engine and the simplicity of the child's domain of the INFANT system help to minimize the adverse effects of the forward chaining.

2   The Informational Network

The Informational Network (Figures 1 and 2) is a propositional knowledge base that provides the basis for computer "understanding" through its interconnected, declar-

```
(ANIM) ((GEN (ANIM)) (SPECS BABY I JOE MARY)
                (ALT (A PERSON)(PEOPLE)))
(anim good anim) ((fuz 7))
(anim happy anim) ((fuz 7))
(anim happy money) ((fuz 9))
(anim happy _) ((fuz 6))
(anim works workobj) ((fuz 8))
(BABY) ((GEN (BABY)(ANIM)))
(baby play playobj) ((fuz 9))
(baby works _) ((fuz 1))
(BALL) ((GEN (BALL)(PLAYOBJ)))
(I) ((GEN (I) (ANIM)))
(JOE) ((GEN (JOE) (ANIM)))
(MARY) ((GEN (MARY) (ANIM)))
(PLAYOBJ) ((GEN (PLAYOBJ) (OBJ)) (SPECS BALL))
(WORKOBJ) ((GEN (WORKOBJ) (OBJ)) (SPECS COMPUTER))

          Uncertainty (FUZZY) Values:
      9 CERTAINLY; ALWAYS
      8 ALMOST CERTAINLY
      7 PROBABLY; USUALLY; FREQUENTLY
      6 POSSIBLY; AT TIMES
      5 UNCERTAIN
      4 POSSIBLY NOT
      3 PROBABLY NOT
      2 ALMOST CERTAINLY NOT
      1 CERTAINLY NOT
      0 NONSENSE
```

Figure 1: Part of the INFANT network

ative structure [3]. The linguistic triplets that make up the propositions are similar to the template forms of Wilks' Preference Semantics [4,5]. In its initial form, prior to expansion during conversation, the knowledge base exists as shown in the network segment of Figure 1. Conceptual data such as ANIM (ANIMATE OBJECT), BALL, MARY, etc. make up the nodes of the semantic network, while conceptual relationships such as (ANIM GOOD ANIM), (BABY PLAY PLAYOBJ), etc. make up the arcs. Concept nodes contain instances of generalization (eg, PLAYOBJ (PLAY OBJECT) for BALL), instances of specialization (eg, BABY, I, JOE, MARY for ANIM), and alternative representations (eg, A PERSON or PEOPLE for ANIM). Arcs encode factual information relevant to ordinary conversation. The attachment of fuzzy uncertainty values to the arcs (see Figure 1 for interpretations) serves to strengthen or moderate the effect of the given facts. For example, the fact (ANIM HAPPY ANIM (fuz 7)) indicates that a person usually (fuzzy 7) is happy with another person; similarly, given that a person works, that person almost certainly works with a

```
                    1. I LOC PARK (Statement 2-1)
(I HAPPY _)              ((fuz 7) (old (8 1)))


                    2. I PLAY JOE (Statement 2-2)
(I HAPPY _)              ((fuz 8) (old (9 2) (8 1)))
(JOE HAPPY _)           ((fuz 8) (old (9 2)))


                    3. JOE -GOOD I (Statement 2-3)
(I HAPPY JOE)           ((fuz 4) (old (1 3) (9 2)))
(I HAPPY _)              ((fuz 6) (old (1 3) (9 2) (8 1)))
(JOE GOOD I)            ((fuz 3) (old (1 3) (9 2)))
(JOE HAPPY I)           ((fuz 4) (old (2 3) (9 2)))


                    4. I HAPPY JOE (Statement 2-4)
(ANIM HAPPY _)          ((fuz 6) (old (7 4) (1 3) (9 2) (8 1)))
(I HAPPY JOE)           ((fuz 7) (old (9 4) (1 3) (9 2)))
(JOE GOOD I)            ((fuz 4) (old (6 4) (1 3) (9 2)))
(JOE HAPPY *)           (( → 6 4 I HAPPY *))
(JOE HAPPY I)           ((fuz 6) (old (7 4) (2 3) (9 2)))
(JOE O-P HAPPY *)       (( → 6 4 * HAPPY I))

                    5. JOE LOC BANK (Statement 2-5)
(I HAPPY MONEY)    ((fuz 8) (old (6 5 4)))
```

Figure 2: The Expanding Network

work object (ANIM WORKS WORKOBJ (fuz 8)), while a baby never works (BABY WORKS _ (fuz 1)). Primitive concepts such as I, JOE, and MARY (animate objects "known" to the computer) begin their existence without any specifically coded relationships with other concepts.

3 Changes to the Network

Figure 2 shows the sequence of changes to the informational network during the sample conversation presented in the introduction. The chosen segments, which can be portrayed as expanding network arcs, reflect the computer's gradually changing opinion of the emotional states of "I," "JOE," and people in general (ANIM). A chronological summary of these changes is presented below. It should be noted that the attempt to represent emotions in the INFANT system has been influenced by similar work in Conceptual Dependency [6] and by the "AFFECT" knowledge structures of Michael Dyer [7].

After Statement 1: I LOC PARK

(I HAPPY _)((fuz 7)(old (8 1)))

"I" am almost certainly (fuz 8) happy about being at the park. Overall, I am probably (fuz 7) happy.

After Statement 2: I PLAY JOE

(I HAPPY _)((fuz 8)(old (9 2)(8 1)))

I am certainly (fuz 9) happy about playing with JOE (Statement 2). Overall, I am almost certainly (fuz 8) happy.

(JOE HAPPY _)((fuz 8)..

For many of the same reasons, JOE is almost certainly (fuz 8) happy.

After Statement 3: JOE -GOOD I

Now INFANT learns something about JOE that changes its opinions.

(I HAPPY JOE)((fuz 4)(old (1 3))..
(I HAPPY _)((fuz 6)(old (1 3))..

I am certainly not (fuz 1) happy about JOE's treatment of I (Statement 3). Overall, I am possibly not (fuz 4) happy with JOE, but I am possibly (fuz 6) still happy in general. Overall opinions change gradually.

(JOE GOOD I)((fuz 3)..
(JOE HAPPY I)((fuz 4)..

JOE is probably not (fuz 3) good to I, and possibly not (fuz 4) happy with I.

After Statement 4: I HAPPY JOE

(I HAPPY JOE)((fuz 7)..

INFANT acknowledges that I probably do like JOE.

(JOE HAPPY I)((fuz 6)..
(JOE GOOD I)((fuz 4)..

Uncertainty abounds about JOE's feelings after INFANT has learned that I like JOE even though he is not good to I.

(ANIM HAPPY _)((fuz 6)..

The majority of "happy" statements (all except Statement 3) leads INFANT to believe that a person is, in general, possibly (fuz 6) happy.

(JOE HAPPY *)((⇒ 6 4 I HAPPY *))
(JOE O-P HAPPY *)((⇒ 6 4 * HAPPY I))

These are inferences stored in the knowledge base after Statement 4. Since (I HAPPY JOE), it is very possible (fuz 6) that if JOE likes something (JOE HAPPY *), then I will like it too (I HAPPY *). The second inference is inverted to facilitate the access of information through the concept "JOE" ("O-P" refers to the Object-Predicate order of the triplet). It states that if someone likes JOE (JOE O-P HAPPY *), then that person will possibly (fuz 6) like I (* HAPPY I).

After Statement 5: JOE LOC BANK

With a hint of moralistic rebuke, INFANT concludes that I might be motivated by something other than concern for JOE.

(I HAPPY MONEY)((fuz 8)(old (6 5 4)))

Given the probabilities that JOE is at the bank (Statement 5) and likes money (Figure 1; Statement 5), and that I like what JOE likes (first inference from Statement 4), INFANT infers a possible (fuz 6) connection between (I HAPPY JOE) and (I HAPPY MONEY).

It must be conceded that INFANT's conclusions about money – and for that matter, all else – may not be realistic; yet in a child's world many concepts are accepted absolutely, without the subtle modifications provided by extenuating knowledge, and this at present is the case with INFANT.

4   Conclusion

The primary goal of the INFANT system is to demonstrate that a simple form of commonsense understanding and conversational interaction can be achieved through the organized interpretation and storage of propositional triplets, which are suggestive of the fragmentary thought patterns of human beings. The INFANT system is presently capable of dealing with single-proposition input statements. That is, a statement such as

MARY IS GOOD TO ME ,

which reduces to the proposition

MARY GOOD I ,

is maintained in such a way that any reference to MARY, I, PERSON, GOODNESS, BADNESS, etc. leads to consideration of the known propositional information that "Mary is good to me." Work on the system has thus emphasized the intricacies of propositional relationships rather than the interpretation of more complex sentences.

However, the continuing development of INFANT necessitates an integration of multi-propositional facts into the existing network. For example, a sentence such as

MARY IS GOOD TO THE MAN WHO WORKS THE COMPUTER

can be interpreted as a pair of propositions:

MARY GOOD MAN...MAN WORKS COMPUTER .

Of course, even such a simple example prompts concern about the logical connection between the two propositions, the entailment of one upon the other, and the intensional or extensional meaning of the word "man" (is it one man, or man in general?). Such problems make it clear that the difficulties involved in multi-phrase analysis greatly outweigh those of single phrases. Yet in either case, the immediate problem remains the need to demonstrate that a network of interlinked propositions is flexible enough to understand the subtle nuances of language that are sure to derive from increasingly more natural conversation.

References

[1] Paul Buchheit and Roger Conant. A Predictive Wait-and-See Parser. Department of Electrical Engineering and Computer Science, University of Illinois at Chicago, P.O. Box 4348, Chicago IL 60680, 1988.

[2] Roger Schank, Neil Goldman, Charles Rieger, and Chris Riesbeck. MARGIE: Memory, Analysis, Response Generation, and Inference on English. *IJCAI-73*, Stanford University, Stanford CA, 1973.

[3] Paul Buchheit, Jeffrey Tsai, Roger Conant, and Thomas Moher. A Discourse-Based Network for a Natural Language System. *Proceedings of SPIE: Applications of Artificial Intelligence VI*, Vol. 937, 1988.

[4] Yorick Wilks. Parsing English II. In Eugene Charniak, and Yorick Wilks (eds.) *Computational Semantics*, North-Holland, Amsterdam, 1976.

[5] Yorick Wilks. Deep and Superficial Parsing. In King, Margaret (ed.), *Parsing Natural Language*, Academic Press, London, 1983.

[6] Roger Schank, and Robert Abelson. *Scripts, Plans, Goals, and Understanding*, Lawrence Erlbaum Associates, Hillsdale, NJ, 1977.

[7] Michael Dyer. The Role of Affect in Narratives. *Cognitive Science* 7, 211-242, 1983.

Formation of Categories in Document Classification Systems[1]

Sanjiv K. Bhatia[2], Jitender S. Deogun[2] and Vijay V. Raghavan[3]

Abstract

Information retrieval systems employ the classification of documents into various categories to facilitate retrieval. The problem of categorization depends on the successful solution to three subproblems: creation of categories, determining the relationship between categories, and maintenance of the categorization system. In existing document categorization systems, the categories are formed by using hit and trial methods. This increases the initial setup period for the system. The initial setup time is further affected by an empirical assignment of relationships between categories.

In this paper, we propose a solution to the problem of developing categories by the application of techniques originating in knowledge acquisition. The approach is based on capturing the knowledge of a user to ensure continuity with the existing categorization system. The use of Personal Construct Theory for knowledge elicitation helps in making explicit the subconscious hierarchical relationships between various categories as perceived by the user.

1   Introduction

In a number of applications, one faces the problem of classification of objects. For example, in a news service environment, a number of stories appear over the wire and need to be routed to an appropriate division within the service which should handle it. In conventional systems, a group of personnel have to read each story as it is received to determine its contents and then, route it to the appropriate division.

In existing document classification systems, for example Text Categorization Shell [2], a set of production rules decide the classification of documents. However, these systems involve a large setup time because of inadequate quantification of uncertain knowledge of the users in the domain of topics addressed by the documents. The quantification of this knowledge is not easy because a person places an object in a particular class based on his experience that might have become part of his subconscious knowledge. The long setup time is due to the inability of the knowledge engineer in determining this quantification. Hence, these systems use hit and trial methods for establishing the proper quantifications of uncertainty for the production rules during the setup period.

In this paper, we describe a system to capture the quantification of uncertain knowledge for classification. Personal construct theory is used for knowledge acquisition. It is shown that the subconscious knowledge can be easily captured and

---

[1]This research is supported by the NSF grant IRI-8805875.
[2]Department of Computer Science and Engineering, University of Nebraska, Lincoln, NE 68588.

[3]Center for Advanced Computer Studies, University of SW Louisiana, Lafayette, LA 70504.

quantified using personal construct theory. Finally, a rule base is developed to classify new documents.

2 Personal Construct Theory

Personal Construct theory was originated in the field of clinical psychology in the mid 50's by George Kelly [4] as a means of capturing subconscious knowledge of the environment of a subject. It was first adapted for automated knowledge acquisition by John Boose [1] in the 70's.

According to personal construct theory, every person has a unique perception of his environment which is made up of other persons and objects having an influence on the person's actions. These objects and persons are known as *entities*. An entity on its own does not directly contribute to a person's action but it is a property possessed by the entity which does so. This property is known as a *construct*. Every entity influences a person's action to some degree. This degree of influence can be quantified on a ranking scale for each entity and construct. This quantification results into a matrix of rankings known as *repertory grid*. The repertory grid shows the degree of presence of each construct in every entity. The entities and constructs can be elicited from a person by an interview. Once they are known, they help in explaining a person's actions in a given environment. We'll illustrate the acquisition of this knowledge for classification in the next section.

3 Categorization System

In this section, we describe the development of the categorization system using personal construct theory. The document categorization system interviews a user showing him a few documents (entities) selected at random from the total collection of documents. The result of this interview process is a list of identifiers representing the topics of the documents (constructs) and the perception of the user about relationship between them. This perception is in the form of a repertory grid which has to be analyzed to extract the relationships in a usable form. The end result from the system is the relationships in the form of a dependence tree which can be transformed into rules. These rules can be directly used to create a production system to categorize documents with the expertise of the user [1].

3.1 Knowledge Acquisition

The categorization system is dependent upon an interview with the user for knowledge elicitation. The interview uses a set of randomly selected documents from the total document collection. This set of documents is known as *learning set*. Learning set is used by the system to elicit user opinion about the documents. During the interview, the user is shown a sample of documents from the learning set and asked to express his opinion about the contents of the documents. The opinion is elicited

	d_1	d_2	d_3	d_4	d_5	d_6	d_7	d_8	d_9	d_{10}	d_{11}	d_{12}	d_{13}	d_{14}	d_{15}	d_{16}	d_{17}	d_{18}	d_{19}	d_{20}
c_1	1	1	1	1	1	1	1	1	5	1	1	5	1	1	1	1	1	1	1	1
c_2	5	1	1	5	1	1	1	1	1	1	1	1	1	1	1	2	1	1	1	2
c_3	1	5	1	1	1	2	1	1	1	1	2	1	2	5	4	1	1	5	1	
c_4	5	1	1	5	1	1	5	1	4	1	1	2	1	1	1	3	5	1	1	
c_5	1	5	1	2	5	5	3	1	3	1	1	1	1	4	5	1	1	5	4	1
c_6	2	5	1	2	5	5	1	2	1	1	1	1	1	1	1	1	1	1	1	5
c_7	1	1	5	1	1	1	1	1	4	1	5	5	1	1	1	1	1	1	1	1
c_8	1	5	1	1	1	2	1	1	1	1	1	1	1	5	5	1	1	5	1	1
c_9	2	5	1	2	2	1	1	1	1	1	1	1	5	4	1	1	1	5	1	1
c_{10}	1	3	1	1	3	1	3	1	3	1	1	4	4	3	3	1	1	5	5	1

Table 1: Repertory grid of the expert's evaluation of documents

c_1	EDUCATION	c_2	HYPERTEXT
c_3	PERSONAL CONSTRUCT THEORY	c_4	INFORMATION RETRIEVAL
c_5	KNOWLEDGE ACQUISITION	c_6	USER-ORIENTED
c_7	INTELLIGENT TUTORING SYSTEMS	c_8	REPERTORY GRID
c_9	DECISION SUPPORT SYSTEMS	c_{10}	CLUSTERING

Table 2: Construct labels for Table 1

by asking the user to categorize this sample of selected documents. This process of categorization forces the user to evaluate the differences between documents.

Following this approach, an experiment was conducted using twenty documents belonging to three broadly defined categories. Before starting the interview, the user is given a brief overview of each document in the learning set. This overview is an abstract for each document and is intended to be a ready reference for the document being evaluated, if need be. In addition, the user can request on-line the abstract of any document in the learning set during the interview process. During the interview, the system selects three documents from the learning set at random and presents them to the user. The user is then asked to differentiate between those three documents in such a way that two of the three documents have some similarity which is not present in the third [3]. The system then asks the user for the property which formed the basis for this categorization. This property or construct, which is a phrase described by the user, is a topic being addressed by the document.

In the next step, the system asks the user to give a ranking to all the documents on a predetermined scale. This ranking describes the extent of confidence which the user has about the document being assigned to the topic just defined. The user is presented with each document identifier one at a time and asked to rank it. If the user has full confidence in the fact that the document represents the topic under review, the user assigns this document a ranking m (on a scale from 1 to m). If the document does not address the topic at all, it is assigned a ranking 1. Other rankings are determined by the confidence the user has in the document addressing the topic. After the user has ranked all the documents, the rankings are collected to form one row of the repertory grid.

The process is now repeated with another set of three documents from the learning set and is continued until the user wants to choose a set of three documents

	c_1	c_2	c_3	c_4	c_5	c_6	c_7	c_8	c_9	c_{10}
c_1	1.00	0.65	0.43	0.45	0.26	0.21	0.98	0.41	0.46	0.40
c_2		1.00	0.58	0.80	0.44	0.41	0.65	0.56	0.66	0.55
c_3			1.00	0.45	0.81	0.79	0.43	0.96	0.89	0.78
c_4				1.00	0.46	0.51	0.45	0.44	0.54	0.63
c_5					1.00	0.90	0.26	0.80	0.73	0.79
c_6						1.00	0.21	0.78	0.73	0.79
c_7							1.00	0.41	0.46	0.40
c_8								1.00	0.90	0.74
c_9									1.00	0.76
c_{10}										1.00

Table 3: Similarity matrix between all the constructs

on his own. The same process elicits more topics and document rankings on those topics in the learning set. Finally, the system asks the user explicitly if there are any more topics to be assigned but missed during the process of interview. The user ranks all the documents on these topics as well. The repertory grid elicited from the user is described in Table 1. The constructs or topics of documents as seen by the user are displayed in Table 2.

3.2 Repertory Grid Analysis

The repertory grid elicited from the user is analyzed to extract the patterns of relationships among different categories. The analysis of grid is based on determination of the dissimilarities between pairs of constructs from user viewpoint. The repertory grid contains the ranking of a set of documents on all the categories. The dissimilarity between any two constructs c_i and c_j for a document d_k is the absolute difference in the ranking of the two constructs in the grid. If r_{ik} and r_{jk} are the rankings of document d_k on constructs c_i and c_j, respectively, then the dissimilarity δ_{ij}^k between the constructs for this document is given by the expression

$$\delta_{ij}^k = |r_{ik} - r_{jk}|$$

The total dissimilarity between the constructs c_i and c_j over all the documents is given by

$$\delta_{ij} = \sum_{k=1}^{n} |r_{ik} - r_{jk}|$$

where n is the number of documents used for eliciting the repertory grid.

The similarity σ_{ij} between two constructs i and j can be determined by using the dissimilarity δ_{ij} as follows:

$$\sigma_{ij} = \frac{-100\delta_{ij}}{(m-1)(p-1)} + 100$$

where m is the maximum value on the ranking scale and p is the number of documents used in eliciting those constructs. These similarities for all the constructs

Rule 01:	if	term = "REPERTORY GRID"
	then	topic = "PERSONAL CONSTRUCT THEORY" cf (0.96) and
		term = "PERSONAL CONSTRUCT THEORY" cf (0.96)
Rule 04:	if	term = "PERSONAL CONSTRUCT THEORY"
	then	topic = "KNOWLEDGE ACQUISITION" cf (0.81)
		term = "KNOWLEDGE ACQUISITION" cf (0.81)
Rule 05:	if	term = "CLUSTERING"
	then	topic = "KNOWLEDGE ACQUISITION" cf (0.79)
		term = "KNOWLEDGE ACQUISITION" cf (0.79)
Rule 05:	if	term = "USER-ORIENTED SYSTEMS"
	then	topic = "KNOWLEDGE ACQUISITION" cf (0.90)
		term = "KNOWLEDGE ACQUISITION" cf (0.90)
Rule 06:	if	term = "KNOWLEDGE ACQUISITION"
	then	topic = "KNOWLEDGE ACQUISITION"

Table 4: Rule base for the class KNOWLEDGE ACQUISITION

in the experiment have been depicted in Table 3 which is also called a *similarity matrix*. The similarity matrix is an upper triangular matrix with all the diagonal elements as 1.00. This is because on the diagonal, the quantity depicted is σ_{ii} - the similarity of a construct to itself. The matrix is upper triangular because $\sigma_{ij} = \sigma_{ji}$.

The similarity matrix is readily convertible into a complete graph whose nodes are constructs and whose edges between nodes i and j are weighted by σ_{ij}. The complete graph can be reduced to a maximum spanning tree [6] by using one of the standard spanning tree algorithms (Figure 1). The maximum spanning tree retains only the most important relationships between constructs and is also called *dependence tree*. As will be shown in the next subsection, other relationships can be extracted from the dependence tree.

After the tree is constructed, it is presented to the user to highlight important categories of topics in it. The categories as formed by the user are highlighted in Figure 1 by dotted boundary. A sub-tree enclosed within the dotted boundary is known as *class-tree*. *Dominant construct* is selected by the user to be a construct that most closely approximates all the constructs constituting the class. The dominant construct is highlighted in Figure 1 by using double circles. Dominant construct forms the root of the class-tree.

3.3 Production Rule Formation

In this subsection, we illustrate the development of a rule base for the classification of new documents. This classification is based on the class-trees developed in the previous subsection.

A class is identified by its dominant construct. The idea of classification is based on the proximity of the constructs representing the document to the dominant constructs. The document is assigned to the class whose dominant construct most closely matches the constructs used to describe the document. This proximity is measured by using the class-trees. Within a class, the class-tree shows the similarity between constructs represented by neighboring nodes. Therefore, if a document is described by the construct PERSONAL CONSTRUCT THEORY, it is also relevant to KNOWLEDGE ACQUISITION with a certainty of 0.81 as shown by user viewpoint captured in the dependence tree. A minimum bound on certainty between non-neighboring nodes X_1 and X_2 is provided by the product of edge weights which lie on the path from the node X_1 to the node X_2. That is, if a document is described by REPERTORY GRID, it is relevant to PERSONAL CONSTRUCT THEORY with a certainty of 0.96 and to KNOWLEDGE ACQUISITION with a minimum certainty given by $0.96 \times 0.81 = 0.78$. A rule-base showing the class-tree represented by KNOWLEDGE ACQUISITION is shown in Table 4.

Whenever a new document is received, it is automatically analyzed to extract index terms [5]. A simultaneous occurrence of two or more terms form a *term phrase* which is equivalent to a construct. A collection of constructs forms the description of the document. Existence of a construct within the document description triggers the rules corresponding to the construct. The document is finally classified to the category for which the certainty of classification is the maximum. As an example, consider a document representing the constructs CLUSTERING and HYPERTEXT. This document triggers rules corresponding to the classes INFORMATION RETRIEVAL and KNOWLEDGE ACQUISITION. It is classified to the class INFORMATION RETRIEVAL because the certainty for the document to belong to INFORMATION RETRIEVAL (0.86) is more than the certainty for it to belong to KNOWLEDGE ACQUISITION (0.79). In a similar manner, any new document can be classified.

4 Conclusion

We have presented a system for categorization of new documents on the basis of user perception. The process of knowledge acquisition and its analysis is described in view of the classification. The use of dependence tree in construction of a production rule base for categorization is discussed.

References

[1] J. H. Boose. *Expertise Transfer for Expert System Design.* Elsevier-Science Publishers, New York, 1986.

[2] Carnegie Group, Pittsburgh, PA. *Text Categorization Shell: Technical Brief,* 1989. 13 p.

[3] A. Hart. *Knowledge Acquisition for Expert Systems.* McGraw-Hill, New York, NY, 1986.

[4] G. A. Kelly. *The Psychology of Personal Constructs.* Norton Publishers, 1955.

[5] C. J. van Rijsbergen. *Information Retrieval.* Butterworth Publishers, Boston, MA, 2 edition, 1980.

[6] C. J. van Rijsbergen, D. J. Harper, and M. F. Porter. The selection of good search terms. *Information Processing and Management,* 17:77–91, 1981.

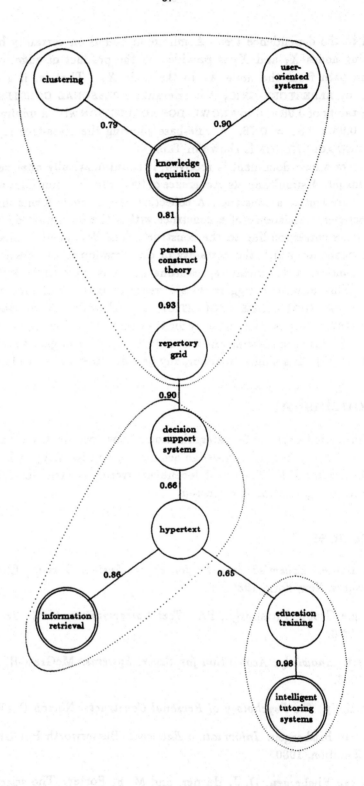

Figure 1: Classification tree corresponding to similarity matrix

An Expert System for Creativity Management

Vipa Ongwisesphaiboon   Ilene Burnstein
Martha Evens   Anjali Puri
Martin E. Ginn
Illinois Institute of Technology
Chicago, Illinois 60616

Abstract

Our expert system for creativity management focuses on the major dichotomies or critical choices found to be present during the creative process. There are two main goals that we plan to accomplish in this project: development of an increased understanding of decision processes employed by creative technologists and construction of a prototype expert system embodying the Ginn model. The expert system serves as a vehicle for expressing ideas about the management of research and development projects in an explicit and testable form and provides a tool so that others can try out these ideas and give us feedback. As our ideas about the system solidify, we will add a rule editor, a rule checking facility, statistical reports, and other improvements in the interface. We plan to refine, test, and validate the system by distributing it to managers in technologically intense research and development laboratories.

1   Introduction

We are building an expert system for creativity management that incorporates the concepts of the Ginn creativity management model. It has been organized into an integrated decision model that focuses on the major dichotomies or critical choices that have to be made by technical personnel and their management during the creative process. As a first step, we have constructed a prototype expert system in Arity/Prolog embodying the Ginn model [1], which was developed after extensive interviews with R&D managers and practitioners. Important issues in developing such a system are how to extract the domain knowledge from the expert and how to represent it in an appropriate form, so the expert can maintain it.

2 The Integrated Decision Model

Based on evidence from the literature, past models, previous study, and analysis of the interview data, an integrated decision model was proposed by Ginn [1,2]. The model incorporates four principal dichotomies represented as separate quadrants. Each quadrant corresponds to a fundamental decision that must be made by the manager or the creative technologist. In order to make a decision, the user must use the decision criteria appropriate for each quadrant.

Quadrant #1: Information Gathering versus Deciding.

The first quadrant examines the question: Is the research project ready to focus on a particular solution, or should more information be gathered, more studies carried out, before commitment to a specific pathway?

Quadrant #2: Individual versus Group Processing.

The second quadrant examines the question: Is the emphasis to be on the individual working alone with self-actualization or on working in a group where peer pressure and mutual support systems are present? Examples shown in the rest of the paper come from quadrant #2.

Quadrant #3: Organic versus Mechanistic Environment.

In this quadrant we will consider the research environment – whether it should be in the organic, loosely structured mode or in the mechanistic, more structured, or rigid mode.

Quadrant #4: Coupled versus Decoupled.

The basic decision to be made in this quadrant is to choose one mode of operation – coupled or decoupled. A choice of a coupled mode means the research group will emphasize linking with the macro environment or corporate culture. A decoupled mode means the present research environment needs to move away from the traditional pattern or culture constraints.

The decision maker first must decide which of the quadrants in the model is of interest, then consider the pertinent criteria in that quadrant. The model allows the decision-maker, who could be a manager or an inventor or a practitioner, to enter whichever decision mode is considered appropriate at a given point. The model emphasizes the premise that creative personnel engaged in new technologies operate with a philosophy that involves a flexible style of management. We plan to refine and expand this model incorporating additional information from a greater variety of industries and cultures, along with input from our panel of experts. We envision a more complex model, covering additional dichotomies, richer in criteria and emphasizing a united global approach [1,3].

3 Why a System for Creativity Management?

Motivation. Corporate management needs tools to assist them in providing a flexible working environment for guiding creative people to produce at their highest potential. Computer scientists are perhaps more in need of creativity management than scientists and engineers in other fields. Since the field is so new, most managers of computer science development projects are not themselves trained in computer science and have difficulties in empathizing with employees. They often feel alienated from those they are trying to manage, while their subordinates feel that the managers do not understand what they are trying to do. We hope to give management a tool that will provide guidance so that decisions to be made in complex managerial situations are systematic, analytical, and objective.

The Benefits of Expert Systems for Creativity Management. Our expert system will fulfill the following functions:

a. Capturing scarce expertise. Our expert system will serve as a store house for the expertise accumulated from years of experience by experts [4]. Often this expertise has never been written down [5].

b. Providing decision support in a systematic rule-based reproducible fashion. By use of the expert system, a manager is encouraged to make his decisions based on identifiable factors rather than purely intuitive feelings and undefined strategies.

c. Serving as a training tool for new managers. By using the system, they have access to the expertise of experienced personnel. They are free to incorporate new knowledge as they discover it during their tenure as managers.

d. Serving as an educational tool for colleges and universities in behavioral and management sciences. Students can gain insights into the creative process and learn techniques to maximize creative potential.

4   Processing Cycle of the Expert System

The system begins by collecting information from the user for a particular quadrant, which it passes to the inference engine. Once the inference engine has completed its work, then the system produces a recommendation and an explanation.

Collecting Information from Users. The first step in the processing cycle is to ask the user for an assessment of the current situation. Assume, for example, that the user has chosen to investigate the portion of model, quadrant #2, where the system helps the user to consider an important decision about mode of operation: whether to work as an individual or work closely with the group. The criteria needed to make the decision according to the model are 1) Prior processing mode, 2) Performance to date, 3) Motivational needs anticipated, 4) Need for creativity, and 5) Need for variety of experiences. The user interacts with the system by giving answers to the questions associated with each criterion (shown below):

Criterion #1: Prior Processing Mode
    1.1 What degree of flexibility has the individual in decision making?
    1.2 What kind of interactions has the individual in the project?
    1.3 What is the availability of slack time?
    1.4 What is the degree of management support?

Criterion #2: Performance to Date
  2.1 Were major scheduled projects completed in the past year?
  2.2 Did completed projects meet budget, time, and quality requirements?

Criterion #3: Motivational Needs Anticipated
  3.1 What is the degree of absenteeism in the group?
  3.2 What are the individual motivational needs in terms of rewards, recognition?
  3.3 Does performance reflect motivational needs?
  3.4 What is the degree of management support?

Criterion #4: Need for Creativity
  4.1 Does the success of the organization depend on technological innovations?
  4.2 What is the need for creativity in terms of prior history?

Criterion #5: Need for Variety of Experiences
This criterion will estimate the need for variety of experiences in the project using the results of criteria #3 and #4.

The rating scales of each question go from 1 to 7 where 1 = nil (no flexibility) or unfavorable, 2 = slight, 3 = some, 4 = medium, 5 = substantial, 6 = high, 7 = extremely high (flexibility) or favorable. The user is prompted to enter a value from 1 to 7. The system will store the query answers in the form of facts in its knowledge base. Calculations are performed on input data for deductions. The system uses these facts along with decision rules to advise the manager as to whether a change is recommended.

Devising these scales was one of the most difficult aspects of building the system. It was necessary to ask our experts to think quantitatively about a problem that they had previously considered only qualitatively, if at all.

Making Deductions. After the user answers all questions, the inference engine combines these values and compares the calculated value with a range already stored in the system.

Criterion 1:	Prior Processing Mode
4 – 8	The working environment operation is solely in group mode
9 – 11	Group mode with inclination towards individual mode
12 – 15	Balance between group and individual but towards group mode
16	Balance between group and individual mode
17 – 20	Balance between group and individual but towards individual mode
21 – 23	Individual mode with inclination towards group mode
24 – 28	Operation solely in individual mode
Criterion 2:	Performance to Date
2 – 4	Extremely poor performance
5 – 9	Rather poor performance
10 – 11	Fair performance
12 – 14	Good performance

Criterion 3:   Motivational Needs Anticipated
 3 – 12   High motivational needs
13 – 14   Some motivational needs
15 – 24   No motivational needs
Criterion 4:   Need for Creativity
 2 – 7   No need for creativity
 8 – 11   Some need for creativity
12 – 14   High need for creativity
Criterion 5:   Need for Variety of Experiences
 2 – 3   No need for variety of experiences
 4 – 5   Some need for variety of experiences
 6 – 7   High need for variety of experiences

Sample Rules for Decision on Mode: Individual versus Group.

RULE1: IF   prior processing mode is GROUP,
                 and performance to date is EXTREMELY POOR,
                 and motivational needs anticipated are HIGH,
                 and NO need for creativity,
                 and SOME need for variety of experiences
         THEN switch from GROUP mode to INDIVIDUAL mode.
RULE2: IF   prior processing mode is GROUP,
                 and performance to date is FAIR,
                 and motivational needs anticipated are HIGH,
                 and NO need for creativity,
                 and NO need for variety of experiences
         THEN stay in GROUP mode.

Explanation Facilities. The system generates simple explanations like this sample explanation for Rule1:

> Switch to the individual mode. Even though the lack of need for creativity would normally indicate a preference for the group mode of operation, the poor performance to date and the need for a larger variety of experiences calls for a change to the individual mode of operation.

5   System Architecture

A Knowledge Base. Our knowledge base consists of a set of rules and facts. Rules are in the form of "IF something is true, THEN perform some action." These rules were derived from previous studies and interaction between Ginn and other expert managers. The domain experts in the prototype development stage include managers of R&D and researchers in creativity. We are assembling an advisory panel of experts from academe and industry. The experts will provide a wide spectrum of knowledge and managerial expertise resulting in the broadening and refinement of our models and the expansion of the knowledge base for the expert system.

The Inference Engine. This routine makes strategic choices for managers based on the facts and rules in the knowledge base. We currently use backward chaining, as provided by the ARITY/PROLOG interpreter.

User Interface. The system prompts for answers to questions about the environment. If the user enters an inappropriate response, the system prompts again for new input. Responses are saved in a file for further use. The main advantage of this kind of interface is that the user does not need to memorize a complex command sequence or undergo any other special training.

6 Future Research

Testing and Validation. At the moment, this system is somewhat primitive. We have plans for improvements in several places. First, we plan to refine, test, and validate the research model by conducting interviews with a set of experts including practitioners and managers at technologically intense R&D laboratories. Decision processes involved in successful and unsuccessful projects will be collected. Finally, the evolving model will be incorporated into an improved expert system.

Knowledge Engineering Tools. Another long term goal of our research is to design software that will allow the human expert to interact directly with the knowledge base to correct and improve it. We plan to develop a knowledge engineering tool with the following functions:

- Rule editor facility will translate structured English into PROLOG rules and Prolog rules back into English.

- Rule checker facility will examine rules for consistency, isolation, and subsumption.

User Interface. Another area for future development is the user interface. We plan to improve the user interface by adding the following:

- Data correction and archiving facility: The first step is to provide the facility for the user to change information already given to the system, as well as to reuse information provided in other quadrants.

- Natural language interface: We hope to provide resources for the user to ask questions and offer information in a subset of English [6].

- Graphic interface: Some users find it easier to communicate via diagrams [7]. We hope to make the system accept information and present it in graphic form.

Performance Tools. We plan to add facilities that collect system statistics. The user interface needs some simple performance tools that measure how long it takes for the system to respond, how often users make errors in each quadrant, and how often users abandon a quadrant without finishing.

7 Summary

We are building an expert system for managers, practitioners, and creative technologists to use as a tool to guide them in accomplishing innovative research projects. Furthermore, we plan to add several facilities: a better user interface, knowledge acquisition tools and monitors to evaluate system performance. Moreover, we have already made arrangements to distribute the expert system to managers and practitioners in technological environments to try out our system. We expect useful feedback that will be the basis for improvements and additions to our system.

References

[1] M. Ginn, I. Burnstein, R. Townsend, Creativity Management: Understanding Behavioral Approaches in Product Design, *Proceedings of the AMS Meeting*, Chicago, June 1987.

[2] M. Ginn, Creativity Management: Systems and Contingencies from a Literature Review, *IEEE Transactions on Engineering Management*, Vol. EM-33, No.2, May 1986, pp 96–101.

[3] M. Ginn, J. Ovitz, Cultural Considerations in Creativity Management: Japanese and American Values, *Proceedings of the Association of the Human Resource Management Organization Behavior Meeting*, New Orleans, Nov. 1986.

[4] E. Turban, Review of Expert Systems Technology, *IEEE Transactions on Engineering Management*, Vol 35, No 2, May 1988, pp 71–81.

[5] G.F. Luger, W. Stubblefield, *Artificial Intelligence and the Design of Expert Systems*, Benjamin/Cummings, Redwood, CA, 1989.

[6] K. Sparck Jones, Natural Language Interfaces for Expert Systems: An Introductory Note, *Proceedings of 4th Technical Conference of British Computer Society Specialist Group on Expert Systems*, University of Warwick, Dec. 1984, pp 85–94.

[7] B. Shneiderman, *Designing the User Interface: Strategies for Effective Human Computer Interaction*, Addison-Wesley, Reading, MA, 1987.

A More Flexible Method for Recognizing Signals Using Back Propagation: Piecewise Linear Regression Vectors

Greg Makowski

Western Michigan University

Computer Science Department

Kalamazoo, MI 49008

email: makowski@gw.wmich.edu

Abstract

Using the neural network architecture of back propagation applied to speech recognition, a new input data structure is developed which improves shift invariance when recognizing signal data in the form such as a formant. The preliminary development of the data structure, piecewise linear regression vectors, is reported. The new input data structure reduces the amount of data presented to the network by as much as an order of magnitude, giving a computational advantage in execution speed.

1 Introduction

Investigations by the author into the limits of generalization of back propagation have lead to the development of a new representation of spectral data that allows back propagation to generalize at a higher level of descriptive parameters. The emphasis of the representation is on modelling the more significant features of the data, while ignoring less useful background data. The individual vectors modelling components of the data are linear, but the overall system model is a non-linear one.

The motivation for this investigation came from experiments conducted by the author with back propagation [10, 9, 3]. Specifically the experiments were testing the limitations of neural net generalization applied to speech patterns [4, 5]. The data consists of a phoneme simulated in the form of a formant track. A formant track is plotted on a frequency versus time matrix, called a spectrogram, with cell values representing energy level. The formant track is the trace of frequency at the highest energy level during each successive time sample. A formant track may be observed after running a speech sample through a Fast Fourier Transform (FFT), which converts the sample from the time domain to the frequency domain [6]. Simulated formant tracks were used for direct control of specific pattern elements for an exhaustive test of the boundaries of generalization.

The experiments were aimed at increasing shift invariance, specifically across the frequency axis. This type of invariance is useful for generalizing a phoneme among higher and lower pitched speakers, such as those who are male, female, young and old. In the experiments, formant test patterns from each class were shifted one frequency band at a time and tested for recognition in that class. Shifted patterns were often incorrectly identified as members of another class, even when the test pattern was the closest to the correct class. Lower resolution matrices lead to a blurring of the spectral data, and allowed a slightly wider recognition tolerance when shifting the formants.

A test for use of shape information was to randomize all training and test patterns with the same mapping function rearranging the matrix cells. This test would then shift a test pattern in frequency, and rearrange the spectrogram cells with the same mapping, and test for recognition. Back propagation recognized the randomized cells with similar accuracy to the original data, from which it may be concluded that back propagation did not use shape information in the same sense that people do. Observing this implies that the amount of cell overlap between the test pattern and a trained class is the significant feature used for recognition. It may be expected that a test pattern shifted outside the set of examples of a trained class would not be recognized. If the test pattern had the same shape as the members of the trained class, it may be possible for some systems to make that generalization. Back propagation is good at generalization, but improvement on shift invariance may be made if geometrical shape information is used.

2 Geometrical Abstraction

The most common representation of speech data to a neural net is a relatively low resolution matrix of spectrogram data. Two of the reasons for the low resolution are computational complexity and a blur effect of the data. Computational complexity is based on the polynomial growth as the data resolution increases, for example from a 8x8 matrix to 16x16. Various research projects have used input data of a size that ranges from 32 to 900 [4, 1, 11, 2, 8]. The input layer is typically the largest layer in speech recognition systems.

The error back propagation phase of learning adjusts connection strength between layers, with the strength of connections between nodes that are significant to the current pattern taking more extreme positive or negative values. The input information being emphasized and de-emphasized is the energy level of each input node. For a given time slice, the energy distribution across frequencies is not understood by the network, because the network has no way to differentiate the shape of a matrix, between an 8x8 or a 2x32 input matrix. The data structure does not use information about the location of a cell relative to the time sample or frequency. Back propagation may generalize at higher levels of the network some relationships between activated cells at the input layer. Information is certainly lost when no details about time or frequency are used when learning on spectral data.

The method employed to try and recover the unused information involves a data representation different than using a low resolution matrix to symbolize and emphasize the information contained in formant tracks in a spectrogram. That data representation consists of modeling the formant tracks with piecewise liner regression vectors, using input parameters such as length and direction. A single vector models a formant moving in a consistent direction on the spectrogram, such as an increasing or decreasing frequency over time, until a directional change causes a new vector to begin. Each vector is a linear regression line through a time-frequency region of formant data. Improvements made by this representation include emphasis on the geometry of a formant which adds shift invariance, as well as fewer input parameters, which speeds up back propagation. The vector representation may be optionally made more detailed by adding a third vector parameter, the standard deviation of each vector. This differentiates otherwise identical vectors modeling data with a wide distribution of values from data with a narrow, high peaked formant. In some instances, the parameter reduction of vector modeling may not represent the data in sufficient detail, and vector modeling would better be suited for spectral envelope modeling over each time slice.

3   Vector Creation

The preprocessing consists of piecewise linear regression of the formant to be modeled, producing vectors with the features of length, direction, and optionally standard deviation. Standard deviation differentiates between a straight line, a smoothly changing curve, or a series of small directional changes that do not vary significantly from the path represented by the vector. The modeling method is based on linear regression, allowing extensions to higher order regression curves and their associated curve parameters. The length of a given vector is the distance along the linear regression line from that vector's starting time slice to its ending time slice.

When input to a neural net is from data representing different types of information, the preferred input to the neural net would be parameters with values ranging from zero to one with an approximately uniform distribution. The network has difficulty to overcome differences in input ranges and distributions to learn patterns, and that difficulty can be efficiently avoided by a preprocessing scaling phase. Data types with values consistently and significantly larger than others will have the same effect to artificially enhanced connection weights before training begins. Data types with extremely spiked distributions may cause longer training times if the neural net needs to differentiate data contained in that spiked range of data. The direction parameter is mapped from 0 to 179 degrees to a range of zero to one, with 0.5 indicating a formant track which is not increasing or decreasing in frequency as time progresses. The heuristic used to map vector length to a similar range is to divide the vector length by one half of the number of time samples used in the spectrogram matrix. The standard deviation range of negative three to positive three deviations is also mapped to the zero to one range. heuristics determine when a directional change becomes significant enough to begin a new vector. Vector segmentation uses thresholds of acceptable variance and direction change to decide when to start the next vector. A single vector models a formant changing at a relatively constant rate over time. The process of vector segmentation uses each local maximum per time slice within the region of the formant track. Advancing from one time slice to the next, each maximum point is used to recompute the overall direction, and a current direction based on the last few points in the vector. The difference between local directions at the end and beginning of the vector are compared with a threshold angle, which was 63 degrees for the simulation studies. If the difference exceeds the threshold angle, a new vector will be started. If the difference between the local end direction and the overall vector direction exceeds the same angle threshold, a new vector will begin. Individual vectors are linear, but the overall system model is non-linear. Future developments of this work include comparison with Dynamic Time Warping (DTW) [7, 12] and application of vector modeling to back propagation architectures such as that of Time Delay Neural Networks (TDNN) [13].

4   Advantages/Disadvantages

Using matrix input, back propagation correctly recognizes test patterns which primarily overlay cells used by the training patters. Matrix input has difficulty recognizing a test pattern which overlaps few of the cells used by the training patterns, or few cells with strong connections. Vector modeling succeeds in this case because there is relatively little difference between the input parameters and the parameters generalized from the class of training examples. The length and direction parameters of the vectors are similar for shifted formants, only the starting frequency of the vectors differs. An extension of shift invariance includes recognition of skewed formants, or the recognition of a formant decreasing more rapidly in time than the examples in the training class. The vector modeling approach may potentially be applied to speech data at the phoneme, syllable or word level for either templates or continuous time models.

When a formant track is modeled with vectors, the number of input parameters is reduced an order of magnitude, from polynomial to linear. For comparison purposes, the size of an n by n matrix would be considered $O(n^2)$, versus $c * n$ or $O(n)$, for c vector parameters. The order of magnitude would remain the same for the more detailed vector modeling of the spectral envelope of each time slice. The computation time for vector formant modeling also reduces significantly when considering that the common architecture completely connects the input and middle layer of the neural net. The middle layer size is heuristically dependant on the size of the input layer, with a practical lower bound being a logarithmic function of the input size, and a typical middle layer size the square root of input size [1, 2, 4, 8, 11]. The output layer size for speech recognition systems is usually small, with a maximum of about forty phonemes. The largest number of connections in the network is clearly between the input and middle layer. A size reduction in the input layer from $O(n^2)$ to $O(n)$ would cause an estimated reduction in connections between the first two layers to change from $O(n^3)$ to $O(n^2)$, implying that the vector modeling approach yields a similar improvement in execution.

This method has certain assumptions and dependencies which may be disadvantages. This data structure has been developed as one possible improvement to back propagation to add shift invariance. The underlying assumption of this model is that the significant features of the spectral data can be modeled with vectors. Actual speech has three formants, which may cross or merge and separate [6]. The isolation of individual formants and tracking of the formants is a significant problem. Only after the formants are isolated can the vector modelling approach be used. Modeling only the formant may not be detailed enough, a tradeoff with faster execution may need to be made to model more details, to model each time slice of data.

5 Conclusions

Advantages of modeling speech formant data with piecewise linear regression vectors include an added degree of shift invariance as a result of the vector input data representation. The vector data structure increases execution speed by reducing the number of input parameters.

References

[1] Y. Bengio and R. De Mori. Speaker normalization and automatic speech recognition using spectral lines and neural networks. In *Proceedings of the 1988 Connectionist Models Summer School*, pages 388–397. Carnegie Mellon University, 1988.

[2] Michael A. Franzini. Learning to recognize spoken words: A study in connectionist speech recognition. In *Proceedings of the 1988 Connectionist Models Summer School*, pages 407–416. Carnegie Mellon University, 1988.

[3] Richard P. Lippmann. An introduction to computing with neural nets. *IEEE ASSP*, Vol 3, No 4:4–22, 1987.

[4] Richard P. Lippmann. Neural network classifiers for speech recognition. *The Lincoln Laboratory Journal*, Vol 1, No 1:107–124, 1988.

[5] Richard P. Lippmann. Review of neural networks for speech recognition. *Neural Computation*, Vol 1, No 1:1–38, 1989.

[6] Thomas W. Parsons. *Voice and Speech Processing*. McGraw-Hill, 1987.

[7] Lawrence R. Rabiner, A.E. Rosenberg, and S. Levinson. Considerations in dynamic time warping algorithms for discrete word recognition. *IEEE Transactions on Acoustics, Speech, and Signal Processing*, VOL ASSP-26, NO. 6:575–582, 1978.

[8] M. L. Rossen and J. A. Anderson. Representational issues in a neural network model of syllable recognition. In *International Joint Conference on Neural Networks*, pages I.19–I.21. IEEE, 1989.

[9] David E. Rumelhart and James L. McClelland. *Explorations in Parallel Distributed Processing*. MIT Press, 1988.

[10] David E. Rumelhart and James L. McClelland. *Parallel Distributed Processing, Vol I,II*. MIT Press, 1988.

[11] Terrence J. Sejnowski and Charles R. Rosenberg. Nettalk: a parallel network that learns to read aloud. Technical Report JHU/EECS-86/01, 32pp., The Johns Hopkins University, Electrical Engineering and Computer Science, Johns Hopkins, 1986.

[12] E. Vidal, H. Rulot, C. Casacuberta, and J. Benedi. On the use of a metric-space search algorithm (aesa) for fast dtw-base recognition of isolated words. *IEEE Transactions on Acoustics, Speech, and Signal Processing*, VOL ASSP-36, NO. 5:651–660, 1988.

[13] Alex Waibel, H. Sawai, and K. Shikano. Modularity and scaling in large phonemic neural networks. Technical Report TR-I-0034, 25pp, ATR Interpreting Telephony Research Laboratories, Japan, 1988.

A COOPERATIVE ALGORITHM
FOR THE DYNAMIC STEREO PROBLEM

Gerald Leonard Gordon
Department of Computer Science
Depaul University
Chicago, Illinois 60604

Abstract

A basic problem in the study of visual motion is determining temporal correspondence, which is commonly called tracking. The psychophysics community suggests that motion and stereo are cooperative processes, each aiding the other in deciding the final correspondences. In this article, we introduce an algorithm which uses a cooperative process between stereo and motion to attack the dynamic stereo problem. The algorithm, after isolating the objects to be tracking in each frame, lists the possible stereo matches in the left and right views which satisfy certain constraints. It then relies on a general smoothness of motion criterion using (1) the center of gravity of each object in each monocular view, (2) the sizes of the objects, as well as (3) the stereo disparities between possible matched stereo objects. Experiments using tennis balls shows the algorithm to be very promising.

1. Introduction.

The motion problem in computer vision (called dynamic image processing), which is to be able to track objects over time, has two major paradigms: (1) image flow and (2) correspondences. The correspondence approach follows from the traditions of the psychological community, which dates back 100 years. The paradigm is to alternately show the human subjects two images with a 50-150 millisecond time between images and ask the respondants to report on the perceived motion. This is referred to as apparant motion. Following this tradition, the computer vision community also started to look at two consecutive frames to detect the motion. Later researchers have tended to increase the number of frames to at least three to detect the motion, Sethi and Jain[9], Yasumoto and Medioni[11], Shariat and Price[10], Gordon[2].

The earliest work in dynamic computer vision was done monocularly. Later work has been done using two cameras at the same time, Jenkins and Tsotos[3], Mitiche[6], Leung,et.al[5].

The results from the psychophysicists research was that location was the dominant cue that humans used to decide which motion occured, Kohlers[4], Antis[1], Ratleff[8]. The changing of shape, color, intensity, or size are not enough to overcome the cue from locations. However, recently Ramachandran[7] has reported a cue, stereo, which will overcome location for the perceived motion. The experiment has the subjects use polarized glasses which induce the stereo affect.

This suggests that to implement a computer vision system using stereo for aiding in tracking, that the metric for depth perception (disparity) should have a larger weight than the metric for location (i.e.,distance), and that the metric for location should have a larger weight than size. We shall report on such an algorithm.

2. A Description of the Algorithm

We use two TV cameras, and tape a motion sequence, yielding a left and right view of the scene. The objects will project onto each of the 2-dimensional image frames of the TV camera, each having its own xy-coordinate system.

For each viewpoint, left and right, the moving objects are isolated (by substracting away the appropriate background). Each connected component of the moving objects (two objects can form one component if they occlude each other) is then assigned three numbers (x, y, s) corresponding to the center of gravity of the x-component, the center of gravity of the y-component, and the size of the object (measured in pixels). These are called the zeroth and first moments, which tend to be robust in the presence of noise.

Let $Pl(i, j)$ denote the ith object in the jth frame of the left frame with coordinates $(xl(i,j), yl(i,j), sl(i,j))$. Suppose that the k objects $Pl(i,j)$, $i = 1, \ldots, k$ are chosen to correspond to one object $Pl(1, j+1)$ in frame$(j+1)$ under the motion observed. (This is referred to as fusion of the $Pl(i, j)$ to $Pl(1, j+1)$ in the psychological literature.) We then form the k vectors of $Pl(i, j)$ to $Pl(1, j+1)$ by

$$vl(1, j+1, i, j) = (xl(1, j+1) - xl(i, j), yl(1, j+1) - vl(i, j), sl(1, j+1, i, j)) \quad (1)$$

where

$$sl(i, j+1, i, j) = \left| rd \left[\left\{ s(1, j+1) - \sum_{i=1}^{k} s(i, j) \right\} \times \frac{s(i, j)}{\sum_{i=1}^{k} s(i, j)} \right] \right| \quad (2)$$

and rd is the round off function. If $k = 1$, then we just take the absolute value of the differences of sizes, else we distribute the total differences in sizes proportionally according to their sizes. A similar formula is given for fission. The motivation for this is discussed in Gordon[2]. This is basically used to help resolve occlusions.

For each frame(j), the stereo correspondence problem is to decide which object is the same when looked at from two different views (the left and the right) at the same time. Let $Pl(i, j)$ denote the ith object in the jth frame for the left view. Suppose we denote its coordinates by $(xl(i,j), yl(i,j), sl(i,j))$. If object $Pl(i, j)$ on the left corresponds to object $Pr(i', j)$ on the right, with coordinates $(xr(i',j), yr(i',j), sr(i',j)$, then define the disparity of the stereo match by

$$z(i, i', j) = xl(i, j) - xr(i', j) \quad (3)$$

Note that $z(i, i', j)$ is greater than or equal to zero by the geometry of the situation. The disparity measures how close or far away an object is to the camera. As an object advances towards the camera, its disparity increases. Conversely, as objects recede from the camera, their disparity decreases. We only consider the x-coordinate, because if the cameras have their viewing axis perpendicular to the ground and are parallel to each other, the y-coordinates of the same object should be nearly equal in both the left and right view.

If, however, there are more than two objects with their y-coordinates sufficiently close, the algorithm must decide which is the stereo match. To further complicate the problem, there might be an unequal number in the left and right view having their y-coordinates sufficiently close to be considered as likely stereo matches.

So our stereo matching algorithm will not necessarily find only one possible stereo match, but might return more than one. We will rely on the motion to resolve these ambiguities.

Suppose we choose a correspondence $C(j)$ from frame(j) to frame($j+1$) yielding the vectors $(vx(t,j), vy(t,j), vs(t,j))$ formed from (1) for each trajectory $t \in C(j)$ for the left or right. Similarly, suppose we choose a correspondence $C(j+1)$ from frame($j+1$) to frame($j+2$) yielding the vectors $(vx(t,j+1), vy(t,j+1), vs(t,j+1))$ for the trajectories $t \in C(j+1)$. Furthermore, suppose we have chosen a stereo correspondence for each of the three frames starting at j, yielding vectors $vz(t,j)$ defined by

$$vz(t,j) = z(t,j+1) - z(t,j) \tag{4}$$

where the $z(t,j)$ are formed from (3). Note that $vz(t,j)$ can be positive or negative as the object approaches or recedes, respectively.

Then we define the cost of the second difference as

$$c(C(j), C(j+1), W) = \sum_{t \in (C,C(j+1))} \sum_{k=1}^{4} vk(t,j,j+1,W) \tag{5}$$

where W is a weighting factor for the size change. In (5), we have

$$v1(t,j,j+1,W) = (vx(t,j+1) - vx(t,j))^2 \tag{6}$$

and

$$v2(t,j,j+1,W) = (vy(t,j+1) - vy(t,j))^2 \tag{7}$$

but

$$v3(j,j+1,t,W) = W \times |vs(t,j+1) - vs(t,j)| \tag{8}$$

and

$$v4(j,j+1,t,W) = |vz(t,j+1) - vz(t,j)|^3 \tag{9}$$

where the vectors are from the same trajectory t from frame(j) to frame($j+2$) via frame($j+1$).

Thus, the differences in position is squared, the differences in disparity is cubed, but the difference in sizes is only linear. But only the size differences uses the weighting factor W.

For the monocular view the difference in position should be the dominating criterion, while the difference in size is a supplementary aid. We want to use the size changes as an improvement over the correspondences chosen, but with the caveat that it minimizes the introduction of new errors. We start with W being zero and we increase W at each set of three frames. As long as the sum of (6) and (7) exceeds (8), the correspondence is accepted. When the sum of (6) and (7) no longer exceeds (8), W is no longer increased. This is discussed in Gordon [2].

However, when we introduce stereo, the stereo should have a larger weight than the location. This is because the psychophysical evidence suggests this.

However, stereo should cooperate with motion. The smoothest two-dimensional motion (via the projection onto the image frame) may not be the smoothest three-dimensional motion. The stereo disparity is introduced to handle this. However, the stereo correspondences can also be chosen incorrectly. The smoothest two-dimensional motion can then correct the stereo correspondences chosen.

So we consider all possible correspondences over time and all possible stero correspondences, and choose the one which minimizes (5). It is possible that the best correspondence for the left view might be different than the best chosen for the right view, and this conflict must be resolved.

3. Experiments

In the experiment that we present here, we throw 6 tennis balls over two TV cameras toward the back wall. We videotape the action, and then grab frames at the rate of 12 frames a second. This sequence lasts 22 frames. We isolate the moving objects and extract their sizes and centers of gravity.

Due to space considerations we only present the action from frames 5 to 9, inclusive, from the right view. The results of the left view are similar. The data for the left and right view for these frames is shown in Table 1 and Table 2, respectively.

During this sequence, ball 1 bounces up and starts down off to the right by itself. Ball 2 hits off the wall and starts going toward the left. Balls 3 and 4 bounce off the floor and rise together, with ball 3 bouncing higher than ball 4. Ball 3 is moving away from the camera. They occlude each other at frame 6. Ball 5 heads down, occludes in front of balls 3 and 4 at frame 6, then bounces toward the camera. Ball 6 bounces off a telephone at the top of the field of vision, and then heads rapidly toward the camera. From frame 6 to frame 7 ball 6 travels half of the frame. The actual trajectories are shown in Figure 1.

If we ignore the stereo contribution and only consider equation (5) for the first three terms (i.e., ignore (8)), the algorithm makes several mistakes, even with the size included. This is because the geometry of the projection of the action onto the two dimensional image. It is a smoother motion to have ball 6 remain at the top, rather than plunge down toward the bottom. With ball 6 being chosen to follow ball 3 after frame 7, the algorithm must deal with ball 3. It does this by having ball 3 stay at the bottom by first switching with ball 2 at frame 6 (so that ball 2 goes into the occlusion). Then ball 3 follows the actual ball 5 at frames 8 and 9. Again, due to the distortions of the projection, it is smoother to have ball 5 bounce farther out (as ball 2) than its actual trajectory. Ball 2 (which switched with ball 3 at frame 6) switches with ball 4 as it leaves the occlusion. The switching is a smoother path for ball 2. Finally, this leaves ball 4 to follow the actual trajectory of ball 5. These trajectories are shown in Figure 2.

However, when we consider the stereo matches, the situation changes. Furthermore, the motion also helps choose the stereo matches. The possible number of stereo matches returned by the algorithm are 1, 1, 12, 4, and 4 for frames 5, 6, 7, 8, and 9, respectively. Here, the left-to-right matching would give the correct matches, but in frames 15 and 16, for example, it would give the wrong matches.

Using our cost function (5) with the stereo disparites included, the algorithm chooses both the correct stereo and motion correspondences.

To give an idea of how the motion mistakes are corrected, we give in Table 3 the stereo disparities for balls 3 and 6 (using the correct stereo matches) for the monocular motion chosen and the actual trajectories. In frames 8 and 9, the monocular motion sent ball 6 to ball 3. It also sent ball 3 to ball 2 instead of the occlusion, and then had ball 3 follow ball 5. These correspondences give that the z-motion (the difference of the disparites) of ball 6 coming towards the camera at increasing speed for frames 5-7, then suddenly move away from the camera at frame 8, and finally be at a constant distance for frame 9. Similary ball 3 starts away from the camera, then slowly toward the camera (this is false due to the occlusion at frame 6 which distorts the x-value), then move toward the camera very rapidly, deaccelerating as it approaches the camera. Comparing these with the disparities of the actual trajectories, we see that the contributions of (8) to (5) forces the algorithm to change the motion correspondences.

4. Conclusion

We have presented an algorithm for tracking moving objects, motivated by the research of the psychophysical community. The motion and stereo cues cooperate to help each other choose the correct correspondences. Stereo is done at the same time, while motion is done over time, but they are not done independently. The stereo modifies what the monocular motion would have chosen by itself, and the motion helps choose among the ambiguous stereo matches. The experimental evidence shows our algorithm to be very promising.

References

[1] S.N. Antis, Phi motion as a subtraction process, *Vision Research*, Vol 10, pp.1411-1430, 1970.

[2] G.L. Gordon, On the tracking of featureless objects with occlusion, *Proceedings of the IEEE Workshop on Visual Motion*, pp. 13-20, Irvine, Ca., 1989.

[3] M. Jenkins and J.K. Tsotsos, Applying temporal constraints to the dynamic stereo problem, *Computer Vision, Graphics, and Image Processing*, Vol. 33, pp. 16-32, 1986.

[4] P.A. Kolers, *Aspects of Motion Perception*, Pergamon Press, Oxford,1972.

[5] M.K. Leung, A.N. Choudhary, J.H. Patel, T.S. Huang, Point matching in a time sequence of stereo image pairs and its parallel implementation on a multiprocessor,, *Proceedings of the IEEE Workshop on Visual Motion*, pp. 321-27, Irvine, Ca., 1989.

[6] A. Mitchie, A computation approach to the fusion of stereopsis and kineopsis, *Motion Understanding: Robot and Human Vision*, ed. by W.N. Martin and J.K. Aggarwal, pp. 81-99, Kluwer Acadmeic Publishers, Boston, 1988.

[7] Ramachandran, Invited Address, *Proceedings of the IEEE Workshop on Visual Motion*, Irvine, Ca., 1989.

[8] A. Ratleff, A Study of visual movements determined by form, color, or brightness, *Acta Physchol*, Vol. 12, pp. 64-70, 1956.

[9] I.K. Sethi and R. Jain, Finding trajectories of feature points in a monocular image sequence, *IEEE Tran. on PAMI*, Vol. 9, pp.56-73, 1987.

[10] H. Shariat and K. Price, Motion Estimation using more than two images, *Motion Understaning: Robot and Human Vision*, ed. by W.N. Martin and J.K. Aggarwal, pp. 143-188, Kluwer Academic Publishers, Boston, 1988.

[11] Y. Yasumoto and G. Medioni, Experiments in estimation of 3-dimensional motion parameters from a sequence of image frames, *Proceedings of IEEE Conference on Computer Vision and Pattern Recognition*, San Francisco, pp. 89-94, 1985.

Frame	Ball 1	Ball 2	Ball 3	Ball 4	Ball 5	Ball 6
5	170, 90, 8	98,122,30	105, 86, 12	118,107,18	115,145,44	96,216,19
6	177,125,28	97, 76,16	113,105,107			93,213,23
7	177,159,15	89,101,26	107,136, 21	121,140,19	95, 95,16	88,187,17
8	176,177,46	59,117,25	115,179, 12	125,160,24	73,118,22	85, 49,44
9	172,159,62	40, 97,29	117,175, 9	125,140,21	65, 84,25	77,103,37

Table 1
This is the right view
The numbers for each ball are the x-coordinate,
then the y-coordinate, and finally the size in pixels.

Frame	Ball 1	Ball 2	Ball 3	Ball 4	Ball 5	Ball 6
5	197, 97,19	127,111,24	144, 78,39	149, 87,29	140,131,19	133,200,47
6	197,133,45	130, 80,33	146,108,98		135, 95,17	137,195,42
7	196,144,78	126,101,25	142,147,29	150,139,28	131,106,29	144,170,55
8	196,165,28	104,114,33	142,162,83	157,151,37	137,112,68	163, 66,63
9	200,144,47	94, 92,38	145,165,25	160,132,27	142, 82,57	168,112,38

Table 2
This is the left view

Frame	true ball 6	monocular ball 6 chosen	true ball 3	monocular ball 3 chosen
5	37	37	39	39
6	44	44	33	33
7	56	56	35	37 *ball2*
8	78	27 *ball3*	27	64 *ball5*
9	91	28 *ball3*	28	77 *ball5*

Disparities

6-5	7	7	-6	-6
7-6	12	12	2	4
8-7	22	-29	-8	27
9-8	13	1	1	13

z-vectors $z(j,t)$

7-6-5	5^3	5^3	8^3	10^3
8-7-6	10^3	41^3	10^3	23^3
9-8-7	9^3	30^3	9^3	14^3

$$v4(j, j+1, t)$$

Table 3

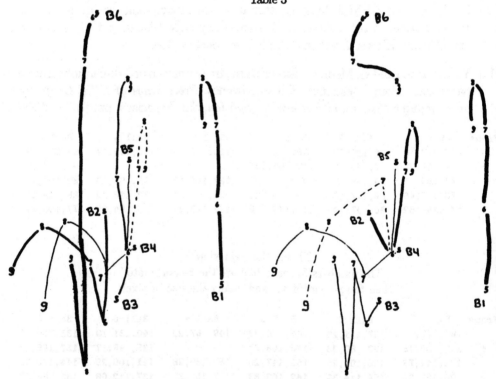

Figure 1
These are the actual trajectories
and the ones chosen using stereo

Figure 2
This are the trajectories chosen monocularly

Both of the Figures are the right view for frames 5-9,inc. The number in the Figure
refers to an object in that frame. The Bi refers to the start of ball i at frame 5.

Design of Hierarchical Classifiers

Richard E. Haskell and Ali Noui-Mehidi
Department of Computer Science and Engineering
Oakland University
Rochester, Michigan 48309

Abstract

Decision trees provide a powerful method of pattern classification. At each node in a binary tree a decision is made based upon the value of one of many possible attributes or features. The leaves of the tree represent the various classes that can be recognized. Various techniques have been used to select the feature and threshold to use at each node based upon a set of training data. Information theoretic methods are the most popular techniques used for designing each node in the tree. An alternate method uses the Kolmogorov-Smirnov test to design classification trees involving two classes. This paper presents an extension of this method that can produce a single decision tree when there are multiple classes. The relationship between this generalized Kolmogorov-Smirnov method and entropy minimization methods will be described. Experiments comparing classification results using this decision tree with results of using a Bayesian classifier will be presented.

Introduction

A long standing problem is that of having a computer learn to recognize complex relationships. A related problem is developing an expert system by showing it examples and having it learn the rules automatically. Decision trees have proved to be a useful approach to these types of problems [1,2]. In a binary tree classifier a decision is made at each non-terminal node of the tree based upon the value of one of many possible attributes or features. If the feature value is less than some threshold then the left branch of the tree is taken, otherwise the right branch is taken. The leaves, or terminal nodes, of the tree represent the various classes to be recognized.

The main problem in designing such hierarchical classifiers is to determine what feature and threshold value to use at each non-terminal node based upon a set of sample training data. A related problem is deciding when to stop splitting the nodes and assigning a class label to a terminal node. The most common methods used to determine the splitting at a tree node are information theoretic methods that try, in some sense, to reduce the uncertainty of the class membership at each node by the largest amount possible [3, 4, 5]. These are often referred to as entropy minimization techniques.

An alternate approach to splitting the tree nodes uses the Kolmogorov-Smirnov (K-S) distance between two distributions [6, 7]. While this method has proved to be useful for two classes, its generalization to the multiclass case has previously involved the generation of multiple decision-trees that separate one class from all the rest. We have recently developed a generalization of this method for the multi-class case that generates only a single decision tree [8]. In this paper we will describe this new method and show how these methods based on the K-S distance are related to entropy minimization methods. Examples of using this new method will also be presented.

Entropy Reduction Approach to Classifier Design

Consider a pattern recognition problem involving M classes. A measure of the uncertainty of class membership C_i, $i = 1, \ldots, M$ is given by the entropy function [9]

$$H(C) = -\sum_{i=1}^{M} P(C_i) \log P(C_i) \tag{1}$$

where $P(C_i)$ is the a priori probability of class C_i.

Let x be the measurement vector x_i, $i = 1, \ldots, N$. At each node of the tree one of the features x_k is selected and a threshold value a_k is chosen. Let X_1^k be the event $x_k < a_k$ and X_2^k be the event $x_k \geq a_k$. Define the conditional entropy $H_k(C \mid X^k)$ as the average entropy of C for each of the two values of X^k weighted accoding to the probability of getting X^k. That is,

$$H_k(C|X^k) = -\sum_{i=1}^{M} \sum_{j=1}^{2} P_k(X_j^k) P_k(C_i|X_j^k) \log P_k(C_i|X_j^k) \tag{2}$$

where $P_k(X_j^k)$ is the probability of getting X_j^k and $P_k(C_i|X_j^k)$ is the conditional probability of the class being C_i given that the measurement x_k falls in the region X_j^k.

The reduction in uncertainty, or entropy, as a result of picking the threshold a_k is called the average mutual information obtained about C_i from the observation X_j and can be written as

$$I(a_k) = H(C) - H_k(C \mid X^k)$$

$$= \sum_{i=1}^{M} \sum_{j=1}^{2} P_k(C_i, X_j^k) \log \left[\frac{P(C_i, X_j^k)}{P_k(X_j^k) \, P(C_{i,})} \right] \tag{3}$$

Sample data can be used to estimate the probabilities in (3). Let

N_S = total number of samples
$n(i,j)$ = number of samples of class C_i in region X_j
$n(i,.)$ = total number of samples of class C_i
$n(.,j)$ = total number of samples in region X_j

Then, for example, the probability $P_k(C_i, X_j^k)$ can be estimated as $n(i,j)/N_S$. Using such estimates in Eq. (3) the mutual information $I(a_k)$ can be written as

$$I(a_k) = \frac{1}{N_s} \sum_{i=1}^{M} \sum_{j=1}^{2} n(i,j) \log \frac{n(i,j) \, N_s}{n(i,.) \, n(.,j)} \tag{4}$$

This value of $I(a_k)$ was used in [3] and [5] to determine the splitting at each tree node. The value of a_k which produced the maximum value of $I(a_k)$ for each feature k is determined. This is done for each feature k. The feature k which produces the overall largest value of $I(a_k)$ is the one selected to split the tree node and the corresponding value of a_k is used as the threshold.

K-S Distance Approach to Classifier Design

In this section we will extend the method of classifier design described in [6] and [7] to handle the multiclass case. Let $p(x|C_i)$ be the state conditional probability density function of x, or the likelihood of class C_i with respect to x. The one-dimensional conditional probability density of the feature vector component x_k is

$$p_k(x_k|C_i) = \int_{x_{n-k}} p(x|C_i)dx_{n-k}$$

where

$$dx_{n-k} = dx_1 dx_2 ... dx_j ... dx_n \qquad j = 1, n \quad j \neq k$$

The one-dimensional conditional cumulative distribution function $F_i^k(a_k|C_i)$ is given by

$$F_i^k(a_k|C_i) = \int_{\infty}^{a_k} p_k(x_k|C_i)\, dx_k$$

In terms of the notation of the last section this cumulative distribution function can be written as

$$F_i^k(a_k \mid C_i) = P_k(X_1^k \mid C_i) \qquad (5)$$

which is the probability that the measurement x_k falls in the region X_1^k given that the class is C_i. Note that

$$P_k(X_2^k|C_i) = 1 - F_i^k(a_k|C_i) \qquad (6)$$

If we let

$$N_i = \text{total number of samples of class } C_i$$

so that

$$N_s = \sum_{i=1}^{M} N_i$$

then $F_i^k(a_k|C_i)$ can be estimated as $n(i,1)/N_i$.

Let M be the number of classes and H^k be the sequence of F_i^k, $i = 1, M$ ordered in ascending order of F_i^k. Let H_q^k be the components of the sequence H^k. That is, H_1^k is the smallest value of F_i^k and H_M^k is the largest value of F_i^k. Let $D_k(a_k) = \max_q | H_q^k - H_{q+1}^k) |$, $q = 1, M-1$. The maximum value of D_k as a function of a_k, denoted by D_k^*, occurs at some value a_k^*. Let the maximum value of D_k^* over all features x_k be denoted by D^*. At each node the feature used is that feature which produces the maximum value D^* and the corresponding value of a_k^* is used as the threshold. In the two class case D_k^* reduces to

$$\max_{a_k} | F_1^k - F_2^k |$$

which is the Kolmogorov-Smirnov distance between the two distributions.

Although this method of classifier design appears to be unrelated to the entropy minimization techniques described in the previous section, it does, in fact, minimize a pseudoentropy function in the two-class case. Watanabe [10] has introduced the pseudoentropy function $U_k(C_1,C_2)$ given by

$$U_k(C_1,C_2) = - \sum_{j=1}^{2} \left[P_k(X_j^k \mid C_1) - P_k(X_j^k \mid C_2) \right]^2 \qquad (7)$$

which is the negative of the polynomial version of divergence.

If we substitute (5) and (6) into (7) and let

$$F_1 = F_1{}^k(a_k \mid C_1)$$

and

$$F_2 = F_2{}^k(a_k \mid C_2)$$

we obtain

$$U_k(C_1,C_2) = - [F_1 - F_2]^2 - [(1-F_1) - (1-F_2)]^2$$

$$= - 2 |F_2 - F_2|^2$$

$$= - 2 \left(D_k^* \right)^2 \qquad (8)$$

which shows that choosing the Kolmogorov-Smirnov distance

$$\max_{a_k} | F_1 - F_2 |$$

is the same as maximizing the divergence or minimizing the pseudoentropy $U_k(C_1,C_2)$.

Experimental Results

The classifier described in the previous section has been successfully applied to a wide variety of applications. To illustrate its classification capabilities a 2-class, 2-feature experiment was run. Samples of each class were selected from a two-dimensional normal distribution with a diagonal covariance matrix and an equal standard deviation of 32 for each feature. The mean vectors $m_i(x_1,x_2)$ for the two classes ($i = 1,2$) were given by:

$$m_1(x_1,x_2) = (x,y)$$
$$m_2(x_1,x_2) = (-x,-y)$$

A series of experiments were run in which the values of x and y in the mean vectors of the two classes were equal and varied from 5 to 40 in steps of 5. This corresponds to the Mahalanobis distance between the two classes varying from 0.195 to 12.50. At each separation distance of the two classes a decision tree was constructed using 250 samples of each class. The splitting of the tree nodes was continued until the region of the feature space corresponding to a node contained samples of only a single class. This class then became the label for the terminal node. In the rare case of a node region containing different class samples with exactly the same values for all features, the node was assigned to the majority class, or arbitrarily if the number of samples of each class was the same. In the absence of this last rare occurrence all of the training samples will then be correctly classified by the decision tree. This, or course, will not be indicative of the results obtained on different test data taken from the normal distributions of the two classes. In constructing the tree the decision surfaces associated with the various tree nodes have warped themselves in such a way as to correctly classify the training data. The number of terminal nodes in the trees varied from a high of 222 when the Mahalanobis distance was 0.195 to a low of 35 when the Mahalanobis distance was 12.50.

The optimum Bayes decision surface is the plane $x_1 = -x_2$. It has been shown in [2] and [11] that improved performance in classifying test data is often achieved by pruning the initial large decision tree. We have developed a tree pruning technique that works as follows. A pruning number is defined equal to the number of training samples in a particular terminal node. The function prune(n) will prune any terminal node with a pruning number of n. By successively pruning the tree with increasing values of n starting at 1 and testing each pruned tree with 1000 test samples of each class we can find the pruned tree with the minimum misclassification error. The trees were pruned and the error rate measured with 1000 test samples for each class. The optimum tree size was determined by selecting the pruned tree that produced the minimum misclassification rate. The effect of the pruned tree size on this error rate is illustrated in Figure 1. As the tree is pruned the number of terminal nodes decreases rapidly and the error rate decreases gradually until the number of terminal nodes reaches a range of 6 to 14. After this the error rate increases rapidly as the number of terminal nodes is reduced to 2. This effect has been described by Breiman, et al. [2] where they refer to the increase in error rate for the unpruned tree as a variance error and the large increase in error rate for the overpruned tree as a bias error.

As an example the original tree produced with a Mahalanobis distance of 9.57 contained 49 terminal nodes. The misclassification error rate was 9.6%. After pruning with a pruning number of 1 the number of terminal nodes was reduced to 19 and the error rate decreased to 8.3%. Further pruning with a pruning number of 2 reduced the number of terminal nodes to 6 and the error rate to 7.4%. Further pruning caused an increase in the error rate. The optimal tree containing 6 terminal nodes results in a staircase decision boundary which is an approximation to the Bayes decision boundary $x_1 = -x_2$. The effect of pruning for different values of the Mahalanobis distance is shown in Figure 2. This shows that the performance of the pruned decision tree classifier can be close to that of a Bayes classifier.

As a further example to illustrate the multiclass capability of the classifier four classes were chosen from the same 2-feature normal distributions used in the previous experiement. The following mean vectors were used for the four classes.

$$m_1(x_1,x_2) = (50 , 50)$$
$$m_2(x_1,x_2) = (-50 , 50)$$
$$m_3(x_1,x_2) = (-50 , -50)$$
$$m_4(x_1,x_2) = (50 , -50)$$

The decision tree was constructed using 250 samples from each class. The initial decision tree contained 168 terminal nodes and produced a misclassification error rate of 17.8% when tested with 100 new samples from each class. The Bayes decision boundary would be the two feature axes. When tested with the test data the Bayes error rate was measured to be 11.6%. After pruning the tree up to a prune number of 10 the number of terminal nodes had been reduced to six and the error rate had been reduced to 12.0% which again approaches that of the bayes error rate.

This decision tree method has been applied to a variety of single-font and multi-font character recognition problems and produced overall average error rates ranging from 13% to 1% [12]. Typical experiments involved 23 features and 26 classes. Training a Bayes classifier with so many features would be out of the question due to the poor estimates of the covariance matrix with any reasonable number of training samples. However, the decision tree method has proved to work well even when the number of training samples is rather limited.

Summary

The algorithm described in this paper can be used to train a multiclass binary tree classifier based on training samples. At each node it selects the feature and threshold which best separates the remaining classes. The method has the advantage that it is not necessary to know beforehand whether a particular feature is important or not. If it is not, the method will simply not select it for any node. By the same token some features may only be important (and therefore only have to be calculated or measured) in certain paths of the tree. By pruning the initially generated tree performance approaching that of a Bayes classifier can be achieved. The performance of the classifier can exceed that of a Bayes classifier in special situations such as multimodal data or cases involving a limited amount of training data. The technique has proved useful for optical character recognition applications.

References

1. G. R. Dattatreya and L. N. Kanal, "Decision Trees in Pattern Recognition," Progress in Pattern Recognition 2, L. N. Kanal and A Rosenfeld (Editors), Elsevier Science Publishers B. V. (North-Holland), 1985.

2. L. Breiman, J. H. Friedman, R. A. Olshen and C. J. Stone, Classification and Regression Trees, Wadsworth & Brooks/Cole, Monterey, CA, 1984.

3. I. K. Sethi and G. P. R. Sarvarayudu, "Hierarchical Classifier Design Using Mutual Information," IEEE Trans. on Pattern Anal. and Machine Intell., Vol. PAMI-4, pp 441-445, 1982.

4. J. R. Quinlan, "Learning Efficient Classification Procedures and their Application to Chess End Games," in Machine Learning. An Artificial Intelligence Approach, R. S. Michalski, et. al. Eds., Tioga Publishing Co., Palo Alto, CA pp. 463-482, 1983.

5. J. L. Talmon, "A multiclass nonparametric partitioning algorithm," Pattern Recognition Letters, vol. 4, pp 31-38, 1986.

6. J. H. Friedman, "A Recursive Partitioning Decision Rule for Nonparametric Classification," IEEE Trans. on Computers, Vol C-26, pp. 404-408, April 1977.

7. E. M. Rounds, "A Combined Nonparametric Approach to Feature Selection and Binary Decision Tree Design," Proc. 1979 IEEE Computer Society Conf. on Pattern Recognition and Image Processign, pp. 38-43, 1979.

8. R. E. Haskell, G. Castelino and B. Mirshab, "Computer Learning Using Binary Tree Classifiers," Proc. 1988 Rochester Forth Conference on Programming Environments, pp. 77-78, June 14-18, 1988.

9. C. E. Shannon, "A Mathematical Theory of Communication," Bell Syst. Tech. J., Vol. 27, pp. 379-423, 1948.

10. S. Watanabe, "Pattern Recognition as a Quest for Minimum Entropy," Pattern Recognition, Vol. 13, pp. 381-387, 1981.

11. J. R. Quinlan, "Decision Trees as Probabilistic Classifiers," Proc. Fourth Int. Workshop on Machine Learning, U. of Cal, Irvine, pp. 31-37, June 22-25, 1987.

12. B. Mirshab, "A Computer-Based Pattern Learning System With Application to Printed Text Recognition," PhD Dissertation, Oakland University, Rochester, MI, 1989.

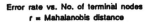

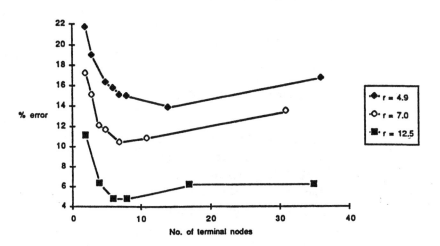

Fig. 1 Misclassification error rate as a function of pruned tree size.

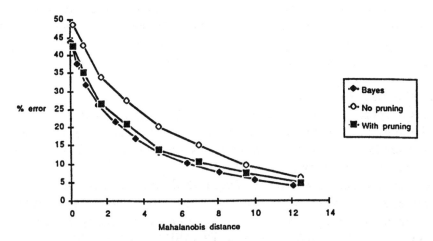

Fig. 2 Error rate vs. Mahalanobis distance showing the effect of pruning.

Designing and Implementing Parallel Constructs

Roy F. Keller

R. Mark Meyer

Thomas L. Seevers

Computer Science and Engineering Department
University of Nebraska-Lincoln
115 Ferguson Hall
Lincoln, NE 68588-0115
email: keller@fergvax.unl.edu

1 Introduction

1.1 Other Languages KL-1, EEL, EL

The work on parallelism started many years ago under the context of construct-ing algorithms. In the early 1970s teaching programming was being identified as something beyond teaching a programming language. Structured programming and "into" programming [4] were taking hold. Keller [3] advocated "into" programming, i.e. the construction of an algorithm to solve a problem completely independent of any programming language and then translating the algorithm into whatever was a most adaptable language to do so.

In the "into" approach, the programmer invented constructs to fit problems to be solved. Some problems naturally have parallel or concurrent things to be done so constructs were invented to state such computational needs. The INCASE and FORCASE constructs were thought of at this time.

Some experimental languages were developed which became known as: 1.) **KL-1**, (Keller-Lindquist), a PASCAL like language which was implemented to experi-ment with proof correctness [5]. Weakest pre-conditions were developed for proce-dures and functions and two case constructs, INCASE and FORCASE, the latter being a parallel construct; 2.) **EEL**, an early experimental language, used to teach compiler writing, was an extension of KL-1; and 3.) **ELC**, experimental language, an extension of C which was used to start the development and experimentation for implementing parallel constructs.

INCASE and FORCASE constructs were derived quite naturally and beginning programming students adapted to them easily. Experienced programmers did not. INCASE was essentially the "case of" in PASCAL, but not exactly the same. The purpose of the INCASE is to select exactly one of many things to do; a natural extension of the "if-then" and "if-then-else." The FORCASE was the selection of many of many things to do and do them independently, i.e. in parallel or concurrently. Algorithms were constructed containing these constructs and students were taught how to translate the constructs, and other ones invented, into many different programming languages, the most common one at the time being FORTRAN. PASCAL had not arrived on the scene yet.

1.2 Experimental Language Based on C (ELC)

The programming language ELC is designed to permit explicit coding of parallel algorithms in a C-like language. ELC is a subset of C which includes five new "case" constructs to specify parallelism. These constructs are INCASE, FORCASE, FORALL, SIMULCASE and SIMULALL, whose complete semantics are explained in Section 2.1. Parallel tasks are specified by caselimbs within the constructs. Caselimbs are sections of code which describe the parallel task. A new type of variable, the "message queue," allows communication between parallel tasks.

A new memory management system is used to facilitate sharing of data and coordination of results during parallel execution of tasks. When a FORCASE (or any parallel construct) begins, each selected caselimb execution gets a copy of memory, including global and heap variables and the automatic (stack) variables that are defined at that point. Each caselimb execution then operates on its private copy of the original environment, possibly changing some values. When it finishes, it sends this modified copy of the environment back to the parent (the task or process which executed the case construct in the first place), and these copies are all merged together to form one new copy of values, which then replaces the original environment. Execution continues in the parent only after all the caselimb executions have finished.

Two or more caselimb executions writing different values to the same memory address is identified as a data integrity error, causing the program to abort. The philosophy of the designers of ELC is that the programmer is writing a deterministic program to solve a specific problem and will carefully code the program to modify only the intended memory cells. In languages based on nondeterminism, the programmer must resort to complicated mechanisms to ensure mutual exclusion, including locks, semaphores, monitors and many other mechanisms to get around the nondeterminism. In ELC, determinism has been made the basis of the semantics, rather than nondeterminism, so that many mutual exclusion problems are handled automatically for the programmer.

2 Syntax and Semantics of ELC

2.1 Syntax of the parallel constructs

ELC's syntax and semantics are identical to that of C, except for the five new constructs, which are: INCASE, FORCASE, SIMULCASE, FORALL and SIMUL-ALL. The first three have the following syntax: (Square brackets denote optional inclusion, braces are part of the syntax)

```
keyword {
    [declarations of variables and message queues]
    1 or more caselimbs
}
```

where each caselimb has the following syntax:

```
[when (expression)] {
    block of declarations and statements
}
```

The syntax of FORALL and SIMULALL is:

```
keyword var = exp1 to exp2 {
    [declarations of variables and message queues]
    1 caselimb
}
```

2.2 Semantics of the parallel constructs

The semantics of the five "case" constructs may be stated as follows:

- INCASE – Select exactly one caselimb, whose "when condition" is true. If none or more than one is true, abort.

- FORCASE – Select any caselimbs whose "when conditions" are true. The caselimbs may all run at the same time, but may be scheduled in any order and combination, even sequentially.

- SIMULCASE – Select any caselimbs whose "when conditions" are true. All the caselimbs must run at the same time, since they may be communicating with each other via message queues. This means the implementation must not require that a caselimb finishes execution before another is started. Thus the caselimbs may not be executed sequentially, although it is not necessary that they start at the same time.

- FORALL – The caselimb is replicated a number of times, once for each value of the control variable. The value of this variable for that caselimb takes on one of the values in the range. Like FORCASE, the caselimbs do not necessarily have to be running at the same time.

- SIMULALL – Like the FORALL, the caselimb is replicated once for each value of the control variable in the range. Like the SIMULCASE, all these caselimbs must run at the same time.

A message queue may be any type of C variable: scalar, structure or array. The purpose of message queues is to communicate between caselimbs within a SIMULCASE or SIMULALL. These are FIFO (first-in, first-out) queues of unspecified length. The operations on them are:

1. **int mque x;** – declares x as a message queue;

2. **putque (x);** – appends a value to the end of the message queue x;

3. **getque (x);** – gets first (i.e. next) value from message queue x;

4. **readque (x);** – reads first (i.e. next) value from message queue x;

5. **sizeofq(x);** – returns number of values in queue x.

Communication between caselimbs through the message queues is done through the parent. ELC is a block-structured language, so message queue variables can be declared in any scope. Thus, the collection of all message queues forms a distributed shared memory for the caselimbs. For a particular instance of a parallel construct, all the message queues declared in its scope are considered the responsibility of that parent process. Inside a caselimb, another parallel construct may declare more message queues to be used privately between the caselimbs of that construct. However, these nested caselimbs must still be able to communicate with "cousins" as well as "siblings," so any messages placed on queues in an enclosing scope must travel to the process that exists at that level.

Deadlock is not automatically eliminated in ELC, however, starvation is, due to the FIFO semantics of the message queues.

3 The Virtual Parallel Machine (VPM)

3.1 Requirements for the support of ELC

There are two essential characteristics of ELC that shape the requirements of the underlying mechanism that must fulfill the semantics of an ELC program. The first is ELC's ability to clearly indicate tasks which may be executed independently without regard to order of inception or completion. Each parallel construct indicates these independent units of work by a "caselimb". In a visual sense, the caselimb is merely a sequence of instructions enclosed by braces and in turn contained within one of the ELC parallel constructs. Based on this, the support requirement is to accept, manage, execute and return results from these units of work.

The second important characteristic of ELC parallel constructs is the absence of directives which stipulate exactly how and where a task will be executed. This characteristic offers the programmer significant simplification in the programming of parallel algorithms. An underlying mechanism assumes this responsibility which includes identification and allocation of processor resources and management of the logically shared memory.

Seevers [6] describes a mechanism referred to as the Virtual Parallel Machine or VPM. The VPM is a logical entity which is dynamically formed based on the requirements of a specific program to be executed. It consists of one or more identical programs, each referred to as a Task Management Module or TMM. A TMM is a program containing an interpreter, a session management layer and a communications management layer. The TMM executes a program or caselimb and controls the functions of other TMMs in a VPM. The VPM is similar in some respects to early versions of Linda [2], which used independent networked processors.

3.2 General Operation

The essence of the VPM is the dynamic formation of a parallel machine by selecting volunteers from a group of interconnected, but otherwise independent processors. At any particular time, multiple VPMs may exist within a physical group of processors. A VPM always begins with a single TMM and adds and releases other TMMs as parallel constructs are encountered and completed. An individual volunteer TMM will be a member of exactly 0 or 1 VPM. If multiple VPMs exist within the same network, a TMM may at various times be an element of any of the VPMs.

VPMs have the ability to cope with nested parallel constructs. The realization of this is a VPM that grows in a "tree like" fashion as additional constructs are encountered. This tree may expand and contract during the life of a VPM.

VPM's also have the ability to resolve differences in the number of available volunteers versus the number of caselimbs that need to be scheduled. All of this is handled by the TMM's session management level and is transparent to the programmer. A TMM can fail or renege without causing the VPM to fail. This ability allows the recovery of work in progress from a volunteer if the parent becomes idle and wishes to assume the child's caselimb execution.

3.3 Task Management Module (TMM)

Once an ELC program is initiated, the TMM handles all phases of execution. It calls upon an attached interpreter to execute non-parallel portions of the program. When parallel portions are encountered, the TMM dynamically enlists other available TMMs to form the VPM. The role of the TMM can be broken down into 5 major tasks:

3.3.1 Control of local execution

The TMM incorporates an interpreter which is necessary to execute the original program, beginning in a serial fashion. The TMM allows the interpreter to execute a specified number of instructions whenever all other TMM duties have been satisfied.

3.3.2 Enlistment of volunteer TMMs

Upon encountering a parallel construct, the interpreter will return to the TMM for assistance in enlisting volunteers. Given n caselimbs, the TMM will attempt to acquire n-1 volunteers. If successful, it will dispatch a caselimb to each of the volunteers. When the dispatch is complete, the parent TMM will execute the remaining caselimb in its own interpreter in exactly the same fashion as it did the original serial code.

3.3.3 Synchronizing the completion of caselimbs

As caselimbs complete, the results are returned to the parent TMM where they are stored in the appropriate variable locations. When all caselimbs have completed, the TMM will ask the interpreter to resume processing the serial code following the parallel section just completed.

3.3.4 Communications and protocol execution

The TMM is involved in communication sessions with its interpreter and other TMMs. This communication is conducted via packets which contain protocol commands and other appropriate information. The TMM will complete necessary processing to respond to arriving protocol commands.

3.3.5 Control of caselimb execution

A TMM may receive a caselimb to be executed even though it did not execute the original program. In this mode it is a volunteer. Execution is identical to the operation of the TMM when functioning as a parent. The TMM may be viewed as a virtual processing element, available for parallel processing in the formation of a VPM. Volunteer TMMs do not differ from a parent TMM. It is merely a role that they assume at a particular point in time.

3.4 Session Protocol

Conceptually, sessions serve to clarify communications. Initially, consider a physical network with some number of TMMs, all in an idle status. As TMMs are added to the VPM, they form sessions in a parent/child relationship. These sessions are used as communications and control channels over which data, instructions and protocol commands are passed. Protocol commands and responses may flow in either direction in any of these sessions. When a child encounters a parallel construct within a caselimb it assumes the dual role of the parent as well as child. These sessions support what Almasi [1] termed a message passing parallel RAM machine. The message passing is not seen at the problem level, where the VPM appears as a shared memory machine.

Protocol commands indicate via an inter-TMM session a request for a TMM to change states. Initially, TMMs are in the IDLE state. Encountering a parallel construct results in execution of the PROPOSE command. PROPOSE establishes necessary information about each of the caselimbs. Ensuing protocol commands such as ENLIST, BIND and DISPATCH cause volunteer TMMs to be added to the VPM. Completed caselimbs in the volunteers cause the COMPLETE protocol to be executed. Caselimb results are returned to their parent and sequential processing continues. If nested parallel constructs are encountered, the VPM is extended and similar protocol commands flow over the new parent/child sessions. The protocol set contains numerous other commands to accommodate such things as abnormal termination of caselimbs, inter-caselimb communication and remote input and output actions.

References

[1] Almasi, George S. and Alan Gottlieb. 1989. *Highly Parallel Computing*. California: Benjamin/Cummings.

[2] Gerlenter David, Ahuja Sudhir and Nicholas Carriero. 1986. "Linda and Friends", *Computer*, Vol. 19, No. 8: 26-34.

[3] Keller, R. F., "On Control Structures for Constructing Programs," *Sigplan Notices*, Vol. 12, No. 9, pp. 36-44, 1977.

[4] Keller, R. F., Boysen, J. P., "On Teaching 'Into' Programming", *Proceedings of the Fifth Joint (AED-IEEE) Workshop on College Curriculum in Computer Science and Data Processing*, 1978.

[5] Lindquist, T. E., Keller, R. F., "The Correctness of Programs Written in the Language KL-1," *Proceedings of IEEE COMSAC77 (Computer Software and Applications Conference)* Chicago, Ill. November, 1977.

[6] Seevers, T. L., "The Virtual Parallel Machine A Dynamically Reconfigurable Approach", *Doctoral Dissertation*, 1989.

Performance of Parallel Consistency Algorithms[1]

Ashok Samal

Department of Computer Science and Engineering
University of Nebraska, Lincoln, NE 68588
e-mail : samal@fergvax.unl.edu

Abstract. Consistency algorithms are used to reduce the overall computation time for consistent labeling problem which is commonly used in computer vision. We have given parallel algorithms to enforce arc consistency, which has been shown to be inherently sequential[3, 6]. Since all three parallel algorithms have the same time complexity on a PRAM, it is necessary to implement them on a parallel processor to determine which one performs best. The results of implementing them on a BBN Butterfly are presented here.

1 Introduction

The *Scene Labeling Problem* is used in computer vision to identify the set of objects in a given scene. The problem has also been referred to as the *Consistent Labeling Problem*[2], the *Satisfying Assignment Problem*[1], the *Constraint Satisfaction Problem*[4], etc. It will be referred to as the Consistent Labeling Problem (CLP) in this paper and is defined below:

1.1 Definitions

- A *unit*, u_i, is an item that has to be assigned a value or a meaning.

- A *label*, l_i, is the value or the meaning that is associated to a unit.

- A unit u_i can be assigned any value from an associated domain D_i. In general, however, there are restrictions on the labels a set of units can have simultaneously in order to be consistent. These are called the *constraints*. Only unary and binary constraints are considered here. The unary constraints R^1 determine the labels a unit may not be given, e.g., u_3 is odd; so even labels may not be given to it. The binary constraints determine the constraints between a pair of units. If $[(u_i, l_i), (u_j, l_j)] \in R^2$, it means the unit u_i cannot have the label l_i, when u_j has the label l_j.

Given a set of units, U, $|U| = n$, a set of domains, D, $|D_i| = a$, and a set R^1 and a binary constraint set R^2, the goal of the consistent labeling problem is to find a complete and consistent (no constraint is violated) labeling.

It is convenient to view the specification of a given CLP as a directed graph, where nodes correspond to the *units*, and the arcs correspond to the constraints. The *domains* for the unit are associated with the graph nodes. Let the set of arcs be E, with $|E| = e$.

[1]This work was done at the University of Utah and was partially supported by NSF Grants MCS-8221750, DCR-8506393, and DMC-8502115.

1.2 The Consistency Algorithms

The consistent labeling problem can be solved in several ways, e.g., *generate-and-test* and *backtracking* (and many variations of it). Another approach to reduce the computation during the backtracking process was taken by Mackworth[4]. Three consistency tests: *node*, *arc*, and *path* consistency tests are given, which when enforced first may reduce the computation time of the backtrack programs drastically.

The consistency algorithms when used in conjunction with search algorithms to reduce the average execution time. The algorithms remove any label that doesn't satisfy minimum consistency criteria. Three types of consistency are defined in [4]: *node*, *arc*, and *path* consistency. In this paper only the first two are used and are defined below:

- A node i is <u>node consistent</u> iff $\forall z(z \in D_i \Rightarrow R_i^1(z))$.

- An arc (i, j) is <u>arc consistent</u> iff $\forall_{z \in D_i}(R_i^1(z) \Rightarrow \exists_{y \in D_j}(R_j^1(y) \land \sim R_{ij}^2(z, y))$.

Several algorithms have been proposed to achieve consistency in a network of constraints. We are concerned only with algorithms that enforce arc consistency. The goal of these algorithms is to make the arcs in the network consistent by removing all the labels from all the nodes that do not have any support from an adjacent node, i.e., a node connected to it by an arc in the graph. The removal of a label from a node may, in turn, make some other arc inconsistent. Thus, this process has to be repeated until no label is removed from the nodes during an iteration. Several arc consistency algorithms have been proposed. Mackworth proposed three sequential algorithms: AC-1, AC-2, and AC-3. Later, Mohr and Henderson[5] gave an optimal sequential algorithm for arc consistency: AC-4.

2 Parallel Arc Consistency Algorithms

Since the main emphasis here is on the performance of the algorithms, we will only briefly describe the algorithms (see [6, 7] for details).

2.1 Enforcing Consistency along an Arc

The algorithm (which takes constant time on a PRAM) to achieve consistency along a single arc is given in below ($\|for$ is used to describe the concurrent execution).

```
function Previse(arc)
begin
    i := arc.start; j := arc.end; change := FALSE;
    ||for each l_i := 1 to a do
        support[l_i] := FALSE;
        ||for each l_j := 1 to a do
            if R_{ij}^2(l_i, l_j) then support[l_i] := TRUE;
        if (¬ support[l_i]) then D_i := D_i − {l_i}; change := TRUE;
end
```

To make a single arc, (i, j), consistent all the labels at i which do not have any support from j must be removed. Support for these labels is checked in parallel in the algorithm.

Parallel AC-1 : In PAC-1 a similar approach to AC-1, i.e., check for consistency along each arc in the graph in each iteration, is taken. However, all the arcs are checked for consistency simultaneously. Checking for consistency along an arc (Previse) can itself be done in parallel. So, the algorithm can utilize up to ea^2 processors; a^2 processors by Previse for each of the e arcs. During each iteration (except the last) at least one label gets removed, because otherwise the algorithm would terminate. Since the total number of labels is na, it follows that the complexity of this algorithm is $O(na)$.

Parallel AC-3 : In PAC-3, only the arcs associated with the nodes whose label sets have changed during the previous iteration are added to the pool of arcs to be checked for consistency. Here, all the arcs in the pool are checked for consistency simultaneously. It also makes use of the **Previse** function to enforce consistency along an arc. During each iteration the pool is constructed from the arcs associated with the nodes whose label sets have changed in the previous iteration. In the worst case it also uses ea^2 processors, although it needs fewer on the average. The worst case time complexity of the algorithm is also $O(na)$.

Parallel AC-4 : The algorithm is based on the notion of support. As long as a label l_i at a node i has some support from one or more labels at all other nodes, l_i is considered a viable label for node i. This information about the support for the labels is stored explicitly in two data structures: *Counter* and *Support*.

The algorithm works in two stages. First the two data structures are constructed in parallel. A list (called *List*) of all the node-label pairs which have no support is also constructed. In the second stage all the labels which have no support are deleted. Initially *List* contains this information. A node-label pair, (j, l_j), is pulled out from *List* and the number of supports (stored in *Counter*) for the node-label pairs which are supported by it is decremented by one. If this makes the number of supports to become zero the label is deleted and this pair is added to *List*. This process continues until *List* is empty. There are two levels of parallelism in the algorithm. First, each unit-label pair in the *List* can be processed in parallel. Also, each element in the support set of the unit-label can also be worked on concurrently. The time taken by PAC-4 is also $O(na)$.

The sequential algorithms (AC-1, AC-3, and AC-4) are $O(ea^3n)$, $O(ea^3)$ and $O(ea^2)$, respectively. However, all three parallel algorithms have the same worst case time complexity of $O(na)$. To determine which algorithm performs best on the average, it is imperative to implement them on a multiprocessor and analyze their performance. The rest of the paper deals with this aspect of the problem.

3   Implementation and Results

The experimental results presented here are obtained using a BBN Butterfly Plus parallel processor which is *MIMD* and has a *shared-memory*. All the processor nodes are connected to an interconnection network called the Butterfly Plus switch. All the application programs in the Butterfly Plus ran under the Chrysalis operating system. To evaluate and compare the performances of the parallel algorithms the most widely used measure, i.e., speedup is used. It is defined as the ratio of time taken by an algorithm on 1 processor and the time taken by the algorithm on k processors.

Three different kinds of problems (described by the underlying graphs) are used here to compare the performance of the algorithms: (1) cyclic graphs, which is sparse ($e = n$), (2) complete graphs, which is very dense ($e = n(n-1)$), and (3) random graphs with $e = n^{1.5}$.

3.1 Implementation

Since the time to create a process on the machine is very large, we take the *multi-sequential* approach. Only one process per processor is created and it performs different computations at different times. The parallel processor used for this work has 16 processors. The task granularity is kept as high as possible, while still keeping the number of tasks large.

Due to the lack of space results for all graphs can not be presented here (See [6] for a complete set of results). Results for only one type of graph is presented for each algorithm. The X-axis shows the number of processors.

The performance of the algorithm using the cyclic graph is shown in Figure 1. In all three problems the maximum speedup obtained is greater than the number of processors used. This is called *super-linear* speedup. This phenomenon will be explained in the next section.

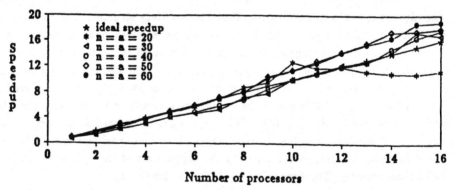

Figure 1: Speedup for the Cyclic Graph Using PAC-1

Figure 2 shows the performance of PAC-3 for the complete graph problem. In general, all the problems have good speedup figures. There is a slow degradation for large number of processors. This is partly due to the memory contention for the task queue. There is only one centralized task queue which results in some memory contention.

The performance of PAC-4 for the random graph problem is shown in Figure 3. In general, good speedup figures are achieved, but there is a slowing down tendency as the number of processors gets large for the same reason as in PAC-3.

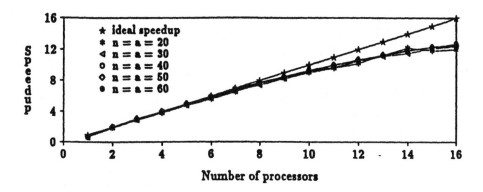

Figure 2: Speedup for the Complete Graph Using PAC-3

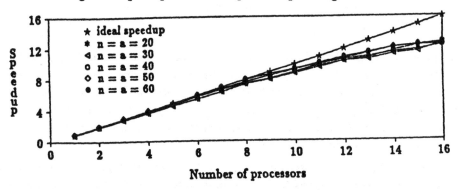

Figure 3: Speedup for the Random Graph Using PAC-4

3.2 Combinatorial Implosion

Here we briefly describe how some algorithms achieved super-linear speedup. It results from the parallel algorithm's ability to work with different parts of the problem and sharing the results. This results in less overall work by the parallel algorithm compared to any sequential algorithm.

Consider the cyclic graph problem with six nodes and only one label per node along with the greater than constraint (Figure 4(a)). In the first iteration every arc, except arc 6, is consistent. So, label 1 at node 1 is deleted after 6 time units (time taken to enforce consistency along one arc). Table 1 shows the sequential execution order.

Now assume that two processors are employed for this task as shown in the Figure 4(b). During the first iteration only label 1 at node 1 is deleted (by P_1). In the second iteration label 2 at node 2 is deleted (by P_1). In the third iteration label 3 at node 3 gets deleted by processor P_1. Since the memory is shared, P_2 sees this change and deletes label 4 at node 4; it no longer has any support from node 3. Finally, the other two labels also get deleted. So, for this problem instance $T_1 = 36$, and $T_2 = 15$, which results in a speedup of greater than 2 with only 2 processors. The parallel execution order is shown in Table 1.

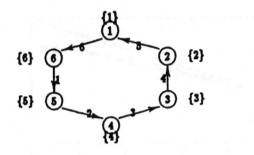
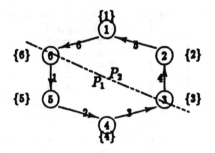

Figure 4: (a) A Network of Constraints   (b) Processor Allocation

4 Summary

The previous sections show the performance of the parallel algorithms for different types of problems. Here the different algorithms for the same problem are compared to see which algorithm performs the best on the Butterfly Plus. Only the best time for each algorithm is used for the comparison. The X-axis here shows the problem size (number of nodes). Again, due to lack of space, only the results for the random graph problem is shown here (Figure 5). Other graphs show similar pattern.

As can be seen, PAC-1 performs better than the other two algorithms, even though the results for PAC-3 are comparable. PAC-4 consistently is worse than the other algorithms. The main reason is that the data structures are very large and use a large amount of memory which leads to memory contention. The results are interesting since the AC-1 (the sequential algorithm) has the worst and AC-4 has the best complexity among the three.

To summarize, while all the arc consistency algorithms have the same worst case time complexity on a PRAM, their performance on a physical multiprocessor differ considerably. It has been proved that enforcing arc consistency in a network is inherently sequential[3, 6] (in total number of labels). However, it is shown here that a large improvement can

Table 1: Sequential and Parallel Execution Orders

ITER No	TIME (sequential)	ACTION (sequential)	TIME (parallel)	ACTION (parallel)
1	6	1 deleted	3	1 deleted
2	6	2 deleted	3	2 deleted
3	6	3 deleted	3	3 and 4 deleted
4	6	4 deleted	3	5 deleted
5	6	5 deleted	3	6 deleted
6	6	6 deleted		
	total = 36		total = 15	

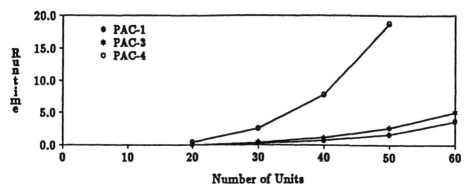

Figure 5: Best Runtimes for the Random Graph

be achieved on reasonably large multiprocessors. In some cases *super-linear* speedup is achieved.

References

[1] John Gaschnig. *Performance Measurements and Analysis of Certain Search Algorithms.* PhD thesis, Carnegie-Mellon University, Department of Computer Science, May 1979.

[2] Robert M. Haralick and Linda G. Shapiro. The consistent labelling problem: Part I. *IEEE Transactions On Pattern Analysis And Machine Intelligence,* PAMI-1(2):173–184, April 1979.

[3] Simon Kasif. On the parallel complexity of some constraint satisfaction problems. In *Proceedings of AAAI-86,* pages 349–353. AAAI, August 11-15 1986.

[4] Alan K. Mackworth. Consistency in network of relations. *Artificial Intelligence,* 8:99–118, 1977.

[5] Roger Mohr and Thomas C. Henderson. Arc and path consistency revisited. *Artificial Intelligence,* 28(2):225–233, March 1986.

[6] Ashok Samal. *Parallel Split-Level Relaxation.* PhD thesis, Department of Computer Science, University of Utah, August 1988.

[7] Ashok Samal and Thomas C. Henderson. Parallel consistent labeling algorithms. *International Journal of Parallel Programming,* 16(5):341–364, 1988.

DELAY ANALYSIS OF THE *N*-CUBE NETWORK

Mokhtar A. Aboelaze*

Computer Science Dept.
York University
N. York, Ontario M3J 1P3 Canada

Catherine E. Houstis**

Computer Science Dept.
University of Crete
Heraklion, Crete Greece

Abstract

In this paper, we analyze the delay of an average message going through an arbitrary link of the *N*-cube. We view each link as an M/M/1 queue and find analytic recursive relations for the arrival rate of messages at an arbitrary link. Then, we calculate the delay per link as a function of the message generation rate at the processor. We investigate two model of communication. The first, uniform communication where each processor communicate with any other processor with the same probability. The second is clustered communication, where neighboring processors communicate more than distant processors do. Finally, we investigate the effect of adding one more link at each node of the cube (*Folded Hypercube*) on the delay and the maximum number of hops.

1. INTRODUCTION

The *N*-cube multiprocessor is a highly parallel multiprocessor architecture consisting of 2^N identical processors. Each processor has its own memory and is connected to N neighbors in the form of a binary *N*-cube network. The hypercube is a message-passing multiprocessor architecture that has the ability to exploit particular topologies of problems in order to minimize communication cost [Fox85], [Ncu86].

In this paper, we report on the performance of the *N*-cube from the point of view of the communication delay incurred by an average message crossing an arbitrary link of the machine. The analysis is based on simple probabilistic relations and the inherent symmetry of the *N*-cube. Analytical recursive relations have been obtained for the message rate of an arbitrary link. Then each link is treated as an M/M/1 queue and a number of performance measures are computed. We also investigate the architecture known as *Folded Hypercube* [LaE89].

Previous work in performance of hypercube [AbP89] concentrated a synchronized system (SIMD) [KuS82], [Bat80]. However, the situation is different in MIMD systems. Where there are N processors, controlled by a single operating system, which provide interaction between processors and their programs [HwB84]. In this case there is no global clock controlling the different processors in the systems, and previous results will not be valid any more.

---
*This work was partially supported by a grant from the Engineering Council of Canada grant number NSERC-OGP0043688.
**This work was completed while the author was with the EE Department of Purdue University. It was supported by NSF grant number DMC-8508685A1.

In Section 2 some basic properties of the N-cube are summarized and a theorem is proved which is used in the delay analysis. In Section 3 the delay analysis is presented. In Section 4 the Folded Hypercube is analyzed and its performance is compared to the N-cube.

2. BASIC PROPERTIES OF THE N-CUBE

The N-cube, is a graph with 2^N nodes numbered from 0 to 2^N-1. A link connects two nodes if the binary representation of their two number differ by one and only one bit. The distance between two nodes a and b is $h(a,b)$, where h is the hamming distance. Let us consider for a moment a link ℓ by its two incident nodes (c,d). Then

Definition : The distance d_1 between a node a and a link ℓ with incident nodes (c,d) is

$$d_1 = \min\left\{ h(a,c), h(a,d) \right\}$$

The above definition is used in the following theorem.

Theorem 1.

In an N-cube the number of nodes at distance f from a link ℓ with incident nodes (c,d), is equal to $\binom{N}{f} - \binom{N-1}{f-1}$ $0 \le f < N$.

Proof: The number of nodes at a hamming distance f from node c is equal to $\binom{N}{f}$. Not all of these nodes are at a distance f from the link (c,d). Since there is one bit in the binary representation of node c that is different from its corresponding bit in the binary representation of node d. Then, some of these nodes are at a distance $f+1$ from node d, and some are at a distance $f-1$ from it. In the first group, the nodes that are at a distance $f+1$ from node d, according to definition 3.2 are at a distance f from link (c,d). The rest of the nodes are at a distance $f-1$ from the same link. The question that remains to be answered is how many nodes are at a distance f from node c and at a distance $f-1$ from node d. Assume that the binary representation of node c is $c_0, c_1, \ldots, c_N$, and that of node d is $d_0, d_1 \ldots, d_N$. Since these two nodes differ in one and only one bit, assume without loss of generality that they differ in the first bit i.e. $c_0 \neq d_0$, and they agree in the rest of the bits. Any node at a distance f from node c and a distance $f-1$ from node d must have the same first bit as node d and differ in $f-1$ of the remaining $N-1$ bits. The number of such nodes is $\binom{N-1}{f-1}$. Therefore the number of nodes at a distance f from (c,d) is $\binom{N}{f} - \binom{N-1}{f-1}$ $\qquad \square$

3. DELAY ANALYSIS OF THE N-CUBE

In our analysis we represent the links of the N-cube as servers in a queueing system [All78], [Kle76a], [Kle76b]. The service rate of each link is its bandwidth. Communication between nodes is accomplished by exchanging messages. We assume that the time between two message generated by the same processor is exponentially distributed with mean $1/\lambda$. We also assume that the length of the message has an exponential distribution with mean $1/\mu$.

Without loss of generality let us assume that a source node is a_0 and that it sends a message to any node with equal probability. Starting at a_0 a message travels through a number of links. We pick an arbitrary link in the path from a_0 to a_N. Let L_i be this arbitrary link. The longest path is composed of a succession of $N+1$ nodes and N links, i.e., $a_0, L_0, a_1, L_1, \ldots, a_i, L_i, \ldots, a_{N-1}, L_{N-1}, a_N$. Notice that the numbering here does not correspond to the binary numbering of the nodes in the N-cube, it simply means that a_0 is the first node in the path, L_0 is the first link in the path a_1 the second node in the path, etc. Figure 1.a shows a 4-cube, and Figure 1.b shows the longest path in the 4-cube

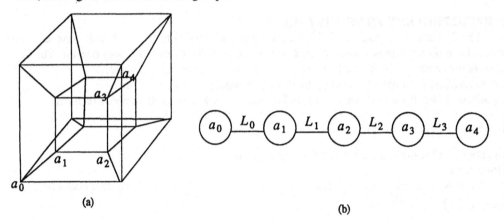

(a)

(b)

Figure 1. A 3-D view of the 4-cube

Next we proceed to define a number of terms pertinent to our analysis. Let

$p_i = prob\,(a_i/L_0 \cap L_1 \cap L_2 \cap, \ldots, \cap L_{i-1})$ = the probability that a message originated at a_0 is destined to node a_i given that it has traveled along the line containing the links $L_0, L_1, L_2, \ldots, L_{i-1}$.

$q_i = prob\,(L_i/L_0 \cap L_1 \cap L_2 \cap, \ldots, \cap L_{i-1})$ = the probability that a message originated at a_0 will travel along link L_i given it has traveled along the path containing the links $L_0, L_1, \ldots, L_{i-1}$.

P_i = probability that a message originated at node a_0 will travel along the link L_i, for $0 \le i \le N-1$

Any message generated at node a_0 will be directed with equal probability to any node in the N-cube, by following any outgoing link of a_0. Since there are N links connected to node a_0 then the probability of this message to choose link L_0 is $1/N$. Thus

$$q_0 = prob\,(L_0) = 1/N \tag{1}$$

Now $p_1 = prob\,(a_1/L_0)$ is the probability that this message is destined to a_1 given that it has traveled along link L_0. Thus

$$p_1 = prob\,(a_1/L_0) = \frac{prob\,(a_1 \cap L_0)}{prob\,(L_0)} \tag{2}$$

Since there is only one route from node a_0 to its neighbor a_1 then $prob\,(a_1 \cap L_0) = prob\,(a_1) = 1/(2^N - 1)$ (all the $2^N - 1$ nodes are equally likely to receive a message from a_0)

$$p_1 = \frac{1/(2^N - 1)}{1/N} = \frac{N}{2^N - 1} \tag{3}$$

Next, we calculate q_1 which is the probability that a message originated at node a_0 will travel along the link L_1, given it has already traveled along the link L_0. This can occur only if the message destination is not a_1. The probability that the message destination is not a_1 is $1-p_1$. Notice also that a message leaving a_1 has $N-1$ nodes to choose from (it can not be forwarded to the link it just arrived from).

$$q_1 = prob\,(L_1/L_0) = \frac{1-p_1}{N-1} \tag{4}$$

We now need to calculate $p_2 = prob\,(a_2/L_0 \cap L_1)$ which is the probability that the message originated at a_0 is designated to node a_2 given that it has traveled along the line containing the link L_0 and L_1. Thus

$$p_2 = prob\,(a_2/L_0 \cap L_1) = \frac{prob\,(a_2 \cap L_0 \cap L_1)}{prob\,(L_0 \cap L_1)} = \frac{prob\,(a_2 \cap L_0 \cap L_1)}{prob\,(L_0)prob\,(L_1/L_0)} \tag{5}$$

Since node a_2 is at a hamming distance 2 from node a_0, there are 2! possible paths between the two nodes. Thus the probability to go to a_2 using one such path and in particular the path containing L_0, L_1 is $prob\,(a_2 \cap L_0 \cap L_1) = \dfrac{1}{2!(2^N - 1)}$. Then

$$p_2 = \frac{\dfrac{1}{2!(2^N - 1)}}{q_0 q_1} \tag{6}$$

In order to calculate q_2 we apply similar thinking as for q_1. Thus, $1-p_2$ is the probability that the message will not have node a_2 as its destination node and since there are $N-2$ paths outbound from a_2, then

$$q_2 = prob\,(L_2/L_0 \cap L_1) = \frac{1-p_2}{N-2} \tag{7}$$

In general, to calculate p_i

$$p_i = prob\,(a_i/L_0 \cap L_1 \cap, \ldots, \cap L_{i-1}) = \frac{prob\,(a_i \cap L_0 \cap L_1 \cap, \ldots, \cap L_{i-1})}{prob\,(L_0 \cap L_1 \cap, \ldots, \cap L_{i-1})}$$

$$= \frac{prob\,(a_i \cap L_0 \cap L_1 \cap, \ldots, \cap L_{i-1})}{prob\,(L_{i-1}/L_{i-2} \cap, \ldots, \cap L_0)prob\,(L_{i-2}/L_{i-3} \cap, \ldots, \cap L_0), \ldots, prob\,(L_0)} \tag{8}$$

Note that we apply the multiplication rule for the probability function in the denominator. Then equation (8) can be rewritten as

$$p_i = \frac{\dfrac{1}{i!(2^N - 1)}}{q_{i-1}q_{i-2}, \ldots, q_0} \tag{9}$$

and

$$q_i = prob\,(L_i/L_0 \cap L_1 \cap, \ldots, \cap L_{i-1}) = \frac{1-p_i}{N-i} \tag{10}$$

This completes the first step in our analysis.

In the second step, we calculate the probability P_i which is the probability that a message originated at node a_0 will travel along link L_i. Since $q_i = prob\,(L_i/L_0 \cap L_1, \ldots, \cap L_{i-1})$ is the conditional probability that this message will travel along the specific path containing $L_0, L_1, \ldots, L_{i-1}$ one can use the total probability formula and find P_i by summing overall possible paths from a_0 to a_i through L_i. This formula is

$$P(A) = \sum_{all\ i} P(A/B_i)P(B_i) = \sum_{all\ i} P(A \cap B_i) \tag{11}$$

where the events A and B_i correspond to the events

$A/B_i = a$ message traveling along $L_i/$has crossed all links $L_0 \cap L_1 \cap, \ldots, \cap L_{i-1}$

Because of the symmetry of the N-cube there are $i!$ such paths between a_0 and a_i, all with the same probability. Thus,

$$P_i = \sum prob\,[L_i \cap \{L_{i-1} \ldots L_0\}] \tag{12}$$

the sum is over all the possible paths $\{L_{i-1} \ldots L_0\}$. since there are $i!$ such paths between L_0 and L_{i-1}, then

$$P_i = prob\,[L_i \cap \{L_{i-1} \ldots L_0\}]\, i! \tag{13}$$

$$P_i = \left[prob\,(L_i/L_{i-1} \cap, \ldots, \cap L_0) \times prob\,(L_{i-1} \cap, \ldots, \cap L_0) \right] i! \tag{14}$$

Using the multiplication rule we obtain

$$P_i = \left[q_i \times prob\,(L_{i-1}/L_{i-2} \cap, \ldots, L_0) \times prob\,(L_{i-2} \cap, \ldots, \cap L_0) \right] i! \tag{15}$$

and finally

$$P_i = [q_i\, q_{i-1}, \ldots, q_0]\, i! \text{ for } 0 \le i < N \tag{16}$$

Thus we have determined the probability that a message originated at node a_0 will travel along link L_i, in other words we have determined the percentage of messages originated at a_0 that will travel across link L_i for $0 \le i \le N-1$.

In the third step of our analysis, we have to determine the contribution of all nodes to L_i, i.e., the total message traffic through L_i. The contribution of all nodes to link L_i will depend on their distance from it. Because of the symmetry of the N-cube all nodes at the same distance, say distance j, $1 \le j < N$, will contribute the same amount of traffic. We need to know how many such nodes exist at distance j from link L_i. According to theorem 1 the number of nodes that are at a distance j from L_i are $\binom{N}{j} - \binom{N-1}{j-1}$. then,

$$S = \sum_{j=0}^{N-1} P_j \left[\binom{N}{j} - \binom{N-1}{j-1} \right] \tag{17}$$

$\lambda_i = \lambda_p \times S$, where λ_i is the effective arrival rate at any link, and λ_p is the message generating rate at the processor.

By treating any link as an M/M/1 queue [All78], the queueing delay T_q, and the total delay T_{total} are

$$T_q = \frac{\rho}{\mu(1-\rho)}, \quad T_{total} = \frac{1}{\mu(1-\rho)}, \quad \rho = \frac{\lambda_i}{\mu} = \frac{\lambda_p\, S}{\mu} \tag{18}$$

This completes our analysis under the assumption that a message is sent from any node to any other node with equal probability.

Now we consider the assumption that a node sends a message to any node with a probability which depends on the hamming distance between the binary labels of the two nodes. Let $f(i)$ be the probability that a message generated at any node will be directed to a node at a distance i from the originating node. Notice that $f(i)$ should be a decreasing function of i, i.e., the further the two processors, the less probable that they will exchange messages. We assume that $f(i)$ will take the form,. $f(i) = k/i$ for $i = 1, 2, \ldots, N$ where k is a constant, such that the sum of the probabilities that a message will be directed to any node is 1. The analysis is as before, except for the calculation of p_i. Since the probability that the message will be directed to a link at a distance i is $f(i)$, then p_i is given by

$$p_i = \frac{f(i)/i!}{q_0 q_1, \ldots, q_{i-1}} \tag{19}$$

The rest of the equations remain the same. This completes our analysis.

To check the validity of our analytical work, we simulated the N-cube and compared our results with the simulation results. The difference between the analytical results and simulation results is less than 7%. Recall, λ_p represents the rate of message generation at any node. Figure 2 shows the delay per link vs λ_p for both the equal probability case and the $f(i) = k/i$ case.

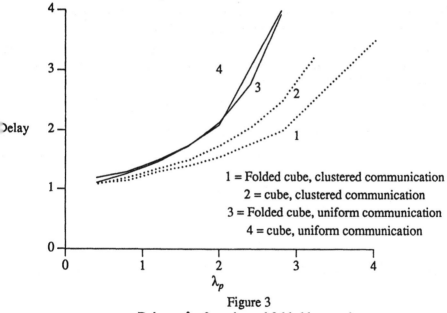

Figure 3
Delay vs λ_p for cube and folded hypercube

4. FOLDED HYPERCUBE

In N-cube the maximum distance between two nodes is N. A modified cube architecture known as *Folded Hypercube* was presented in [LaE89]. The basic differences between this modified cube and the ordinary hypercube architecture is the addition of some extra links known as the complementary links. To derive the folded hypercube from the ordinary N-cube, it is sufficient to add N bi-directional links (known as complementary links) to connect two nodes that differ in all their bits, i.e., a link is added to connect node $(a_{N-1}, a_{N-2}, \ldots, a_0)$ and node $(\bar{a}_{N-1}, \bar{a}_{N-2}, \ldots, \bar{a}_0)$. The number of the added links is N. In the rest of this section we study the effect of the added links on the average message delay.

4.1. Delay Analysis

The basic idea of routing in the modified cube is as follows. Assume that a message is directed from node a to node b, recall that the hamming distance between a and b is $h(a,b)$. Then, if $h(a,b) \leq \lceil N/2 \rceil$ then the ordinary routing is used. If $h(a,b) > \lceil N/2 \rceil$ then the message is sent to the node that differs in all the bits in its binary representation from the source node via the complementary link, and then ordinary routing is used. Thus, the maximum number of steps to send messages between any two nodes is $\lceil N/2 \rceil$.

To calculate the delay at each link, it will be very hard to follow the individual messages from node to node as we did with the ordinary cube, henceforth a simpler approach is used. Since the added link is used once at the beginning of the routing if the hamming distance is greater than $\lceil N/2 \rceil$ and never used again we can calculate the effective arrival rate for the ordinary links and the added links separately as follows. If we define the arrival rate at the ordinary links as $\lambda_{ordinary}$, then.

$$\lambda_{ordinary} = \lambda_p \times \frac{number\ of\ nodes \times Average\ number\ of\ hops\ per\ message}{Total\ number\ of\ links} \quad (20)$$

Notice that, the nodes that are at a distance of $i \leq \lceil N/2 \rceil$ from the source node, require i hops. However, the nodes that are at a distance of $i \geq \lceil N/2 \rceil$ from the source node require one hop via the complementary link and $N-i$ hops via the ordinary links to reach its destination

$$Average\ number\ of\ hops = \frac{\sum\limits_{i=1}^{\lceil N/2 \rceil} i \times \binom{N}{i} + \sum\limits_{i=\lceil N/2 \rceil+1}^{N} (N-i) \times \binom{N}{i}}{\sum\limits_{i=1}^{\lceil N/2 \rceil} \binom{N}{i} + \sum\limits_{i=\lceil N/2 \rceil+1}^{N} \binom{N}{i}} \quad (21)$$

$$\lambda_{ordinary} = \lambda_p \frac{\left[\sum\limits_{i=1}^{\lceil N/2 \rceil} i \times \binom{N}{i} + \sum\limits_{i=\lceil N/2 \rceil+1}^{N} (N-i) \times \binom{N}{i}\right] \times 2^N}{\left[\sum\limits_{i=1}^{\lceil N/2 \rceil} \binom{N}{i} + \sum\limits_{i=\lceil N/2 \rceil+1}^{N} \binom{N}{i}\right] \times N 2^N} \quad (22)$$

For the complementary link, the traffic that crosses it is the part of the traffic directed to a node at distance greater that $\lceil N/2 \rceil$

$$\lambda_c = \frac{\lambda_p}{2^N - 1} \times \sum\limits_{i=\lceil N/2 \rceil+1}^{N} \binom{N}{i} \quad (23)$$

Table 1 shows the relation between $\lambda_{ordinary}$ (the arrival rate at the ordinary links in the Folded hypercube), λ_c (arrival rate at the complementary link for the folded hypercube), and λ_i (arrival rate for links in the hypercube) for different values of N. Figure 2 shows the delay vs λ_p for the folded hypercube.

N	$\lambda_{ordinary}$	λ_c	λ_i
2	0.500	0.333	0.667
3	0.500	0.143	0.571
4	0.357	0.333	0.533
5	0.400	0.194	0.516
6	0.355	0.349	0.508
7	0.389	0.228	0.504
8	0.366	0.365	0.501
9	0.392	0.254	0.501
10	0.378	0.377	0.500

Table 1. $\lambda_{ordinary}$, λ_c, and λ_i ($\lambda_p = 1$)

5. CONCLUSION

In this paper, we studied the average message delay per link in an N-cube. We assumed that the system is running asynchronously, the rate of message generation in each processor is Poisson and the length of the message is exponentially distributed. We established recursive relations for the rate of message arrival at each link. Knowing that, we calculated some performance measures such as the average message delay per link and the average queue length at each link. We also studied the delay in the Folded Hypercube, and we showed that the average message delay in the Folded Hypercube is much less than the average message delay in the ordinary cube. Simulation results were shown to validate our analysis, the difference between the simulation results and our analysis is less than 7%.

6. REFERENCES

[AbP89]   S. Abraham and K. Padmanabhan, "Performance of the Direct Binary n-Cube Network for Multiprocessors," *IEEE Transactions on Computers,* Vol. 38, No. 7, July 1989, pp. 1000-1011.

[All78]   A. O. Allen, *Probability, Statistics, and Queueing Theory,* Academic Press, 1978.

[Bat80]   K. E. Batcher, "Design of a Massively Parallel Processor," *Trans. on Computers,* Vol. C-29, N 9, Sept. 1980, pp. 836-840.

[Fox85]   G. Fox, *The Performance of the Caltech Hypercube in Scientific Calculations,* Caltech Report CALT-68-1298, Caltech, 1985.

[HwB84]   K. Hwang and F. A. Briggs, *Computer Architecture and Parallel Processing,* McGraw-Hill, 1984.

[Kle76a] L. Kleinrock, *Queueing Systems, Volume 1: Theory,* John Wiley and Sons, 1976.

[Kle76b] L. Kleinrock, *Queueing Systems, Volume 2: Computer Applications,* John Wiley and Sons, 1976.

[KuS82]   D. J. Kuck and R. A. Stokes, "The Burroughs Scientific Processor (BSP)," *IEEE Transactions on Computers,* Vol. C-31, May 1982, pp. 363-376.

[LaE89]   S. Latif and A. El-Amawy, "On Folded Hypercubes," *Proc. of International Conference on Parallel Processing,* 1989.

[Ncu86]   NCUBE Corp., *NCUBE Handbook, version 1.0,* NCUBE Corp., Beaverton, Oregon, 1986.

A Note on Conway's Parallel Sorting Algorithm

Kazem U. Ahmed   Der-Yun Yeh

Computer Science Department
Arizona State University
Tempe, Arizona 85287

Abstract

This paper presents an improved lower bound on Conway's parallel sorting algorithm. It is shown that Conway's parallel sorting algorithm sorts N keys in $(N+\lceil N/2 \rceil-2)$ cycles, where $\lceil X \rceil$ denotes the smallest integer which is larger than or equal to X. The original result proposed by Warshauer is $(2N-3)$ cycles. With this improvement it can be saved $(N-\lceil N/2 \rceil-1)$ cycles for N keys. Consequently it is shown that $50(1-2/N)$ percent of cycles can be saved on the sorting process. Also with this improvement the modified algorithm for average behavior proposed by the authors in an earlier paper will become more efficient.

1   Introduction

Parallelism is a fairly common concept in everyday life. One of the most important application of the parallelism is parallel sorting algorithm that have been receiving much attention since last decade. In this paper an improved lower bound on Conway's parallel sorting algorithm is proposed. It is shown that Conway's parallel sorting algorithm sorts N keys in $(N+\lceil N/2 \rceil-2)$ cycles, where $\lceil X \rceil$ denotes the smallest integer which is larger than or equal to X. The original result proposed by Warshauer [3] is $(2N-3)$ cycles. With this improvement it can be saved $(N-\lceil N/2 \rceil-1)$ cycles for N keys. Consequently it is shown that $50(1-2/N)$ percent of cycles can be saved on the sorting process. Also with this improvement the modified algorithm for average behavior proposed by the authors [1] in an earlier paper will become more efficient.

This paper is organized as follows. In section 2, the Conway's original sorting algorithm is restated. In section 3, modifications of the processor and the algorithm for average behavior proposed by the authors is restated. In section 4, the proof for the improved lower bound is presented.

2   Conway's Parallel Sorting Algorithm

The parallel processor suggested by Conway consists of N-1 finite state machines (FSM'S) to sort N number of keys, K_1, K_2, ... , K_N, stored as m-bit binary words. The ith finite state machine, denoted by FSM_i (see Fig. 1) is responsible for comparing the ith and (i+1)th words. In one cycle, comparisons and exchanges are made between pairs of adjacent keys and the ith finite state machine FSM_i will swap or not swap between $Word_i$ and $Word_{i+1}$. If either FSM_{i+1} or FSM_{i-1} assumes the swap state on a given cycle, then FSM_i must assume the no swap state because a given word can only swap with one neighbor on a given cycle. A cycle is composed of m phases.

The function of each phase is to compare each bit of the words. On the first phase of a given cycle, the leading bit of $Word_i$ is sent to FSM_i and FSM_{i-1}. $Word_1$ only sends a bit to FSM_1 and $Word_N$ only sends a bit to FSM_{N-1}.

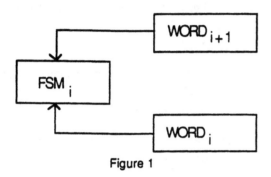

Figure 1

By analyzing the ith finite state machine FSM_i, it can assume one of the three states and they are as follows:

(1) no swap state denoted by N_i

(2) swap state denoted by S_i

(3) undecided state denoted by U_i

All the finite state machines initially are in the undecided states. The functions performed by each finite state machine during a phase of a cycle are follows:

(1) each FSM_i receives a new bit Bit_t from $Word_i$ and Bit'_t from $Word_{i+1}$, where $1 \leq t \leq m$;

(2) changes its state according to the following transition table :

OLD STATE	NEW STATE
N_i	N_i
S_i	S_i
U_i	(1) if S_{i-1} or S_{i+1}, or if $Bit'_t > Bit_t$, then N_i
	else (2) if $Bit_t > Bit'_t$, then S_i
	else (3) U_i

The ith finite state machine on each successive phase will receive the next largest bits of the words $Word_{i+1}$ and $Word_i$. All the previous bits of words $Word_{i+1}$ and $Word_i$ are equal as long as FSM_i is in the undecided state U_i. By receiving the new bits, FSM_i will assume a new state according to the above transition table. And therefore, as long as the finite state machines FSM_{i+1}, FSM_i, and FSM_{i-1} are in the undecided state the words $Word_{i+1}$ and $Word_i$ will circulate in place. If FSM_i ever assumes the swap state S_i then successive bits of $Word_{i+1}$ and $Word_i$ are swapped. As the earlier bits are equal, swapping these remaining bits will interchange $Word_{i+1}$ and $Word_i$.

We next examine how many cycles this process requires to ensure that the keys are arranged in descending order. Some notation is established below. We denote the keys by $K_1, K_2, \ldots \ldots \ldots, K_N$. The position of K_i after cycle s can be denoted by $K_i(s)$. Our sorting procedure is finished after cycle s provided $K_i(s) > K_j(s)$ whenever $K_i > K_j$.

Definition 1 [3]

The key K_i is attractive up after cycle s if either of the following conditions is satisfied:

Condition 1. The key in position $K_i(s)+1$ is larger than K_i.

Condition 2. The key in position $K_i(s)+2$ is larger than K_i.

Definition 2 [3]

The key K_i is attractive down after cycle s if either of the following conditions satisfied:

Condition 1. The key in position $K_i(s)-1$ is smaller than K_i.

Condition 2. The key in position $K_i(s)-2$ is smaller than K_i.

Lemma 1 [3]

Suppose key K_i is attractive up (respectively down) after cycle s. Then key K_i is attractive up (respectively down) after each cycle $t > s$.

Lemma 2 [3]

After $(N + \lceil N/2 \rceil - 3)$ cycles, every key is attractive up and down.

Theorem 1 [3]

After at most $(2N-3)$ cycles, all keys will be sorted.

3 Modifications of the Processor and the Algorithm

The original algorithm proposed by Warshauer was modified by the authors in an earlier paper to investigate the average behavior of the original algorithm.

With the modifications it is shown that in average the number of phases can be saved in a cycle is at least

$$\sum_{r=1}^{m-1} \{1 - (1 - 2^{-r-1})^{n-1}\}(m-r-1).$$

In this section we restate the modifications of the processor and the algorithm. The reason for restating is explained at the end of section 4.

3.1   Modification of the Processor

In analyzing this algorithm we find that during execution, some of the phases in some cycles, all the finite state machines repeat their same states (either swap or no swap) until the next cycle begins. It is not the case if one of the finite state machines is in the undecided state. Because if FSM_i is in the undecided state in a phase then all the previous bits of $Word_{i+1}$ and $Word_i$ are identical and according to the original algorithm in the next phase, FSM_i will be either in the undecided again, or swap state, or no swap state. But if none of the finite state machines is in the undecided state then in the successive phase, FSM_i will be repeting their same states either no swap state or swap state until the next cycle begins. As a result, we realize that this repetition makes the algorithm inefficient.

In order to eliminate this repetitions, the parallel processor and the algorithm are modified. To achieve our objective, we add an "Inclusive OR" hardware logic to the parallel processor as shown in figure-2. The parallel processor is connected with these wired-or lines which sets "off" when none of the finite machines are in the undecided state. Otherwise wired-or line is set "on" when at least one of the finite state machines is in the undecided state.

The "on" or "off" signal is checked along with the execution of each consecutive phase. If the wired-or lines set "off" then the controller sends the signals to all the finite state machines so that the algorithm would go to the next cycle and then the execution must be resumed. But if the wired-or lines set "on", then the controller will resume the normal operation as described in the original algorithm.

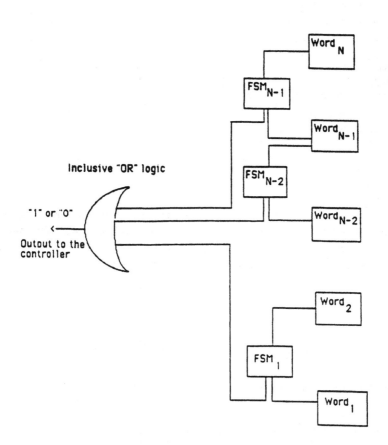

Fig. 2 Modification of the Conway's parallel
processor

3.2   Modification of the Algorithm

Transition table:

OLD STATE	NEW STATE
N_i	N_i
S_i	S_i
U_i	(a) if S_{i-1} or S_{i+1} or
	if $Bit_{i+1} > Bit_i$ then N_i
	else (b) if $Bit_i > Bit_{i+1}$, then S_i
	else (c) U_i

1:     Initialize cycle=1;
Initialize all FSM_i are in undecided state;
2:     Initialize phase=1;
while cycle<(2N-3) do
3:     Execute transition table;
4:     If phase = m or signal = "off"
    then
        cycle=cycle+1;
       phase=1;
       initialize all FSM_i are in undecided state;
    else   { signal = "on" }
     phase=phase+1;
    endif;
   endwhile.

Theorem 2 [1]
Suppose we have n number of keys to be sorted and they are stored as m-bit binary words. The probability of having at least two consecutive rows with their 1st r bits equal and the (r+1)th bit different is $P_r = 1-(1-2^{-r-1})^{n-1}$ and consequently we show that the average number of phases to be saved in a cycle is

$$\sum_{r=1}^{m-1} \{1-(1-2^{-r-1})^{n-1} \}(m-r-1).$$

4   Improvement of the Lower Bound

In this section, the improvement of the lower bound for Conway's parallel sorting algorithm is proposed.

Theorem 3
After at most $(N+\lceil N/2 \rceil -2)$ cycles, all keys will be sorted.
Proof: After $(N + \lceil N/2 \rceil -3)$ cycles all keys are attractive up and attractive down by Warshauer [3].
Let $p = (N + \lceil N/2 \rceil - 3)$.
Claim: After at most (p+1) cycles all the keys will reach their final positions.

Assume we first apply p cycles.

(A) This part of the proof divides into two: one deals with attractive up (see 1.a and 1.b) and the other deals with attractive down (see 2.a and 2.b). We use K_i to denote $K_i(p)$ throughout this proof.

Now consider K_i (without loss of generality, we assume $3 \le i \le N-2$). Since every key is attarctive up after p cycles then by definition either $K_i < K_i + 1$ or $K_i < K_i + 2$.

1(a). Suppose $K_i < K_i + 1$. Then $K_i + 2$ must be greater than or equal to or less than K_i. But if $K_i + 2 \le K_i$ then $K_i + 2$ will not be attractive down. If $K_i + 2 > K_i$ then either $K_i + 2 = K_i + 1$ or $K_i + 2 > K_i + 1$ or $K_i + 2 < K_i + 1$. And we swap between $K_i + 1$ and $K_i + 2$ only when $K_i + 2 < K_i + 1$ otherwise no swap.

Also when $K_i < K_i + 1$ then $K_i - 1 < K_i$ or $K_i - 1 = K_i$ or $K_i - 1 > K_i$. If $K_i - 1 \le K_i$ then no swap between $K_i + 1$ and K_i and no swap between K_i and $K_i - 1$. But if $K_i - 1 > K_i$ then $K_i - 1 < K_i + 1$ otherwise $K_i - 1$ will not be attractive up. Therefore, if $K_i - 1 > K_i$ then there is a swap between K_i and $K_i - 1$ otherwise no swap.

1(b). Suppose $K_i < K_i + 2$ then $K_i + 1$ must be greater than or less than or equal to K_i. If $K_i + 1 = K_i$ then there is no swap between $K_i + 2$ and $K_i + 1$ and no swap between $K_i + 1$ and K_i. If $K_i + 1 > K_i$ then we will have to compare between the keys $K_i + 2$ and $K_i + 1$. And if $K_i + 2 < K_i + 1$ then there is a swap between $K_i + 1$ and $K_i + 2$ otherwise no swap. If $K_i + 1 < K_i$ then there will be a swap between K_i and $K_i + 1$ but no swap between $K_i + 1$ and $K_i + 2$ (as $K_i + 2 > K_i + 1$). Also if $K_i + 1 < K_i$ and since every key is attractive down therefore $K_i + 1 > K_i - 1$. Now since $K_i + 1 > K_i - 1$ and $K_i > K_{i+1}$ therefore $K_i > K_i - 1$. So there will be no swap between K_i and $K_i - 1$.

Again we consider K_i. since every key is attractive down after p cycles, then by definition either $K_i > K_i - 1$ or $K_i > K_i - 2$.

2(a). Suppose $K_i > K_i - 1$ then K_i must be greater than or less than or equal to $K_i - 2$. If $K_i \le K_i - 2$ and since $K_i > K_i - 1$ then $K_i - 2$ will not be attractive up. So $K_i > K_i - 2$. Now we have to compare between $K_i - 1$ and $K_i - 2$. If $K_i - 1 < K_i - 2$ then there is a swap between $K_i - 1$ and $K_i - 2$ otherwise no swap. Also if $K_i > K_i - 1$ then $K_i - 1 < K_i + 1$ or $K_i - 1 = K_i + 1$ or $K_i - 1 > K_i + 1$. But if $K_i - 1 \ge K_i + 1$ then $K_i + 1$ will not be attractive down (as $K_i > K_i - 1$). Therefore, $K_i - 1 < K_i + 1$. Now when $K_i - 1 < K_i + 1$ then we are to compare between $K_i + 1$ and K_i. And if $K_i > K_i + 1$ then there is swap between K_i and $K_i + 1$ otherwise no swap.

2(b). Suppose $K_i > K_i - 2$ then K_i must be less than or equal to or greater than $K_i - 1$. If $K_i < K_i - 1$ then there is swap between K_i and $K_i - 1$ otherwise no swap. And if $K_i - 2 > K_i - 1$ then there is swap between $K_i - 2$ and $K_i - 1$ otherwise no swap.

(B) If K_i be the largest key not in its final position after p cycles then K_i must be one place below its final position even if the largest key placed in the position 1 before the sorting began otherwise K_i will not be attractive up. Similarly, if K_i be the smallest key not in its final position after p cycles then K_i must be one place above its final position even if the smallest key placed in the position N before the sorting began otherwise K_i will not be attractive down.

Hence from the above explanations (A) and (B) we conclude that after applying p cycles if any key is not in its final position then it must be either one place below or one place above its final position and consequently we verify that after at most (p+1) cycles all the keys will reach their final positions.

i.e. $p+1 = (N + \lceil N/2 \rceil - 3) + 1 = (N + \lceil N/2 \rceil - 2)$ cycles.

Proposition 2

If the sorting process requires $(N + \lceil N/2 \rceil - 2)$ cycles to sort N keys then $50(1-2/N)$ percent of cycles can be saved compare to the original result (i.e. 2N-3 cycles).

Proof: In order to sort N keys, the original result proposed by Warshauer is (2N-3) cycles. But the proof we have shown in this paper that require $(N + \lceil N/2 \rceil - 2)$ cycles to sort N keys.

Therefore to sort N keys the number of cycles can be saved

$$= (2N-3) - (N + \lceil N/2 \rceil - 2)$$
$$= (N - \lceil N/2 \rceil - 1)$$

Hence the number of cycles can be saved in percentage

$$= 100 (N - \lceil N/2 \rceil - 1)/N$$
$$= 100(1/2 - 1/N)$$
$$= 50(1 - 2/N)$$

The purpose for restating the modifications of the Conway's parallel processor and the algorithm in this paper is to make the reader aware that the sorting process in the modified algorithm was based on (2N-3) cycles but now on it will be based on $(N + \lceil N/2 \rceil - 2)$ cycles (as per our improvement). Hence we conclude that the proposed modified algorithm with this improvement will become more efficient.

Conclusions

The results of recent research have caused to be more optimistic about the cost-effectiveness of parallel computers for selected classes of computations. In this paper, an improved lower bound on Conway's parallel sorting algorithm was proposed. We showed that after at most $(N + \lceil N/2 \rceil - 2)$ cycles all the N keys will be sorted. The original result proposed by Warshauer is (2N-3) cycles. Consequently we showed that $50(1-2/N)$ percent of cycles can be saved on the sorting process. Also with this improvement we concluded that the modified algorithm proposed by the authors for average behavior will become more efficient.

References

[1] K. U. Ahmed and D. Y. Yeh. Time Efficient Implementation of Conway's Parallel Sorting Algorithm. 1988 International Computer Symposium, Tamkang University, Taipei, Taiwan, Dec 15-17, 1988.

[2] D. E. Knuth. Sorting and Searching. In the Art of Computer Programming Vol 3, Addison-Wesley, Reading, Mass. 1973.

[3] M. L. Warshauer. Conway's Parallel Sorting Algorithm. Journal of Algorithms 7 (1986), 270-276.

Visualization of Program Performance on Concurrent Computers

Diane T. Rover
Ames Laboratory, Applied Mathematical Sciences
email: *rover@alisuvax.bitnet*

G. M. Prabhu
Computer Science Department

Charles T. Wright
Electrical Engineering and Computer
Engineering Department

Iowa State University
Ames, Iowa 50011

Abstract

Evaluation of program performance on concurrent computers requires methods and tools that are part of an integrated environment for observing, analyzing, and displaying system performance. This paper describes a unique graphical approach for presenting performance data of concurrent computer systems, possibly having large numbers of processors. Performance data is generated and collected via instrumentation, reduced via conventional cluster analysis techniques, and converted into a graphical form to highlight important performance measures. A novel kind of data plot is introduced to visually display both temporal and spatial information describing system activity. A prototype implementation applied to two case studies is described.

1 Introduction

Consider the following question with respect to Figure 1: How can we evaluate program performance on this computer system? Figure 1 illustrates a parallel computer representative of the class of *distributed memory concurrent computers*. A distributed memory concurrent computer involves the collective and simultaneous interaction of many nodes engaged in computation and communication activities. The objective is to organize interactions among the nodes so that computations are performed concurrently and communication occurs locally within the system. Within the realm of sequential computers, a programmer is concerned only with sequences of instructions in time. However, with the advent of parallel computers, a programmer also must contend with sets of communications distributed in space. Because of the additional complexity and overhead incurred during program execution, programmers (and hardware designers) require methods and tools that will offer insight into the development of concurrent algorithms and architectures.

For the work reported here, we focus on a family of concurrent computers called *multicomputers* [1], which originated with the Cosmic Cube [10]. This paper prescribes an approach for observing, analyzing, and displaying program execution on concurrent computer systems and illustrates the approach on a hypercube multicomputer.

Figure 1. A distributed memory concurrent computer

2   Visualization of Program Performance

To study the dynamics of a concurrent program, we need to monitor the activities of the system. A program monitor (implemented in software or hardware) for a complex multicomputer system typically generates very large amounts of performance data [3, 6, 7, 9]. The visualization field offers effective techniques for presenting performance data in a meaningful format. A four-step approach for studying program execution on a concurrent computer is prescribed:

(1) Observe and measure program performance via instrumented execution of actual and synthetic benchmark programs.
(2) Analyze and reduce performance data via appropriate techniques.
(3) Generate aggregate measures of system behavior.
(4) Visually display program performance via a computer graphics format that illustrates computation and communication activities in time and space within the machine.

Events occur during program execution and trigger the instrumentation (i.e., the monitor) to non-invasively generate and store event records. Events describe important program activities and demarcate states of the concurrent computation. The event records are collected from individual processors and merged into a global event trace, either during or after program execution. The global event trace is used to reconstruct the state of the system at particular instants in time and to calculate useful performance statistics.

The state of the system can be viewed from three possible perspectives: (1) the program, (2) the architecture, or logical network, and (3) the machine, or physical network. A program perspective shows the flow of control and data in terms of algorithm entities (e.g., processes or data structures) [2]. An architecture perspective highlights the logical structure and interaction of the components in the computer system (e.g., processors and channels) [3,6]. A machine perspective focuses on the implementation of the architecture in two- or three-dimensional space. Figure 2 contains an example illustrating the relationships among the three perspectives. The machine is a two-dimensional geometrical layout, where each cell in the layout denotes a node within the computer system. The two-dimensional array of cells forms an *image* of the system. Figure 2 also portrays the process that maps a program onto a machine to achieve optimal performance. There should be a good match between the computational systems.

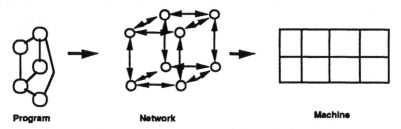

Program   Network   Machine

Figure 2. Graphical formats for viewing program states

An image displays spatial and temporal information extracted from performance data. Spatial data are shown by labeling the image axes with positional values, where processor numbers in the logical network are associated with grid coordinates in the physical network. A cell is color-coded (or shaded) to indicate the value of a performance parameter for the processor. Intensity variations of the parameter across the system are depicted. Thus, an image illustrates the spatial distribution of values of a parameter over all processors at a particular time.

The *machine perspective* distinguishes this approach to presenting performance data. It achieves four essential objectives. First, in this format, a system with hundreds or thousands of processors can be displayed at once. Secondly, a two- or three-dimensional image is appropriate because: (1) a network of any (logical) dimension must be implemented physically in two or three dimensions, and (2) future large multicomputers may require an architecture based on a two-or three-dimensional mesh [1]. Thirdly, the flow of granules of computation and communication throughout the system, over both time and space, can be shown. Finally, the format provides a *surface* upon which we can overlay program and network graphs in order to analyze the mapping between the computational systems.

3   Case Studies in Visualization

A prototype implementation was developed which focuses on the visual performance analysis steps and incorporates the following: (1) images, (2) profiles, and (3) statistics. Rover [7] has specified these features in detail. Several case studies were performed using the prototype implementation in order to demonstrate the feasibility of the approach for presenting performance data. An instrumented simulator was developed and used to generate the event traces for programs executing on a hypercube multicomputer. Post-processing of the event traces transforms performance data into system states that are graphically displayed in the form of images.

For the two case studies presented here, the simulator is configured as an eight-dimensional (256-node) hypercube multicomputer (although the approach to analyzing and visualizing program states is independent of any specific architecture). The hypercube is mapped onto a two-dimensional grid using a gray code mapping function [4]. The assignment of logical processor numbers to locations in the grid is specified in Figure 3. Observe that Processor 0 is mapped to the lower left cell at location (0,0). Its hypercube neighbors reside either in row 0 or in column 0, and include processor numbers 1, 2, 4, 8, 16, 32, 64, and 128, as illustrated.

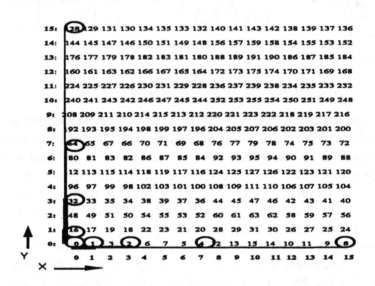

Figure 3. Gray code mapping of a 256-node hypercube onto a two-dimensional grid

The simulated hypercube is configured with hardware parameters taken from a first generation NCUBE hypercube machine [5]. Coupled with the simulator is a program library that consists of a collection of synthetic programs that drive the simulation. The two case studies presented are Broadcast and Quicksort. The images generated for the case studies were created via a graphics software package called *Image* (from NCSA, the National Center for Supercomputing Applications, University of Illinois). Within *Image*, data may be displayed in the form of a raster graph, where the value of the variable of interest is denoted by color. An alternative representation, a dither plot, is used here, replacing color with shades of gray. *Image* also interpolates the data via a local averaging operation to create a smoother picture. Thus, when viewing the images, superimpose a 16-by-16 grid on the image to identify individual cells, or processors.

3.1 Broadcast

Broadcast is a collective communication routine. A common broadcast algorithm distributes the data using a tree-like processor communication graph [5]. The basic operation of Broadcast is graphically depicted in Figure 4 (for the simplified case of an eight-node hypercube). Processor 0 initiates the broadcast by sending messages to its hypercube neighbors.

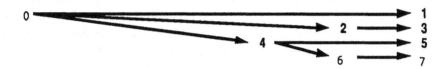

Figure 4. Basic operation of Broadcast

In the simulation, performed on a 256-node hypercube, a 100-byte message was broadcast among the processors. Two images of program execution are depicted in Figure 5. The displayed parameter represents the cumulative amount of local traffic, in number of bytes, resulting from message passing activities (sends and receives) of the processor at the indicated time. The first image corresponds to a state of the system near the beginning of the simulation (7.2 msec.), and the second image, near the end of the simulation (14.4 msec.). Observe how the traffic of the broadcasted message spreads throughout the system. It is apparent that Processor 0 and its hypercube neighbors, especially those neighbors at the higher levels of the broadcast tree, account for the largest amounts of traffic. The region surrounding Processor 255 is void of any traffic, since it is the last node to receive the broadcasted message. In practice, an animated sequence of images brings the program's traffic patterns to life.

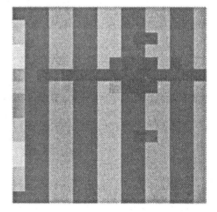

Figure 5. Pictures of performance: Broadcast on a 256-node hypercube

3.2 Quicksort

Quicksort is an application program that uses a divide-and-conquer approach to sorting a list of numbers [4]. The basic operation of Quicksort is graphically depicted in Figure 6 (for the case of an eight-node hypercube). Processor 0 initially has the original list.

In the simulation, performed on a 256-node hypercube, a 4096-byte list was sorted on the processor ensemble. An image of program execution is depicted in Figure 7 (27.9 msec.). The displayed parameter represents the cumulative amount of work, in number of operations, done by the processor at the indicated time. The range is 0 to 16,352 operations. Observe how the work emanates from Processor 0 into the rest of the system. Most of the work is localized around Processor 0, as might be expected. In fact, because the length of the original list is small compared to the size of the system (only sixteen numbers remain to be sorted on each processor), we see that the bulk of the system has relatively little work to do. Tables of statistics are associated with images [7].

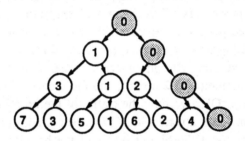

Figure 6. Basic operation of Quicksort

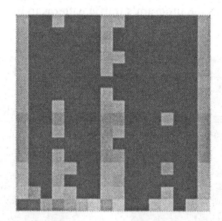

Figure 7. Picture of performance: Quicksort on a 256-node hypercube

4   Conclusions

We have developed a framework in which to study patterns in program execution. Patterns are visual and offer insight into the behavior of concurrent algorithms and the systems that execute them. An objective of our ongoing efforts is to effectively couple *qualitative* observations and *quantitative* measurements of the system into a coherent representation of performance. Furthermore, we are only beginning to understand the importance of structure in concurrent computing: the structure of the problem, the program, the network, and the machine, and the relationship among these structures. The proposed view of performance should be a useful tool for investigating these structures.

References

[1] Athas, W. and Seitz, C. "Multicomputers: message-passing concurrent computers." *IEEE Computer*, 21, No. 8 (August 1988): 9-23.

[2] Brown, Marc H. "Exploring algorithms using Balsa-II." *IEEE Computer*, 21, No. 5 (May 1988): 14-36.

[3] Couch, A. "Graphical representations of program performance on hypercube message-passing multiprocessors." Ph.D. dissertation, Department of Computer Science, Tufts University, April 1988.

[4] Fox, G., Johnson, M., Lyzenga, G., Otto, S., Salmon, J., and Walker, D. *Solving Problems on Concurrent Processors*. Englewood Cliffs: Prentice- Hall, 1988.

[5] Gustafson, J., Montry, G., and Benner, R. "Development of parallel methods for a 1024-processor hypercube." *SIAM Journal on Scientific and Statistical Computing*, 9, No. 4 (July 1988): 609-638.

[6] Reed, D. A. "Instrumenting distributed memory parallel systems: a report." In *Instrumentation for Future Parallel Computer Systems,* edited by Bucher, Simmons, and Koskela. Reading, MA: Addison-Wesley, 1989.

[7] Rover, D. T. "Visualization of program performance on concurrent computers." Ph.D. dissertation, Iowa State University, 1989.

[8] Rover, D. T., Prabhu, G. M., and Wright, C. T. "Characterizing the performance of concurrent computers: a picture is worth a thousand numbers." *Proceedings of the Fourth Conference on Hypercubes, Concurrent Computers, and Applications*. 1989.

[9] Rudolph, D. "A performance evaluation tool for the Intel iPSC/2." M.S. thesis, University of Illinois, Urbana-Champaign, July 1989.

[10] Seitz, Charles L. "The Cosmic Cube." *Communications of the ACM*, 28, No. 1 (1985): 22-33.

Minimum Odd Neighbourhood Covers for Trees

Robin W. Dawes
Queen's University, Kingston, Ontario

Abstract: *Finding the smallest odd neighbourhood cover (odd N-cover) of an arbitrary graph is known to be NP-complete. We observe that there exist trees with an exponential number of odd N-covers, and present a polynomial-time algorithm to determine a minimum cardinality odd N-cover of a tree.*

Introduction

Covering problems for graphs are well known and much studied. The literature on these and related domination problems is extensive; see [4] for an excellent survey. The particular problem addressed here has its roots in a problem of cellular automata: the "all-ones" problem [6]. Linear cellular automata have been proposed as a useful model for massively parallel computation [5], and their behaviour under various rule systems has been extensively studied and catalogued [8,9].

Definition: The *closed neighbourhood* of a vertex v is the set of all vertices adjacent to v, plus v itself.

Definition: Let G be a graph with vertex set V, $|V| = n$. (All graphs are assumed to be simple and undirected). An *odd neighbourhood cover (odd N-cover)* of G is a set $X \subseteq V$ such that each vertex of G is included in an odd number of the closed neighbourhoods of the vertices in X.

We shall use $d_G(v)$ for the degree of v in G.

For notational simplicity, when X is a vertex set, we will use X to represent both the set itself, and its representative 0-1 vector, where $x_i=1$ iff $v_i \in X$. If v is in X and w is a member of v's closed neighbourhood, we will say w is *covered* by v's closed neighbourhood under X.

For other notation the reader is referred to Bondy and Murty [1].

Odd N-Covers of Graphs

In [6], Sutner demonstrates that every graph has an odd N-cover. His proof can be summarised as follows:

a) an odd cover Z of G satisfies the matrix equation $(A + I) \cdot Z = 1$ where A is the adjacency matrix of G, I is the $n \times n$ identity matrix, 1 is the vector of length n with all elements equal to 1, and all arithmetic is carried out over GF(2).

b) For any symmetric 0-1 matrix A, there exists a solution to $(A + I) \cdot Z = 1$.

Sutner [7] observes that for arbitrary G, determining an odd N-cover of minimum cardinality is an NP-complete problem.

The definition and observations in this paragraph are drawn from elementary linear algebra. The *kernel* of the transformation $g(X) = (A + I) \cdot X$ is the set of all vectors Y such that $g(Y) = 0$, where 0 is the vector of length n with all elements equal to 0. If X is an odd N-cover and Y is an element of the kernel, then $X + Y$ is also an odd N-cover. Furthermore, if X and Z are two odd N-covers, then there exists a kernel element Y such that $Z = X + Y$.

Definition: Let Y be a kernel element of the transformation $g(X) = (A + I) \cdot X$. We call the subgraph H induced by Y a *kernel subgraph*.

Lemma 1: Let G be a graph. H is a kernel subgraph of G iff each vertex of H has odd degree in H, and each vertex in G - H is adjacent to an even number of vertices in H (possibly 0).

Proof: Let H be the kernel subgraph induced by some kernel element Y. Let X be an odd N-cover, and consider the odd N-cover $Z = X + Y$. For each $y_i = 1$, $z_i = 1$ iff $x_i = 0$.

Let v be any vertex of H. Suppose v has even degree in H. Then v's closed neighbourhood Q in H has odd cardinality. Let $r = |Q \cap Z|$ and let $s = |Q \cap X|$. Since $|Q| = r + s$ is odd, $r - s$ is also odd. If v is covered by p closed neighbourhoods under X, then v is covered by $p + r - s$ closed neighbourhoods under Z. We know p is odd, so $p + r - s$ is even. This establishes a contradiction.

Similar arguments suffice to complete the proof. ∎

Odd N-Covers of Trees

Consider a tree T defined as follows:

Let v be a vertex adjacent to vertices $u_1, u_2, ..., u_t$. Let each u_i also be adjacent to vertex w_i. Each odd cardinality subset S of $\{1, ..., t\}$ corresponds to the odd N-cover $\{u_i \mid i \in S\}$ $\cup \{w_i \mid i \notin S\}$. Since $\{1, ..., t\}$ has 2^{t-1} odd cardinality subsets, T has an exponential number of odd N-covers. More complex trees with similar properties can be constructed by taking two such trees and identifying a leaf from one with a leaf from the other. Thus we can construct trees of arbitrarily large diameter and average degree with an exponential number of odd N-covers.

Galvin [3] gives a constructive algorithm to determine an odd N-cover of a tree in linear time. The algorithm is non-deterministic and can easily be shown to fail to find a minimum cardinality odd N-cover on many trees. We now present an algorithm to find a minimum odd N-cover in polynomial time.

This new algorithm, given any odd N-cover X, finds a minimum cardinality odd N-cover Z by constructing the kernel element Y such that $X + Y = Z$.

Definition: An *o-tree* is a tree in which each vertex has odd degree. With respect to a tree T, an *external o-tree* of T is a subtree S of T such that S is an o-tree, and S is connected to T - S by a single edge. An *internal o-tree* of T is a subtree R of T such that R is an o-tree, and R is connected to T - R by more than one edge.

Lemma 2: Let T be a tree, and let Y be an element of the kernel of $g(X) = (A + I) \cdot X$, other than $Y = 0$. Then the kernel subgraph H induced by Y is a non-empty set of o-trees with the following properties:

i) Each vertex in T - H is adjacent to an even number of o-trees in H.

ii) The o-trees in H and the vertices of T - H adjacent to vertices of H can be represented by a forest with a bipartition $\{U,W\}$ such that all the o-trees are represented by vertices of U, all the neighbours of o-trees are represented by vertices of W, and all leaves of the forest are vertices of U.

Proof: Suppose some component of H is not an o-tree. Then it contains a vertex of even degree in H, which contradicts Lemma 1.

Property i) also follows immediately from Lemma 1.

To justify property ii), consider the bipartite graph F defined as follows. Let U contain one vertex u_i for each o-tree O_i in H. Let W contain each vertex w in T - H adjacent to at least one vertex in H. Make u_i adjacent to $w \in$ W iff w is adjacent to a vertex of O_i. Clearly F is a forest, and by property i), each vertex in W has degree at least 2. Hence every leaf in this forest must represent an o-tree in H. Since any internal o-tree will also be represented by a vertex of degree ≥ 2, each leaf must represent an external o-tree. ∎

Restrictions on the ways in which o-trees can intersect are important in the proof of correctness for the algorithm. We summarise the important points in three lemmas.

Lemma 3: No external o-tree of a tree T is a subtree of any other o-tree of T.

Proof: Suppose R is an o-tree properly containing external o-tree S. Let v be the vertex of S which is connected to T - S. Then $d_R(v) = d_S(v) + 1$, which is even. ∎

Lemma 4: Let S be an external o-tree of T, connected to vertex x of T - S. Then x cannot be in any o-tree of any kernel subgraph H.

Proof: Suppose the lemma is false. Let R be the o-tree of H that contains x. By Lemma 3, S is not a subtree of R, so some vertex w in S - R is adjacent to some vertex in R. Since H is a kernel subgraph, w must be adjacent to another o-tree, which clearly must be a subtree of S. This implies that some subtree of S must be an external o-tree, which is forbidden by Lemma 3. ∎

Lemma 5: Let S and R be different external o-trees of kernel subgraphs H_1 and H_2. Then $S \cap R = \varnothing$.

Proof: Follows immediately from Lemmas 3 and 4. ∎

These lemmas allow the construction of a forest which contains the forest representation of every kernel subgraph of T.

Theorem 1: It is possible to construct a forest B from a tree T in polynomial time such that each kernel element of g(X) corresponds to a subforest of B.

Proof: We will first discuss the construction of B, then demonstrate that it contains each forest described in Lemma 2. The vertex set of B consists of two sets K and L, where each vertex of K represents an o-tree of T, and each vertex of L represents a vertex of T adjacent to two or more o-trees.

If T is an o-tree, it is trivial to show that the kernel contains only the vectors $Y = 0$ and $Y = 1$. K (and B) consists of a single vertex; X and $1 - X$ are the only odd N-covers.

Assume T is not an o-tree. Represent each external o-tree O of T by a vertex k_O in K, and represent each vertex v of T adjacent to an external o-tree by a vertex l_v in L. Delete each external o-tree and its adjacent vertex from T, and recursively apply the process to each tree in the remaining forest. Lemmas 3, 4, and 5 show that this a well-defined process.

For each l_v in L, make l_v adjacent to each vertex of K representing an o-tree in T to which v is adjacent. B is clearly a forest with fewer vertices than T.

Let H be a kernel subgraph of T. By Lemma 2, the o-trees and adjacent vertices of H correspond to a forest F, of which all the leaves are external o-trees of T, and hence leaves of B. Deleting the leaves and their adjacent vertices from F produces a smaller forest F', in which all the leaves are again o-trees. These o-trees are the external o-trees of the forest T' derived by deleting all external o-trees and their adjacent vertices from T. Therefore the o-trees of H are exactly the o-trees determined by repeatedly removing external o-trees and adjacent vertices from T. Thus B will contain the forest representation of H.

The algorithm to construct B is based on a single traversal of the tree T. Details are given in [2]. We note here that B must be pruned: any non-o-tree vertex l_v of B which has degree $= 1$ in B is adjacent to only one o-tree in T. Hence this o-tree cannot be in a kernel subgraph, and l_v and its neighbour may be deleted from B. If B is now empty, 0 is the only kernel element. ∎

Since the trees in B are clearly independent of one another with respect to membership in kernel subgraphs, we will assume without loss of generality that the forest consists of a single tree.

For an o-tree O in T, we can easily determine the effect of including O in a kernel element Y: if $|O| = t_O$, and r_O vertices of O are in X (the given odd N-cover), then X+Y will contain $t_O - r_O$ vertices of O. The gain is then $r_O - (t_O - r_O)$, i.e. $2 \cdot r_O - t_O$. Let $s_O = 2 \cdot r_O - t_O$.

Definition: The *value* of a kernel element Y is $\sum_{O \in Y} s_O$.

Finding a minimum odd N-cover Z is thus equivalent to finding a kernel element Y such that the value of Y is maximum. We determine Y by choosing a root for B, then examining the rooted subtrees. From this point, B will be assumed to be rooted at an arbitrarily chosen vertex k_Q.

Lemma 6: Let B_O be the subtree of B rooted at vertex k_O. Let T_O be the subtree of T corresponding to B_O. For the transformation $g_O(X) = (A_O + I) \cdot X$ where A_O is the adjacency matrix of T_O, there is a kernel element containing O, and one not containing O.

Proof: Clearly the empty kernel element satisfies the second requirement. We can construct a kernel element Y containing O by choosing one other vertex of B_O adjacent to each vertex l_v adjacent to k_O, then recursively working down to the leaves of B_O by applying the same process to each just-chosen vertex of K. ∎

The following two results permit the efficient selection of combinations of o-trees to form an optimal kernel element.

Lemma 7: Let $\{(a_i, b_i)\}$, $1 \le i \le k$ be a set of pairs of integers. The set $M \subseteq \{1,...,k\}$ such that $|M|$ is even and $F(M) = \sum_{i \in M} a_i + \sum_{j \notin M} b_j$ is maximum over all even cardinality subsets of $\{1,...,k\}$, can be found in polynomial time.

Proof: Let $\delta_i = a_i - b_i$. Without loss of generality, assume $\delta_i \ge \delta_{i+1}$, $1 \le i < k$. If $\delta_1 + \delta_2 \le 0$, $M = \emptyset$ satisfies the lemma. Suppose $\delta_1 + \delta_2 > 0$. Let P be any non-empty even cardinality subset of $\{1,...,k\}$, and let r and s be any elements of P.

Let $P' = P - \{r,s\} + \{1,2\}$.

$$F(P') = F(P) - (a_r + a_s) + (b_r + b_s) + (a_1 + a_2) - (b_1 + b_2)$$
$$= F(P) - (\delta_r + \delta_s) + (\delta_1 + \delta_2)$$
$$\ge F(P)$$

Thus there exists an even cardinality sum-maximising set M such that $\{1,2\} \subseteq M$. The problem reduces to finding M', an even cardinality subset of $K = \{3,...,k\}$ that maximises $\sum_{i \in M'} a_i + \sum_{j \in K - M'} b_j$. Again, M' is either empty or $\{3,4\} \subseteq M'$.

Thus we arrive at $M = (\{i,i+1\}| \text{ i is odd, and } \delta_i + \delta_{i+1} > 0)$ ■

Corollary 1: An odd cardinality subset M of $\{1,2,...,k\}$ that maximises F(M) can be found in polynomial time. ■

Definition: Let k_O be a vertex of B, representing o-tree O in T. Then define a_O to be the maximum value of any kernel element of T_O containing O. Similarly, let b_O be the maximum value of any kernel element of T_O not containing O.

Definition: Let l_v be any vertex of L, and let C be the set of l_v's children in B. Let $odd(l_v)$ be the maximum of $\sum_{O \in D} a_O + \sum_{O \in C-D} b_O$ over all odd-cardinality sets $D \subseteq C$. Let $even(l_v)$ be similarly defined.

Lemma 8: Let k_Q be the arbitrarily chosen root of B. The larger of the two values

$$a_Q = s_Q + \sum_{l \text{ a child of } k_Q} odd(l) \qquad \text{or} \qquad b_Q = \sum_{l \text{ a child of } k_Q} even(l)$$

is the cardinality of an optimal kernel element.

Proof: Q is either contained in an optimal kernel element, or not. ■

The a and b values for the subtrees are found recursively; in fact, the resulting traversal of the tree is a modified post-order traversal, in which alternating generations are treated differently. This requires only a polynomial amount of work at each vertex of B. Hence the entire process requires only polynomial time.

Theorem 2: A minimum cardinality odd N-cover of a tree T can be determined in polynomial time.

Proof: The algorithm outlined above yields only the cardinality of the minimum odd N-cover. The kernel element Y can be created by associating with each a and b value a list of the o-trees used in arriving at that value. These lists can be joined by simple concatenation, which requires only constant time for each concatenation.

The algorithm thus consists of five phases:

1. Find an odd N-cover X.
2. Construct the forest B.
3. Compute s_O for each o-tree in B.
4. Traverse B to compute Y.
5. $Z = X + Y$.

Phases 1, 2, 3, and 5 are each $O(n)$ in complexity. Phase 4 requires a sort of a total of $O(n)$ δ values at each of $O(n)$ vertices, and is therefore $O(n \cdot \log n)$. ∎

References

[1] J.A. Bondy and U.S.R. Murty, *Graph Theory with Applications*, Macmillan Press, London (1976).

[2] R.W. Dawes, Neighbourhood covers for trees, Queen's University Technical Report 90-266.

[3] F. Galvin, Solution, *Mathematical Intelligencer* **11 No.** 2(1989), 32.

[4] S.T. Hedetniemi and R. Laskar, Recent results and open problems in domination theory,*Technical Report* 543, Clemson University, 1987.

[5] N. Margolus, Emulating physics with cellular automata, *Colloquium, Queen's University*, 1989.

[6] K. Sutner, Linear cellular automata and the garden-of-eden, *Mathematical Intelligencer* **11 No.** 2(1989), 49-53.

[7] K. Sutner, Linear automata on graphs, to appear.

[8] S. Wolfram, Statistical mechanics and cellular automata, *Rev. Modern Physics* 55(1983), 601-644.

[9] S. Wolfram, Computation theory of cellular automata, *Comm. Math. Physics* 96(1984), 15-57.

CASCADING LZW ALGORITHM WITH HUFFMAN CODING:
A VARIABLE TO VARIABLE LENGTH COMPRESSION ALGORITHM

Yehoshua Perl, Ashish Mehta
Institute of Integrated Systems, Department of Computer Science
New Jersey Institute of Technology, Newark, NJ 07102
email : perl@mars.njit.edu, ashish@mars.njit.edu

Abstract

Two common schemes in data compression are fixed to variable length coding and variable to fixed length coding. Higher compression is expected from the more flexible scheme of variable to variable length coding. In such a scheme a compression dictionary is used to transfer variable length strings over the text alphabet into variable length strings over the coding alphabet. The compression is achieved due to matching longer more frequent text strings with shorter coding strings.

To obtain a variable to variable length coding we choose to cascade the LZW, variable to fixed, coding with the Huffman, fixed to variable, coding. In this work we consider the effective way of performing this cascading, to optimize the compression using limited time resources.

I. Introduction

In text compression we typically replace strings of characters of the given text alphabet by strings over the coding alphabet. To faciliate the transformation many compression algorithms use a compression dictionary matching strings over the text alphabet with the coding strings replacing them.

We distinguish between two different schemes in dictionary coding. One scheme is fixed to variable length coding and the other is variable to fixed length coding. In fixed to variable length coding , strings of fixed length over the text alphabet are replaced by strings of variable length over the coding alphabet. A known example of such coding scheme is Huffman[H] coding , described later , where each character of the text alphabet is replaced by variable length bit string. The compression is achieved by assigning shorter coding strings for frequent characters.

In variable to fixed length coding , strings of variable length over the text alphabet are replaced by fixed length coding strings , typically the index to the dictionary entry containing the variable length text strings. Compression is obtained due to selecting long frequent text strings for the dictionary. The most known example of such coding is the LZW algorithm [ZL1] [ZL2] described later.

BMoreover, the problem of constructing a compression dictionary of variable length character strings from the text has received considerable attention in the literature. Heuristic experiments are reported by Lynch [L]. The problem of finding such an optimum dictionary maximizing the compression is considered in Storer and Szymanski [SS1] [SS2]. They model the dictionary as one long string, where each substring constitutes an entry in the dictionary, and show that finding an optimum dictionary is an NP-hard problem, that is, probably not solvable in polynomial time. A dynamic version of this model called the Sliding Dictionary is used in Smith and

Storer [SS3] for parallel data compression.

Choueka Fraenkel and Perl [CFP] show that if the dictionary is limited to contain only prefixes or only suffixes of words in the text, then it is possible to construct an optimum dictionary in polynomial time by a dynamic programming algorithm. On the other hand if both prefixes and suffixes are permitted in the dictionary then the problem is shown by Fraenkel, Mor and Perl [FMP] to be NP-Hard. They describe experiments with heuristics for constructing dictionaries with only prefixes and both prefixes and suffixes. The LZW algorithm differs from all these algorithms except the sliding Dictionary of [SS3] in that it is adaptive, while all the others are based on preprocessing of the text.

Naturally one would like to consider variable to variable length coding where longer and more frequent text strings are replaced by shorter coding strings. Such a scheme can be expected to yield higher compression than the above two schemes as it is more flexible than they are. However this flexibility makes the selection of such a compression dictionary a very complicated task as there are more degrees of freedom in this case.

One possibility to achieve variable to variable length coding and still keep the process of constructing the compression dictionary under control is by cascading two compression techniques one a variable to fixed length coding and the other a fixed to variable length coding. In such a combination we can still keep the construction of the compression dictionary under control since each of the two parts is controllable. On the other hand higher compression ratio can be expected due to the higher flexibility of this scheme.

In this work we choose to cascade the LZW variable to fixed compression algorithm with the Huffman fixed to variable coding to obtain a variable to variable length coding scheme.

In the next two sections we introduce the LZW and Huffman compression algorithms. The problem of how to perform the cascading of these two algorithms in the best way is considered in section IV. In section V experiments are performed in search of the proper parameters for the cascading process.

II. The LZW Compression Algorithm

One of the known compression algorithms is the algorithm of Lempel and Ziv [ZL1], [ZL2]. Welch[W] described an implementation of this algorithm known as the LZW algorithm. This algorithm has the advantage of being adaptive. That is, the algorithm does not assume any advance knowledge of the properties of the input and builds the dictionary used for the compression only on the basis of the input itself, as the input is read. This property is especially important in compression for communication.

The LZW algorithm starts with a dictionary containing entries for each character in the alphabet. The algorithm scans the input matching it with entries in the dictionary. The matching is finished, when we read from the input a string Y, not in the dictionary, such that Y=X.a, where X is a string already in the dictionary, "a" is a character and "." denotes the concatenation operation. The compression algorithm then sends the code for X (an index into the dictionary table) and inserts Y into the dictionary. The encoding of the input continues from the character "a" that follows X. The decoder builds an identical dictionary to the one built by the encoder.

Note that the entries for the LZW dictionary satisfy the property that if a string X is in the dictionary then every prefix of X is also in the dictionary. Another property is that for every code sent by the encoder a new entry is added to the dictionary. Since the dictionary size is finite and may be limited for practical reasons, the dictionary may fill up fast.The LZW algorithm then continues by encoding according to the existing dictionary without adding new entries to the dictionary.Experiments show that after a while a significant decline in the compression ratio is observed. The compression ratio is defined as the difference between the number of characters in the original text and the compressed text divided by the number of characters in the original text. This decline is typically due to a change in the properties of the text, so the dictionary is no longer appropriate. At this point the LZW algorithm forgets the old dictionary and starts from scratch, usually obtaining a higher compression ratio.

Totally ignoring the old dictionary and building the new one from scratch is wasteful. Even though the decline in the compression ratio may indicate that the dictionary is no longer adequate, there are probably parts of it which will appear in the new dictionary. Dynamic variations of the LZW algorithm using updates of the dictionary are considered in [PCM]. An attempt to find an upper bound for the compression ratio possible by the LZW approach is discussed in [PGS].

III. The Huffman Coding Method

Huffman[H] coding is a data-compression technique whose employment will minimize the average code length used to represent the characters of an alphabet. This algorithm replaces each character by a variable length code according to the frequency of that character in the text.

The Huffman code is an optimum binary code since it results in the shortest average code length of all fixed to variable encoding techniques when the frequencies are given. In addition Huffman code is a prefix code which means that no short code word appears as the prefix of a longer code word.

The Huffman code can be developed through the utilization of a tree structure. The binary tree produced by Huffman's algorithm minimizes the weighted external path length $\Sigma_j w_j l_j$ among all binary trees, where w_j is the weight of the jth leaf, and l_j is its distance from the root in the tree. Huffman's algorithm uses an optimum static code, in which each occurrence of a_j, for $1 \leq j \leq k$, is encoded by the l_j bits specified by the path in the Huffman tree from the root to the jth leaf, where "0" means "to the left" and "1" means "to the right".

Huffman's method makes two passes over the data: one pass to collect frequency counts of the characters in the text, followed by the construction of a Huffman tree ; and a second pass to encode and transmit the characters themselves, based on the static tree structure.

Huffman presented a greedy algorithm for the construction of the tree representation of the optimum code.

The Huffman length of a code word is the number of its bits. We define the term Average Huffman Length (AHL) as the weighted (according to frequencies) average length of the code words for the characters.

Consider the case that the frequencies used in the calculations of AHL are the actual frequencies of the characters in the text obtained for example by a preliminary scanning of the text. Then the Average Huffman Length(AHL) is equal to the ratio of total number of bits sent to the total number of messages sent.

IV.   How to Cascade the LZW and Huffman Algorithms

The LZW algorithm builds up a dictionary of 2^k entries from the text. In the encoding of the input text we match a maximum length prefix which appears in the dictionary and replace it by the index of k bits of the appropriate entry in the dictionary of size 2^k.The encoding then continues with the rest of the input string similarly. This way each entry from the text is replaced by a fixed length bit string. However not all entries of the dictionary have the same frequency in the text, some may be more often than others and some may never occur. We can use the difference in the frequencies to replace the fixed length bit string by variable length bit strings according to the frequencies and obtain some extra compression. We call the original compression obtained by the LZW algorithm primary compression and the extra compression obtained due to the different frequencies, secondary compression. As we know the Huffman algorithm is guarnteed to yield the maximum compression for a variable length code where the frequencies are given. Thus it is natural to cascade the LZW algorithm with the Huffman algorithm to maximize the overall compression.

As usual in Huffman algorithm we have the problem from where do we know the frequencies. This question is even more difficult in this case as we consider entries of the LZW dictionary rather than frequencies of given characters. For text compression by Huffman Coding for the characters the exact frequencies can be found by a preliminary scanning of the text collecting the frequencies. This simple solution is not applicable for the entries of the LZW dictionary as an occurance of an entry in the text is not sufficient. This occurance of the entry will be encoded by the LZW algorithm only if this occurance will appear in the parsing performed by the algorithm. Hence for collecting the frequencies we need to have a preliminary LZW encoding of the input to account for the frequencies of the entries only those occurances which are actually sent by the LZW algorithm.

Such a preliminary LZW encoding is very expensive and in cases of compression for communication is not possible at all.Hence we can use this method only as a theoretical bound to measure the effects of other methods for obtaining the frequencies which we are using for the actual encoding.

A common solution for avoiding the preliminary scanning of the text for Huffman coding is using some known information about frequencies of characters in general texts of a similar nature. This solution is not applicable for the frequencies of the LZW algorithm as there is no given set of entries but every text generates a different LZW dictionary.

However a possible solution is counting the frequncy of the entries during the process of constructing the dictionary. Each entry in the dictionary is sent to the decoder each time a child is added to the vertex representing the entry in the tree representation of the dictionary discussed in section 2. Hence when the dictionary gets full the frequency of each entry is the number of children of the corresponding vertex in the tree representation of the dictionary. It seems natural to pick the frequencies obtained during the construction of the dictionary as a good prediction relative to the actual frequencies to be encountered during the encoding. The reasoning behind this assumption is that a more frequent entry of the dictionary appears also more during the construction of the dictionary.

There is a problem how to deal with the 0 frequency entries which were put into the dictionary but were never sent. We must allocate to them a positive frequency for the case that they occur during the encoding.

To resolve the difficulty we realize that when the first occurance of an entry occured it is entered into the dictionary, but the frequency is initialized as a 0 since another entry, that of the parent in the tree representation of the dictionary is sent. However since such an entry appeared once and may appear again it is appropriate to allocate to it some frequency. But if we allocate say frequency 1 to such an entry due to its first occurance then it will have the same frequency as an entry which is sent once during the construction of the dictionary, a misleading assumption as such an entry has a higher chance of reccurance. A better solution is to assign a value ε , $0 < \varepsilon \leq 1$ for the 0 frequency entries. This way we credit these entries for their first occurance, enable coding of 0 frequency entries and still keep the relative frequencies of all entries.

The approximate value for ε should be determined experimentally. Note that some of the 0 frequencies entries will probably never occur in the encoding and their number has an impact on the appropriate value for ε. Having a too large ε implies having shorter code words for some entries which never appear for the price of longer code words for other entries.

We have several possible ways to measure the average Huffman length (AHL) for a given text. The first one which is equal to the one defined in the previous section is calculated by the Huffman algorithm for the set of frequencies found by a preliminary scanning of the whole text. If we send the messages according to the corresponding Huffman code than the total number of bits sent divided by the number of messages sent is equal to the Average Huffman length.

The second measure which we call the estimated average Huffman length (EAHL) is calculated by applying Huffman algorithm to a set of approximated frequencies where 0 frequencies are replaced by ε values and taking the average length over the (estimated) Huffman code obtained.

The third measure which we call the practical average Huffman Length (PAHL) is the number of bits used to send the text by the estimated Huffman code divided by the number of messages sent. Note the last two measure are not necessarily equal. Actually the estimated average Huffman length is estimating the practical average Huffman length on the basis of partial information.

TABLE : 1
AHL = 8.43

ϵ	EAHL	PAHL
0.1	8.35	10.25
0.2	8.66	9.95
0.3	8.89	9.94
0.4	9.08	9.67
0.5	9.20	9.68
0.6	9.31	9.68
0.7	9.40	9.68
0.8	9.48	9.68
0.9	9.56	9.68

TABLE : 2
AHL = 8.43
SAMPLE = 1024

ϵ	EAHL	PAHL
0.1	8.22	9.07
0.2	8.51	9.05
0.3	8.71	8.95
0.4	8.89	8.95
0.5	9.05	9.05
0.6	9.14	9.05
0.7	9.23	9.05
0.8	9.31	9.05
0.9	9.38	9.05

TABLE : 3
AHL = 8.43
SAMPLE = 2048

ϵ	EAHL	PAHL
0.1	8.25	8.79
0.2	8.40	8.71
0.3	8.53	8.71
0.4	8.64	8.68
0.5	8.73	8.67
0.6	8.81	8.67
0.7	8.89	8.67
0.8	8.96	8.67
0.9	9.03	8.67

TABLE : 4
AHL = 8.43
SAMPLE = 3072

ϵ	EAHL	PAHL
0.1	8.25	8.59
0.2	8.35	8.52
0.3	8.44	8.48
0.4	8.51	8.48
0.5	8.59	8.48
0.6	8.66	8.45
0.7	8.71	8.47
0.8	8.76	8.47
0.9	8.81	8.47

TABLE : 5
Secondary Compression
AHL = 8.43 $\epsilon = 0.5$

SAMPLE	EAHL	PAHL	Compression (%)
1024	9.04	9.05	7.85
2048	8.73	8.67	10.08
3072	8.58	8.48	10.49
4096	8.48	8.29	10.80
5120	8.37	8.12	10.79
6144	8.52	7.95	10.93

TABLE : 6
Primary, Secondary and Overall Compression
Maximum Overall compression = 54.04

$\epsilon = 0.5$

SAMPLE	Primary Compression (%)	Secondary Compression (%)	Overall Compression(%)
1024	45.58	7.86	49.86
2048	45.58	10.08	51.07
3072	45.58	10.49	51.29
4096	45.58	10.80	51.46
5120	45.58	10.79	51.45
6144	45.58	10.93	51.53

V. Experimental Results

First we perform an experiment to determine which ε value should we use. We used two test files , one is a textbook in engineering of 151305 characters and the second is a UNIX manual of 202792 characters. The results for both test files are similar. Due to space limitation we report the results only for the first text file. The dictionary is of size 2^{10}. The frequencies for the entries of the LZW dictionary were accumulated during the construction of dictionary until it got full. We tried values of ε from 0.1 to 0.9. The results are given in Table 1.

First observation is that the AHL is smaller than the EAHL and PAHL. This is because in AHL we work with full information on the frequencies in the text rather than an estimate. The other reason is that in AHL we do not have to allocate ε frequency for the 0 frequencies since we know they do not appear in the text. The difference between EAHL and PAHL is expected since in PAHL we examine the estimation of EAHL in practice.

From the PAHL we see that the best compression is obtained for ε values around 0.5. The best PAHL obtained is around 9.7 , only a small saving in comparison with the 10 fixed length of the LZW algorithm for a 2^{10} size dictionary. In contrast the potential compression is demonstrated by the value of AHL = 8.43.

This observation leads us to reconsider our estimated frequencies. Looking into the actual dictionary we found typical cases of high frequency entries with low (mostly 0) frequency children for which the following phenomenon occurs: Since the rule of the LZW coding is to send the longest matching string available, the children entries are sent in the coding after dictionary gets full , rather than the parent entry . The parent entry was sent during the dictionary construction because the children were not in the dictionary at that time but then they were added to the dictionary and they are the ones which will be usually sent (unless they have their own children in the dictionary). Hence we conclude that the frequencies accumulated during the process of the dictionary construction are not appropriate for the process of the coding once the dictionary gets full. Thus we try to accumulate frequencies after the dictionary gets full during the process of coding a sample of 1024 messages according to the LZW coding only. This implies that during the process of coding the sample, we do not get the extra compression from the Huffman secondary coding. However we expect the better approximation of the actual frequencies encountered during the coding process to compensate later for this loss.

In Table 2 we bring results for frequencies accumulated during a sample of 1024 messages for a dictionary of size $2^{10} = 1024$, for the above file.

The results are verifying our prediction that frequencies accumulated during the coding of a sample of the text, after the dictionary gets full, are better than the frequencies accumulated during the construction, in approximating the frequencies in the whole text. The optimal PAHL was obtained for $\varepsilon = 0.5$. However the PAHL value 9.05 is still disappointing in comparison with the AHL value 8.43.

We realize that for better approximation of the frequencies for a table of size 1024 we need a larger sample. We try samples of size 2048 and 3072 which are twice and thrice the size of the dictionary. The results are summarized in Tables 3 and 4. The optimal PAHL is obtained for $\varepsilon = 0.5$. Thus we shall continue with $\varepsilon = 0.5$ in all our following experiments. The values of PAHL for a sample of 2048 is 8.67 and for a sample of 3072 it is 8.48. Hence we see a significant improvement obtained by doubling the size of the sample and only slight extra improvement obtained when the sample size is trippled. These results are quite close to the AHL = 8.43 which is using frequencies obtained in a preliminary scanning of the text. Thus showing a good approximation of the sample results to the optimal result using full knowledge about the text.

However, as we mentioned before there is a loss in compression in case of a larger sample due to the delay in applying the secondary coding. Thus we have to compute the actual compression ratio obtained for each cycle for the whole file and not only after the coding of the sample as we did in the previous experiments measuring the PAHL.

We experiment now with the actual secondary compression ratio obtained for different sample sizes with $\varepsilon = 0.5$. The results are summarized in Table 5. We see a large increase in the compression when doubling the size of the sample from 1024 to 2048. There are smaller increases when we further increase the sample. The compression ratio 10.80 for a sample of size 4096 is close enough to the best results obtained. Thus there is no point in taking larger samples. However samples of size 2048 give ratio of 10.08, quite close to this value and will satisfy users which do not insist on the maximum compression.

Table 6 summarized the compression ratios for the primary , secondary and overall compression ratios obtained. The Huffman secondary compression adds slightly more than 5% to the primary compression. This is quite close to the potential secondary compression using Huffman as is indication by the optimal average compression ratios 54.04 obtained according to the AHL values.

References

[CFP] Y. Choueka, A.S. Fraenkel, Y. Perl.: *Polynomial construction of optimal prefix tables for text compression.* Proc. 19th Annual Allerton Conferences on Communication, control and Computing, 1981, 762-768.

[FMP] A. S. Fraenkel , M. Mor , Y. Perl. : *Is text compression by prefixes and suffixes practical ?* Acta Informatica 20 , 1983 , 371-389.

[H] D.A. Huffman.: *A method for the construction of minimum redundancy codes.* [A In Proc. IRE 40 (1951). 1098-1101.

[L] M.F. Lynch.:*Compression of bibliographic files using an adoption of run-length coding.* Infor. Stor. Retr. 9, 1973, 207-214.

[PCM] Y. Perl, S. Chatterjee, T. Mahapatra.: *Incorporating updates into the LZW compression algorithm.* N.J.I.T. Technical report.

[PGS] Y. Perl, S. Gupta, A. Shrivastava, *Towards a bound for the compression of the LZW algorithm.* N.J.I.T. Technical report.

[SS1] J.A.Storer, T.G. Szymanski.:*The macro model for data compression. Extended Abstract. Proc. Tenth Annual ACM symposium on theory of computing,* San Diego, CA, 1978, 30-39.

[SS2] J.A.Storer, T.G. Szymanski.:*Data compression via textual substitution.* JACM 29, 1982, 928-951.

[SS3] M.E.G. Smith, J.A. Storer.: *Parallel Algorithms Data Compression,* JACM, Vol. 32 No. 2 , April 1985.

[W] T.A. Welch.: *A technique for high performance data compression,* IEEE Computer Journal, 1984, 8-19.

[ZL1] J. Ziv, A. Lempel.: *A universal algorithm for sequencial data compression.* IEEE Trans. on Info. theory, Vol.IT-23, 1977, 337-343.

[ZL2] J. Ziv, A. Lempel.: *Compression of individual sequences via variable-rate coding.: IEEE Trans. on Info. Theory, Vol.IT, 1978, 530-536.*

DENDROGRAMS AND IRREDUCIBLE PREFIX CODES

John McAlpin and Christos Nikolopoulos
Department of Computer Science
Bradley University
Peoria, IL 61625

Abstract

Dendrograms have been used in cluster analysis and in hierarchical classification problems. In this paper we note that the Huffman method for producing optimal binary codes also produces only dendrograms.

We define an equivalence relation on codes and give an algorithm to produce a prefix code in each class. We also define minimal and maximal total length functions and by exploiting the relationship between irreducible codes and dendrograms, we derive formulas for them. We also derive a measure of code extensibility.

1. Dendrograms.

Definition 1.1 A dendrogram is a tree in which each nonleaf node has exactly two children.

Definition 1.2 The potency $P(t)$ of a dendrogram t is the number of its leaves. The potency of a node is the potency of the subtree rooted at that node.

For $0 \leq j \leq$ height (t), let n_j be the number of nodes in the tree t at level j, and let k_j be the number of leaves at level j. Obviously, $P(t) = \Sigma k_j \leq 2^{\text{height}(t)}$.

Moreover, for $1 \leq j \leq$ height(t), we have $n_j = 2 (n_{j-1} - k_{j-1})$ and, by mathematical induction, we have the following.

Proposition 1.1 $n_j = 2^j - \sum_{i<j} 2^{j-i}k_i$, for all j.

If $r =$ height(t) then we have the following proposition and corollary.

Proposition 1.2 $\Sigma k_i 2^{r-i} = 2^r$.

Proof. By Proposition 1.1, $k_r = n_r = 2^r - \sum_{i<j} 2^{r-i}k_i$.

Corollary. $\Sigma k_i / 2^i = 1$

Definition 1.3 Two dendrograms t_1 and t_2 are <u>equivalent</u> ($t_1 \sim t_2$) if and only if height$(t_1) =$ height (t_2) and at each level they have the same number of nodes. i.e., $n_i(t_1) = n_i(t_2)$ for all $i \geq 0$.

Proposition 1.3 $t_1 \sim t_2$ if and only if $k_i(t_1) = k_i(t_2)$ for all i.
Proof. This is an immediate consequence of definition 1.3 and proposition 1.1

2. Binary Codes

Given an alphabet $A = \{a_1, \ldots, a_n\}$ consisting of n letters, let F(A) denote the set of all strings that can be formed from A. F(A) is a free semigroup generated by A. Its elements are called the messages written in A.

Let $C: A \to F(\{0,1\})$ be any mapping of A into the set of binary strings. C has a unique extension as a homomorphism from F(A) into F($\{0,1\}$), which we will also denote by C. Let $C_i = C(a_i)$ for $i = 1, \ldots, n$. For C to be useful as an unambiguous code, it must have the property that any bitstring can be interpreted in at most one way as the concatenation (product) of C_i's. Thus the coding problem is to find one to one homomorphisms C from F(A) into F($\{0,1\}$). In this case, we call the C_i the code words for the characters in the alphabet A. In the following, when we refer to codes we will always mean unambiguous codes.

Definition 2.1 The _length_ $L(C_i)$ of any codeword is the number of bits in it.

Definition 2.2 The _total length_ of a code C is given by $T(C) = \Sigma\, L(C_i)$.

For each i, let k_i denote the number of codewords of length i. Let $r = \max\{L(C_j)\}$. Then obviously, $M = \Sigma\, k_j \leq 2^r$ since the maximal number of distinctions we can make with r (or fewer) bits is 2^r.
We have, in fact, the following much stronger result.

Proposition 2.1 $\Sigma_{i \leq j}\, 2^{j-i} k_i \leq 2^j$ for all j.

Proof. While there are codewords of length less than j, repeat the following process:

Let g be the smallest integer such that there are codewords of length $g \leq j$ and codewords of length $i < g$. For each string s of length $g-i$, define

$C'(a,s) = C_a s$, if $C_a s$ in _not_ a codeword,
   $s C_a$, otherwise.

Note that if $C_a s$ is a codeword C_b then since $C(F(a)) = F(C(A))$ is freely generated from the $C(A) = \{C_1, \ldots C_n\}$, there cannot exist products P_1 and P_2 of codewords such that $sP_1 = P_2$. Otherwise we would have $C_b P_1 = C_a s P_1 = C_a P_2$. (In particular, sC_a is not a codeword). We now replace C_a by the 2^{g-i} member set $\{C'(a,s)\}$ and create a new code (on a larger alphabet). Since this code satisfies the same conditions as the original one, we can repeat the process until all the codewords with length less than g have been exhausted.
At this time, we will have $\Sigma_{i \leq j}\, 2^{j-i} k_i$ codewords of length j. Since we cannot exceed totality of such words which is 2^j, this completes the proof.

Note that if equality holds for any j, then $k_i = 0$ for all $i \geq j$.
We also have the following corollary.

Proposition 2.2 $\Sigma\, k_i / 2^i \leq 1$.

Definition 2.3 Given two binary codes C and C' on the same alphabet A, the code C' is said to _reduce_ the code C if and only if $T(C') < T(C)$ and, for all i,

$L(C'_i) \leq L(C_i)$. We call two codes <u>equivalent</u> iff $k_i(C) = k_i(C')$ for all i.

<u>Definition</u> 2.4 A code C is irreducible if and only if there is no code which reduces it.

For many applications the code itself is unimportant, only the lengths are of consequence. In such cases, we usually seek irreducible codes. In some applications, however, we have a code given for a small alphabet and wish to keep those codewords fixed while adding more to extend the code to a larger alphabet.

<u>Definition</u> 2.5 Given an alphabet A' which contains A and the codes C' on A' and C on A such that C'|A = C, we say that C' is an <u>extension</u> of C.

<u>Definition</u> 2.6 A code C is called <u>extensible</u> if and only if it has an extension. It is inextensible if it cannot be extended.

In general it is not too easy to determine if a given set of binary strings $\{C_1, \ldots, C_n\}$ defines an (unambiguous) code. Moreover, even if it does, its deciphering may not be trivial. There is, however, one class of strings which obviously define codes and which are easily decoded, namely strings with the prefix property.

<u>Definition</u> 2.7 We say that $\{C_1, \ldots, C_n\}$ satisfies the prefix condition or has the prefix property if no C_i is the prefix to another C_j.

<u>Definition</u> 2.8 A code defined by a set of codewords with the prefix property is called a prefix code. Irreducible prefix codes are called Huffman codes.

The following set $\{1, 101, 1001, 10001, 10101\}$ defines a code for a five letter alphabet. It is not a prefix code. However, there is a prefix code in every equivalence class of codes. E.g., $\{0, 110, 1110, 11110, 11111\}$ is equivalent to the above.

<u>Proposition</u> 2.3 Given any finite sequence of integers $\{k_i\}$ such that $\Sigma \, k_i/2^i \leq 1$, there is a prefix code on $\Sigma \, k_i$ letters with exactly k_i codewords of length i.

Proof. Let $r = \max\{i : k_i \neq 0\}$ and $n = \Sigma \, k_i$. For $1 \leq i \leq k_r$, Let $L_i = r$. In general, for $\Sigma_{p>j} k_p < i \leq \Sigma_{p \geq j} k_p$, let $L_i = j$.

Consider the following algorithm:

```
C₁:=2ʳ-1;
i:=1;
Repeat
C_{i+1}:=C_i·2^{L_{i+1}} - L_i-1;
i:= i + 1
until i = n;
```

The binary representations of the C_i defined by this algorithm, considered as strings of length L_i, give a prefix code on n letters with the desired lengths.

When considered as integers, the C_i represent the number of additional characters that could be encoded with L_i bits while keeping the codes $\{C_1, \ldots C_i\}$ fixed. Moreover if we define $L_{n+1} = 0$ and $R_i = C_i \bmod 2^{L_i - L_{i+1}}$, for all i, then the R_i represent the number of additional codewords of length L_i which would be added to the $\{C_1, \ldots, C_n\}$.

Proposition 2.4 C extensible if and only if $\Sigma R_i \neq 0$.

A prefix code can be uniquely associated with a binary tree. Starting with the root, let 0 indicate the path to the left subtree and 1 the path to the right subtree. Then the leaves of the tree will represent the codewords. Let us call this the canonical representation of the code by a tree. Obviously, if two codes C and C' are equivalent then their canonical trees are also equivalent.

Proposition 2.5 The following conditions are all equivalent for prefix codes:
  (1) C is irreducible.
  (2) C is inextensible.
  (3) The tree representing C is a dendrogram.
  (4) $\Sigma k_i 2^{r-i} = 2^r$.
  (5) $\Sigma k_i / 2^i = 1$.
  (6) $\Sigma R_i = 0$.

Proof. Let t be the canonical tree representing C. If t contains a node which has only one child then
  (a) by identifying that node with its child we can eliminate one bit from all the codewords corresponding to the node's descendent leaves. Hence, if the tree is not a dendrogram, the code is reducible.

  (b) by creating a new branch from the node with only one child, we can increase the potency of the tree without changing any of the older branches. Hence, if the tree is not a dendrogram, it is extensible.

If, however, the tree is a dendrogram, then the identities (4) and (5) follow from proposition 1.2 and its corollary. (6) is equivalent to (4) and (5) and is equivalent to (2) by Proposition 2.4. In addition, if $R_i > 0$ for some i, then we have a pair of codewords from the algorithm in the proof of proposition 2.3, C_i and C_{i+1}, say, such that $C_i = sR_i$ and $C_{i+1} = s'$ where s and s' (= s - 1) have $L_{i+1} < L_i$ bits and $R_i > 0$ a string of $L_i - L_{i+1}$ bits. Since $R_i \neq 0$ the string $C_i' = sR_i'$ where $R_i' = R_i - 1$ is another potential codeword which could be included without violating the prefix condition. Hence, the common prefix of C_i and C_i' (which is shorter than C_i) could replace C_i giving a reduction of the code.

3. Irreducible codes with minimal and maximal total length.

Definition 3.1 For every positive integer N, let
  $m(N)$ = min $\{T(C)\}$ where C is a code for N letters, and
  $M(N)$ = max $\{T(C)\}$ where C is an irreducible code for N letters.

Definition 3.2 A code C on N letters such that $T(C) = m(N)$ is called a minimal code. Obviously any minimal code is irreducible. We will call an irreducible code C for which $T(C) = M(N)$ a maximal code.

Proposition 3.1 $T(C) = \Sigma i k_i$ where k_i is the number of codewords of length i and r is the maximal codeword length.

Proposition 3.2 Let t be the canonical tree representation of C. Let LC be the code defined by the left subtree of t and RC be the code defined by the right subtree. Then $T(C) = P(t) + T(LC) + T(RC)$.

Proposition 3.3 If we modify a tree t to create a new tree t' by replacing a node Q of t at level i by a new node Q' which has a leaf as left child and a node identical with Q as right child, then the resulting change in the total length is $\Delta T = i + 1 + P(Q)$.

A couple of special cases are of interest: if Q is the root then $\Delta T = 1 + P(t)$, and if Q is a leaf then $\Delta T = 2 +$ length of the codeword corresponding to the leaf.

Proposition 3.4 $\Delta M(N) = N + 1$, for all N.

Proof. Note that for any dendrogram, the level of a node plus its potency is always less than or equal to the potency of the tree, so $M \leq N + 1$. However, the increase $N + 1$ is achieved when are split the root and by making the larges possible increase to M(N) we must achieve M(N+1).

Proposition 3.5 $M(N) = (N-1)(N+2)/2$, for all N.

Proof. By direct observation, the formula is seen to hold for N=2. Now suppos the formula to hold for N=k, i.e., $M(k) = (k-1)(k+2)/2$. Then $M(k+1) = M(k) + \Delta M(k) = (k-1)(k+2)/2 + (k+1) = (k^2+3k)/2 = ((k+1)-1)((k+1)+2)/2$.
Thus, by mathematical induction, the formula is valid for all N. Note that as one would expect this maximal value is achieved with the most unbalanced tre possible.

Of greater interest, however, are the minimal codes, which we will address now. For convenience, we define m(1) to be 0. Then, as a corollary of Proposition 3.2, we have $m(N) = N + m(i) + m(N-i)$ for some i such that $1 \leq i \leq [N/2]$, where [ ] denotes the greatest integer function.

The following proposition illustrates a standard optimization principle: i order to minimize a result one should seek to maximize the balance.

Proposition 3.6 We have the following recursive formula for N.
  (1) $m(N) = N + m([n/2]) + m(N - [N/2])$, for all $N \geq 2$.

Moreover,
  (2) $\Delta m(N) = [\log_2 (N)] + 2$, for all $N \geq 1$.

Proof. We have observed that $m(1) = 0$, $\Delta m(1) = m(2) = 2$. $\Delta m(2) = 3$ and $m(3) = 5$, whence the proposition holds for N<3. Suppose now that it holds for N<k. Then $m(k) = k + m(i) + m(k-i)$, for some i such that $1 < = i \leq [k/2]$. Let $f(i) = m(i) + m(k-i)$. The value we seek is the minimal value of f(i). But since both i and k-i are less than k, we have $\Delta_i m(i) = [\log_2(i)]+2$, and $\Delta_i m(k-i) = -([\log_2(k-i)]+2)$, so that $\Delta f(i) = [\log_2(i)]-[\log_2(k-i)] \leq 0$ for $i<[k/2]$. But $\Delta f(i) \geq 0$ if $i>[k/2]$. Hence the minimal value is achieved when $i = [k/2]$. This demonstrates (1). To demonstrate (2), we suppose that $2^r \leq N < 2^{r+1}$, so that $r = [\log_2(N)]$. Now $2^{r-1} \leq [N/2] \leq N - [N/2] \leq 2^r$, so that applying Proposition 3.3 to a leaf Q of minimal level (r), we get $\Delta m(N) = \Delta T = 2 +$ lengt of the branch leading to $Q = 2 + r = 2+[\log_2(N)]$.

We can now express m in closed form.

Proposition 3.7 Let $r = \lceil \log_2 (N) \rceil$ then $m(N) = N(r + 2) - 2^{r+1}$. In the case $N = 2^r$ this reduces to $m(N) = Nr = r \cdot 2^r$.

Proof. Direct calculation shows that the formula holds for $N \leq 2$. Suppose now that it holds for $N = k$. Furthermore, assume that $2^i \leq k < 2^{i+1}$. Then, $m(k) = k \cdot (i+2) - 2^{i+1}$ and $\Delta m(k) = i+2$, so that $m(k+1) = m(k) + \Delta m(k) = (k+1)(i+2) - 2^{i+1}$. If $k+1 < 2^{i+1}$, this is the correct expression for $m(k+1)$; moreover, if $k+1 = 2^{i+1}$, then this formula reduces to $(i+1)2^{i+1}$. Thus the proof is complete.

Definition 3.3 A tree has a _heap shape_ if all its leaves appear on at most two consequential levels $r-1$ and r, and all its leaves on level r are as far to the left as possible.

Proposition 3.8 There is a tree with the heap shape corresponding to any equivalence class of codes of minimal total length.

Proof. The preceding shows that a tree corresponding to a minimal for N letters can be derived from that for one for N-1 letters by replacing any leaf on the lower level by a node with 2 children. We merely have to choose the leftmost such node each time in order to produce trees with the heap shape.

4. Optimal Codes

Given $A = \{a_1, \ldots, a_m\}$ as before, let p_i denote the probability of a_i's occurence. Then for any code C on A the expected codeword length is $E = \Sigma \, p_i * L(C_i)$.

Definition 4.1 A code is optimal for the distribution p if E is minimal.

Proposition 4.1 Every irreducible prefix code (Huffman code) is optimal for some distribution (and obviously a reducible code cannot be optimal for any strictly positive distribution).

Proof. Let $p_i = 1/2^{L(C_i)}$. Then, by Proposition 2.5, $\Sigma \, p_i = \Sigma \, 1/2^{L(C_i)} = \Sigma \, k_j/2^j = 1$. There p is a distribution. Since all p_i are negative powers of 2, Shannon's binary fission process gives optimality.

Note that even a maximal code (in the sense of total code length for the letters) is optimal for some distribution in this sense of minimizing the expected length of codewords, hence of transmitted messages.

References

M.R., Anderberg, "Cluster Analysis for Applications," Academic Press, New York, NY, 1973.

M.A. Harrison, "Introduction to Formal Language Theory," Addison-Wesley, Menlo Park, CA, 1978.

D. Huffman, "A Method for the Construction of Minimal Redundancy Codes," Preceedings IRE 40, 1952.

Massively Parallel Implementations of Adaptively Subdividing Fractal Generating Algorithms with Parameter Extensions

Michael S. Wainer
Dept. of Computer Science, Southern Illinois University at Carbondale

Abstract. *Fractal approximations are used to generate data to mimic natural objects for realistic image synthesis. While many algorithms for generating fractal data for this purpose exist, the adaptive subdivision methods are in widespread use because of their computational efficiency. This paper discusses the adaptation of the triangular and rectangular subdivision algorithms originally described in [1] to massively parallel SIMD architectures. In addition, the algorithms are enhanced to permit more control over the characteristics of the surfaces.*

Triangular and Rectangular Subdivision

The creation of a realistic terrain model requires the specification of a very large number of graphics primitives. Paradoxically, the actual details of this data are usually far less important than the collective characteristics of the data. Ideally the image creator will specify only the general characteristics (rocky, flat, etc.) and coarse features of the terrain leaving the multitude of nuances essential to conveying the illusion of reality to the computer. This is exactly what fractal subdivision techniques do. As pointed out in [1], they are, stochastic interpolation techniques.

Input to a stochastic subdivision algorithm is a relatively sparse number of input patches used to define the gross features of the terrain along with a few parameters which influence the characteristics of the final surface. The algorithm subdivides the input patches recursively, producing output patches which are rendered by the graphics system. The subdivisions are halted when the details that would be created by further subdivision would not add to the visual realism of the scene. This usually occurs when the output primitives have become approximately pixel sized.

A time complexity proportional to the number of output primitives produced often makes the subdivision method preferable to other more time consuming methods. It is not unreasonable to expect a single input patch to be subdivided to produce in excess of several thousand output patches. Using massive parallelism, the time complexity can be reduced to the logarithm of the number of output patches produced. Special purpose hardware has previously been designed for triangular [6] and rectangular subdivision methods [5]. The general purpose massively parallel SIMD approach permits more flexibility in the algorithms and avoids a potential I/O bottleneck since rendering can be done on the same hardware as modeling [7].

The two forms of adaptive subdivision algorithms discussed here, triangular and rectangular subdivision, were introduced in [1]. Both methods use input patches to loosely define surface features. Input patches are subdivided to create finer details by stochastically interpolating the initial vertex values across the surface of the patch. The two interpolation methods are in many ways similar but they differ in one key aspect aside from the obvious use of different primitives. The triangular method subdivides an edge shared by two neighboring patches using only information from the edge itself. In contrast, the rectangular method uses not only edge information but information from the interiors of adjacent patches. Thus the triangular subdivision process is Markov while the rectangular subdivision process is nonMarkov.

The parameters as defined in [1] are used to control the stochastic interpolation process and thus the characteristics of the final surface. The parameter h determines the surface's roughness or an approximation to its fractal dimension. A scaling parameter, s, is used to express the influence of randomness in the interpolation process. Equation 1 will help to clarify the use of these parameters. Level refers to the depth of the subdivision.

$$std = s \times 2^{-h \times level} \qquad \text{(Equation 1)}$$

A normally distributed random number with mean 0 and standard deviation std forms the stochastic component used to dither the deterministic midpoint. Deterministic midpoints are computed using averaging from adjacent patch vertices. The final value used for the stochastic interpolant is the sum of the deterministic midpoint and the stochastic component. It is easy to see that if we set s to 0 we remove the stochastic component entirely.

If the stochastic component is not constrained, rifts may be created along edges between input patches. The rifts result from dithering the midpoint of an edge differently in one adjoining patch than in the other. To avoid this problem the pseudorandom numbers which determine the stochastic components are generated using seeds formed from the positions of the deterministic midpoints. Since shared edges have exactly the same endpoints and are using the same parameters they will always produce the same midpoints. For terrain modeling, altitude is generally the characteristic to be interpolated so the stochastic component can be seeded using the midpoint x and y.

Parameter Enhancement

Natural terrain varies a great deal in its characteristics depending on its substrate and the impact of various eroding processes. A limitation in previous subdivision methods is that in order to prevent rifts in the surface from forming due to mismatched interpolants, the parameter values of every adjacent patch must be identical. This constraint forces all objects created with these subdivision methods to have constant parameters (i.e. surface characteristics) throughout the entire object [4]. It is not clear how to vary terrain from one texture to another since even with the addition of new input patches the parameters must be preserved to prevent surface gaps. Postprocessing techniques [4] have been used to massage surface data after its generation but many of the desired surface characteristics can be generated directly by associating parameters with individual vertices rather than entire patches. Thus a triangular patch will not have a single set of parameters but instead three sets, one for each vertex.

The interpolation process now requires an additional step which interpolates the parameter values of the new vertices being created. The midpoint parameter values are created using the same communication and averaging processes as the deterministic interpolation component. For triangular subdivision this means the process stays Markov and the new h and s parameters are merely the averages of the endpoint vertices' h and s values. Specifying equal values of h and s respectively at each vertex will generate the same subpatches as the original algorithm. The cost for this extra flexibility is a modest increase in execution time along with the additional memory required to store h and s parameter values at each vertex.

The Opportunities for Massive Parallelism

The large number of primitives produced by stochastic subdivision, potentially tens of thousands for a single input patch, afford many opportunities for parallelism. Massively parallel SIMDs match well with data generating algorithms since the generating process is likely to be synchronous, have fine granularity and produce a number of output primitives approximately equal to the number of processing elements. Massively parallel machines which may be suitable targets for these algorithms are the MPP and the Connection Machine [3, 7].

Most of the parallelism achieved on SIMD machines is due to the large number of processing elements, PEs, operating in parallel on problem data. To facilitate sharing of local PE data items, PEs route data over an interconnection network. In the parallel subdivision algorithms to be considered, PEs will be associated with patch data. Effectively this means that for the triangular subdivision process, which is Markov, the interconnection network will not have to be used to communicate between adjacent patches. The rectangular method, being nonMarkov, does require use of the interconnection network since interior patch data needs to be shared. Hence, we will discuss the triangular subdivision algorithm first then briefly outline the rectangular method. The rectangular method is more thoroughly explained in [3, 8].

Massively Parallel Triangular Subdivision

Input to the triangular algorithm is an input triangle and a parameter set. The major consideration for efficiently adapting this procedure to a massively parallel SIMD machine is the correspondence of the patch information to PE memory. Obvious choices to consider are individual vertices, edges or patches. On a sequential machine, vertices are a logical choice because we eliminate redundant storage and calculation of new vertex values. On a PE array, to minimize routing, data are best stored as entire patches not broken across PEs.

At each subdivision, every parent patch subdivides to produce four distinct child patches as labeled in Figures 1 and 2. Child patches of type 3 are defined using three new vertices. Children 0 through 2 are defined to each have one vertex retained from the parent at the same vertex position as found within the parent. For example, children of type 0 have vertex A defined to be the same vertex as their parent's vertex A. Accordingly, if the child patches 0 through 2 copy their parent's data they have already obtained one of their three vertices. The remaining vertices are shared by at least two other subpatches, one of which is always a type 3.

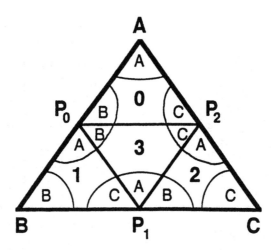

Figure 1: Labeling of child subpatch types 0 through 3 and parent and child vertices. The temporary vertex variables P_0, P_1 and P_2 are also shown.

Rather than treating the calculation of new vertices as a special case for each child type, let all children calculate each new vertex and store the results in temporary variables P_0, P_1, P_2. Since all PEs will be performing the same calculation no PEs will be idle and maximum parallelism can be obtained. Because triangular subdivision is Markov the child patches can obtain all the data they need from their parents without any need to communicate with adjacent patches. Children obtain parent data trivially since parent patches are composed of their child PE groups.

All PEs initially belong to the input patch and are initialized to contain all of its vertex and parameter data. After the first subdivision, four patches will exist corresponding to each of the four child types. Each PE must decide which child patch it will become based on an identity code. This code is easily derived and need only be computed once even if many input patches are to be subdivided. The only assumption is that each PE can obtain a unique integer ranging from 0 to the number of PEs minus one. The identity code for each level of subdivision, the PE's *level_id* , is obtained by treating this unique integer as a string of base four digits and examining a different base four digit position at each level of the subdivision. See Figure 2.

After $log_4(M)$ subdivisions each PE of an SIMD machine with M PEs will contain a single patch. Every level of the subdivision breaks the existing PE groups into PE groups of one-fourth the size. No matter what the subdivision level is there are always equal numbers of the four child types. Each parallel subdivision takes constant time and is composed of the steps shown in Listing TRI. Step 2 of Listing TRI is a series of assignment statements which move the contents of the temporary vertex variables to the actual vertex memory locations. The assignments are all within each PE's local memory so the execution time of step 2 should be minimal in comparison to that of step 1. Even so, more parallelism in step 2 is possible if PEs are permitted to access local memory via independent array indexes. Using tables to specify source temporaries and destination vertices, all PEs would participate in two parallel copy commands after which type 3 children would do one more parallel copy for a total of three parallel copy steps.

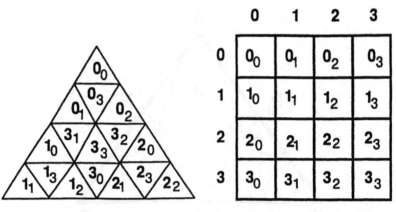

Triangular patches

A 2D mesh array showing the identifiers of the patches for each PE

Figure 2: Correspondence between PE groups and triangular patches.

1.   **For all PEs do in parallel**
     P_0 = interpolate(A,B); P_1 = interpolate(B,C); P_2 = interpolate(C,A)

2.a **For all PEs with level_id of child type 0 or 3 do in parallel**
     copy P_0 to vertex B; copy P_2 to vertex C

2.b **For all PEs with level_id of child type 1 do in parallel**
     copy P_0 to vertex B; copy P_2 to vertex C

2.c **For all PEs with level_id of child type 2 do in parallel**
     copy P_2 to vertex A; copy P_1 to vertex B

2.d **For all PEs with level_id of child type 3 do in parallel**
     copy P_1 to vertex A

Listing TRI: Pseudocode for performing a triangular subdivision

Interpolants are computed with the *interpolate* function of Listing TRI. Interpolation uses
the values of the two vertices defining the edge being interpolated over. PEs each contain a patch
data structure composed of three vertices within their local memories. Each vertex contains fields
for the coordinates x, y, z and the parameters h and s. The values for z are to be stochastically
interpolated in a direction parallel to the z-axis. Interpolation for each edge is similar. Listing
INTER describes the interpolation function which uses two input vertices A and B and returns the
stochastically interpolated vertex.

Because parallelism is expressed using data parallelism, the interpolation routine in listing
INTER is also suitable for a sequential implementation. The parameter enhancements necessitate
extra fields h and s in each vertex and the parameter interpolation of step 2. This interpolation need
not be a simple average and, in fact, the parameters themselves could be stochastically interpolated.

```
    /* Compute deterministic midpoint */
1.  P.x = average(A.x, B.x);  P.y = average(A.y, B.y);  P.z = average(A.z, B.z);

    /* Compute interpolated parameters */
2.  P.s = average(A.s, B.s);  P.h = average(A.h, B.h);

    /* Use interpolated s and h to calc. stochastic component */
3.  stoch = P.s * pow2(-P.h * level) * norm(x,y);

    /* Stochastic interpolation of z is completed */
4.  P.z = P.z + stoch; return(P);
```

Listing INTER: Pseudocode description of interpolate(A,B)

We have assumed that the current subdivision level is contained in the variable *level* and that *norm(x,y)* produces a normally distributed pseudorandom number with mean 0 and standard deviation 1. This pseudorandom number is seeded using the x and y coordinates so adjacent patches will obtain the same stochastic component when interpolating across a common edge.

Both computation of the interpolants and assignment of the temporary vertex values to the actual vertex positions are steps that are accomplished in constant time. The complexity of the algorithm will be proportional to the number of parallel subdivisions taken. PEs work independently on this problem so multiple instances of triangular subdivision can also be performed in parallel.

Massively Parallel Rectangular Subdivision

Rectangular subdivision also produces four child patches for every parent patch subdivided. Child patches are classified into the four basic types and assigned to PE groups using level identifiers as was done in the triangular subdivision method. Subdivision is accomplished by first computing each parent patch's center point interpolant. Center point interpolants can be computed using only the vertex values of the parent patch. Edge interpolants are then computed using not only the shared edge vertices of adjacent patches but also the center point interpolants of both parents [3,8]. The use of the center point interpolants in this manner makes the process nonMarkov and so requires the SIMD algorithm to use the PE interconnection network.

Each child patch, PE group, must use the network to receive center point interpolation data from patches which share an edge with it. The four different child types require four different sets of source destination pairings. Consequently the parallelism in these steps may be restricted depending upon the routing capabilities of a given machine. The Connection Machine uses an intelligent router which permits routing operations to occur simultaneously in multiple directions throughout the network in nearly constant time [2]. Since this is the case rectangular subdivision on a machine like the Connection Machine can be accomplished in time proportional to the number of parallel subdivision steps or simply $log(M)$ for an M processor machine. A simple two dimensional mesh, as used on the MPP, can only route data in one direction at a time thus the routings for the four directions must be done as four separate steps. More importantly, routings which are not of distance one will have to be accomplished by a succession of routings passing data through intermediate PEs. On a mesh connected machine routing will incur a cost of $\sqrt{M}$ where M is the number of PEs or final number of subpatches produced.

Summary

The algorithms for triangular and rectangular subdivision have been extended in a useful and intuitive manner by giving the modeler more control over the parameters defining the characteristics of the model. Both algorithms have been successfully adapted to massively parallel SIMD machines. Triangular subdivision can be performed without the use of an interprocessor communications network in order $log(M)$ where M is the number of patches produced. Similar results are obtained with rectangular subdivision on a machine which has an intelligent routing network such as the Connection Machine. Without an intelligent router an additional communications complexity must be considered. For a two dimensional mesh this cost is proportional to the square root of the number of patches produced. Even so, the communications cost may be so small on actual machines that the computational cost continues to dominate for practical problem sizes.

Acknowledgements

Some of the ideas in this paper were developed or clarified with the support of a NASA Graduate Student Researchers Grant and also the Argonne Summer Institute on Parallel Processing.

References

[1]   Fournier, A. Fussel, D. and Carpenter, L. Computer rendering of stochastic models. *Comm ACM* 25, 6, 1982, pp. 371-384.

[2]   Hillis, D. and Steele, G., Data parallel algortihms. *Comm ACM* 29, 12, 1986, pp. 1170-1183.

[3]   McAnulty, M. and Wainer, M. Algorithmic commonalities in the parallel environment. *Proc. 1st Symp. on the Frontiers of Massively Parallel Proc.* , edited by J. Fischer, NASA Goddard Space Flight Center, 1986

[4]   Musgrave, K., Kolb, C., Mace, R. The synthesis and rendering or eroded fractal terrains. *Computer Graphics (SIGGRAPH)* 23, 3, 1989, pp. 41-50.

[5]   Piper, T.S. Fournier, A. A hardware stochastic interpolator for raster displays. *Computer Graphics (SIGGRAPH)* 18, 3, 1984, pp. 83-92.

[6]   Stepoway, S.L., Wells, D.L. and Kane, G.R. A multiprocessor architecture for generating fractal surfaces. *IEEE Trans on Comp.* C-33, 11, 1984, pp. 1041-1045.

[7]   Wainer, Michael S. Generating fractal-like surfaces on general purpose mesh-connected computers. *IEEE Trans. on Comp.* C-37, 7, 1988, pp. 882-886.

[8]   Wainer, Michael S. Massively parallel implementations of adaptively subdividing fractal generating algorithms with parameter extensions. *Tech. Rept., Dept. of Computer Science, Southern Illinois University*, Carbondale, Il, 1989.

A Simple and Powerful Representation of Binary Search Trees

Si-Qing Zheng

Department of Computer Science
Louisiana State University
Baton Rouge, LA 70803-4020

I. Introduction

It is well known that if a binary search tree of n nodes is height balanced, then the operations of search, insertion and deletion of a tree node can be carried out in $O(\log n)$ time. There are several efficient dynamic tree balancing methods that can be used to balance a binary search tree in $O(\log n)$ time after every insertion and deletion ([K1][K2]). Due to the logarithmic time efficiency of these operations, binary search trees and their variations are the most important data structures in computer algorithms.

Many algorithms are based on tree traversing, which is a systematic way of examining the nodes in a binary search tree. The three principle tree traversal schemes are called preorder, inorder and postorder traversals. Commonly, a stack is used to facilitate traversing a binary tree. This method requires additional space for the stack. It is known that if the "wasted" link fields of the tree nodes are used as threads, then the use of stack, which in the worst case requires $O(n)$ space when the tree is not height balanced, for tree traversal can be avoided. This type of binary search trees are called threaded binary search trees. In addition to the space efficiency, inorder traversal of a threaded binary search tree is 25% faster in average than the stack method ([B][BK]). However, in a threaded binary search tree, to distinguish between threads and branches, additional space for tags are needed. Recently, Cheng, Haq and Zheng ([CHZ]) gave algorithms for operations as search, insertion, deletion, and inorder tree traversal for threaded binary search trees without tags. They showed that these algorithms are as simple and efficient as their counterparts for threaded binary trees with tags. The implication of their results is that untreaded binary search trees and threaded binary search trees can be unified without additional space requirement when the above mentioned operations are considered.

In the conventional representation T of a binary search tree, each node p in T

consists of three fields: KEY[p], which is the key value stored in p, L[p] and R[p], which are pointers pointing at the left child node and right child node of p, respectively. Consider the following operation: for a given node p in T, find the parent node of p. Can this operation be carried out in $O(1)$ time? Certainly not. This is because that finding the parent node of p requires searching from the root of T. A trivial solution to this problem is to associate with each node a pointer pointing at its parent node. Clearly, this representation of a binary search tree requires n additional pointers in total. Now the question is: Can we design a representation of binary search trees such that finding the parent node of a given node in a binary search tree can be done in $O(1)$ time without introducing additional space, and all other tree operations as search, insertion, deletion, dynamic tree balancing , and tree traversals can be implemented at least as efficient as the best algorithms for conventional binary search trees? In this paper, we introduce a simple representation T_G of binary search trees and show that the answer for this question is positive. In fact, our conclusion is much stronger than this. We show that *any* algorithm on conventional binary search trees T with time and space complexities $O(t(n))$ and $O(s(n))$ can be converted into algorithms performing the same operation with time and space complexities $O(t'(n))$ and $O(s'(n))$ on their corresponding representations T_G such that $O(t'(n)) \leq O(t(n))$ and $O(s'(n)) \leq O(s(n))$, and show that $O(t'(n)) < O(t(n))$ or $O(s'(n)) < O(s(n))$ for certain operations.

II. The Results

We present a simple graph representation T_G of binary search trees. As conventional binary search trees, each node p in our representation T_G of a binary search tree consists of three fields: KEY[p], L[p] and R[p]. Let T be the conventional representation of a binary search tree. We assume that for a node p in T L[p] = null (R[p] = null) if and only if p has no left (right) child node, where *null* is a special value that can not be used as a normal pointer. Referring to T, our representation T_G is defined as follows:

(1) if p is the root of T, then R[p] = null in T_G;

(2) if p is the only node of T, then R[p] = p;

(3) if p does not have any child in T, then L[p] = null in T_G;

(4) if p has a left (right) child q but p does not have a right (left) child, then L[p] = q and R[q] = p in T_G; and

(5) if p has a left child q and a right child r, then L[p] = q, R[q] = r and R[r]

$= p$ in T_G.

Graphically, if we consider every node of T_G as a vertex and every non-null link of nodes in T_G as an arc, then T_G is a strongly connected directed graph, i.e. there exists a directed path from any vertex u to any other vertex v in T_G. Note that T_G uses exactly same amount of space as its corresponding T. In figure 1(b) we give our representation T_G for the binary search tree T shown in figure 1(a). Assuming that all key values in T_G are distinct, it is easy to verify the following properties of T_G, comparing with its corresponding conventional binary search tree T:

(i) p is the root of T iff $R[p] = $ null in T_G;

(ii) p is a leaf in T iff $L[p] = $ null in T_G;

(iii) p has exactly one child node in T iff $L[p] \neq $ null and $R[L[p]] = p$ in T_G, and this child node is $L[p]$ in T_G; furthermore, if p has a left child node in T, then $KEY[L[p]] < KEY[p]$ in T_G, otherwise p has a right child node in T;

(iv) p has a left child node in T iff $L[p] \neq $ null and $KEY[L[p]] < KEY[p]$ in T_G, and furthermore, this node in T_G is $L[p]$;

(v) p has both left child node and right child node in T iff $L[p] \neq $ null and $KEY[L[p]] < KEY[p] < KEY[R[L[p]]]$ in T_G, and furthermore, these child nodes are $L[p]$ and $R[L[p]]$, respectively, in T_G;

(vi) q is the parent node of p and p is the right child node of q in T iff $q = R[p] \neq $ null and $KEY[p] > KEY[q]$ in T_G;

(vii) q is the parent node of p and p is the left child node of q in T iff one of the following conditions holds:

(a) $q = R[p]$, $KEY[p] < KEY[q]$, and $R[q] = $ null;

(b) $q = R[p]$ and $KEY[p] < KEY[q] < KEY[R[q]]$;

(c) $q = R[p]$, $KEY[R[q]] < KEY[p] < KEY[q]$; and

(d) $q = R[R[p]]$, $KEY[p] < KEY[R[p]]$ and $KEY[q] < KEY[R[p]]$.

All of these properties of T_G can be easily proved by using the linear order of the keys associated with the nodes of T. For example, for property (vii), the situations corresponding to (a), (b), (c) and (d) are shown in (a), (b), (c) and (d) of figure 2, respectively. These properties can be divided into three groups. The first group, Group I, which consists of (i) and (ii), can be used to determine whether or not a given tree node is the root or a leaf. The second group, Group II, which consists of (iii), (iv) and (v), can be used to find the left and/or the right child node of a given node. The third group, Group III, which consists of the remaining properties, can be used to find the parent node of a given node and determine the given node is a left or right child node of its parent. By these properties, one can show that T_G is more powerful than its corresponding T. Now let us make the following comparisons between T_G and its corresponding T:

(I) As mentioned earlier, for a given node p in T finding its parent node requires $\Omega(m)$ time, where m is the length of the path from the root of T to p. For the same operation on T_G, $O(1)$ time is sufficient by the properties in Group III. Note that this efficiency is achieved without sacrificing space.

(II) Other operations on T_G can be implemented by mimicking their counterparts on T. For operations as search, insertion and deletion, its is easy to see that the properties in groups I and II are sufficient. Thus, these operations on T_G have the same time complexities as their counterparts on T. Similarly, any tree balancing algorithm for conventional binary search trees can be converted into an algorithm for T_G with the same complexity. Therefore, $O(\log n)$ time for search, insertion and deletion (including the tree balancing after updating T_G) is attainable for T_G.

(III) All above listed properties of T_G allow us to convert a recursive operation on T into a non-recursive one on T_G without using stacks. For example, AVL tree rebalancing operations can be easily implemented in a recursive way. For programming languages which do not support dynamic storage allocation and recursive procedures, such as standard FORTRAN, a non-recursive implementation without using stacks is not always easy. However, properties of T_G can be used to convert recursive AVL tree balancing operations into non-recursive ones trivially. Consequently, not only the space for the implicit stack is saved, the system overhead for executing a recursive program is also reduced.

(IV) Using all above listed properties of T_G, one can develop $O(n)$-time inorder, preorder and postorder tree traversal algorithms using $O(1)$ additional space in straightforward ways. In fact, these three traversal algorithms are trivial using recursion. By (III), these recursive operations can be transformed into non-recursive ones. To the author's knowledge, no algorithms for preorder and postorder traversing conventional binary search trees using $O(n)$ time and $O(1)$ additional space without altering and recovering the original tree links during the tree traversal have been reported.

III. Concluding Remarks

We introduced a new simple representation T_G for binary search trees. By the properties of T_G, one can be easily convinced that any algorithm using conventional binary search trees T with time and space complexities $O(t(n))$ and $O(s(n))$ can be converted into algorithms performing the same functions with time and space complexities $O(t'(n))$ and $O(s'(n))$ using their corresponding representations T_G such that $O(t'(n)) \leq O(t(n))$ and $O(s'(n)) \leq O(s(n))$. That is, T_G is more powerful than T. This time and space efficiency are achieved without introducing additional space and information to the tree nodes. In particular, the operations of finding the parent node of a given node, and preorder and postorder tree traversals on T_G outperform their counterparts on T.

The main idea behind our representation T_G is to utilize the semantics of the data stored in the tree nodes, i.e. the linear order of the key values. We assumed that all key values are distinct. This assumption holds for most applications of binary search trees. One generalization of this representation is to allow duplicated keys. A possible approach to accommodating duplicated keys is to construct a two-level data structure. The first level is a T_G, which contains all distinct keys, each is a representative of a set of identical keys. The second level consists of clusters of keys, each cluster corresponds to a set of identical keys. Finally, we would like to point out that our representation T_G for binary search trees can be generalized to a rich set of variations of binary search trees. For examples, 2-3 trees, B-trees, interval trees, segment trees, multidimensional binary search trees, range trees, etc. (see [AHU] [B][K1][K2][PS] for details). We believe that similar results on these trees can be obtained.

IV. References

[AHU] Aho, A.V., J.E. Hopcroft and J.D. Ullman, *"Data Structures and Algorithms"*, Addison-Wesley, 1983.

[B] Bentley, J.I, Multidimensional Binary Search Trees Used for Associative Searching, *CACM*, 18, 9, 1975.

[Br]

Brinck, K., The Expected Performance of Traversal Algorithms in Binary trees, *Comput. J.*, 28, 4, 1985.

[BK]   Brinck, K. and N.Y. Koo, Analysis of Algorithms on Threaded Trees, *Comput. J.*, 24, 2, 1981.

[CHZ]   Cheng, Y., E. Haq and S.-Q. Zheng, "Threaded Binary Search Trees Without Tags", *Proc. of International Conference on Computing and Information*, Toronto, 1989.

[K1]   Knuth, D.E., *The Art of Computer programming*, Vol. 1, Addison-Wesley, Reading, Mass., 1973.

[K2]   Knuth, D.E., *The Art of Computer programming*, Vol. 3, Addison-Wesley, Reading, Mass., 1973.

[PS]   Preparata, F.P. and M.I. Shamos, *Computational Geometry*, Springer-Verlag, 1985.

V. Figures

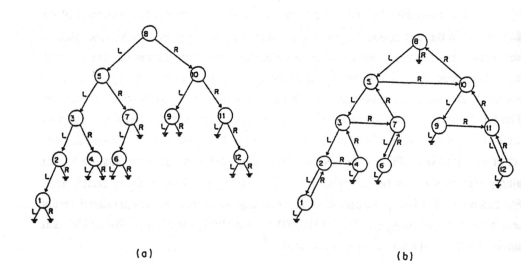

(a)   (b)

Figure 1: Representations T and T_G.

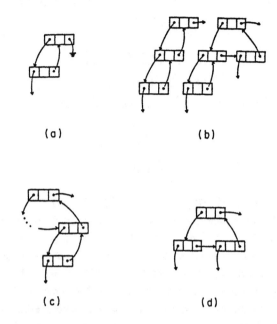

(a)   (b)

(c)   (d)

Figure 2: Conditions for finding parent node.

Random Permutations from Logarithmic Signatures

Spyros S. Magliveras
Nasir D. Memon
University of Nebraska - Lincoln

Abstract

A cryptographic system, called PGM, was invented in the late 1970's by S. Magliveras. PGM is based on the prolific existence of certain kinds of factorization sets, called *logarithmic signatures*, for finite permutation groups. Logarithmic signatures were initially motivated by C. Sims' bases and strong generators. A logarithmic signature α, for a given group G, induces a mapping $\hat{\alpha}$ from $Z_{|G|}$ to G. Hence it would be natural to use logarithmic signatures for generating random elements in a group. In this paper we focus on generating random permutations in the symmetric group S_n. Random permutations find applications in *design of experiments, simulation, cryptology, voice-encryption* etc. Given a logarithmic signature α for S_n and a seed s_0, we could efficiently compute the following sequence : $\hat{\alpha}(s_0), \hat{\alpha}(s_0 + 1), \ldots, \hat{\alpha}(s_0 + r - 1)$ of r permutations. We claim that this sequence behaves like a sequence of random permutations. We undertake statistical tests to substantiate our claim.

1 Introduction

If G is a finite group we call an ordered collection $\alpha = \{B_i : i = 1, \ldots, s\}$ of ordered sets $B_i = \{\alpha(i, j) : j = 1, \ldots, r(i)\}$ a *logarithmic signature* of G if each element g of G can be expressed uniquely as a product of the form

$$g = q_s \cdot q_{s-1} \cdots q_2 \cdot q_1 \tag{1}$$

with $q_i \in B_i$. The elements q_i are not necessarily elements of G, but could belong to a much larger group in which G is embedded. The B_i are called the *blocks* of α and the vector of blocklengths $\alpha = (r(1), \ldots, r(s))$ is called the *type* of α. The logarithmic signature is called *non-trivial* if $s \geq 2$ and $r(i) \geq 2$ $(1 \leq i \leq s)$. A logarithmic signature is called *tame* if the factorization (1) can be achieved in time polynomial in the degree n of G and *supertame* if (1) can be achieved in time $O(n^2)$. A logarithmic signature is called *wild* if it is not tame. If G is a given permutation group other than the symmetric or alternating group of degree n then the number of blocks is often bounded and the factorization (1) can be achieved in time $O(n)$ with respect to a supertame logarithmic signature. We denote by Λ the collection of all logarithmic signatures of G. In [3] it is shown that Λ is a very large set.

An example of a supertame logarithmic signature for a permutation group is obtained as follows: let G be a permutation group on the letters of a set Ω, let $\{b_1, \ldots, b_s\} \subset \Omega$, and let $\gamma : G = G_0 > G_1 > \ldots > G_s = 1$ be the chain of *stabilizer subgroups* corresponding to $\{b_1, \ldots, b_s\}$. Thus, G_i is the set of all elements of G_{i-1} fixing b_i. Replacing the above chain by another subgroup chain where the subgroups are not necessarily stabilizers yields a log signature which we call *transversal*. By taking the sets of right coset representatives of G_i in $G_{i-1}, 0 < i \leq s$, one gets a logarithmic signature of G. Efficient algorithms for obtaining such logarithmic signatures are known [8] [1].

Given a group G and a logarithmic signature α of type $(\alpha) = (r(1), \ldots, r(s))$, running through the products $\alpha(p_1, \ldots, p_s) = \alpha(s, p_s) \ldots \alpha(1, p_1)$, $0 \leq p_i < r(i)$ in an orderly manner gives us a listing of the elements of the group. Choosing a different logarithmic signature β yields the elements of the group in a different order. So we see that a logarithmic signature induces a mapping from $Z_{|G|} \to G$. We now define such a mapping in more formal manner. If $\alpha = (r(1), \ldots, r(s))$ is the type of a logarithmic signature α, define the integers m_i, $i = 1, 2, \ldots, s$ by :

$$m_1 = 1, \quad m_i = \prod_{j=1}^{i-1} r(j), \quad i = 2, \ldots, s.$$

Let λ be the bijection from $Z_{r(1)} \times \cdots \times Z_{r(s)}$ onto $Z_{|G|}$, defined by

$$\lambda(p_1, \cdots, p_s) = \sum_{i=1} p_i m_i$$

then for $x \in Z_{|G|}$, $\lambda^{-1}(x)$ is efficiently computable by successive subtractions [representation of x with respect to mixed base $(r(1), \ldots, r(s))$]. For a group G and a logarithmic signature $\alpha = \{\alpha(i, j) : i = 1, \ldots, s; j = 1, \ldots, r(i)\}$ define the bijection $\Theta_\alpha : Z_{r(1)} \times \cdots \times Z_{r(s)} \to G$ by $\Theta_\alpha(p_1, \cdots, p_s) = \alpha(s, p_s) \cdots \alpha(2, p_2) \cdot \alpha(1, p_1)$. Finally, define the map $\hat{\alpha} : Z_{|G|} \to G$ by $\hat{\alpha} = \lambda^{-1} \Theta_\alpha$. The function $\hat{\alpha}$ is always efficiently computable, but $\hat{\alpha}^{-1}$ is not unless α is tame. When α is supertame $\hat{\alpha}^{-1}$ is computable with great efficiency [4]. Two logarithmic signatures α, β are said to be *equivalent* if $\hat{\alpha} = \hat{\beta}$.

Suppose that $\beta = \{B_i : i = 1, \ldots, s\}$ is a transversal logarithmic signature of a group G with respect to the chain of subgroups $\gamma : G = G_0 > G_1 \cdots > G_s = 1$. Note that while $\beta = \{B_i : i = 1, \ldots, s\}$ is a logarithmic signature for $G = G_0$, the set of blocks $\beta(k) = \{B_{k+1}, \ldots, B_s\}$ is a logarithmic signature for G_k. If the element $\alpha(i, j) \in B_i$ of $\beta(k)$ is replaced by $h \cdot \alpha(i, j)$, where $h \in G_i$, the resulting collection $\beta(k)^*$ forms a new logarithmic signature for G_k. Moreover, any rearrangement of the elements of a block $B_i \in \beta(k)$ yields a new logarithmic signature for G_k. We call this procedure *shuffle*. Procedure *shuffle* for generating new logarithmic signatures from a a given one can be concisely described by a certain group action. Other transformations, namely, *sandwiching, translation, inversion, fusion* and *refinement* are described in [4], [5]. An enumeration of logarithmic signatures up to equivalence has been carried out in [4], [5].

2 Random Permutations

We have seen that a logarithmic signature α, for a given group G, induces a mapping $\hat{\alpha}$ from $Z_{|G|}$ to G. Hence it would be natural to use logarithmic signatures for generating random elements in a group. In this paper we focus on generating random permutations in the symmetric group S_n. Random permutations find applications in the *design of experiment, simulation, cryptology, voice–encryption* etc. Several methods of constructing random permutations have been proposed in literature [2], [6], [7]. In our case, given a logarithmic signature α for S_n and a seed s_0, we could efficiently compute the sequence $\hat{\alpha}(s_0), \hat{\alpha}(s_0+1), \ldots, \hat{\alpha}(s_0+r-1)$ of r permutations. We claim that this sequence behaves like a sequence of random permutations. In the rest of this paper we proceed to substantiate our claim. Before we proceed, we wish to make a few observations. Our method for generating random permutations gives us more control over the types of permutations which are generated. In some application, it may be desirable to avoid permutations with too many fixed points. By choosing a logarithmic signature for an appropriate subgroup or coset of a subgroup or union of conjugacy classes of S_n, this is possible. Secondly, multiplication of permutations can be done very efficiently in parallel. Hence, our scheme is well suited to parallel implementation. Finally, since a logarithmic signature induces a permutation on $Z_{|G|}$, we can use it to generate permutations of degree $| G |$, simply compute $\hat{\alpha} \cdot \hat{\beta}^{-1}$ for $\alpha, \beta \in \Lambda$.

3 Tests for Randomness

Given a set of permutations from S_n, how can we test if these permutations are random? This problem has not been studied as intensely as the corresponding question for random numbers [2]. However, the combinatorial properties of permutations have been studied extensively and a number of tests can be constructed from them. In the rest of this section we list a few such tests. In the next section we use them to test the randomness of permutation sequences generated by logarithmic signatures.

Cycles test: A permutation on n objects has k cycles with probability $S(n,k)/n!$ where $S(n,k)$ denote the Stirling numbers of the first kind [2]. Stirling numbers of the first kind are given by the recurrence $S(n,m) = (n-1)S(n-1,m)+S(n-1,m-1)$ with boundary values $S(0,n) = S(n,n) = 1$, $S(n,0) = 0$. So given a set of random permutations, we can count the number of permutations with k cycles, $1 \leq k \leq n$, and compute a chi-square statistic for the difference between the expected and observed frequencies.

Run test: Let $a_1 a_2 \cdots a_n$ be a permutation on the set $\{1, 2, \cdots n\}$. A *run* is defined to be a maximal monotone subsequence of $(a_1, \ldots, a_n)$, and its *length* the number of elements in the subsequence. Denote the number of permutations of degree n

which have exactly k ascending runs by $E(n,k)$. These numbers are called *Eulerian Numbers* [2] and satisfy the recurrence relation $E(n,k) = kE(n-1,k) + (n-k+1)E(n-1,k-1)$, where n and k are integers and $n \geq 1$. By convention we set $E(0,k) = 1$ and by definition it follows that $E(n,0) = 0$, $E(n,1) = E(n,n) = 1$ Given a set of random permutations, we can count the number of permutations with k runs, $1 \leq k \leq n$, a compute the chi–square statistic for the difference between the expected and observed frequencies.

Inversions test: Let $a_1 a_2 \cdots a_n$ be a permutation on the set $\{1, 2, \cdots n\}$. If $i < j$ and $a_i > a_j$, the pair (a_i, a_j) is called an *inversion* of the permutation. The number of permutations of degree n with exactly k inversions is given by the coefficient of the $k'th$ term of the generating function $(1 + z + \cdots + z^{n-1}) \ldots (1+z)(1)$ [2]. Again, given a set of random permutations, we can count the number of permutations with k inversions, $0 \leq k \leq \binom{n}{2}$, and compute the chi–square statistic for the difference between the expected and observed frequencies.

Type test: The relation of conjugacy under G induces a decomposition of a group G into disjoint conjugate classes. The number of conjugacy classes for S_n is $p(n)$, the number of partitions of the natural number n. Two permutations in S_n are conjugate if and only if they have the same cycle type. We use the notation $1^{k_1} 2^{k_2} \cdots n^{k_n}$ to mean k_1 cycles of length 1, k_2 cycles of length 2 etc. Then the number of permutations with cycle type $1^{k_1} 2^{k_2} \cdots n^{k_n}$ is given by :

$$\frac{n!}{\prod_{i=1}^{n} i^{k_i} k_i!}$$

where $\sum_{i=1}^{n} i \cdot k_i = n$. As before, given a set of random permutations, we can count the number of permutations with cycle type $1^{k_1} 2^{k_2} \cdots n^{k_n}$ and compute a chi–square statistic for the difference between the expected and observed frequencies.

4 Experimental Results and Conclusions

In this section we describe the experiments performed to test the randomness of sequences of permutations generated by logarithmic signatures. We specify all the parameters necessary for their reconstruction. The symmetric group on 12 points, S_{12}, was chosen as the underlying group. Let $\gamma : S_n = G_0 > G_1 > \cdots > G_n = 1$ be a chain of nested stabilizers in S_n, where for $i \geq 1$, G_i fixes pointwise the letters $1, 2, \ldots, i$. Let $\{B_i : i = 1, \ldots, n\}$, be an ordered collection of subsets in S_n where $B_i = \{((i\ j)) : j = i+1, \ldots, n)\}$. It is easily seen that B_i is a complete set of right coset representatives of G_i in G_{i-1}. Hence $\{B_i\}$ forms a logarithmic signature for S_n. We call this logarithmic signature the *canonical* one for S_n. Let α be the canonical logarithmic signature for S_{12}. We specify the logarithmic signature β used in the experiments in terms of α by listing its elements in Figure (1). To list an element

Block Size	Block Elements				
12	292748502	2282248	230710104	302007663	99910315
	91349265	705889	437720342	204020564	358004134
	427511849	376213595			
11	296549605	317948821	417427873	6501037	128858929
	28431577	328220089	204264265	195438337	242957833
	238003405				
10	418001365	244344145	193842661	421915957	114538249
	457469893	472507201	286206229	290348257	435243073
9	386869561	258219721	349831681	296506321	426779761
	227437321	216024601	213055921	255625921	
8	347727601	431719201	318312721	201021481	96311161
	382785481	35544961	469485721		
7	139708801	409907521	261740161	210798721	423308161
	57689281	430816321			
6	380540161	407816641	19293121	329313601	401829121
	83825281				
5	475009921	359251201	311351041	387192961	203575681
4	79833601	119750401	219542401	419126401	
3	239500801	319334401	159667201		
2	1	239500801			

Figure 1: The Logarithmic Signature β

$g \in G$, we simply list the integer x, where $x = \hat{\alpha}^{-1}(g)$. The reader can recover g by computing $g = \hat{\alpha}(x)$. Next, we select a set of random seeds $\{S_i : 1 \leq i \leq 50\}$ such that when $i \neq j$, we have $| S_i - S_j | > 2000$. The seeds are listed in Figure (2).

To produce a sequence of pseudorandom permutations we used the transformation $x \to \hat{\beta}(x)$ and compute $\hat{\beta}(S_i), \hat{\beta}(S_i + 1), \ldots, \hat{\beta}(S_i + 1999)$ for a given random seed S_i. We obtain 50 sequences, X_i, of length 2000 from the seeds listed in Figure (2). In the rest of this section we describe the results of applying the tests listed in section 3 to the test data.

Cycles+KS: For each of the random sequences X_i, a chi–square statistic was computed from the observed number of permutations with k cycles and the expected value. However, for a random set of 2000 permutations, the expected number of permutations with more than 8 cycles is very small. Hence, although the number of cycles in a random permutation from S_{11} could be between 1 and 12, we considered only the categories 1 through 8. We then apply the Kolmogorov–Smirnov test, to the 50 chi–square variates to determine the closeness of fit with the theoretical chi–square distribution for 6 degrees of freedom. The results are tabulated in Fig (3).

17046660	2412040	778600	31112470	10047900
1439460	19857840	27843400	29765990	7545900
33516620	20405730	16386460	18419150	26084140
36087900	25524720	6608700	16101600	38941760
13476190	21529870	2450960	36921700	16213970
25554940	25335040	10051900	25505650	28636220
23256850	16347410	39866150	29264320	36426270
39173980	12409150	31421610	1008160	15484200
17529730	31270320	18168680	18523840	13500670
24236850	36260100	13818710	23837970	33911610

Figure 2: The Seeds S_i used in the experiment

Run+KS: For each of the random sequences X_i, a chi–square statistic was computed from the observed number of permutations with k runs and the expected value. However, for a random set of 2000 permutations, the expected number of permutations with 1, 2, 10, 11 and 12 runs is very small. Hence, although the number of runs in a random permutation from S_{12} could be between 1 and 12, we considered only 7 categories. We then apply the Kolmogorov–Smirnov test, to the 50 chi–square variates to determine the closeness of fit with the theoretical chi–square distribution for 6 degrees of freedom. The results are tabulated in Fig (3).

Inversions+KS: For each of the random sequences X_i, a chi–square statistic was computed from the observed number of permutations with k inversions and the expected value. However, for a random set of 2000 permutations, the expected number of permutations in some categories is very small. Hence, although the number of inversions in a random permutation from S_{12} could be between 0 and 55, we excluded the categories 0 through 6 and 50 through 55. We then apply the Kolmogorov–Smirnov test, to the 50 chi–square variates to determine the closeness of fit with the theoretical chi–square distribution for 42 degrees of freedom. The results are tabulated in Fig (3).

Type+KS: For each of the random sequences X_i, a chi–square statistic was computed from the observed number of permutations with a given cycle structure and the expected value. The number of different conjugacy classes in S_n is 56. However, we excluded the identity as it was never generated. We then apply the Kolmogorov–Smirnov test, to the 50 chi–square variates to determine the closeness of fit with the theoretical chi–square distribution for 54 degrees of freedom. The results are tabulated in Fig (3).

Test	Statistic	Value	Probability
Cycles+KS	KS_{50}^{+}	0.59315	$0.50 < p < 0.75$
	KS_{50}^{-}	0.79059	$0.50 < p < 0.75$
Run+KS	KS_{50}^{+}	0.78434	$0.50 < p < 0.75$
	KS_{50}^{-}	0.67701	$0.50 < p < 0.75$
Inversions+KS	KS_{50}^{+}	0.60797	$0.25 < p < 0.50$
	KS_{50}^{-}	0.42376	$0.50 < p < 0.75$
Type+KS	KS_{50}^{+}	0.94579	$0.75 < p < 0.95$
	KS_{50}^{-}	0.14142	$0.05 < p < 0.25$

Figure 3: Summary of Statistical Results

References

[1] M. Furst, J. E. Hopcroft, and E. Luks. Polynomial-time algorithms for permutation groups. In *Proceedings of the 21'st IEEE Symposium on Foundations of Computation of Computer Science*, pages 36–41, 1980.

[2] D. E. Knuth. *The Art of Computer Programming*. Addison-Wesley, 2'nd edition, 1981.

[3] S. S. Magliveras. A cryptosystem from logarithmic signatures of finite groups. In *Proceedings of the 29'th Midwest Symposium on Circuits and Systems*. Elsevier Publishing Company, August 1986.

[4] S. S. Magliveras and N. D. Memon. Algebraic properties of cryptosystem PGM. In *Advances in Crptology, Crypto 89*. Springer-Verlag, 1989.

[5] N. D. Memon. On logarithmic signatures and applications. Master's thesis, University of Nebraska at Lincoln, May 1989.

[6] E. S. Page. A note on generating random permutations. *Applied Statistics*, 16:273–274, 1967.

[7] C. R. Rao. Generation of random permutations of given number of elements using random sampling numbers. *Sankhya*, 23:305–307, 1961.

[8] C. C. Sims. Some group-theoretic algorithms. In M. F. Newman, editor, *Topics in Algebra*, pages 108–124. Springer-Verlag, 1978. Springer Lecture notes in Math. Vol 697.

Novel Design Techniques for RNS Systolic VLSI Arrays

Paruvachi V.R. Raja
Department of Computer Science and Engineering
Oakland University,
Rochester, Michigan 48309 , USA

Abstract

This paper presents novel design techniques for Residue Number System based systolic arrays for arithmetic computation useful in digital signal processing applications. Design of a 5-bit pipelined adder is explained with emphasis on the basic systolic cell design, use of clocks, pipeline techniques, simulation, and layout optimization. This pipelined adder can be used to build systolic multipliers, correlators, computational structures for DFT, etc.

1. Introduction

There are three levels of parallelism that we encounter in the design of high speed VLSI architectures: 1) mathematical level, 2) architectural level, and 3) implementation level. Residue Number System (RNS) provides mathematical level of parallelism. RNS arithmetic operations such as additions and subtractions have no inter-digit carries or borrows, and multiplication doesnot need the generation of partial products. The RNS exhibits the property of separability since the arithmetic operations can be decomposed into a set of parallel sub-operations.

2. RNS review

RNS is a means of representing a number in a nonweighted number system. The base of RNS is a set of $\{m_1, m_2, ..., m_L\}$, where each individual member of the set is called a modulus and the set elements are pairwise relatively prime [1].

For any given base(moduli set), the residue representation of an integer X in L-tuple is $(X_1, X_2, ..., X_L)$, where the $\{X_i\}$ are least positive residues of X modulo m_i and are defined by

$$X_i = |X|_{m_i} \quad \text{for } i = 1, 2, ..., L$$

The total number of integers that may be unambiguously encoded in an RNS is:

$$M = \prod_{i=1}^{L} m_i$$

2.1. RNS Arithmetic

In the RNS, binary operations of addition, subtraction and multiplication based on modulo m between numbers X and Y have the following property:

$$Z = |XoY|_M \text{ if } X>0$$

$$|Z|_{m_i} = Z_i = |x_i o y_i|_m$$

where o is one of addition, subtraction, or multiplication operations.

3. Implementation of RNS architectures

A common implementation approach for arithmetic operations is to store RNS functions in ROM based look-up tables. The advantages of this approach are: 1) hardware savings can be achieved if some of the operands are fixed; constants can be pre-multiplied or added and stored along with the binary operation being implemented, and 2) ease of pipelining for high-speed and large throughput rate.

For mod M, the storage capacity of each ROM is $W*M^2$; where $W = \log_2 M$. Early architectures used commercially available ROM packages for implementation of arithmetic operations. Recent developments in VLSI technology allow RNS architectures to be implemented on a single die using custom designed ROM standard cells. Also, reevaluating the existing RNS architecture in the form of array architectures such as systolic arrays opens a new avenue of interesting implementations.

The major design issue in the ROM based systolic cell is the design of ROM itself. The ROMs have to be small, fast, simple, reconfigurable, programmable, pipelinable, and suitable for implementaion using available CMOS fabrication technology. The other issues involve selection and use of proper latches, use of proper clocks for synchronization of operations, optimization of circuit and layout, etc.

4. Design of a 5-bit adder

We will discuss the design of a ROM based building block, a pipelined 5-bit adder, which can be used to realize higher level DSP algorithms and arithmetic, as an example. The basic principle behind the bit-level addition of two numbers A and B in the RNS medium can be explained using the bit-level arithmetic as follows:

$$(A+B)\text{mod } M = (2^0 A_0 + 2^1 A_1 + 2^2 A_2 + 2^3 A_3 + 2^4 A_4 + B)\text{mod } M \quad --(1)$$

The above operation can be performed in 5-stages. A schematic diagram of a 5-bit adder using the two non-overlapping clocks, CL1 and CL2, is shown in Figure 1.

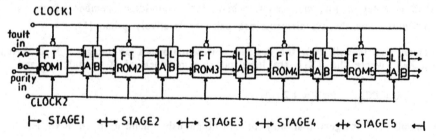

Figure 1: Schematic of the 5-stage pipelined adder

Each stage consists of a block as shown in Figure 2. This block consists of a ROM with fault-tolerant capabilities and 12 latches. The ROM uses dynamic CMOS techniques which employ precharge/discharge logic. The major components in this ROM are a column decoder, a row decoder, a precharge block which has a set of p-channel transistors, and an array of 7-bit 32 words. Among the seven bits, the least two bits are used for fault-tolerance. The sixth bit stores the content parity and the seventh bit stores the address parity [5].

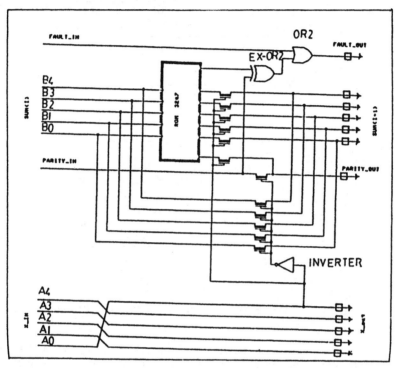

Figure 2: Schematic of the fault-tolerant ROM
based systolic cell

The cell structure of the ROM is shown in a representative circuit shown in Figure 3. N-channel enhancement mode transistors are used as memory cells. If there is a transistor in the selected location, then a logic '0' is stored. A logic '1' is stored if there is no transistor. Clock CL1 is to precharge the ROM and Clock CL2 is used to evaluate the ROM. Let us assume that the input is present on the address lines and neither clock is high at initially. When the clock CL2 is high, the row decoder selects a particular row of n-channel memory cells. The selected n-channel transistors discharges the nodes ND1s through N2,N4, and N7 selected by the column decoder since the ground is connected to their sources. Hence the output of the output lines will be low. If there is no n-channel transistor in the selected location, then the output line will remain precharged and the output will be high. Thus it is possible to program '1's and '0's using n-channel transistors.

The row decoder uses domino CMOS AND gates for the purpose of implementing a gated decoder to be used with the clock CL2. The row decoder remains inactive until the clock CL2 goes high. The column decoder is implemented in static CMOS so that it would become active before the row decoder inorder to allow precharge go to the nodes of ND2s. Allowing the nodes ND2s to get precharged during the precharge phase eliminates the potential charge-sharing problem between nodes ND1s and ND2s.

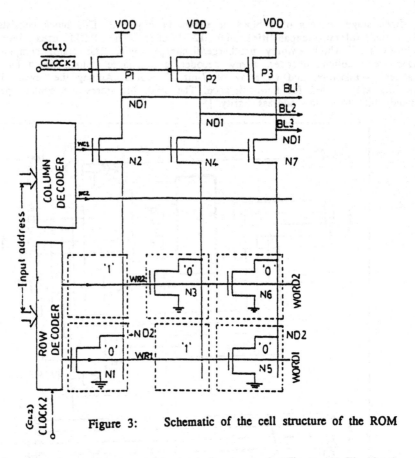

Figure 3:   Schematic of the cell structure of the ROM

The schematic of two-phase testable latch is shown in Figure 4. The latch uses two clocks for operation. The clocks CL1 and CL2 used for the dyanmic ROM are used to operate the latches. Clock CL1 turns on the precharge transistors and the section LB of the latch when it is high. When the clock CL2 goes high, it evaluates ROM bit lines and stores the output.

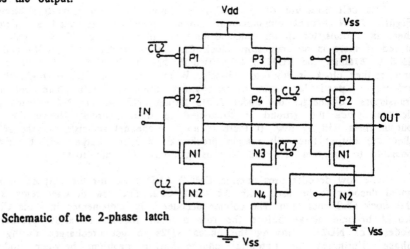

Figure 4:   Schematic of the 2-phase latch

4.1. The layout of the 5-bit adder

The layout of the ROM based systolic cell is shown in Figure 5. The layout uses CMOS 3-micron double metal technology. The advantages of this technology are reduced resistance and capacitance of the metal lines. Several measures have been taken to prevent latch-up and delay due to parasitics. The layout of the pipelined adder is shown in Figure 6.

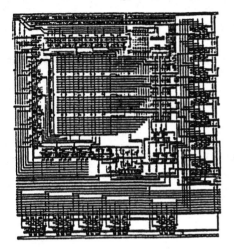

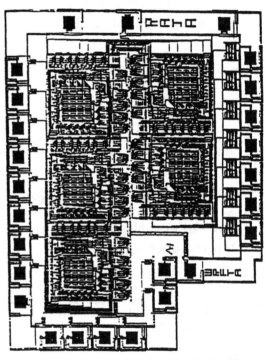

Figure 5:   Layout of the ROM

based systolic cell

Figure 6:   Layout of the pipelined adder

For circuits that donot use dynamic techniques, a complementary cell based static CMOS ROM could be used; however, this complementary cell occupies much larger area than the dynamic CMOS ROM of the same size. The design of such a static CMOS ROM is well documented in [2].

5. Simulation and Analysis

Simulation of VLSI circuits involve two types: 1) switch level simulation and 2) transistor level simulation. In the switch level simulation, transistors are regarded as switches. The switch level simulation has been done using LOGCAP and ICAP modules.

Transistor level simulation was used to predict the delay time or latency time of a circuit. The capacitances and the resistances of the circuit were extracted from the layout using a separate electrical parameter extraction module under the MASKAP environment. The values obtained from this module were used in the SPICE and RELAX simulators. The access time of the 32*7 dynamic CMOS ROM is 13.3 NS, the 32*7 static CMOS ROM is 21.7 NS, and the systolic cell is 26.7 NS. The static ROM is slower than the dynamic CMOS ROM because it has more capaciatnces and resistances than the dynamic ROM.

5.1. Optimization

Area*Time product optimization for the systolic cell has been done using two optimization techniques   given in [3,4]. The techniques involve arranging the memory cells and sizing of the p- and n-channel transistors.

6. Implementation of a FFT butterfly using the pipelined adder

Using the pipelined adder, it is possible to implement a FFT butterfly[5]. The computation of a radix4 butterfly is as follows:

$$X_k = \sum_{n=0}^{3} +(X_n * W^{k\,n})$$

with $j= \sqrt{-1}$ and $W=e^{j2\Pi/N}$, $k \in [0,4]$ --(2)

The above equation can be recursively computed using intermediate variables A and B as shown below:

$X_k = A^{[k]} \oplus (W^{2k} \otimes B^{[k]})$ where $A^{[0]} = x_0 o x_1$ and $B^{[0]} = x_2 o x_3$

and the set of

$A^{[k+1]} = A^{[k]} \otimes x_1 \otimes (W^{k+1} \otimes [-W^k])$ ----(3)

$B^{[k+1]} = B^{[k]} \otimes x_3 \otimes (W^{k+1} \otimes [-W^k])$ ----(4)

to compute $A^{[k]}$ and $B^{[k]}$ for k=0,1,2,3,4

Equations 2,3, and 4 can be computed using the systolic architecture. Figure 7 shows a butterfly based on 15 modulo 5-bit adders. The throughput rate of butterfly is found to be 37 MHz.

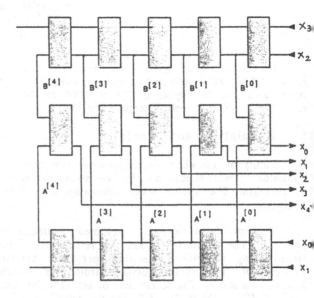

Figure 7:   Schematic of the

FFT butterfly

7. Conclusion

The RNS systolic arrays use ROM based cells. The cell can be designed using fast ROMs with fault-tolerant capabilities. Feasibility of employing static and dynamic CMOS transistor techniques is explored. Use of dynamic CMOS techniques simplifies the design of ROMs with regular layout techniques and provides speed. Static CMOS ROMs are slower and bigger than the dynamic CMOS ROMs. Two phase clocks can be used to coalesce the ROM operations with the pipeline operations. The ROMs use novel techniques to reduce the layout size, latch-up, delay, and charge redistribution. Using these unique ROM based cells, it is possible to design a building block like pipelined adder which is used to build higher level DSP and arithmetic architectures. The throughput of the pipelined adder is found to be sufficiently high.

8. References

[1] G.A. Jullien," Residue Number Scaling and Other Operations Using ROM Arrays", IEEE Transactions on Computers, Vol.C-27, No.4, pp.191-201, April 1977.

[2]. Paruvachi V.R. Raja, "Custom Design of CMOS ROMs for VLSI RNS hardware", Thesis, University of Windsor, Ontario, Canada, 1988.

[3]. S.M. Kang, "A design of CMOS poly cels for LSI circuits", IEEE Transactions on Circuits and Systems, Vol.CASS-28, No.8, August 1981, pp.8388-842.

[4]. M.A.Bayoumi, G.A. Jullien, and W.C.Miller, "Models for VLSI implementation of Residue Number Systems", Proc. of 6th symposium on Computer arithmetic, 1983, pp.174-182.

[5]. G.A. Jullien, et.al, "A VLSI Systolic Quadratic Residue DFT with fault tolerance", ISCAS'88, pp.2271-2274, Glascow, Scotland, 1988.

A COMPOUND DECISION THEORY APPROACH
TO DIGITAL SIGNAL RECONSTRUCTION

K. L. D. Gunawardena

Department of Mathematics, University of Wisconsin Oshkosh
Oshkosh, WI 54901

Abstract. A compound decision theory approach is described for the reconstruction of digital signals with Markov chain structure. The decision rules suggested are based on the construction of the Γ^k decision problem. Simulation results are provided to assess the performance of these rules when compared with MAP rules.

1. Introduction

In this paper, the problem of decision making about one dimensional digital signals is considered. In most instances, the one dimensional digital signal is assumed to be a Markov chain corrupted by independent noise. Some of the early work in decision making on one dimensional digital signals is due to Cover and Shenar [3], Raviv [7,8] and, Scharf and Elliott [10]. Most of the work involves maximizing the joint likelihood function of the data and the Markov state sequence, which yields the maximum a posteriori (MAP) estimate.

In this paper we use techniques developed in compound decision theory to classify digital signals. An important development in compound decision theory is the idea of Γ^k construct introduced by Gilliland and Hannan [4]. This involves the incorporation of more stringent standards for the compound risk. The advantages of using these "extended" rules in classification problems is due to the fact that these rules benefit from empirical dependencies in the state sequence. Ballard and Gilliland [2], Vardeman [12,13] have studied the finite risk performance of extended decision procedures for sequence versions of Robbins [9] component decision problem.

2. Statement of the Problem

Let $\{X_i\}$ denote the random observations and $\{\theta_i\}$ the unknown but fixed classifications. The $\{X_i\}$ are conditionally independent given $\{\theta_i\}$ with $X_i \sim P_{\theta_i}$, where P_{θ_i} is the normal distribution with mean $2\theta_i - 1$, variance 1 and $\theta_i \in \theta = \{0,1\}$, $i = 1,2,\dots$. Let f_θ denote the density of P_θ. The sequence of states $\{\theta_i\}$ is assumed to be a realization of a two state stationary Markov chain with initial probability distribution

$$P(\theta = 0) = p = 1 - P(\theta = 1), \qquad 0 < p < 1$$

and transition matrix

$$\underline{P} = \left[p_{ij} \right], \qquad i,j = 0,1$$

where $p_{00} = \delta$, $p_{01} = 1-\delta$, $p_{10} = \dfrac{p(1-\delta)}{1-p}$, $p_{11} = 1-p_{10}$, and $0 < \delta < 1$.

3. Empirical Maximum A Posteriori Probability Rule

The MAP rule chooses a state sequence which maximizes $f(\underline{\theta}|\underline{x})$. The MAP rule is Bayes with respect to the loss function

$$L(\theta,\hat{\theta}) = [\; \theta \neq \hat{\theta} \;]$$

where $[A]$ denotes the indicator of the set A.

The induced density on $\underline{\theta}$ is

$$p(\underline{\theta}) = p \; p_{00}^{n-1} \left[\frac{1-p}{p}\right]^{\theta_1} \prod_{i=2}^{n} \left[\frac{p_{10}}{p_{00}}\right]^{\theta_{i-1}} \left[\frac{p_{01}}{p_{00}}\right]^{\theta_i} \left[\frac{p_{00} \; p_{11}}{p_{01} \; p_{10}}\right]^{\theta_{i-1}\theta_i}. \qquad (1)$$

Since we assume X_i to be conditionally independent given θ_i, we have

$$f(\underline{x}|\underline{\theta}) = \prod_{i=1}^{n} \left[\frac{1}{\sqrt{2\pi}} \exp\left\{- \tfrac{1}{2}(x_i - 2\theta_i + 1)^2\right\}\right]. \qquad (2)$$

From (1) and (2)

$$\log f(\underline{x},\underline{\theta}) = a + \sum_{i=1}^{n} b_i \theta_i + c \sum_{i=2}^{n} \theta_{i-1}\theta_i, \qquad (3)$$

where a, b_i, and c are functions of x_i, p, δ.

Maximizing $f(\underline{\theta}|\underline{x})$ is equivalent to maximizing (3) and is done by dynamic programming recursion.

The MAP rule is given by

$$d_1: \quad \text{decide} \quad \theta_i = \begin{cases} 1 & \text{if } A_i^1 \geq A_i^0 \\ 0 & \text{otherwise} \end{cases}, \quad 1 \leq i \leq n,$$

where $A_{i+1}^0 = \max(A_i^0, A_i^1)$, and $A_{i+1}^1 = \max(A_i^0 + b_{i+1}, \; A_i^1 + b_{i+1} + c)$.

In order to implement the MAP rule d_1 we need to obtain estimates for the unknown parameters of $\underline{P}$. The proposed estimates are based on $\underline{X}$. When plugged into the MAP rule d_1 the result is an empirical MAP rule (EMAP).

Proposition 1

(i) $U_n = \frac{1}{2}(1 - \bar{X}_n)$, where $\bar{X}_n = \frac{1}{n}\sum_{i=1}^{n} X_i$, is an unbiased estimate for p.

(ii) $V_{n-1} = a\bar{Z}_{n-1} - b$ is an unbiased estimate for $p(1-\delta)$, where

$$\bar{Z}_{n-1} = \frac{1}{n-1}\sum_{i=1}^{n-1} Z_i, \; Z_i = [\text{sgn } X_i \neq \text{sgn } X_{i+1}], \; a = .5[\Phi(1) - \Phi(-1)]^{-2}$$

$\simeq 1.0731$ and $b = 2a\Phi(1)\Phi(-1) \simeq .2865$.

Proof

(i) Since $E(X_i|\theta_i) = 2\theta_i - 1$ and $E(\theta_i) = 1-p$ the proof of (i) is immediate.

(ii) We have $EZ_i = 2P(X_i \geq 0, X_{i+1} < 0)$ and by partitioning on (θ_i, θ_{i+1}) it can be shown that

$$P(X_i \geq 0, X_{i+1} < 0) = p(1-\delta) [\Phi(1) - \Phi(-1)]^2 + \Phi(1)\Phi(-1).$$

Thus,

$$E\left[\frac{Z_i - 2\Phi(1)\Phi(-1)}{2(\Phi(1) - \Phi(-1))^2}\right] = p(1 - \delta),$$

and this completes the proof. □

Since $0 \leq p$, $\delta \leq 1$, it is natural to truncate U_n and V_{n-1} at 0 and 1 and use the modified estimators

$$U'_n = U_n[0 < U_n < 1] + [U_n \geq 1]$$
$$V'_{n-1} = V_{n-1}[0 < V_{n-1} < 1] + [V_{n-1} \geq 1].$$

4. Extended Rules

We begin this section with a brief review of the Γ^k construct introduced by Gilliland and Hannan [4] when applied to the finite-state, finite-action compound decision problem. Ballard and Gilliland [2], Vardeman [12,13] have used the concept of Γ^k construct to obtain extended rules for the two-state compound decision problem with Robbins component.

Consider a component decision problem with states $\theta \in \Theta$ indexing possible distributions $P_\theta \in P$ where $P_i \in P$ are distinct probability measures on (X, B) and $i \in \Theta$ $(i=1,2,\ldots,m)$. Let the actions $a \in A$ and the loss function $L(\theta, a)$ be such that

$$0 \leq L(\theta, a) < \infty \quad \text{for all } \theta \in \Theta \text{ and } a \in A.$$

For the above description of the component decision problem, we will now describe the Γ^k construct. The Γ^k decision problem has states $\underline{\theta}_k = (\theta_1, \theta_2, \ldots, \theta_k) \in \Theta^k$, observations $\underline{X}_k = (X_1, X_2, \ldots, X_k)$ distributed as $P_{\underline{\theta}_k} = P_{\theta_1} \times P_{\theta_2} \times \ldots \times P_{\theta_k} \in P^k$ and θ_k is to be classified. The loss matrix L^k is $m^k \times n$ with $L^k(\underline{\theta}_k, a) = L(\theta_k, a)$.

Let $R^k(\underline{\theta}_k, \varphi)$ denote the risk of a decision rule φ in the Γ^k decision problem at state $\underline{\theta}_k$. Then

$$R^k(\underline{\theta}_k, \varphi) = E[L(\theta_k, \varphi_j(\underline{X}_k))] = \int [\sum_{j=1}^{n} L(\theta_k, j) \; \varphi_j(\underline{x}_k) f_{\underline{\theta}_k}(\underline{x}_k) d\mu^k(\underline{x}_k)$$

where $f_{\underline{\theta}_k}(\underline{x}_k) = \prod_{i=1}^{k} f_{\theta_i}(x_i)$.

Letting $R^k(G,\varphi)$ denote the Bayes risk of φ versus a prior G on θ^k, we have

$$R^k(G,\varphi) = \int \{ \sum_{j=1}^{n} \varphi_j(\underline{x}_k) [\sum_{\theta_k} L(\theta_k,j) f_{\theta_k}(\underline{x}_k) G_{\theta_k}] \} d\mu^k(\underline{x}_k). \qquad (4)$$

The Bayes envelope in the Γ^k decision problem is given by

$$R^k(G) = \inf_{\varphi} R^k(G,\varphi).$$

From (4) it follows that a Γ^k Bayes rule has all of its mass placed on the j's which minimize $\Delta_j(\underline{x}_k)$, where

$$\Delta_j(\underline{x}_k) = \sum_{\theta_k} L(\theta_k,j) f_{\theta_k}(\underline{x}_k) G_{\theta_k}. \qquad (5)$$

The criterion for the classification rules is minimizing the risk and the concept of the Γ^k decision problem is useful for constructing rules for this purpose. The rules thus obtained will be termed extended rules. Since $\{\theta_i\}$ is assumed to be a Markov chain we consider Γ^3 Bayes rules. For the application of Γ^3 to the compound decision problem the θ_i are grouped as $\underline{\theta}_i^3 = (\theta_{i-1}, \theta_{i+1}, \theta_i)$ with θ_i to be classified. For each $\{\theta_i\}$ and n let G_{n-1}^3 be the empirical distribution of $\underline{\theta}_2^3, \underline{\theta}_3^3, \ldots, \underline{\theta}_n^3$. The loss function considered is $L(\theta,a) = [\theta \neq a]$.

For the Γ^3 decision problem, the state space

$$\theta^3 = \{(i, j, k): i, j, k = 0, 1\}$$

and we let $p^3 = \{p_{ijk}: i, j, k = 0, 1\}$ be a probability measure on θ^3. In this case (5) gives the Γ^3 Bayes rule versus p^3 as

$$d_2: \text{ decide } \quad \theta_\ell = \begin{cases} 1 \\ 0 \end{cases} \quad \text{if}$$

$$f_1(X_\ell) \sum_{i=0}^{1} \sum_{k=0}^{1} p_{i1k} f_i(X_{\ell-1}) f_k(X_{\ell+1}) \overset{\geq}{<} f_0(X_\ell) \sum_{i=0}^{1} \sum_{k=0}^{1} p_{i0k} f_i(X_{\ell-1}) f_k(X_{\ell+1}).$$

The estimation of the Γ^3 Bayes rules, d_2, versus empirics in the compound problem depends on the construction of estimates for G^3_{n-1}. The estimates for these empirical distributions are then plugged in place of $\underline{p}^3$ yielding extended compound Bayes rules, ER3. We follow Hannan [6], Robbins [9], Van Ryzin [11] and Ballard [1] in the construction of unbiased estimates, and use Robbins [9] kernel function $\underline{r}(x) = (r_0(x), r_1(x))$ where $r_0(x) = \frac{1}{2}(1 - x)$ and $r_1(x) = \frac{1}{2}(1 + x)$ to produce estimators for the components of G^3_{n-1} as follows:

$$\hat{G}^3_{n-1;ijk} = \frac{1}{n-1} \sum_{\alpha=2}^{n} r_i(X_{\alpha-1}) r_j(X_\alpha) r_k(X_{\alpha+1}) , \quad n \geq 2 . \tag{6}$$

These estimators are unbiased and consistent for the components of G^3_{n-1}. The extended compound rule ER3 is formed by substituting (6) for p_{ijk} in d_2 and letting $\ell = 2, 3, \ldots, n$.

5. Simulations and Results

In our simulation studies the $\underline{\theta}$ sequence was generated as a Markov chain with parameters (p, δ). A total of 84 different combinations of (p, δ) were considered. The observables X_i were generated as $X_i = Z_i + 2\theta_i - 1$, where Z_i, $(i = 1, 2, \ldots, n+1)$ is i.i.d. standard normal . For each (p, δ), 100 replications were performed with $n = 50$ and $n = 200$.

In 100 simulations for each of 84 different (p, δ) combinations, in all the cases ER3 rules have a higher PCC than the EMAP rule. In simulations with $n = 50$ components the improvement of ER3 over EMAP rule, denoted IMP ER3 [= PCC of ER3 - PCC of EMAP] has a mean of 8.70 with standard deviation 4.47. In simulations with $n = 200$ components IMP ER3 has a mean of 10.42 with standard deviation 7.34. See Gunawardena [5] for more details.

REFERENCES

[1] R. J. Ballard. *Extended rules for the sequence compound decision problem with m×n component.* Ph.D. dissertation, Department of Statistics and Probability, Michigan State University, East Lansing, 1974.

[2] R. J. Ballard and D. C. Gilliland. *On the risk of performance of extended sequence compound rules for classification between N(-1,1) and N(1,1).* J. Stat. Comput. Simul., vol 6, pp 265-280, 1978.

[3] T. M. Cover and A. Shenhar. *Compound Bayes predictors for sequences with apparent Markov structure.* IEEE Trans. Syst., Man, Cybern., vol SMC-7, pp 421-424, June, 1977.

[4] D. Gilliland and J. Hannan. *On the extended compound decision problem.* Ann. Math. Statis., vol 40, pp 1536-1541, 1969.

[5] K. L. D. Gunawardena. *Extended rules for the classification of dependent parameters.* Ph. D. dissertation, Department of Statistics and Probability, Michigan State University, East Lansing, 1988.

[6] J. Hannan. *Approximations to Bayes risk in repeated play.* Contributions to the Theory of Games, vol 3, pp 9-139, 1957.

[7] J. Raviv. *Decision making in Markov chains applied to the problem of pattern recognition.* IEEE Trans. Inform. Theory, vol IT-3, pp 536-551, Oct, 1967.

[8] J. Raviv. *Decision making in incompletely known stochastic systems.* Int. J. Engng. Sci., vol. 3, pp 119-140, 1965.

[9] H. Robbins. *Asymptotically subminimax solutions of compound statistical decision problems.* Proc. Second Berkeley Symp. Math. Stat. Probability, Berkley, CA, University of California Press, pp 131-148, 1951.

[10] L. L. Scharf and H. Elliott. *Aspects of dynamic programming in signal and image processing.* IEEE Trans. Automat. Control. vol AC-26, pp 1018-1029, Oct 1981.

[11] J. Van Ryzin. *The compound decision problem with m×n finite loss matrix.* Ann. Math. Statist.,vol 37, pp 412-424, 1966.

[12] S. Vardeman. *Admissible solutions of k-extended finite set and sequence compound decision problems.* Journ. Multivariate Anal., vol 10, pp 426-441, 1980.

[13] S. Vardeman. *On the small N performance of bootstrap and Bayes extended and unextended set compound rules for classification between N(-1,1) and N(1,1).* J. Statist. Comput. Simul., vol 13, pp 255-271, 1981.

REAL-TIME PARAMETER CONTROL IN SPACE VEHICLES: A PARALLEL ARCHITECTURE AND THE PROTOCOLS

Sarma R. Vishnubhotla

Department of Computer Science and Engineering
Oakland University, Rochester, Michigan 48309-4401

ABSTRACT: *A parallel processor architecture is presented in this paper for the real-time engine and vehicle guidance control in a modern spacecraft. The system is designed to be fault-tolerant and will give diagnostic messages to aid repair. The architecture is based on the multiple shared bus concept. Multiple buses increase fault-tolerance and will enable computation of complex control equations within the required time frame. Each processor stage has a priority queue and any process that requires processing is inserted into the priority queue, if the current process under execution has a higher priority than the new process. Protocols are designed to run various routines on different processor stages under a prioritized system.*

1. INTRODUCTION

Space vehicle control requires computation of complex equations in real-time. These equations depend upon numerous dynamic parameters. These computations become more complex by the severity of time requirements. The possibility of some processors, buses, sensor units, bus controllers etc., developing hardware faults will add another dimension to the challenge of multiprocessor design. There are numerous operations within a spacecraft that require dynamic controlling. Sometimes these operations are unrelated at the actuator level, even though they might share the data measured by the sensory system. Computational needs aboard a spacecraft are extremely critical both for successful completion of the mission and the safety of the personnel aboard the vehicle. Among the many units to be controlled, some may not be directly connected to each other. For example, there are a set of engine controls and vehicle guidance related controls. These two sets of controls are related. There are other controls such as the life support system control, temperature and pressure controls, processing of the fluids, lighting controls, and controls to conduct various commercial and military experiments etc. These operations are not related to the engine and guidance controls.

System engineers have been debating whether it is prudent to have one larger fault-tolerant computer system for all the controls aboard the spacecraft or to have many smaller independent computer systems for the control of various unrelated operations. Some of these operations may be large enough to warrant a dedicated computer system, while others are not. For example, engine control and vehicle guidance are both related, complex, and important enough to warrant a dedicated computer system [1,2]. Controls such as internal lighting, temperature and pressure controls, entertainment etc., can all be controlled by one computer system. Similarly there can be different computer systems for the controls of various experiments. Studies on multiprocessor architectures have shown [3] that the over all system efficiency will come to a saturation as the number of processors increase. Instruction and data transfers and the limitations of a shared bus will act as a bottle neck, causing system saturation.

Providing parallel buses will increase the efficiency. There is another important factor against the use of one centralized system. Most controls use the parameter values measured by the sensory system [4,5,6]. A centralized computer system would require that wires are run throughout the spacecraft, bringing the measured data from the sensor units to the central processor. Experience has shown that this is highly prone to errors. We will therefore assume that different computer systems are used for unrelated sets of controls. Throughout this paper we shall assume that the multiprocessor system to be designed is intended for engine control and vehicle guidance.

2. ARCHITECTURE DECISIONS

While deciding upon the system architecture, the real-time computational demands on the system are to be analyzed first. The system must be able to monitor the sensor data, activate various software routines, execute them, and send the results to the actuators fast enough during the most critical times. Faults may develop in the computer system, or in various data paths from sensor units to the computer system and from the computer system to the actuators. In view of the importance of the controls, maximum fault-tolerance must be provided. The speed of computation of equations depend upon their complexity, which in turn depends upon factors such as the number of parameters, size of the vehicle, speed of the vehicle etc. During normal course of the vehicle, control equations are computed at some frequency. At critical times, these computations must be completed within a time frame. It is the time frame that is most crucial and it is for this reason, we have to go to a multiprocessor system.

2.1　Fault-tolerance requirements

The sensory system measures various parameter values, digitizes them and sends the readings to the computer system. If a sensor unit fails, the computer system will have an important parameter missing. In automobiles, the system will use a default value in such a case. But in spacecraft control, a default value may not be of much use. Normally some fault-tolerance is provided by simply using many replicas of the same sensor and comparing the data measured by these units using coincidence circuitry [7]. Each unit will have a valid line, which is activated when the value measured by this unit coincides with the maximum number of measurements. Otherwise this line will be turned off. During diagnostic phase, the address of each unit with an invalid signal will be printed.

Each processor is supplemented by identical replicas of the processor to form a processor stage. All processors within a stage will simultaneously execute the same code. The values produced by various processors are continuously compared and the values of maximum coincidence are taken as valid. The units producing invalid values are marked invalid . During diagnostic phase, addresses of these faulty processors are printed. Faults may develop in bus arbitration circuits, bus controllers etc. Parallel buses are provided to increase the system performance and this will also add to the fault-tolerance.

2.2   Analysis of Parameters

The parameters influencing the engine control and guidance system may be classified as 1) Engine parameters, 2) Guidance parameters, and 3) ride parameters. All these are dynamic parameters and are continuously monitored by the computer system through the sensory system.

Engine Parameters: All parameters such as temperature and pressure measurements, fuel consumption rates etc., fall into this category.

Guidance Parameters: All parameters related to maintaining the course of the vehicle fall into this category. Vehicle guidance is implemented by continuously computing the error in the vehicle course. This error is a measure of the deviation of the present path from the desired path. The engine will get the commands to increase or decrease the fuel consumption, to accelerate or decelerate the vehicle respectively, or to change the vehicle course, depending on the error value.

Ride parameters: These parameters are related to the smoothness of the journey. Sudden fluctuations in the vehicle direction, wobbling etc fall into this category.

3. SYSTEM ARCHITECTURE AND PROTOCOLS

The organization of processor stages, shared memory modules, and the multiprocessor system architecture are presented in this section.   Consider the organization given in Figure 1. P1, P2, ..., Pm are m processor stages.   M1, M2,...., Mk are k shared memory modules. B1, B2, ..., Bq are q parallel buses. The sensor data comes to the processors either through a dedicated bus. The computed values will go to various actuators through demultiplexers, from one of the shared buses. All built-in routines are stored in ROM areas of the memory modules.   Shared memory modules and processor stages communicate through multiple shared buses.   All high priority computations that may have to be executed simultaneously during crucial times are stored in different memory modules.   Parallel sections within a computation are also stored in different memory modules so that if some free processor stages are available, then these sections can be executed simultaneously. All sections of software are prioritized.

3.1 Priority Queue

There is a priority queue associated with each processor stage. Each routine to be executed by the processor stage is considered as an interrupt service routine. When a request to execute a routine arrives into a processor stage, the request will be processed immediately if the processor stage is free. If it is not free, then the priority of the new process is compared against the priority of the current process being executed. If the new process has a lower priority than the current process, then the new process is inserted into the priority queue. Otherwise, the current process is interrupted, and the new process is executed. There can be different implementations for this. For example, in some implementations the current process is not interrupted, and the new process is started only after the execution of the current process is completed. The advantage of this method is that the profile of hardware registers holding partially computed values of the current process need not be saved for eventual restoration. However, the time frame of execution of the new process must permit this delay caused by waiting for the completion

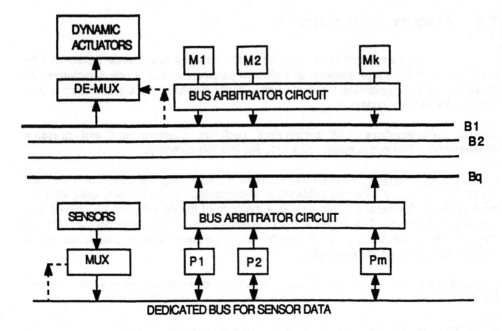

Figure 1., Multiple Shared Bus Architecture for Engine Control and Vehicle Guidance

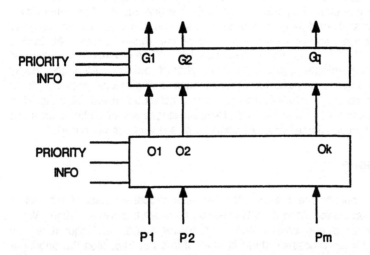

Figure 2., Intelligent Bus Arbitrator Circuit to Connect m Processors to q Buses

of the current process. If such a delay is not permitted, then current process is interrupted, the hardware profile is saved on the stack, and the new process is started.

3.2 Shared Bus Architecture

The architecture shown in Figure 1, is a shared multiple bus architecture. A single shared bus architecture can support up to 15 processor stages. Beyond this number, the bus contention might become so severe that further increase in the number of processors will not add proportionally to the system efficiency. Multiple bus architecture will provide better throughput and facilitate fault-tolerance as explained earlier. We further assume that each processor has adequate instruction cache and private memory. The sensory data can be transferred to the private memories of each processor stage through a dedicated bus.

When a processor (say P1) is executing a routine, it may have to use the data computed by another processor (say P2). Assume that P2 has written the new data into the RAM area of memory module M2. If P2 is still busy with the computation, then the process on P2 will be interrupted, if the process on P1 has higher priority. Otherwise P1 waits until P2 completes the execution. If both processes on P1 and P2 need the data in a memory module simultaneously, then which ever has higher priority will get the data first and the other request will be queued and processed later.

Priority bus arbitrators are used to connect memory modules to processors. For example, if all processors want M1, then they send the request to the arbitrator circuit, which will select the processor executing the highest priority process. Now, one of the multiple buses should be allocated to connect these two units, and there are only q buses. If a bus is free, then it will be allocated. Otherwise, a low priority transfer is interrupted and the bus is allocated for the higher priority transfer. This architecture uses a bus arbitrator with m inputs and k outputs. The m inputs come from the m processors and the k outputs correspond to the k highest priority requests. However, only q of these k requests can be connected to the buses at a given time. Another priority bus arbitrator with k inputs and q outputs is used to select the q highest priority processes. Figure 2 shows such a priority bus arbitrator organization. The first stage m inputs come from the m processor stages P1, ..., Pm. O1, O2, ..., Ok correspond to the k highest priority requests among the m requests. Another priority bus arbitrator circuit with k inputs O1, O2, ..., Ok and q outputs G1, G2, ..., Gq is used to select the q highest priority processes among the k highest priority processes. The k shared memory modules are connected to the q buses through another k input q output bus arbitrator. It should be noted that we are assuming that k > q , which is normally the case. These priority values are stored in the ROM and are read from the ROM locations at cold start. From this point onwards, these values can change dynamically with the changes in the environment.

3.3 System Operation

Consider Figure 1. One of the processor stages is used as a central processor stage (CPS). This is responsible for executing the kernel of the real-time software based on the sensory data, to allocate various processes to the free processors, keeping track of the computed values, and routing these values to various dynamic actuators through a set of demultiplexers. If the CPS becomes unreliable, then a default program is activated to run on another processor and mean while another processor is chosen as the new CPS. There is a dedicated line in the bus called "CPS active" (CPA). This line will be high so long as the CPS is active. If this line is turned off for some reason, a watchdog timer becomes active and counts for how long the CPS remains inactive. When the count reaches a level, the system decides that the current CPS is unreliable and another processor stage is chosen as the new CPS. Thus, this architecture assures that the engine and guidance control operations still continue, at a degraded level. The level of degradation caused by one inoperative processor stage will be smaller for larger values of m.

A processor status register (PSR) with one bit for each processor stage, is stored in the memory. A bit is **zero** if the corresponding processor stage is not busy and the bit is **one** otherwise. The CPS will dynamically alter these values as processor stages become busy and free. When the CPS decides to allocate a process to a processor, the value of the corresponding bit in the PSR register will indicate whether the processor stage is busy or not. When the CPS wishes to allocate a process to Pi, the protocol is as follows.

1. Let Pi be free. Pi is interrupted, the starting address of the routine to be executed is passed through one of the buses, and ith bit of PSR is set to **one**. If this process is not further interrupted, then at the end of execution of the current process, Pi will check the priority queue for processes waiting for Pi. If this queue is empty, then it becomes free and the ith bit of PSR is reset to **zero**. If the queue is not empty, then it will start executing the next process in the queue and the PSR ith bit will remain **one**. If the process itself is interrupted by a higher priority process then all hardware registers are saved, control given to the new process and the control is passed back to the interrupted process after the execution of the high priority process is completed. This architecture permits many levels of such interruption, the depth being limited only by the stack space.

2. Let no processor be free. The CPS will check whether any processor is executing a process of lower priority. If so, it will interrupt this process and will execute the new process. If all processors are busy with processes of higher priority, then it will enter the new process in the priority queue of a processor stage whose process has a priority nearest to the new process.

The CPS also checks all other processors, bus controllers, bus segments etc., to determine whether they are functioning properly or not. Diagnostic tables are maintained in the memory, to keep track of the faulty nature of the units, if any. This diagnostic information is printed and the technicians can use this information to replace the faulty units.

4. CONCLUSION

Multiple shared bus architecture is chosen because money is not the primary concern in the space applications and reliability is. There are many hardware and software implementations for fault-tolerance. It is normal to run programs written with different algorithms for the same computation and to compare the results for software fault-tolerance. In the hardware fault-tolerance, it is not necessary that the readings of majority of stages should coincide. It is acceptable to select the values of maximum coincidence, provided the number of values coinciding is not below a predefined lower bound. This will be reliable because it is very unlikely that erroneous values will coincide at all.

REFERENCES

[1]. "Engine and Drive-line Control Systems", Published by SAE, SP-739, March 1988.

[2]. R. Kober and C. Kuznia, "SMS-A Multiprocessor Architecture for High Speed Numerical Calculations", Proc. of the 1978 International conf. on Parallel processing, pp 18-23, 1978.

[3]. K. Hwang and F. Briggs, "Computer Architecture and Parallel Processing", McGraw-Hill, 1984.

[4]. Kamal N. Majeed, "Dual Processor Automotive Controller", Proc. of Workshop on Automotive Applications of Electronics, pp 39-44, October 19, 1989, Dearborn, Michigan.

[5]. Sarma R. Vishnubhotla and Syed M. Mahmud, "A Centralized Multiprocessor-based control to Optimize Performance in Complex Vehicles", Proc. of Workshop on Automotive Applications of Electronics, pp 52-56, October 19, 1989, Dearborn, Michigan.

[6]. S. Ganesan and R. P. Sharma, "Engine Control using DSP Microprocessors", The eleventh Annual Fall Technical Conf. of the ASME, pp 105-110, October 15-18, 1989, Warren, Michigan.

[7]. F. Ozguner and M. L. Kao, "A Re-configurable Multiprocessor Architecture for Reliable Control of Robotic Systems", IEEE Int. Conf. on Robotics and Automation, pp 802-806, 1985.

A MICROINSTRUCTION BASED PROCEDURE TO DIAGNOSE HARDWARE FAILURES IN INDUSTRIAL ROBOTS

Sarma R. Vishnubhotla
Department of Computer Science and Engineering
Oakland University, Rochester, Michigan 48309-4401

ABSTRACT: *Modern industrial robots contain substantial amount of electronic hardware both analog and digital. When an internal hardware fault develops, robot operations will be adversely effected. This paper presents three different diagnostic strategies, to locate hardware faults at the lowest replaceable integrated circuit level. First method is based on enumerating all paths in the circuit and designing test sequences for each path enumerated. Second method is based on identifying sets of test sequences with individual microinstructions of the robot controller and designing microinstruction routines for diagnosis. Third method is based on running software routines, designed exclusively to move the robot arm through pre-defined diagnostic moves. The data during these dummy arm movements are collected and compared with the expected data. Discrepancies between these two data sets will yield another set of diagnostic information. Diagnostic information obtained from each method is refined using the information from the other methods to give the fault location information at the desired level. In the presence of multiple faults, these three methods are applied repeatedly, after replacing the faulty chip located during the previous application.*

1. INTRODUCTION

In a robot system, any deviation of the arm movement from the desired profile is called an abnormality. Some examples are [1]: end-effector unable to close/open the grip, failure to synchronize arm movements with the movement of parts, motors stuck at joints, failures in servo loops, missing parts, etc. Some of these abnormalities are due to hardware failures, some due to unexpected environment, and the rest due to both. Abnormalities due to unexpected environment are called operational errors [2,3,4], and robot arm can be recovered from these abnormalities by running appropriate error recovery routines. Missing part, disorientation of part or tool, misfit or faulty part etc. fall into the category of operational errors. There can be no error recovery if there is a hardware failure. Some of these failures are, faults in the sensory units/paths, faults in motors, wires getting stuck at zero (s-a-0) or at one (s-a-1), signal decay in analog circuitry etc. The only hardware faults that are easily visible are motors getting stuck. We assume that such faults are repaired before going into the diagnostic phase.

Traditionally, stuck-at-type fault models were considered adequate for most of the hardware fault diagnosis work [5,6,7,8]. However, in robot hardware, the circuits are hybrid. For example, if the fault is due to a decaying signal measured by a sensor unit, then it does not fall under the stuck-at-type model. This signal when digitized by the A/D convertor, may represent an unexpected reading different from readings caused by either s-a-0 or s-a-1 faults. The present method will at least identify the paths along which signals are decaying due to a hardware failure.

228

An **abnormality handler(AH)** hardware unit works in conjunction with the robot controller for diagnosis. When a set of point-to-point end-effector readings deviate from the set of values that define the trajectory beyond the tolerance limits, an abnormality is detected, and the control is passed from the robot controller to the AH. The first task of the AH is to determine whether the abnormality is due to an operational error or due to a hardware failure. If it is due to a hardware failure, then it will stop all robot application tasks, retract the arms to safe positions and will activate the off-line diagnostic phase which is the main topic of this paper. Otherwise, it will activate the built-in error recovery routines that are written at different levels of the software development [3,4]. The AH must have adequate intelligence to distinguish between these two types of abnormalities. This is provided by the sensory system. For example, consider the case when the controller fails to receive a reading from a camera indicating that a part has come to the station. This indicates an abnormality. But this may be due to either a missing part or due to a hardware failure either in the camera or in the paths that take the camera readings to the controller. Suppose there is another camera on the conveyor belt mounting. If this camera also fails to read the presence of a part, then it is very probable that the abnormality is due to a missing part. In this case, appropriate error recovery routines are activated. Once the service of these routines is completed, the AH will pass the control back to the robot controller. On the other hand, if the camera on the conveyor belt does read a part, then it is very likely that the failure is in the hardware. The flowchart in Figure 1, explains how these two types of abnormalities are distinguished. Intelligent sensory system will not only give robot the ability to handle more complex tasks, it will help diagnosis also.

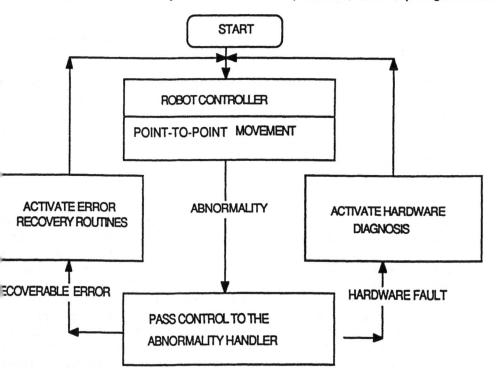

Figure 1., Distinguishing Recoverable Errors from Hardware Faults

2. ANALYSIS OF DIAGNOSIS PROBLEM

The software for various robot tasks are run on an external computer system. These software routines are compiled, optimized and loaded into the robot controller for execution. These lowest level routines are run by the controller. In the event of an abnormality, the AH will decide whether it is due to a recoverable error or a hardware fault. If it is due to a hardware fault, it will retract the robot arms to safe positions and will go into an off-line diagnostic phase. During the diagnostic phase, we assume the following:

1. No motors are stuck at any joints.
2. There are no software errors.
3. Controller, AH, and the external computer are fault-tolerant
4. All hardware faults are deterministic, i.e., once a fault develops, it remains in the circuit until repaired.
5. The faults, single or multiple are detectable, i.e., the fault must cause an abnormal robot behavior at least once, or equivalently, the fault must cause erroneous output to at least one unit. In other words, we shall exclude the faults on redundant wires.
6. All faults in the digital circuitry are stuck-at type. This need not be the case for analog circuitry. For example, consider an amplifier stage not being able to boost sensor signal adequately. This is not a stuck-at type fault. Such cases are also located by the present strategy.

3. DIAGNOSIS PROCEDURE

We shall classify the robot circuits into two classes, end-effector circuits and sensor circuits. End-effector circuits are those that will take the values supplied by the controller to various end-effectors. Values coming through the controller output ports are the inputs and the analog values supplied to the end-effectors are the outputs to these circuits. If there is a hardware fault in these circuits, some of the end-effector moves will be erroneous. For sensor circuits, the analog values measured by the sensors are the inputs and the digitized version of these readings that are sent to the controller input ports are the outputs. Controller will read erroneous sensor readings, if there is a hardware fault in these circuits or in the end-effector circuits.

The diagnosis procedure consists of three distinct approaches. Diagnostic information obtained by these three approaches are superimposed to extract the lowest level fault location information. The **first** method is based on enumerating all paths in the circuit along which signals flow from the controller to the end-effectors and from the sensor units to the controller. Test sequences are built based on the structure of these paths. A set of test sequences are identified with each path and are used to check the path for correct operation. The **second** method is based on using the same test sequences built in the first method and identifying them with various microinstructions of the controller. Diagnostic routines are written at the microinstruction level. All test sequences associated with a microinstruction are applied to the circuit when this microinstruction is active and the diagnostic information is gathered. The **third** method is based on using a different type of diagnostic software. This software is designed to a). force the end-effectors through dummy moves designed exclusively for diagnostic purposes and b). to send fake sensor values to the sensor circuits and to compare the measured values with the expected values.

$.1 Path Enumeration Method

All paths in the circuit are enumerated [6,7,8] and test sequences are built or each path by sensitizing the path. These test sequences are used to check each path for correct operation. Let $P1$, $P2$, ..., Pn be n paths in the circuit and let Pi has ti test sequences. The set of all single faults detected by a test sequence is called its range and the union of these ranges of ti will give the range of Pi. It should be noted that the range of Pi will include some of the faults not in Pi besides all the detectable faults in Pi. During the diagnostic phase, the ti test sequences are applied to the circuit if Pi is one of the suspected paths.

Consider the simple combinational circuit shown in figure 2. There are four paths, $P1 = (1,5,7)$; $P2 = (2,5,7)$; $P3 = (3,6,7)$; and $P4 = (4,6,7)$. $c1$ and $c2$ are two micro signals and a and b are some data values. There are seven wires numbered from 1 to 7 giving fourteen faults $f1$, $f2$, ... , $f14$ as follows.

fi is the s-a-0 fault on wire numbered i, if $i <= 7$, and
fi is the s-a-1 fault on wire numbered $(i - 7)$, if $i > 7$.

The 5 test patterns $t1$, $t2$, $t3$, $t4$, and $t5$ will locate all single faults in this circuit.

$t1 : c1\ a\ b\ c2 = 0\ 1\ 0\ 1$ $t2 : c1\ a\ b\ c2 = 1\ 1\ 0\ 1$ $t3: c1\ a\ b\ c2 = 1\ 0\ 0\ 1$
$t4 : c1\ a\ b\ c2 = 0\ 1\ 1\ 1$ $t5 : c1\ a\ b\ c2 = 1\ 0\ 1\ 0$

The matrix in the table 1 is the fault dictionary. There is a row for each distinguishable group of faults and there is a column for each of the test patterns. The entry at ith row and jth column is zero, if the fault(s) in the ith row is not detected by tj. Otherwise, the entry will be a one. Let $r1$, $r2$, $r3$, and $r4$ be the ranges of $P1$, $P2$, $P3$, and $P4$ respectively.

$r1 = \{(f1,\ f2,\ f5),\ f7,\ f8,\ f10,\ (f12,\ f13,\ f14)\}$
$r2 = \{(f1,\ f2,\ f5),\ f7,\ f9,\ f10,\ (f12,f13,f14)\}$
$r3 = \{(f3,\ f4,\ f6),\ f7,\ f9,\ f10,\ (f12,\ f13,\ f14)\}$
$r4 = \{(f3,\ f4,\ f6),\ f7,\ f9,\ f11,\ (f12,\ f13,\ f14)\}$

.2 Microinstruction based method

The circuit in figure 2 has two control signal inputs $c1$ and $c2$. This method is based on identifying a set of test sequences with each microinstruction. It should be noted that some microinstructions may activate more than one control signal at a time. All test sequences associated with a microinstruction I will have all control signals associated with i active. The union of the fault ranges of the test sequences of a microinstruction will form the range of the microinstruction. The location of the faults in these ranges may be spread all over the hardware and may not include all the faults in any path. In other words, the ranges of paths and the microinstructions will be pair wise incomparable. Microinstruction level routines are designed exclusively for diagnosis. These routines are designed so that a microinstruction will remain active while all the test sequences associated with this microinstruction are applied one by one to the circuit. Once this is completed the next microinstruction is activated and so on. The disparities in the monitored and expected output values will indicate the occurrence of faults in the range of the microinstruction.

In the example of figure 2, patterns $(t2, t3, t5)$ are associated with $c1$, ($t1$, , $t3$, $t4$) are associated with $c2$, and $(t2, t3)$ with both $c1$ and $c2$. There must be

microinstructions that will activate c1 and c2 simultaneously, besides activating them on
at a time. Let i1, i2, and i3 be the microinstructions that activates c1, c2 and both c1 an
c2, respectively.The ranges R1, R2, and R3 of i1, i2, and i3 respectively are as follows.

$$R1 = \{(f1, f2, f5), f7, f9, f10, f11, (f12, f13, f14)\}$$
$$R2 = \{(f1, f2, f5), (f3, f4, f6), f7, f8, f9, f10, (f12, f13, f14)\}$$
$$R3 = \{(f1, f2, f5), f7, f9, f10, (f12, f13, f14)\}$$

Table 1., A Fault Dictionary

FAULTS	t1	t2	t3	t4	t5
f1,f2,f5	0	1	0	0	'
f3,f4,f6	0	0	0	1	'
f7	0	1	0	1	'
f8	1	0	0	0	'
f9	0	0	1	0	
f10	1	0	1	0	'
f11	0	0	0	0	
f12,f13,f14	1	0	1	0	

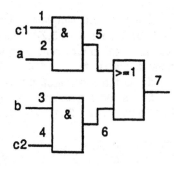

Figure 2., A Simple Logic Circuit

3.3 End-effector movement method

This method consists of two strategies, one for the end-effector circuits an
the other for the sensor circuits. For end-effector circuits, mechanical movements ar
designed for each end-effector such that it is taken through the full range of its motion alon
all axes over which the end-effector movements are defined. The sensors read the value
during these movements and are fed back to the controller. When there are no faults, th
sensor readings will correspond to the expected readings within the tolerances. In th
presence of a fault, the measurements during at least one motion of an end-effector must b
adversely effected. Each movement of an end-effector is divided into a well defined sequenc
of sub-motions. All hardware paths that could possibly cause an error in a sub-motion ar
identified with the sub-motion. During the diagnostic phase, erroneous paths are identifie
by identifying the erroneous sub-motions. Erroneous sub-motions are identified when th
values sent back to the controller during a sub-motion do not correspond to the expecte
values. The most important thing in this method is that the set of movements must b
complete in the sense that no robot movement outside this set is defined. Software i
designed for each sub-motion and the corresponding paths are stored in the diagnostic table
of the AH's ROM. When this software is executed, values generated by it are sent to th
relevant end-effector(s) through D/A convertor(s). The magnitude of the movement mus
correspond to the value supplied. In other words, there is a one-to-one correspondenc
between the values and the extent of the end-effector move.

The above method will also check the paths of sensor circuits indirectly
because the movements of the end-effectors are continuously monitored by the sensor units
These values are sent back to the controller through A/D convertors. However, when th
controller receives an erroneous value back from the sensors, the error may be due to
fault in the end-effector circuits or in the sensor circuits or both. The first task is t

determine which of the two types of the circuits has the fault. The AH will disengage
sensors from rest of the circuitry electronically and will send predetermined analog
values as inputs to the sensor circuitry. If the values monitored by the AH correspond to
the correct values, then no fault is assumed in any of the corresponding paths. Otherwise
one of these paths must contain a fault. This process is repeated at every sensor unit and the
set of all suspicious paths are listed.

4. ABNORMALITY HANDLER ORGANIZATION AND DIAGNOSIS

During the diagnostic phase, the AH will serve as the master and the robot
controller as the slave. All paths in the circuits, their ranges, test sequences, their ranges,
all microinstructions, their ranges, all microinstruction level routines for diagnosis, all
software routines to move end-effectors for diagnosis, the parameters that will determine
the magnitude of the analog signals needed to test the sensor circuits, various fault
dictionaries etc., are all stored in the AH ROM. The AH unit will also have access to the
controller so that while running the diagnostic software, it can use the hardware resources
of the controller. The schematic of AH is given in figure 3.

The third method explained in section 3.3 is applied first. All erroneous
movements, and the movements end-effectors were unable to make are listed in the AH RAM.
The paths identified by this method are further tested by the test sequences built for them as
explained in section 3.1. Finally, the microinstruction level diagnostic routines are
executed and ranges of the microinstructions containing faults are marked. The diagnostic
information gathered is now pooled by the AH to locate the faulty chips. The main technique
used is the principle of inclusion and exclusion which is used for any fault dictionary
construction. While this method works for single faults, there are problems when there are
multiple faults especially in the same path or in the related paths. Some times these faults

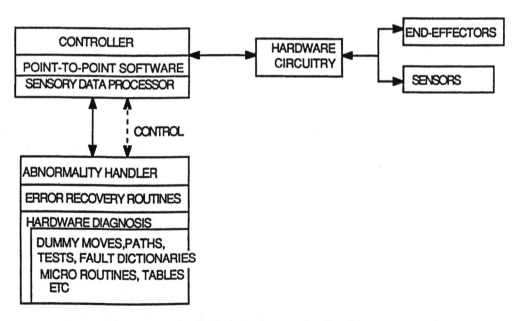

Figure 3., Organization of Abnormality Handler

may nullify each other with respect to the test sequences chosen, while for some other input values they may not. The path enumeration technique [6,7,8] will address this problem. It has been shown that the test sequences built will detect all multiple faults also. However, multiple faults will some times behave in such a way that a fault on a wire can not even be detected unless the fault(s) masking this are first repaired. Consequently, the diagnostic methods given in section 3 may have to be applied many times adaptively in order to locate all faults.

Faults such as the decay in analog signals can also be located by these methods. For example, if the signal in a end-effector path is decaying, then the end-effector move will be erroneous as measured by the sensors. However, the AH can not determine whether the decay is in this path or in the sensor circuit path feeding the sensor value back to the AH. The analog signals supplied to test the sensor circuits will first test the sensor paths. If fault is found, then it must be repaired first before the end-effector circuit path can be checked.

5. CONCLUSION

Using path enumeration method alone will make the diagnosis very tedious, as there are many hundreds of paths in a typical robot hardware. Forcing the robot to make some dummy moves for diagnostics does not require any extra hardware. The outcome will drastically reduce the area of search for faults. This area under suspicion is further refined by the diagnostic information gathered in the other two methods. The only extra hardware required for this method is the ability to generate analog signals, besides the AH unit. All the methods described in this paper are algorithms and can be automated to give valuable diagnostic information.

REFERENCES

[1]. John J. Criag, "An Introduction to Robotics", Addison Wesley, 1986.

[2]. S.R. Vishnubhotla, "An Expert System to Diagnose Failures in Industrial Robots", Proc. of Third Int. Conf. on CAD/CAM, Robotics, and Factories of the Future, Southfield, Michigan, August 1988.

[3]. M. Gini, R. Doshi, M. Gluch, R.E. Smith, and I. Zualkerman, "The Role of Knowledge in the Architecture of a Robust Robot Control", IEEE Int. Conf. on Robotics and Automation, 1985, pp 561-567.

[4]. R.E. Smith and M. Gini, "Robot Tracking and Control Issues in an Intelligent Error Recovery System", IEEE Int. Conf. on Robotics and Automation, 1986, p 1070-1075.

[5]. A. Miczo, "Digital Logic Testing and Simulation", Harper and Row, 1986.

[6]. S.R. Vishnubhotla, "Fault Diagnosis in Computer Systems", D.Sc Dissertation, May 1973, Washington University, St. Louis, Mo.

[7]. S.R. Vishnubhotla and O.D. Altan, "A Structure Based Procedure to Build Test Sequences for the Diagnosis of Asynchronous Sequential Circuits", 23rd Midwest Symp. on Circuits and Systems, University of Toledo, Ohio, pp 165-169, August 1980.

[8]. S.R. Vishnubhotla and Y.H. Chuang, "A Theory and A Procedure for the Detection of Multiple Faults in Combinational Circuits", 10th Annual Allerton Conf. on Circuit and System Theory, pp 133-142, October 1972, University of Illinois at Urbana, Illinois.

A SPECIFICATION AND VERIFICATION TOOL
FOR COMMUNICATION PROTOCOLS

Harbans Kaur, James Brown Grier and Graham Campbell
Department of Computer Science
Illinois Institute of Technology
Chicago, IL 60616

Abstract

This paper describes Protype, a prototyping tool for communication protocol specifications. The tool is based on extended finite state machine augmented with context variables and procedural information. The tool helps a protocol designer in developing error free protocols. It also helps protocol implementors in verifying protocols.

Introduction

The complexity and size of communication protocols necessitates the use of formal methods for their specification and verification. Although complete verification of the communication software is almost impossible, even partial verification that helps isolate bugs has been always found useful. Processes executing communication protocols are distributed entities whose behavior is guided by the protocol specifications. Since protocols are complex and large pieces of software and are executed on distant machines, unless formal methods are used to verify them, total chaos can reign in the system. Protocols guide the behavior of processes during their interaction with other processes. The behavior of a process depends not only on the messages received from the remote process but also on the state of the variables defining the process locally. Two popular models form specification of communication protocols are the finite state machine (FSM) model and the programming language model. Each of these methods has it's own advantages and disadvantages. Communicating processes are analogous to FSMs in their behavior and hence FSMs seem to be a natural method to represent protocols. Reachability analysis, a method used to verify FSM specifications generates state space explosion. While language models do not have this problem, a protocol specifier can very easily get into the implementation details of the protocol very early in the development stage. Hybrid models with a small state machine to capture the essence of the protocol augmented by procedural information provides the advantages of both the approaches. Readers are referred to [2,6,14] for a exhaustive reading. SDL [9], Estelle [8], Ina Jo [1], Paisley and LOTOS are some of the specification languages in use.

Finite State Machine

A finite state machine FSM, can be defined by a set of six tuples
$M = (Q,S,R,f,g,q1)$ where

Q is a finite set of internal states, S is a finite input alphabet
R is a finite output alphabet
f is the state transition function f: $Q * S \rightarrow Q$
g is the output function $g : Q * S \rightarrow R$, $q1 \in Q$ is the initial state

An FSM like the one described above where output symbols are based on transactions between states is called the Mealy automaton. The Moore automaton is another automaton where output symbols are state assigned rather than transition assigned. A state diagram is a directed graph, with each node of the digraph corresponding to each state in the state machine and the arcs between nodes corresponding to the transitions between states. If a system consists of m state machines and each can be in any of the N states, then the total number of possible states that can be generated is N^m. The state of the system will then be represented by a state vector with the states of each o. the m state machines. (q1,q1,q3,...,qm).

Communicating processes are similar in their behavior to FSMs. Their behavior depends on the messages they receive from the remote processes which are represented by remote interactions. Certain internal conditions like expiry of timers and flag values also cause change of states. These are represented by spontaneous interactions. To represent a process completely, all the parameters that define the process need to be specified in the state vector e.g. state name, channels, flags, counters. Hence communicating processes need extended finite state machines to represent them. A change in any variable changes the state vector and hence defines a different state. This escalates into state space explosion during reachability analysis, a method use fo verification of FSM specifications. For example, if the timer value can vary from 0 to 200 then other variables remaining the same, then just a change in the counter value can lead to approximately 200 different states although in a real system the possibility of just one variable changing, is quite improbable.

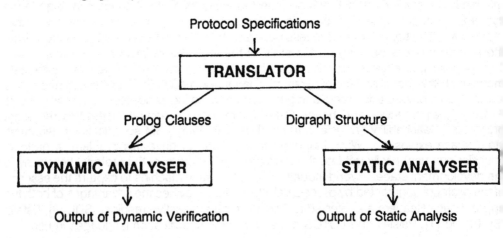

Fig. 1 Modules of Protype

Protype

Protype is a prototyping tool for communication protocols. It consists of two components, the translator and the analyser. The user specifies the protocol specifications in a user-friendly language, based on the extended FSM model. These are translated into Prolog clauses by the translator. The translator also generates a digraph representation of the protocol. These are analysed by the static analyser, the Prolog clauses are analysed by the dynamic analyser.

```
PROTOCOL_NAME poll
PROTOCOL_TYPE unbalanced
NUMBER_OF_PROCESSES 2

PROCESS_DEF node_1
STATE_NAME norm,await,reset,error
CHANNEL_NAME C12,C21
QUEUE_NAME Iq1,Oq1
SIGNAL_NAME data_req,data,i_cmd
TIMER_NAME Rt1,Pt1,Bt1,At1,Jt1
COUNTER_NAME Rc1,Rs1,Rn1,Vs1,Vr1
FLAG_NAME Pf1,Ch1,Bi1,Rb1,Si1,Ss1
END_DEF node_1

PROCESS_DEF node_2
STATE_NAME norm,await,reset,error
CHANNEL_NAME C12,C21
QUEUE_NAME Iq2,Oq2
SIGNAL_NAME data_req,data
TIMER_NAME Rt2,Pt2,Bt2,At2,Jt2
COUNTER_NAME Rc2,Rs2,Rn2,Vs2,Vr2
FLAG_NAME Pf2,Ch2,Bi2,Rb2,Si2,Ss2
END_DEF node_2

ASSERTION ((nonvar(Rc1),Rc1>2);(nonvar(Rc2),Rc2>2)),
        n1,write('Retry Counter greater than 2'),
        n1,n1,!,fail.
END_ASSERTION

PROCESS node_1
STATE norm
INPUT Msg FROM Iq1
TASK split1(Msg,M),M=data_req,nonvar(Rb1),nonvar(Pf1),Rb1=0,Pf1=0
OUTPUT ['i_cmd,Vs1,Vr1,1,0] TO C12
TASK Rn1x=0,Pflx=1,Pt1x=1,At1x=1,Id='9.2 S1'
NEXT_STATE norm
```

```
TASK nonvar(Pf1),Pf1=1
INPUT Msg FROM C21
TASK split5(Msg,M,S,R,P,F),M=rr_rsp,F=1.Pf1x=0,Pt1x=0
TASK Rn1x=R,Rc1x=0,ifrec(R,Vs1,At1x),Rb1x=0,Bt1x=0,Id='I5.2S1'
OUTPUT [not_bsy] TO Oq1
NEXT_STATE norm
                          :

END_STATE norm

END_PROCESS node_1
                          :

PROCESS node_2
                          :

END_PROTOCOL poll
```

Fig. 2 Protocol Specification in Protype Specification Language

Specification Language

The specification language of Protype is based on the hybrid model, Fig.2 has the partial specifications of the polling phase of the Triiner protocol, developed at IIT, for Metropolitan area needs. The translator translates user-specifications into Prolog clauses Fig.3. Prolog was first proposed by Sidhu [10] for verifying protocols. Prolog is a logic programming language based on Horn clauses which is a sub-set of first order predicate calculus. It provides an excellent theorem-proving mechanism with back-tracking and pattern-matching with unification. The language of Protype is based on SDL, formalized by CCITT.

Two types of protocols can be specified:
1. balanced protocol specifications, where the communicating processes have an equal peer-to-peer relationship. In this case if the specifications of one process are entered by the user, the specifications of the other process are generated by the translator.
2. unbalanced protocol specifications, where the processes have an unequal relationship. In this case, the user needs to specify the behavior of the processes himself.

Referring to Fig.2, the protocol definition is followed by the process definitions where all the parameters defining that process need to be specified. These are required to generate the Prolog clauses. The process definitions are then followed by the state transitions for each of the processes. Of special interest is the TASK definition. The procedural processing in each state goes into the TASK definition. Several predicates that we have defined and predicates that the user defines can all go into the TASK definition.

Prolog has case dependence and type independence. Both these can lead to errors in generating Prolog clauses. The translator helps eliminate many of these errors. In Fig.3

the connect predicate has two lists, the first one defines the current state of the system and the second defines the next stated of the system if the goals after ':-' are satisfied, Id defines trace of states visited, for debugging. The language also helps specify assertions that need to be true for proper functioning of the protocol. Assertions global to the protocol, assertions local to an individual process and assertions local to an individual state can be specified. States in which these assertions are not true will not be visited during reachability analysis.

PROTOCOL VERIFICATION

While the Prolog clauses generated by the translator constitute the data portion of the Prolog program, the verifier constitutes the control portion. The verifier consists of two modules, the static verification module and the dynamic verification module. The static verification module verifies the connectivity of the digraph while the dynamic verification module generates an execution trace of the Prolog clauses, using reachability analysis. Protype is a tool that helps incremental development of protocols, which is an essential requirement of large and complex systems. At each stage of development, the user can specify and verify specifications in an incremental manner and isolate errors. Static analysis should be conducted before dynamic analysis since each error encountered in the protocol can generate many more errors during reachability analysis. For example, West in [12] describes that in verification of the OSI Session Layer, 40000 states were reached, 20 errors in the protocol were discovered and each of these errors generated approximately 1000 error states. Boehm and Papaccio describe in 'Pareto Analysis' [3], that 20% of errors cause 80% of rework cost. Isolation of errors during the early development stage of the protocol, leads to lesser development costs. Static analysis checks the digraph for

- existence of a path from a given initial state to a given final state
- connectivity of the digraph that indicates reachable and non-reachable states from a given initial state.

Finding the existence of transitions that lead from an initial state to the final state should be the first step towards dynamic analysis. Although errors in static analysis always imply errors in dynamic analysis, the reverse is not true.

```
connect([STATEnode_1,C12,C21,Iq1,Oq1,Rc1,Rs1,Rn1,Vs1,Vr1,
        Pf1,Ch1,Bi1,Rb1,Si1,Ss1,Rt1,Pt1,Bt1,At1
        Jt1,STATEnode_2,Iq2,Oq2,Rc2,Rs2,Rn2,Vs2,Vr2,Pf2,
        Ch2,Bi2,Rb2,Si2,Ss2,Rt2,Pt2,Bt2,At2,Jt2],
        [STATEnode_1,C12,C21,Iq1,Oq1,Rc1,Rs1,Rn1,Vs1,Vr1,
        Pf1,Ch1,Bi1,Rb1,Si1,Ss1,Rt1,Pt1,Bt1,At1,
        Jt1,STATEnode_2,Iq2,Oq2,Rc2,Rs2,Rn2,Vs2,Vr2,Pf2,
        Ch2,Bi2,Rb2,Si2,Ss2,Rt2,Pt2,Bt2,At2,,Jt2],Id) :-
        ((nonvar(Rc1),Rc1>2);(nonvar(Rc2),Rc2>2)),
        nl,write('Retry counter greater than 2'),nl,nl,!,fail.
```

```
connect([STATEnode_1,C12,C21,Iq1,Oq1,Rc1,Rs1,Rn1,Vs1,Vr1,
        Pf1,Ch1,Bi1,Rb1,Si1,Ss1,Rt1,Pt1,Bt1,At1
        Jt1,STATEnode_2,Iq2,Oq2,Rc2,Rs2,Rn2,Vs2,Vr2,Pf2,
        Ch2,Bi2,Rb2,Si2,Ss2,Rt2,Pt2,Bt2,At2,Jt2],
        [STATEnode_1x,C12x,C21,Iq1x,Oq1,Rc1,Rs1,Rn1x,Vs1,Vr1,
        Pf1x,Ch1,Bi1,Rb1,Si1,Ss1,Rt1,Pt1x,Bt1,At1x,
        Jt1,STATEnode_2,Iq2,Oq2,Rc2,Rs2,Rn2,Vs2,Vr2,Pf2,
        Ch2,Bi2,Rb2,Si2,Ss2,Rt2,Pt2,Bt2,At2,Jt2],Id) :-
        STATEnode_1=norm,
        receive(Iq1,Msg,Iq1x),
        split1(Msg,M),M=data_req,nonvar(Rb1),nonvar(Pf1),Rb1=0,Pf1=0,
        send(C12,[[i_cmd,Vs1,Vr1,1,0]],C12x),
        Rn1x=0,Pf1x=1,Pt1x=1,At1x=1,Id='9.2 S1',
        STATEnode_1x=norm.


connect([STATEnode_1,C12,C21,Iq1,Oq1,Rc1,Rs1,Rn1,Vs1,Vr1,
        Pf1,Ch1,Bi1,Rb1,Si1,Ss1,Rt1,Pt1,Bt1,At1,
        Jt1,STATEnode_2,Iq2,Oq2,Rc2,Rs2,Rn2,Vs2,Vr2,Pf2,
        Ch2,Bi2,Rb2,Si2,Ss2,Rt2,Pt2,Bt2,At2,Jt2],
        [STATEnode_1x,C12,C21x,Iq1,Oq1x,Rc1x,Rs1,Rn1x,Vs1,Vr1,
        Pf1x,Ch1,Bi1,Rb1x,Si1,Ss1,Rt1,Pt1x,Bt1x,At1x,
        Jt1,STATEnode_2,Iq2,Oq2,Rc2,Rs2,Rn2,Vs2,Vr2,Pf2,
        Ch2,Bi2,Rb2,Si2,Ss2,Rt2,Pt2,Bt2,At2,Jt2],Id) :-
        STATEnode_1=norm,
        nonvar(Pf1),Pf1=1,
        receive(C21,Msg,C21x),
        split5(Msg,M,S,R,P,F),M=rr_rsp,F=1,Pf1x=0,Pt1x=0,
        Rn1x=R,Rc1x=0,ifrec(R,Vs1,At1x),Rb1x=0,Bt1x=0,Id='15.2 S1',
        send(Oq1,[[not_bsy]],Oq1x),
        STATEnode_1x=norm.
```

DYNAMIC ANALYSIS

Reachability analysis is the process of exploring all states that can be reached from a given initial state. FSM specifications are analysed using reachability analysis. Since the reachable states in an extended FSM can be unmanageably large, the limitation on the cpu time and on memory size make reachability analysis an undecidable problem. Different approaches have been taken to verify protocol specifications [6,13]. Protocol partitioning is used to partition a protocol into logical sub-units and each sub-unit is verified separately [2], random walkthrough approach to test complex protocols [12], use of test sequences for conformance testing [4,11]. A more recent approach for exhaustive search mechanism, is the use of parallel database machines for protocol verification [5]. Dynamic analysis in Protype helps detect livelocks, deadlocks, unspecified receptions, non-executable interactions, liveness, termination, boundedness and initialization of variables (timers, counters). We have limited state space explosion during verification by:

1. using high level abstractions of states and refining them incrementally.
2. gradually increasing number of reties from initial value of zero.
3. gradually increasing channel size from an initial value of 1.
4. focussing seach using the static representation of the digraph and pruning the digraph.
5. cutting of branches of the digraph as soon as error is encountered, to avoid error propagation.

Fig.4 gives the results of verification of a sub-set of a polling phase of Triinet. Most of the errors were detected without generation all the reachable states. Most errors encountered in this protocol were due to late arriving messages and uninitialized timers. The former was corrected by setting the timer to a reasonable value and the latter by resetting expired timers.

Total number of reachable states : 377
Reachable states with no retries : 9
Reachable states with 1 retry : 36
Reachable states with channel size 1 : 19
Reachable states with pruning (without error and reset states) : 66

Fig.4   States generated during polling phase of Triinet

CONCLUSION

A prototyping tool for specification and verification of communication protocols has been developed. The tool helps a protocol designer to incrementally develop protocols wherein the specifications are verified at each stage of modification and errors are isolated as early in the design phase as possible to enable early detection and avoid error propagation.

REFERENCES

1 Berry, D.B., "Towards a Formal Basis for the Formal Development Method and the Ina Jo Specification Language," IEEE Trans. Software Eng.,SE-13 (2), Feb. 1987, pp. 184-201.

2 Bochmann, G.V. and Chung, R.J., "A Formalized Specification of HDLC Classes of Procedures," in Proc.Nat. Telecommn.Conference, Los Angeles, CA, Dec. 1977.

3 Boehm, B.W. and Papaccio, P.N., "Understanding and Controlling Software Costs," IEEE Trans.Soft.Eng., pp.1462-1467, Oct.1988.

4 Chang, W.Y.L., Vuoung, S.T. and Ito, M.R., "An Improved Test Generation Procedure based on UIOS," in Communications, Architectures and Protocols, SIGCOMM, '89,pp.283-294, Texas, Sept.1989.

5 Frieder, O.and Herman, G.E., "Protocol Verification using Database Technology," IEEE JSAC, April 1989, Vol.7, No.3.

6 Gouda, M.G. and Yu, Y.T., "Protocol Validation by Maximal Progress State Exploration," IEEE Trans. Commn., Jan, 1984.

7 Information Processing Systems - Open Systems Interconnection, "LOTUS (formal description technique based on temporal ordering of observational behavior)," ISO 8807, International Organization for Standardization, Aug.1987.

8 ISO TC97/SC21/WG1, "Estelle - A Formal Description Technique based on an Extended State Transition Model," DP9074, May 1985.

9 Rockstrom, A. and Saracco, R., "SDL - CCITT Specification and Description Language," IEEE Trans. Commn., Vol.COM - 30, No.6, pp.1310-1318, June 1962.

10 Sidhu, D.P., "Protocol Verification via Executable Logic Specifications," in Protocol Specification, Testing and Verification, III, Rudin H. and West, C.H., Eds., North Holland, 1983, pp.237-248.

11 Sidhu, D.P. and Chang, C.S., "Probabilistic Testing of Protocols," in Communications, Architectures and Protocols, SIGCOMM '89, Texas, pp. 295-302, Sept. 1989.

12 West, C.H., "Protocol Validation in Complex Systems," in Communications, Architectures and Protocols, SIGCOMM '89, Texas, pp. 303-312, Sept.1989.

13 West, C.H. and Rubin, J., "An Improved Protocol Validation Technique," Computer Networks, Vol.6, No. 2, pp.65-74, May 1982.

14 Zave, P., "An Operational Approach to Requirement Specifications for Embedded Systems,"pp. 250-269, May 1982.

Structured On-Line Directory and File Organization

Phil G. Richards   Meng-Chun Chao

Department of Computer Science
University of Alabama in Huntsville
Huntsville, AL 35899

Abstract

This paper describes the concepts and methodologies regarding personal directory and file management. It also presents a software system (SIFO), which provides a structured environment for program developers using an on-line template that provides guidance during program initiation and modification. This system can assist both experienced and inexperienced programmers in organizing and documenting files in a structured manner.

1   Introduction

Users of mainframe computers and personal computers with a hard disk soon accumulate a large collection of files. Recalling a file that has not been accessed recently is made difficult because most operating systems accept relatively short file names and offer only a crude directory listing. If a directory is divided into subdirectories, the problem is compounded.

This problem has been discussed recently by Miastkowski [6] who described the benefits of DOS shells. Many other utilities are available to help locate lost files for personal computers by doing directory searches but if similar utilities exist for mainframe computers, they are expensive. It is our contention that, on a properly organized disk, files would be easily and efficiently located. In this paper we suggest that the problem of disk file organization is very similar to program design and apply the principles of structured programming to the problem. The change directory command has the undesirable property that it allows the user to jump between subdirectories at will and is analogous to the GOTO statement or to having multiple entry and exit points from a module in programming languages. This undesirable property could be controlled by insisting that access to a subdirectory must always be through the parent directory.

We are not concerned in this paper with the development of large software projects by teams of programmers such as Chief Programmer Team Management described by Baker [1]. Instead, we deal with the problem of file organization as encountered by individual users and small groups of semi-autonomous program-mers. Whereas large programming projects require strict adherence to procedures, individual users may put an emphasis on flexibility.

A well organized user may keep a paper record of the location of all files but a software system could not only have the computer keep a record of where files are located but also help in providing a logical structure to the whole directory. In this paper, we describe a system that guides the user in file organization and also helps the experienced user maintain a structured and documented disk. The system was developed for use in a VAX VMS programming environment where a manager supervises several programmers working on mostly individual programming assign-ments. In this environment the project supervisor faces two major problems (1) monitoring the progress of program development and, (2) employees leaving. Our system improves monitoring by allowing the manager to actually perform hands on testing. If the manager cannot find her way around a directory or run a program, she can take appropriate action. A well organized disk also helps a new employee take over.

2 Requirements

A good file organization system should have the following attributes,

1. Provide sufficient on-line documentation for the user to locate a required file knowing only the general contents of the file. This can be implemented through a combination of menus and documentation files on each subdirec-tory. For example, logging on to a system would automatically provide a menu listing of all the level 1 subdirectories and their contents. Changing di-rectory would automatically provide a similar menu for the subdirectory. This is similar to the methodology of CONTEXT [7]; an On-line Documentation System, which provides an on-line document preparation and delivery system for Control Data-supplied on-line manuals as well as user-developed manuals.

2. Help organize the directories and files in a logical manner. For example, assist in deciding when to create a new subdirectory and automatically provide a menu and documentation file for the subdirectory.

3. Provide an updating capability. The system will detect the addition of new files and changes to old files and demand updates to menus and documentation files.

4. Show relationships between files. If a number of files are related to single program or project, these relationships must be defined and documented.

5. Be flexible. The typical individual programmer may need to use several differ-ent programs or utilities (word processing, communications, integrated pro-

gram environments). Thus, a file organization system should not be unduly restrictive.

Many of the above requirements can be implemented by the user without the need for complicated software. For example, a rudimentary menu system can be implemented on a PC and VAX-VMS system by creating simple batch files that are responsible for changing the directory and typing a menu file. This implementation provides maximum flexibility and can easily be incorporated into introductory programming classes along with the general principles of file organization. The conscientious user will provide additional on-line documentation for each project as required. The advantage of a software system is that it provides a stable framework, standardizes the procedures (requirements 2 and 3), and is especially helpful to the inexperienced user.

If a user is also a software developer rather than purely a user, a systematic approach must be adopted as described by Hsia and Petry [4]. There are software management tools available but most apply to large software projects and may not be appropriate for the development of small programs.

3 Concepts and Principles

The concepts of our Structured Interactive File Organization (SIFO) system are based on the principles of structured programming namely, top-down design, modularity, and structured documentation.

Top-down design and modularity are promoted through a tree structure organization. Such a system could, in principle, be implemented on a single directory but we use subdirectories because they provide a convenient and efficient organizational tool. The main directory is at level 0 on this tree and different projects are located at level 1. Various utilities are also located at level 1. The main program development takes place at level 2 and lower levels. When a PC is booted or the user logs on to a main frame computer, a main menu is displayed which summarizes the purpose of each of the projects at level 1. The user may choose one of the existing projects or elect to create a new project. If an existing project is chosen, control is transferred to that project and a level 1 menu is displayed which offers similar options. If the user opts to create a new project our system automatically performs several tasks. First, it updates the root menu then it creates a new subdirectory and a menu for the new subdirectory. Finally, the SIFO creates a documentation file that is used to provide more detailed on-line documentation for a project. At the lowest level the menu describes the contents of individual files.

To provide flexibility, actual program development is done by exiting SIFO and using software development tools preferred by the user. However, this flexibility has the undesirable property that it allows the creation of undocumented programs. SIFO enforces proper documentation by detecting the presence of undocumented files and requesting the missing documentation each time the user changes directories.

In the VAX system that we are developing for relatively inexperienced programmers writing moderately complex FORTRAN programs, SIFO provides a template for program development. This template is based on the creation of command files for compiling and linking source files, and for running the programs. Interactive programs are probably best for people who merely use short applications programs but command files are superior for the programmer because they provide additional documentation relating to the relationships between modules and data requirements. Command files are also very useful for large programs because they can be submitted to batch queues in addition to being run interactively.

What distinguishes this system from other systems is that it it is designed to provide assistance in actually organizing the disk storage and also in requesting the provision of on-line documentation. It does not assume that the user is already familiar with file organization and only needs an efficient means of locating files.

4 Strategies in SIFO

The SIFO system was developed with the following strategies which reflect the requirements and principles described in the above sections,

1. The Technique of Subdirectory -

   In the SIFO system, we use the subdirectory technique to categorize different projects and different project activities. The file organization in the system is a tree structure organization as the block diagram showed in Figure 1. The highest level is the main directory. The second level consists of all individual project subdirectories. The third level is composed of different project activities which are implemented by their corresponding command files and the documentation file used to provide information regarding the project. The bottom level shows all of the individual files that are the elements of each project activity.

2. The User Interface Dialogue -

   In the SIFO system, We employ two user interface dialogues - Menu and Command Language. The features of these two dialogue types were described by Kantorowitz and Sudarsky [5]. The system will automatically display the required menu whenever users enter into a point represented by one of the boxes in Figure 1, which means the system will provide enough information for users to follow the procedures or understand the functions of the operation that users want to or have to implement. In the development of SIFO system, we use command files for users to understand the detailed procedures of all project activities, not just to implement them, so we adopt the features of a command file to achieve this purpose. The SIFO system will aid programmers

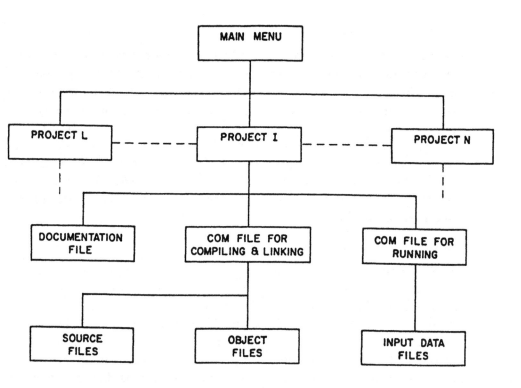

Figure 1: A Hierarchical Tree Structure File Organization

in organizing their files by advising them to create a series of ordered well-documented command files step by step and then save them in the appropriate subdirectory in the system, so the whole system will become a well-structured file organization.

3. Flexibility -

A programmer may frequently have to develop his program or use other software utilities during the operations of managing files. The SIFO system creates an flexible environment for users to work between this managing system and the operating system by communicating with users interactively. It will prompt users to leave or not when it reaches to an appropriate point, for example the point of compiling and linking in Figure 1, where users may want to develop their programs. Under such a structured environment, users can organize their files and develop their programs back and forth without affecting the operations of SIFO.

5 Operating Modes

The operations of three operating modes in the SIFO system are described as following,

1. Initiating a new project -

   It is necessary to create a new project in the system every time when programmers want to develop a new project. The SIFO system will create a new subdirectory for each new project automatically, and then ask programmers to create a series of command files which are necessary to implement the project just created by providing a series of corresponding standard-format command files for programmers to edit to fit the need of this project. The programmers can also have the option to leave the system to develop their programs on the operating system and all programs developed by programmers at this point will be located under the subdirectory just created for this project automatically.

2. Updating an existing project -

   The SIFO system provides an updating mechanism for programmers to modify or edit any command file or documentation file in the system. Programmers can access any file that they want to update by locating the associated subdirectory and file from the different level menus showed on the screen. In addition, a very important function of the SIFO system is it can detect the addition and modification of files and prompt programmers to update the associated command files and documentation files. This is different from the function of MAKE [3], which automatically executes a sufficient sub-sequence of the commands after checking which files have changed.

3. Using a project -

   This operating mode is designed for users who just want to check or implement any particular project without changing the contents in the system. For example, a new user or project supervisor may need to understand or monitor the status of a project through an efficient way. Under such situation, the SIFO system will provide sufficient on-line information for them to reach out their purposes. users can locate the desired project and essential command files simply by choosing them on menus, and then read through or run them.

6   Conclusion

Personal directory and file management will become an important issue with the increasing functions and usage of PC and increasing individual projects developed in mainframe systems. Instead of dealing with the development of large software systems, the SIFO system was developed for managing a large variety of files under individual users or small groups. The focus of SIFO is to construct a well-structured file organization by advising users interactively, such as providing on-line documentation through menus and command languages, assisting users to update file organization by supporting standard formats and allowing users to work between the SIFO system and operating system flexibly without affecting the operations of management. It does not concentrate on automated management, such as the automated techniques of APMIS described by Bratman [2] and a automated software tool which performs a variety of software management tasks using a single structure model in a system [8]. The features of structured construction and interactive management in the SIFO system demonstrate that it is efficient and flexible to organize a wide variety of files in a structured on-line environment.

References

[1] F. T. Baker. Chief Programmer Team Management of Production Programming. IBM Systems Journal, Vol.11, No.1, 1972, pp.56-73.

[2] H. Bratman. "Automated Techniques for Project Management and Control", in Practical Strategies for Developing Large Software Systems, ed. E. Horowitz. Addison-Wesley, Reading Mass., 1975, pp.193-211.

[3] S. I. Feldman. Make- A Program for Maintaining Computer Programs. Software-Practice and Experience, Vol.9, No.4, April 1979, pp.255-265.

[4] P. Hsia and F. E. Petry. A Systematic Approach to Interactive Programming. Computer, Vol.13, No.6, June 1980, pp.27-34.

[5] E. Kantorowitz and O. Sudarsky. The Adaptable User Interface. Communications of the ACM, Vol.32, No.11, Nov. 1989, pp.1352-1358.

[6] S. Miastkowski. Looking Beyond the DOS Prompt. BYTE IBM Special Edition, Vol.14, No.11, Fall 1989, pp.105-114.

[7] R. R. Ragan. CONTEXT: An On-line Documentation System. Software-Practice and Experience, Vol.16, No.3, Mar. 1986, pp.217-224.

[8] R. C. Waters. Automated Software Management Based on Structural Models. Software-Practice and Experience, Vol.19, No.10, Oct. 1989, pp.931-955.

Genetic Algorithms and the Search for Optimal Database Index Selection

Farshad Fotouhi and Carlos E. Galarce

Computer Science Department
Wayne State University
Detroit, MI 48202, U.S.A.

Abstract

The problem of the search for an optimum database index selection problem is an NP-complete problem. Genetic algorithms have been shown to be robust algorithms for searching large spaces for optimal objective function values. Genetic algorithms use historical information to speculate about new areas in the search space with expected improved performance. The feasibility of the application of genetic algorithms to the optimal database index selection is studied in this paper.

1. Introduction

In a database file with records that have several attributes, an index mechanism to the file will decrease the cost of transactions to the file. The problem of determining an optimum index, the optimum index selection problem (OISP), has been shown to be NP-complete. [Comer 78, Piatetsky 83].

Genetic Algorithms (GA's) are designed for searching large spaces for optimal function values [Holland 75]. GA's are based on the mechanics of natural selection and combine survival of the fittest among string structures with randomized information exchange to form a search algorithm. Even though GA's are random, they are not a simple random walk. They use historical information to speculate about new areas in the search space with expected improved performance [Goldberg 89]. GA's are part of the rule discovery mechanism used by a machine learning system called classifier systems [Booker 87, Holland 86].

In this paper, an explanation of the theory behind GA's is described, the difficulty of Optimum Index Selection is discussed, a machine learning model that learns about database indexes is presented, and an implementation of such a model using GA's is shown.

2. Genetic Algorithms

The work on genetic algorithms is based on the area of adaptation in natural and artificial systems [Holland 75]. Adaptation is defined as the change that any process undergoes where the structures of the process are progressively modified to improve the performance of the process.

An adaptive system is essentially an optimization process that employs an adaptive plan to locate high performance structures under a variety of environmental conditions. Examples of adaptive systems are Economic Planning, Genetics and Game Theory.

An adaptive system has the following components:

- A set of attainable structures, A
- A set of operators for modifying structures, Ω
- A set of possible inputs to the system from the environment, I
- An adaptive plan, T

The set A is the space of structures that is being searched for optimal structures. The set of operators Ω is the way to generate new structures during the search and is defined as: o $\in$ Ω, o: $A{\rightarrow}P$, where P is some set of probability distributions over A. The set I is often defined as a payoff function, an objective function that evaluates a generated member of A. It represents an environmental response. T is the strategy for searching the problem space. T is a function $IxA{\rightarrow}\Omega$. Given a member of A and the current environmental response at time t, T determines what operator from Ω is to be applied to A at time t.

An example of an adaptive system are genetic algorithms.The genetic algorithms components are mapped as follows:

- A A set of structures called chromosomes
- Ω A set of genetic operators: reproduction, crossover and mutation
- I A objective function measuring the fitness of a chromosome
- T A generated plan that varies with a particular area of application

In GA's a chromosome is a concatenation of finite-length strings over an alphabet Σ $\{0,1,\#\}$. With this representation, each finite string, called a gene, represents a particular characteristic of members of the structure space. The symbol # is a metasymbol that represents either of the other two symbols. The genetic algorithm does not process the metasymbol; it will bind it to a symbol before processing.

The operators of Ω are reproduction, crossover and mutation. The operators reproduction and crossover are applied in one functional step. In crossover, two chromosomes are selected randomly based on their observed payoff from the current population A. If the length of chromosome strings is N, then a random number from 1 to N is selected. This is the crossover point. The mutation operator introduces a random change at a random point in a chromosome. Mutation is an operator that normally has a low utilization probability.

The genetic algorithm is executed in the following steps:

> Generate a population A at random
> For a determined number of generations
> do begin
> > evaluate A's fitness using I
> > Apply crossover/mutation/reproduction to generate new A
>
> end
> Report plan T

Genetic algorithms differ from more traditional search methods in the following ways [Goldberg 89]:

- GA's work with a coding of the parameter set, not the parameters themselves.
- GA's search from a population of points, not a single point.
- GA's use payoff (objective function) information, not auxiliary knowledge.
- GA's use probabilistic transition rule, not deterministic rule.

3. Schema

From the description of genetic algorithms above, there is nothing that suggests anything more than an exhaustive search of the structure space. In the reproductive phase, the most fit chromosome string in the initial random population will come to dominate, unless by mutation or crossover this chromosome is destroyed. This seems to indicate something better than trial and error.

The question of what information contained in a given population of strings guides the search for improvement is answered with the concept of schema.

A schema [Holland 75] is a similarity template that describes a subset of strings with similarities at certain string positions. A schema can be thought of as a pattern matching device that behaves in the following fashion: A schema matches a particular string if at every location in the schema a "1" matches a "1" in the string, a "0" matches a "0" in the string, and a # matches either. For example, consider the strings and schemata of length 4. The schema #1111 matches the strings { 01111, 11111 }, the schema #11# describes a string set { 0110, 0111, 1110, 1111 }.

The number of possible schemata is based on the cardinality of the alphabet Σ and the length l of the string and schema being considered. The schemata space is given by: $(\text{cardinality}(\Sigma) + 1)^l$. In general, a population of structures of size n contains between 2^l and $n*2^l$ schemata.

Since the schemata grows exponentially with the length of the chromosome, it is not possible to keep a list of the possible schemata and their average measure of fitness. The power of the genetic algorithm is derived from the ability to manipulate a large flow of information in a manner that is algorithmically feasible. This is accomplished by the reproduction, mutation and crossover operators of the genetic algorithm.

Reproduction has a very simple effect in the schemata population. Since more highly fit strings have a higher probability of selection, a chromosome with a good schema will have a high reproductive rate, and with that an ever increasing number of chromosomes will occur in the population that carry this schema.

Crossover leaves the schema intact if it doesn't cut through the schema, but will affect the schema if it does. For example, consider the schemata 1###0 and ##11#, crossover will very likely affect the former while the latter is not likely to be destroyed. As a result, schemata of short defining length are most likely unaffected by the crossover operator and reproduced at a good rate by the reproduction operator.

Mutation being a low probability operator does not affect the particular schema very frequently. Mutation has the effect of introducing change to particular gene positions that may have become fixed in value and help to prevent loss of potentially important genetic material.

With the genetic operators, highly short-defining-length schemata, called building blocks [Goldberg 89], are propagated from generation to generation by exponentially increasing samples of the observed best. It is this propagation of building blocks combined with the crossover operator that gives the genetic algorithm its ability to achieve improved performance.

4. The Optimal Index Selection Problem

Given a file on secondary storage where records in the file have several attributes, it is often necessary to build an index mechanism to decrease the cost of accessing the file. The index selection is dependent on the usage of the file and may not be static. The usage demands on the file change with the set of queries using the information in the file. For the purposes of this paper, it is assumed that the type of queries being made to the file are unknown.

Formally the Optimum Index Selection Problem (OISP) is defined as: Given a file F with n records and k attributes, and an integer p, does there exist an indexing set for F with size no more than p?

The OISP problem has been shown to be an NP-Complete problem for files of degree d, d ≥ 2 [Comer 78]. A program to solve OISP on a file of k attributes might require 2^k steps (or worse). And by adding just 1 more attribute to the file it may take twice as long. This program will be practical only for small values of k.

Genetic algorithms have been applied to optimization problems known to be NP-complete problems. These problems include the Traveling Salesman Problem, [Grefenstette 85], Set Covering Problem, and Job Shop Scheduling.

5. A system that learns about Database Indexes

In traditional database management systems (DBMS), the user query is sent directly to the *Query Processor* unit which determines the best access method (i.e., an access method which minimizes the transaction cost) for processing the query. To determine the best access method, this unit will look at the existing set of indexes which is specified by the user at the time the database is created. The problem with this strategy is that through the life cycle of the database, the user pattern of the request might change. Therefore, the existing set of indexes may need to be changed dynamically with the change in the users request pattern. Here we will present a model of a *Learning System* which observes the pattern of the user request and decides on which attributes indexing is profitable. This information is then passed to the Query Processor unit. Figure 1 demonstrates this concept.

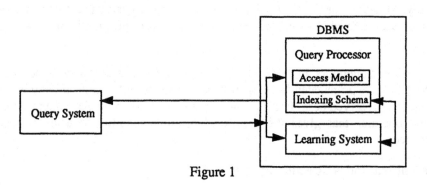

Figure 1

6. An implementation

In order to utilize GA's in an empirical approximation for a solution of the optimal index set problem, a computer model of a library database was created. The following tables describe the physical and logical specifications of the database, where:

Attribute Name	NIV	NRIV
Classification	100	10000
ISBN	1	1000000
Title	30	10000
Subject	1000	60000
Author	10	100000

NIV is the number of occurrences of particular item type in the database and
NRIV is the expected number of records containing a particular item value

The genetic code utilized by the system was based on a simple five bit long chromosome string. This string has a one-to-one relationship between a chromosome bit, an allele and the status of an index to an attribute such that chromosome string 01011 would indicate the

254

presence of an index on attributes ISBN, Subject and Author. Note that the user query is also represented a five bit long chromosome string. For example, the query "Find the ISBN of the book titled 'Introduction to Databases' by J.D. Ullman," is represented by 00101.

To model the performance of the GA, the fitness function that assigns a reward to the proper chromosome is defined as follows:

Payoff = 1-(number_of_no_index_matches* PENALTY) - (error_indexes * .5 * PENALTY),

where PENALTY = 1/# of attributes, number_of_no_index_matches is the number of attributes in the user query which have no index. Error_indexes is the number of attributes which have indexes, but are not included in the query. For example, for the index schema 01011 and the query 00101, the number_of_no_index_matches=1 (no index for the attribute Title), and the error_indexes=2 (unused indexes on ISBN and Subject attributes). Note that Payoff function is maximum if number_of_no_index_matches and error_indexes are both zero.

A query is generated against the database with variable probabilities and these probabilities are entered at runtime. A query generated using the probabilities may access more than one attribute in the database. For the above database we have considered the following set of probabilities for the attributes: P(Classification)=P(ISBN)=P(Author)=P(Subject)=0.01, and P(Title)=0.96.

The computer model used the previous parameters to generate a simulation for the utilization of such a database. Every time a chromosome string was evaluated, a query was generated by the system and then matched against the alleles of the chromosome. This is how an objective value was assigned to the chromosome string based on the fitness function described above.

The result of the above experiment along with others where the probability attributes are changed are shown in Figure 2. The X-axis is the number of generations, and the Y-axis is the average Payoff for each set of secondary indexes.

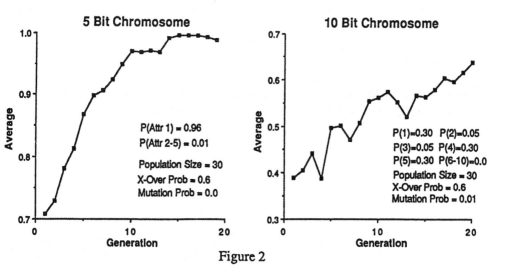

Figure 2

7. Conclusions

The application of genetic algorithms to the search of optimal indexes was explored in this study. The results provide some insight into the application of adaptive, if not machine learning systems to dynamic database systems. One can envision a database system attached to a GA like system to perform physical and logical optimization of the database. This system may use the GA's as the basis for the discovery of rules that affect the database performance. Given the length of genetic memory needed to maintain appropriate reasoning about indexes, the encoding of chromosome structure must be made more sophisticated. The results obtained in this study should motivate further study of the application of adaptive planning and machine learning to database optimization.

References

[Booker 87], Booker, L.B., Goldberg, D.E., Holland, J.H., *Classifier Systems and Genetic Algorithms. Cognitive Science and Machine Learning Laboratory*, Technical Report No. 8. The University of Michigan, Ann Arbor, MI.

[Comer 78], Comer, D. The difficulty of optimum index selection. *ACM Transactions on Database Systems*, 3(4), 440-445.

[Goldberg 89], Goldberg, D.E. *Genetic Algorithms: In search optimization & machine learning*. Reading, MA: Addison-Wesley.

[Grefenstette 85], Grefenstette, J.J., Gopala, B.J., & D.V. Gucht, Genetic Algorithms for the Traveling Salesman Problem. In *Proceedings of an International Conference on Genetic Algorithms and Their Applications* (pp 136-140), Carnegie-Mellon University, Pittsburgh, PA.

[Holland 75], Holland, J.H. *Adaptation in natural and artificial systems*. The University of Michigan Press, Ann Arbor, MI.

[Holland 86], Holland, J.H. Escaping brittleness: The possibilities of general purpose learning algorithms applied to parallel rule-based systems. In R. S. Michalski, J.G. Carbonell, & T. M. Mitchell (Eds.), *Machine Learning II* (pp. 593-623). Los Altos, CA: Morgan Kaufmann.

[Piatetsky 83], Piatetsky-Shapiro, G. The Optimal Selection of Secondary Indices is NP-Complete. In *SIGMOD Record, Vol 13-N2*, (pp 72-75).

An Object-Based Approach to the Specification of Office Entities

Hossein Saiedian

Mathematics and Computer Science
University of Nebraska, Omaha, Nebraska 68182

Abstract

Office-specific systems are often difficult and costly to implement and/or prototype. One reason for this difficulty is the unavailability of an appropriate office specification language. In this paper, we introduce an object-based language to formally specify the externally observable behavior of office objects as well as their computations. This language is called ABSL and is based on the actor model. The overall structure of ABSL objects as well as some of their properties are presented.

1 Introduction

Office automation is the body of knowledge that is concerned with the analysis, design, implementation and efficiency of the systems that transform information within an office. Office-specific systems for use in an office are often costly and difficult to implement and/or prototype. One reason for such difficulty is the unavailability of an appropriate specification methodology that an office analyst can use to formally describe the externally observable behavior of such systems at a high-level of abstraction. As a result, a great deal of effort, time and money is spent on "re-enventing" the wheel whenever a new office system concept is to be developed.

Computations in an office are often very difficult to specify using the traditional techniques because office computations are diverse [3], inherently concurrent [5], asynchronous [5] [12], distributed [7], nondeterministic [5], and event-driven [12]. Thus, to be effective, a specification methodology should be powerful and expressive enough to precisely and clearly express all aspects and relevant behavior of a system to be used in an office environment. We believe that if the support of an adequate specification methodology is provided, then the development of an office system can greatly be accelerated, many of the design difficulties can significantly be simplified and the design cost substantially reduced.

To address the above problem, we have developed a specification language for the formal specification of office objects. This language is called ABSL (for **A**ctor-**B**ased **S**pecification **L**anguage). As its name implies, ABSL is principally based on the formal theory of the actor model [4] with certain extensions. Our approach to designing a formal office specification language has emerged from research on models of concurrency and distributed computations. In addition to the actor model, we considered several other well-defined models as a semantic basis for an office specification language, including the Petri nets model [9] and CSP [6]. But we decided to take advantage of the fact that

```
object object-name --Object header
      with clause --List of parameters this object my be initialized with
      copy clause --Data types to be imported to this object;
      env-def     --Object environment definition
            define section
            state section
      end-env
      behavior-def  --Behavior definition of an object
            behavior-rule 1
            behavior-rule 2
            ...
            behavior-rule n
      end-behavior
end object-name
```

Figure 1: The Overall Structure of an Object in ABSL

the actor model not only provides a mathematically precise abstract machine [1] for the analysis of concurrent, asynchronous and non-deterministic computations but captures as well the abstraction power of *object-oriented* modeling techniques.

2   Object Representation

ABSL supports an *object-based* approach to the specification of office computations. In this approach, virtually every entity, whether abstract or concrete, that appears in an office is uniformly viewed as an object that can send or receive messages.

Each object consists of a local memory (or environment) containing tightly coupled data that are used to define the *state* of that object as well as all the operations that act on the local data. These operations are referred to as *behavior rules*. Thus an object consists of (1) a local memory definition called *environment definition* defining features and important properties of an object, and (2) a *behavior definition* that defines the actions or functions performed by the object when it receives a message. In particular, the behavior definition (analogous to actor's *script*) specifies the type of messages accepted, operations performed on the local data, the new objects created, and/or the messages sent in response to the incoming messages. The behavior definition consists of a set mutually independent behavior rules. The overall structure of objects in ABSL is shown in Figure 1 while the general format of a behavior rule is shown in Figure 2. (ABSL keywords are **typed**.)

ABSL has several distinctive characteristics. First, it allows one to specify the behavior of office entities independent of their physical representation in an abstract and non-procedural fashion. Since all computations are represented as patterns of message passing among the objects, the only things that are important to the users (and the implementors)

accept [message-tag(*message parameters*) delegate-to: d-path, sender: sender-name]
      requires: *set of pre-conditions that must be true*
           send-to, send-wait, reply *and/or* new *statements*
      become: *set of post-conditions about the state of object that will be true*
end-accept

Figure 2: The General Format of a Behavior-Rule

about an object is what kind of messages that object may receive and what it does in response to the accepted messages. No attempt is made to describe how an object perform its actions; only the kind of messages it accepts. Such descriptions are abstract and independent of any implementation bias.

Second, since office applications constantly evolve, one of our main goals in developing ABSL has been to facilitate one with a notation to conveniently develop partial description of behavior of an object which describes the known properties of that object and to further specify additional features (*i.e.*, behavior rules) of that object in an incremental fashion. This goal becomes specially important if one considers the facts that (1) it is usually difficult and often impossible to arrive at a complete specification for complex systems and (2) properties of objects in an office are not available all at once; they often evolve with time.

Third, since ABSL specifications are structured as a collection of objects with well-defined interfaces, they can directly be mapped into an object-oriented implementation via an object-oriented language. Object-oriented programming is one of most active areas of research in computer science [11] and interest in this area continues to increase.

3 Event-Driven Semantics

The actor morel [4] [1] is a model of distributed computing in which every computational entity is represented as an autonomous object called actor. The only means by which an actor may affect the behavior of another actor is by sending a message to it. All computations in the actor model are thus represented as message transmission. A message transmission is refereed to as an *event*. Thus the only things that happen in an actor system are events. An event marks the arrival of a message. Events are ordered in two ways: messages arriving at a given actor have a unique linear order called the *arrival order* while an event causing other events precedes those events in the *activation order*. The transitive closure of these two ordering provides a partial order of events called the *combined order* [4]. The laws associated with the combined ordering include:

- No event precedes itself in the combined ordering,

- If event E_1 precedes event E_2, then there are only finitely many events between E_1 and E_2,

- Each event has finitely many immediate successors,

- No event can cause infinitely many events,

- Each event is generated by the sending of at most a single message.

The purpose of the actor laws is to restrict a system of actors to those computations that are physically realizable and to ensure that an actor system can physically be implemented. For a complete description, analysis and implication of actor law see [4].

As mentioned earlier, the design of ABSL is based on the formal theory of the actor model. Each object in ABSL, with some extensions and modifications (see [10]) is essentially an actor as defined in that model. Although the actor theory has traditionally been used in the area of artificial intelligence, we believe that it can effectively be used in the area of office automation. Office activities exhibit a great deal of parallelism, its computations are event-driven and involve asynchronous communications through message passing. Similarly, the computations in the actor model are event-driven, imply an overwhelming amount of parallelism, and involve asynchronous communications through message passing. Objects in ABSL coordinate their activities by participating in events, where an event has the same semantics as in the actor model: the arrival of a message. This definition of event resembles the activities in an office. Normally, the arrival of a message (*e.g.*, arrival of an invoice form) will result in some activities to be performed by office objects (*e.g.*, processing the invoice). All computations in ABSL are thus triggered by events (or arrival of messages).

4 Formal Definition of an ABSL Object

The definition of an ABSL object is given as follows:

Definition 1 *Object — An object θ is a 2-tuple (ξ, β) where*

- *ξ is the local environment of object θ (ξ in particular is the union of Σ and $\overline{\Sigma}$, object θ's states before and after processing a message), and*

- *β is object θ's behavior.*

The local environment of object θ defines the *state* of θ at various time references. Object θ's behavior, on the other hand, defines the set of messages the θ accepts and its response to the accepted messages. Formally, the behavior of an object θ is a function that maps the incoming messages to a set of created objects, a set of communications sent to other objects, and the new state of object θ which results from processing the accepted message:

Definition 2 *Behavior — An object θ's behavior, β, is a function*

$$\beta : \Sigma^\theta \times \Gamma \rightarrow (\Theta \times \gamma\prime) \times \overline{\Sigma}^\theta$$

where

- *Σ^θ represents the state of object θ before the arrival of message $\gamma \in \Gamma$;*

- Γ is a universal set of messages that object θ can accept;

- Θ represents the finite set of objects created as a result of processing message γ;

- $\gamma\prime$ represents the communications sent to other objects in respond to message γ and,

- $\overline{\Sigma}^{\theta}$ represents the state of objects θ after processing γ.

The above definition implies that an object θ may exhibit a new state after processing a message γ, which may not be the same as its state before it accepting γ. An object which may change state is said to be *serialized*. The state of *unserialized* objects remains the same regardless of the number of messages processed:

Definition 3 *Unserialized Object* — *An object θ with behavior β and state Σ is an unserialized object if*

$$\forall \gamma \in \Gamma, \Sigma^{\theta} \times \gamma \to (\Theta \times \gamma\prime) \times \overline{\Sigma}^{\theta} \Rightarrow \Sigma^{\theta} = \overline{\Sigma}^{\theta}.$$

5 History of Computations

Acceptance of a message by an object is called an event. The behavior involving only a single object is a totally (linearly) ordered sequence of events. Thus the history of computations of an object can be viewed as a sequence of events. Events in this history are distinguished by their place in the total ordering of events. The state of an object can be captured by recording the events in which it participates. Given a history of computations for an object, one can determine whether the object has participated in a particular event or not. Suppose S represents a sequence of events that an object has participated in:

Definition 4 *Sequence* — *S is a sequence of events occurring at an object θ if $S = < e_1, e_2, ..., e_n >$ and $e_1 \succ e_2 \succ ... \succ e_n$ (where $\succ$ means means "happened before").*

Using this definition, one can determine whether a given event e_i belongs to the computation history of an object θ.

The behavior of an object can be described by specifying the set of operations that it performs once it receives a message. Furthermore, given the past history of events an object has participated in, one can determine the reaction (response) of that object to the next event. This implies that the set of past messages that an object θ has accepted must be recorded to predict its future behavior. For practical purposes, however, it may not be desirable to keep such a record. Alternatively, one can apply the concept of *state* from the sequential systems to define an object's response to incoming messages. In the context of sequential systems, the concept of state allows the future behavior of the system to be completely predicted by *abstract* state of the system at the time of an event instead of the whole past history of the system [2]. The above concept of abstract state can be used to define the state of individual objects: the state of an object will be defined by the abstract state of that object at the time of a message arrival. Thus if an object θ is in state Σ, then θ can accept a message γ and exhibit a new state shown as $\overline{\Sigma}$.

ABSL supports a first order predicate logic sublanguage to express Σ and $\overline{\Sigma}$, (the state of object θ before and after processing a message). The predicates of this language express the state of an object in terms of pre- and post-conditions (or I/O predicates) where pre-conditions are assertions about state (Σ) of an object before accepting a message and post-conditions are assertions about state ($\overline{\Sigma}$) of an object that will be obtained or will prevail after the processing completion of γ.

As discussed previously, each object has a well-defined local time which linearly orders the events as they occur at that object. These local orderings can be related to each other by the *activation ordering*. The activation ordering specifies the causal relationship between events happenings at different objects. The causal relationship is a partial ordering relationship in which events occurring at different objects are unordered unless they are connected by direct or indirect causal links. Thus, the computational history of a system of objects is a partially ordered set of events obtained by the transitive closure of *activate* and *arrival* ordering relations. The partial ordering relation approach to semantics of computations is well suited to specify the behavior of objects in a distributed system: Instead of recording the current state of system, changes in state are reflected in change over time in behavior of individual objects. In other words, since the causal relation ordering among the events in a distributed environment does not specify a unique total orderings of events [1], the notion of computations are generalized from a total ordering of events to a partial orderings of events. As a result, two events are ordered only if they are related. In other words, as long as the changes made to an object at a given time do not affect other objects, the state of those objects need not be considered when an object receives a message. That is, one needs only to consider the effects of an event e on the local state of object θ and those events that will be generated once θ participates in event e.

6 Configuration of a System of Objects

The description of a system of objects in some frame of reference is referred to as a *configuration*. That is, a configuration represents a *snapshot* of objects and events in a system of objects. Configurations may be used to analyze a system of objects. A configuration is defined as follows:

Definition 5 *Configuration* — *A configuration δ is a 2-tuple (Θ, Γ^p) where Θ is the finite set of objects in the system, and Γ^p is a finite set of pending events (i.e., messages that have been sent but not yet received). Objects of δ are symbolically denoted as δ'objects while its events are denoted as δ'events.*

Objects in a system of objects are created during the course of computation unless they existed at the beginning of the computation. The objects that exist at the start of the computation are called *primordial* objects. For the purpose of uniformity and completeness, one may assume that the *creation* event for the primordial objects corresponds, for example, to turning a switch on. Such an event is considered the *initial* event and it marks the beginning of the computations. Each system starts in an *initial* configuration:

Definition 6 *Initial Configuration — An initial configuration consists of a finite number of primordial objects which are a subset of Θ, and a single event called the* initial *event, shown as γ_0.*

Once the initial event has occurred and its message is received by one of the primordial objects, then objects' *computations* conceptually will begin. Configuration δ_i is said to have evolved into a new configuration, δ_j, once a message of configuration δ_i has been received by its recipient (*i.e.*, an event has occurred). Changes between configurations is referred to as *transitions*:

Definition 7 *Transition — Let δ_i and δ_j be two configurations. δ_i is said to have a transition to δ_j after occurrence of event e, symbolically, $\delta_i \longmapsto^e \delta_j$ provided that $e \in \delta_i$'events.*

The following theorem establishes the *liveness* property of the computations, *i.e.*, every pending event (message) will eventually occur (arrive) at its target, causing a transition to occur:

Theorem 1 *As long as events (messages) exist in a configuration, transitions will take place and the system continues to evolve. (This theorem essentially expresses the* liveness *property of this message passing scheme, i.e., each message sent by an object will "eventually" be received by its expected recipient). Note: Two important assumptions are made: (1) The arbiter associated with each object is fair and (2) the underlying communication network is reliable. (The proof this theorem can be found in [10].)*

Each event may cause additional events and as a result many *intermediate* configurations may be attained before a *final* configuration is reached. Thus during a course of computations, a configuration may evolve into a new configuration through many transitions:

Definition 8 *Possible Evolution — A configuration δ is said to possibly evolve into a configuration $\overline{\delta}$, symbolically, $\delta \longmapsto^* \overline{\delta}$, if there exists a (finite) set of events $e_1, e_2, ..., e_n$, and a sequence of configurations $\delta_0, \delta_1, ..., \delta_n$ for some $n \geq 1$, such that*

$$\delta = \delta_0 \longmapsto^{e_1} \delta_1 \longmapsto^{e_2} ... \longmapsto^{e_n} \delta_n = \overline{\delta}$$

During each transition, a pending event is caused to occur. If the set of pending events becomes empty, the computation is then completed, leading to the *final* configuration:

Definition 9 *Final Configuration — A final configuration is a configuration in which the set of pending events is empty.*

In other words, the final configuration will be reached when all events have occurred (*i.e.*, all messages have been delivered). The final configuration is indicative of the end of computation.

7 Conclusion

An object-based language for the specification of office computations was introduced. This language is called ABSL and is based on the actor model.

Computations in ABSL are event-driven. For an object to participate in an event, certain *pre-conditions* must be true. The state of an object after participating in an event is captured via the *post-conditions*. It was stated that the state of an object is consistent and well-defined before and after participating in an event. This was achieved by appeals to the *indivisibility* of an object's operations in response to an accepted message and the *atomic* state change property of objects. As a result, the specification of objects in both concurrent and non-concurrent environments can be given in a similar fashion in terms of the kind of messages they accept and the operations they perform in response to the accepted message. This property of objects frees the office analyst of concerns about the specification of such low-level issues as mutual exclusion, synchronization and safety of objects' computations. Other semantic aspects of ABSL as well as the formal definition of its syntax were not presented due to lack of space but can be found in [10].

References

[1] Agha, G.: *Actors: A Model of Concurrent Computation in Distributed Systems,* MIT Press, 1986.

[2] Baker, H.: *Actor Systems for Real-Time Computations,* PhD Dissertation, MIT, Cambridge, Mass., 1978.

[3] Bracchi, G. and Pernici, B.: *"The Design Requirements of Office Systems,"* ACM TOOIS, Vol. 2, No. 2, April 1984.

[4] Hewitt, C. and Baker, H.: *"Actors and Continuous Functionals,"* in Formal Description of Programming Concepts, E. Neuhold (Editor), North-Holland, 1977.

[5] Hewitt, C.: *"Offices are Open Systems,,"* ACM TOOIS, July 1986.

[6] Hoare, C.A.R.: *"Communicating Sequential Processes,"* CACM, Vol. 21, No. 8, 1978.

[7] McBride, R.A. and Unger E.A.: *"Modeling Jobs in a Distributed System,"* in Proc. of ACM Symp. on Small and Personal Computers, 1983.

[8] Peterson, J.L.: *"Petri nets,"* Computing Surveys, Vol. 9, No. 3, Sept. 1977.

[9] Saiedian, H.,: *An Object-Oriented Approach to the Specification of Applications for Office Automation,* PhD Dissertation, Kansas State Univ., 1989.

[10] Shriver, B. and Wegner, P. (Editors): *Research Directions in Object-Oriented Programming,* MIT Press, 1987.

[11] Zisman, M.D.: *Representation, Specification and Automation of Office Procedures,* PhD Dissertation, Wharton School, Univ. of Pennsylvania, Philadelphia, 1977.

Lexical Acquisition for Lexical Databases [1]

Sumali Pin-Ngern   Robert Strutz   Martha Evens
Department of Computer Science
Illinois Institute of Technology
Chicago, Illinois 60616
(312)-567-5153, csevens@iitvax.bitnet

Abstract

This paper describes our lexical acquisition system, which supplements knowledge in the lexical database with knowledge acquired from human informants. The database is organized to support the needs of natural language processing applications and facilitate the operation of acquisition system.

1 Introduction

Lexical Databases are central parts of Natural Language Processing systems. Most applications, such as parsing, language understanding, and text generation systems, need a large amount of syntactic and semantic information about words and how to combine them into sentences.

Currently, most natural language processing systems have vocabularies of a few hundred words. We are building a Lexical Database for English which contains information about 50,000 words. This database is designed to support information retrieval, natural language understanding, and text generation applications. To make the lexicon useful, information in the lexicon must be complete, explicit, and extendable so that users can add to or modify the database conveniently. Our system allows users to extend the lexicon with a dialogue between system and expert. The answers that are provided by users give clues to the system to modify the database so that it is more appropriate to the specific application.

We have combined information from many sources to make the lexicon more complete. Our database is stored in the Oracle Relational Database Management System. Oracle is embedded in the programming language C and provides a facility

---
[1]This Research was supported by the National Science Foundation under grant IRI-8704619. Our thanks also to G&C Merriam Company, Collins, and Oxford University Press for permission to use their dictionary tapes.

called SQL Forms. The acquisition system is developed in C which accesses data in the database by using the language SQL on an Oracle system.

2   Information in the Database

We have included semantic and syntactic information from various sources in our database. Three machine readable dictionaries, *Webster's Seventh Collegiate Dictionary* (W7) [1], *Collins English Dictionary* (CED) [2], and the *Oxford Advanced Learners Dictionary* (OALD) [3] are our primary sources. We have extracted syntactic and semantic information semi-automatically from definitions in these dictionaries by using parsers and other text processing methods. The word *kitten*, for example, has the following definitions in W7.

| kitten | 1 | 0 | n | a young cat; also :an immature individual of various other small mammals |
| kitten | 2 | 0 | vi | to give birth to kittens |

This indicates that *kitten* belongs to two parts of speech; it is both a noun and an intransitive verb. After parsing and analyzing these definitions, we have been able to add explicit information about semantic relations to the lexical database as follows:

kitten	CHILD	cat
kitten	TAXONOMY	mammal
kitten	GIVE-BIRTH	kitten

We can further classify *kitten* as an animate, concrete, countable, common, regular (plural form is kittens) noun. The syntactic information that we achieve from this is that, for example, kitten can be the subject of verbs that require an animate noun (e.g., *eat, move, walk*).

Ahlswede [4] and Evens [5] have found more than 100,000 relationships between words by analyzing definitions from machine- readable dictionaries. We have also found much word classification information as well as other syntactic information from machine readable dictionaries.

Analyzing definitions from machine readable dictionaries gives us both syntactic and semantic information, but it is not complete. In order to make natural language processing systems understand and generate sentences, more sophisticated syntactic information about each word and where it can be put in a sentence needs to be prepared. We have included syntactic information from other sources such as the Indiana Corpus [6], the Brandeis Verb Lexicon [7], the lexicon from Sager's Linguistic String Parser (LSP) [8], grammatical information that has been compiled by Quirk et al. [9], and the dictionary of adverb placements by Sven Jacobson [10; 11].

The process of collecting information from more than one source leads to many problems. These problems include incompleteness of the information in the original sources and conflicts between different sources. To solve these problems, we have built a system which lets human informants (sometimes linguists or native speakers) help us [12]. This system combine knowledge from informants and information in the database. Since the Lexical Database is very large, it is difficult to handle a system that requires users to work on every detail. Thus, to achieve an efficient system, we had to organize the database for this purpose.

Since the Lexical Database contains a large amount of sophisticated information, we have been careful to organize it in a systematic way. Our database is organized based on part of speech. The database organization includes noun, verb, adjective, and adverb sections. Each part of speech contains information such as word classification, lexical semantic information, and grammatical information. A good database organization helps us handle the lexical acquisition system more easily. The following shows the broad structure of our database:

> Nouns
>> Classifications (e.g., human, animate, or inanimate)
>> Semantic relations (e.g., *kitten* CHILD *cat*)
>> Grammatical information
>
> Verbs
>> Classifications (e.g., dynamic or stative)
>> Semantic relations (e.g., *run* TAXONOMY *move*)
>> Case frames with selectional restrictions
>> Grammatical information
>
> Adjectives
>> Classifications (e.g., inherent or noninherent)
>> Semantic relation (e.g., *comical* SYNONYM *funny*)
>> Grammatical information
>
> Adverbs
>> Classification (time, manner, degree, etc.)
>> Adverb placement information

Our Lexical Database contains information with some sample sentence structures for each part of speech. These examples came from sample sentences that are provided in sources. List 5 in the Indiana adverb list, for example, contains the following information:

List 5   Post-modifying a predicate (verb-phrase or verb-phrase + object noun-phrase).

Example: She bought it CHEAPLY.

Word lists: already, bravely, equally, evenly, etc.

3 Example: Database Information for Adverbs

Adverbs are very complicated and difficult to understand. They may modify adjectives, verbs, other adverbs, or even the whole sentence. The following shows example entries from our adverbial lexicon containing classification and adverb placement information.

1) Adverb classification: contains information about whether an adverb is an adverb of time (*then*), manner (*fast*), direction (*forward*), degree (*quite*), or hedge (*sort of*). This type of information comes from analyzing definitions from machine readable dictionaries. The adverb classification table in the database looks like this:

```
ADV_MAIN(WORD,HOMO#,SENSE#,CLASS)
         enough   2     1    degree
         often    0     0    time
```

Each class has its own database table containing information about what types of verb, adjective, adverb, and sentence an adverb can modify. Here are some example entries in the table for adverbs of time,

```
ADV_TIME(WORD,     VERB,     SENTENCE, POSITION)
         again    dynamic action      F,M,E
         annually dynamic action      M,E
```

2) Position of adverbs: We have included information about adverb placements from four sources. Jacobson [10] has particularly helpful information about adverb placement. Positions are Front (F), Middle (M), and End (E). There also are sub-positions for each position.

```
ADV_JACOBSON(WORD,        CLASS,   POSITION)
             enough      degree   E1,E4,E5
             normally    time     F1,F2,M1,M3
             otherwise   manner   M3,E1,E4,E5
```

The Indiana Adverb lists [6] contain two types of information: general frame structures including examples and also word lists:

```
ADV_INDIANA_FRAME(LIST#,PATTERN,EXAMPLE)
  1  Sentence-linking        Yet you lent him money?
  2  Premodifying an object  He said PRECISELY that.
     noun-phrase or pronoun
```

```
      ADV_INDIANA_FRAME(WORD,        LIST#)
                        accordingly  1
                        briefly      2c
                        really       2b
```

4 The Lexical Acquisition System

The acquisition system allows users or human informants to add missing information or update the lexicon. Since the database is so large, we have to avoid working with information unrelated to the group that we want to deal with. The system eliminates the irrelevant groups of information by asking information from users interactively. The answers that the system gets from users help the system to focus on the smaller set.

In this discussion, we describe the acquisition system for the Indiana Adverb Lists. We have used sentence examples that are provided in the Indiana adverb lists and information from other sources to help us build this system.

The first question that the system asks users is what part of speech the word belongs to. If that word belongs to more than one part of speech, users will have to decide which part of speech of that word he wants to work on. The system starts by asking user to input a word that he wants to work on. Suppose user wants to work on the word *enough* with part of speech *adverb*. The following shows how the first step users see:

```
System: Please enter a word that you want to work on
User:   enough
System: Here are the parts of speech that {\it enough} belongs to
```

WORD	HOMO-GRAPH#	SENSE#	POS
enough	1	0	adjective
enough	2	1	adverb
enough	2	2	adverb
enough	2	3	adverb
enough	3	1	noun
enough	3	2	noun

```
System: What part of speech would you like to work on?
User:   Adverb
```

The system then eliminates information which is related to other parts of speech (noun and adjective). After searching through the database, the system presents information about *enough* as follows:

1) It is an adverb of degree (from ADV_MAIN table)

2) It can be put into position E1, E4, and E5 and it can be used as a modifier (from ADV_JACOBSON table)

3) It belongs to list 5 in the Indiana Adverb Lists. The information in frame 5 is:

```
Post-Modifying a predicate (verb-phrase or
verb-phrase + object noun-phrase)
```

If the user wants to know what other lists of adverbs the word *enough* should be added to, the system searches through other groups of information that are closely related to the list that the word *enough* belongs to and presents them to user.

In the Indiana Adverb Lists, there are nine frames for adverbs. Some frames are subdivided into subframes. List 5 in the Indiana adverb lists belong to subframe A4a. The following sentences are sample sentences in frame A4a:

```
Frame A4a: The girl answered the question foolishly.
           The engineer joined the ends inseparably.
           He read the passage aloud.
```

There are three sub-frames which are A4a, A4b, and A4c in Frame A4. Only subgroup A4a has an adverb list. The system guesses that *enough* can also applied to some sub-frames in frame A4. Thus, the system lists the sample sentences that are presented in each subframe and lets the user judge whether it is possible to add *enough* or not. The following are lists of sentences which the system presents to the user:

```
Frame A4b: He altered the facts, unfortunately.
           The scientists found a solution, incidentally.
           They moved the sign, apparently.

Frame A4c: My friend likes the overture particularly.
           Children hate spinach, too.
           We bought cigarettes instead.
           They shot the leader first.
```

If the user agrees to add *enough* to frames A4b and A4c then the database is updated.

Our lexical acquisition system has been able to handle most types of syntactic information but we are still experimenting with techniques for adding semantic information. This system does not require users who have strong backgrounds in computer science or linguistics, but they must know English well enough to modify the lexical database.

5   Conclusion

Effective natural language processing systems need well organized lexical databases that contain systematic information. We have shown that it is possible to add lexical acquisition facilities to a well designed database in such a way that users can easily extend the database to meet their needs. The key idea is to include in the database itself definitions and examples of all the attributes and categories that it uses.

References

[1] J. Olney. To All Interested in the Merriam Webster Transcripts and Data Derived from them. System Development Corporation Document L-13579. 1968.

[2] D.J. Carver (ed.) *Collins English Dictionary*. Collins Publishers, Birmingham, 1974.

[3] A.S. Hornby (ed.) *Oxford Advanced Learners Dictionary*. Oxford University Press, Oxford, 1974.

[4] T. Ahlswede. *Syntactic and Semantic Analysis of Definitions in a Machine Readable Dictionary*. Unpublished doctoral dissertation, Department of Computer Science, Illinois Institute of Technology, Chicago, 1988.

[5] M. Evens (ed.) *Relational Models of the Lexicon*. Cambridge University Press, Cambridge, 1988.

[6] F. Householder, W. Wolfgang, and J. Matthews. *Preliminary Classification of Adverbs in English*. Indiana Linguistic Club, Indiana University, Bloomington, Indiana, 1965.

[7] J. Grimshaw and R. Jackendoff. Report to NSF on grant IST-81-20403 (Brandeis Verb List). Department of Linguistics, Brandeis University. 1985.

[8] N. Sager. *Natural Language Information Processing*. Addison-Wesley, Reading, Massachusetts, 1981.

[9] R. Quirk, S. Greenbaum, G. Leech, J. Svartvik. *A Comprehensive Grammar of the English Language*. Longman, London, 1985.

[10] S. Jacobson. *Adverbial Positions in English*. Dissertation, Uppsala, AB Studentbok, Stockholm, 1964.

[11] S. Jacobson. *On the Use, Meaning, and Syntax of English Preverbial Adverbs*. Almqvist & Wiksell International, Stockholm, 1978.

[12] M. Evens, S. Pin-Ngern, T. Ahlswede, S.M. Li, and J. Markowitz. Acquiring Information from Informants for a Lexical Database. In *Proceedings of the First International Lexical Acquisition Workshop*, Detroit, Michigan, 1989.

A Search for Good Lattice Rules Based on the Reciprocal Lattice Generator Matrix*

James N. Lyness   W. Newman

Mathematics and Computer Science Division
Argonne National Laboratory
9700 South Cass Avenue
Argonne, IL 60439-4844 U.S.A.

Abstract

The search for cost-effective lattice rules is a time-consuming and difficult process. After a brief overview of some of the lattice theory relevant to these rules, a new approach to this search is suggested. This approach is based on a classification of lattice rules using "the upper triangular lattice form" of the reciprocal lattice generator matrix.

1 Background

A lattice rule is a numerical quadrature rule for integrating over an s-dimensional hypercube. It is a generalization of the one-dimensional trapezoidal rule using a subset of the nodes that would be used by the Cartesian product trapezoidal rule. Number theoretic rules, associated with Korobov (1959), Hwalka (1962), and Niederreiter (1988) form a major subset of the set of lattice rules.

Since their inception, several large-scale searches for good number theoretic rules have been reported in the open literature. Among the most successful are those of Maisonneuve (1972), Kedem and Zaremba (1974), and Bourdeau and Pitre (1985). The number of potential candidates is vast and the construction and organization of these searches has proved to be a challenging task. Using the most up to date computers available, scientists have taken advantage of every available mathematical property to streamline their program.

---

*This work was supported by the Applied Mathematical Sciences subprogram of the Office of Energy Research, U.S. Department of Energy, under Contract W-31-109-Eng-38.

In this paper we draw attention to a particular form of the generator matrix of the reciprocal lattice. While this form has proved to be useful in the general theory of lattice rules, here we emphasize only its use as the basis for a search which includes all lattice rules.

We begin by describing some of the underlying theory; in Section 1 we define lattices, lattice rules, and the reciprocal lattice. In Section 2, we introduce the upper triangular lattice form of its generator matrix and propose that this be used to classify lattice rules. In Section 3, the relation between the discretization error in terms of Fourier coefficients and the reciprocal lattice is briefly reviewed; and a standard criterion for assessing the quality of a rule is described. In Section 4, searches for "good" rules are put into perspective and some preliminary results, based on a pilot version of our search, are presented.

Without loss of generality, we treat quadrature over the s-dimensional unit hypercube $[0,1)^s$. In the sequel, all vectors are s-dimensional having rational elements. In particular, e_j denotes the j-th unit vector (whose components coincide with those of the j-th row of the $s \times s$ unit matrix I).

DEFINITION 1.1. *The unit lattice* Λ_0 *comprises all points* $\lambda = (\lambda^{(1)}, \lambda^{(2)}, \ldots, \lambda^{(s)})$ *all of whose components* $\lambda^{(i)}$ *are integers.*

This familiar array of points is the most fundamental lattice. A general definition follows.

DEFINITION 1.2. *A set of points form a lattice* Λ *when*

$$p, q \in \Lambda \Rightarrow p+q, \ p-q \in \Lambda$$

and there exists ε *such that*

$$p \neq q \Rightarrow |p-q| \geq \varepsilon.$$

Given c_i, $i = 1, 2, \ldots, u$, the set of points

$$p = \Sigma \lambda^{(i)} c_i \quad \forall \text{ integer } \lambda^{(i)} \tag{1.3}$$

clearly form a lattice. Here, the vectors c_i are known as *generators*. The same s-dimensional lattice Λ may be generated in many ways, but does not *require* more than s generators. These may be assembled in an $s \times s$ matrix A. Then (1.3) takes the form

$$p = \lambda A \quad \forall \ \lambda \in \Lambda_0. \tag{1.4}$$

The matrix A is termed a generator matrix of Λ, and its rows a_r are, of course, a set of generators of Λ. When $\det A \neq 0$, these are linearly independent and are collectively known as a *basis* for Λ.

The lattice rule $Q(\Lambda)$ is constructed using an *integration lattice*.

DEFINITION 1.5. *An integration lattice* Λ *is one that contains* Λ_0 *as a sublattice.*

Given $z_i \in \Lambda_0$ and integers n_i and t, it is clear that the points

$$\mathbf{p} = \sum_{i=1}^{t} j_i \mathbf{z}_i / n_i + \sum_{i=1}^{s} \mu^{(i)} \mathbf{e}_i \quad \forall \text{ integer } j_i \text{ and } \mu \in \Lambda_0 \tag{1.5}$$

form an integration lattice. Note that an integration lattice Λ satisfies

$$d^{-1} \Lambda_0 \supseteq \Lambda \supseteq \Lambda_0 \tag{1.6}$$

for some integer d.

DEFINITION 1.7. *The lattice rule* $Q(\Lambda)$ *defined when* Λ *is an integration lattice is one that assigns an equal weight* N^{-1} *to every point*

$$\mathbf{p} \in \Lambda \cap [0,1)^s .$$

When Λ is given by (1.5), this lattice rule may be written as

$$Q(\Lambda)f = \frac{1}{n_1 n_2 \dots n_t} \sum_{j_1=1}^{n_1} \sum_{j_2=1}^{n_2} \cdots \sum_{j_t=1}^{n_t} \bar{f}\left[\sum_{i=1}^{t} j_i \mathbf{z}_i / n_i \right] . \tag{1.8}$$

Here $\bar{f}(\mathbf{x})$ is a periodically continued version of $f(\mathbf{x})$ that coincides with $f(\{\mathbf{x}\})$ when $\{\mathbf{x}\} \in (0,1)^s$. For details, see Lyness (1989). Expression (1.8) is termed a t-cycle form of the lattice rule. It is not unique, and may be repetitive (i.e. include each point k times). One can always express a rule in this form with $t \leq s$. The *rank* r of a rule is the smallest value of t for which it may be written in this form. Thus a rule of rank 1

$$Qf = \frac{1}{N} \sum_{j=1}^{N} \bar{f}(j\mathbf{z}/N) \tag{1.9}$$

coincides with the number theoretic rule of Korobov. The joint publications of Sloan and Lyness in 1989 and 1990 are devoted to obtaining properties of lattice rules based almost exclusively on this definition. Exploiting finite Abelian group theory, we have made significant headway in classifying lattice rules. However, many problems remain unresolved.

A fundamental concept in lattice theory is the reciprocal lattice or polar lattice (denoted by $\Lambda^{\perp}$) of a lattice Λ.

DEFINITION 1.10. *The reciprocal lattice of* Λ, *denoted by* $\Lambda^{\perp}$, *comprises all* $\mathbf{r}$ *such that*

$$\mathbf{p} \cdot \mathbf{r} = \text{integer} \quad \forall \, \mathbf{p} \in \Lambda .$$

It can be shown that when A is a generator matrix of Λ, then $B = (A^T)^{-1}$ is a generator matrix of $\Lambda^{\perp}$. The reciprocal lattice $\Lambda^{\perp}$ occurs naturally in expansion (3.1) below for the discretization error. However, it also provides a simple criterion for whether the lattice Λ defined in terms of A is an integration lattice, i.e., $\Lambda \supseteq \Lambda_0$.

THEOREM 1.11. Λ *is an integration matrix if and only if any generator matrix B of $\Lambda^{\perp}$ is an integer matrix, i.e., all its elements are integers.*

It can be shown that when Λ is an integration matrix, and $B = (A^T)^{-1}$,

$$N = |\det A|^{-1} = |\det B| \qquad (1.12)$$

is the number of lattice points in $[0,1)^s$, which is, of course, the number of distinct function values $f(\mathbf{x})$ required by the rule $Q(\Lambda)$. Moreover, it is the smallest value of d for which (1.6) is valid and

$$N\Lambda_0 \subseteq \Lambda^{\perp} \subseteq \Lambda_0 . \qquad (1.13)$$

2 The Upper Triangular Lattice Form (utlf) of B

A pervasive source of difficulty in all these results is the extreme lack of uniqueness. The same lattice Λ may be defined by using many different sets of generators in (1.3), (1.4), or (1.5) and the same rule may be defined by using different $\mathbf{z}_i, n_i$ in (1.8) or (1.9) even when t coincides with the rank of $Q(\Lambda)$. Much of the work based on (1.8) has been in search of uniqueness. So far as generator matrices A or B are concerned, it is almost self-evident that adding one row to another while altering the matrix has no effect on the lattice Λ. The same lattice Λ is now described using a different set of generators. Such an integer row operation may be described in terms of pre-multiplication by a unimodular matrix U. This is an integer matrix having $|\det U| = 1$. Thus, B and UB generate the same lattice so long as U is unimodular. This may be exploited to transform B into *upper triangular lattice form* defined below; we find there is a (1-1) correspondence between each distinct integer matrix of this form and each distinct integer lattice $\Lambda^{\perp}$.

DEFINITION 2.1. *An $s \times s$ integer matrix B is of upper triangular lattice form (utlf) if and only if*

(a) *All elements below the diagonal are zero, i.e.,*

$$b_{r,c} = 0 \quad r > c ;$$

(b) *All diagonal elements are positive integers, i.e.,*

$$b_{c,c} \geq 1 ;$$

(c) *All elements are nonnegative, and the unique maximum element in any column is the diagonal element, i.e.,*

$$0 \leq b_{r,c} < b_{c,c} \quad r = 1,2,,...,s .$$

The principal theorem of this paper follows.

THEOREM 2.2. *Every integer lattice Λ has one and only one generating matrix B of upper triangular lattice form.*

A version of this theorem is given in Cassells (1959), Section I.2.2. As it applies to integer matrices, this result is classical and the utlf is essentially the Hermite Normal Form. An excellent description of this part of elementary lattice theory is given in Section 4 of Schrijver (1986). A useful discussion and algorithm is given in G. Bradley (1971).

This classification is dealt with in considerable detail in an ANL report, Lyness and Newman (1989), which is a preliminary and extended version of the present article. In particular, a straightforward triangularization algorithm is described. Other relations between the utlf of B and the lattice rule with which it is associated are given. And attention is drawn to a major drawback to classification using the generator matrix A of Λ directly.

We have found the utlf of B useful also in developing the general theory of lattice rules. See, for example, Lyness and Sørevik (1989) and Lyness, Sørevik, and Keast (1990). In this article we treat only the application to the search.

3 The Good Lattices

The error made by any quadrature rule may be expressed in terms of the s-dimensional Fourier coefficients $a_{\mathbf{m}}$ of the integrand function using a generalization of the Poisson Summation Formula. (This is the basis of much of the theory of number theoretic rules. A discussion in the context of lattice rules appears in Lyness (1988).) For lattice rules $Q(\Lambda)$, it can be shown that the Poisson Summation Formula reduces to

$$Q(\Lambda)\bar{f} - \bar{If} = \sum_{\substack{\mathbf{m} \in \Lambda^{\perp} \\ \mathbf{m} \neq 0}} a_{\mathbf{m}} . \tag{3.1}$$

Here $a_{\mathbf{m}}$ is the multivariate Fourier coefficient and $\Lambda^{\perp}$ is the reciprocal lattice of the lattice Λ on which the rule is based. This suggests a criterion for choosing from the many available N-point lattice rules those that may be cost effective. Specifically, one chooses Λ so that the larger Fourier coefficients on the right drop out. Before we are able to apply this, we have to decide which are the more significant Fourier coefficients. This issue is discussed in detail in Lyness (1988). The conventional wisdom is to proceed as follows. Let

$$\rho(\mathbf{m}) = \rho(m_1, m_2, ..., m_s) = \prod_{i=1}^{s} \max(|m_i|, 1) \quad \mathbf{m} \in \Lambda_0 ;$$

then define the Zaremba rho-index of an integer lattice by

$$\rho(\Lambda^{\perp}) = \min_{\substack{\mathbf{m} \in \Lambda^{\perp} \\ \mathbf{m} \neq 0}} \rho(\mathbf{m}) .$$

The "good" lattice rules $Q(\Lambda)$ are those for which $\rho(\Lambda^{\perp})$ is largest.

4 Some New Lattice Rules

The theory of this paper may be used to construct a search program to find cost-effective lattice rules. Previous searches for "good lattice rules" are described by Maisonneuve (1972), Kedem and Zaremba (1974), and Bourdeau and Pitre (1985). Between them, these authors have considered number theoretic rules in dimensions $s = 3$, 4, and 5 with N up to $N = 6066$, 3298, and 772, respectively. They have demonstrated that a clear appreciation of the problem and sophisticated coding technique can lead to significant economy and speedup. All these searches, of course, were confined to number theoretic rules which are of form (1.9) above and were based on treating in turn different parameters $\mathbf{z}$ for given values of s and N.

On the other hand, we have used Theorem 2.2 above as the basis for an exhaustive search for cost effective lattice rules. For given values of s and N, such a program employs an outer loop in which all sets of positive integers $v_1, v_2, ..., v_s$ for which $v_1 v_2 \cdots v_s = N$ are included. Then for a given set $v_1, v_2, ..., v_s$, all combinations of off-diagonal elements $b_{r,c}$ $r = 1, 2, ..., s-1$; $c = 2, 3, ..., s$ are treated for which

$$0 \le b_{r,c} < v_c .$$

We expect that the organization of such a search, and the number of distinct lattice rules $v_s(N)$, will form the topics of other articles (Lyness and Sørevik (1989)).

In this search, as in the other searches, a critical feature concerns the possibility of avoiding separate treatment of different lattices that are related by affine transformation. In the various search procedures we have encountered, this is handled in a somewhat *ad hoc* manner, which relies partly on theory and partly on inelegant and sometimes cumbersome algorithms. The present search is no exception in this respect. It seems to be just as bad or good as the previous searches. It is this sort of theoretically peripheral but practically vital circumstance on which an ultimate choice of methods is likely to depend.

At this point we have carried out only a primitive search, as a pilot scheme, with $s = 3$ and $N < 150$. Even this limited search has uncovered new rules, mainly of academic interest. The list in Table 1 gives the additional entries required to extend Maisonneuve's list to include all lattice rules, following the convention introduced by her for listing these rules. That is, one includes a rule if there is no rule having a smaller value of N and the same value of ρ; but one does not include rules that can be obtained from rules already on the list by an affine transformation of the cube into itself.

Table 1. Some New Three-Dimensional Lattice Rules

N	ρ	n_1	z_1	n_2	z_2	n_3	z_3
16	4	4	(1,1,1)	2	(0,1,0)	2	(0,0,1)
42	6	42	(2,3,16)				
54	8	18	(1,2,10)	3	(0,1,0)		
54	8	18	(1,5,5)	3	(0,1,2)		
96	12	48	(3,9,28)	2	(0,1,0)		
144	16	36	(1,11,5)	2	(0,1,0)	2	(0,0,1)

These rules are given in the canonical form of Sloan and Lyness (1989), specifically

$$Qf = \frac{1}{n_1 n_2 n_3} \sum_{j_1=1}^{n_1} \sum_{j_2=1}^{n_2} \sum_{j_3=1}^{n_3} \bar{f}\left[\frac{j_1 z_1}{n_1} + \frac{j_2 z_2}{n_2} + \frac{j_3 z_3}{n_3}\right],$$

where n_i divides n_{i-1} and $N = n_1 n_2 n_3$. We note that rules of ranks 1, 2, and 3 appear. Those of rank 3 are 2^3–copy versions of lattice rules having $N/8$ abscissas.

The 42-point rule is interesting because it is a rank 1 (number theoretic) rule, which was not discovered by Maisonneuve. Her search omits a relatively small class of number theoretic rules that can be expressed in number theoretic form (1.9) only with all components of z_1 greater than unity.

References

G. H. Bradley, 1971. "Algorithms for Hermite and Smith Normal Matrices and Linear Diophantine Equations," Math. Comput. 25 (1971), pp. 897-907.

Marc Bourdeau and Alain Pitre, 1985. "Tables of good lattices in four and five dimensions," Numer. Math. 47 (1985), pp. 39-43.

J. W. S. Cassels, 1959. *An Introduction to the Geometry of Numbers*, Springer.

E. Hlawka, 1962. "Zur angenäherten Berechnung mehrfacher Integrale," Monatsh. Math. 66 (1962), pp. 140-151.

Gershon Kedem and S. K. Zaremba, 1974. "A table of good lattice points in three dimensions," Numer. Math. 23 (1974), pp. 175-180.

N. M. Korobov, 1959. "The approximate computation of multiple integrals," (in Russian), Dokl. Akad. Nauk. SSSR 124 (1959), pp. 1207-1210.

J. N. Lyness, 1988. "Some comments on quadrature rule construction criteria," in International Series of Numerical Mathematics, vol. 85, *Numerical Integration III*, ed. G. Hämmerlin and H. Brass, Birkhauser Verlag, Basel, 1988, pp. 117-129.

J. N. Lyness, 1989. "An introduction to lattice rules and their generator matrices," to appear in IMA JNA (1989).

J. N. Lyness and W. Newman, 1989. "A classification of lattice rules using the reciprocal lattice generator matrix," (1989), Argonne National Laboratory Report ANL-89/20, Argonne, Illinois.

J. N. Lyness and T. Sørevik, 1989. "The number of lattice rules," BIT 29 (1989), 527-534.

J. N. Lyness, T. Sørevik, and P. Keast, 1990. "Notes on integration and integer sublattices," preprint MCS-P34-1288, Argonne National Laboratory; to appear in Math.Comput. (1990).

J. N. Lyness and I. H. Sloan, 1989. "Some properties of rank-2 lattice rules," to appear in Math. Comput. (1989).

D. Maisonneuve, 1972. "Recherche et Utilisation des 'Bons Treillis'. Programming et Resultats Numeriques," in *Applications of Number Theory in Numerical Analysis*, S. K. Zaremba, ed., Academic Press (1972) [QA 297 .S995], pp. 121-201.

H. Niederreiter, 1988. "Quasi-Monte Carlo methods for multidimensional numerical integration," in International Series of Numerical Mathematics, vol. 85, *Numerical Integration III*, ed. G. Hämmerlin and H. Brass, Birkhauser Verlag, Basel, 1988, pp. 157-171.

A. Schrijver, 1986. *Theory of Linear and Integer Programming*, Wiley.

I. H. Sloan and J. N. Lyness, 1989. "The representation of lattice quadrature rules as multiple sums," Math. Comp. 52 (1989), pp. 81-94.

I. H. Sloan and J. N. Lyness, 1990. "Lattice rules: projection regularity and unique representations," Math. Comput. (to appear). Also MCS-P75-0489, Argonne National Laboratory.

S. K. Zaremba, 1966. "Good lattice points, discrepancy and numerical integration," Ann. Mat. Pura Appl. 73 (1966), pp. 293-317.

An Adaptive Numerical Integration Algorithm for Simplices

Alan Genz

Computer Science Department

Washington State University

Pullman, WA 99164-1210

email: acg@cs2.cs.wsu.edu

Abstract

A globally adaptive algorithm for numerical multiple integration over an n-dimensional simplex is described. The algorithm is based on a subdivision strategy that chooses for subdivision at each stage the subregion (of the input simplex) with the largest estimated error. This subregion is divided in half by bisecting an edge. The edge is chosen using information about the smoothness of the integrand. The algorithm uses a degree seven-five integration rule pair for approximate integration and error calculation, and a heap for a subregion data structure. Test results are presented and discussed where the algorithm is used to compute approximations to integrals used for estimation of eigenvalues of a random covariance matrix.

1 Introduction

The problem considered in this paper is the numerical evaluation of integrals in the form

$$I(f) = \int_S f(\mathbf{x})dS,$$

where $\mathbf{x} = (x_1, x_2, ..., x_n)$ and S is an n-simplex with vertices $\mathbf{v}_0$, $\mathbf{v}_1$, ..., $\mathbf{v}_n$. There has been only limited work done on practical algorithms for this general problem. Much of the research has considered the $n = 2$ case, where S is a triangle. For this case there has been work on the development of integration rules (see [1], [18], and [21]), and algorithms ([2], [6], [11], [12] and [15]). For the $n = 3$ case, where S is a tetrahedron, there has been more limited work on rule development ([14] and [21]) and little algorithm development work. For $n > 3$, the three main rule development papers are by Silvester [19], Grundmann and Möller [10] and Lyness and Genz [17]; some other rules are described and referenced in the books by Stroud [21] and Engels [8]. The only general algorithm currently available [18] is an automatic algorithm that uses a sequence of increasing polynomial degree Grundmann and Möller rules, although an experimental algorithm was developed by Kahaner and Wells [13].

In the following sections a globally adaptive algorithm for the general problem will be described. The general algorithm is based on successive refinements or subdivisions of S, where each subdivision is used to provide a better approximation to I(f). These subdivisions are designed to dynamically concentrate the computational work in the subregions of S where the integrand $f(\mathbf{x})$ is most irregular, and thus adapt to the behavior of the integrand. While algorithms of this type have been extensively used for numerical integration [5] over hyper-rectangular regions, an outstanding problem for simplical regions has been the development of a subdivision method that allows for a controlled increase in the computation as the algorithm proceeds. This paper describes a subdivision method which solves this problem.

2　The Basic Globally Adaptive Algorithm

Subregion adaptive algorithms for numerical integration have a general structure that consists of a sequence of stages. Each stage has the following four main steps:
　　i) select some subregion(s) from the current set of subregions;
　　ii) subdivide the selected subregion(s);
　　iii) apply an integration rule to new subregions and update the subregion set;
　　iv) update the global integral and error estimates, and check for convergence.
The initial subregion set for these algorithms is usually the set that contains only one region, the whole integration region for I(f). The required input for such an algorithm is a description of the integration region, the integrand $f(\mathbf{x})$ and a requested error tolerance ϵ. The algorithm terminates when the estimated global error is less than ϵ.

Globally adaptive algorithms make the subregion choices in step i) based on information about the estimated integration errors in all of the subregions in the current subregion list. The basic algorithm that will be used for the simplex is similar to a globally adaptive algorithm for integration over hyper-rectangles that was first described by van Dooren and de Ridder [7], and improved by Genz and Malik [9], and Berntsen, Espelid and Genz [3]. With this algorithm, the subdivision strategy involves subdividing (at each stage) a subregion with largest estimated error. This subregion is divided in half, in a direction (chosen from some finite set of directions) where the integrand is more irregular. The algorithms for hyper-rectangular regions use possible subdivision directions that are parallel to the coordinate axes. An error-keyed heap is used for a subregion data structure, and this allows the subregion list to be efficiently maintained throughout the calculation.

The basic integration rules that are used for the subregion adaptive algorithms take the form

$$B(f) = \sum_{i=1}^{N} w_i f(\mathbf{x}_i) \simeq \int_R f(\mathbf{x}) d\mathbf{x},$$

for a subregion R. With these rules, the points x_i and weights w_i are chosen to make the rule exact for all polynomials of degree d or less, for some fixed d and n, with N small. The rules that are used in practical calculations typically have degrees in the range 5-13, with N a polynomial in n. The points and weights are obtained for some standard hyper-rectangle, (e.g. the unit n-cube), and then the linear structure of the rule allows an affine transformation, preserving the polynomial degree, to any other n-dimensional finite hyper-rectangle. The use of polynomial integrating rules ensures rapid convergence once the subdivision is fine enough so that the integrand is reasonably smooth locally. The basic error estimate used for the subregion adaptive integration algorithms is a difference of two integration rules

$$E(f) \; = \; |B(f) \; - \; B'(f)| \; \simeq \; |\int_R f(\mathbf{x})dx \; - \; B(f)|.$$

The rule $B'(f)$ usually has degree $d' < d$ (the degree of $B(f)$) and may use a subset of the points for $B(f)$. In this case $E(f)$ is usually a better estimate for the error in $B'(f)$, but because $d > d'$ the error in $B(f)$ should usually be smaller than the error in $B'(f)$, and so $E(f)$ is usually a conservative bound for the actual error in $B(f)$.

In order to use the globally adaptive algorithm for the simplex, an appropriate family of simplex integration rules is needed and a method of selecting directions for further subdivision is needed. The integration rules that are used in the modified algorithm are the degree seven Grundmann-Möller rules [10] for $B(f)$ and the degree five Grundmann-Möller rules for $B'(f)$. The degree five rules use a subset of the points for the degree seven rules, which have $N = (n+4)(n+3)(n+2)/6$. For $n > 3$ these rules are currently the most efficient rules available.

3   Subdivision Method

At each stage in the algorithm for hyper-rectangles a selected subregion is divided by halving along edges in a direction chosen from the n possible directions parallel to the n coordinate axes. A simplex has $n(n + 1)/2$ possible edge directions; the algorithm modified for the simplex chooses a subdivision direction from one of these directions. If the chosen edge is bisected, then two new simplices can be produced. One simplex has all of the vertices of the selected largest error simplex, except that the left endpoint of the chosen edge is replaced by the midpoint; the other simplex replaces the right endpoint of the selected simplex with the midpoint. Each of the new simplices has half of the volume of the original selected simplex subregion. This subdivision strategy, which uses division of the largest error subregion into only two new pieces at each stage, allows the algorithm to proceed from one stage to the next in a controlled manner. A simpler subdivision method divides the selected subregion into 2^n pieces by bisecting all of the edges. This method has been used in several algorithms for triangles, but becomes much more expensive for larger n values. It is also not as adaptive as the method discussed here because subdivision will usually be done in some directions where the integrand is smooth; the relatively large error for the integral over the selected subregion is often due to irregularity of the integrand in only a small number of directions.

With the hyper-rectangle algorithm the integrand irregularity in the different edge directions is estimated by using the fourth difference of the integrand in those directions. Each fourth difference requires integrand values from from five symmetrically placed points that are centered at the center of the selected hyper-retangle and lie along a line through the center, in the appropriate direction. The algorithm modified for the simplex also uses fourth differences; these are centered at the centroid of the selected simplex. Let $v_{k,0}$, $v_{k,1}$, ..., $v_{k,n}$ be the vertices of the current largest error simplex subregion S_k, and let the edge directions be given by $d_{i,j} = v_{k,j} - v_{k,i}$, for $0 \leq i < j \leq n$. Now define $f_{i,j}(\alpha) = f(c_k + \alpha d_{i,j}/(4(n+1)))$, with $c_k = \sum_{i=0}^{n} v_{k,i}/(n+1)$ (the centroid of S_k). Then a fourth difference operator for the $(i, j)^{th}$ direction is given by

$$D_{i,j} = 16f_{i,j}(0) - 9(f_{i,j}(1) + f_{i,j}(-1)) + (f_{i,j}(3) + f_{i,j}(-3)).$$

This difference (times as constant) is an approximation to the fourth derivative of $f(\mathbf{x})$ in the $(i, j)^{th}$ direction. All of the points where $f(\mathbf{x})$ is computed for these differences lie within S_k. The direction $d_{l,m}$ for subdivision is a direction where $|D_{l,m}| = \max_{i<j} |D_{i,j}|$. If $v_c = (v_{k,l} + v_{k,m})/2$, then the two new simplical subregions have the same vertices as S_k does except that the l and m vertices are respectively replaced by the c vertex. Measures other than the fourth differences could also be used to measure the irregularity of the integrand for this type of algorithm, but since the degrees of the rules used for error estimation are seven and five, the size of the fourth difference may be comparable to the size of the terms in the actual integration error. The cost of determining the direction indices l and m is $2n(n+1)+1$ integrand evaluations; this is small compared to the cost of computing $B(f)$.

4   Some Test Results

The algorithm described in the previous sections has been implemented in Fortran by making appropriate modifications to a Fortran subroutine developed by Berntsen, Espelid and Genz [4] for vectors of hyper-rectangles. As an example of the usefulness of the algorithm, the Fortran code was used to determine approximate values for a family of integrals that are used for estimating the eigenvalues of a random covariance matrix [16]. Define $I_{s,n}(g)$ by

$$I_{s,n}(g) = C_{s,n} \int_S e^{-\sum y_i/2} \prod_{j<i}(y_i - y_j) \prod_{i=1}^{n} y_i^{(s-n-1)/2} g(y) dS,$$

where S is the infinite simplex defined by $0 \leq y_n \leq y_{n-1}\cdots \leq y_1 \leq \infty$, and $C_{s,n}$ is chosen so that $I_{s,n}(1) = 1$. The integral is needed for various polynomial g's, and $1 < n < s$. The algorithm that has been described applies only to finite simplices so a transformation is needed. The transformations $y_i = (x_i/(1 - x_i))^2$, that take the infinite simplex S to the finite simplex defined by $0 \leq x_n \leq x_{n-1}\cdots \leq x_1 \leq 1$, were used for the test of the algorithm. The algorithm was used for n in the range 3-5 and $s < 15$, with $g(y) = 1$ and $g(y) = y_i$, $i = 1, 2, ..., n$. The following table gives the results.

Eigenvalue Integrals

n	s	$g's$	$I(1)$	$I(y_i)/(ns)$, $i = 1, ..., n$				
3	4	6251	0.9973	0.6903	0.2495	0.0555		
	5		0.9995	0.6559	0.2669	0.0763		
	6		1.0004	0.6284	0.2782	0.0933		
	7		1.0007	0.6067	0.2861	0.1075		
	8		1.0012	0.5892	0.2919	0.1194		
	9		1.0015	0.5745	0.2963	0.1295		
	10		1.0011	0.5618	0.2999	0.1383		
	11		1.0003	0.5507	0.3027	0.1459		
	12		0.9996	0.5410	0.3051	0.1528		
	13		0.9992	0.5327	0.3072	0.1590		
	14		0.9992	0.5254	0.3091	0.1646		
	15		0.9993	0.5187	0.3108	0.1697		
4	5	34124	1.0008	0.5901	0.2756	0.1090	0.0250	
	6		0.9997	0.5591	0.2792	0.1242	0.0367	
	7		0.9998	0.5354	0.2814	0.1357	0.0471	
	8		1.0000	0.5161	0.2827	0.1448	0.0562	
	9		1.0000	0.5000	0.2834	0.1522	0.0643	
	10		1.0000	0.4865	0.2838	0.1585	0.0714	
	11		1.0002	0.4750	0.2840	0.1638	0.0777	
	12		1.0004	0.4649	0.2839	0.1683	0.0835	
	13		1.0005	0.4559	0.2836	0.1722	0.0887	
	14		1.0006	0.4480	0.2834	0.1757	0.0935	
	15		1.0009	0.4410	0.2832	0.1788	0.0979	
5	6	310650	1.0000	0.5132	0.2760	0.1402	0.0573	0.0133
	7		0.9997	0.4876	0.2744	0.1487	0.0683	0.0205
	8		0.9997	0.4673	0.2726	0.1553	0.0772	0.0272
	9		1.0002	0.4508	0.2709	0.1604	0.0847	0.0334
	10		1.0005	0.4368	0.2692	0.1644	0.0910	0.0390
	11		1.0002	0.4247	0.2673	0.1676	0.0964	0.0441
	12		0.9999	0.4142	0.2655	0.1703	0.1011	0.0488
	13		0.9998	0.4050	0.2639	0.1726	0.1053	0.0531
	14		1.0000	0.3969	0.2625	0.1746	0.1090	0.0570
	15		1.0003	0.3899	0.2612	0.1764	0.1123	0.0607

All of the integrals for each n value were computed as a vector, and the same subdivision was used for all of those integrals. The requested absolute accuracy was only $\epsilon = 0.05$. The integrals I(1) should have value 1, but the results show that the absolute accuracy is usually less than 0.0005. An additional theoretical check on these results is $\sum_{i=1}^{n} I(y_i)/ns = 1$. For comparison, the n = 3, s = 15 integral $I(y_1)$ has been computed using a Monte-Carlo method [16]. In that calculation 30,000 g values were needed to achieve 0.001 accuracy.

5 Concluding Remarks

A globally adaptive algorithm for numerical integration over simplices has been described. The most novel feature of the algorithm is the subdivision method. This allows the largest error subregions in the subregion list to be further subdivided in a controlled way that allows the algorithm to efficiently and dynamically take account of the local irregularities of the integrand. Test results were produced to illustrate the effectiveness of a vector implementation of the new algorithm.

References

[1] J. Berntsen and T. O. Espelid, Degree 13 Symmetric Quadrature Rules for the Triangle, submitted to *BIT*, 1989.

[2] J. Berntsen and T. O. Espelid, An Algorithm for Adaptive Cubature over a Collection of Triangles, Dept. of Inf., Univ. of Bergen, 1989.

[3] J. Berntsen, T. O. Espelid and A. Genz, An Adaptive Algorithm for the Approximate Calculation of Multiple Integrals, to be published in *ACM Trans. Math. Soft.*.

[4] J. Berntsen, T. O. Espelid and A. Genz, An Adaptive Multiple Integration Routine for a Vector of Integrals, to be published in *ACM Trans. Math. Soft.*.

[5] P. J. Davis and P. Rabinowitz, *Methods of Numerical Integration*, Academic Press, New York, 1984.

[6] E. de Doncker and I. Robinson, An Algorithm for Automatic Integration over a Triangle Using Nonlinear Extrapolation, *ACM Trans. Math. Soft.*, 10(1984), pp. 1-16.

[7] P. van Dooren and L. de Ridder, An Adaptive Algorithm for Numerical Integration over an N-Dimensional Rectangular Region, *J. Comp. Appl. Math.* 2(1976), pp. 207-217.

[8] H. Engels, *Numerical Quadrature and Cubature*, Academic Press, New York, 1980.

[9] A. C. Genz and A. A. Malik, An Adaptive Algorithm for Numerical Integration over an N-Dimensional Rectangular Region, *J. Comp. Appl. Math.*, 6(1980), pp. 295-302.

[10] A. Grundmann and H. M. Möller, Invariant Integration Formulas for the N-Simplex by Combinatorial Methods, *SIAM J. Numer. Anal.* 15(1978), pp. 282-290.

[11] A. Haegemans, An Algorithm for Automatic Integration over a Triangle, *Computing*, 19(1977), pp. 179-187.

[12] D. K. Kahaner and O. W. Rechard, TWODQD: An Adaptive Routine for Two-Dimensional Integration, *J. Comp. Appl. Math.* 17(1987), pp. 215-234.

[13] D. K. Kahaner and M. B. Wells, An Experimental Algorithm for N-Dimensional Adaptive Quadrature, *ACM Trans. Math. Soft.*. 5(1979), pp. 86-96.

[14] P. Keast, Cubature Formulas for the Sphere and Simplex, Department of Computer Science Technical Report 1985CS-2, Univ. of Toronto. *J. Inst. Maths. Applics.* 23(1979), pp. 251-264 .

[15] D. P. Laurie, CUBTRI: Automatic Integration over a Triangle, *ACM Trans. Math. Soft.*, 8(1982), pp. 210-218.

[16] V. Luzar and I. Olkin, Comparison of Simulation Methods in the Estimation of Ordered Characteristic Roots of a Random Covariance Matrix, Stanford University Statistics Preprint, 1989.

[17] J. N. Lyness and A. C. Genz, On Simplex Trapezoidal Rule Families, *SIAM J. Numer. Anal.*, 17(1980), pp. 126-147.

[18] J. N. Lyness and D. Jesperson, Moderate Degree Symmetric Quadratue Rules for the Triangle *J. Inst. Maths. Applics.* 15(1975), pp. 19-32.

[19] D01PAF: An Automatic Integration Subroutine for Integration over an N-Simplex, Numerical Algorithms Group Limited, Wilkinson House, Jordan Hill Road, Oxford, United Kingdom OX2 8DR.

[20] P. Silvester, Symmetric Quadrature Formulas for Simplices, *Math. Comp.*, 24(1970), pp. 95-100.

[21] A. H. Stroud, *Approximate Calculation of Multiple Integrals*, Prentice-Hall, Englewood Cliffs, New Jersey, 1971.

The HK Singular Value Decomposition of Rank Deficient Matrix Triplets

L. Magnus Ewerbring [1]

Mathematics and Computer Science Division
Argonne National Laboratory
Argonne, Illinois 60439

Franklin T. Luk [2]

School of Electrical Engineering
Cornell University
Ithaca, New York 14853

Abstract

In this paper we consider a simultaneous reduction of three matrices. The described method is extended from the work presented in [3] to include rank deficient data. It is shown how, via an initial reduction, the problem becomes one of diagonalizing a product of three matrices. We compare three different algorithms for its computation and show why one is preferred over the others.

1 HK-SVD

The HK-Singular Value Decomposition (HK-SVD) concerns the simultaneous diagonalization of three matrices. We are given the matrices A ($n \times p$), H ($n \times n$) and K ($p \times p$), where H and K are symmetric and positive semi-definite, and

$$\text{rank}(H) = r, \quad \text{rank}(K) = s \quad \text{and} \quad r \geq s.$$

For simplicity, we assume that all data are real. Our aim is to find an $n \times r$ transformation Y and a $p \times s$ transformation Z, such that

$$\begin{pmatrix} Y^T & 0 \\ 0 & Z^T \end{pmatrix} \begin{pmatrix} H & A \\ A^T & K \end{pmatrix} \begin{pmatrix} Y & 0 \\ 0 & Z \end{pmatrix} = \begin{pmatrix} I_r & D \\ D^T & I_s \end{pmatrix},$$

where $D = \text{diag}(d_1, d_2, \ldots, d_s)$. The diagonal entries in D may be ordered such that

$$d_1 \geq d_2 \geq \cdots \geq d_q > 0 \quad \text{and} \quad d_{q+1} = \cdots = 0 .$$

Hence $\text{rank}(Y^T A Z) = q$. We refer the reader to [2] for a detailed discussion of the many applications of the decomposition, e.g., weighted least squares, linear prediction, and canonical correlation analysis, as well as for a proof of its existence.

[1]Supported by the Applied Mathematical Sciences subprogram of the Office of Energy Research, U.S. Department of Energy, under Contract W-31-109-Eng-38

[2]Supported by Army Research Office Grant DAAL 03-86-K-0109

2   Problem Reduction

To compute the HK-SVD we proceed as follows. Since both H and K are symmetric semi-definite, we find their square roots as upper trapezoidal matrices, viz., $H^{1/2}$ $(r \times n)$ and $K^{1/2}$ $(s \times p)$, respectively, satisfying

$$H = (H^{1/2})^T H^{1/2} \quad \text{and} \quad K = (K^{1/2})^T K^{1/2} .$$

The combined data matrix is then reduced as follows:

$$\begin{pmatrix} (H^{1/2})^+ & 0 \\ 0 & (K^{1/2})^+ \end{pmatrix}^T \begin{pmatrix} H & A \\ A^T & K \end{pmatrix} \begin{pmatrix} (H^{1/2})^+ & 0 \\ 0 & (K^{1/2})^+ \end{pmatrix} = \begin{pmatrix} I_r & B \\ B^T & I_s \end{pmatrix} , \quad (1)$$

where

$$B = ((H^{1/2})^+)^T A (K^{1/2})^+ . \quad (2)$$

Next, we wish to diagonalize the $r \times s$ matrix B without disturbing I_r and I_s, a feat accomplished by a singular value decomposition (SVD) of B, i.e.,

$$B = U \Sigma V^T ,$$

where U $(r \times r)$ and V $(s \times s)$ are orthogonal and Σ $(r \times s)$ is diagonal. The desired transformations are given in product form by

$$Y = (H^{1/2})^+ U \quad \text{and} \quad Z = (K^{1/2})^+ V .$$

It follows that the problem simplifies to an SVD of a product of three matrices. For obvious numerical reasons, we seek to avoid finding pseudo-inverses and forming explicit matrix products. As in [3] we utilized implicit Jacobi-SVD methods for a product of three matrices.

Consider $H^{1/2}$ and $K^{1/2}$. In equation (2), we notice that their pseudo-inverses are required. We compute their RQ factorizations:

$$H^{1/2} = R_H Q_H \quad \text{and} \quad K^{1/2} = R_K Q_K , \quad (3)$$

where R_H $(r \times r)$ and R_K $(s \times s)$ are upper triangular with full rank, and Q_H $(r \times n)$ and Q_K $(s \times p)$ have orthonormal rows. Greville [4] examined conditions under which the relation

$$(MN)^+ = N^+ M^+ ,$$

holds for arbitrary matrices M and N. For instance, a sufficient condition is when M has full column rank and N has full row rank. This is why we have chosen to compute RQ factors in (3), for we now get

$$(H^{1/2})^+ = (R_H Q_H)^+ = Q_H^+ R_H^+ = Q_H^T R_H^{-1} \text{ and } (K^{1/2})^+ = Q_K^T R_K^{-1} . \quad (4)$$

Thus, equation (2) becomes:

$$B = ((H^{1/2})^+)^T A (K^{1/2})^+ = (R_H^{-1})^T Q_H A Q_K^T R_K^{-1} .$$

Since the rows of Q_H and Q_K are orthonormal, we can safely form the product $\tilde{A} = Q_H A Q_K^T$, and so

$$B = (R_H^{-1})^T \tilde{A} R_K^{-1} ,$$

where the dimensions of R_H, $\tilde{A}$ and R_K are $r \times r$, $r \times s$ and $s \times s$, respectively. We discussed in [3] how to reduce the matrix product B to one where all three factors have equal dimensions (here $s \times s$). Our goal now is to find an SVD of C, where

$$C = E^{-1} F G^{-1} , \tag{5}$$

and E, F and G are all $s \times s$ and upper triangular.

3 Implicit SVD

To diagonalize the product in equation (5), we build on a Jacobi-type algorithm developed especially for triangular matrices [6]. The main idea is to simultaneously diagonalize a number of two-by-two submatrices. By applying the transformations and data permutations in some special order (the so called *outer rotations* and *odd-even ordering* [6]), we can guarantee convergence of the overall algorithm [7].

Let $\hat{E}$, $\hat{F}$ and $\hat{G}$ be three two-by-two matrices extracted from the ith and $(i+1)$st rows and columns of the matrices E, F and G, respectively, and let $\hat{C}$ denote the corresponding submatrix of C. Since the matrices are upper triangular, it follows that $\hat{C}$ may be found directly as

$$\hat{C} = \hat{E}^{-1} \hat{F} \hat{G}^{-1} . \tag{6}$$

In a Jacobi-type method, we find two-by-two orthogonal transformations to diagonalize the extracted matrix. For the purpose of finding the rotations we may further simplify equation (6) by replacing each inverse by its adjoint (abbrev. adj), an approach advocated in [8] for the generalized singular value decomposition (GSVD). Hence, we form the product using adjoints and find two-by-two rotations $\hat{U}$ and $\hat{V}$ such that

$$\hat{U}^T [\mathrm{adj}(\hat{E}) \hat{F} \, \mathrm{adj}(\hat{G})] \hat{V} = \mathrm{diag}(d_1, d_2) . \tag{7}$$

The transformations are applied on the individual data matrices. The products $\hat{E}\hat{U}$ and $\hat{V}^T \hat{G}$ are formed. But they are no longer triangular. Using two orthogonal transformations, say $\widehat{W}$ and $\hat{Q}$, we can ensure that

$$\hat{E} \leftarrow \widehat{W}^T \hat{E} \hat{U} \quad \text{and} \quad \hat{G} \leftarrow \hat{V}^T \hat{G} \hat{Q}$$

are both upper triangular relative to machine precision. The middle matrix $\hat{F}$ is updated accordingly. We now have

$$(\hat{U}^T \, \mathrm{adj}(\hat{E}) \widehat{W})(\widehat{W}^T \hat{F} \hat{Q})(\hat{Q}^T \, \mathrm{adj}(\hat{G}) \hat{V}) = \mathrm{diag}(d_1, d_2) . \tag{8}$$

Since the right hand side in equation (8) is diagonal and the updated $\hat{E}$ and $\hat{G}$ are upper triangular, the updated $\hat{F}$ matrix must be upper triangular as well. Hence, by introducing *two* extra orthogonal transformations, we can theoretically maintain the triangularity of the *three* matrices. As explained in [3] the iteration is continued until C is diagonalized. We refer to the overall algorithm as Method Truncate, since it automatically truncates the (2,1) element of the updated matrix $\widehat{F}$ to zero.

We now present an example showing why the truncation error in $\widehat{F}$ can be quite large. Let

$$E = I, \quad F = \begin{pmatrix} 1 & 1 + \sqrt{\epsilon} \\ 0 & 1 - \sqrt{\epsilon} \end{pmatrix} \quad \text{and} \quad G = \begin{pmatrix} 1 & 1 \\ 0 & \sqrt{\epsilon} \end{pmatrix},$$

the case of a GSVD. We wish to find transformations such that the product FG^{-1} is diagonalized. As a first step, we form the product

$$C = F \operatorname{adj}(G) = \begin{pmatrix} \sqrt{\epsilon} & \sqrt{\epsilon} \\ 0 & 1 - \sqrt{\epsilon} \end{pmatrix}.$$

Following scheme USVD of [1], we find a rotation, Q say, to symmetrize C. Consider the matrix

$$Q = \begin{pmatrix} 1 & \sqrt{\epsilon} \\ -\sqrt{\epsilon} & 1 \end{pmatrix},$$

which is orthogonal relative to the machine precision. When Q is applied to C, we find that

$$C \leftarrow \mathrm{fl}\left(Q^T C\right) = \begin{pmatrix} \sqrt{\epsilon} & \epsilon \\ \epsilon & 1 - \sqrt{\epsilon} \end{pmatrix}, \tag{9}$$

which is accepted by us as numerically diagonal. Hence, no further calculation is required and the rotations are $U = Q$, and $V = I$. The transformations are applied separately on the data matrices, i.e.,

$$F \leftarrow \mathrm{fl}\left(U^T F\right) = \begin{pmatrix} 1 & 1 \\ \sqrt{\epsilon} & 1 \end{pmatrix} \quad \text{and} \quad G \leftarrow \mathrm{fl}\left(V^T G\right) = \begin{pmatrix} 1 & 1 \\ 0 & \sqrt{\epsilon} \end{pmatrix}.$$

We see that although both G and C are upper triangular relative to the machine precision, F is not.

An alternative scheme enforcing that all updated matrices are upper triangular is an extension from a GSVD scheme of Hammarling [5]. Again, consider the two-by-two subproblem. We form the explicit matrix product, and compute its SVD. But now we keep only $\widehat{U}$ and discard $\widehat{V}$. A QR decomposition of $\widehat{E}\widehat{U}$ yields $\widehat{W}$, which in turn is applied to $\widehat{F}$. The effect of doing so is that $\widehat{F}$ loses its triangularity, which is restored with the application of $\widehat{Q}$. Finally, the product $\widehat{G}\widehat{Q}$ is forced to triangularity by another QR decomposition, yielding $\widehat{V}$. Hence, the difference between the two methods lies in that the first ensures diagonality of the product, while the second ensures triangularity of each updated matrix. A potential disadvantage of the latter, to be called Method QRD, is that it may not diagonalize the two-by-two matrix product. Other slightly different schemes have been suggested and examined in [2].

4   Numerical Comparisons

In this section we compare the two implicit schemes against an explicit approach coded in *Matlab*. As input data, we used 8×8 matrices, M say, which were either constant with random entries or ones with singular values

$$\sigma_1 = \sigma_2 = \sigma_3 = \kappa(M) , \quad \sigma_4 = \sigma_5 = \sqrt{\kappa(M)} \quad \text{and} \quad \sigma_6 = \sigma_7 = \sigma_8 = 1 ,$$

where $\kappa(M)$ is the condition number of M. All matrices were of full rank. During one test run, the matrix M would vary. To be able to compare the different SVD algorithms, the square root factors were given explicitly. The error measure was

$$\| A - (Y^T)^{-1}DZ^{-1} \|_F ,$$

where the transformations Y and Z were kept in product form. This error measure is useful, since it tells us how well the computed transformations diagonalize A, and does not require us to form any inverses.

In the first test run, we let both $H^{1/2}$ and A remain constant, where

$$\kappa(H^{1/2}) = 55 , \quad \| H^{1/2} \|_F = 4.5 , \quad \kappa(A) = 1.1 \cdot 10^2 \quad \text{and} \quad \| A \|_F = 4.7 .$$

The simulation results for various values of $K^{1/2}$ are shown in Table 1.

		$\| A - (Y^T)^{-1}DZ^{-1} \|_F$		
$\| K^{1/2} \|_F$	$\kappa(K^{1/2})$	Explicit	Truncate	QRD
$1.73 \cdot 10^{+04}$	$1.00 \cdot 10^{+2}$	$2.32 \cdot 10^{-13}$	$9.39 \cdot 10^{-14}$	$2.68 \cdot 10^{-14}$
$1.73 \cdot 10^{+08}$	$1.00 \cdot 10^{+4}$	$3.49 \cdot 10^{-12}$	$4.52 \cdot 10^{-12}$	$1.89 \cdot 10^{-14}$
$1.73 \cdot 10^{+12}$	$1.00 \cdot 10^{+6}$	$9.82 \cdot 10^{-10}$	$3.81 \cdot 10^{-10}$	$1.45 \cdot 10^{-14}$
$1.73 \cdot 10^{+16}$	$1.00 \cdot 10^{+8}$	$1.81 \cdot 10^{-07}$	$4.00 \cdot 10^{-08}$	$2.54 \cdot 10^{-13}$
$1.19 \cdot 10^{+18}$	$1.00 \cdot 10^{+9}$	$7.45 \cdot 10^{-07}$	$4.94 \cdot 10^{-07}$	$1.93 \cdot 10^{-11}$

Table 1. Error comparison

A second set of runs is presented in Table 2. Here, both $H^{1/2}$ and $K^{1/2}$ are modified while the middle matrix is kept constant. The norms and condition numbers of the square root factors are $\kappa(A) = 1.1 \cdot 10^2$ and $\| H^{1/2} \|_F = 4.7$.

		$\| A - (Y^T)^{-1}DZ^{-1} \|_F$		
$\| H^{1/2} \|_F$ $=\| K^{1/2} \|_F$	$\kappa(H^{1/2})$ $= \kappa(K^{1/2})$	Explicit	Truncate	QRD
$1.73 \cdot 10^{+2}$	$1 \cdot 10^{+2}$	$1.77 \cdot 10^{-13}$	$7.46 \cdot 10^{-14}$	$6.94 \cdot 10^{-14}$
$1.73 \cdot 10^{+4}$	$1 \cdot 10^{+4}$	$1.68 \cdot 10^{-09}$	$5.28 \cdot 10^{-12}$	$4.82 \cdot 10^{-12}$
$1.73 \cdot 10^{+6}$	$1 \cdot 10^{+6}$	$1.25 \cdot 10^{-05}$	$9.21 \cdot 10^{-10}$	$8.74 \cdot 10^{-08}$
$1.73 \cdot 10^{+8}$	$1 \cdot 10^{+8}$	$8.37 \cdot 10^{-02}$	$7.00 \cdot 10^{-08}$	$6.89 \cdot 10^{+07}$

Table 2. Error comparison

In Table 1, the implicit methods always perform better than the explicit one. As expected, Method QRD generates the best accuracy since it minimizes the truncation errors. However, in Table 2 we find that its error term increases dramatically for the most ill-conditioned case. The other two methods perform according to our expectations, i.e., the error of the explicit approach is at worst proportional to the condition number of the matrix triplet, while errors in Method Truncate are at worst proportional to the condition number of the individual data matrices. This behavior was observed in other simulations as well [2].

The unexpected large error in Method QRD causes nonconvergence. Recall that the last rotation $\widehat{V}$ only ensures that the updated version of $\widehat{G}$ be upper triangular. The drawback is that the two-by-two product may not be diagonalized. To illustrate this problem consider an example extracted from the ill-conditioned case of Table 2. At some step during execution of the algorithm, we extracted the two-by-two matrices $\widehat{E}$, $\widehat{F}$ and $\widehat{G}$, and calculated the product

$$\mathrm{adj}(\widehat{E})\widehat{F}\,\mathrm{adj}(\widehat{G}) = \begin{pmatrix} 8.744691048073930 \cdot 10^3 & 7.764944105437424 \cdot 10^1 \\ 0 & 4.150648572814645 \cdot 10^{11} \end{pmatrix}.$$

After one set of rotations to the three matrices, the product became

$$\mathrm{adj}(\widehat{E})\widehat{F}\,\mathrm{adj}(\widehat{G}) = \begin{pmatrix} 4.15064857281464 \cdot 10^{11} & -1.467379403422819 \cdot 10^2 \\ 1.864297754699555 \cdot 10^{-6} & 8.744691048073930 \cdot 10^3 \end{pmatrix}.$$

The off-diagonal mass of the product has in fact increased! Indeed it was observed how this scheme may quickly raise the off-diagonal mass by several orders of magnitude. The observed effect also applies to the GSVD, which was verified in experiments [2]. Due to this possible loss of convergence, we advocate the use of Method Truncate for the product SVD problem.

5 Conclusions

We introduce a matrix decomposition of three rank deficient matrices, and show how it can be determined via an SVD of a product of three upper triangular matrices. We compare three algorithms for the product SVD problem and show that one of them produces the best numerical results.

6 References

[1] R.P. Brent, F.T. Luk and C. Van Loan, "Computation of the singular value decomposition using mesh-connected processors," *J. VLSI Computer Systems*, 1 (1985), pp. 250-260.

[2] L.M. Ewerbring, "A new generalization of the singular value decomposition: algorithms and applications," Ph.D. dissertation, School of Elec. Eng., Cornell Univ., 1989.

[3] L.M. Ewerbring and F.T. Luk, "Canonical correlations and generalized SVD: applications and new algorithms," *J. Comput. Applied Math.*, 27 (1989), pp. 37-52.

[4] T.N.E. Greville, "Note on the generalized inverse of a matrix product," *SIAM Review*, 8 (1966), pp. 518-521.

[5] S.J. Hammarling, Personal Communication.

[6] F.T. Luk, "A triangular processor array for computing singular values," *Lin. Alg. Applics.*, 77 (1986), pp. 259-273.

[7] F.T. Luk and H. Park, "A proof of convergence for two parallel Jacobi SVD algorithms," *IEEE Trans. Computers*, 38 (1989), pp. 806-811.

[8] C.C. Paige, "Computing the generalized singular value decomposition," *SIAM J. Sci. Statist. Comput.*, 7 (1986), pp. 1126-1146.

Approximate Integration Using Iterated Levin Transformations

Ricolindo Cariño
La Trobe University
Bundoora VIC 3083
Australia
carino@latcs1.oz.au

Elise de Doncker [1]
Western Mich. Univ.
Dept. of Comp. Science
Kalamazoo MI 49008
elise@cs.wmich.edu

Ian Robinson
La Trobe University
Bundoora VIC 3083
Australia
ian@latcs1.oz.edu

Abstract

The efficiency of a quadrature scheme based on iterated Levin U transformations and composite rule approximations for a harmonic sequence of mesh ratios is demonstrated for typical problem classes. Numerical results indicate a favourable comparison with the well known nonlinear extrapolation procedures applied to a sequence of composite quadrature rule sums for a geometric progression of the mesh ratios.

1 Introduction

Extrapolation methods used in approximate integration can be classified as linear or non-linear. These methods take as input a sequence of quadrature sums generated according to some interval subdivision scheme and combine these sums to produce new sequences which converge to the value of the integral faster than the original sequence. Linear methods include Romberg integration, the Neville algorithm and modified Romberg integration [4,5]; while non-linear methods include Aitken's Δ^2 process and the ε algorithm [2,6,9].

For standard linear extrapolation methods to be effective, the related quadrature error expansion for the rule and integral under consideration must be an asymptotic series in integer powers of h, the subdivision stepsize. Modified Romberg integration is effective for series involving non-integer powers of h, but one must know in advance the exponents of these powers. This is not necessary in the case of the ε algorithm and Aitken's Δ^2 process, each of which can accomodate non-integer powers and logarithmic terms without advance knowledge of the exponent values. However, for these methods it is essential that a geometric subdivision sequence be followed (usually the sequence $G : 1,2,4,8,16,\ldots$). Thus, linear methods have a limited scope of applicability, and non-linear methods may be costly in terms of the number of function

[1]On leave at: California Institute of Technology, Caltech Concurrent Supercomp. Fac., Mail stop 158-79, Pasadena CA 91125; dedonker@wega.caltech.edu

evaluations required. It should be mentioned that the ε algorithm can be applied in an adaptive manner to reduce the number of function evaluations needed [3].

In [1], the Levin U transformation, a non-linear extrapolation method based on the harmonic sequence (H : 1,2,3,4,5,...) is shown to be efficient and effective for integrals of the form $\int w(x)g(x)dx$, where $g(x)$ is analytic and $w(x)$ is $w_1(x) = 1$ or $w_2(x) = [x(1-x)]^\lambda$, $\lambda > -1$. For the weight functions $w_3(x) = x^\lambda$ and $w_4(x) = x^\lambda(1-x)^\mu$, ($\mu, \lambda$ non-integer ≥ -1, $\mu \neq \lambda$), it has limited effectiveness, with only the first one or two steps of the transformation producing significant improvement (depending on the values of λ and μ).

In this paper we identify the equivalence of an iterated form of the Levin T transformation (based on sequence G) with the iterated Aitken's Δ^2 process, and by analogy, we demonstrate that results better than those using the U transformation (with sequence H) can be obtained for integrals with weight functions w_3 and w_4 by iterating the first few steps of the Levin U transformation. It is also shown that these results of the iterated Levin U transformation are better than the corresponding results of the ε algorithm.

2   Theoretical considerations

We briefly review the general Levin transformation (see [7,8] for a fuller exposition). Let S_r, $r = 1, 2, \ldots$ be an infinite convergent sequence with limit S. Assume that S_r has the form

$$S_r = S + R_r f(r), \ r = 1, 2, \ldots, \tag{1}$$

where R_r is a first-order estimate of the error in S_r, and where $f(x)$, considered as a function of the continuous variable x, is continuous for all $x \geq 1$, including $x = \infty$, and as $x \to \infty$, $f(x)$ has a Poincaré-type expansion in inverse powers of x, given by

$$f(x) = \sum_{i=0}^{\infty} \beta_i/x^i, \ as \ x \to \infty, \ \beta_0 \neq 0.$$

The limit S, and the coefficients β_i, $i = 0, 1, \ldots, k-1$ can be approximated by T_{kn}, and the constants γ_i, $i = 0, 1, \ldots, k-1$, respectively by solving the $k+1$ linear equations

$$S_r = T_{kn} + R_r \sum_{i=0}^{k-1} \gamma_i/r^i, \ r = n, n+1, \ldots, n+k.$$

A closed-form solution for T_{kn} is given by

$$T_{kn} = \frac{\sum_{j=0}^{k}(-1)^j \binom{k}{j}(n+j)^{k-1}(S_{n+j}/R_{n+j})}{\sum_{j=0}^{k}(-1)^j \binom{k}{j}(n+j)^{k-1}(1/R_{n+j})}. \tag{2}$$

In particular, the T and U transformations of Levin correspond to the choices $R_r = \Delta S_{r-1}$ and $R_r = r\Delta S_{r-1}$ respectively, where $\Delta S_{r-1} = S_r - S_{r-1}$. For sequences of quadrature approximations, it can be shown ([1]) that the form of R_r used in the T transformation is appropriate for the elimination of the dominant error term in the quadrature error expansion when the interval subdivision scheme follows a geometric sequence (i.e., G). The form used in the U transformation is appropriate when the harmonic sequence H is used as the subdivision scheme.

It is easy to show the equivalence of the first step of the Levin T transformation (call this $T1$) to Aitken's Δ^2 process. In (2), let $R_r = \Delta S_{r-1}$ and let $k = 1$. Then

$$T_{1n} = \frac{S_n/\Delta S_{n-1} - S_{n+1}/\Delta S_n}{1/\Delta S_{n-1} - 1/\Delta S_n} = S_{n+1} - \frac{(\Delta S_n)^2}{\Delta^2 S_{n-1}}, \tag{3}$$

which is the standard Aitken's Δ^2 formula. It follows that reapplying the $T1$ transformation on the new sequence T_{1n} will also be equivalent to the iterated Aitken's Δ^2 process. Some properties of this process when applied to sequences of quadrature approximations are discussed in [6]. Briefly, the iterated Aitken's Δ^2 process, in the limit, successively eliminates the dominant term in the error expansion, but due to its non-linear nature, it also introduces new error terms. For the weight functions w_1 and w_2, these introduced terms do not change the form of the error expansion; but for w_3 and w_4, the form of the error expansion is changed and will require extra elimination steps. Nevertheless, the method is still an improvement over the single use of (3), albeit marginally for the latter pair of weight functions, especially in the later steps.

Motivated by the above equivalence, we show that, at least for the types of integral under consideration, the first step of the Levin U transformation (call this $U1$) is an analogue of the Aitken's Δ^2 process based on the harmonic sequence of interval subdivision, i.e., that it eliminates the dominant term in the error expansion. In the remainder of this section, we present results obtained by symbolic manipulation. Assume a sequence has the form $S_r = S + p(r)$ and apply the $U1$ transformation:

$$U_{1n} = \frac{S_n/n\Delta S_{n-1} - S_{n+1}/(n+1)\Delta S_n}{1/n\Delta S_{n-1} - 1/(n+1)\Delta S_n}.$$

It follows that

$$U_{1n} - S = \frac{p(n+1)[p(n) + np(n-1)] - (n+1)p^2(n)}{(n+1)p(n+1) - (2n+1)p(n) + np(n-1)}. \tag{4}$$

We consider the error expansions appropriate for the weight functions w_1, w_2, w_3 and w_4: (i) Substituting

$$p(n) = a_0/n^s + a_1/n^{s+1} + a_2/n^{s+2} + a_3/n^{s+3} + \dots, \quad 0 < s \tag{5}$$

into (4) (for $w = w_1$, s integer, or $w = w_2$, s non-integer), yields

$$U_{1n} - S = \frac{An^{-2s-1} + \mathcal{O}(n^{-2s-2})}{Bn^{-s} + \mathcal{O}(n^{-s-1})},$$

where $A = a_0 s(s+1)/2 + a_1$ and $B = s^2$. In the limit as $n \to \infty$,

$$U_{1n} = S + Cn^{-s-1} + \mathcal{O}(n^{-s-2}),$$

where $C = (a_0 s(s+1) + 2a_1)/(2s^2)$.

(ii) If $w = w_3$ or $w = w_4$, then $p(n)$ is of the form

$$p(n) = a_0/n^s + a_1/n^{s+1} + \ldots + b_0/n^t + b_1/n^{t+1} + \ldots. \tag{6}$$

For example, under the assumption that $0 < s < t < s+1$, we deduce that

$$U_{1n} - S = \frac{An^{-t-s} + Bn^{-2s-1} + Cn^{-t-s-1} + \mathcal{O}(n^{-2t-1})}{Dn^{-s} + En^{-t} + \mathcal{O}(n^{-s-1})},$$

where A, B, C, D, E are constants, with $A = b_0(t-s)^2$ and $D = s^2$. In the limit for $n \to \infty$ we have

$$U_{1n} = S + Kn^{-t} + \begin{cases} \mathcal{O}(n^{-2t+s}) & 2s+1 \geq 2t \\ \mathcal{O}(n^{-s-1}) & 2s+1 \leq 2t \end{cases}$$

where $K = b_0(t/s - 1)^2$.

We conclude that for error expansions of the form (5) and (6), in the limit, the *U1* transformation eliminates the dominant error term. For 'mixed-term' error expansions like (6), new terms with powers of $(1/n)$ not present in the original expansion are introduced. Thus, by iterating the *U1* transformation, we expect at least the first few iterations to be effective in decreasing the error.

We can go further: since a higher-order transformation eliminates more terms (although not necessarily the dominant ones), we expect for example the iterated *U4* to attain accuracies better than the iterated *U1*. As an illustration, given six original approximations, the *U1* transformation can be iterated twice, effectively eliminating one term from the original expansion in the first application and eliminating a term from the intermediate expansion in the second. The *U4* transformation, although applied only once, effectively eliminates four terms from the original expansion.

3 Numerical results

We concentrate mainly on integrals with weight functions w_3 and w_4, choosing as particular examples $I_3 = \int_0^1 x^{1/2} dx$ and $I_4 = \int_0^1 x^{1/2}(1-x)^{3/4} dx$. Quadrature approximations are generated using the m-copy midpoint rule with m following the H sequence. All computations are performed in quadruple precision on a VAX8800 (approximately 32 decimal digits). After each extrapolation step, the exact relative error is plotted against the cumulative number of function evaluations.

When $w = w_1$ or $w = w_2$, the iterated *U4* gives results only slightly inferior to those of the straight Levin U transformation; the accuracy attained in both cases is limited by round-off introduced during the computations. Compared with the ϵ algorithm, the U transformation and iterated *U4* are far more economical up to the point where round-off becomes significant (~ 250 function evaluations in Figure 1).

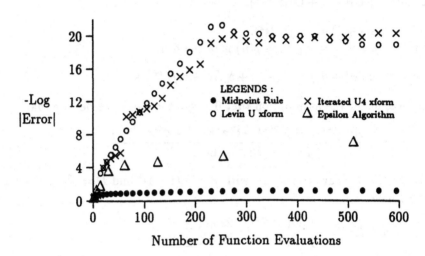

Figure 1. Levin U vs. Iterated U4 vs. Epsilon Algorithm for
$$I_2 = \int_0^1 [x(1-x)]^{-1/2}dx$$

For the integrals I_3 and I_4, comparisons of the U transformation, the iterated $U1$ and iterated $U4$ are given in Figures 2 and 3. The superiority of the iterated $U4$ over the other two transformations is evident (especially for I_4). Note that in this range, all three methods reach a 'plateau' in performance. This is not yet due to round-off, but rather, in the case of the U transformation, to the existence of uneliminated terms in the error expansion, and for the iterated $U1$ and $U4$ transformations, the limit is imposed by an accumulation of introduced terms. Though the performance of the U transformation is limited by the non-elimination of the dominant term, the fact that some terms are nevertheless being eliminated is indicated by the greater slope in its performance curve compared to that of the original midpoint rule approximations.

The iterated $U4$ transformation and the ε algorithm are compared in Figures 4 and 5. For these examples and range of accuracies, the iterated $U4$ is more efficient

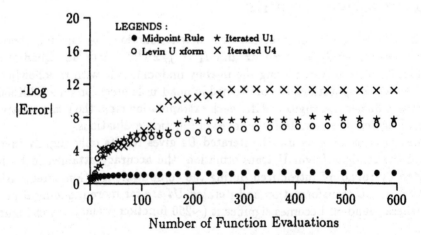

Figure 2. Levin U vs. Iterated U1 vs. Iterated U4 for
$$I_3 = \int_0^1 x^{-1/2}dx$$

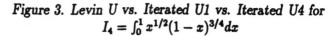

Figure 3. Levin U vs. Iterated U1 vs. Iterated U4 for
$I_4 = \int_0^1 x^{1/2}(1-x)^{3/4}dx$

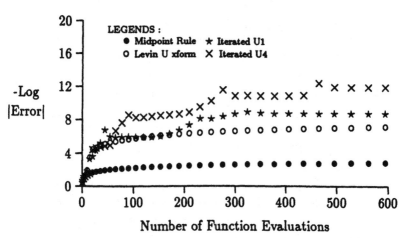

than the ε algorithm. The ε algorithm may eventually attain better accuracies than the iterated $U4$ but after a far greater number of function evaluations. Further, the existence of a greater number of extrapolated results makes the determination of an effective error estimate easier for an automated version of the iterated $U4$ than for the ε algorithm. The cost of conservative error estimation is certainly much lower.

4 Concluding Remarks

Based on the theoretical and numerical evidence, the iterated $U4$ transformation shows promise for general use and for inclusion in an automatic quadrature routine.

Figure 4. Iterated U4 vs. Epsilon Algorithm for
$I_3 = \int_0^1 x^{-1/2}dx$

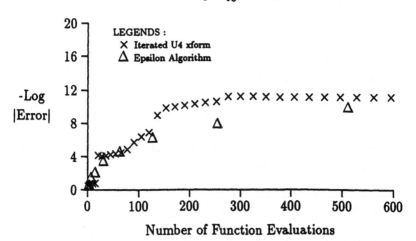

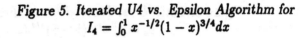

Figure 5. Iterated U4 vs. Epsilon Algorithm for
$$I_4 = \int_0^1 x^{-1/2}(1-x)^{3/4}dx$$

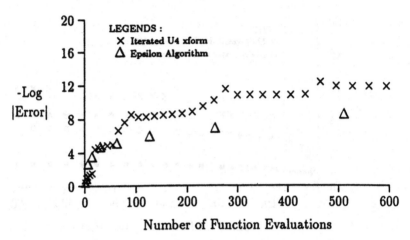

Number of Function Evaluations

This is especially true for multi-variable integration where error expansions similar to those considered here are common and for which the advantage of using the harmonic sequence as subdivision scheme will be even more pronounced.

References

[1] R.L. Cariño, I. Robinson, and E. de Doncker (1989), Approximate integration by the Levin transformation, *In preparation*.

[2] J.S.R. Chisholm, A. Genz and G.E. Rowlands (1973), Accelerated convergence of quadrature approximations, *J. Comp. Phys.*, v. 10, pp. 284-307.

[3] E. de Doncker (1978), An adaptive extrapolation algorithm for automatic integration, *SIGNUM Newsl.*, v.13, pp. 12-18.

[4] L. Fox (1967), Romberg integration for a class of singular integrands, *Comput. J.*, v. 10, pp. 87-93.

[5] L. Fox and L. Hayes (1970), On the definite integration of singular integrals, *SIAM Review*, v. 12, pp. 449-457.

[6] D. Kahaner (1972), Numerical quadrature by the ϵ algorithm, *Math. Comp.*, v. 26, pp. 689-693.

[7] D. Levin (1973), Development of non-linear transformations for improving convergence of sequences, *Intern. J. Computer Math.*, v. B3, pp. 371–388.

[8] A. Sidi (1979), Convergence properties of some nonlinear sequence transformations, *Math. Comp.*, v. 33, pp. 315-326.

[9] P. Wynn (1956), On a device for computing the $e_m(S_n)$ transformation, *Math. Comp.*, v. 10, pp. 91-96.

Recent Advances in
Shape Preserving Piecewise Cubic Interpolation

Thomas Sprague

Department of Mathematics and Statistics
Western Michigan University
Kalamazoo, Michigan 49008

Abstract

A number of recent papers have addressed the problem of constructing monotone piecewise cubic interpolants to monotone data. These have focused not only on the monotonicity of the interpolant, but also on properties such as "visual pleasure", and optimal order error bounds. We review some of these results, and generalize them by constructing C^1 piecewise cubic polynomial interpolants to non-monotone data. These interpolants have a minimum number of changes in sign in the first derivative and approximate an underlying function and its first derivative with optimal order.

1 Introduction

The problem of constructing accurate interpolants without unnecessary oscillations is very old. The use of piecewise polynomials, especially the cubic spline functions, partially solve this problem. These of course may also oscillate, and a number of modifications, including the choice of end-point conditions (e.g. Akima's interpolation) or more sophisticated approaches such as the taut spline have been suggested.

More recently, the restriction of the problem to finding monotone interpolants to monotone data has received considerable attention. Fritsch and Carlson [6], in their fundamental paper of 1980, demonstrated that monotone piecewise cubics could be characterized in terms of the slopes of the interpolant at adjacent knots. The slopes scaled by the first divided difference in the data over the interval, (α, β), must lie in a certain region in the first quadrant. This suggested that an initial cubic spline interpolant could be modified to force monotonicity by projecting (α, β) onto this region. By choosing certain subsets of this region, Fritsch and Carlson were able to construct interpolants that were not only monotone, but were "visually pleasing."

Eisenstat, Jackson, and Lewis [5] subsequently analyzed these and other "fit and modify" algorithms, and showed that those of Fritsch and Carlson were only third order accurate to an underlying C^3 monotone function. They also produced a new fourth order algorithm. Yan [7] improved on the accuracy of the algorithms of Fritsch and Carlson by adding knots to his interpolant. Finally, Beatson and Wolcowicz [2] gave algorithms with the *optimal order approximation property*. That is, the error in approximating an underlying function $f \in C^j$ with the piecewise cubic interpolant s satisfies

$$\|f^{(l)} - s^{(l)}\| \le K\delta^{j-l}\omega(f^{(j)}, \delta), \quad 1 \le j \le 3, \ 0 \le l \le 1$$

This was achieved by adding at most one knot to the interior of each interval—a refinement of the device employed by Yan. They also illustrated how one may retain the "visually pleasing" property of Fritsch and Carlson by projecting the endpoint slopes slightly into the interior of the monotonicity region, and still retain the optimal order approximation (1).

This work greatly improved the situation for monotone functions. But one frequently desires to reduce the number of oscillations in an interpolant to non-monotone data, while preserving (1). In this paper, we generalize the algorithm of Beatson and Wolcowicz to produce C^1 piecewise cubic interpolants to non-monotone data that satisfy (1) and have no unnecessary changes in direction (i.e. the sign of the first derivative).

More specifically, if $D = \{(x_i, f_i) \mid x_1 < x_2 < \cdots < x_n, \, y_i = f(x_i), \, f \in C^j\}$ is a data set detecting all changes in direction of f then the algorithm given below produces a C^1 piecewise cubic interpolant satisfying (1), which is monotone wherever f is known to be monotone, and has no more changes in direction than the piecewise linear interpolant to the data.

2 Some earlier results

The algorithm developed below depends heavily on four previous results of Fritsch and Carlson [6], Beatson [1], and Beatson and Wolcowicz [2].

LEMMA 1 (F.N. Fritsch and R.E. Carlson). *Let p be a cubic polynomial on $[a, b]$, $a < b$, and let $p[a, b] = \frac{p(b) - p(a)}{b - a}$. Then necessary and sufficient conditions for p to be monotone on $[a, b]$, are:*

(i) *If $p[a, b] = 0$, then $p' \equiv 0$ on $[a, b]$.*

(ii) *If $p[a, b] \neq 0$, and $(\alpha, \beta) = \frac{1}{p[a,b]}(p'(a), p'(b))$, then $(\alpha, \beta) \in \mathcal{M}$, where*
$$\mathcal{M} = \{(\alpha, \beta) \mid 0 \geq (\alpha - 1)^2 + (\alpha - 1)(\beta - 1) + (\beta - 1)^2 - 3(\alpha + \beta - 2)\}$$
$$\cup \{(\alpha, \beta) \mid 0 \leq \alpha, \, 0 \leq \beta, \, \alpha + \beta \leq 3\}.$$

For the algorithms below, we shall need to produce optimal order error estimates for the derivatives of a function f on $[a, b]$. The following result of Beatson shows that this may be accomplished with a cubic spline function. (Beatson's result is more general than reported here).

LEMMA 2 (R.K. Beatson). *Let $a = t_0 < t_1 < \cdots < t_n = b$, and let $f \in C^j[a, b]$, $j = 2$, or 3. Let $s \in C^2$ be the cubic spline interpolant determined by the not-a-knot end condition of deBoor, or by putting $s^{(l)}(x_m)$ equal to the corresponding values of local fourth order interpolants for l fixed at 1 or 2, and $m = 0$, and n. Then, if $f \in C^j[a, b]$ for $j = 2$ or 3 where $n \geq 3$ ($n \geq 5$ for the not-a-knot condition), there exists a constant C so that*

(5) $$\|(f - s)^{(k)}\|_{[t_i, t_{i+1}]} \leq C h_i^{2-k} \delta^{j-2} \omega(f^{(j)}, \delta), \qquad 0 \leq i \leq n-1, \quad k = 0, 1, 2.$$

LEMMA 3 (R.K. Beatson). *Let p be a polynomial of order 4 interpolating $f \in C^j[c, d]$ at c and d, and satisfying*

(6) $$|p'(x) - f'(x)| \leq \epsilon, \quad \text{for } x = c, d.$$

Then,

$$(7) \qquad \|f^{(l)} - p^{(l)}\|_{[c,d]} \leq \frac{7}{2^{j-l+1}}(d-c)^{j-l}\omega(f^{(j)},\delta) + \epsilon\left(\frac{d-c}{2}\right)^{1-l}, \quad l = 0,1.$$

In particular, lemma 3 shows that if one has an optimal order algorithm to produce estimates of f' at nodes of interpolation, then the piecewise cubic hermite interpolant constructed from these slopes must satisfy (1).

LEMMA 4 (R.K. Beatson and H. Wolcowicz). *Let* $k \geq 3$. *Let a mesh* $t : t_0 < t_1 < \cdots < t_n$ *be given with mesh size* $\delta = \max\{t_{i+1} - t_i \mid 0 \leq i \leq n-1\}$. *Let* $r : r_0 \leq r_1 \leq \cdots \leq r_m$ *be a superset of* t *with* $r_{i+k-2} > r_i$ *for* $0 \leq i \leq m - k + 2$. *Further suppose that each interval* $[t_i, t_{i+1}]$ *contains at least* k *knots* r_l. *Let* $1 \leq j \leq k-1$. *Then for each monotone* $f \in C^j[t_0, t_n]$, *there exists a piecewise polynomial function* $s \in S_{r,k} \subset C^1[t_0, t_n]$ *such that*

$$(8) \qquad \begin{aligned} &(i) \quad s(t_i) = f(t_i), \quad 0 \leq i \leq n; \\ &(ii) \quad s \text{ is monotone on } [t_0, t_n]; \\ &(iii) \quad \|f^{(l)} - s^{(l)}\|_{[t_o, t_n]} \leq C_3\delta^{j-l}\omega(f^{(j)},\delta), \quad l = 0,1. \end{aligned}$$

Furthermore, if g *is a* (C^2) *cubic spline function satisfying the hypotheses of lemma 2, then there exists an algorithm to construct such interpolants* s *so that* $|s'(x_i)| \leq |g'(x_i)|$ *for each* i.

3 Extensions to Previous Results

We now turn our attention to the problem for arbitrary direction determining data sets. We shall first establish the existence of optimal order co-monotone piecewise cubic interpolants for these data sets, and then consider an algorithm for their construction.

Suppose that a direction determining data set $D = \{(x_i, y_i) \mid x_1 < x_2 < \cdots < x_n, y_i = f(x_i)\}$ has been given. Suppose further that we have a set of optimal order approximations to the derivatives $g_i = f'(x_i)$. Now if for any i, $g_i f'(x_i) < 0$, replace g_i by $-g_i$, so that all of the signs of the g_i are correct. Then we may infer from D and the g_i whether f is monotone on subinterval I. On all subintervals where f is monotone, construct a monotone interpolant s (lemma 4), perhaps further modifying some of the g_i. We claim that if on the remaining subintervals, we take s to be the piecewise cubic hermite interpolant to the values (x_i, y_i, g_i), then s will be both co-monotone with D, and satisfy (1).

To see this, consider a subinterval $I = [x_i, x_{i+1}]$, where f is not monotone. Now either $g_i g_{i+1} < 0$, or f' changes sign twice on I. In the former case, since s' is a quadratic on I, and has an odd number of zeros in I, it has exactly one zero in I. In the latter case, the piecewise cubic hermite interpolant will also change direction twice on I. So the hermite interpolant has no unnecessary changes in direction. Thus setting s equal to the piecewise cubic hermite interpolant on subintervals I where f is not monotone yields a co-monotone interpolant. Finally, we note that at each step, the initial derivative estimates g_i are altered in such a way that the $|g_i|$ either remain constant, or are reduced. Furthermore they were changed either to correct errors in sign, or according to an algorithm yielding optimal order monotone interpolants. Thus, by lemma 3, s approximates f' with optimal order. We formalize these remarks with the following theorem.

THEOREM 1. *Let D be a direction determining data set for f on $[a, b]$, and let $G = \{g_i \mid i = 1, 2, \dots, n\}$ be a set of optimal order approximations to $f'(x_i)$, $i = 1, 2, \dots, n$. Then there exists a C^1 piecewise cubic interpolant s, interpolating and co-monotone with D, satisfying*

$$(9) \qquad |s^{(l)}(x_i) - f^{(l)}(x_i)| \leq K\delta^{j-l}\omega\left(f(j), \delta\right) \text{ for } i = 1, 2, \dots, n, \text{ and } l = 0, 1$$

and

$$(10) \qquad\qquad |s'(x_i)| \leq |g_i|, i = 1, 2, \dots, n$$

Having established the existence of the desired interpolant s, we now turn to the problem of its construction. Before formally presenting an algorithm, however, observe that we have reduced the problem to the following search problem.

Consider the set of data points (x_i, y_i) for which the sign of f' cannot be inferred from D; we shall refer to such points as *critical data points*, or simply as critical. Each critical point presents us with two options: start the interpolation with $f'(x_i) \approx g_i$ or $-g_i$. Once these decisions have been made, an essentially unique interpolant s is determined. At least one of these is guaranteed by theorem 1 to have the desired properties. Our task then is to be able to recognize a desirable interpolant, and to be able to locate one efficiently.

As for the recognition of a desirable interpolant, we simply apply the triangle inequality. Since both a desirable interpolant s and the initial estimates g_i approximate f', we need only choose s so that $\max_i |s'(x_i) - g_i|$ is, in some sense, "small". To search for this interpolant, we will construct a multistage graph G, so that there is a one-to-one correspondence between paths through G, and the choices $f'(x_i) \approx g_i$ or $-g_i$. A weighting function will be constructed so that a path of minimum weight corresponds to an interpolant which changes the original estimates g_i in a controlled—though not necessarily minimal—way.

4 Algorithm

We now turn to the problem of efficiently locating a desirable interpolant. As indicated above, this algorithm depends on the construction of an appropriate graph, and a weighting function for it edges.

The construction of the multistage graph G is quite simple. The graph contains n stages S_i, corresponding to the data points of D. Stage S_i corresponds to $P_i = (x_i, y_i)$ it contains a single vertex v_i if P_i is not critical, and two vertices v_i^+ and v_i^- otherwise. In the case that P_i is critical, the vertices correspond to the choices $f'(x_i) \approx \pm g_i$ in the obvious way. The edge set of G contains all edges between adjacent stages S_i and S_{i+1} and no others. Hence there will be either one, two, or four edges between any two adjacent stages. Finally, we associate an interpolant s with each $v_1 - v_n$ path $\mathcal{P}$ through G (simply "path" in the sequel). This interpolant is one obtained as in the proof of theorem 1. An example of a typical data set D, and the associated graph G appears in figure 1.

We construct a weighting function $w(e)$ for the edges of G so that these weights bound the value $|g_i - s'(x_i)|$. Before constructing any of the weights, we modify the derivative estimates g_i so that s is an optimal order monotone interpolant, on subintervals

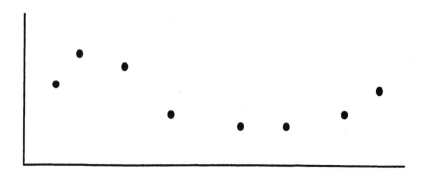

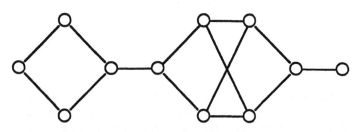

figure 1. A data set D and associated graph G.

where f is known to be monotone. Let e be an edge between stages S_i and S_{i+1}, corresponding to initial slope estimates $h_i = \pm g_i$ and $h_{i+1} = \pm g_{i+1}$. If h_i, h_{i+1}, and $f[x_i, x_{i+1}]$ all agree in sign, find a local optimal order monotone piecewise cubic interpolant t to $x_i, y_i)$, (x_{i+1}, y_{i+1}), h_i and h_{i+1}, and set $w(e) = \max_{j=i,i+1} |h_j - t'(x_j)|$. Otherwise, set $w(e) = \max_{j=i,i+1} |h_j - g_j|$.

Now consider a path $\mathcal{P}$ through G. Let the *cost* of $\mathcal{P}$ be given by $\text{cost}(\mathcal{P}) := B(s) := \max_{e \in \mathcal{P}} w(e)$. There may be significant interactions between the subintervals, but since an algorithm to construct monotone interpolants cannot change the sign of the slope estimates s_i, it can be shown that

11) $$\frac{1}{2} B(s) \leq \max |g_i - s'(x_i)| \leq B(s).$$

So that $B(s)$ is a good approximation to the quantity we wish to control. Thus, if we choose s so that $B(s)$ is minimized, s should be a good approximation to f.

Once this graph has been constructed, we can find a minimum cost path through it in time linear in n. A minimum cost path from stage S_1 to S_2 is trivial. Given a minimum cost path from S_1 to S_i it can be extended to S_{i+1} by examining at most four edges, since all possible edges exist between stages. Hence, we must examine at most $4(n-1)$ edges to construct $\mathcal{P}$.

THEOREM 2. *Let a direction determining data set D, and initial optimal order error estimates g_i to $f'(x_i)$ be given. Let G be the multistage graph associated with D, and s*

the interpolant corresponding to a minimum cost path $\mathcal{P}$ through G. Then s is an optimal order co-monotone interpolant to D.

PROOF: It follows from the discussion preceding Theorem 1, that every interpolant s corresponding to a path through G is co-monotone with D. We need only show that inequality (1) holds. We obtain this from the triangle inequality, and inequality (11).

Let s be an interpolant with minimum bound $B(s)$. Let s^* be an interpolant with minimum error $\max |(s^*)'(x_i) - f'(x_i)|$. Then

$$\max_i |s'(x_i) - f'(x_i)| \leq \max_i |s'(x_i) - g_i| + \max_i |g_i - f'(x_i)|$$

$$\leq 2 \max_i |(s^*)'(x_i) - g_i| + \max_i |g_i - f'(x_i)|$$

$$\leq 2 \max \left\{ 2 \max_i |(s^*)'(x_i) - g_i|, \ \max_i |g_i - f'(x_i)| \right\}$$

$$\leq 4C\delta^{j-1}\omega\left(f^{(j)}, \delta\right)$$

We summarize our results in a formal algorithm.

ALGORITHM. *Given a direction determining data set D, and algorithms to construct optimal order estimates g_i to $f'(x_i)$, and monotone piecewise cubic interpolants to monotone data satisfying (1), we construct a co-monotone piecewise cubic interpolant to D as follows.*

1.) Compute initial optimal order estimates g_i to $f'(x_i)$, and correct their signs wherever the signs of f' can be inferred from D.
2.) Modify the g_i to correspond to a monotone piecewise cubic interpolant on each subinterval I where f is known to be monotone.
3.) Construct the weighted multistage graph G, corresponding to D and the g_i.
4.) Find a minimum cost path $\mathcal{P}$ through G.
5.) The desired interpolant is s, where s corresponds to $\mathcal{P}$.

5 Implementation

The above algorithm provides a method for computing the *slopes* for an interpolant to the data set D. While this certainly prescribes a unique piecewise cubic interpolant, it may not be convenient for some implementations. Namely, if there exist long regions in which the values of the initial slopes g_i are unchanged, and if a one uses a C^2 cubic spline to compute the g_i, then specification of s in terms of hermite data is not efficient in storage. For if one wants to express the interpolant in terms of B-splines, hermite data is most naturally expressed with double knots everywhere, while only single knots are necessary on intervals where s has two continuous derivatives. It is therefore suggested that one keep track of which slopes g_i have been changed, and which break points x_i were added in the construction of the interpolant. At such points assume that a double knot is needed for the B-spline representation. If however the initial slope g_i is retained, then s will have two continuous derivatives at x_i, and a single knot will suffice.

We may use this information to construct a knot sequence t, a superset of x,

$$t : t_o = \cdots = t_3 = x_1 < t_4 \leq t_5 \cdots \leq t_{m-3} = \cdots = t_m = x_n$$

satisfying $t_i < t_{i+2}$. One may then use the output of the above algorithm to construct the B-spline coefficients.

References

[1] R.K. Beatson, *On the convergence of some cubic spline interpolation schemes*, SIAM J. Numer. Anal., 22(1985) pp. 1220-1237.

[2] R.K. Beatson and H. Wolcowicz, *Post-processing piecewise cubics for monotonicity*, SIAM J. Numer. Anal., 26(1989), pp 480 - 502.

[3] Carl de Boor, *A Practical Guide to Splines*, Springer–Verlag: 1978.

[4] S.D. Conte and Carl de Boor, *Elementary Numerical Analysis*, 3rd ed., McGraw–Hill: 1980.

[5] S.C. Eisenstat, K.R. Jackson, and J.W. Lewis, *The order of piecewise cubic interpolation*, SIAM J. Numer. Anal., 22(1985), pp. 1220-1237.

[6] F.N. Fritsch and R.E. Carlson, *Monotone piecewise cubic interpolation*, SIAM J. Numer. Anal., 17(1980), 238-246.

[7] Z. Yan, *Piecewise cubic curve fitting algorithm*, Mathematics Department, University of South Carolina, Columbia, SC, 1986.

Structured Graph Models: An Efficient Tool for VLSI Design

M. Ancona
Instituto per la Matematica Applicata
16132 Genoa, Italy

K. S. Bagga
Department of Computer Science
Ball State University
Muncie, Indiana 47306 U.S.A.
BITNET: 00ksbagga@bsuvax1

E. Bruzzone   L. De Floriani
Instituto per la Matematica Applicata
16132 Genoa, Italy

J. S. Deogun
Department of Computer Science
University of Nebraska
Lincoln, Nebraska 68588 U.S.A.

Abstract

Hierarchical graph models are a powerful tool for describing VLSI circuits. They combine the representation of a hierarchical decomposition of a circuit with a graph description of its topological structure in terms of components and connections. *Structured Graphs* are an example of such models. In this paper we consider the graph-theoretic problems of spanning trees and Steiner trees in structured graphs. These have connections with the global routing problems in VLSI circuits.

1   Introduction

The motivation for defining structured graphs is provided by the increasing complexity of integrated circuits, and the task of developing designs and specifications for them. One way to consider VLSI design problems is to do hierarchical decomposition to reduce the circuit complexity to a manageable size. Our proposed model is the *structured graph* which is a hierarchical graph model. It provides a graph theoretic description of the design object as a hierarchy of interconnected nets of components. Thus one can represent the object at different levels of abstraction. Also one can keep track of the design process, make local updatings and consistency checks of the design efficiently.

A structured graph $\hat{G}$ may be regarded as a hierarchical description of a *flat* graph G, called the *expanded graph* defined by $\hat{G}$. The expanded graph G associated with $\hat{G}$ provides a description of the circuit at the lowest level of detail and is obtained from S by replacing each module of the circuit by its detailed description.

The definition of a structured graph leads to the concept of structured solution. A *structured solution* to a problem in a structured graph is a solution which reflects the hierarchical organization in such a way that a confinement of this solution to any graph in the model is a well-defined solution to the same problem for that graph. The basic objective of using a structured graph model is to try to solve the computation problem associated with each graph component of the model as much independently as possible from the others.

In this paper we consider the spanning tree and the Steiner tree problems in the framework of structured graphs. Both of these problems have important applications in the global routing of VLSI circuits. A minimum cost spanning tree is employed in algorithms for global routing as an approximation to the Steiner minimum cost tree, and also in the placement of the components of a circuit to decide individual block locations without trying the actual routing. In the latter case, a simpler route is sufficient, and thus a minimum spanning tree algorithm is often employed, since it performs better in terms of efficiency compared to any heuristic for Steiner tree computation. If a hierarchical graph-based description of an IC is adopted, the computation problem is reduced to that of finding a structured spanning tree of minimum cost.

2   Structured Graphs

The concept of a structured graph is based on the notion of condensation of a connected subgraph of a graph. For several properties of structured graphs and their applications to PERT/CPM networks, and to communication and computer networks the reader is referred to [1], [2], and [4].

Here we review the definition of a structured graph as applied to undirected graphs. The standard graph theoretic terminology may be found in [5]. All the graphs we consider are connected. Given a graph $G = (V,E)$, and a subgraph $G' = (V',E')$ of G a vertex $x \in V'$ is called a *boundary vertex* of G' if there is a vertex $y \in V - V'$, such that $xy \in E$. Figure 1 on the next page shows a graph G, a subgraph G' induced by the inner five vertices, and the shaded boundary vertices of G' in G. We define the *reduced graph* R given by G and G' as the graph obtained from G in which G' is replaced by a single vertex m(called a *macrovertex*), and this vertex m is joined to those vertices of G - G' which have edges incident with the boundary vertices of G'. R is in general a multigraph. Figure 2 shows the graph obtained when the subgraph G' of G in Figure 1 reduced to a vertex.

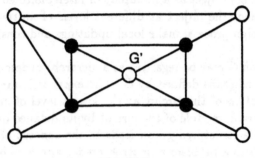

FIGURE 1

The relationship between m and the graph G' it replaces can be maintained by keeping track of the adjacencies of the neighboring vertices of m in R with the boundary vertices in G'. This can be done by labeling the edges in R incident with m with labels which name the appropriate boundary vertices of G'.

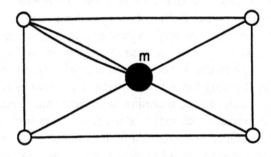

FIGURE 2

In the other direction, given a graph R with a macrovertex m, and given a graph G', R can be *expanded* to a graph G by replacing m by G' and by joining the neighboring vertices of m in R by specified vertices of G'. G' is called the *replacement graph* of m.

The repeated application of reductions to a given graph G gives a hierarchical representation of G, called a structured graph. More formally, a *structured graph* consists of a family $\hat{G} = \{G_0, G_1, G_2, ..., G_n\}$ of graphs $G_i = (V_i, E_i)$ such that for every G_i in $\hat{G} - \{G_0\}$, there exists exactly one G_j in $\hat{G}$, $j \neq i$, such that G_i is the replacement graph of a macrovertex m_i in G_j with the edges in G_j incident with m_i appropriately labeled as explained earlier.

In such a setting, G_j is called the *parent graph* of G_i, and G_i is called the *child graph* of G_j. G_0 is called the *root graph* of the structured graph $\hat{G}$. This gives a tree description of $\hat{G}$ in terms of its components G_k.

A structured graph $\hat{G}$ is thus a hierarchical representation of a graph at different levels of abstraction. A structured graph $\hat{G}$ can be obtained from a given graph G through a sequence of reductions, or it may be built directly as the result of a hierarchical design process. The graph G represented by a given structured graph $\hat{G}$ is called the *completely expanded graph* defined by $\hat{G}$.

3   Spanning Trees

In this section we introduce the definition of a spanning tree of a structured graph. Suppose $\hat{G} = \{G_0, G_1, G_2, ..., G_n\}$ is a structured graph. Also suppose that for $i = 0, 1, 2, ..., n$, S_i is a spanning tree of G_i. We define a structured graph $\hat{S} = \{S_0, S_1, S_2, ..., S_n\}$ as follows. If G_i is the replacement graph of a macrovertex m_i in G_j, then define S_i to be the replacement graph of the macrovertex m_i in S_j, with the labels of edges in S_j incident with m_i the same as those in G_j. Then $\hat{S}$ is called a *spanning tree* of $\hat{G}$. Let G and S be the completely expanded subgraphs of $\hat{G}$ and $\hat{S}$ respectively. Some basic properties of S are given by the following theorem.

Theorem 1 *With G, $\hat{G}$, S, $\hat{S}$ as above, we have*
i. The tree description of $\hat{S}$ is the same as that of $\hat{G}$.
ii. S is a spanning tree of G.

Proof *i.* This follows from the definition of $\hat{S}$.
ii. Clearly, S is a spanning subgraph of G. Also, since each macrovertex in S is replaced by trees, a cycle in S would imply the existence of a cycle in some S_i, a contradiction. $\square$

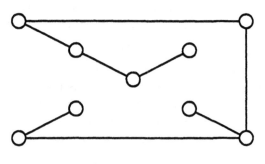

FIGURE 3

We thus have a method of computing the spanning tree of G by recursively expanding the macrovertices of a spanning tree $\hat{S}$ of $\hat{G}$. A spanning tree $\hat{S}$ of $\hat{G}$ can be obtained by applying standard graph traversal algorithms. This also implies that any modification on a component of $\hat{G}$ does not cause the recomputation of the whole spanning tree of $\hat{G}$.

We observe, however, that there are spanning trees of G which cannot be obtained by expanding spanning trees of $\hat{G}$. Figure 3 shows such a spanning tree of the graph G of Figure 1.

4   Steiner Trees in Structured Graphs

In this section we consider the Steiner tree problem in structured graphs. We first briefly review the Steiner problem in graphs. Given a graph $G = (V, E)$, and a subset B of V, a connected subgraph G' of G containing B is called a *Steiner subgraph* of

G for B. The vertices of B are called *base vertices*. For a weighted graph G any minimum weight Steiner subgraph of G for B is a tree called the *minimum weight Steiner tree* of G for B. The problem of finding a minimum weight spanning tree for a given G and B is NP-complete. See [6] for a survey of exact or heuristic algorithms for this problem.

Now consider a weighted structured graph $\hat{G} = \{G_0, G_1, G_2, ..., G_n\}$. A structured graph $\hat{H}$ is called a *structured subgraph* of $\hat{G}$ if every component of $\hat{H}$ is a subgraph of a component of $\hat{G}$. For $i = 0, 1, 2, ..., n$, let B_i be a nonempty subset of vertices in G_i such that B_i contains all the macrovertices and boundary vertices of G_i. A structured subgraph $\hat{S} = \{S_0, S_1, S_2, ..., S_n\}$ is a *Steiner subgraph* of $\hat{G}$ for the family $\mathcal{B} = \{B_0, B_1, B_2, ..., B_n\}$ if S_i is a Steiner subgraph of G_i for B_i for $i = 0, 1, 2, ..., n$.

The assumption that the macrovertices and the boundary vertices of each component of a structured graph are base vertices of that component is natural due to the application of structured graphs to global routing of VLSI circuits.

Just as in the case of graphs, it turns out that with all weights being positive, a minimum weight Steiner subgraph of $\hat{G}$ for the family $\mathcal{B}$ is a tree, that is, each component of the subgraph is a tree. Moreover we have the following result. Its proof is straightforward and is therefore omitted.

Theorem 2 *Suppose $\hat{S}$ as above is a minimum weight Steiner tree of $\hat{G}$ for a family $\mathcal{B}$. Then every component S_i of $\hat{S}$ is a minimum weight Steiner tree of G_i for B_i.* □

Finally we describe a structured solution to the Steiner problem in a graph G. Suppose G is the completely expanded graph of a structured graph $\hat{G}$, $\mathcal{B} = \{B_0, B_1, B_2, ..., B_n\}$ is a family of base vertices, M_i is the set of macrovertices in G_i, and $B_G = \bigcup_{i=0}^{n}(B_i - M_i)$. Also suppose that $\hat{S}$ is a Steiner minimum cost tree of $\hat{G}$. Then the completely expanded graph S of $\hat{S}$ is called a *Steiner minimum weight strutured subgraph* of G for B_G. When all the weights are positive, this subgraph is a tree.

We now state a sufficient condition for S to be a Steiner minimum weight subgraph of G for B_G. First we need a definition. Let $diam(G_i)$ denote the weight of a longest simple path in the component G_i of $\hat{G}$. Then $\hat{G}$ is said to satisfy the *diameter property* if for every G_i, and every G_j which is a child graph of G_i, with m_j being the corresponding macrovertex of G_i, $diam(G_i)$ is less than the weight of all the edges incident to m_j.

We state our last theorem without proof. A slightly more general version of it may be found in [3].

Theorem 3 *With G, $\hat{G}$, $\mathcal{B}$, and B_G as above, if $\hat{G}$ satisfies the diameter property, then a Steiner minimum weight structured graph of G for B_G is a Steiner minimum weight subgraph of G for B_G in the usual sense.* □

We thus have a structured solution to the Steiner graph problem.

References

[1] M. Ancona, L. De Floriani. Computational Algorithms for Hierarchically Structured Project Networks, *Operations Research Letters*, vol. 1, no. 5, 1982.

[2] M. Ancona, L. De Floriani, J.S. Deogun. Path Problems in Structured graphs. *The Computer Journal*, vol. 29, no. 6, 1986.

[3] M. Ancona, E. Bruzzone, L. De Floriani. The Steiner Problem in structured Graphs. *Tech. Rep. I.M.A.*, 28-88, Genova, 1988.

[4] L. De Floriani, J.S. Deogun. Structured Graphs and Spanning Trees. *Proceedings IEEE COMPSAC'83*, Chicago, November 1983.

[5] F. Harary. *Graph Theory*. Addison Wesley, Reading, Mass., 1977.

[6] P. Winter. Steiner Problem in Networks: A Survey. *Networks*, vol. 17, 1987, pp 129-167.

A STOCHASTIC ALGORITHM FOR
CIRCUIT BI-PARTITIONING

Youssef Saab and Vasant Rao

Coordinated Science Laboratory
and Department of Electrical and Computer Engineering
University of Illinois at Urbana-Champaign
1101 W. Springfield Avenue,
Urbana, Illinois 61801.

ABSTRACT

Circuit bi-partitioning is an important step in placement algorithms based on the min-cut paradigm. In this paper, we present a stochastic algorithm for circuit bi-partitioning (BIPART) which minimizes the number of nets cut while maintaining a tight control on the sizes of the two parts. BIPART performs better than simulated annealing and the Fiduccia-Matheyses algorithm, and runs in linear time per iteration.

1. INTRODUCTION

Circuit bi-partitioning has several applications in VLSI layout such as floorplanning and module placement [1-3]. The majority of existing bi-partitioning algorithms [4-6] fail to adequately represent the real problem because they assume a unit size for all modules and/or use a graph (edge) model rather than a net model which is known to be better for electrical networks [7]. Furthermore, when modules of different sizes are considered, most bi-partitioning methods can only exercise loose size control. BIPART, the algorithm presented in this paper, minimizes the number of nets cut, maintains a tight control on the sizes of the two parts, and uses an appropriate net model to represent the circuit.

2. PRELIMINARIES

In this section we establish the notations and definitions that will be used in this paper :

$M = \{1, 2, \cdots, m\}$: a set of modules.

$N_1, ..., N_n$: a collection of nets.

(M_1, M_2) : a partition of M into two parts.

$c_{ij} = |N_i \cap M_j|$: the number of modules shared between net N_i and part M_j. A net N_i is *cut* if $1 \leq c_{i1} < |N_i|$ and is *uncut* otherwise.

$C(M_1, M_2) = |\{N_i : 1 \leq c_{i1} < |N_i|\}|$: number of nets cut.

$size(i)$: the size of module i.

$size(A) = \sum_{i \in A} size(i)$: the total size of $A \subseteq M$.

$S(j) = size(M_j)$: the size of the j-th part.

$$b(i) = \begin{cases} 1 & \text{if } i \in M_1 \\ 2 & \text{if } i \in M_2 \end{cases} : \text{part to which } i \text{ belongs.}$$

$$g(i) = \begin{cases} C(M_1,M_2) - C(M_1-\{i\},M_2\cup\{i\}) & if\ i\in M_1 \\ C(M_1,M_2) - C(M_1\cup\{i\},M_2-\{i\}) & if\ i\in M_2 \end{cases}$$: the gain of i which is the decrease in the number of nets cut when module i is moved from its current part to the complementary part.

$B(M_1,M_2) = |size(M_1) - size(M_2)|$: balance of the partition.

$COST(M_1,M_2) = (B(M_1,M_2),C(M_1,M_2))$: cost of partition.

$(v_1,v_2) < (w_1,w_2)$ if $v_1 < w_1$ or $(v_1 = w_1$ and $v_2 < {}'w_2)$: lexicographic ordering of vectors.

$d(i) = |\{N_l : i\in N_l\}|$: number of nets connected to i or the number of pins of module i.

$p = \sum_{i=1}^{m} d(i) = \sum_{i=1}^{n} |N_i|$: the total number of pins which is taken as the problem size.

A mathematical formulation of the bi-partitioning problem considered in this paper is as follows :

> Given M, $N_1,...,N_n$, find a partition (M_1,M_2) of M which minimizes $COST(M_1,M_2)$.

The cost function is a vector of two components : the balance of the partition, and the number of nets cut. Because the lexicographic order is used for vectors, the minimization of the size difference between the two parts is given higher priority than the minimization of the number of nets cut.

3. THE ALGORITHM

BIPART belongs to the class of adaptive heuristics [8]. An adaptive algorithm uses a set of parameters that can be modified either by the user or the algorithm itself. Hence, the algorithm adapts to the particular problem at hand. The adaptation of the parameters influences the course of the algorithm. Consequently, the quality of the resulting solution is affected. An outline of BIPART is given below :

```
Let (M1,M2) be an initial partition;
(P1,P2) = (M1,M2);      /*save partition*/
γ = 0; p = po;     /*initialize*/
REPEAT
        (M1,M2) = PERTURB(M1,M2,p);
        UPDATE(p);
        IF ( current-cost < best-cost ) THEN {
                (P1,P2) = (M1,M2);      /*save best partition*/
                γ = γ - R;
                }
        ELSE
                γ = γ + 1;
UNTIL  γ > R; /* R is specified by user */
RETURN (P1,P2); /* report best partition */
```

BIPART retains the best partition among those generated by the function PERTURB. In the remainder of this section we describe the details of this algorithm.

The initial partition

To generate the initial partition, we scan the modules in decreasing order of size, and when a module is being scanned it is put in the currently smaller part. The following code is used :

```
Let l_1, ..., l_m be the modules in decreasing order of size;
S(1) = S(2) = 0;
FOR i=1 TO m DO {
        IF ( S(1)<S(2) ) THEN {
                b(l_i) = 1;
                S(1) = S(1) + size(l_i);
                }
        ELSE {
                b(l_i) = 2;
                S(2) = S(2) + size(l_i);
                }
        }
```

The function PERTURB

This function consists of two steps : *selection*, and *exchange*.

Selection : This step begins by scanning all the modules in *decreasing order* of size and initializing two sets A_1 and A_2 to empty sets. when module i is being scanned, the gain g_i is compared to a random integer r on the interval $[p,0]$, where p is a parameter whose value is controlled by UPDATE. If $g_i > r$ the module i "wishes" to move to its complementary part. In this case, if $i \in M_1$ then i is included in A_1; else if $i \in M_2$ then i is included in A_2, and the gains g_j of all modules are updated as if the module i were already in the complementary part. Therefore after all modules are scanned, the set A_1 contains a subset of modules from M_1 that "wish" to move to M_2, while A_2 contains a subset of modules from M_2 that "wish" to move to M_1. The goal of this step is to minimize the number of nets cut;

Exchange : In this step, only a subset B_k of modules from A_k are allowed to move to their complementary part for each $k=1,2$. The sets B_1 and B_2 are chosen so that the new partition $(M_1 \cup B_2 - B_1, M_2 \cup B_1 - B_2)$ has a better size balance than the old partition (M_1, M_2). We now describe the function BALANCE which is the core of the exchange step.

The function BALANCE : The goal of this function is to produce a new partition that has better size balance. More precisely, let (M_1, M_2) be a given partition. Without loss of generality, suppose that M_1 is the larger part and let $S(1) - S(2) = x > 0$. It is desired that BIPART chooses for exchange a subset $B_1 \subseteq A_1$ and $B_2 \subseteq A_2$ such that $|size(B_1) - size(B_2) - x|$ is as small as possible. This leads us to the following problem :

Given two sets Y and Z and an integer x, find subsets $Y_1 \subseteq Y$ and $Z_1 \subseteq Z$ that minimize $|\, size\,(Y_1) - size\,(Z_1) - x\,|$.

The decision version of the above problem can be shown to be NP-Complete [9]. Consequently, we do not expect to be able to solve it in polynomial time. BALANCE solves a special version of this problem by realizing that in the selection step a module that is selected to move to its complementary part affects the gains of other modules. Hence, BALANCE prefers earlier selected modules over the later ones for exchange. Moreover, if $A_1 \cup A_2 \neq \varnothing$ then *BALANCE* insures that $B_1 \cup B_2 \neq \varnothing$. Consequently, the difference between the sizes of the two parts might increase, but this gives BIPART a higher chance of escaping local minima. BALANCE takes as input two arrays $Y[\,]$ and $Z[\,]$ of modules sorted in *decreasing order* of size, and an integer x. Let $y =$ the number of elements in array $Y[\,]$ and $z =$ the number of elements in array $Z[\,]$. It is *assumed* that the array $Y[\,]$ contains modules from the part of larger size, while $Z[\,]$ has modules from the complementary part. BALANCE finds the best non-negative integers k and l such that $|\, size\,(Y_1) - size\,(Z_2) - x\,|$ is minimized where $Y_1 = \{Y[1], ..., Y[k]\}$ and $Z_1 = \{Z[1], ..., Z[l]\}$. Ties are broken by choosing the largest possible k and l. If $k = 0$, then this indicates that the subset Y_1 is empty. Similarly, if $l = 0$, then the subset Z_1 is empty. The outline of BALANCE is as follows :

```
BALANCE(Y,Z,x)
{
SY = 0; SZ = 0; MIN = ∞; k = 0; l = 0; j = 0;
FOR i = 1 TO y DO {
    SY = SY + size (Y[i]); min = |SY - SZ - x|;
    IF ( z ≠ 0) THEN improve = true;
    WHILE ( (j ≤ z) and (improve) ) DO {
        improve = false;
        w = |SY - SZ - x - size (Z[j+1])|;
        IF ( w < min) THEN { min = w; j = j+1; SZ = SZ + size (Z[j]); improve = true }
        }
    IF ( min ≤ MIN ) THEN { MIN = min; k = i; l = j }
    }
RETURN(k,l);
}
```

Note that BALANCE requires linear time since i and j are never decremented. The reason that j is never decremented is as follows : Suppose that for a given i, we found j that yields the minimum of $|SY - SZ - x|$. Then, for $i' > i$, the integer j' that minimizes $|SY - SZ - x|$ must necessarily satisfy $j' \geq j$.

In the selection step, the modules are scanned in decreasing order of size so that arrays Y and Z can be constructed in linear time without sorting and so that their orders reflect the order in which the modules were picked during the selection step. The modules are initially sorted as a preprocessing step using a bucket sort which require linear time if the size of the largest module is $O(m)$. An outline of PERTURB is as follows :

```
                /* Selection */
        y = z = 0 ; x = S (1) - S (2);
        Let l₁, ..., lₘ be the modules of M in decreasing order of size;
        FOR i=1 TO m DO {
            IF ( g (lᵢ) > RANDINT(p ,0) ) {
                IF ( b (lᵢ) = 1) THEN { y = y+1; Y[y] = lᵢ } ELSE { z = z+1; Z[z] = lᵢ }
                Move i to its complementary part;
                }
            }
                /* Exchange */
        IF ( x ≥ 0 ) THEN   (j,k) = BALANCE(Y,Z,x)   ELSE   (k,j) = BALANCE(Z,Y,-x);
        Move each of Y[j+1], ..., Y[y], Z[k+1], ..., Z[z] back to its original part;
```

The function UPDATE

This function controls the parameters p which is used in the selection step of PERTURB. If the number of nets cut has not changed, then p is decremented; otherwise, p is reset to its initial value p_o (in our implementation we used -1 for p_o). Our experience with circuit bipartitioning indicates that as the partition becomes better the gain values of the modules become negative and get clustered around 0. Therefore, in the selection step, we are allowing only the modules with the largest gains to move to the complementary part. Also, we decrement p when we suspect that BIPART is trapped in a local minimum, so that in the next iteration an uphill climb is favored.

The iteration bound R : The iteration bound R acts as the expected number of iterations the algorithm needs until an improvement takes place. If an improvement occurs at $\gamma < R$ iterations then the remaining $R - \gamma$ iterations are added to the next R iterations to be performed. Therefore, if T is the total number of iterations performed by the algorithm, then T/R is the number of improvements encountered. Consequently, the quality of the final partition obtained increases with the running time of the algorithm.

4. FEATURES AND LIMITATIONS OF BIPART

BIPART retains the best partition among those found by the function PERTURB. In the selection step, PERTURB tries to minimize the number of nets cut, and in the exchange step, it tries to improve the size balance. Therefore, the current partition is perturbed into a new one that "hopefully" will have a better size balance and a lesser number of nets cut. The use of random numbers in the selection step renders BIPART nongreedy, and enables it to overcome local optima in the quest of a globally optimal partition.

The quality of partitions found by BIPART depends on the choice of the user-defined parameter R. If R is chosen too small, then the optimization capability of BIPART is severely restricted. If R is chosen too large, then too much CPU time is consumed. Moreover, there is no guarantee that BIPART will always find a "best" partition even if we choose a very large value for R.

5. TIME COMPLEXITY

Each iteration of BIPART consists of a call to PERTURB, a call to UPDATE, and a saving of the new partition if it is found to be better than the current best one. Clearly, UPDATE requires constant time and saving a partition requires $O(m)$ time. Therefore, in order to compute the time required per iteration, we have to determine the time requirement of PERTURB.

Definition 1 : Given a partition (M_1, M_2) of M, a net N_j is i-critical if

(1) $i \in N_j$, and

(2) either $b(i) = b(k)$ $\forall k \in N_j - \{i\}$ or $b(i) \neq b(k)$ $\forall k \in N_j - \{i\}$.

If N_j is i-critical, then moving i from its current part to the complementary part renders N_j cut (uncut) if it were uncut (cut).

In the implementation of BIPART, each module has a linked list of its nets, and each net has a linked list of its modules. Therefore, a module i can access all of its nets in $O(d(i))$ time, and a net N_j can access all of its modules in $O(|N_j|)$ time,

Consider a situation in which module i is being moved to its complementary part, and let N_{ic} be the set of i-critical nets. Clearly, such a move affects only the gains of the modules of the i-critical nets. To perform this move we need to update :

(1) COST(M_1, M_2), and $g(i)$. This can be done in $O(1)$ time.

(2) c_{j1}, c_{j2} of every net N_j that contains i. This can be done in $O(d(i))$ time.

(3) $g(k)$ for each $k \in \bigcup_{N \in N_{ic}} N$. This can be done in $O(\sum_{N \in N_{ic}} |N|)$ time.

It, therefore, takes $O(d(i) + \sum_{N \in N_{ic}} |N|)$ to move module i to the complementary part.

Definition 2 : Given a partition (M_1, M_2) of M, a net N_j is critical if it is i-critical for some $i \in M$.

Observation 1 : Given a partition (M_1, M_2) of M, if net N_j is critical then c_{j1} is equal to 0, 1, $|N_j| - 1$, or $|N_j|$.

Let A be a set of modules such that a net N_j were i-critical for each $i \in A$ during a sequence of modules moves in which each module is moved once.

Proposition 1 : $|A| \leq 4$.

Proof : If c_{j1} increases (decreases) and then decreases (increases) during a sequence of moves in which each module is moved once, then N_j remains cut for the remaining moves. Consequently, N_j cannot be i-critical for any module i which appears later in the sequence. Therefore, proposition 1 is true by observation 1. □

Proposition 2 : A sequence of moves in which each module is moved once requires $O(P)$ time.

Proof : Let $l_1, ..., l_k$ be a sequence of modules that are moved in this order. Let N_{ic} be the set of l_i-critical nets after the $(i-1)$th move. The sequence of moves requires :

$$O(\sum_{i=1}^{k}(d(l_i) + \sum_{N \in N_{ic}} |N|)) = O(P + \sum_{i=1}^{k}\sum_{N \in N_{ic}} |N|) = O(P + 4\sum_{i=1}^{n} |N_i|) = O(P). \ \square$$

In the selection step, PERTURB scans the modules in decreasing order of size and per forms a sequence of moves in which each module is moved once. In the exchange step, PER TURB calls BALANCE which requires linear time and then perform a sequence of moves in which each module is moved once. Therefore, PERTURB requires $O(m + P) = O(P)$ time. It is assumed that each module is contained in at least one net so that $O(m) = O(P)$. We conclude that each iteration of BIPART requires $O(P)$ time.

6. EXPERIMENTAL RESULTS

All our experiments were performed on a SUN 3/50 workstation. BIPART was compared to the algorithm of Fiduccia and Mattheyses (FM) [6]. In the implementation of FM, we only allowed moves from the larger part to the smaller part. Both algorithms used the same initial partition. The results are given in Table 1 which gives the execution time in seconds, the number of nets cut (Cut), and the difference (Diff) between the sizes of the two parts, for each algorithm. The results indicate that FM is faster than BIPART. However, the partitions found by BIPART are of better quality.

BIPART was also compared to a double loop simulated annealing (SA) algorithm [10]. For the purpose of this comparison, we assumed a unit size for all the modules, required the number of modules to be even, and enforced that the partitions found be perfectly balanced (i.e., an equal number of modules in both parts). The move strategy used by the SA algorithm is the interchange of two random modules from different parts. The remaining details of the SA algorithm are briefly described below.

Let Δ, and δ be the maximum and minimum of the absolute difference in cost between any

TABLE 1 : Comparison of FM and BIPART

Circuit		Time(s)		Cut		Diff	
m	n	FM	BIPART	FM	BIPART	FM	BIPART
60	60	0.6	1.8	17	11	58	2
183	165	1.4	21.2	12	10	75	15
200	300	5.2	23.8	56	51	0	0
286	307	2.9	28.8	25	17	720	0
752	829	11.3	106.3	61	69	200	0
800	684	8.1	74.8	71	62	16	14
1000	1000	48.0	104.7	294	159	0	0
2081	1793	32.1	333.7	118	82	30	2
2776	2995	27.6	453.7	200	143	6	2
2976	3027	41.1	403.3	119	96	6	2

TABLE 2 : Comparison of SA and BIPART

Circuit		Cut		Time(s)	
m	n	SA	BIPART	SA	BIPART
200	300	61	54	146.1	4.8
286	307	24	16	185.4	8.8
752	829	113	66	387.8	12.1
800	684	124	59	433.6	76.8
1000	1000	650	159	516.3	52.0
2776	2995	407	153	1385.5	376.7
2976	3027	333	81	1544.5	206.7
3060	3123	354	177	1697.4	115.7

two neighboring[†] partitions, respectively. Then, the following choices for the parameters of SA were made.

1) The initial temperature T_o was chosen so that $e^{-\Delta/T_o} > 0.8$ in order to allow even moves with large negative gains[††] to be accepted.

2) The final temperature T_f was chosen so that $e^{-\delta/T_f} < 0.1$. At this temperature hardly any move with negative gain is accepted.

3) The temperature was reduced by a factor 0.95 after each iteration of the outer loop.

4) The inner loop was repeated $me^{\delta/T}$, where m is the number of modules. Consequently, more iterations are performed at lower temperature.

5) The outer loop was repeated until $T < T_f$.

The results, shown in Table 2, indicates that BIPART generates better partitions than SA in less computation time. In other words, if BIPART and SA were given the same amount of time, then BIPART will produce better partitions.

REFERENCES

[1] A. Dunlop and B. Kernighan, "A Procedure for Placement of Standard-Cell VLSI Circuits," *IEEE Trans. Computer-Aided Design,* vol. CAD-4, no. 1, pp. 92-98, Jan. 1985.

[†] A partition (P_1,P_2) is a *neighbor* of (M_1,M_2) if $P_1 = M_1 \cup \{j\}-\{i\}$ and $P_2 = M_2 \cup \{i\}-\{j\}$ for some $i \in M_1$ and $j \in M_2$.

[††] the gain of a move is equal to the reduction in the number of nets cut when the move is performed

[2]   D. La Potin and S. Director, "Mason: A Global Floorplanning Approach for VLSI Design," *IEEE Trans. Computer-Aided Design,* vol. CAD-5, no. 4, pp. 477-489, Oct. 1986.

[3]   M. Breuer, "Min-Cut Placement," *J. Design Automation and Fault-Tolerant Computing,* vol. 1, no. 4, pp. 343-362, Oct. 1977.

[4]   B. W. Kernighan and S. Lin, "An Efficient Heuristic Procedure for Partitioning Graphs," *Bell System Technical Journal,* vol. 49, pp. 291-307, February 1970,

[5]   Earl E. Barnes, " An Algorithm for Partitioning the Nodes of a Graph," *IBM Technical Report RC8690,* 1981.

[6]   C. M. Fiduccia and R. M. Mattheyses, "A Linear-Time Heuristics for Improving Network Partitions," *Proceedings of the 19th Design Automation Conference,* pp. 175-181, January 1982.

[7]   D. Schweikert and B. Kernighan, "A Proper Model for the Partitioning of Electrical Circuits," *Proceedings of the 9th Design Automation Workshop,* pp. 57-62, 1972.

[8]   S. Nahar, S. Sahni, and E. Shragowitz, "Simulated Annealing and Combinatorial Optimization," *Proc. 23rd Design Automation Conference,* pp. 293-299, June 1986.

[9]   Y. G. Saab and V. B. Rao, "Some NP-Complete Problems in the Physical Design of Digital Integrated Circuits," *Report UILU-ENG-90-2218,* Coordinated Science Laboratory, University of Illinois at Urbana-Champaign, June 1990.

[10] S. Kirkpatrick, C. Gelatt, and M. Vecchi, "Optimization by simulated annealing," *Science,* vol. 220, pp. 671-680, May 1983.

An Optimal Channel-Routing Algorithm
for a Restricted Class of Multi-Terminal Nets

Dee Parks

Abstract. We are given a channel-routing problem in which all nets have either (1) all their terminals on the same side of the channel, or (2) all but their rightmost terminal on the same side. This is the only class of multi-terminal nets for which an optimal algorithm has been found. Our paper describes an algorithm that routes the channel in knock-knee mode using D tracks, where D is the channel density and is a trivial lower-bound for channel width. Our implementation has complexity $O(n \log_2 D)$, where n is the number of columns in the channel.

Description of the Problem

Routing wires through rectangular regions of a printed circuit board is part of the VLSI design process that follows the placement of chips onto the board. Chips of similar size that have all their terminals on two opposite sides are often placed next to each other in rows, forming *channels* between the rows. Wires are routed through these channels to make the necessary electrical connections between chips.

We model the channel as a rectangular region of a unit grid having t horizontal lines called *tracks*, and c vertical lines called *columns*. Tracks are numbered $1, 2, \cdots, t$ from top to bottom. We label the vertices at the top and bottom of the columns $v_1^t, v_1^b, v_2^t, v_2^b, \cdots, v_c^t, v_c^b$ from left to right, where the superscripts t and b refer to top and bottom. For example, the leftmost column will have v_1^t at the top and v_1^b at the bottom. A *net* is a collection of terminals that must be electrically connected, and is given as an ordered list of vertex labels. If a net has two terminals in the same column, the top terminal is given before the bottom. We distinguish between *2-terminal* and *multi-terminal* nets (those nets having more than 2 terminals). We also distinguish between nets that have their first terminal at the top (*top* nets), and those with their first terminal at the bottom (*bottom* nets).

A *routing* is a collection of pairwise edge-disjoint subgraphs of the grid, one for each net. The subgraph corresponding to a 2-terminal net is a path, while that of a net with more than two terminals is a tree. The algorithm given in this paper produces a routing in knock-knee mode, but not a wiring. Brady and Brown[1] have shown, however, that any layout containing knock-knees can be wired in four layers.

Our objective is to electrically connect the terminals of each net using a minimum of horizontal tracks. A primary characteristic of a channel-routing problem is its density D, defined as the maximum over all columns x, $1 \le x \le c$, of the local density of x. Local density of column x is the number of nets that have their leftmost terminal at or to the left of column x, and their rightmost terminal to the right of x. Intuitively, local density is the number of nets that must cross the space between columns x and $x+1$. Clearly, density is a trivial lower bound to the number of tracks required for a routing. An optimal channel-routing algorithm is one that routes in D tracks.

This paper describes an optimal channel-routing algorithm for a restricted class of multi-terminal nets. There is no known optimal algorithm for the general multi-terminal net channel-routing problem, although Mehlhorn, Preparata, and Sarrafzadeh[2] give an approximation algorithm that comes within a factor of 2 of the optimum. On the other hand, various optimal algorithms for 2-terminal nets are known.[2-4] Our algorithm routes a class of multi-terminal nets that have either (1) all their terminals on the same side of the channel, or (2) all but their rightmost terminal on the same side. Such nets are similar to 2-terminal nets in that they cross the channel at most one time, but the class is slightly more general. We know of no other class of multi-terminal nets that can be routed in D tracks.

Although the algorithm given here is similar in style to the algorithms of Mehlhorn et al.,[2] significant differences exist. The problem we solve requires a new approach because of the multiple connections that may have to be made to a net before it ends. Some of those connections may occur in columns where a second net crosses the channel, and in that case we must ensure that the two nets do not overlap. Connections to a net of the type routed by our algorithm always occur on the same side of the channel as the starting terminal of the net. The algorithm maintains each of the two groups of nets (top, bottom) in sorted order by their ending terminals to ensure that no vertical overlap occurs between nets. The resulting layout is more complex than that produced by the algorithms for 2-terminal nets.[2-4] Nets have more bends and the routing contains more knock-knees. Although nets routed by the algorithm of Preparata and Lipski[3] have at most four bends, nets routed by our algorithm may have $2D$ bends.

It is interesting that we have not been able to find an optimal algorithm for problems in which nets may have either their first or last terminal on one side, and their remaining terminals on the opposite side. Including both types of nets in the problem increases the difficulty substantially. Of course, the present algorithm can be applied to problems in which all nets have their first terminal on one side, and the remainder on the opposite side. We simply reverse the order in which columns are processed.

Description of the Algorithm

Our algorithm processes the channel from left to right, one column at a time. If the current column is empty or contains both terminals of a 2-terminal net, the only layout action required is to extend all horizontal wires rightward one column and, in the latter case, make a vertical connection between the two terminals. Therefore, we assume in the remainder of this paper that no such columns exist. In a layout produced by the algorithm given here, no net occupies tracks to the left of its leftmost terminal. However, a net may have to be extended past its rightmost terminal, so it is possible that a routing produced by our algorithm will require more than c columns.

If the current column being processed by the algorithm is between the leftmost and rightmost terminals of a net, that net is called *active*. If the current column is to the right of the rightmost terminal of a net and the net still occupies tracks, that net is referred to as *extended*. A terminal is called *starting* (resp. *ending*) if it is the leftmost (rightmost) terminal of a net, and is called *continuing* otherwise. A net may have its last two terminals in the same column. In that case, the terminal on the same side of the channel as the starting terminal is called continuing; the other is called ending.

We maintain the same invariant throughout our algorithm as that given in Mehlhorn et al.[2] for 2-terminal nets:

I1. Active nets use one track; extended nets use two tracks.

I2. $d+2e \leq D$, where d is the local density of the current column (also the number of active nets) and e is the number of extended nets.

The optimality of the algorithm is evident from the invariant.

A column in our restricted channel-routing problem may be in one of 16 different states, shown in Figure 2. These states are a subset of those used in Sarrafzadeh and Preparata.[5] The symbols illustrate the type of terminals found at the top and bottom of the column, and are classified with a left-to-right scan in mind. Figure 1 shows symbols corresponding to top and bottom starting terminals, top and bottom continuing terminals, and top and bottom ending terminals. The first five states in Figure 2 are *density-increasing*, the second five are *density-preserving*, and the last six are *density-decreasing*. In a left-to-right scan, a column c is density-increasing (resp. density-preserving, density-decreasing) if the local density of column c is greater than (the same as, less than) that of column $c-1$.

$$\llcorner \quad \ulcorner \quad \perp \quad \top \quad \lrcorner \quad \urcorner$$

Figure 1

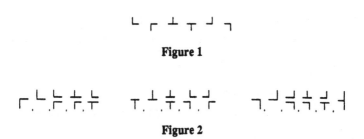

Figure 2

The algorithm maintains a three-part partition of the channel with top nets on the topmost tracks, bottom nets on the bottommost tracks, and any extended nets in the middle. This arrangement ensures that no active net occupies a track between the two strands of any extended net. Top (resp. bottom) nets are kept in sorted order by their ending terminals, with the net that ends soonest being on the lowest (highest) track of those in the group. The order of nets in the top (bottom) group is maintained by inserting each new net on its correct track, and moving those that end sooner down (up) one track. In either the top or bottom group, if two nets both end in the same column, the one that ends at the top is placed above the one that ends at the bottom. Figure 3 illustrates two possible configurations of the topmost tracks and the resulting layout actions. In the first case all the nets end in different columns, but in the second case nets **a** and **b** both end in column 19.

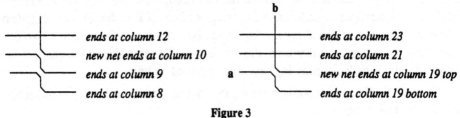

Figure 3

Once a net enters the channel, it remains on its starting track unless some later start-ing net pushes it down (or up) one track. The crucial step in the algorithm is determining the appropriate starting track for each net. In the algorithm for 2-terminal nets given in Mehlhorn et al., [2] a net may start on the next available track since it is not necessary to keep the nets in sorted order.

Our algorithm closes the two strands of an extended net as soon as the current column contains no ending terminal. Closing an extended net and ending a net in the same column may cause vertical overlap if the ending net crosses the channel. Even if the ending net has all its terminals on the same side of the channel, the present algorithm does not close the extended net. This modification would produce slightly shorter wires, but would not alter the complexity of the algorithm. If two nets end in the current column and one net has all its terminals on the same side of the channel, we end both nets. If not, then one net is ended and one is extended. We arbitrarily choose the net to end, and use its track for the second strand of the extended net.

In the following description of the layout actions, we verify the algorithm invariant for each case. As in Mehlhorn et al.,[2] we use d to denote local density before the current column and d' to denote local density after the current column, and the same for e.

Case 1. No ending terminal in current column.

> **if** there is extended net N **then**
>> (if more than one extended net, choose N to be the outermost)
>> close N;
>> **case** current column of

> $\llcorner$,$\ulcorner$:   Place new net in proper order in its group.
>   ($d'= d+1,\ e'= e-1$)

⊢ :   Place top net in proper order in its group, bottom
      net in proper order in its group.
      $(d'= d+2, e'= e-1)$

⊥,⊦ :   Make the connection to the continuing net, and place
      the new net in proper order in its group.
      $(d'= d+1, e'= e-1)$

⊥,⊤,⊥ :   Make the connection(s) to the continuing net(s).
      $(d'= d, e'= e-1)$

   end (case)
else (no extended net)
   case current column of

⌐,⌐,⊢ :   Place new net(s) in order in the correct group(s), using
      new tracks.
      (Since active nets use one track,
      $d' \leq d_{max}, e'= 0$)

⊥,⊦ :   Make the connection to the continuing net, and use a
      new track to place the new net in order in its group.
      $(d' \leq d_{max}, e'= 0)$

⊥,⊤,⊥ :   Make the connection(s).
      $(d' \leq d_{max}, e'= 0)$

   end (case)

Case 2. At least one ending terminal in current column.

Let N be a net that ends in the current column. If two nets end and one has
all its terminals on the same side, choose N to be that one; else choose N
arbitrarily. Let N' be the other net with a terminal in the current column.

case current column of

⌐,⌐ :   Terminate N.
      $(d'= d-1, e'= e)$

⌐ :   Terminate N.
      if N has all terminals on the same side **then**
            terminate N'
            $(d'= d-2, e'= e)$

else
> extend N' using N's track for
> the second strand of N'.
> $(d'= d-2, e'= e+1)$

$\dfrac{}{}\,,\,\dfrac{}{}$:   Terminate N and connect N'.
          $(d'= d-1, e'= e)$

$\dashv$:   Terminate N.
          $(N= N', d'= d-1, e'= e)$

$\vdash\,,\,\llcorner$:   Terminate N and use its track to make room for N'
          to be brought in. Place N' in order in its group.
          $(d'= d, e'= e)$

Implementation and Complexity

Suppose the channel-routing problem contains k nets, $N_1, N_2, \cdots, N_k$. Nets are given as ordered lists of vertex numbers. As the nets are input we update two structures, *Nets* and *Columns*. *Nets* is an array of k net records, each having two fields. One field contains the ending vertex of the net, and the other indicates whether the net is top or bottom. *Columns* is an array of c records, each containing four fields. The first two contain the number of the net that has a terminal at the top of the column and the type of that terminal (starting, continuing, or ending). The second two contain the corresponding information for the bottom terminal.

Clearly, the outer case statement of the algorithm is processed n times, once for every column in the channel. If we output D numbers for every column to show which net occupies every track, we obtain a complexity of $O(nD)$. We will show that the algorithm requires $O(n\log_2 D)$ time to determine a routing; therefore, we must reduce the output necessary to describe the routing. As we mentioned previously, a net remains on its starting track unless some later starting net causes it to shift up or down one track. We can uniquely describe a routing by outputting for each net the track on which it starts, and the column in which it ends. If the net is a top net (resp. bottom net), we assume that any nets already occupying both that track and the lower tracks in the topmost group (higher tracks in the bottommost group) are pushed down (up) one track. It is not necessary to output any extra information for extended nets. If a net does not end in the column containing its ending terminal, then it is extended. Its second strand enters the channel on the track freed by the other net that ended in its ending column. A routing is easily constructed from our output together with the input to the algorithm. We output a total of $4k$ numbers. Connections of continuing terminals to their respective nets can be assumed to occur wherever continuing terminals exist.

A net is extended only when two nets both end in the same column. Even though $\lfloor k/2 \rfloor$ nets can be extended, only $\lfloor D/2 \rfloor$ can be extended at one time since each takes two tracks. This bounds the number of columns used in a routing at $c + \lfloor D/2 \rfloor$.

It remains to show that complexity of the algorithm is $O(n \log_2 D)$. Channel density D can be calculated with one scan of the *Columns* array so it takes $O(n)$ time to determine the number of tracks to use. We maintain two balanced trees of active nets, one for the top nets and one for the bottom. Each node of the tree is a record with four fields: (1) the net number, (2) the ending column of the net, and (3) a count of the number of nodes in the right subtree of this node.

When a net starts we must output the track number on which it enters the channel. To calculate the track number we perform an insertion into the appropriate tree using the ending column of the net as a key. Note that v_i^t is considered smaller than v_i^b. We update the count in the nodes along the insertion path as we go. Then we traverse this path once more to count the number of nets with ending columns larger than the inserted net; call this count nl (number larger). If the net is a bottom net, its entering track is always $D - nl$. If the net is a top net, the track on which it enters the channel is $nl + 1$ unless another top net that ends in the same column is already in the tree. In that case, the track number depends on whether the net just inserted ends at the top or the bottom of the channel. If it ends at the top, the track number is nl; if it ends at the bottom, the track number is $nl + 2$.

When a net ends or becomes extended, its node is deleted from the appropriate tree and the counts along the deletion path are adjusted. We keep a linked list of extended nets, inserting newly extended nets at the front of the list. We always close the net at the front, and delete that node from the list. Then the handling of extended nets takes $O(k)$ time; clearly $k \le n$. Both insertions and deletions into balanced trees take logarithmic time yielding our $O(n \log_2 D)$ complexity.

References

1. M. L. Brady and D. J. Brown, "VLSI routing: Four layers suffice," *Advances in Computing Research*, vol. 2, pp. 245-257, JAI Press, Inc., 1984.

2. K. Mehlhorn, F. P. Preparata, and M. Sarrafzadeh, "Channel routing in knock-knee mode: Simplified Algorithms and Proofs," *Algorithmica*, pp. 213-221, 1986.

3. F. P. Preparata and W. Lipski, Jr., "Optimal three-layer channel routing," *IEEE Transactions on Computers*, vol. C-33, no. 5, pp. 427-437.

4. R. L. Rivest, A. E. Baratz, and G. Miller, "Provably good channel routing algorithms," *Proceedings CMU Conference on VLSI Systems and Computations*, pp. 151-159, October, 1981.

5. M. Sarrafzadeh and F. P. Preparata, "Compact channel routing of multiterminal nets," *Annals of Discrete Mathematics*, vol. 25, pp. 255-280, 1985.

Correct and Provably Efficient Methods
for Rectilinear Steiner Spanning Tree Generation

F. D. Lewis
N. Van Cleave
University of Kentucky

Abstract. *Two rectilinear Steiner spanning tree algorithms are presented, proven to be correct, and examined with regard to their complexity. It is shown that their worst case efficiencies are merely 1.5 times the optimum solution. These algorithms, when experimentally compared to existing algorithms, excel. They in fact produce the best solutions over 80% of the time and are never more than 1% from the best solution found.*

1. INTRODUCTION

The original Steiner Problem is to find the shortest tree spanning a set of given points in the Euclidean plane. Additional points (called Steiner points) may be introduced where the edges of the tree meet one another. Replacing the Euclidean metric with a rectilinear metric, produces the Rectilinear Steiner Problem (RSP). Rectilinear Steiner Trees (RST's) have a variety of practical applications such as wire layout for integrated circuits, and layout of electrical and mechanical systems in buildings and along streets.

If we focus on integrated circuit design problems, we find that Rectilinear Shortest Steiner Trees (RSST's) can be used for the global or loose routing phase of this design process where the path (which channels to use) is chosen for wires, but not the specific track in each channel. Steiner Trees have been used in the work of Imai and Asano [ImAs86], Larson and Li [LaLi81], Li and Marek-Sadowska [LiMa84], Ng, Raghavan and Thompson [NRT86], and Vecchi and Kirkpatrick [VeKi83], among others.

Garey and Johnson [GaJo77] have proven that determining the minimum length of an RST for a set of points in the plane is NP-complete. Thus, finding an optimal solution is itself NP-complete and heuristic solutions must be explored for applied research.

Many algorithms are given in the superb surveys of Winter [Wi87] and Richards [Ri89]. Some, employing Prim's minimal spanning tree (MST) algorithm are due to: Takahashi and Matsuyama [TM80], Lee, Bose, and Hwang [LBH76], and Hwang [Hw79]. Others founded upon Kruskal's MST algorithm [Kr56] were proposed by: Rayward-Smith [Ra83] and Bern, et. al. [BC85, NRT86]. And, geometric methods have surfaced in the work of: Richards (after Hanan) [Ri89], Komlos and Shing [KoSh85], Smith, Lee, and

Liebman [SLL80], and Ho, Vijayan, and Wong [HVW89]. Worst case complexities for these methods range from O(n) to O(n³). Also, complex and precise analyses are presented. While claims as to correctness and optimality are often made (and in fact are true), informal arguments are used to justify them.

In this paper we take two classic minimal spanning tree algorithms (from Prim [Pr57] and Kruskal [Kr56]), extend them so that they form hueristics for the RSST problem, and show that they are indeed correct and produce solutions no more than 1.5 times the optimum. We close with an empirical comparison of these new algorithms to the algorithms mentioned above.

2. PRELIMINARIES

Given a set of points in the plane there are trees which span the points in several ways if a rectilinear or Manhattan metric is employed. For example,

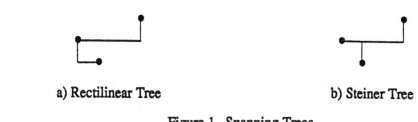

a) Rectilinear Tree   b) Steiner Tree

Figure 1. Spanning Trees

The spanning trees of figure 1 both span the three points. That on the left is a *Rectilinear Minimal Spanning Tree* (RMST) and the tree to the right is a *Rectilinear Shortest Steiner Tree* (RSST). Obviously the RSST is smaller.

Definition. *A **Rectilinear Shortest Steiner Tree** (RSST) over a set of points in the plane is a collection of vertical and horizontal lines of shortest possible total length which spans the set of points and contains no cycles.*

Investigation of the RRST problem began with the work of Hanan [Ha66]. He set forth several conditions which are necessary to any solution of the problem. In addition he also proved that there always exists a solution in which the Steiner points are located at a predetermined finite set of possible locations, namely the intersections of lines through all of the points drawn parallel to the x and y axes, imposing a grid on the plane. This result provides a connection between the RST problem and the Steiner problem for graphs (GST) and thus all of the work done on the GST problem is applicable to the RST or RSST problems.

Another of Hanan's theorems provides an optimum solution to the RSST problem over any three points. (Introduce a Steiner point at the median x-coordinate and median y-coordinate of the three points. Connect as illustrated in figure 1b.) This result has proven useful in finding heuristic solutions to problems with larger numbers of points. Another useful result follows, which links the RMST problem to the RSST problem.

Theorem 1. (Hwang [Hw76]) *A rectilinear minimum spanning tree for a set of points is no larger than 1.5 times the size of the rectilinear shortest Steiner tree.*

3. ALGORITHMS

Since the search space (original points and possible Steiner points) indicated by Hanan's theorem is of size n^2, most of the algorithms based on the algorithms of Prim and Kruskal seek to prune this space in order to achieve complexities lower than n^3. For example, Lee, Bose, and Hwang begin with a three point tree and then add points using Hanan's optimal three point connection algorithm. Hwang modified this algorithm by deciding the order of connections in a preprocessing step. Thompson's Kruskal-based algorithm (examined by Bern and associates) combines trees by sliding the connecting edge up and down the closest parts of the trees to be combined.

We modify the basic algorithms of Prim and Kruskal in a straightforward manner, utilizing Hanan's grid. First we present an extension of Prim's algorithm.

ExtendedPrim(P,T)
PRE: P is a set of points $\{p_1, p_2, \dots, p_n\}$
POST: T is a Steiner Spanning Tree over P

$S := \{p_1\}$
$T := \emptyset$
D := table of distances from points in S to points in P-S

repeat n-1 times
       a) select the shortest edge <u, p_k> from S to P-S
       b) add this edge <u, p_k> to T
       c) add p_k to S
       d) add any grid points on edge <u, p_k> to S
       e) update distance table D for points added to S

Figure 2. Extended Prim Rectilinear Steiner Tree Algorithm

Two notes about specifics in the algorithm must be made. When the edge <u, p_k> is added to the tree T it is drawn as an *L shaped line* (if necessary), not as a set of stair steps. In addition it is drawn towards the center of gravity of the set of points.

Since as many as n-1 grid points may be added to S during each iteration of the loop, it can require $O(n^2)$ steps to update the distance list used to select the shortest edge. And since the loop is repeated n-1 times the time complexity for this algorithm is $O(n^3)$.

Kruskal's MST algorithm provides the basis for two algorithms: EK1 and EK2 (figure 3). These algorithms follow Kruskal and connect closest objects (line segments, corners, nodes, or points) as long as they are in different subtrees (or sets). The difference between them lies in the choice of corners when joining two non-collinear objects. In EK1, all grid points along the two connecting line segments are considered, and the corner which adds the line segment nearest a third set or point is chosen. In the second case, for EK2, we choose the corner which itself lies nearest a node in a third set.

ExtendedKruskal(P,T)
PRE: P is a set of points $\{p_1, p_2, \dots , p_n\}$
POST: T is a Steiner Spanning Tree over P

$S_1 = \{p_1\}, S_2 = \{p_2\}, \dots , S_n = \{p_n\}$
$T_1 = \varnothing, T_2 = \varnothing, \dots , T_n = \varnothing$

repeat n-1 times
      a) select shortest edge $<u,v>$ where $u \in S_i$, $v \in S_j$, and $i \neq j$
      b) merge S_i and S_j giving S_i
      c) merge T_i, T_j, and $<u,v>$ giving T_i
      d) add any Steiner points on $<u,v>$ to S_i

Figure 3. Extended Kruskal Rectilinear Steiner Tree Algorithm

---

As before, when a connection is made, it is drawn as an *L shaped line* (if necessary), not as a set of stair steps. Since as many as n-1 Steiner points may be added to S_i during each iteration of the loop, it can require $O(n^2)$ steps to update the distance list used to select the shortest edge. This makes the complexity $O(n^3)$.

4. VERIFICATION AND OPTIMALITY

Verification of these algorithms depends upon lemmas which are used to prove that they construct rectilinear Steiner spanning trees over P. We shall follow the sequence of results which leads to the correctness and optimality of the Extended Prim algorithm. A more intricate sequence would be involved in the proofs for Extended Kruskal.

Definition. *The quadruple (P, E, S, T) is a **mixed rectilinear spanning** tree over a set of points P = {p₁, ... , pₙ} if and only if:*

    a) T is a rectilinear Steiner tree spanning S ∩ P.
    b) S contains points in P and grid points on the edges of T.
    c) The edges of E go between points in P ∪ S.
    d) The edges of E have at least one end in P-S.
    e) E ∪ T is a rectilinear Steiner spanning tree for P.

Figure 4 is an example of a mixed rectilinear spanning tree. The Steiner tree T is in the ellipse and the set S = {p_4, p_5, p_7, p_9, q_1, q_2, q_3, q_4}. Note that there are no grid points on the edge <p_6, q_3> since this edge is in E and not T. Likewise for the edges <p_2, q_1>, <p_3, p_5>, and <p_{10}, p_7>.

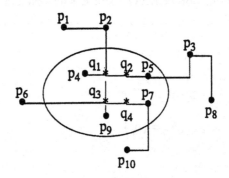

Figure 4. Mixed Rectilinear Spanning Tree

The lemma needed for the proof of correctness for the algorithm employs this mixed tree concept and is an extension of the standard lemma used to prove Prim's MST algorithm correct.

Lemma. *Let P be a set of points. Let T be a rectilinear Steiner tree spanning S (which contains some points from P and the grid points of T). Let <u, p_k> be the shortest edge leading from S to P-S. Then among all of the mixed rectilinear spanning trees (P, E, S, T) over the set of points, there is a minimal one which contains <u, p_k>.*

Theorem 2. *The Extended Prim Algorithm is correct and produces a rectilinear Steiner spanning tree no larger than the rectilinear minimal spanning tree for the set of input points.*

Combining this result with theorem 1 provides us with a bound on the optimality of the ExtendedPrim algorithm for generating Steiner spanning trees over a set of points.

Corollary *The Extended Prim Algorithm always provides a Steiner spanning tree no larger than 1.5 times the optimal shortest Steiner spanning tree for a set of points.*

5. EMPIRICAL RESULTS

Experimental testing consisted of executing the new algorithms (EP, EK1, and EK2) and that of Lee, Bose, and Hwang as well as Hwang's modification on all three and four point nets and sixty larger nets. Maximum net size was thirty. A full and detailed analysis appears in the complete paper, but some of the major points of interest follow.

From our observations we note that in general, EP generates the shortest trees for five or fewer points, while a combination of the EK1 and EK2 algorithms to produces the best trees for larger nets. Over 79% of the time at least one of the EK algorithms found the shortest tree. And, on the average, when the EK algorithms did not produce the best tree they were very close, in fact, less than 1% off.

The table below provides a comparison of these new algorithms with the *reported* results of other methods. (We note that on our test cases the EK's performed better than Hwang which in turn was better than Lee, Bose, and Hwang. Possibly EP and the EK's should be raised by a percentage point!) At any rate, the table provides percent improvement over MST's for each algorithm as well as the basis of each method.

Researchers	Method	Complexity	Improvement
Lee et. al.	Prim	n^2	9
Hwang	Prim	$n\log n$	9
EP	Prim	n^3	7
Bern et. al.	Kruskal	$n^2\log n$	9
EK1	Kruskal	n^3	8
EK2	Kruskal	n^3	8
Richards (Hanan)	line-sweep	$n\log n$	4
Smith et. al.	Geometry	$n\log n$	8
Ho et. al.	edge-flip	n	9

We also note that Hwang's algorithm as well as that of Ho, Vijayan, and Wong involved constructing a minimal spanning tree which was not counted in the complexity.

Our closing remarks concern worst case complexity. The new, straightforward algorithms were $O(n^3)$. This seems like a lot when compared to $O(n\log n)$ or $O(n)$. But with today's readily available machines (such as Vaxen) these algorithms compute 20 point nets in less than a second and 40 point nets in under 5 seconds. This is not excessive. (Besides, the constant in the $O(n)$ algorithm was 2^6.) Thus simple, verifiable, and easily modifiable algorithms may well be preferable to more complicated yet theoretically faster methods.

6. References

BC85   Bern, M. W., and M. de Carvalho. "A Greedy Hueristic for the Rectilinear Steiner Tree Problem." *Univ. California at Berkeley TR*, (1985).

GaJo77   Garey, M. R., and D. S. Johnson. "The Rectilinear Steiner Tree Problem is NP-Complete." *SIAM J of Applied Mathematics*, 32 (1977), 855 - 859.

Ha66   Hanan, M. "On Steiners Problem with Rectilinear Distance." *SIAM Journal of Applied Mathematics*, 14:2 (1966), 255 - 265.

HVW89   Ho, J., G. Vijayan, and C. K. Wong. "A New Approach to the Steiner Tree Problem." *Proc. 26th ACM/IEEE Design Auto. Conf.* (1989), 161 - 166.

Hw76   Hwang, F. K. "On Steiner Minimal Trees with Rectilinear Distance." *SIAM Journal of Applied Mathematics*, 30 (1976), 104 - 114.

Hw79   Hwang, F. K. "An $O(n\log n)$ Algorithm for Sub-optimal Rectilinear Steiner Trees." *IEEE Trans. on Circuits and Systems* CAS-26:1 (1979), 75 - 77.

ImAs86   Imai, H., and T. Asano. "Efficient Algorithms for Geometric Graph Search Problems." *SIAM Journal of Computing*, 15:2 (1986), 478 - 494.

KoSh85   Komlos, J., and M. T. Shing. "Probabilistic Partitioning Algorithms for the Rectilinear Steiner Problem." *Networks*, 15 (1985), 413 - 423.

Kr56   Kruskal, J. B. "On the Shortest Spanning Subtree of a Graph." *Proceedings of the American Mathematical Society*, 7 (1956) 48 - 50.

LaLi81   Larson, R. C., and V. O. Li. "Finding Minimum Rectilinear Distance Paths in the Presence of Barriers." *Networks*, 11 (1981), 285 - 304.

LBH76   Lee, J. H., N. K. Bose, and F. K. Hwang. "Use of Steiner's Problem in Suboptimal Routing in Rectilinear Metric." *IEEE Trans. on Circuits and Systems*, CAS-23:7 (July 1976), 470 - 476.

LiMa84   Li, J. T., and M. Marek-Sadowska. "Global Routing for Gate Arrays." *IEEE Trans. on Computer Aided Design of Integrated Circuits and Systems*, CAD-3:4 (Oct 1984), 298 - 308.

NRT86   Ng, A. P-C, P. Raghavan, and C. D. Thompson. "Experimental Results for a Linear Program Global Router." manuscript submitted to: *Computers and AI* and *1986 ACM Design Automation Conference*, (November 1985).

Pr57   Prim, R. C. "Shortest Connection Networks and Some Generalizations." *Bell System Tech. J* 36 (1957), 1389 - 1401.

Ra83   Rayward-Smith, V. J. "The Computation of Nearly Minimal Steiner Trees in Graphs." *Int. J of Math. Education in Sci. and Tech.* 14 (1983), 15 - 23.

Ri89   Richards, D. "Fast Heuristic Algorithms for Rectilinear Steiner Trees." *Algorithmica* 4 (1989), 191 - 207.

SLL80   Smith, J. M., D. T. Lee, and J. S. Liebman. "An $O(n\log n)$ Heuristic Algorithm for the Rectilinear Steiner Minimal Tree Problem." *Eng. Optimization* 4 (1980), 179 - 192.

TM80   Takahashi, H. and A Matsuyama. "An Approximate Solution for the Steiner Problem in Graphs." *Mathematica Japonica* 24 (1980), 573 - 577.

Va87   Van Cleave, N. "Rectilinear Steiner Tree Algorithms for the Global Routing Phase of VLSI Design.", *M.S. Thesis*, University of Kentucky, Lexington, KY (1987).

VeKi83   Vecchi, M., and S. Kirkpatrick. "Global Wiring by Simulated Annealing." *IEEE Trans. on Computer-Aided Design*," CAD-2:4 (Oct 1983), 215 - 222.

Wi87   Winter, P. "Steiner Problem in Networks: A Survey." *Networks*, 17 (1987), 128 - 167.

A Three-Phase
Task Scheduling Scheme in A
Hard Real-Time Distributed Environment

Ghasem S. Alijnai
Computer Science Department
University of Wyoming
Laramie, WY 82071

Horst F. Wedde
Computer Science Department
Wayne State University
Detroit, MI 48202

Abstract

The incentive of the local task scheduling scheme developed here is to guarantee a maximum number of unpredictable critical tasks locally. In order to guarantee the execution of a critical task within a requested time frame, a Safety Time Factor (STF) is defined based on the estimated worst-computation time of the task and added to its execution time. A three-phase local task scheduling is designed to take advantage of accumulative safety times and provide alternatives for scheduling the critical tasks locally. At each phase a different class of critical tasks is scheduled. The performance of the model has been ested using the most recent task scheduling scheme as a baseline model.

1. Introduction

Real-time distributed systems are characterized by the execution of each task having time constraints. The importance of meeting a task execution deadline makes the scheduling scheme a central issue for the correctness and reliability of real-time distributed systems. Generally, task scheduling methods are much influenced by the physical specification. In single-processor environment a *local* task scheduling scheme is required to utilize the CPU time-slices for execution of assigned tasks. Whereas in a distributed environment since the use of a single-processor scheduling scheme may produce unexpected results [8], both *local* and *global* scheduling policies should be established with respect to the overall system goals.

Recently, a great deal of research work was directed toward global task scheduling leaving local task scheduling to traditional single-processor scheduling methods. Due to the unpredictable behavior of a dynamic environment, the optimal solutions are computationally intractable [3,4]. Therefore, there has been an increased interest in heuristic solutions to the local task scheduling problem. A guaranteed procedure is presented in [6] in which a newly arrived task is only considered guaranteed if it can be scheduled without jeopardizing other already scheduled tasks. Otherwise, the new task will be sent to a remote node for execution. Another heuristic scheme utilizes imprecise results of periodic and iterative processes [5]. An interesting heuristic approach that combines the concepts of deadline and criticalness for processing aperiodic tasks can be found in [2]. In this approach, if a task arrives at a node with an already full schedule an attempt is made to remove enough lower priority tasks in order to guarantee the new task. However, this method relies on surplus computation time of the system which may not be available.

The method presented in this paper provides an alternative to the existing local task scheduling schemes by using flexible worst-case computation time. If the current scheduled tasks and the deadline of the new task allow, an STF will be estimated based on worst-case computation time and added to the new task execution time. The Accumulative safety times are utilized to schedule critical tasks. In a real-time environment, minimizing the computation overhead which is caused by the scheduler, is a crucial issue. The three-phase scheme incorporates this goal by making the level of the scheduling depend on the criticalness of tasks and using windowing techniques to reduce the search domain.

2. System Specification

The entire system here is collection of nodes connected to each other via a communication subsystem. Each node in the system is functioning independently and arranged in some arbitrary topology using broadcasting protocol such as token bus. Since a complete description of internal structure of the model is beyond the scope of this paper, only the local scheduler is described here. Further detail can be found in [1, 7]. Development of a task scheduling requires some knowledge of the characteristics of the task. This information helps to identify a task based upon the local and global scheduling policies. We assume that at time t_1, the system contains a set of tasks, T, where each task, $T_j \in T$ ($1 \le j \le s$, where s is a positive integer) and can be characterized as $T_j = (i , AT_j , WT_j , DT_j , CR_j , ST_j , STF_j)$.

where i   is the task identification
AT_j is the arrival time of T_j based on the local clock
WT_j is the worst-case computation time of T_j
DT_j is the deadline of T_j
CR_j is the degree of criticalness of T_j
ST_j is the start time of T_j , which will be set up by the local scheduler
STF_j is the safety-time factor that is added to WT_j , $0 \le STF_j \le WT_j$

During the operation, a node can be in one of two possible states:*local* or *remote* . A node is in the local state if it is using its own resources to schedule local or remote tasks by invoking the local scheduler. However, if the current status of the scheduled tasks does not allow for local execution of a new task, the local node must switch its state and request for remote service by invoking the global scheduler.

3. Local Scheduler

The success of scheduling a new task depends on the deadline, worst-computation time as well as the current status of scheduled tasks. The current status of each scheduled task is stored in a schedule list defined as S-LIST. To find an available time , AVT_i , for a new task a search should be conducted within a window frame. The size of the window at time t is equal to deadline of a new task minus the present time. Thus, AVT_i can be found as follows:

AVT_i = S-LIST [i].ST - (S-LIST [i-1].ST + S-LIST [i-1].WT + S-LIST [i-1].STF) , $1 < i \leq n$

Where n is number of slots within the window. The scheduler maintains S-LIST in which the tasks are ordered according to start times. The tasks are executed in an Earliest-Start-Time next scheme. The local task scheduler presented in this paper contains three phases. At each phase a certain class of tasks will be scheduled using an appropriate algorithm.

First Phase : In this phase, each new task is examined and possibly processed without using the accumulated safety times. This phase will activate the second phase if a new critical task meets the *threshold* (it will be explained later), and it cannot be scheduled based on the current schedule without further manipulation of the tasks already scheduled. The algorithm for this phase can be expressed as follows:

```
Phase-1 ;
Begin
 For every task , Tj, in the Input_Buffer Do
 Begin
  Set  STFj = WTj * C ;          /* where C is a constant factor set by the system */
  Set  STj = DTj - STFj - WTj ;
  If Tj cannot be inserted at the end of the list then
    Begin
     Find if there is an AVT in the list such that ;
     S-List [i] .DTj < STj and DTj < S-List [i+1] .ST
     If such an entry exists then
        insert Tj
     Else activate the second phase of the local scheduling
    End
  Else insert Tj at the end of the list
 End;
End;
        Local Scheduler, First Phase
```

Second Phase : In this phase, the scheduler tries to guarantee a new critical task by manipulating the tasks within a window frame and utilizing the accumulated safety times of already scheduled tasks. A metric is defined in order to decide whether a task is "critical enough" to activate the second and third phases of the scheduler. The scheduler compares a new task criticalness, CR_j, with a flexible threshold, TH, set by the system. If CR_j is greater than TH, then the new task is considered as a critical task. Otherwise, it is classified as non-critical task. Within the window frame a *Forward Shifting* is performed to utilize the STFs for scheduling the new task. If the provided time frame is less than the WT_j, the third phase of the scheduler will be activated. The second phase of the local task scheduling algorithm can be sated as follows:

```
Phase_2 ;
 Begin
  If  CR_j ≤ TH    Then
      Activate the global scheduler for remote execution ;
  Else
    Begin
      Create a window from  DT_j to the present time ;
      Add  the STFs and AVTs of n tasks within the window frame;

         If  Σ STF_i + Σ AVT_i ≥  WT_j Then
            i=0       i=0

         Begin
         change the ST of the task(s) from which the STFs and AVTs were taken ;
         insert  T_j ;
         End
      Else activate the third phase of the local scheduling algorithm
      End;
   End;
```

Local Scheduler, Second Phase

Third Phase : The critical tasks that are not processed by the second phase will be passed to the third phase for further consideration. Removal of one or more non-critical tasks from the list is performed in order to schedule a new critical task. The idea for the third phase of the scheduling algorithm is taken from a well established policy used in [2]. However, a provision is made in order to reduce the search domain of victim tasks by combining the concepts of threshold with window frame. In our model, the non-critical tasks are guaranteed to be executed in the absence of critical tasks, or when the schedule has enough accumulated time due to the safety times for incorporating the critical tasks. The critical tasks are always guaranteed to be executed once they are in the scheduler list. The third phase of the local task scheduling algorithm can then be expressed as follows:

Phase_3 ;
  Begin
    For non-critical tasks in the window frame, add WTs and the respective
    STFs and AVTs by moving from future towards the present time, such that

   If $\sum_{i=0}^{n} WT_i + \sum_{i=0}^{n} STF_i + \sum_{i=0}^{n} AVT_i \geq WT_j$ then

    Begin
      remove the non-critical task (s) ;
      activate the global scheduler after the new task, T_j, is accepted
    End
    Else Activate the global scheduler to find a remote node and
          send T_j to be serviced
  End ;

Local Scheduler, Third Phase

4. Experimental Results

Since the emphasis of this research is on maximizing the number of critical tasks processed locally, an attempt was made to reflect this goal in the presented experimental model and monitored results. The major parameters used is this experimental model can be characterized as follows :

- CR, criticalness ranging from 1 to 10
- TH, the threshold for evaluating the degree of criticalness with value of 5
- WT, estimated worst-case computation time between 10 to 50 time units
- DT, deadline with range 20 - 200 time units beyond the WT and task arrival time
- AT, arbitrary arrival time
- AR, arrival rate ranging from 0 to 15 tasks per time unit
- R, ratio of critical tasks to the total tasks generated by the system with value of 1/2.

As previously stated, to evaluate the performance of our local scheduler, an appropriate baseline model had to be constructed. Since the model presented in [2] integrates the concepts of criticalness and deadline, it was used as a baseline model for comparison. Hereafter we refer to the three-phase model as model-1 and the baseline model as model-2. Comparing the algorithms given for model-2 with the ones established for model-1, the model-2 can be implemented by eliminating phase two of our local task scheduler and excluding the safety time feature.

In this experiment, both models using identical tasks generated by the system where 50 percent of them considered as critical tasks. The value of STF was selected as 10 percent of the WT and tasks were generated in the rage of 0 to 12. The figures 1 and 2 show the number of critical tasks scheduled by each phase of the scheduler using model-1 and model-2, respectively.

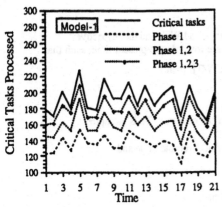

Figure 1 : Critical tasks processed by model-1

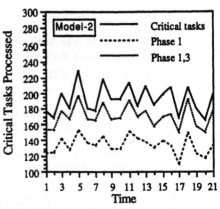

Figure 2 : Critical tasks processed by model-2

A Comparison was then made with respect to the total number of critical tasks scheduled by model-1 and model-2. As results indicate in figure 3, model-1 which contains all three phases outperformed model-2 during the entire experiment. Finally, we look at the total number of tasks processed by the two models. As the result in figure 4 shows, the total number of tasks which were processed by model-1 is higher than model-2. However, the studied performance depends upon the value of system parameters.

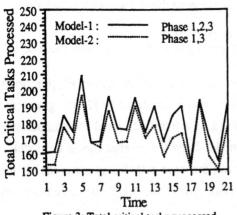

Figure 3: Total critical tasks processed

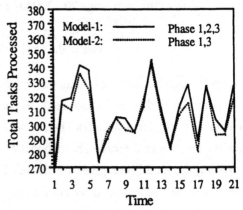

Figure 4 : Total tasks processed

5. Conclusion

In order to obtain the inherent performance of distributed computing systems over conventional computing systems, it is essential to develop efficient distributed task scheduling schemes. The research presented in this paper offers a new approach for processing unpredictable critical tasks in a hard real-time distributed environment. Several experiments were conducted to evaluate the performance of our proposed model versus a base model simplify the relative comparisons. Under the assumed conditions studied, our model outperformed the base model in terms of the number of critical and the total number of tasks scheduled.

Acknowledgment

We deeply appreciate Tom A. Skeie's contribution to the design and implementation of the three-phase task scheduling algorithms.

References

[1]   G.S. Alijani, "Object Mobility in Distributed Computing Systems", *Ph.D Thesis, Wayne State University*, 1988.

[2]   S.R. Biyabani, J.A. Stankovic and Ramamritham, " The Integration of Deadline and Criticalness in Hard Real-Time Scheduling", *Proc. Real-Time Sys. Sym.*, December 1988.

[3]   M.R. Garey and D.S. Johnson, " Two-Processor Scheduling with Start-Times and Deadlines", *SIAM Journal , Compt., Vol. 6, No. 3,* 1977.

[4]   R.L. Graham et al. , "Optimization and Approximation in Deterministic Sequencing and Scheduling: A Survey", *Ann. Discrete Math., Vol. 5,* 1979.

[5]   J.W.S. Liy, K-J. Lin and S. Natarajan, "Scheduling Real-Time Periodic Jobs Using Imprecise Results", *Proc. Real-Time Sys. Sym.*, December 1987.

[6]   J.A. Stankovic, K. Ramamrithm and S. Cheng, "Evaluation of Flexible Task Scheduling Algorithm for Distributed Hard Real-Time Systems", *IEEE Trans. on Computers, Vol. c-34, No. 12,* December 1985.

[7]   H.F. Wedde, G.S. Alijani and et al., "Operating Support for Adaptive Distributed Real-Time Systems in DRAGON SLAYER", *ACM Operating Systems Review Vol. 23 No. 3*, pp. 126-140, July 1989.

[8]   C.M. Woodside and D.W. Craig, "Local Non-Preemptive Scheduling Policies for Hard Real-Time Distributed Systems", *Proc. Real-Time Sys. Sym.*, December 1987.

A Broadcast Protocol:
Functional Properties and Specification

Sub Ramakrishnan
Department of Computer Science
Bowling Green State University
Bowling Green, Ohio 43403
rama@andy.bgsu.edu

Abstract

This paper concerns a reliable broadcast protocol which we have been investigating within the context of programming distributed systems [Ram1989(a)]. The protocol can be used to simplify the design of distributed computation algorithms. We prove certain important properties of this protocol and provide a concise functional specification of this protocol. The specification is required in order to help understand the behavior of the protocol.

1.   INTRODUCTION

The design and analysis of point-to-point and multipoint protocols have received considerable attention in the literature [Moh1988, ChL1986]. In the case of multipoint communication there is one sender and a number of receivers. An extension of this problem leads to broadcast communication between multiple senders and multiple receivers. Protocols for reliable broadcast communication are just emerging [ChM1984] The authors have designed one such protocol (known as global message ordering protocol for broadcast communication. The protocol resides at the Transport Layer. The design philosophy of this protocol is discussed in [Ram1989(a)].

Reliable message broadcast opens up the possibility of reaching unknown destinations, either to advertise or locate resources. Broadcast is used as an underlying mechanism in at least one distributed system [Che1988]. We have developed a distributed computation algorithm [Ram1989(b)] using reliable broadcast as an underlying communication primitive.

In this paper, we prove some important properties of the global message ordering protocol and provide a concise functional specification of this protocol. Specifically interactions within the protocol layer, with the Client layer above and the Transmission layer (or, Data layer) below are identified. In Section 2, we describe the environment and give an overview of the protocol. Proof of properties of the protocol are taken up in

Section 3. The functional specification of the protocol is given in Section 4. The paper concludes with a summary in Section 5. Due to length restriction, the functional specification and the proof methodology described here is very concise. A full exposition of the specification is available elsewhere [Ram1990].

2. THE ENVIRONMENT

Consider a distributed system consisting of P nodes of which Q, Q ≤ P is the set of nodes engaged in broadcast communication. The set Q is logically partitioned (possibly disjoint) into two subsets R and T that denote the group of receivers and senders respectively. Let M, N denote the size of these sets. The receivers need to know the order in which the messages from various senders are to be delivered to their client-layer. However, in a system with multiple senders, it is difficult to determine which message was generated first, second and so on. This is due to the fact that a distributed system has no global clock to synchronize the various events of the system.

This paper concerns the functional properties of a broadcast protocol proposed by the authors. The approach used in the design of the broadcast protocol is similar to Chang's protocol [ChM1984] in that a many-to-many communication is viewed as consisting of two one-to-many modes of communication. A designated node, henceforth referred to as the Token Site (TS), acts as an intermediate agent between the senders and receivers. Any node from the set R may elect to function as TS. The system description of our protocol [Ram1989(a)] is given by Figure 1.

2.1. The Broadcast Protocol: An Overview

The protocol operates in cycles; each cycle is composed of a maximum of three phases, viz: (1) Solicit, (2) Confirm, and (3) Sequence. The start of a cycle and the phases therein, are determined by TS.

In Solicit phase, TS issues a Poll and requests at most one time stamped message from each of the senders. This phase ends when all senders respond with either a Data or a Null message. The data messages are buffered at TS for later retransmission (if necessary). The TS also maintains a variable MaximumClock - the maximum time stamp of all messages received thus far. The poll is timer driven and carries the value of MaximumClock. Phase 2 is used to handle last minute message transmissions by one or more senders and to determine order of message delivery. For example, a sender that sent a Null message in Phase 1 may subsequently generate a data message. If this message bears a time stamp less than MaximumClock, then the message is accepted as part of the current cycle. At the end of Phase 2, TS establishes the order of all messages (based on their time stamps). The ordering information is broadcast to all the receivers in the Sequence phase. The receivers deliver data messages to their client in this order. The receivers may also seek message retransmission from TS when necessary.

At the end of a cycle, a new node is elected to function as TS for the following cycle. TS buffers data messages that are received from the time it became TS to the time it elects its successor (or a new TS). A node may become TS provided it has received, and buffered all messages that have been transmitted since it relinquished TS status the previous time. Transfer of TS responsibility is carried out as in Chang's protocol [ChM1984] using an election process.

3. PROTOCOL PROPERTIES

There are some fundamental differences between our protocol and the one proposed by Chang (1984). Our protocol satisfies some important properties as conveyed by the following two theorems.

Theorem 1 (Ordering Property)

All receivers deliver incoming messages to their client layer in the same sequence. This sequence corresponds to the sequence in which these messages are generated by the various senders.

Proof To satisfy Theorem 1, we construct a virtual ordering of the sender nodes, based on Lamport's [Lam1978] mechanism. Each node maintains a local (not necessarily physical) clock: LocalClock. The only requirement is that the clock values be *monotonically* increasing. The sender sends Data messages in response to a Poll from TS. Each such message from the sender carries the value of LocalClock. Recall that TS maintains an updated clock value: MaximumClock. This value which is the maximum of all 'LocalClock' values received so far is broadcast in the next Poll. The senders update LocalClock when a message is received from any other sender or when a subsequent Poll is received from TS.

Thus, the individual clock sources are synchronized (when two time stamps are equal the node identifier is used as a tie-breaker) without the use of a global clock. Further, TS instructs all receivers to deliver messages to their client layer in this time stamp order. Thus, our scheme (a) provides a total ordering of all messages that are generated by members of T; and (b) ensures that each member of R ultimately delivers incoming messages (to the layer above), in the same sequence; this sequence being the order perceived in step (a). This completes proof of the Theorem.

Theorem 2 (Fairness Property)

Between the completion of two consecutive message transmissions from any sender, one transmission from other waiting (if any) senders will be completed.

Proof This property is readily enforced as a direct consequence of the way Phase 1 and Phase 2 have been defined. To see this, let sender X generate two messages A & B with time stamp T_a and T_b in this order.

Case 1. No other sender has a message bearing a time stamp T_c such that $T_a < T_c < T_b$. TS knows of this fact at the end of Phase 2. Thus, every receiver receives messages A & B in this order (without any intervening message). This scenario does not violate Theorem 2.

Case 2. Some sender Y has a message C bearing a time stamp T_c such that $T_a < T_c < T_b$. We shall prove this case using proof by contradiction. Suppose a receiver delivers messages A & B in this order to its client without the intervening message C. This implies that TS entered Phase 3 (since ordering information is conveyed only in Phase 3). That is, TS ends Phase 2 (since Phase 3 follows Phase 2) without any knowledge of message C. (Note that if message C has been lost in transmission, TS would not end Phase 2.) This can happen only if node Y sent a Null message in Phase 1 & 2. (And, node Y has updated its clock to be greater than the maximum time stamp of the current cycle.) This contradicts the hypothesis that node Y sent a message with time stamp T_c in the current cycle. This proves the theorem.

It can be argued that Theorems 1 and 2 may not be satisfied by Chang's [ChM1984] protocol. We illustrate this fact using an example: Let node X, node Y, node X generate messages, A, B, and C respectively in this order (with time stamps T_a, T_b, T_c such that $T_a < T_b < T_c$). Suppose the message from node Y is lost. Then, TS sequences the messages in the order: A followed by C. Theorem 1 is violated since the order of delivery is inconsistent with the order in which messages are generated at the senders. Theorem 2 is not satisfied since two consecutive messages from the same sender have been delivered to the client layer, even though there is a waiting sender (Node Y).

Suppose round robin transfer of TS functions is enforced. Then, in the absence of permanent node failures, the maximum required buffer size can be readily computed. This leads to the following theorem.

Theorem 3 (Buffer Size)

The maximum buffer size at any receiver node is bounded above by M*N.

Proof Suppose node D_i, $D_i \in R$ is TS for the current cycle C_i. In this cycle (and any other cycle) there may be at most N new messages (one from each sender). At the end of C_i, let D_i elect node D_{i+1} to be TS. This marks the beginning of cycle C_{i+1}. At this point no messages are buffered at node D_i (by definition). From then on, in each of the following M-1 cycles, node D_i will hopefully receive (and buffer) at most N new messages. Continuing this argument it is clear that at the end of cycle C_{i+M-1}, node D_{i+M-1} will solicit node D_i to be TS. If node D_i has received, and buffered all messages that have been transmitted between C_{i+1} and C_{i+M-1} (both cycles included) D_i accepts TS responsibility at once. Otherwise, it will ask node D_{i+M-1} to retransmit missing messages. In any case, when D_i is ready to assume TS role, the number of buffered messages is bounded above by (M-1) * N. In cycle C_{i+M} TS (D_i) will receive and buffer at most N additional messages. Thus, between any two successive TS roles by the node D_i, number of messages buffered is ≤ M*N. This proves the theorem.

4. FUNCTIONAL SPECIFICATION
4.1 Process Organization

The model consists of six cooperating entities: Sender, Receiver, TS, Timer, Client and Data layer. Four of them reside at the Transport layer The other two reside at adjacent layers. The Sender process receives messages from its Client through the Client Layer interface. It then time stamps the message before its final broadcast on the channel. The Receiver process delivers incoming messages to its Client Layer in the order specified by TS. It also seeks message retransmission from TS when such messages are known to be lost. The primary responsibilities of TS include soliciting message transmission from senders and global clock synchronization. TS sends out message retransmission as required and sends ordering information to receivers. The Timer process is responsible for timer maintenance, and notification when it runs out. The Client acts as producer and consumer of data messages, interfacing with the Sender and Receiver respectively. The Data Layer is responsible for transporting messages across the channel using an appropriate channel access medium at the layer below.

4.2. Interface Description

The interface that exists within and across Transport Layer is described in subsequent sections.

4.2.1. The Sender Entity

Client-Transport

The sender invokes Client Layer using a stop and wait protocol. The Sender when ready to accept client data invokes the primitive: *Enable ClientDataInterrupt;* similarly when it is not ready to accept data invokes *Disable ClientDataInterrupt*. The client notifies the Transport Layer of the pending message using the event *ClientDataReady*. The Sender then receives the client message by invoking *GetClientData (incomingBlk : .., Node..; Status:..)*. *Status* provides a completion code for the call and can be either *InError* or *ErrorFree*. The variable *Node* denotes the sender *id* of the client. incomingBlk is a record structure with several fields.

Transport-Data Layer

The two primary services points between the Data Layer and Transport Layer are (Figure 2): *TxDataLayer (outgoingBlk:.., Status: ..)*, and *RxDataLayer (incomingBlk:.., Status: ..)*. These forms are used to send/receive outgoing/incoming blocks to/from Data Layer. Again, *Status* provides the required completion code. The Data Layer enables the event *TxnLayerData* to notify the Transport Layer of the incoming block.

Every sender receives and interprets commands from TS. A sender *i* performs two actions upon receiving this message.

(1)   LocalClock <-- Max (MaximumClock, LocalClock) + 1. Herein incomingBlk.MaximumClock is the maximum clock value field of the incoming command.
(2)   Inspect the field incomingBlk.MsgReceived[i]. This field is an indication of the status of this node as perceived by TS. Possible values of this field are: Empty, Null, or Data. If field = Empty then invoke TxDataLayer and send the pending message (if ClientDataReady is True) or send a Null message (if ClientDataReady is False). If the field is Null and Phase = Confirm, then invoke TxDataLayer and send the pending message (if

ClientDataReady is true and ClientData.TimeStamp < incomingBlk.MaximumClock) or send a Null message.

4.2.2. The Receiver Entity

The receiver entity receives data messages from sender nodes. In addition, it receives the _Sequence_ command and also message retransmission from TS. Message reception is handled using the RxDataLayer primitive (see Section 4.2.1), leading to the following actions (Figure 3):

1) _Buffer messages_ Data messages are buffered invoking the _QHandler_ primitive. The specific function on the queue is specified as a parameter; it is one of *(Flush, Get, Put, GetCopy)* . Message are filed based on the cycle number and the message sequence number.

2) DetectLoss: if loss of a data message is detected this procedure is invoked to seek its retransmission(s). (Multiple retransmissions may be requested in one call.) This procedure, in turn, uses _TxDataLayer_ to send the block out. The retransmission requests are timer driven.

3) PutClientData The receiver part of the Transport layer delivers incoming data messages to the Client Layer through the interface *PutClientData (outgoingblk : .., site:..; Status:..)*. Messages are delivered only in sequence, as conveyed in the _Sequence_ message from TS.

4.3. The Token Site

A node, in addition to being a receiver may function as TS. The functional diagram of TS is depicted in Figure 4. The primitives _TxPoll / LastCall_ and _TxSequence_ are used in Phases 1/2 and 3 respectively. Upon receiving a message from a Sender, TS invokes *UpdateStatus (incomingBlk)* to update MaximumClock value and to note the message type. Further, *DecideNextPhase(incomingBlk)* is called to check if the Phase is to be changed. Upon receiving a request for retransmission, the primitive *Schedule Retxn(outgoingBlk)* schedules retransmission of the corresponding message(s).

Other functions including fault detection and network reconfiguration are performed by various protocol entities. For brevity, we do not include those details in this paper. Full specification details can be found elsewhere[Ram1990].

5. CONCLUSION

Broadcast is considered an essential mechanism for most distributed systems. In this paper we specified and proved some important functional details of a broadcast protocol proposed by the authors. Ordering property is very useful, as in the case of distributed mutual exclusion algorithms. The protocol was also proved to be starvation free. A concise description of the protocol was also presented.

REFERENCES

[ChM1984]   J. Chang, N.F. Maxemchuk, *Reliable Broadcast Protocols*, ACM ToCS,, 2(3), August 1984, pp. 251-273.

[ChL1986]   S.R. Chandran, S. Lin, *A Selective Repeat ARQ Scheme for Point- to-Multipoint Communication and its Throughput Analysis*, Computer Communication Review, 16(3), August 1986, pp. 293-301.

[Che1988]   D. Cheriton, *The V Distributed System*, CACM, Vol 31(3), March 1988.

[Lam1978]   L. Lamport, *Time, Clocks and the Ordering of Events in a Distributed System*, CACM, 21(7), July 1978, pp. 558-564.

[Moh1988]   S. Mohan, J. Qian et al, *Efficient Point-to-Point and Point-to-Multipoint Selective-Repeat ARQ Schemes with Multiple Retransmissions: A Throughput Analysis*, SIGCOMM Proceedings, 1988, pp. 49-57.

[Ram1989(a)]   S. Ramakrishnan, *A Protocol for Global Message Ordering*, XX Annual Simulation & Modeling Conference, PA, May 1989, 7.

[Ram1989(b)]   S. Ramakrishnan, *A Protocol for Program Migration*, XIV IEEE Conference on Local Computer Networks, MN, October 1989, pp. 219 224.

[Ram1990]   S. Ramakrishnan, *Procedural Specification: Global Message Ordering Protocol*, ICCC '90, submitted for publication.

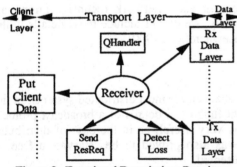

Figure 1 System Description

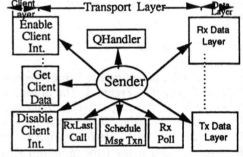

Figure 2. Functional Description: Sender

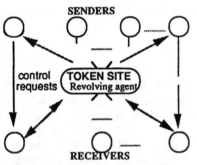

Figure 3. Functional Description: Receiver

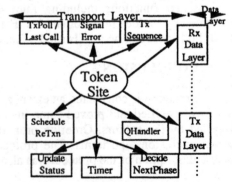

Figure 4. Functional Description: TS

Leader Election in Distributed Computing Systems

Mohamed El-Ruby   James Kenevan   Robert Carlson

Department of Computer Science
Illinois Institute of Technology
10 W 31st Street,
Chicago, IL 60616

Khalid Khalil

Bell Communications Research
444 Hoes Lane,
Rm. RRC-1J217,
Piscataway, NJ 08854

Abstract

In a distributed computing system, a change in the state of the system usually requires that the new state be propagated to all active nodes so that they can correctly perform cooperative tasks. Since more than one node may detect a status change, conflicts in state determination and propagation are possible. In order to ensure that all nodes of a communicating group are at the same state, all nodes of the group must agree upon the election of a single leader (coordinator).

In this paper, we present an Election Protocol for General Configuration networks (EPGC). The protocol was tested on different well known configurations and its performance was studied using simulation modeling techniques. The simulation study showed a trade off between the election time and the number of exchanged messages. A technique to minimize the number of messages was then introduced. Both positive and negative effects of this technique were observed.

Introduction

The election protocols that were developed in the past were often dependent upon the network topology. In particular, a considerable amount of work has been done for systems in which node are arranged in a ring and messages are passed from node to node around the ring.

But in general network, a protocol developed for a ring network may not be adequate, since messages may circulate rather slowly in a system with irregular node

connections. Several protocols have been proposed for such systems [1, 2, 3, 4], bu
they were largely developed under the assumption that messages are not lost durin
the election process. Lost messages can cause undetected multiple candidacies an
hence can introduce unnecessary groupings that must later be resolved [4]. I
addition, these protocols have no known performance.

In this paper, we present an election protocol that does not assume an underly
ing ring structure and that tolerates failures, including lost messages and networ
partitioning, during the execution of the protocol itself.

2 System Model

Node failures and communication link failures are both taken into account in ou
protocol. A node failure occurs when a node in the network goes down, and
communication link failure occurs due to a transmission medium fault. When
node failure occurs, it is assumed to be *pure*, meaning that the processor simpl
stops running and no garbage messages are produced. Similarly, a transmissio
medium failure causes lost messages, but not garbled ones. Also, a transmissio
medium failure may cause partition in the network.

In our system, we assume the following properties:
1. Random configuration of n processors, except each has its own unique identifie
2. The maximum number of nodes is known a priori.
3. All nodes cooperate and use the same election protocol.
4. Election messages have higher priorities than other messages.
5. No central controller is considered.
6. If a node i receives a message M from node j, then that message M was ser
by node j to node i at some earlier time. That is, we assume the communicatio
subsystem will not spontaneously generate messages.
7. If a message is received, it is guaranteed not to have been damaged. Th
assumption means that if node i sends a message to node j, then if the message
not lost, j receives exactly the same message that i sent.
8. Message delivery is not guaranteed. The communication subsystem can fail s
that messages between nodes can be lost.

3 The EPGC Protocol

In this section a protocol for electing a leader (coordinator) in general network
presented. The unique I.D. of each processor is an integer number.

The protocol is initiated by individual processors that decide independently t
wake up. The processors need not wake up at the same time. When a proce
sor wakes up (henceforth called a participating processor), it broadcasts the ha
message over all its links. This protocol is designed so that the processor wit
the smallest I.D. number (from the set of the active processors) will be eventuall

lected to be the coordinator.

Before describing the protocol, we will introduce the different states and the types of messages used by the protocol.

States:

There are three different states that any node (processor) can be in at any instant of time. These states are:

) N.O. State:

This is the *Normal Operation State* where the nodes perform their normal tasks.

) Halt State:

This is the *Halt State* where the nodes halt their normal operation and be ready to start the election process.

) Elect. State:

This is the *Election State*. This is the state where all the nodes are participating in the election of the new coordinator.

Messages Types:

There are three different messages that are used by the protocol. These messages are:

) H Message:

This is the halt message. The node(s) that first detects a failure, changes its state from N.O. state to Elect state. Then it broadcasts the H message to all the neighboring nodes. This will cause all the operating nodes to halt their normal operation and changes their state to the Elect state and be ready for the election process.

) E Message:

This is the election message. It is used during the election process. This enables all the participating nodes in the election process to communicate together for the election of the new leader (coordinator).

) EE Message:

This is the End of Election message. As soon as one of the participating nodes knows the I.D. of the elected leader. It changes its state to the N.O. state and broadcast the EE message to the rest of the nodes, informing them with the new leader identity and that the election process ended successfully.

The formats of the above messages are shown in figure 1. All different type messages have checking fields equal to the number of the nodes in the network. All checking fields are initially set to zero. As the message traverses through the network, active nodes set their corresponding checking fields to 1. The checking fields corresponding to the failed nodes are set to -1 by their neighboring nodes. The checking fields technique was introduced to assure the consistency in the nodes states and to avoid the case of a node unaware of the election process.

4 The Protocol Description

The protocol is initiated by individual processors that detect a status change. This occurs when a node is not able to communicate with another node either because this node has failed or the communication subsystem that allows them to communicate has failed. The protocol state diagram is presented in figure 2.

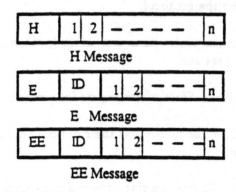

Figure 1. The Messages Format.

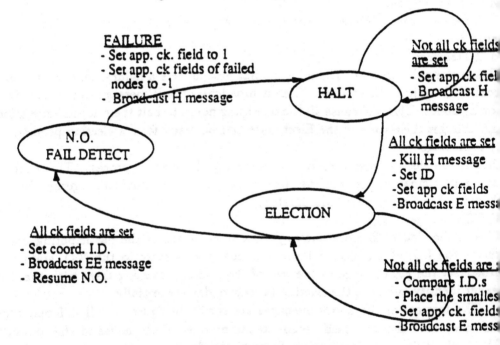

Figure 2. The Protocol State Diagram.

When a node detects a status change, it suspends locally executing processes (halt state) and broadcasts the halt message with its corresponding checking field set to 1, and the checking fields of all failed nodes set to -1. The nodes receiving the halt message, checks the checking fields. If all checking fields are not set, it will perform as above. If all the checking fields are set, it will kill the halt message change its state to the election state and broadcast the election message with its I.D. and its corresponding checking field set to 1 and the checking fields of all failed nodes set to -1.

A node receiving the election message, checks the checking fields. If not all of them are set. it compares both its own I.D. and the message I.D. Then, it places the smallest I.D., sets the appropriate checking fields in the election messages, and then broadcasts the new election message. If all the checking fields were set, it compares both its own I.D. and the message I.D. Then, it places the smallest I.D., sets the appropriate checking fields in the end of election message, and then broadcasts the end of election message.

A node receiving the end of election message will know the coordinator I.D., set the appropriate checking fields, broadcast the end of election message, and resume normal operation. Eventually one of the nodes will receive the end of election message with all checking fields set. It will kill the message and by that time all the active nodes will know the I.D. of the coordinator and all of them will be in the normal state.

5 Message minimization techniques

To minimize the number of the floating messages in the network, we introduced two techniques. The first is, a node receiving any message keep a copy of it in its memory. Then when it receives another message of the same type it compares both messages and create a new message with the information from both messages. Then it broadcasts the newly created message instead of the one received. The second is the window mechanism. A node queues all the incoming messages it receives for a certain period of time (the window size period), then processes the batch and respond with one message only.

6 Multiple candidacy resolution

Most of the previous algorithms allow more than one coordinator to be elected and then resolve the multiple candidacy situation after the subgroups are formed. Usually, if this problem can be resolved during the election process, it will save the cost of merging subgroups and reduce the time for the nodes in a physical partition to form a single group under one coordinator.

The EPGC protocol resolves the multiple candidacy problem during the election process itself. A candidate receiving an election message with I.D. smaller than its own, is forced to give up its candidacy. This will ensure the election of a single coordinator in the case of no message loss.

However. if messages can be lost, the smallest ranking candidate cannot be sure that all other candidates will withdraw. Thus resolution of multiple candidacies must involve the non-candidates nodes. One possibility (and the approach adopted here) is that non-candidate nodes receiving an election message with higher I.D. than the message I.D. it has in its memory, kills the message and do not respond to it. This technique will ensure the election of a single coordinator with the smallest I.D.

7 The Experimental Model: ELECTO

The distributed system is modeled as multiple instances of submodels. Each submodel represents a node. Each submodel has the protocol information embedded in it. The communication links connecting the nodes are represented by delay lines

This modeling design has the following advantages:

1. High flexibility in reconfiguring the network, so the protocol can be tested on different configurations with the minimum changes in the model.
2. Flexibility in updating and making changes in the protocol.
3. Minimum debugging effort.

This model allows the modeler to conduct many different experiments. The modeler has the capability to specify the number of nodes, the status of each node and the configuration of the network for each experiment. Moreover, which node(s) detects the failure occurrence to start the election process, can also be specified.

In our model, the transmission time over the communication links are assumed to be constant and equal to ONE time unit. Also, the processing time at the node is assumed to be ZERO.

In addition to this design philosophy, the model has two more features. First the nodes have the capability of memorizing all the information it received through the messages that was sent to it earlier in one updated message. This feature was added to the model design to simulate the technique to minimize the number of messages floating in the network. The second feature is the window mechanism This mechanism can be modeled in two different ways.

1. By allowing each node to process the incoming messages as they arrive, and then holds the response message for a specific period of time (the window size) before broadcasting it, or,
2. By queuing all the incoming message for the period of the window size, the process this batch and respond with only one message. This alternative was chosen for its simplicity.

8 Experiments And Results

The protocol was simulated on an eight node model with different configuration It was tested on random configurations and it performed correctly and the election ended successfully. A set of experiments to determine the maximum time and the maximum number of messages needed by the protocol were conducted on different well known configurations. This made it easier to study the protocol behavior, and on certain configurations manual verification could be done. These configurations were, Bus, Star, Hypercube, Bidirectional Ring, Unidirectional Ring, and Full Connected. The results showed that there is a trade off between the election time nd the number of messages expanded.

The effect of the window mechanism was studied on each of these configurations.)n certain configurations (Bus, Star, Hypercube, and Bidirectional Ring) the winlow mechanism had strong positive effect on reducing the number of messages and aused the election time to be slightly higher. Other configurations (Unidirectional Ring and the Fully Connected) had negative effect. The time was increased slightly nd the number of messages was not affected.

9 Conculsion

n this paper, we introduced an Election Protocol for the General Configuration aetwork, (EPGC). The simulation results showed that this protocol performed corectly and efficiently.

An experimental model (ELECTO), was developed to evaluate the performance of the protocol using simulation modeling. Experiments were conducted to study he behavior of the protocol. It was observed that there was a trade off between he time and the number of messages. So, depending on the application performed by the system. the system manager can determine which is more important. The EPGC protocol was designed to allow the system manager the choice. Also, the vindow mechanism were simulated. Both positive and negative results were observed depending on the configuration. Therefore, this technique should not be ised directly on any configuration network.

The election protocol is an important component for recovery in distributed systems, but it is just one of the many such components. The election protocol nteracts with the rest of the application components in various ways, and it is impossible to implement a complete election protocol without designing the rest of the system. In this paper we only introduced an election protocol, and more work is required before this idea can be properly integrated into a complete system.

References

[1] H. Garcia-Molina. "Elections in A Distributed Computing System," *IEEE Trans. on Comp.*, vol. C-31, no. 1, pp. 48—59, 1982.

[2] W. Kim. "AUDITOR: A Framework for High Availability of DB/DC Systems." *IBM Res. Rep. RJ3512*, 1982.

[3] P. Bernstien, V. Hadzilacos, and N. Goodman. *Concurrency Control and Recovery in Database Systems*, Addison–Wesley, 1987.

[4] J. Kim and G. Belford. "A Robust, Distributed Election Protocol," *7th Symp. Reliable Distributed Systems*. (Colombus, Ohio), IEEE, vol. CH2612, pp. 54—60, 1988.

A New Approach to System-Level Fault-Tolerance in Message-Passing MultiComputers

Guy W. Zimmerman
Abdol-Hossein Esfahanian
Michigan State University

Abstract. *The loop is a commonly used interconnection network for computer systems. In this paper we consider the problem of making a loop network fault-tolerant. Previous solutions employ the absolute minimum number of redundant components, for a specified level of fault tolerance. In our approach, "extra" redundancy is used to reduce the size and complexity of the interconnection network. Designs based on chordal rings are presented which can tolerate one and two processor failures. The examples given indicate that for large scale systems, the approach can produce improved designs, which are more in accord with the limitations of current technology.*

1. Introduction.

A *MultiComputer* (MC) is a collection of linked autonomous processors in which each processor has its own local memory. Processors may communicate by exchanging messages and a message may have to go through several intermediate processors before reaching its destination. These systems have also been referred to as *message-passing* or *point-to-point* networks [7]. The advances in technology have made it possible to construct MCs with large numbers of processors, and the goal of a number of research and development projects has been to construct MCs that will deliver high performance for selected applications, at a relatively low cost [6, 11]. A fundamental design consideration for an MC is the choice of the topology of the interconnection network, as this significantly influences the types of applications which can be efficiently executed. Over the years many topologies have been proposed [2, 8, 9].

In this paper we consider the problem of designing *fault-tolerant* MC topologies. For an MC, fault-tolerance at the *system level* implies that the type of faults to be tolerated are processor and/or link failures, and an MC is said to be fault-tolerant if it can remain *functional* in the presence of such failures. It is, however, the topological requirements of the application that essentially determine when an MC is considered to be functional. Here, an MC is considered to be functional as long as a *desired* topology is contained in the system. In the past few years much work has been done in developing parallel algorithms and the best MCs for their executions [10]. For these algorithms, the existence of certain topologies is a significant factor in delivering the desired performance. Thus, for such applications, the system should be able to provide a specific topology throughout the execution of the algorithm. The basic approach in achieving fault-tolerance in the above sense, is to employ system-wide redundancy. The existing work on fault-tolerant (in the above sense) topologies has mainly considered processor failures only and we will do likewise here.

In designing such a fault-tolerant topology, the number of faults to be tolerated is specified *a priori*. Given this value, say k, a topology is determined such that the desired sub-topology can be realized given any set of k faults. Fault-tolerant topologies have been proposed for many desired topologies including the loop, binary tree, cube connected cycles and hypercube [3, 5]. In the existing work, the primary design criteria has been to employ the minimum number of redundant processors in deference to other parameters, such as the number of communication links, ease of layout, etc. The overriding rationale for this choice has largely been economic; processors being usually the most expensive component. However, using the absolute minimum number of spare processors has typically forced these designs to incorporate a very large number of redundant communication links; in graph theoretic terms each vertex has very "high" degree. From a practical perspective this presents a problem in that processors have only a finite (usually quite small) number of communication ports.

In this paper we present an alternate primary design criteria and employ it in the design of fault-tolerant loop topologies. The basic idea is to place a bound on the maximum number of connections at each processor and determine the number and configuration of redundant components required to achieve a specified level of fault-tolerance. Loops are a common interconnection topology and are important in their own right. However, as many other topologies have loops "embedded" within them, results relating to the construction of "low" degree fault-tolerant loops can give insight into the feasibility of such constructions for other topologies. In the next section, we present terminology and a formal statement of the problem. In section 3, we present a design for fault-tolerant loops based on a class of graphs called *Chordal Rings*. Section 4 gives a comparison of our approach with previous work and concludes the paper.

2. Background.

The topology of an MC is modeled as a graph $G(V,E)$, with the vertex set $V = V(G)$ representing the processors and the edge set $E = E(G)$ representing the passive, bidirectional communication links between processors. Graph theoretic terms not defined here can be found in [4]. Let $G(V,E)$ be a finite graph without loops or multiple edges. If an edge $e = (u,v) \in E$, then vertices, u and v are said to be *adjacent*, the edge e is said to be *incident* to these vertices. The degree of a vertex v, $d(v)$, is the number of edges incident to v. The *minimum* and *maximum* degrees of a graph G are: $\delta(G) = \min \{ d(v) | v \in V \}$ and $\Delta(G) = \max \{ d(v) | v \in V \}$, respectively. A *subgraph* D of G, denoted $D \subseteq G$, is a graph having all of its vertices and edges in G. A graph G is *r-regular* if for all $v \in V$, $d(v) = r$. Graphs that are 3-regular are also referred to as *cubic* graphs. A *Hamiltonian* graph contains a cycle passing through all its vertices. The length of a shortest cycle in a graph G, called the *girth* of G, is denoted $g(G)$. The cycle of order N, also called an N-cycle, will be denoted as C_N. When convenient, a cycle will be specified by listing, in order, the vertices in the cycle. Example: x_0, x_1, x_2, x_3, x_0 defines a 4-cycle. For a set $X \subset V$, the notation $G - X$ represents the subgraph of G obtained by removing from G the vertices in X and the associated incident edges. We will use the graph theoretic terms cycle, vertex, and edge interchangeably with the terms, loop, processor and link, respectively. The failure of a processor in an MC is represented by the removal of the corresponding vertex and its incident edges in the graph.

As previously mentioned, in this model an MC is functional as long as a desired structure is contained within the system. This criterion was first formulated by Hayes and can be stated formally as follows [5]. Let $G(V,E)$ represent the topology of an MC and $D(V,E)$ be a desired structure. Then, G is k-fault-tolerant (k-ft) with respect to D, if for any set of faulty vertices $F \subset V(G)$, with $|F| = k$, the graph $D \subseteq G - F$. We also say that G is a k-ft D graph. Thus G is a 1-ft N-cycle means that $C_N \subseteq G - \{v\}$ for each $v \in V(G)$. It is clear from this definition that G is a k-ft D graph implies $|V(G)| \geq |V(D)| + k$. For a given graph D, and specified integers k and m, the set of all k-ft D graphs G, with $|V(G)| = |V(D)| + m$ will be denoted by $\Gamma_k[D,m]$.

Using the above definition, several classes of problems can be formulated by imposing certain requirements on the graph G. The problem originally proposed by Hayes can be stated as: Given a graph D and a positive integer k, construct a graph G such that:

(a) $D \subseteq G - F$ for any set $F \subset V(G)$ with $|F| = k$,

(b) $|V(G)| = |V(D)| + k$, and

(c) no graph H satisfying (a) and (b) above has fewer edges than G.

In [5], two designs for 1-ft cycles were presented (one each for graphs of odd and even orders) and also two general designs for k-ft cycles, where $k > 1$. These designs use the minimum number of spare vertices, that is they belong to the class $\Gamma_k[C_N,k]$.

The criteria (b), dictates that the number of spares be exactly equal to the desired level of fault-tolerance. When no additional restriction is placed on the set of faulty vertices, it is not difficult to conclude that $\delta(G) \geq \delta(D) + k$; for the case of $D = C_N$, this gives $\delta(G) \geq k+2$. Thus the degree of each vertex in G is at least proportional to the number of faults to be tolerated. Since current technology limits the number of connections at each processing node (and it seems this constraint will persist for some time to come [2],) the above optimality criteria may not be viable in certain situations.

To address the above concern, we propose the following modified version of the above problem. Given a graph D and a positive integers k and r, construct a graph G such that:

(a) $D \subseteq G - F$ for any set $F \subset V(G)$ with $|F| = k$,

(b) G is r-regular, and

(c) no graph H satisfying (a) and (b) above has fewer vertices than G.

It is clear that this problem may not have any solution for certain choices of D, k, and r. A case in point, when $r=2$ and $D = C_N$ there is no solution G for any k. Thus 3 is the smallest value of r for which a solution may exist for the case of $D = C_N$.

In the sequel we will consider the modified problem for the case $r=3$ and $D = C_N$, N even. We will show that no solutions using exactly k spares exist; thus we must incorporate "extra" redundancy into the design. In fact, we show that the minimum number of spares required is bounded by $2k$, that is $|V(G)| \geq |V(D)| + 2k$, and we will exhibit a class of graphs for which the lower bound is achievable for $k=1,2$.

3. Chordal Rings as k-ft Cycle Topologies.

We begin with some additional definitions.

Definition. A *fault set* F is a set of faulty vertices.

Definition. Given a graph G and a desired graph D, a vertex v is *unusable* with respect to a given fault set F, if no subgraph of $G - F$ isomorphic to D contains v.

Example: Let G be 3-regular and the desired graph D be a cycle. Let $\{u_1, u_2, u_3\} \subset V(G)$ and $\{(u_1,u_2),(u_2,u_3)\} \subset E(G)$. Then the fault set $\{u_1,u_3\}$ makes u_2 unusable because u_2 has (at most) one edge connected to a non-faulty vertex in G, implying that u_2 can not be a vertex in any cycle. It is "trapped" between two faulty vertices. Note that by this definition any faulty vertex is unusable.

Definition. A vertex is *usable* if it is not unusable.

Definition. Given a graph G, a fault set F, and a desired graph D, the set of all unusable vertices induced by F will be denoted $U(F)$ or simply U.

Clearly, a necessary condition for a graph to be k-ft for C_N, is that there be N usable vertices for every fault set F of order k. In other words, the maximum cardinality of an unusable set may not exceed the total number of spare vertices. As we have noted, the tradeoff in using cubic graphs as k-ft cycles is that we must include "extra" spare vertices in the design. Theorem 1 establishes the lower bound (cited earlier) on the amount of redundancy required.

Theorem 1: Let $G \in \Gamma_k(C_N, m)$ be 3-regular and connected. Then $m \geq 2k-1$.

Proof. By definition, there is an N-cycle in G. Label the vertices of this cycle $v_0, v_1, ..., v_{N-1}$ and consider the fault set $F = \{v_1, v_3, ..., v_{2k-1}\}$. As in the example above, the failure of the vertices v_{2i-1} and v_{2i+1} $1 \leq i \leq k-1$ "traps" the vertex v_{2i}, making it unusable. Thus all the vertices "between" such pairs of vertices in F are unusable. This gives $\{v_1, v_2, ..., v_{2k-1}\} \subset U$ and hence $|U| \geq 2k-1$, proving the theorem. ∎

As we are considering designs for even N, theorem 1 and the fact that there exists no cubic graph of odd order, imply that the minimum number of spares is at least $2k$. Hereafter we restrict our attention to cubic graphs having this minimum number of spares, i.e., those in the class $\Gamma_k(C_N, 2k)$. In addition, we will consider only the cases where $k < N/2$. This seems a reasonable requirement for large scale systems and eliminates many special cases in the proofs.

The Chordal Ring class CR(N,w).

A chordal ring of degree three, hereafter referred to simply as a chordal ring, is a 3-regular Hamiltonian graph. Clearly, chordal rings are of even order. Following [1] we define a specific class of chordal rings, $CR(N, w)$ as follows. Construct a cycle of order N; index the vertices $v_0, v_1, \cdots, v_{N-1}$ around the cycle. For each even vertex, v_{2i} $0 \leq i < (N-1)/2$ add the edge (v_{2i}, v_j) where $j = (2i + w) \bmod N$. The parameter w is called the *chord length* and it is required to be odd and at least 3. Note that $CR(N, w)$ is *bipartite* with v_i and v_{i+1} being in different partitions. Without loss of generality, we will assume that $w \leq N/2$. The chordal ring $CR(20, 3)$ is shown in figure 1. (For sake of readability, we have labeled the graphs in the figures using integral labels, i.e., vertex v_i is labeled simply i.)

Fault Tolerance of CR(N,w)

As we noted earlier, two solutions for 1-ft cycles were given in [5]. The solution for even cycles has $\Delta = 4$, while the solution for odd cycles is cubic. We have noticed that that Hayes' solution for 1-ft C_{2j+1} (using one spare) can also serve as a 1-ft C_{2j} (using two spares). In fact Hayes' design is the chordal ring $CR(2j+2, 3)$. Thus such chordal rings belong to $\Gamma_1[C_{2j}, 2]$. The following theorem establishes a stronger result for 1-ft cycles.

Theorem 2: For any even $N \geq 4$, $CR(N+2, w) \in \Gamma_1[C_N, 2]$, where w is as defined above.

Proof. Let N be given and let the vertex set of $CR(N+2, w)$ be $V = \{v_0, v_1, \cdots, v_{N+1}\}$.

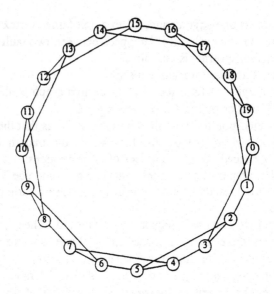

Figure 1. The chordal ring CR(20,3).

Without loss of generality, let $F = \{v_0\}$. Then it is not difficult to see that the N-cycle: $v_1, v_2, v_3, \cdots, v_{N+1-w}, v_{N+1}, v_N, \cdots, v_{N+3-w}, v_1$, is contained in $CR(N+2, w) - F$. ∎

For the 2-ft case, we have proved (by exhaustion) that no such cubic graph can exist for $N=4$, and we thus consider $N \geq 6$. The next theorem establishes that for such N, the chordal rings $CR(N+4, 3)$ are 2-ft for C_N.

Theorem 3: For any $N \geq 6$, $CR(N+4, 3) \in \Gamma_2[C_N, 4]$.

Proof. Let N be given and let the vertex set of $CR(N+4, 3)$ be $V = \{v_0, v_1, \cdots, v_{N+3}\}$. To establish the result, we must show that for any fault set $F = \{u_0, u_1\} \subset V$, $C_N \subseteq CR(N+4, 3) - F$. Since the design uses 4 spare vertices, for any fault set F as above, two additional vertices will not be used in the resulting cycle. The two faulty vertices and the two additional ones will be referred to as the *unused* vertices for the fault F. Without loss of generality, we let $u_0 = v_0$ and consider the possibilities for u_1. There are 3 cases:

Case 1. $u_1 = v_1$ Consider the paths:

$$v_3, v_4 , \quad v_7, v_8 , \cdots, v_{4i-1}, v_{4i} , \cdots, v_{N-1}, v_N, v_{N+1}$$

$$v_2, v_5 , \quad v_6, v_9 , \cdots, v_{4i-2}, v_{4i+1} , \cdots, v_{N-3}, v_{N-2}, v_{N+1}$$

These two paths have only the vertex v_{N+1} in common. A cycle of order N can be formed by concatenating the two paths and including the edge between v_2 and v_3. Note that the vertices v_{N+2} and v_{N+3} are unused in this cycle.

In the remaining two cases we will exploit the Hamiltonian cycle highlighted by solid lines in figure 2, to establish the result. This cycle is made up of paths of the form $v_{2i}, v_{2i+3}, v_{2i-1}$; that is, an edge from the "peripheral" cycle followed by a chord in the "opposite" direction. It is clear that such a cycle always exists in CR(M,3). Note that a cycle with two fewer vertices may be obtained by removing the endpoints v_{2i}, v_{2i+3} of any chord and then using the edge connecting v_{2i+1} and v_{2i+2} to "reconnect" the cycle.

Case 2. $u_1 = v_j$, $j \neq 1, 3$ In this case, an N-cycle can be obtained by removing the chords (i.e. their endpoints) corresponding to the faulty vertices as discussed above.

Case 3. $u_1 = v_3$ Here, the two faulty vertices are the endpoints of a chord. To obtain a cycle of the correct size, we choose the endpoints of any other chord in the graph, with the exception of the pair v_1, v_{N-3} and remove them as in case 2.

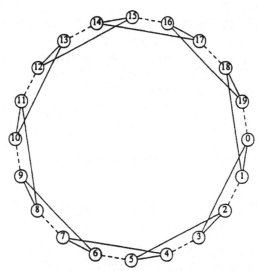

Figure 2. A Hamiltonian cycle in CR(20,3).

Thus for all combinations of 2 failures we can obtain a cycle of order N and the theorem is proved. ∎

We have shown that $CR(N+2k,w) \in \Gamma_k(C_N,2k)$ for $k=1,2$. We will next show that the 3-ft is the best that can be achieved using chordal rings with the minimum number of spare vertices. To do this we need the following result which we state without proof.

Theorem 4: Let G be a 3-regular and connected graph. Further, let $G \in \Gamma_k(C_N,2k)$. Then $g(G) \geq k+2$. ∎

We are now ready to state the following theorem.

Theorem 5:

Proof. $CR(N+2k,w) \notin \Gamma_k(C_N,2k)$ for any $k \geq 4$.

For any values of N and w as defined above, the graph $CR(N,w)$ contains the cycle induced by the edge set:

$$\{(v_0, v_1), (v_1, v_2), (v_2, v_{w+2}), (v_{w+2}, v_{w+1}), (v_{w+1}, v_w), (v_w, v_0)\}$$

This implies that $g(CR(M,w)) \leq 6$ and therefore from theorem 4 the conclusion holds for $k \geq 5$. For $k=4$, consider the fault set $F = \{v_0, v_2, v_4, v_{N+2k-w+2}\}$. The vertices in the set $F' = F \cup \{v_1, v_3, v_{N+2k-w+1}, v_{N+2k-w+3}\}$ are all unusable. Since 5 of these vertices all belong to one set of a bipartition of $CR(N+2k,w)$, the largest cycle that can exist in $CR(N+2k,w) - F'$ is $C_{N+2k-10}$. This gives the desired result for $k=4$. ∎

4. Concluding Remarks.

For the 1-ft case, we have exhibited a class of 3-regular graphs which are in the class $\Gamma_1[C_N,2]$. Previously known results have $\Delta=4$ and do not have the advantages of being regular. In the 2-ft case, our design is 3-regular, requires 4 spare vertices and $3(N+4)/2$ edges. Previously known results are 4-regular, use 2 spare vertices and require $2(N+2)$ edges. Thus the savings in edges is $O(N)$, while the cost in vertices is fixed (and small). So for large N, our designs yield improvements in terms of numbers of edges and are more in accord with the limitations of current technology. In addition since these designs have "extra" redundancy, they have the ability to tolerate certain specific patterns of greater than k failures.

Finally, it has been shown in this paper that 3-ft is the best that can be achieved from chordal rings when using the minimal number of spares. We have shown that a class of chordal rings exists which achieves this upper bound. In particular, we have verified that $CR(N+6,7) \in \Gamma_3[C_N,6]$ for $26 \leq N \leq 50$. Part of the focus of our current research is to extend this result to all even $N > 50$.

REFERENCES

[1]   B. Arden and H. Lee, "Analysis of Chordal Ring Network," *IEEE Trans. on Comput.*, Vol. C-30, pp. 291-295, April 81.

[2]   D.V. Chudnovsky, G.V. Chudnovsky, and M.M. Denneau, "Regular Graphs with Small Diameter as Models for Interconnection Networks," *Proc. of the 3rd International Conf. on Supercomputing*, Vol. III, pp. 232-239, 1988.

[3]   S. Dutt and J.P. Hayes, "Design and Reconfiguration Strategies for Near-Optimal k-Fault-Tolerant Tree Architectures," *FTCS-18*, June 1988.

[4]   F. Harary, *Graph Theory*, Addison Wesley, 1972.

[5]   J.P. Hayes, "A Graph Model for Fault-Tolerant Computing Systems," IEEE Trans. on Comput., Vol. C-25, No. 9, pp. 875-884, September 1976.

[6]   J.P. Hayes, T.N. Mudge, Q.F. Stout, S. Colley, S. and J. Palmer, "Architecture of a hypercube Supercomputer," *Proc. of 1986 Int'l Conf. on Parallel Processing*, August 1986, pp. 653-660.

[7]   K. Hwang and F.A. Briggs, *Computer Architecture and Parallel Processing*, McGraw-Hill, 1984.

[8]   K. Hwang and J. Ghosh, "Hypernet: A Communication-Efficient Architecture for Constructing Massively Parallel Computers," *IEEE Trans. on Computers*, pp. 1450-1466, December 1987.

[9]   D.K. Pradhan, "Interconnection topologies for fault-tolerant parallel and distributed architectures," *Proc. 10th Int'l Conf. on Parallel Processing*, pp. 238-242, August 1981.

[10] M.J. Quinn, *Designing Efficient Algorithms for Parallel Computers*, McGraw-Hill Book Company, 1987.

[11] C.L. Seitz, W.C. Athas, C.M. Flaig, A.J. Martin, J. Seizovic, C.S. Steele and W. Su, "The Architecture and Programming of the Ametek Series 2010 Multiprocessor," *Proc. of The 3-rd Conf. on Hypercube Concurrent Computers and Applications*, pp. 33-38, January 1988.

A Functional Language with Classes

Mike Beaven   Ryan Stansifer   Dan Wetklow
Department of Computer Sciences
Purdue University
West Lafayette, IN 47907
mwb@cs.purdue.edu   ryan@cs.purdue.edu   dww@cs.purdue.edu

1   Introduction

Recent advances in type reconstruction algorithms for type systems with subtyping hold out the possibility of a strongly-typed, object-oriented language in which type declarations are redundant. We propose a language that includes an object construct, which, following Cardelli, we model as a typed record. The methods of the object are modeled as fields with functional types. The advantage of this approach is in the elimination of the "method not found" run-time error, in addition to other benefits of strong typing. The elegance of the language ML [Mil84], which has an expressive type system and the property that all types can be inferred at compile-time, motivates us to ensure that there is a type reconstruction algorithm for our language.

We propose a design of a typed, functional language that supports objects, classes, multiple inheritance and parametric polymorphism. We give the syntax of the language and a discussion of subtyping in the language along with examples of programming with classes to illustrate the different flavor of typed object-oriented languages, and some of the subtleties.

In [Car84], Cardelli showed that it was possible to model objects and inheritance with records and subtyping respectively. Records can account for all of the basic features of objects, a method of an object being modeled as a record field with functional type. Inheritance was modeled by expanding the fields of a record. Wand [Wan89] gave a concrete modeling of objects, classes and inheritance in terms of the typed lambda calculus augmented with records. Objects were modeled with records and classes were modeled with functions that mapped a set of instance variables to an object.

The type of a record consists of information about its fields, specifically what fields are present and the type of each of these fields. Since we can statically determine which fields must be present in a record, we can determine the set of messages supported by an object. This means that the error message *method not found* will never appear during the execution of a type correct program, since this would be an error in field selection.

2   Syntax

We first give the syntax of the language we wish to consider in this paper. The syntax is given in tabular form. Key words are in typewriter font, while slanted font is used for syntactic categories such as identifiers. We use $\emptyset$ to denote the empty sequence.

Value Bindings	Expressions
valbind $\Rightarrow$	*expr* $\Rightarrow$
id = *expr*	*id*
rec *id* = fn *id* => *expr*	con
valbind and *valbind*	self
Types	(*expr*)
type $\Rightarrow$	*expr* . *id*
basetype	*expr* : *type*
typevariable	*expr expr*
type -> *type*	let val *valbind* in *expr* end
object { *extension*	if *expr* then *expr* else *expr*
field $\Rightarrow$	fn *id* => *expr*
Absent	class *id* methods *valbind* end
Pres (*type*)	class *id* inherits *inherit* end
extension $\Rightarrow$	class *id* inherits *inherit* methods *valbind* end
id : *field* , *extension*	*inherit* $\Rightarrow$
} Empty	*id* from *id* with *expr*
} *rowvariable*	*inherit* and *inherit*
Declarations	
decl $\Rightarrow$	
val *valbind*	
decl ; *decl*	

For the sake of discussion, we present a fairly simple language without lists or functions with multiple arguments. Furthermore, the let val expression is used instead of the more general let expression, no side effects are allowed in expressions, objects may have only one instance variable, and inheritance of methods from the same object must be listed seperately. All these restrictions can easily be removed, but we wish to focus on the more important aspects of the class expression. We do not specify the entire set of *basetype* but we assume that a type boolean is present and we use the type int when convenient. Identifiers are used to denote several different things, such as value variables, type variables, row variables, method names, and so on. We have chosen disjoint classes of identifiers for each kind of use. Each class is distinguished by the initial characters specified in the following table.

Class of Identifier	Starting Character
Value Variable	(alphabetic character)
Type Variable	'
Row Variable	&
Method Names	#

3 Examples

In this section we give some simple examples of the language. We will assume that the environment contains some predefined functions or constants such as $+, -, *, 0, 1$, and others as needed.

Defining a class of objects with an instance variable, x, and methods #a and #b, is accomplished by using the **class** construct.

```
val C = class x methods #a = x and #b = (fn z => x+z) end;
```

This defines a class value C which has the following type:

```
C: int -> object{#a:Pres(int),#b:Pres(int->int)}Empty
```

The type of C is a function type. Instantiation of classes is accomplished through function application. The following example creates two distinct instances of the class C.

```
val O = C 0;
val O' = C 1;
```

In the first instance, the instance variable x has value 0; in the second it has 1.

A definition utilizing **self** is as follows.

```
val C' = class x methods #a = x and #b = fn z => (self.#a)+z end;
```

This has the same type and behavior as C. To illustrate inheritance, we create a new class C'' which inherits methods from C and C'.

```
val C'' = class x
            inherits #a from C with x and #b from C' with 1
            methods #c = self.#a + (self.#b 3)
          end;
```

The type of the value of C'' is

```
C'':int->object{#a:Pres(int),#b:Pres(int->int),#c:Pres(int)}Empty
```

A computationally equivalent definition of C'' that does not inherit methods from C and C' is

```
val C''' = class x
            methods #a = x
                and #b = fn z => 1+z
                and #c = self.#a + self.#b
        end;
```

Note that in all class definitions, any method name not explicitly appearing in the methods list or in an inheritance clause is assumed to be absent. This information is contained in the extension Empty. One can think of Empty as representing the infinite sequence

$$l_1 : \textbf{Absent}, l_2 : \textbf{Absent}, \ldots$$

where the labels $l_1, l_2, \ldots$ are all *other* labels. Therefore, in values of type

```
object{#a:Pres(int)}Empty
```

we can infer that the object has only one method, namely #a which has type int and that all other methods are absent.

Row variables are used primarily when an object is passed as a parameter to a function, as in the following example.

```
val f = fn x => (x.#m)+3;
```

Here x is an object with a method #m of type int. The row variable shows that x may or may not have methods other than #m. We cannot infer any information about the existence, nonexistence, or type of any other methods of x. In the type of f, the row variable is denoted by &a:

```
f:object{#m:Pres(int)}&a->int.
```

Next, we consider a slightly more complicated example, the class Int of objects modeling the integers. Each object has methods returning the value of the object, the objects representing the successor and predecessor of the object, and the functions #Plus.

```
val Int = class x
            methods #Val  = x
                and #Succ = Int (x+1)
                and #Pred = Int (x-1)
                and #Plus = fn y => if x = 0 then y
                                    else self.#Pred.#Plus y.#Succ
        end;
```

4   Subtyping

In this section we give examples of how subtype polymorphism manifests itself in the language. The basic idea of a subtype is that τ_1 is a subtype of τ_2 if an expression of type τ_1 can be used anywhere that an expression of type τ_2 is used without causing an error. Another way of viewing it is that an expression having type τ_1 also has type τ_2. We denote the fact that τ_1 is a subtype of τ_2 by $\tau_1 \leq \tau_2$.

One way of expressing subtype polymorphism would be to add a typing rule:

(SUB) $\dfrac{A \vdash e_1 : \tau'}{A \vdash e_1 : \tau} \quad \tau' \leq \tau$

where "$\leq$" defines a subtype relation between types, or to have the type system set up so that adding this rule to the existing type rules has no effect on the typing of expressions. Typing rule (SUB) states that if an expression has type τ' and τ is a supertype of τ', then that expression is also of type τ.

Cardelli [Car84] defined a subtype relation on functions and records. In the context of the type system introduced in this paper the subtype relation is defined in terms of functions and objects. The subtype relation for objects states that object O_1 is a subtype of object O_2 if and only if every method in O_2 is also a method in O_1, and for each of these methods #m, the type of O_1.#m is a subtype of the type of O_2.#m. It is easily seen that an object O_1 can be used anywhere that O_2 can be used since the extra methods of O_1 can simply be ignored. The subtype relation for functions states that a function f_1 is a subtype of a function f_2 if and only if the domain of f_2 is a subtype of the domain of f_1 and the range of f_1 is a subtype of the range of f_2.

In [BSW90] we give typing rules for the entire language. The typing rules are similar to those in [DM82], with the modification that there is one typing rule for each construct in the language, as per [CDDK86]. There are also additional rules that allow object-oriented programming. The type system comes from [Rem89] and [Wan89]. There is one typing rule for each construct in the language. The rule for typing function applications specifies that the types of the formal and actual parameters must be the same. The rule for typing expressions of the form: e.#m demands that e be of type object and that it have a method #m. Another construct that must be mentioned is the let expression, which has the form: let val v=e in e' end. This is semantically equivalent to: (fun v=>e') (e). The difference is that in the let expression, the type of the actual parameter e is known when deriving the type of e'. This has certain advantages in type reconstruction. In particular, this additional information allows the type of the actual parameter to be universally quantified. In other words, v can be used polymorphically in e'.

The advantage of adding subtyping to the type system is that it gives us a richer type structure. Consider a function that demands its parameters be objects with methods #a:Pres(int->int) and #b:Pres(bool->string). Should we be able to apply this function to an object that has appropriate #a and #b methods and also has a method #c of some type? It will not present any problems with correctness in the execution of the program; the extra methods will simply be ignored by the function. However, the rule for typing function applications states that the formal and actual parameters must have the same type. If we have no notion of subtype polymorphism, then an object with two methods cannot have the same type as an object with three methods, therefore the function cannot be applied to objects with extra methods. The typing rules seem unduly restrictive in this case. If we add rule (SUB) with Cardelli's subtype relation, then the function can be applied to objects with extra methods. One way of viewing it is that we use typing rule (SUB) to coerce the actual parameter to a supertype that only has methods #a and #b, and then use the rule for typing function application.

In our system, subtyping is obtained by the use of row variables. Row variables are used to add fields to objects. The subtyping present in our type system is not as powerful as Cardelli's subtype relation. In other words, adding rule (SUB) where "$\leq$" is defined as Cardelli's subtype relation to our typing rules would permit us to derive types for expressions that are currently untypable under our set of typing rules. Consider the following expression:

```
val f = fn v => v.#m(3)+4
```

From the typing rules, we can derive that f has the following type:

```
object{#m:Pres(int->int)}&a -> int
```

If x and y have types

```
object{#m:Pres(int->int),#l:Pres(bool->bool)}Empty
object{#m:Pres(int->int),#w:Pres(str->str)}Empty
```

in the type environment, then the expression

```
(fn f => f(x)+f(y))(fn v => v.#m(3)+4)
```

cannot be typed using the typing rules. To type f(x), the row variable &a must have #l:Pres(bool->bool), while at the same time &a must have #l:Absent to type f(y). Since it cannot have both, we cannot type the expression. However, if we added typing rule (SUB) to our typing rules with Cardelli's subtype relation this expression would be typable since both x and y have a method #m of type int->int, which is really all that function f requires.

This does not mean that there is no subtype polymorphism present in our type system. Note that in the above example f has type object{#m:Pres(int->int)}&a -> int. This means that it can be applied to any object that has a method #m of type int->int, i.e., it can be applied to all and only subtypes (using the subtype relation defined by Cardelli) of object{#m:Pres(int->int)}Empty, since the row variable &a can be instantiated to include any additional methods. This is an example of subtype polymorphism.

The reason that we could not type the expression in the first example was because of the presence of both f(x) and f(y). We could not instantiate the row variable, &a, two different ways in the same context. Note that if we rewrote the above expression in the computationally equivalent form:

```
let val f = fn v => v.#m(3)+4 in f(x)+f(y) end
```

then this expression can be typed with our typing rules because the row variable &a is universally quantified. For subtype polymorphism, as well as parametric polymorphism, the let-expression is required if we wish to use a parameter polymorphically in an expression. The reason for this is that we are using the same technique to obtain subtype polymorphism (row variables) as we used to obtain parametric polymorphism (type variables).

5 Concluding Remarks

In [BSW90] we have a full discussion of the relation between subtyping and inheritance. Our conclusion is that the subclass mechanism should not be the same as subtyping. We also provide an ML implementation of the language, as well as the typing rules, a type reconstruction algorithm, and semantics using reduction rules. We also discuss single and multiple inheritance, the resolution of method name conflicts in multiple inheritance, and means of modeling multiple inheritance along with a discussion of Wand's [Wan89] modeling.

References

[BSW90]   Michael Beaven, Ryan Stansifer, and Dan Wetklow. A functional language with classes. Technical Report CSD-TR-946, Purdue University, 1990.

[Car84]   Luca Cardelli. A semantics of multiple inheritance. In *Proc. Int. Symp. on Semantics of Data Types, Sophia-Antipolis(France), Springer LNCS 173*, pages 51–68, 1984.

[CDDK86] D. Clement, J. Despeyroux, T. Despeyroux, and G. Kahn. A simple applicative language: Mini-ML. In *Conf. Proc. 1986 ACM Symposium on LISP and Functional Programming*, pages 13–27, 1986.

[DM82]   Luis Damas and Robin Milner. Principal type-schemes for functional programs. In *Conference Records of the Ninth Annual ACM Symposium of Principals of Programming Languages*, pages 207–212, 1982.

[Mil84]   Robin Milner. Proposal for standard ML. In *Conf. Proc. 1984 ACM Symposium on LISP and Functional Programming*, pages 184–197, 1984.

[Rem89]   Didier Remy. Typechecking records and variants in a natural extenstion of ML. In *Conference Records of the 16th Annual ACM Symposium of Principals of Programming Languages*, pages 77–88, 1989.

[Wan89]   Mitchell Wand. Type inference for record concatenation and multiple inheritance. In *Proc. Fourth IEEE Symposium on Logic in Computer Science*, pages 92–97, 1989.

Using ML as a Command Language

Steve J. Chapin   Ryan Stansifer

Department of Computer Sciences
Purdue University
West Lafayette, IN 47907
sjc@cs.purdue.edu   ryan@cs.purdue.edu

1   Introduction

We consider using a typed, functional language as the command line interpreter. Often the user interface to the operating system, or shell, is ad hoc in design. There is an increasing tendency to add on baroque extensions to shells, resulting in an inconsistent and confusing command language. Frequently these extensions are constructs that have analogs in programming languages. In the interest of regularity it seems appropriate to move towards a monolingual environment, i.e., one in which the user issues commands and constructs programs in the same language. In order to implement such a shell, we choose an existing programming language, ML. ML is a logical choice due to its conceptual simplicity and perspicuity.

In this paper, we examine the purpose and use of shells as the interface to UNIX[1]. We determine which features of shells are already present in ML, and which need to be added. We are modifying the underlying abstract machine for our own ML interpreter to include these capabilities as an integral part of the language.

2   What Is a Shell?

The user interface to the operating system is usually in the form of a command line interpreter. The following list enumerates the capabilities generally associated with command line interpreters. Most shells will:

1. provide the ability to invoke arbitrary programs named by the user as processes.

2. provide control structures, such as looping and conditionals, for the combination of shell primitives.

3. interpret programs written in the command language, also known as *shell scripts*.

---

[1] UNIX is a trademark of AT&T.

4. run tasks asynchronously, allowing tasks to run concurrently with the shell, as well as providing some control over the execution of these tasks.

5. compose programs to form more complex functions via the connection of the output of one program to the input of the next.

6. perform I/O redirection, allowing files to be used in place of input and output devices.

7. allow the user to customize the operational environment for programs the shell will invoke.

8. provide reasonable performance and a concise syntax.

9. perform path searching, wildcarding, and filename completion. Path searching is the act of looking for a named file in a list of directories, often in anticipation of executing the file. Wildcard expansion refers to the ability of the shell to translate an expression representing several file names into the actual names. Filename completion allows the user to type a unique prefix of the name and have the shell fill in the rest.

10. provide a history mechanism to allow the user to repeat often used commands easily.

The UNIX shell delivers a remarkable amount of power for a minimum effort. Its notion of a stream of characters as the only I/O data type makes function composition intuitive and relieves the programmer of type considerations.

A major advantage of using an existing programming language as the basis for a command interpreter is that we gain all the flexibility and power of the existing language. As noted in [HK85], the user has only one language to learn for both programming and for issuing commands. Most programming languages, including ML, have features that are analogous to items 2, 3, 4, and 5. The other items will have to be added to the ML interpreter if it is to act as a shell. We have available the ML conditional and iteration structures, structured data types, and the ability to write scripts to perform complex tasks.

We therefore will combine the desirable aspects of the UNIX shell with the ML programming language. The result will have the versatility of the shell with ML's powerful typing system and control structures.

3 Operating System Service Requirements

Before defining the shell primitives that will allow a user to access operating system services, we must first determine which services are of interest. This information will help guide our selection of primitives and their semantics.

Some of the items listed in section 2 are operating system issues. Both the ability to run an arbitrary program and the composition of programs fall into this category. Input/output redirection and job control also require operating system access.

Several common shell features require knowledge of and access to the file system. A function similar to the UNIX stat system call that reports information on a selected file will be of use for writing the ML function to do filename completion, wildcarding, and path searching.

The concept of the *working directory* as a reference point in the file system for relative path operations, such as a call to open_in "datafile"; is important. Since a complete path name is not specified, the file datafile is opened relative to the working directory. The shell needs a mechanism to set this working directory for itself. Although UNIX provides a default mechanism to propagate the working directory to child processes, it would be useful to allow the shell to explicitly set the working directory for a child process.

When a file is created, it usually inherits a default set of access rights. In UNIX, this is called the umask, and the shell should be able to set the value of this operating system variable.

4   The CML Shell

CML is an implementation of the Core ML language, written at Purdue University. We are extending CML to make it suitable for use as a command interpreter. One very important feature is the stream data type, as presented in [Har85]. This solves the problem that ML has with emulating a command interpreter on the computation of function values in composition. A stream of characters can be thought of as a possibly infinite sequence of characters. Streams come in two types: instreams are streams that can be read, and outstreams can be written. Our ML shell has two predefined data types for streams, instream and outstream.

Without the stream type, ML must wait for the value of a function to be completely computed before it can pass that value to another function; e.g. in the function composition $f(g())$, ML must wait for g to complete computation before it knows the value of the argument for f. Streams allow ML to pass partially computed sequences of characters between functions.

We have also defined several functions for file I/O, as listed in table 1.

Several of the upcoming examples will use the definition

```
val sio = (std_in, std_out, std_err);
```

It is a notational convenience that represents the common UNIX triple of the standard input stream, the standard output stream, and the standard error stream. We intend to provide access to operating system features via extended CML primitives and to allow the programmer to use the ML language features to customize the interface to these features. The following sections contain examples of these extensions.

4.1   exec

CML has an exec function of type

item	description	type
open_in	function to open an input file	string -> instream
open_out	function to open an output file	string -> outstream
open_append	function to open an output file in append mode	string -> outstream
close_out	function to close an outstream	outstream -> unit
close_in	function to close an instream	instream -> unit
std_in	standard input	instream
std_out	standard output	outstream
std_err	standard error	outstream

Table 1: Input/Output features of CML

```
string ->
    instream * outstream * outstream ->
        (string * string) list ->
            string ->
                unit
```

The first argument is a string representation of a UNIX program name to be run, the second is a triple of streams for input and output, the third is the environment list, and the last is a string containing the arguments for the program. An example might be

```
exec "/bin/ls" sio environ "foo.c";
```

exec would locate the file /bin/ls in the file system, execute it and return unit if it could find the file, otherwise it would raise an exception. The environ argument is a list of name/value pairs comprising the UNIX program's environment.

If we were to make the definitions

```
val ls = exec "/bin/ls" sio environ;
fun ll (args) = ls ("-l " ^ args);
```

we could then pass arguments with short statements such as ls "foo.c"; or ll "foo.c", providing an easy shorthand while still allowing the user the ability to construct complicated commands if required.

The definitions of our shell primitives are intended to allow the programmer the maximum control over the shell functions, while using ML code to build higher level functions. This leaves the programmer with a wide range of choices for power and convenience.

The exec function is a good example of this philosophy. exec does not itself do any path searching or wildcard expansion with its arguments. We have left these mechanisms to be defined at a higher level (resolve_cmd and expand_args above),

```
val path = [ ".", "/usr/sjc/bin", "/bin", "/usr/bin" ];

fun docmd cmd io env s =
    let
        val cmd2 = resolve_cmd(cmd);
        val args = expand_args(s);
    in
        exec cmd2 io env args
    end;

fun ls = docmd ls sio [];

ls "*c";
```

Figure 1: Example use of the **exec** function

so that the user can customize the shell. Default functions are provided to perform these tasks. An example of using the power of the **exec** function while retaining flexibility is in figure 1.

4.2   Error Handling

UNIX error handling is primitive in comparison with ML error handling. By convention, UNIX processes return an integer code, with 0 representing successful completion, and any non-zero value indicating an error. **exec** could be written to return an integer instead of the unit value, but to encourage the use of the exception mechanism provided in ML, **exec** raises an exception when the UNIX process returns a non-zero value.

4.3   pipe

In order to aid function composition between UNIX programs, we have added the pipe function to CML. It is of type **unit -> instream * outstream**. Given the standard form for UNIX commands, we can then define a piping mechanism shown in figure 2. Note that pipe returns a pair of streams that are connected, and that Pipe uses this call to connect successive commands together. We place the I/O streams as the first argument to both the UNIX commands and the Pipe call. This allows us to curry these operators to achieve a desirable conciseness of syntax.

4.4   Shell Variables

In the past, there has been some confusion in the treatment of shell variables in command interpreters. We feel that there are two kinds of variables that a shell must deal with, intended for completely different purposes. First, there are variables

```
fun Pipe (s1, s2, s3) env (f, a1) (g, a2) =
    let
        val (i,o) = pipe();
        val () = docmd f (s1, o, s3) env a1;
        val () = docmd g (i, s2, s3) env a2;
        val () = close_in(i);
        val () = close_out(o);
    in
        ()
    end;

Pipe sio environ;
```

Figure 2: sample ML definition and use of piping function

local to the shell that are not intended to affect the shell's children; second, there are variables that are used to modify the environment of child processes but which are not needed by the shell. The second type of variable is often referred to as an environment variable.

Past shells have used a lookup mechanism that has clouded this distinction. Most shells will look for a variable in the environment if it is not found locally. Our shell keeps these two issues separate by using ML variables for local variables and making the environment for children an explicit parameter of the exec call.

The environment is intended to model the UNIX environment, supplying a list of variables that a program can access to customize the interface for the user. The shell's environment can be accessed through a predefined constant environ, which has type (string * string) list. Since we explicitly name the environment for all UNIX commands, it is easy to supply a different environment to commands by passing a modified copy of the local environment. Therefore, we can simulate a subshell by using a let statement to modify the environment that will be passed to UNIX commands; this will not affect our local environment.

5 Conclusion

We have shown that ML can be used as the basis for a command interpreter for UNIX. A functional shell has many advantages over a conventional shell, and ML provides much of the mechanism for implementing such a shell at essentially no cost. We feel that the gain in expressive power far outweighs the slight degradation in speed, and note that a distributed implementation of ML could provide an increase in speed substantial enough to offset the additional overhead our shell incurs.

Although it is not the primary goal, we intend to add many of the convenience features of other command line interpreters to CML. The readline package distributed by the Free Software Foundation implements emacs-style command editing and history mechanism for general use.

CML has all of the essential features of a command line interpreter except job control. The addition of job control would require a new data structure for the shell containing pertinent information about jobs such as their status, name, and arguments. This could be bound to the symbol jobs in the initial environment. Job suspension is a desirable feature, and could be invoked using the UNIX convention of control-Z to cause an interrupt and suspend the currently executing process, returning control to the shell. We would also need commands to change job state (e.g., suspend, foreground, background). The shell would have to be modified internally to handle the SIGTSTP signal and to do the correct I/O handling.

This paper is a condensed version of [CS90]. [AM87] describes the Standard ML of New Jersey compiler which has some shell features. An implementation of the UNIX shell written in Standard ML appears in [KM87].

References

[AM87]   Andrew W. Appel and David B. MacQueen. A Standard ML Compiler. In Gilles Kahn, editor, *Functional Programming Languages and Computer Architecture*, pages 301–324. Springer-Verlag, 1987.

[Bou]   S. R. Bourne. *An Introduction to the UNIX Shell.*

[CS90]   Steve J. Chapin and Ryan Stansifer. Using ML as a Command Language. Technical report, Purdue Univerity, January 1990.

[Har85] Robert W. Harper. Standard ML Input/Output. Technical report, Edinburgh Univerity, June 1985.

[HK85]   J. Heering and P. Kint. Towards Monolingual Programming Environments. *ACM Transactions on Programming Languages and Systems*, April 1985.

[Joy]   William Joy. *An Introduction to the C shell.*

[KM87]   Yogeesh H. Kamath and Manton M. Matthews. Implementation of an FP-Shell. *IEEE Transactions on Software Engineering*, SE-13(5):532–539, May 1987.

[Kor]   David Korn. *Introduction to KSH (Issue 2).*

[McD89] Cristopher S. McDonald. An Executable Formal Specification of a UNIX Command Interpreter. In *IFIP W2.7 Working Conference on Engineering for Human-Computer Communication*, August 1989.

An Interactive System for Generating Hospital Progress Notes [1]

Huei-Ning Natasha Ma   Martha Evens
Illinois Institute of Technology
Chicago, Illinois 60616

David A. Trace   Frank Naeymi-Rad
University of the Health Sciences/Chicago Medical School
North Chicago, IL 60064

Abstract

Research has shown that physicians find a medical expert system much more attractive if the system can provide in addition to diagnostic support some relief from the heavy burden of responsibility for daily record keeping required in hospital practice. This paper introduces a sophisticated interactive system for generating daily progress notes designed to function as an integral part of MEDAS (the Medical Emergency Decision Assistance System). MEDAS is a pattern-recognition expert system, using multi-membership Bayesian inference. At hospital admission, the MEDAS diagnosis module and severity module produce a problem list and assign a severity code to each problem. In many hospitals, physicians are expected to provide daily progress notes discussing the patient's condition with respect to each problem area. For each problem, they need to consider subjective and objective information, assessment and make a plan for handling the problem. The items to be considered depend on the specific problem: remembering these items is a huge memory load; writing it all down is very time-consuming. Our system presents the physician with a series of problem-specific menus, making data entry easy and rapid. Finally, it automatically generates the necessary output for the patient record.

1   Introduction

Many hospitals and clinics have been partly computerized during the last decade. They use commercially available computer systems to handle daily administrative tasks, pharmacy control, equipment inventory, laboratory test reports, patients' demographic profiles, third party insurance claim forms, and billing information. While all these systems are widely used by medical care providers, and have become

---

[1]We want to thank Dr. Daniel Woodard of Bionetics and Dr. Paul Buchanan of NASA for their advice and support.

part of their regular tools in coping with the increasing complexities of their daily jobs, progress notes and other medical record information must still be written manually by physicians at every encounter with patients in most institutions.

A few medical record systems, however, attempt to help physicians in preparing progress notes or record summaries. Some significant systems are RMIS (Regenstrief Medical Information System) [12]; TMR (The Medical Record) [9, 18]; STOR (Summary Time-Oriented Record) [16]; COSTAR (Computer-Stored Ambulatory Record) [1]; ODISY (Online Deaconess Information SYstem) [15]. However, these systems merely provide a word processor or part of a database record, and the scope of the disorders are specified in a particular area, such as obstetrics [17], pediatrics [6], rehabilitation [19], or psychiatry [13]. Consequently, either physicians or record clerks have to type in much essential information in order to get a complete medical record [15].

2   Problems with Existing Medical Records

Today's medical records have become more and more detailed and complex. Often 40 years ago only a few lines were recorded, but now medical records commonly contain notes from various primary-care physicians, nurses, specialists and other health-care providers in association with reports from different laboratory tests and physical examinations.

The primary-care physicians or nurses typically identify and report most of the relevant information for the medical record. Yet their traditional hand written notes, with too many nonstandard abbreviations or vocabulary items, too many incomplete sentence and no specific headings or sub-headings, sometimes make it difficult for subsequent specialists or other physicians to identify the data they need and interpret it correctly. Manually written records, tend to have difficulties in of: 1)availability, 2)retrievability, 3)legibility and 4)organization [13]. These unorganized medical records definitely have negative effects on 1) clinical judgment, 2) patient-care plans, 3) medical record audits 4) medical education, and even 5) evaluations of physician performance [20].

Most so-called called "automated record systems," Barnett [1, p.1645] explains, "include the name of the diagnosis or problem and only a minimal amount of detail in coded format; and the bulk of the descriptive information which is stored in narrative form." Unfortunately, these forms have to be filled out or dictated by the physician. There are major problems in locating, reentering, translating, transferring and interpreting of this narrative information. Performing such data transformations is not only very time and energy consuming but also prone to errors [1].

3 Problem-Oriented Medical Records

The Problem-Oriented Medical Record (POMR)), described by Weed is our basic guideline in developing the progress note system introduced in this paper. Weed says, "...the basic criterion of the physician is how well he can identify the patient's problems and organize them for solution" [20]; thus, he designed the structure for better record-keeping and maintenance. When he first proposed the POMR many physicians disagreed with him [4]; some even conducted research to prove the POMR was no better than the SOR (Source Oriented Record) [5, 7]. However, Weed had some supporters from the first [10], and this support has grown steadily with more sophiscated software and hardware devices and with the dramatic drop in the price of computers. Now Weed's POMR has largely supplanted the traditional methods for medical record-keeping [8].

In his original statement about progress notes, Weed says, "The progress notes should be written in a form which relates them clearly and unmistakably to the problem" [20]. His design has two parts: the first is a problem list, which is a "table of contents" and an "index" combined. Items that must be inserted in the problem list include the patient's present and past problems. The contents of the list should not be limited to medical problems; social and psychiatric problems must be considered as well [20].

The second part is the statement by the physician. Weed suggests that each note should be preceded by the number and title of the appropriate problem. For each problem, four basic elements compose the structure of the note, they are: (S) Subjective data – the patient's chief complaints; (O) Objective data – actual clinical findings, X-ray or laboratory results; (A) Assessment – the patient's progress as viewed by the physician; (P) Plan – treatment program for the problem plus further test plans, if any.

4 Interface with the MEDAS Expert System

Our progress note system is originally designed both as an integral part of a medical expert system – MEDAS, and a stand alone system. As research has shown that a medical expert system will be more attractive for physicians if it can provide not only the diagnostic function but also generation of progress notes [3], we here put more emphasis on integration with an expert system.

MEDAS is a probabilistic diagnostic consultant employing pattern-recognition in its inference engine and relational database technology for its knowledge base maintenance. The system was developed by Ben-Basset and Weil [2], as a decision assistance system for emergency rooms in the late 1970's at the University of Southern California and the Institute of Critical Care with support from NASA. The diagnostic process is based on disorders and features (patient health status, clinical data, signs, symptoms, laboratory tests, x-rays, etc...). MEDAS moved to Chicago in 1981 and has grown from 70 disorders and approximately 700 features to 150 disorders defined by 4500 features. It has now evolved to work as a complete system with a Hypercard front end for data acquisition, a feature dictionary for data sharing and translation among different knowledge bases [14], treatment protocols, severity for measurement of the patient's condition, and now finally an intelligent progress note system.

5 System Design Goals

The National Center for Health Services Research [11] has sponsored a review of automated medical-record systems being developed in different types of ambulatory health-care settings, and concluded that the important issues to be addressed in the further development of automated medical record systems for ambulatory practice are as follows:

(1) getting the practitioner more involved in using the system, (2) developing more efficient methods of data capture and entry, and (3) improving user interaction with the system. [11]

Considering these problems and others raised by local physicians, we have set up the following goals:

(1) Reducing the time spent in data input

(2) Providing a reminder to prompt physicians. Some argue that information overload is responsible for many medical errors and have used a computerized reminder system to reduce such errors [12]; others go further and show evidence to suggest that reminders generated by computers have a positive effect. McDonald claims that this happens because the computer prompts the physician for some proper procedure that he or she intended to carry out but simply forgot [12].

(3) Producing acceptable progress notes that meet the JCHSO criteria and are accepted by most physicians. Clearly, the format of the report is very important.

6 Methods

Predictive Check-off Sheet as a Reminder. In order to fulfill our goals, we propose the following method to solve the problems of most automated record systems. Before the physician encounters the patient, the system will generate a patient-specific check-off sheet or screen for each problem mentioning all items that should be considered. When the patient is seen, the physician marks items that are present or not present.

Special Interface. Types of interface under consideration include an electronic clip board, a scanner, and menu selection.

Different Formats for Different Data. We feel srongly that data of different natures should be presented differently. For example, the subjective data should be expressed by narrative text, while numeric values and other objective data should be presented in tabular form. In our system, the physician does not have to type in all the narrative text, the system will supply text for stereotyped situations.

7 System Architecture

Input for the System. Our progress note system is basically an expert system, with knowledge base, inference engine, special interface for input and a smart editor with a pool of sentences. The input to the system is the problem list, which is derived from the chief complaint, the system review, the past history, and the current active illnesses. The problem list can be obtained by running the diagnostic module and severity module from MEDAS or by asking the physician for information using the special front end.

Knowledge Base: Disorders and Features. The knowledge base of the system consists of disorder patterns and feature patterns, which are stored in a realational database system. The features are marked to indicate whether they are subjective or objective for use in the progress note system.

Inference Engine. The inference engine of the progress notes system applies forward chaining. The key part of the changing relationship is the severity [28]. The severity varies over time as laboratory test results are reported or new findings appear. When severity changes, the relationsip between disorder and features will be redefined; some features will be added or ruled out for this particular disorder.

A Smart Editor with a Pool of Sentences. Our system will automatically generate a brief narrative as well as a tabular report in accordance with data input by our intelligent interface. In case the physicians are not satisfied with the text produced by the system, a smart editor is provided for physicians to modify the text. They can either write their own text or select phrases or whole sentences from a pool provided by the system. There is still an open question regarding the editor; we are not sure whether we should use an existing word processor or build our own editor.

Assessment and Treatment. An assessment is provided by the system automatically, but the physician will have the option to modify it using a series of menus. The treatment plans are produced by calling the treatment module from the MEDAS system. Again the physician can easily moidify the treatment plan using a menu interface.

Final Report and Security. Before the final report is generated, the physician always has the right to modify the progress note. However, if the final report is printed out, for security reasons, the file should not be modified. A hardcopy printout should be signed by the physician and kept in the patient's medical file. Finally, the progress note should be compressed and saved in the patient's portable file.

8 Conclusion

This paper describes a Progress Note System that attempts to reduce data input time and produce the a satisfactory medical report. Once we have a working system, we need to investigate its actual reception by physician users. Some questions we need to investigate are: How do the progress notes produced by our system compare with hand written notes in terms of physician approval and usability? How much input time can be saved? Are our different formats suitable?

References

[1] G.O. Barnett. The application of computer-based medical-record systems in ambulatory practice. *N Engl J Med.* 1984;310:1643–1650.

[2] M. Ben-Bassat, R.W. Carlson, V.K. Puri, M.D. Davenport, J.A. Schriver, M.H. Weil. Pattern-based interactive diagnosis of multiple disorders: The MEDAS system. *IEEE Transactions in Pattern Analysis and Machine Intelligence.* 1980;148–160.

[3] M.B. Bischoff, E.H. Shortliffe, A.C. Scott, R.W. Carlson, C.D. Jacobs. Integration of a computer-based consultant into the clinical setting. *Proceedings of the Seventh Annual Symposium on Computer Applications in Medical Care,* IEEE, 1983:149–152.

[4] A.R. Feinstein. The problems of the "problem-oriented medical record." *Annals of Internal Medicine.* 1973;78:751–762.

[5] W.J. Fessel, E.E. Van Brunt. Assessing quality of care from the medical record. *N Engl J Med.* 1972;286:34–38.

[6] N.N. Finer, A.J. Fraser. Neonatal data base and automated discharge summary using a personal computer and proprietary software. *Pediatrics.* 1985;76:(2) 269–273.

[7] R.H. Fletcher. Auditing problem-oriented records and traditional records: a controlled comparison of speed, accuracy, and identification or errors in medical care. *N Engl J Med..* 1974;290:829–833.

[8] H.H. Friedman. *Problem-Oriented Medical Diagnosis.* Little Brown and Company, Boston, 1987.

[9] W.E. Hammond, W.W. Stead, M.J. Straube, F.W. Jelovsek. Functional characteristics of a computerized medical record. *Methods Inf Med.* 1980; 19:157–162.

[10] J.W. Hurst. Ten reasons why Lawrence Weed is right. *N Engl J Med.* 1971, 284:51–52.

[11] I.M. Kuhn, G.W. Wiederhold. The evolution of ambulatory medical systems in the U.S. In: H.G. Heffernan, (ed.) *Proceedings of the Fifth Annual Symposium on Computer Applications in Medical Care.* IEEE, 1981:80–85.

[12] C.J. McDonald, S.L. Hui, D.M. Smith. Reminders to physicians from an introspective computer medical record. *Annals of Internal Medicine.* 1984. 100:130–138.

[13] M.J. Meldman, D. Harris, J.P. Robert, E.A. Johnson. A computer-assisted, goal-oriented psychiatric progress note system. *Am J Psychiatry.* 1977;134:38–41.

[14] F. Naeymi-Rad. A feature dictionary for a multi-domain medical knowledge base. *Proceedings of the Twelfth Annual Symposium on Computer Applications in Medical Care,* IEEE, 1988:212–217.

[15] M.S. Roberts, J.D. Zibrak, A. Siders. The development of an on-line, partially automated discharge summary and core clinical data-base in an existing hospital information system. *Proccedings of the Thirteenth Annual Symposium on Computer Applications in Medical Care.* IEEE, 1989:649–653.

[16] D.W. Simborg, Q.E. Whiting-O'Keefe. Summary time oriented record (STOR) - a progress report. *Proceedings of the Fifth Annual Symposium on Computer Applications in Medical Care.* IEEE, 1981:100–103.

[17] R.P. Smith, G.B. Holzman. The application of a computer data base system to generation of hospital discharge summaries. *Obstetrics and Gynecology.* 1989;73:(5), 803–807.

[18] W.W. Stead, W.E. Hammond, M.J. Straube. A chartless record - is it adequate? *Proceedings of the Sixth Annual Symposium on Computer Applications in Medical Care.* IEEE, 1982:89–94.

[19] P.H. Stern, B.S.Rubin. Computerized discharge sumaries. *Arch Phys Med Rehabil.* 1979;60:25–29.

[20] L.L. Weed. *Medical Records, Medical Education, and Patient Care. The Problem-Oriented Record as a Basic Tool.* Chicago, Year Book Medical Publishers, Inc., 1970.

[21] Q.E. Whiting-O'Keefe, D.W. Simborg, W.V. Epstein, A.A. Warger. A computerized summary medical record system can provide more information than the standard medical record. *JAMA.* 1985;254:1185–1192.

Biological Evolution as A Paradigm
for Performance Driven Design Processes

Mateen M. Rizki
Department of Computer Science and Engineering
Wright State University
Dayton, Ohio 45435

Louis A. Tamburino
WRDC/AAAT
Wright-Patterson Air Force Base
Dayton, Ohio 45433

Michael A. Zmuda
Department of Computer Science and Engineering
Wright State University
Dayton, Ohio 45435

Abstract

The application of evolutionary processes to the problem of automated design is explored. A feature detector component for a pattern recognition system is used as an example of the automated design process. Results obtained from applying the resultant detector system to the problem of character recognition are discussed.

1 Introduction

The structure and function of a biological system result from interaction between genetic information and the environment. The genetic material encodes the design for a biological structure whose function is modulated by environmental forces. Using design terminology, a population of biological organisms may be considered a collection of genetic designs competing to exploit constraints imposed by the environment. Natural evolution drives the design process through an endless cycle of reproduction, variation, and selection. During reproduction, changes to the genetic makeup resulting from mutations and recombinations modify the design transmitted from parent to offspring. Modified offspring then compete with other members of the population for limited resources. Successful individuals survive to pass their designs on to the next generation. As a result of the evolutionary process, populations of new designs gradually emerge.

We can mimic the evolutionary process for the design of man-made systems as a means to automate the design process. Genetic algorithms [4], abstractions of biological evolution, have been used in a variety of engineering applications [1,3]. To apply evolutionary learning processes, it is necessary to develop representations for a genetic code, techniques to vary the code, performance measures to evaluate populations of designs, and strategies to apportion resources among the candidate designs.

A few of the differences between biological systems and man-made systems are listed in Table 1. For example, in nature DNA (RNA) encodes all genetic information, but a customized code is required to use the evolutionary process for machine learning. In natural systems, new structures and functions emerge during the evolutionary process, but there are limitations to simulated evolution. Simulated evolution is a performance driven search process in which the set of structures that can be generated is pre-defined. Although dynamic interactions between modelled components can lead to interesting and unexpected behavior, no new structures can appear.

Evolutionary Features	Biological Systems	Man-Made Systems
Genetic Coding	DNA	Selected representation
Genetic Expression (Decoding)	DNA specified	Externally specified
Individual Fitness	Emergent property	Evaluation function pre-determined
Resource Allocation	Determined by competitive interactions	Determined by fitness function
Mutation/Recombination Rate	Inherent	Selected

Table 1. Differences between biological and man-made systems.

In this paper, we examine the application of evolutionary processes to automated design. Section 2 describes the automated design problem, and section 3 examines the application of evolutionary learning to the automated design of a pattern recognition system. In section 4, we summarize observations and review the value of an evolutionary approach to automated design.

2 Principles of Automated Design

An automated design process locates an acceptable design in a set of potential designs termed the design space. Typically, the design space is sufficiently large to preclude an exhaustive search so we must develop techniques to control this search process. Our system for automated design has two basic subsystems: a design subsystem and a learning subsystem. The design subsystem consists of two components: a design representation and a set of processing algorithms. The algorithms operate on the current state of the representation to perform an input-output task. The design process consists of altering the current state of the design representation and/or the behavior of the processing algorithms. The learning subsystem guides the design process by evaluating the current output of the design subsystem with respect to a user-specified design goal and then sends control signals to the design subsystem to modify the current state of the design.

The choice of representation for the design space is critical. The representation must be amenable to search and easily expressed in a finite format suitable for computation. Unfortunately, there are no well developed theories or techniques for creating a representation so human expertise and intuition are often the best guides. The development of search strategies must be coordinated with the representation to exploit properties of the design space. In addition, resource allocation strategies are required to apportion computational resources among different phases of the design process. Finally, evaluation criteria and performance measures are necessary to guide the design process. These measures must reflect the design constraints and goals.

3 Pattern Recognition System Design

A pattern recognition system detects features in images and then assigns each image to a specific class. Figure 1 presents an overview of a system for the automated design of a pattern recognition system. The feature detector subsystem used in our design problem is based on the principles of mathematical morphology [6]. The morphological analysis is limited to erosion operations that utilize structuring elements to evaluate binary images. Image erosion is the systematic removal of pixels from an input image as it is compared to a structuring element, or second image. The structuring element is a collection of pixels serving as a template that is translated across the surface of the input image. For each coincidence between the foreground and background pixels of the template and image, a reference pixel in the structuring element is used to mark a pixel position in a third, or resultant, image. The ultimate result of eroding an image by a specific structuring element is the production of a smaller set of pixels in the resultant image. The images selected for the study described below were alphabet letters; Figure 2 illustrates the hit-or-miss (erosion) operation on the letters L and T. If the detector defined by a structuring element produces a non-null resultant image after an erosion, then the input image contains the feature embodied by the detector and a binary response is recorded.

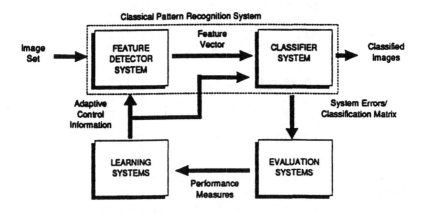

Figure 1. Automated Design of a Pattern Recognition System.

For our preliminary experiments, we investigated a two-class identification problem that requires the design of global structuring elements capable of discriminating between two sets of training images, target and non-target. The design objective in this problem was to locate a single design point or global structuring element that responded to a selected character in the set (A-Z) and did not respond to the remaining characters.

In this problem, the two-dimensional structuring elements serve as a convenient representation of a genetic substrate. The evolutionary process operating in the system proceeds through a cycle of variation, evaluation, selection and resource allocation. The variation appears in the form of point mutations that alter the state of the structuring elements. The parent structuring element reproduces an offspring template that is a mutated copy containing an additional foreground or background point at a random location. The offspring is evaluated using a performance measure that weights the difference in number of correct responses and incorrect responses. A design constraint imposed on this process is that the performance of offspring templates must exceed those of their parents to survive. If the offspring survives, the parent is eliminated. In this way, only the most discriminating templates are preserved. The sequence of templates generated can be visualized as a trajectory of improving designs moving through a design space (Figure 3). In this simple experiment, a fixed amount of computational resource was allocated to each line of template development so at some instant time expires and the design process terminates. Competition was limited to evaluating final designs using an independent set of test images to decide if the final designs could enter the population of acceptable designs.

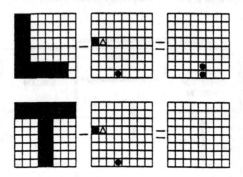

Figure 2. Hit-or-Miss Operation. Images of characters L and T (left) are eroded by the same structuring element (middle) producing a footprint in the resultant image (right). The hit-or-miss template fits into the letter L but not the letter T. Foreground point (solid box), background point (open triangle), and reference or mark point (solid circle).

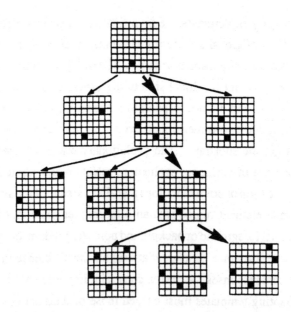

Figure 3. Design Trajectory. From an initial point (top), random mutations produce templates with two points. Poor performing templates are eliminated and the best template is extended to level three. A successful trajectory (bold arrows) consists of a series of templates having increased power of discrimination.

4 Observations and Discussion

For two-class character recognition problems, the evolutionary learning process described above is capable of generating efficient global detectors. These detectors perform extremely well (100% accuracy) on training sets of images and achieve good results on independent image test sets (80-90% accuracy). The detectors generated using the automated design process were sensitive to the resource allocation strategies used to control the design process [9]. An overabundance of resource tended to produce detectors customized to the training set that did not perform well when applied to the test set. Limited resource allocations did not allow structuring elements to reach their full potential with respect to performance. This behavior is similar to that of a natural system where favorable environmental conditions and an abundance of resources promote diverse genotypes and specialists while uncertain environmental conditions and poor resource availability tend to remove marginal genotypes and favor generalists [5].

The size of the structuring element influences the rate of image recognition. Experiments using different sizes of structuring elements indicate that large structuring elements perform better on training sets. However, performance on the training set is not the only indicator of test set performance. Large structuring elements can become too complex and perform poorly on test sets.

Results from these studies on the design of a feature detector component of a pattern recognition system clearly demonstrate that evolutionary learning processes can be employed as tools to automate the design process. A process reminiscent of natural evolution has been used to design local feature detectors [2,11] and global feature detectors [7,8,10]. It is our expectation that the techniques developed for simple two-class design problems will transition to more complex design problems such as multi-class recognition tasks.

Acknowledgement

This work was supported by the Air Force Office of Scientific Research, Directorate of Electronic and Material Sciences under task 2305R5 and contracts F33615-C-1416 and F49620-88-C-0053.

References

[1] L. Davis, *Genetic Algorithms and Simulated Annealing*, Pitman, London, 1987.

[2] A. M. Gillies, "Machine learning procedures for generating image domain feature detectors", Ph.D. Dissertation, University of Michigan, Ann Arbor, 1985.

[3] D. E. Goldberg, *Genetic algorithms in search, optimization, and machine learning*, Addison-Wesley, Mass., 1989.

[4]   J. H. Holland, *Adaptation in natural and artificial systems*, University of Michigan Press, Ann Arbor, 1975.

[5]   M. M. Rizki and M. Conrad, "Computing the theory of evolution", Physica 22D, 1986.

[6]   J. Serra, *Image Analysis and Mathematical Morphology*, Academic Press, London, 1982.

[7]   F. W. M. Stentiford, "Automatic feature design for optical character recognition using an evolutionary search procedure", IEEE PAMI-7, No. 3, 1985.

[8]   L. A. Tamburino, M. M. Rizki, "Automatic generation of binary features", IEEE Aerospace and Electronics Magazine, September 1989.

[9]   L. A. Tamburino, M. M. Rizki and M. A. Zmuda, "Computational resource management in supervised learning systems", NAECON, Vol. 3, 1989.

[10] L. A. Tamburino, M. M. Rizki, W. VanValkenburgh, "Automated feature detection using evolutionary learning processes", NAECON, Vol. 3, 1989.

[11] L. Uhr and C. Vossler, "A pattern-recognition program that generates, evaluates, and adjusts its own operators", in *Computers and Thought*, ed. E. A. Feigenbaum and J. Feldman, Krieger Publishing Co., Malabar, FL., 1981.

PREDICTING CHEMICAL REACTIONS
WITH A NEURAL NETWORK

David W. Elrod Gerry M. Maggiora
Computational Chemistry
The Upjohn Company
Kalamazoo, Michigan 49001

Robert G. Trenary
Computer Science Department
Western Michigan University
Kalamazoo, Michigan 49008

Abstract. This project is an attempt to use neural networks to extract relevant features from data about the reactivity and product distribution in a chemical reaction in order to predict the percentages of products formed in the reaction. Electrophilic aromatic substitution reactions were chosen because they have been well studied and a fairly large amount of data is available about the percent of each of three resultant isomers formed when various chemical substituents were present. Different representation schemes and network architectures were used, and results achieved are comparable to results obtained from existing programs and from the intuition of chemists.

1. Introduction

Predicting the products of a chemical reaction is one aspect of organic retrosynthesis -- finding a chain of reactions which will yield a desired product. If predictions of steps in the synthesis are good, fewer hours of laboratory work will be required to disprove or refine poor predictions. Since a reaction is determined by many competing factors, the problem of reaction prediction seems reasonable for a neural network application. We chose a textbook reaction called electrophilic aromatic substitution (EAS) for which there is a fair amount of data available. The EAS reaction (Figure 1) involves the substitution of a hydrogen atom attached to an aromatic ring by an electrophile. When the reaction is limited to one substitution there are five possible products, corresponding to the substitution of each of the five hydrogen atoms on the aromatic ring. However, only three different products can be measured because of the symmetry of the system. Replacement of hydrogen atoms adjacent to the X substituent results in a single product called the ortho product. Replacement of the hydrogens at positions 3 and 5 are considered as a single product, the meta product. The third product, the para product, is due to replacement of the hydrogen atom at position 4. The ratio of the various products formed depends on the nature of the substituent X, which is already attached to the ring. First semester organic chemistry students are taught some general principles to predict the reaction. Substituents are divided into two main classes, the ortho-para directors and the meta directors, named for the position of substitution. The meta directing groups tend to accept electrons from the ring while the ortho-para directors tend to donate excess electrons to the ring. The size of the

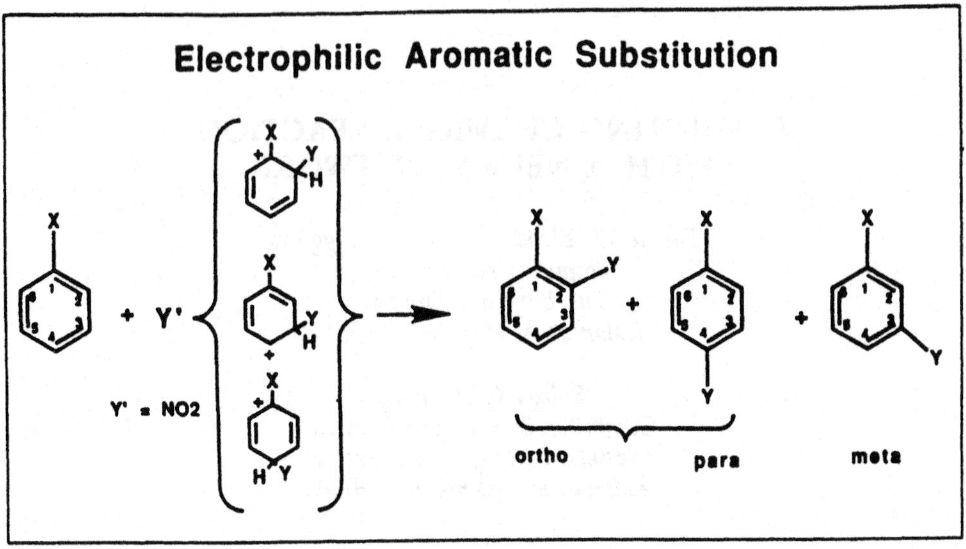

Figure 1 - The electrophilic aromatic substitution (EAS) reaction of a monosubstituted benzene ring with an electrophile, Y', yields three possible products called ortho, para, and meta corresponding to substitution position of the electrophile on the ring.

substituent can affect the reaction by blocking the adjacent ortho positions. After gaining some experience chemists tend to be able to predict the major products in EAS by simply looking at the substituent and classifying it as ortho-para directing or meta directing. This project had as a goal the prediction of the products which would be formed in an EAS reaction for any substituent X already on the ring and to predict the percent of each product solely on the basis of the molecular structure of the X substituent.

2. Methods

2.1 Network Configuration

A Back Propagation network (BP) was used to associate an input pattern (chemical structure) with an output pattern (product percentage). All networks used had three layers: input, hidden and output. The output layer was a vector of product percentages. Initially, the output of the net was a three component vector corresponding to the fractions of each of the three products formed. Later, to speed up the network and to make the predictions more similar to what chemists try to do, the fractions of ortho and para products were combined to a single number and just two output units were used.

Two different input layers were used. These reflected two distinct approaches to representing the reaction which was being predicted. One method directly represented the substituent X with a matrix containing information such as atomic number and bonds between atoms in X. This was termed a Connectivity Representation. A second method used as input the charges at the 6 locations on the aromatic ring (Charge Vector Representation). The rationale for this approach is that these charges play a key role in determining where the substitution will take place.

2.2 Data

A set of data for 54 substituents was taken from the literature [2, 3, 5, 6, 8] and used to train and test our networks. The 54 compounds were split into a training set of 45 compounds and a test set of 9 compounds. The test set was chosen to be representative of both the types of chemical substituents and the range of product ratios. Since some initial networks using this data set proved to be too large and slow, the larger members of both sets were removed in order to allow us to operate with a smaller network (since the input representation was then smaller). For simplicity, the network results shown in Tables 1 and 2 are reported only as the percent of meta product predicted. Experimentally, the sum of the meta and ortho-para products was 1.0. So the amount of ortho-para products can be derived from the percentage of meta product.

In addition to the 7 test compounds, four other test examples were constructed by making trivial structural changes in four of the training set compounds. The structural changes were deemed trivial if a chemist would expect the resulting compound to react the same way the parent compound would. The experimental values given for the four additional compounds were the same as those for the parent compounds.

2.3 Testing and Training

The performance of networks was judged based on overall measures such as root mean square error (RMS) with training inputs, and on more detailed measures. In particular, the prediction of the meta percentage on testing samples was used as a basis for determining whether the net made a correct or incorrect prediction of the tendency of the reaction (meta-directing or ortho-para directing). If a meta prediction was within 20% of the experimental data it was deemed to be predicting the correct tendency. This is reasonable given the variability of experimental data and conditions. We also used the average meta percentage error for deciding that one net was a better predictor than another.

3. Connectivity Representation

The most versatile of the commonly used methods of representing chemical structures for computer manipulation is the connectivity matrix or connection table. [1]. It is a straightforward encoding of a chemical structure in machine readable form and can be extended to incorporate additional chemical information. A connection table is only a crude approximation to the reality of a chemical compound and may not contain sufficient information on which to train a neural network but is it is a convenient choice because it is easy to obtain and unambiguous.

A compact connection table (Figure 2) was used to represent the chemical structure for the neural network. Since the benzene ring was the same in every case only the atoms in the substituent were described. The initial connectivity representation was four times as large as the final one so this preceding convention was used to speed up the network learning by reducing the size of the network.

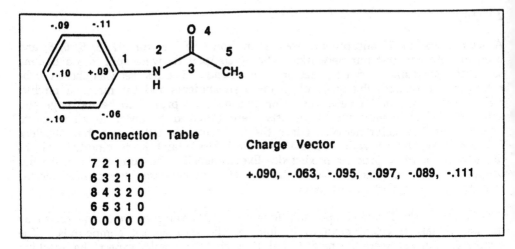

Figure 2 - Each bond in the substituent attached to the ring generates a row in the connection table. Atoms are numbered from the ring and each row encodes a bond as (source atom atomic number, source atom identifier, destination atom identifier, bond type, and charge). The charge vector representation is composed of the charges on the atoms of the ring, beginning with atom 1 and proceeding clockwise.

Atom identifiers were assigned starting with atom 1 for the atom in the ring where the substituent is attached. The rest of the atom identifiers were assigned sequentially from the ring out with the atom connected to the ring being atom 2. The hydrogen atoms were ignored, only non-hydrogen atoms were numbered. The connection table was kept more concise by citing only the bonds to lower numbered atoms and thus starts with atom 2. The first column contains the atom type of the atom with the higher identifier number in a bonded pair by giving its atomic number. The second and third columns indicate which two atoms are connected. The fourth column is the bond type: 1 for single bonds, 2 for double bonds, and 3 for triple bonds, and the fifth column is the charge on the atom, either -1, 0 or +1. Using the last column for the charge on the atom allows the hydrogen atoms to be ignored. This results in a very compact 5 by 5 connection table. In order to accommodate the largest substituent, a 7 by 16 table was required. Since most of the substituents were smaller most of the tables consisted of zeroes. Later experiments used a smaller 5 by 11 table which could accommodate 40 of the 54 substituents for which experimental data was available. It was this set of 40 compounds which were used to compare the connectivity and charge vector representation.

The best predictions were obtained with the 3 layer network designated CON5 with 5 X 5 input units, 5 hidden units and 2 output units was trained on the 33 compound training set for 36,000 training cycles. The total RMS error of the trained network was 0.045 with a maximum output unit error of 0.14. This network correctly predicted 33/33 (Table 2, Column 2) in the training set with an average error of 2.5 percent. When the net was tested on 11 compounds that it had not been trained on it predicted 8/11 or 73% within a 20% error. A 20% error was chosen based on the range of predictions by chemists.

The effect of changing the number of hidden units was investigated using several networks which had a 5 by 11 connectivity matrix as input. The network with 10 hidden units was trained to a total RMS error of 0.098 and predicted 32/33 of the training set but only 3/7 of the test set. The network with only 5 hidden units was trained to a total RMS error of 0.073. It correctly predicted 32/33 training examples but this time 5/7 of the test set were correctly predicted. A network with 4 hidden units also predicted 32/33 training examples and 5/7 test cases but it had larger errors on the ones that it predicted incorrectly. With 10 hidden units the network seemed to be able to do a table lookup for cases it had seen before but could not generalize well to cases that it had not previously seen.

4. Charge Vector Representation

Instead of representing the substituent directly, the effect that the substituent has on the aromatic ring can be represented by the charge at each carbon atom on the ring (Figure 2). This charge pattern can be used to explain, in part, how a reaction will proceed. These charges can be calculated using MOPAC [7], a quantum mechanics program which allows a molecular structure to be specified and then calculates charges on all atoms. The data from MOPAC was used to create a vector of 6 charge values which was used as the input representation to train and test a 3 layer back propagation network with the same data used for the Connectivity Representation. Hidden layers of both 5 and 10 hidden units were used.

A number of networks were trained with this representation and architecture. Generally these networks could be trained to within a RMS error of less than 0.1, usually 0.06 to 0.07. Maximum output unit error was never lower than 0.16 and usually remained above 0.2.

The best network, with 10 hidden units, was trained so that it had a RMS error of 0.05 with a maximum output unit error of 0.16. When the network was used to predict the tendency of the reaction (meta or ortho-para) the training set was correctly predicted in 30 of 33 examples and the test data was correctly predicted in 5 out of 7 items.

5. Discussion

Tables 1 and 2 show the results of the best networks using the connectivity and charge vector representation. CON5 was a network using the connectivity representation and a hidden layer with 5 units. VEC10 used the vector representation using 10 hidden units. These results are compared to the actual experimental data, the results of a program called CAMEO, and the averaged predictions of three chemists with a background suited to this kind of problem. The CAMEO program is a rule based program [4] which will predict either a meta or ortho-para result for the EAS reaction. This program is used as a practical tool in a number of companies and can be considered a good representative of the current ability of artificial intelligence approaches to this problem. It will not predict actual percentages of each product.

The two networks compare well with the CAMEO program in the number of correct predictions it can make. According to the 20% criteria CAMEO predicted 7/11 (64%) of the test cases but only got 21/33 of the training set correct. However, CAMEO, like most chemists, predicts that the products will be either all meta-product or all ortho-para-products so intermediate cases will appear as error here. The best network predicted 8/11 correctly and got 33/33 correct on training data.

The chemists, however, outperform all three artificial methods, predicting 10/11 (91%) correctly. This result is to be expected because the chemists are operating with a more developed intelligence. They are also trained to consider a number of factors in making this prediction. The networks, however, have been trained with a limited set of information − either the connectivity which represents the variable substituent or the resulting charge vector. Other dynamic considerations which might determine this reaction and which might be used by a trained chemist are entirely missing.

6. Conclusions

One of the key questions in this project is how to represent chemical information or neural network applications. Through training and experience a chemist constructs an internal representation of what an atom or collection of atoms mean chemically. An important cognitive question asks what, if any, information is contained in a chemical structure and whether a neural net can extract that information. In other words, is there any chemical information intrinsic in a representation of a chemical structure or do chemical structures just provide a nominal focus around which a chemist associates other information. If a neural net can predict reactivity from chemical structures alone, then the structural representation must contain sufficient information. A back-propagation network with 5 hidden units that was trained on structural representations of 33 mono-substituted benzenes gave very good predictions of the products formed in 5 out of 7 electrophilic aromatic substitution reactions involving substituents that the network had not been trained on. An alternate charge vector representation was designed to deal with a factor which is taken to be important in dealing with the EAS problem. Yet the network did no better with this representation than with the more descriptive, yet less specific connectivity information. This result suggests the difficulties that exist in choosing representations of (chemical) data for network applications.

On the basis of these results we conclude that that a neural network can extract information from chemical representations and use it to predict the outcome of EAS reactions 70 percent of the time for unknown compounds. Further work will attempt to find a more compact structure representation that would also allow extension of this network to the prediction of substitutions of other substrates and to other reaction types.

References

[1] J.E. Ash, P.A. Chubb, S.E. Ward, S.M. Welford, and P.Willett, Communication, Storage and Retrieval of Chemical Information. Chichester, UK: Ellis Horwood Limited, 1985, pp.128-156.

[2] F.A. Carey and R.J. Sundberg, Advanced Organic Chemistry, 2nd ed., Part A, New York: Plenum Press, 1984, pp. 481-503.
[3] P.D.B. De La Mare and J.H. Ridd, Aromatic Substitution: Nitration and Halogenation, New York: Academic Press, 1959, pp.80-93, 236-237.

[4] A.J. Gushurst and W.L. Jorgensen, "Computer-Assisted Mechanistic Evaluation of Organic Reactions. 14.", J. Org. Chem., vol. 53, pp. 3397-3408, 1988.

[5] D.R. Harvey and R.O.C. Norman, "The ortho:para Ratio in Aromatic Substitution.", J. Chem. Soc., pp. 3606-3611, 1961.

[6] J.G. Hoggett, R.B. Moodie, J.R. Penton and K. Schofield, Nitration and Aromatic Reactivity, London: Cambridge University Press, pp. 166-183, 1971.

[7] MOPAC, A General Molecular Orbital Program Package V4.0, QCPE, Department of Chemistry, Indiana University, Bloomington,IN, 47405.

[8] R.O.C. Norman and R. Taylor, Electrophilic Substitution in Benzenoid Compounds, Amsterdam: Elsevier Publishing, pp. 72-85, 1965.

Table 2
Neural Network Predictions for Training Set Compounds

Compound	Error (exp - predicted)		
	CON5	VEC10	CAMEO
Total Error	81	204	595
AVG % Error/cmpd	2.5	6.2	18.0
Correct Predictions	33/33	30/33	21/33

Table 1
Neural Network Predictions For Unknown Test Compounds

Compound	Error (exp - predicted)			
	CON5	VEC10	CAMEO	Chemist
Total Error	112	99	100	55
AVG % Error/cmpd	16.0	14.1	14.3	7.9
Number Correct	5/7	5/7	5/7	7/7
Results with 4 additional unknowns tested				
Total Error	165		224	114
AVG % Error/cmpd	15.0		20.3	10.4
Number Correct	8/11		7/11	10/11

Mutation and Recombination Effects on the Adaptability of Sexual and Asexual Organisms

Mateen M. Rizki
Department of Computer Science and Engineering
Wright State University
Dayton, Ohio 45435

Jong Chen
Department of Computer Science
Wayne State University
Detroit, Michigan 48202

Abstract

EVOLVE III, an evolutionary ecosystem simulation program, is used to study the relationship between genetic variation and adaptability of organisms in constant and fluctuating environments. The simulation runs suggest that point mutations increase genetic diversity while gene recombination acts as a stabilizing force for phenotypic variability.

1 Introduction

An evolutionary ecosystem consists of a set of organisms in an environment that serves as a selective force. Each organism contains genetic information that determines its physical structure and behavioral characteristics. The phenotype, the appearance of an organism, results from interactions between the genotype and the environment. During reproduction, organisms transmit genetic information to their offspring. This information may be modified by mutation and gene recombination so that the resultant genotypes of the offspring are variants of the parent genotypes. Competition among individuals in an ecosystem results in the increased probability of survival of the individuals that are better adapted to the environment.

We observe the results of evolution in nature. However, study of the evolutionary process requires monitoring multiple generations of organisms over large time scales. For this reason, models of evolutionary ecosystems are valuable tools to gain insight into the dynamics of evolution. Many mathematical models of this process have been developed, but the approach we have taken differs from these models in its algorithmic specification of the evolutionary process. EVOLVE III [3,4] is the third model in a series of interactional models [1,2] designed to provide a software environment suitable for conducting controlled experiments of evolutionary processes.

In this paper, we describe an extension to EVOLVE III and use the model to investigate the relationship between variability and adaptability of organisms having sexual and asexual reproduction.

Overview of EVOLVE III

EVOLVE III abstracts three levels of organization: genotype, phenotype, and population. The model of the genotype includes abstractions of the DNA molecule, transcription, translation to produce proteins, and the process of protein folding. The genetic makeup of each organism consists of a set of genes which is represented by a string of symbols. Each element in the string is one of four possible values {00, 01, 10, 11}, mimicking the four nucleic acid bases of a DNA molecule {adenine, thymine, cytosine, guanine}. To model protein folding, regions of the protein molecules that correspond to active sites on real proteins (enzymes) are designated as critical and modifier sections. Each of these sections is large enough to hold a triplet of string symbols that are mapped to real values during the decoding process. The final value of a gene is the weighted sum of the mapped values. Sets of values of the genes in each organism are combined to encode different phenotypic traits.

The phenotypic traits of the organisms are classified into fourteen categories (Table 1). Categories involving temperature and light intensity specify an environmental range suitable for the survival of an organism. Energy related traits define the metabolic activities of the organism. Aging and development traits determine the lifespan and the onset of reproductive capability. The reproduction trait specifies the rate of reproduction and the energy expended during the reproduction process. Finally, the protection and aggression traits allow the organism to interact with other organisms in the environment. The value of each trait is determined by one or more genes as illustrated in Table 1. In some cases, the same gene participates in the encoding of multiple traits. A total of 23 genes was used in the experiments described in this paper.

Phenotypic Trait	Gene Number				
Optimum Temperature	1	2			
Temperature Tolerance	3	4			
Optimum Light Intensity	5	6	7		
Light Intensity Tolerance	8				
Rate of Energy Intake	9	10			
Rate of Energy Outflow	11	12			
Minimum Energy Required	3	4	8	20	21
Maximum Energy Desired	13	14	15		
Development Time	16				
Adult Lifespan	9	17	18		
Rate of Reproduction	19				
Reproduction Energy	22	23			
Protection Mechanisms	20				
Aggression Mechanisms	21				

Table 1. Genotype-to-Phenotype Coding Table.

The environment is a two-dimensional grid of cells each of which can hold several organisms and a supply of resources and waste products. Each cell is subject to variations in temperature and light intensity. Organisms migrate through these cells collecting resources and depositing waste products. The resource supply is limited, so organisms compete and adopt dynamic strategies to exploit the available supply. Since competition occurs locally within a single environmental cell, no global fitness function is used to assign an arbitrary ranking to the organisms. An organism's probability of surviving a local conflict is proportional to its ability to protect its position, attack invaders, and match to the environmental attributes of temperature and light. Successful individuals gather sufficient resources to reproduce.

Two types of reproduction mechanisms were incorporated in the version of EVOLVE III used to conduct the experiments reported here. One population of organisms had asexual reproduction while the second population reproduced sexually. The genetic information of the asexual organisms is subject to variation in the form of point mutations which occur as random alterations of string elements in the gene model when these organisms transmit a copy of their genetic structure to their offspring. If the mutated element is located in a critical section of a gene, the value for the gene will be altered significantly; mutation within a modifier section results in a slight alteration of the gene value. In either case, the phenotypic traits that depend on the gene will have a modified expression. A mutation that affects a string element outside the critical and modifier sections is not immediately expressed.

The genetic material of organisms that reproduce sexually is also subject to point mutation but, in addition, it may acquire alterations as a result of gene recombination. In the process of recombination, genes that originated in the two parents of an organism are reshuffled during their transmission to the next generation. In this way, new combinations of genes arise in the absence of mutational events.

EVOLVE III was implemented using a discrete event simulation formalism [5]. Each organism was simulated as a set of processes of the form: collect resources, reproduce, migrate, and die. During the life of a simulated organism, the activities of resource collection, reproduction, and migration are repeated many times. The simulated time of occurrence of each event is the result of interactions of the phenotypic traits of the organism and its environment. To permit controlled experiments, temperature and light intensities in different regions of the environment are adjustable. Also, collections of grid cells can be isolated for periods of simulation time. These facilities can be used to impose environmental constraints and allow the user to establish barriers restricting migration of organisms from one cell to neighboring cells.

3 Experiments and Results

For each experiment the environment was divided into two regions by a migration barrier. Twenty organisms having an asexual reproduction mechanism were placed in the first region and ten pairs of sexually-reproducing organisms were placed in the other region. Each region was subjected to the same environmental conditions of temperature and light. These conditions were either held constant throughout the simulation run or they were allowed to randomly fluctuate within defined intervals. The barrier between the two environmental regions was maintained for 2000 time steps to allow the two populations to stabilize in their respective environments. At simulation time 2000 the migration barrier between the populations was removed so that the organisms could move between the regions. The sexually-reproducing and asexually-reproducing organisms were thus forced to compete for resources with each other in addition to individuals of their own kind. The simulation continued for an additional 160 time steps. At the end of each simulation run, the numbers of organisms in the asexual and sexual populations were tabulated to determine the predominant group.

Series of experiments were performed using different levels of mutation rates for the sexual and asexual populations. The mutation rate for the sexually-reproducing organisms ranged from 0.1 to 0.3 in steps of 0.05. For each of these rates, a simulation experiment was performed in which mutation rates of 0.4, 0.6, and 0.8 were assigned to the asexually-reproducing organisms. These mutation rates are higher than rates calculated for organisms in nature, but they were used in this study to compress simulation time. The entire series of experiments was completed using either a constant or fluctuating environment, giving a total of 60 simulation runs.

In 22 of the 30 runs in fluctuating environments, sexually-reproducing organisms were the predominant population while in 21 of the 30 runs using a constant environment the asexual organisms were predominant. The major difference between the asexual and sexual organisms was the existence of gene recombination in the latter group. Therefore, the results are consistent with the known behavior of the recombination operation in nature. Recombination tends to increase the rate of adaptation. Figure 1 illustrates the dynamic behavior of a single phenotypic trait (reproduction resource) during a simulation run in a fluctuating environment, using a mutation rate of 0.6 for asexual organisms and 0.3 for sexual organisms. Notice, the asexual organisms have a large spread of marginal phenotypes particularly early in the evolutionary development, while the sexual organisms rapidly converge to a small range of phenotypes. This result is expected since each mutation in an asexual population creates a new genotype and a potentially new marginal phenotype. The sexual organisms exhibit transient polymorphisms during the early part of the simulation that disappear under stabilizing selection.

In a fluctuating environment, the sexual organisms prevailed over the asexual organisms (sexual predominated in 10 out of 10 runs) when the asexual mutation rate was high (0.8), but this relationship was reversed (asexual predominated in 6 out of 10 runs) when the asexual mutation rate was low (0.4). This result is readily understood. As mutation rate increases the chance of maintaining a well-adapted trait decreases. Also, as the mutation rate decreases, the chance of losing a useful genotype also decreases. It can be reasoned

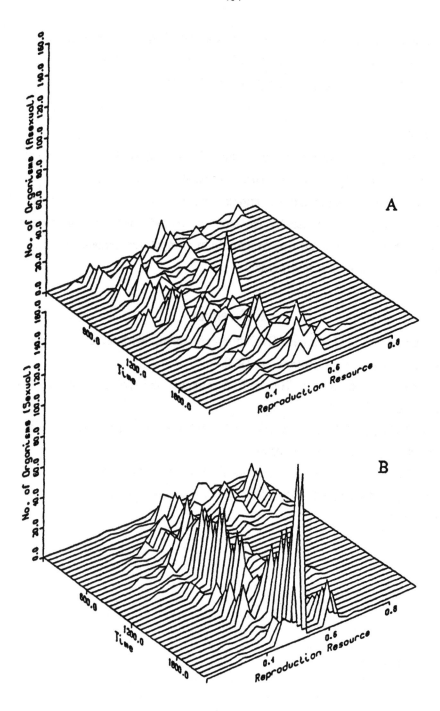

Figure 1. Comparison of the phenotypic trait of reproduction
resource.   A - asexual organisms;   B - sexual organisms.

that the asexual organisms dominated over sexual organisms as the rate dropped from 0.8 to 0.4 because the adaptive advantage afforded by sexual recombination was offset by the additional resource costs required to support two parents.

4 Discussion

EVOLVE III is an effective tool for the study of evolutionary theory. In this paper, we examined the relationship between asexual and sexual reproduction mechanisms with their corresponding variation operators of mutation and recombination. The adaptability of organisms is strongly influenced by the mode of reproduction and the corresponding variation, but there are subtle influences induced by competitive demands such as resource requirements afforded by the environment.

References

[1] M. Conrad and H.H. Pattee, "Evolution experiments with an artificial ecosystem", Journal of Theoretical Biology 28, 1970.

[2] M. Conrad and M. Strizich, "Evolve II: A computer model of an evolving ecosystem", BioSystems 17, 1985.

[3] M. M. Rizki and M. Conrad, "EVOLVE III: A discrete events model of an evolutionary ecosystem", BioSystems 18, 1985.

[4] M. M. Rizki and M. Conrad, "Computing the theory of evolution", Physica 22D, 1986

[5] B. P. Zeigler, *Multifacetted Modelling and Discrete Event Simulation*, Academic Press New York, 1984.

Logical Structure of Neurobiological Information Processing

William P. Coleman

MIEMSS, UMAB; Baltimore, MD 21201,
Department of Mathematics, UMBC; Baltimore, MD 21228,
and St. John's College; Annapolis, MD 21404

David P. Sanford

Aeronautical Radio, Inc.; 2551 Riva Road, Annapolis, MD 21401

Andrea De Gaetano

C.N.R. Centro di Studio per la Fisiopatologia dello Shock,
Istituto di Clinica Chirurgica, Università Cattolica del Sacro Cuore;
Via Pineta Sacchetti, 644, I-00168 Roma, Italia

Fred Geisler

Division of Neurosurgery, UMAB; Baltimore, MD 21201,
and Department of Neurosurgery, Patuxent Medical Group;
Columbia, MD 21045

Abstract

In a series of papers, we have developed a logical model, using category theory, for neurobiological processing. A schema is a functor $C : \mathbf{C} \to \mathbf{Set}$ It is essentially an action of a category $\mathbf{C}$ on $\mathbf{Set}$. A model $M = \langle F, \alpha \rangle$ of $C' : \mathbf{C}' \to \mathbf{Set}$ in $C : \mathbf{C} \to \mathbf{Set}$ is given by a functor $F : \mathbf{C}' \to \mathbf{C}$, and a natural transformation $\alpha : C \circ F \xrightarrow{\cdot} C'$. In this paper, we develop a set of simple psychophysical *gedankenexperiments* and apply the general theory to work out some of the logic of the perceptual process.

1. Introduction

We have previously [1] [2] suggested an architecture for processing in neural networks. The mathematical structure is based on a general theory [3] of computational processes called "computational logic," and its particular features are based on the following assumptions. A neural network can be viewed as a modular system of subnetworks. This can be done at different levels of granularity, but the logic is the same at any level. A subnet is a black box computing output states from input states. Thus the net can be viewed as a system of sets and functions. Computational logic uses category theory to describe this as a *schema*, a functor $C : C \rightarrow$ **Set** from a category C to the category of sets. The machinery of category theory is then available to help analysis.

Although the general principles on which the architecture is based appear sound and biologically well-motivated, the result is (as it should be) a sophisticated layered structure whose properties are hard to visualize without examples. The purpose of the present paper is to develop a set of examples, realistic enough to be used as input to a neural network software emulation, that can clarify the several dimensions in which processing takes place.

We try to analyze the structure of computations in the network by using algebraic techniques to represent the logic of the functions it can compute. We illustrate [1] this by the simplified network $\mathcal{N}$ shown in figure 1. $\mathcal{N}$ has three neurons: f, g and h. The axon

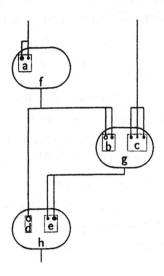

Figure 1: A simple network $\mathcal{N}$ of neurons and some functions it computes.

of neuron f terminates in a set b of synapses to g and a set d of synapses to h. Similarly neuron g has a set e of synapses to h. There is a set of synapses a to f, and a set c to g.

Each set of synapses can assume various states, depending on activity in the presynaptic neuron. We call such a set of states a *type*. For example, in $\mathcal{N}$, the set of synapses a can assume states in the type a, and the other sets of synapses similarly. Thus f computes a function $f : a \rightarrow b \times d$, while g computes a function $g : b \times c \rightarrow e$.

Also, f and g could be lumped together and considered as a subnetwork [f.g] that computes a function $[f, g] : a \times c \rightarrow d \times e$. At any level of granularity, we can regard a subnet as a black box for computing output states from input states, and we can use the same principles to analyze its logic, the system of functions that it is capable of computing.

There is a third way of looking at the functions computed by $\mathcal{N}$. Given a fixed $b \in b$, g computes a function $g_b : c \rightarrow e$, defined by $g_b(c) = g(b, c)$. There is an ambiguity between the use of "b" as the name of a state of the synapses b and its use as the name of the function g_b computed by g.

2. Computational Logic

Computational logic is based on the mathematical theory of categories [4], discovered by EILENBERG and MAC LANE, which has been used, particularly in work deriving from LAWVERE, to provide a foundation for logic. (There is an accessible presentation in [5].) The automata theory books [6] [7] are also very relevant to the present work.

In this section we give a brief and informal review of some elementary notions. An example of a category is Set, the category of sets. It contains *objects*, namely sets, and *arrows* or *morphisms*, namely ordinary functions between sets. An arrow goes from its *domain* to its *codomain*. For each object c, there is an *identity function* i_c, and for suitable pairs of arrows $f : c \rightarrow d$ and $g : b \rightarrow c$ there is the *composition* $f \circ g : b \rightarrow d$. These obey the rules, $i_d \circ f = f = f \circ i_c$, and $f \circ (g \circ h) = (f \circ g) \circ h$, for any $h : a \rightarrow b$.

More generally, a *category* is any system of objects and arrows that obeys these rules. The objects might be sets with some structure, and the arrows functions that preserve that structure. Or, the category might just be a system of dots and arrows.

A *functor* from a category C to a category D is a mapping F between them, carrying objects and arrows in C correspondingly to objects and arrows in D. Structure must be preserved: $F(i_c) = i_{F(c)}$, for all $c \in$ C, and $F(f \circ g) = F(f) \circ F(g)$, for composable f and g.

A *natural transformation* is a way of converting one functor $F :$ C $\rightarrow$ D into another one, $G :$ C $\rightarrow$ D between the same categories. This is done by supplying a set of arrows in D that drag the image of F across to the image of G. For each $c \in$ C, one gives an arrow $\alpha_c : F(c) \rightarrow G(c)$ in D. This is to be done in such a way that applying these functions to the image $F(d)$ and $F(c)$ of the domain and the range of any arrow $f : c \rightarrow d$ of C converts $F(f)$ to $G(f)$. Thus, $G(f) \circ \alpha_c = \alpha_d \circ F(f)$: One writes this as $\alpha : F \overset{\cdot}{\rightarrow} G$.

We try to capture the notion of a system of neural processes. Let C be a category freely generated from a diagram indicating a finite number of types and a finite number of arrows – "basis" arrows – between them. C shows schematically the connectivity of the system. Let $C :$ C $\rightarrow$ Set be the functor that sends each type to the set of states that it comprises, and each arrow to a function between the corresponding sets. Thus C lets the logic of C act on Set. We call C a *schema*.

Next, we have to distinguish between a schema, which is a template according to which certain processes can occur, and an instance in which such a process actually does occur. A *development* of C is a functor from a finite totally ordered category $C_1 :$ C$_1 \rightarrow$ C that maps basis arrows of C$_1$ to basis arrows of C. The development induces a schema $C \circ C_1 :$ C$_1 \rightarrow$ Set. It is evident that a development of C corresponds to a path of C. As any instance, or *particle*, of the process unfolds, it corresponds to successively longer developments.

We hypothesize that part of the semantic power of cognitive processes comes from the fact that a development can function simultaneously in several schemata. We need a notion of how one system of processes can be modeled by a simplified version. A *model* $M = \langle F, \alpha \rangle$ of $C' : \mathbf{C'} \to \text{Set}$ in $C : \mathbf{C} \to \text{Set}$ is given by a functor $F : \mathbf{C'} \to \mathbf{C}$, and a natural transformation $\alpha : (C \circ F) \overset{\cdot}{\to} C'$. Intuitively, we think of C' as a simplified version of C in which the states have been relabeled by α. To discover the effect of some process $f : c \to d$ in C' on a state c of a type $C'(c)$, find a state that α_c sends to c, do the corresponding process $F(f)$ on it, and then use α_d to relabel.

A *conceptual schema* is a schema $C : \mathbf{C} \to \text{Set}$ together with a system $\{C_i : \mathbf{C}_i \to \mathbf{C}\}$ of schemata with models between them and from them to C. A *development* of a process is a development of one of the schemata $C \circ C_i : \mathbf{C}_i \to \text{Set}$.

Some cognitive processes describe natural processes outside the mind. Some cognitive processes describe other cognitive processes. We use the notion of 'model' to capture how one process can describe another. Let $C : \mathbf{C} \to \text{Set}$ and $C' : \mathbf{C'} \to \text{Set}$ be the conceptual schemata of two processes. An *interpretation of C' in C* is a model $M = \langle F, \alpha \rangle$, together with some extra data. For each schema $\{C'_i : \mathbf{C'}_i \to \mathbf{C}\}$ of C there must be selected a schema $\{C_i : \mathbf{C}_i \to \text{Set}\}$ and a functor $F_i : \mathbf{C'}_i \to \mathbf{C}_i$, and there must be a function assigning to each particle of $\mathbf{C'}_i$ a particle of $\mathbf{C}_i$.

3. Theory of Cognition

Using these ideas, we can begin to see a way to express how the influences of sensory data, working from bottom up, and of conceptual schemata, working from top down, cooperate in the neural network. It will be helpful to illustrate this by using a character recognition example, some features of which are suggested by work [8] of RUMELHART and MCCLELLAND, in their interactive activation model, although the analysis given is different.

Much has been done [9] [10] [11] [12] to work out the neurological structure of visual processing. Prominent in the architecture of the early stages is a series of maps — in the retina, in the lateral geniculate nucleus, and in the visual cortex — of the visual field. However, for the purposes of the present paper, this system of maps contains too much detail, and we shall find it convenient to simplify considerably. We regard a visual map as an array,

of pixels. This one happens to contain an F. Of course, the F need not be presented in any privileged position:

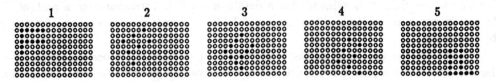

With this understanding in mind, we now denote such a pixel array, containing a cnaracter in some arbitrary position, by a symbol such as $\boxed{\text{F}}$.

The letter F is an example of a conceptual schema. It is a system of horizontal and vertical bars that themselves derive from (but do not *denote*) pixels in a visual map. 'Horizontal bar' and 'vertical bar' are two schemata whose types are sets of pixels. F is also a schema whose types are sets of pixels, but it is specified by requiring that its states be made up of instances of horizontal and vertical bars, with certain required incidence relations.

F is detectable from any of the above pixel arrays, as well as from many others. Some pixel arrays, like $\boxed{\text{H}}$, could belong to more than one character, depending on which direction is understood to be horizontal. Other arrays, like $\boxed{\Gamma}$, cannot be understood as belonging to any character, at least by speakers of english. We hypothesize that there is a relatively small number of schemata in the network's repertory at any one time, and from these can be generated a relatively large number of states, but by no means all the states that would be mathematically possible. This fact is central to the semantics. Not every brain state is possible without rebuilding the schemata, but the number of them is large and depends on the possible combinations of schemata. The states that are possible are semantically linked by the relationships of the schema processes that can generate them — the brain doesn't find them by searching, but by using a pattern to generate them.

The processing of $\boxed{\text{FOX}}$ involves recognizing F, O, X, and FOX. However, these concepts do not apply to the visual field as a whole but to different parts of it. Above, we considered a series of pixel displays, each of which had an F. Our discussion was naive in the sense that we made no attempt to relate the F's in the different pictures and spoke as if they were five different instances of the concept F. However, in the more usual perceptual situation we are presented with successive views of the same object, and our ability to identify it is closely bound up with the ordered differences between these presentations. In our terms, there is an *object* F that is an instance, a particle, of the concept F; the five pixel displays are the states of different levels of development of the particle.

It seems necessary to distinguish between *field-oriented* and *object-oriented processing*. The concept F is a state of a set of synapses in some subnetwork where it is activated by simultaneous mutual reinforcement with other concepts in the same subnet, the whole subnet getting its input from the senses (from the visual cortex) or from memory. There is also a logical operation in which the brain identifies an *object* to which the concept (or location in physical space) can be attributed. There must as well be an object-oriented memory store, able to retain *facts*, the conceptual information thus associated with specific objects.

This approach to cognition can be contrasted to that of artificial intelligence, in that schemata — rules — are not found by sequential search, but are generated by the data that they apply to. Further the state space that has to be searched is small and structured. The structures can evolve in time through a larger space, but at any one time they are sparse.) On the other hand, this approach can be contrasted to that of non-modular neural networks in that the modularity provides a structure for the state space, and this structure gives the states and processes their semantic meaning.

References

[1] William P. Coleman, David P. Sanford, Andrea De Gaetano, and Fred Geisler. Functional models of neurobiological processes. In Xavier J.R. Avula, editor, *Mathematical and Computer Modeling in Science and Technology* (in press), Pergamon Press, 1990.

[2] William P. Coleman, David P. Sanford, Andrea De Gaetano, and Fred Geisler. Modularity of neural network architecture. In *Proceedings of the International Joint Conference on Neural Networks, Washington DC* (in press), 1990.

[3] William P. Coleman. Computational logic of network processes. In Martin D. Fraser, editor, *Advances in Control Networks and Large Scale Parallel Distributed Processing Models*, Ablex Publishing Company, 1989. In press.

[4] Saunders Mac Lane. *Categories for the Working Mathematician*. Springer-Verlag, New York, 1971.

[5] Robert Goldblatt. *Topoi: The Categorial Analysis of Logic*. North-Holland Publishing Company, Amsterdam, revised edition, 1984.

[6] Samuel Eilenberg. *Automata, Languages, and Machines*. Volume A, Academic Press, New York and London, 1974.

[7] Samuel Eilenberg. *Automata, Languages, and Machines*. Volume B, Academic Press, New York and London, 1976.

[8] David E. Rumelhart and James L. McClelland. *Parallel Distributed Processing*. Volume 1, MIT Press, Cambridge, Massachusetts, 1986.

[9] E.R. Kandel and J.H. Schwartz. *Principles of Neural Science*. Elsevier, New York, second edition, 1985.

[10] S.W. Kuffler, J.G. Nichols, and A.R. Martin. *From Neuron to Brain*. Sinauer, Sunderland MA, second edition, 1984.

[11] Oswald Steward, editor. *Principles of Cellular, Molecular and Developmental Neuroscience*. Springer-Verlag, New York, 1989.

[12] E. Bruce Goldstein. *Sensation and Perception*. Wadsworth Publishing Company, Belmont, California, third edition, 1989.

Development of an Experimental Setup for Studying Parallel Processing

Gretchen Vogel, Diane Rover, Charles Wright, Gurpur Prabhu
Department of Electrical Engineering and Computer Engineering
Iowa State University

Abstract

The teaching of the fundamentals of parallel processing is becoming increasingly important in undergraduate Computer Engineering and Computer Science programs. This paper discusses the development of a simple laboratory environment designed for the study and testing of principles governing the performance of parallel processors. The laboratory environment is structured to be simple enough for undergraduate use, flexible enough to test the many facets of parallel processing, and sophisticated enough to give results applicable to larger scale parallel processors. Particular emphasis in this paper is placed on tests that were run to examine the suitability of the laboratory to support experimentation with shared memory multi-processors. The main test involved investigating the influence of communication and calculation times on the amount of synchronization overhead in the system.

1 Introduction

Parallel processors are becoming increasingly popular alternatives to meet the demand for faster, more powerful computers. Computer systems consisting of multiple processors are, no doubt, going to play an important role in the computer world of the future. Two needs arise from this situation: first, methods must be developed to properly evaluate the performance of the new systems, and second, educators must prepare future computer engineers to work with this new facet of computing. Both these needs require an appropriate laboratory support environment and such an environment is the subject of this paper.

One goal of the laboratory described here is to provide a flexible experimental setup to be used in testing, teaching, and researching principles governing the performance of parallel processors. Ideally, the setup would be simple enough to use in an undergraduate laboratory experience, flexible enough to test many of the varied facets of parallel processing, and sophisticated enough to give results applicable to larger scale parallel processors. We present here an experimental setup we've developed for the study of parallel processing and illustrate the suitability of that setup as an experimental framework within which to teach various fundamental principles.

This work is part of an ongoing effort to develop a laboratory for studying and teaching parallel processing. The laboratory consists primarily of Hewlett Packard engineering workstations and microprocessor emulation systems connected to single board computer systems housed in VME bus card cages. The workstations support activities ranging from VLSI design to microprocessor emulation. The microprocessor emulation tools provide an excellent environment for investigating microprocessor-based computer systems. Although the lab has been used to design several kinds of systems, two projects, one by Rover [3] and another by Helfter [2], have involved parallel processing. Rover dealt with the number of processors that can be used efficiently. Helfter investigated how communication overhead affects efficiency and scaled the problem size to attain high efficiency.

The focus of this paper is the creation of an experimental setup to be used in an instructional setting and a demonstration that the setup is suitable for parallel processing experiments. To show the suitability of the setup, several tests were performed. These tests involved the amount of synchronization overhead incurred when multiple processors access a shared resource, such as memory. Because communication between processors is one of the factors that makes parallel processing systems less than 100% efficient, much effort has been put into trying to quantify and control the relationship between the amount of time parallel systems spend in communication and calculation. An ideal parallel system would give a speedup equal to the number of processors added (see Helfter's work [3]). However, just as a group of people working together must communicate, processors in parallel systems must pass data back and forth. This requires time and therefore speedup is less than ideal. But not all of the time spent "communicating" is spent passing data. When a group of people work together, each person must take turns talking, otherwise no one understands anything. This means that the rest of the group must spend time waiting for turns to speak. This situation also exists in parallel computer systems. Synchronization coordinates communication and determines who speaks when.

A critical section within a program is an instruction sequence that gives one processor exclusive access to a resource and excludes all other processors [1]. Often, this is time spent accessing a shared memory. A critical section corresponds to time spent talking in the above analogy. While one processor is in its critical section, no other processor may enter its critical section. The tests described here investigated the time that processors spent waiting to enter their critical sections. These tests are explained in more detail below.

2 Experimental Setup

The experimental setup consists of both hardware and software components. The hardware is configured as a simple two-processor, single-bus system. Each processor node consists of a Motorola 68000 Single Board Computer (SBC) connected via an emulator to a Hewlett Packard 64000 microprocessor development workstation. The emulators on the HP 64000 replace the actual microprocessors on the SBCs. This lets us control and observe the operation of the SBC. (Measurements will be described later.) The processor nodes, along with a memory module, are attached to a VME bus backplane. The memory module is included to provide a shared memory. Each SBC has access to its own local memory and to the shared memory. Each SBC is also connected to a CRT terminal.

The software used in our experiments consists of two COPY programs, a "parent" and a "child," each residing in its own processor node. These programs are identical except for an extra initialization step included in the parent program. The processor nodes have equal priority.

The programs, written in Motorola 68000 assembler code, consist of four parts: LOCK, GET, UNLOCK, and FILTER. Each part is contained in a subroutine so it can be easily isolated for timings. The program reads an array from shared memory (subroutine GET) and runs it through a filter (subroutine FILTER). This program structure is illustrated as follows:

```
LOOP:
        LOCK
        GET DATA
        UNLOCK
        FILTER DATA
        GOTO LOOP
```

Only one node can access shared memory at one time, so the GET subroutine includes a critical section. The synchronization protocol used in this experiment is a semaphore-based, busy wait subroutine called LOCK. This LOCK routine, when called, repeatedly checks the "lock" semaphore on the shared memory. When the semaphore is cleared, the waiting processor can access the memory and get the array. When the processor is finished getting the array, it jumps to the UNLOCK subroutine (to clear the semaphore) and lets the other processor into shared memory.

Two delay functions are built into the GET and FILTER subroutines to accommodate experimentation. The lengths of the delays are controlled by inputting values for "tuning" variables. Changing the length of the delay in GET simulates changing the size of the array. Changing the delay within FILTER simulates changing the size of the array or changing the amount of work to be done on each element of the array.

3 Experimental Method

One concern of ours was the validity of our experimental setup and methodology. Several experiments were run on the setup to investigate its workability. First, the linearity of each delay function was tested by taking multiple timings of the GET and FILTER subroutines with different values in the tuning variables. Second, we investigated the effect of using different "amounts of data" versus "work spent on data" on the time each processor spent in the various subroutines (especially LOCK).

Using the emulation and measurement capabilities of the HP 64000 system to obtain timing data, we studied GET and FILTER delays with the tuning variables assuming values from 0 to 1000. The results from these experiments are shown in the following table. The results were linear enough to judge our tuning mechanism sufficiently reliable for use in subsequent investigations.

	Tune	Time in GET (μs)	Time in FILTER
1	0	6	5
2	1	6	6
3	5	12	11
4	10	18	17
5	20	31	30
6	40	55	54
7	50	68	68
8	80	106	105
9	100	131	130
10	200	256	255
11	300	381	380
12	500	631	630
13	750	944	942
14	1000	1287	1288

To investigate the effect on synchronization overhead of time spent in GET and FILTER, several timings (using the HP 64000 system) were performed. The parent program was first run in a single processor configuration to provide a control and then both programs were run in a two-processor, shared memory configuration. For each configuration, three cases were run as follows:

Case 1: GET variable set at 1000

   FILTER variable set at 300

   (This caused the program to spend three times as much time in GET as in FILTER.)

Case 2: GET set at 300

   FILTER set at 1000

   (This caused the program to spend three times as much time in FILTER as in GET.)

Case 3: GET set at 650

   FILTER set at 650

   (The program spent equal amounts of time in GET and FILTER.)

4   Results

Single Processor - Proc 0	Two Processors - Proc 0	Two Processors - Proc 1
Case 1	**Case 1**	**Case 1**
LOCK: 11-12 µs	LOCK: 897-899 µs	LOCK: 899-900 µs
GET: 1261 µs	GET: 1261 µs	GET: 1261 µs
FILTER: 385-419 µs	FILTER: 385 µs	FILTER: 385 µs
COPY: 1668-1702 µs	COPY: 2525-2591 µs	COPY: 2556-2559 µs
Case 2	**Case 2**	**Case 2**
LOCK: 11-12 µs	LOCK: 11-12 µs	LOCK: 10-12 µs
GET: 385-387 µs	GET: 385 µs	GET: 385 µs
FILTER: 1260-1296 µs	FILTER: 1260 µs	FILTER: 1260 µs
COPY: 1668-1702 µs	COPY: 1666-1700 µs	COPY: 1666-1700 µs
Case 3	**Case 3**	**Case 3**
LOCK: 11 µs	LOCK: 17-24 µs	LOCK: 17-24 µs
GET: 823 µs	GET: 823 µs	GET: 822 µs
FILTER: 822 µs	FILTER: 822 µs	FILTER: 822 µs
COPY: 1668-1702 µs	COPY: 1668-1715 µs	COPY: 1668-1716 µs

The table above summarizes the results of this experiment. There was little time spent busy waiting in LOCK except when both processors were spending a relatively large amount of time in the shared memory and relatively little time outside of it.

5   Discussion

As a result of the timings, the setup was judged as legitimate. Overall, the times obtained from the measurements are reasonable and may be expected. Several things about the results of the second test give legitimacy to the setup. First, if there had not been a significant increase in the time spent waiting when GET was large and FILTER was small, it would be suspected that the programs were not running correctly. Second, the timings for the GET and FILTER subroutines were constant for constant variables. Third, each timing for COPY was the sum of the four subroutines contained in COPY. Fourth, the timings for Processor 0 and Processor 1 were almost identical for identical variables. Finally, when there was little contention for the shared memory, time spent in COPY was constant when the sum of the tune variables was constant.

The results of the second experiment show that synchronization overhead is linked very closely to the relationship between time spent inside the critical section and time spent outside of the critical section. This is particularly evident if one studies the time spent in LOCK for both configurations. Notice that the relative time spent in LOCK is much larger in Case 1 than it is in either Case 2 or Case 3. Since the time spent in LOCK represents synchronization overhead, this suggests that such overhead is quite large when time in the critical section is large relative to time outside it (Case 1) and is quite small otherwise (Cases 2 and 3). This is exactly what we would expect.

6   Conclusions

Our work so far has certainly indicated our experimental setup is suitable for the study and teaching of parallel processing systems. We hasten to add, however, that most of our time spent so far has been on developing the experimental setup, and therefore the potential of the setup has not been fully explored or utilized. Possibilities for the use of the setup are practically endless. A few possibilities are: investigating processor efficiency; testing new, more complicated software on the hardware setup; investigating the merits of communicating through message passing as opposed to shared memory; and further investigating the effect of changing time spent in the various subroutines. For all the timings taken so far, both processors were tuned identically. However, each processor is tuned individually, so this does not have to be the case. All of these possibilities are further expanded with the option of adding more processors to the hardware system.

Because parallel processing is currently a young but relatively advanced field, it is expected that the setup will at first be utilized primarily by graduate students or undergraduates working on individual projects. However, as the use of parallel processing becomes more and more common, the need to educate our future electrical and computer engineers about the fundamentals of parallel processing will grow. This setup could help meet that need through its possible use in an undergraduate laboratory experience. It is hoped and expected that the use of the setup will grow with the expanding field of parallel processing.

References

[1] Denning, A. "A Survey of Synchronization Methods for Parallel Computers." *Computer* Vol.22, No 7. (July 1989): 66-77.

[2] Helfter, S. "An Analysis of the Effect of Problem Scaling on the Efficiency of a Parallel Processor." Technical Report, Iowa State University Women in Science and Engineering Program, July 1988.

[3] Rover, D. "Investigation of a Multiple Processor Architecture for Boundary Value Problems." M.S. Thesis, Iowa State University, May 1986.

Compiler Course with a Semi-Challenging Project

Roger Yim and Gongzhu Hu
Department of Computer Science
Central Michigan University
Mt. Pleasant, MI 48859

Abstract

This paper describes a semi-challenging compiler project appropriate for Compiler Construction course at the advanced undergraduate-graduate level at a non-PhD-granting institution. The compiler project is centered around a table-driven parser and associated syntax-directed semantic routines for a real programming language. Our experience indicates that the curriculum can be strengthened by putting students into the most challenging learning environment in which they can succeed.

1. INTRODUCTION

Programming language syntax and semantics concepts and compiler construction, as one of the core areas in computer science, have been developed for more than three decades since FORTRAN was introduced in the 1950's. Because of its theoretical significance to computer science and its availability in every computer system, compiler design has long been in the curriculum of almost every computer science department in colleges and universities. Yet for predominantly undergraduate institutions (i.e. those which offer no Ph.D's), the level at which the compiler course should be taught remains a question.

Usually a compiler course would cover basic formal language theories and translation techniques, with a compiler project for the entire semester [1,2,3]. What is not so clear is the way the project is designed and implemented. It seems that compiler projects have been done in many schools at the *simple* level for undergraduate seniors and at the *simple-intermediate* level for senior-grad mixtures. These terms are clarified in the results of a survey we have conducted about teaching compiler courses.†

The survey involved ten universities, most of them being non-PhD-granting institutions. Table 1 shows part of the results of the survey. From the table, we see that almost all of them (except one PhD-granting school) use simple/intermediate level projects for the compiler course. About half of the schools who responded to our questionnaire used a table-driven approach for lexical and/or syntax analysis. The language features implemented by their students include simple data types (integer, real, char), arithmetic expressions, and simple control structures (e.g. if statement); a few had more advanced language features implemented.

---

† with the help of the Benjamin/Cummings Publishing Company, Inc.

Item surveyed		number of schools
course level	senior	4
	senior-grad	4
	grad	2
project level	simple	5
	intermediate	4
	challenging	1
language features implemented	simple scalar types	6
	table-driven scanner	3
	hard-wired scanner	2
	top-down table-driven parser	5
	recursive descent parser	3
	bottom-up parser	1
	simple expressions	6
	read-write	3
	strings	1
	if ... then ... else	5
	for, while, loop	5
	case	2
	block structure	2
	subprograms (no parameters)	4
	subprograms (parameters)	3
	user-defined types (arrays, records, etc.)	1

Table 1. Results of a survey of computer science dept. at 10 schools about compiler courses

To strengthen our computer science curriculum, we have been revising the materials of the *Compiler Construction* course (a senior-grad level course) at Central Michigan University. Using the textbook *Crafting a Compiler* [2] and the associated compiler writing tools, we introduced a semi-challenging project to our students — implementation of a compiler for a substantial subset of a real Pascal-like language. Although the students were extremely busy, they appreciated the knowledge gained in the class more than ever before. We feel that it is appropriate to have a quite challenging project for the compiler course at non-PhD-granting schools like Central.

2. THREE CATEGORIES OF COMPILER PROJECTS

The course is often taught around a compiler project. There are primarily three kinds of compiler projects: simple, intermediate, and challenging. Table 2 outlines the three categories, although there are no clear cut lines separating them.

	simple	intermediate	challenging
language	toy	extended toy or reduced subset of real	real language
scanner	instructor provides code framework	hard-wired or table-driven	table-driven
parser	operator precedence, or recursive descent	recursive descent, or table-driven	LL or LR table-driven
semantics	basic data type, expressions	simple semantics plus control structures	intermediate semantics plus user-defined data types, subprograms (without-with parameters), recursion
execution	assembly language, no execution	tuple language, no execution	tuple language or code for a virtual machine, executed via an interpreter

Table 2. Three kinds of compiler projects

3. AUTOMATION OF SCANNER AND PARSER

Although the theory of formal languages covered in the compiler course is usually not very deep, the basic aspects such as regular languages, context-free languages, and semantic specifications are rather thoroughly studied in the course. The importance of the theory lies in the fact that some components of a compiler can be automated, independent of the language to be compiled. Typical compiler components that can be automated are the lexical analyzer and the syntax analyzer, since the relevant theories are well-defined and understood, and they are relatively easy to implement. In order for the students to understand the theory and the implementation, we need to employ the automation mechanism of these compiler components. We shall discuss these components in turn in this section.

3.1 Lexical Scanner

Lexical analysis groups input sequence of characters into *tokens*. A hard-wired approach to lexical analysis is to test the validity of specific characters for particular tokens and to determine where a token terminates. A very simple example is to scan an integer-token that is just a sequence of digit-characters of arbitrary length. The scanner must test if the next character is a digit. It is very easy for the students to understand this kind of hard-wired approach, since it requires students to have no more knowledge than is needed for basic programming and data structure courses. Many textbooks discuss lexical analysis in the hard-wired way, even with the code for the entire scanner.

We feel that the hard-wired lexical analysis method has a severe drawback — it separates the theory of regular languages from its implementation mechanism. The lexical scanner is nothing but a regular language recognizer, which is in fact an finite state automaton (FA). So we prefer to emphasize the natural connection between an FA and a scanner rather than separate the two. We adopted the lexical table generator, ScanGen, provided by the authors and the publisher of the textbook, which inputs token definitions in terms of regular expressions and outputs an finite state automaton represented in the form of a transition table. The scanner a student is to implement is just a table-driven routine whose actions are totally determined by the transitions from one state to the other in the FA. From our experience, such implementation has shown the following advantages over hard-wired scanners from the students' point of view:

- understood the theory better;
- appreciated the relationship between theory and implementation;
- became familiar with compiler writing tools via language-independent scanner;

The reason we selected ScanGen rather than *lex* (available on UNIX) was that ScanGen exposes regular expressions and FA's more directly. It requires students to really understand the transitions between states in the FA to use the ScanGen tool. The source code is available to the instructor too.

3.2 Parser

A parser answers the question "Is the input a syntactically legal program of a language?" If yes, it finds the syntactic structure of the program. Because the syntax of almost all "typical" programming languages (e.g. Pascal, Ada, etc.) can be described by context free grammars (CFG), parsers for these languages can and should be implemented using a push down automaton (PDA). A simple parsing approach is the *recursive descent* method, which requires the students to understand the CFG and derivation. The good thing about recursive descent is that the parsing procedures are so "trivial", strictly obtained from the productions (rewriting rules) of the CFG. But the semantic interpretation that is triggered at various places in the syntax analysis process is hard to incorporate with recursive descent procedures. Another old but still used parsing approach is the *operator precedence* method that doesn't really involve much of the theory about CFG.

With the same purpose as in the case of lexical processing — to gain an understanding of the relevant theory, parsing should and can be done directly from the CFG, which is the formal description of the language. LL and LR parsing techniques should be studied in the classroom and one of the two should be used in implementing the parser. Our experience indicated that LL(1) parsing is best suitable to the students' projects. This top-down parsing method involves the understanding of CFG and associated theories about predictive parsing (FIRST, FOLLOW and PREDICT). Although LL is in general not as powerful as LR, we see several advantages in the LL approach:

- Top-down is much simpler to understand and implement than bottom-up;
- Almost all typical programming languages have LL(1) grammars, so we need not worry about the "power" of the parsing method to handle, say, left-recursion;
- LL is more natural than LR for incorporating semantic procedures;
- Bottom-up approaches (LR, LALR, etc.) have proved difficult for students.

We feel that LR techniques, especially LALR(1), should be studied in the classroom since they are more involved in the theory about CFG's, but should not be used in students' project.

With the help of LLgen, an LL(1) parse table generator provided by the authors and the publisher of the textbook *Crafting a Compiler* [2], we were able to offer our students a predictive parsing tool. LLgen inputs an LL(1) CFG of a language and outputs the PREDICT sets of the productions with 1-token lookahead. After completely understanding the underlying theory of the CFG and the parse table, the students can write a working parser in a few days.

4. SEMANTIC PROCESSING

The semantics of a programming language is usually specified informally, i.e. in English. Formal approaches to semantics, such as *attribute grammar, denotational semantics,* and *axiomatic approach* ought to be briefly discussed in class so that students will have a clear idea of how difficult it is to define the semantics formally. Semantics is implemented using *semantic routines*, which may or may not be a separated phase of a compiler. If the entire parse tree can be constructed (which is very unlikely for a non-toy language), the semantic processing can be isolated from the parsing. But for a moderate sized subset of a real programming language, it is impossible to construct the entire parse tree. *Syntax-directed* semantic analysis becomes the only feasible way for students to implement a compiler.

The cooperation between parsing and semantic routines is achieved via so-called *action symbols* embedded in the productions of the CFG. LL(1) provides a very flexible way to place the action symbols anywhere in the right-hand side of the productions. This is another advantage of LL over LR since LR requires that action symbols be placed only at the extreme right of a production. Students had no difficulty understanding the syntax-driven approach to semantic processing.

The most difficult part of semantic processing is the communication between semantic routines, which is achieved through a *semantic stack*. The semantic stack contains information about each syntactic structure (e.g. id, <expr>, <stmt>, etc.), which is typically a variant record because different syntactic structures have different semantic information. Our experience indicated that the majority of students had a very hard time understanding this issue. Once they understood the flow of semantic information, which took about 3 to 4 weeks, the students came to a turning point: At this point the students felt it became much easier to add more language features to their compilers.

Language features that may be implemented by the students should include not only simple scalar types and arithmetic expressions (as is usually the case in courses taught at many schools) but also other features of many real programming languages:

- logical operations and boolean expressions
- formatted writing
- string types with I/O
- arrays (multi-dimensional, static and/or dynamic range)
- records (with an arbitrary-level of nesting)
- enumeration types
- subrange type
- control statements — **if, for, while, case**
- procedures and functions
- parameters (various passing modes)
- nesting procedures and functions, blocks (like in Algol)
- recursion
- labels and exits

In our class, a majority of students implemented boolean expressions, formatted writing, strings, one-dimensional arrays, **if** and **for** statements, and procedures without parameters. Several students did **case**, label/exit, parameters, nesting procedures and functions (recursive). One student implemented dynamic arrays, records and enumeration types. Although a few students experienced great difficulties and withdrew from the course, the students who survived felt a great accomplishment at the end of the semester. They were very proud of the language features they had implemented. We believe that providing the students with the opportunity to implement a real language will be rewarding.

5. CODE GENERATION AND EXECUTION

It is essential to "execute" the code generated by students' compilers so that the students will have a real feeling about a working project. The target machine language into which the code is generated can be one of the following:

(a) an assembly language of a real machine,

(b) a tuple language that can be converted to a machine language separately, or

(c) a machine language of some virtual machine that can be "executed" directly by an interpreter.

We feel that choice (c) would be most appropriate for the following reasons:

(1) With assembly language as the target machine, students won't be able to implement run-time storage allocation because the allocation in the address space is handled by the assembler. This is especially important when dealing with dynamic run-time storage allocation for, say, recursion. So, assembly language is not suitable for code generation, if run-time storage allocation is considered an important issue in students' project, which in fact would be the case.

(2) Tuple language is good if a separate code generation phase is planned after the semantic processing is done. But it will add too much extra work to the project that may not be crucial. Code can be generated directly by the semantic routines without further processing or modification.

(3) With an interpreter that simulates the hardware of a virtual machine, students are provided with an instruction set of a "hardware" machine. Not only the address computation for allocating space for variables of various sizes (scalars, arrays, records, parameters, function return-values, etc.) is made explicit, but also the code is generated directly by the semantic routines without a separate code generation phase. By executing the code via the interpreter, students can achieve a deep understanding of the semantic processing.

We have used the Ada/CS virtual machine interpreter provided by the authors and the publisher of the textbook *Crafting a Compiler*, for testing the students' compiler. The students all greatly appreciated this approach. It served as a tool or "debugger" to help the students to gain more knowledge about the relationships between high-level and low-level languages.

6. CONCLUSIONS

At a non-PhD-granting institution like Central Michigan University, a compiler construction course at the senior-graduate level can be quite challenging with concentrations in the following aspects:

(1) Automated lexical analysis and parsing.

(2) Syntax-directed compiler.

(3) LL(1) parsing.

(4) Semantic stack and semantic routines.

(5) Code generation and execution.

We believe that it is very appropriate to have the students to implement a challenging compiler project. The theoretical aspects of programming languages and compilers can be grasped by the students only through the implementation of a "real" compiler. Students can do it, and they will be glad they did.

REFERENCES

[1] Aho, A.V., Sethi, R. and Ullman, J. D. "Compilers, Principles, Techniques, and Tools", Reading, Massachusetts: Addison-Wesley, 1986.

[2] Fischer, C. N. and LeBlanc, R. Jr. "Crafting a Compiler", Benjamin/Cummings, Inc., 1989.

[3] Hansen, J. C. and Yim, R. "Undergraduate Compiler Construction", *Interface: The Computer Education Quarterly*, Vol. 11, No. 1, Apring 1989, 54–59.

Report on a PC Based System Designed to Enhance the Teaching of IBM 370 Assembly Language

Bill E. Swafford

Department of Applied Computer Science
Illinois State University
Normal, Illinois 61761

Abstract

This is a report on the current capabilities and status of the EAS system, an integrated editor, assembler, and emulator for IBM 370 assembler language that runs on PC and AT machines. EAS has been placed in the public domain by the author.

1 Introduction

The EAS system is intended as an educational support vehicle to simplify, and soften, the introduction to IBM 370 assembly language programming. It consists of a full screen program editor, an assembler that converts IBM 370 assembler source code into IBM 370 machine code, and an emulator that emulates a subset of the instruction set of the IBM 370 family of computers. These three software subsystems are integrated to provide a complete programming environment designed to make the beginning IBM 370 assembler language student more successful. A major design consideration has been to provide simple tools that allow students to check what their programs are actually doing in much the same way as DEBUG does for DOS.

In the spirit of simplifying the introduction of assembly language programming, ASSIST style I/O has been emulated as opposed to the DCB, GET, and PUT instructions of the IBM system. XDECI, XDECO, XPRNT, and XREAD are provided to support input and output, as well as conversion between binary and character formats. XREAD assumes the input file to be in ASCII format and automatically converts all input characters to their EBCDIC equivalent. Similarly, XPRNT converts EBCDIC coded character streams to ASCII character streams for output.

2 Project History

After teaching IBM 370 assembler language programming for more than ten years using the IBM assembler and ASSIST on IBM OS systems, it became clear that there should be a better way. The introduction of CP/M with DDT, and DOS with DEBUG, had made that abundantly clear. Replacing the language with 8086 assembly language was an option, but not the most desirable one for two reasons. First, an assembler is an extra cost option with DOS. This is a real problem since most universities never have enough money for software. The second reason is simply that little knowledge about IBM 370 data types, particularly packed decimal, would be learned by the student of Intel 8086 assembly language. Since most students who are required to take a course in IBM 370 assembly language programming are so required in order that they develop a functional model of a real computer on which they will most likely be programming in a high level language in the future, this reason seems most important.

Thus it was decided to emulate a subset of the IBM 370 instruction set on a microcomputer in order to gain access to the interactive capabilities required to support the kind of debugging facilities provided by DEBUG. C was chosen as the programming language, and has proven to be a good choice. However, there is a small amount of assembler code and several tables. The current version is written in Turbo C, V2.0.

Coding began in 1985 and the system was first used by students in the fall of 1988. Control and experimental sections were taught using the ASSIST assembler and EAS. The two sections were back-to-back, and consequently they received the same lectures, wrote the same programs, and took the same tests, except for the final exam. Both sections had a final programming assignment consisting of a COBOL driver and multiple external assembler subroutines using the IBM VM assembler. Statistical comparison of the student results showed that there was no difference in the overall achievement, but the experimental class had a better attitude toward some aspects of the course, notably the instructor and the text [1]. However, some achievement differences favoring the experimental class were observed on individual test questions, suggesting that improving the software might lead to better results.

EAS was originally designed with a main menu from which the three subsystems had to be accessed, as well as an options menu from which to specify input and output files. The editor was a mode editor patterned after, but less capable than, the SEE editor that is supplied with the Desmet C package. The system has now been extensively modified in the direction of currently available integrated environment systems such as Turbo C. The editor has been converted to a Wordstar type editor with pull down menus and function key access to the other two subsystems. The emulator now supports a register window, a program/storage window for storage dumps and disassemblies, and an output window. The single-step, trace, and run-until execution modes of DEBUG have been retained, and in addition it is now possible to suspend execution when specified storage addresses or registers are modified. This new version is now undergoing testing, again using control and experimental sections.

3 The EAS Editor

When EAS is started, the editor is invoked. If a file was named on the DOS command line, this file is read and displayed with the cursor positioned at the beginning. Otherwise a filename is requested, and must be given before a user can continue. It is ok if the file is empty or even if it does not exist, but it must be given. All activity is directed from this display with access determined by pull down menus or function keys. For example, a displayed source program can be assembled by pressing the F9 key, and then the emulator can be invoked to run the object module by pressing CTRL-F9.

The EAS editor is a full screen Wordstar style program editor which supports records of a maximum length of 80 characters. All records are held in memory for the entire editing process. In addition to the normal cursor movement keys (arrow keys), the editor supports PgUp and PgDn, and Del and the back Del

key in the normal way.   CTRL--→ moves the cursor to the
beginning of the next word, and CTRL-←- moves the cursor to
beginning of the previous word.   CTRL-PgUp causes the top of
the file to be displayed, and CTRL-PgDn causes the bottom of
the file to be displayed. The Home key causes the cursor to
be moved to the first character of the current line, while the
End key causes the cursor to be moved to the column after the
last character on the current line.   If the editor is in
insert mode the tab key will insert blanks up to columns 10,
16 or 32, depending on the position of cursor when the tab key
is pressed. If the editor is not in insert mode, the tab key
will position the cursor in either column 10, 16, or 32,
depending on its original position.

The term "Wordstar like" is used above to describe the spirit
of the EAS program editor. However, not all Wordstar commands
are implemented, and those that are implemented are not always
provided in their fullest form.   For example, The CTRL-Q
commands F and A (Find and Replace) are implemented but are
only performed once. But, CTRL-L is implemented and can be
used to repeat the find and replace commands as many times as
necessary. The CTRL-K block commands are implemented but can
be used only on blocks of complete lines. The commands to
copy, move, delete, read, and write blocks are implemented in
the usual way.

4 The EAS Assembler

The EAS assembler is a two pass system. On the first pass
through the source code, addresses are assigned to labels and
the symbol table is built. On the second pass the instruction
operands are decoded and machine code is produced. If an
error is observed in either pass, the assembly process is
immediately terminated and the editor is invoked. The source
line in error is displayed at the top of the editor display
with the cursor in column 1. An error message detailing the
error is displayed on the bottom line of the console.

The assembler produces listings of the symbol table and
program. The symbol table listing is produced by the first
pass and consists of the equates with their values and the
variables with their assigned offsets. The program listing
is intended to look much like an IBM assembly listing with
the offset, generated machine code, and source statement all

on the same line. These listings are always sent to the console each time an assembly is requested. From a pull down menu, one can request that the listing also be sent to an attached printer. It is the author's intent that the assembler should produce correct translations for instructions of types RR, RX, RS, SI, and SS. The only data types currently supported by the EAS assembler are: A, C, F, H, P, and X. These data types are supported with DC, DS, and literals. However, each data type can have only one argument; i.e. A(ONE,TWO) is not supported. Support for the type D is provided for DS only, in order that the CVB and CVD instructions can be used in a natural way.

Currently, only a weak form of operand expression is supported. The form "variable+constant" is supported to provide for references like

        L   R4,ARRAY+4(R2).

However this is the limit of the complexity allowed. As the example suggests, symbolic reference for registers is supported, but the EQU statements that define R0 through R15 must be included in the source file. A file containing only these statements can be saved on a disk and easily copied into any source file under edit with the use of the CTRL-K R command.

5 The EAS Emulator

The emulator determines the actual 370 instructions that can be used in a program that is to run in the EAS system. Unlike the assembler that can mostly be programed to handle classes of instructions, there must be a segment of code for each instruction that is to be emulated. EAS provides support for all instructions required to perform standard IBM linkage, most fullword binary arithmetic and compare instructions, all conditional branch instructions, loop control instructions, MVI and CLI, and MVC and CLC. The RR, RX, and SI instructions for the bitwise operators AND, OR, and XOR are supported, as are also CVB, CVD, ED, and all packed decimal arithmetic instructions.

The emulator initializes all 16 of the GPR's, but only two of the values actually matter. GPR 14 and GPR 15 are both initialized to zero for specific purposes. GPR 15 is set to zero pursuant to IBM's policy of guaranteeing that a problem program can assume that when it gets control, GPR 15 contains the address of its first instruction. GPR 14 is set to zero to enable the emulator to recognize the combination of this value and the instruction BR 14 as program termination. Thus, for programs to terminate gracefully in the EAS system, GPR 14 must be preserved (or loaded with zero) and the instruction BR 14 must be issued. Of course, if standard linkage practices are followed, the desired result will occur.

When the emulator is invoked, it first opens the input file. The output file is also opened if the user has requested that program output be sent to a file instead of the console. The input file name is defaulted by EAS to the source file name with the extension "DAT". The input file name can be changed from the Run menu and the output file name can be specified there also. After the file is opened the registers are displayed in the register window at the top of the screen, the program/storage window is cleared, the output window is cleared, the command prompt '*' is displayed on the last line of the screen, and the first instruction is disassembled. At this point, the emulator waits for a command defining what action is required.

The commands that direct program execution allow combinations of single step execution, execution until a specified address is encountered, and execution until program termination. When an execution request is completed, the register window is updated and the next instruction is disassembled. All output generated by the program is either displayed in the output window or sent to the output file.

Program/storage commands provide facilities to dump storage in the traditional hexadecimal and character format, and to disassemble machine code into source statements. There are also commands to display and modify the registers. The command Q causes the emulator to close the files and return to the editor.

The most recent debugging feature of the emulator provides the user the ability to request that program execution be suspended in the event certain storage areas and/or registers are modified. This service is requested from the Debug menu before the emulator is invoked. Once requested, if an executing program modifies storage that is on display in the program/storage window, or modifies a register in a specified range, the storage is redisplayed, the register window is updated, the instruction causing the modification is disassembled, and execution is suspended.

6 Student Acceptance and the Future

Students have been very positive in their acceptance of EAS. Since it has been placed in the public domain, all students have their own copy of the system and are free to use it any where that they have access to a PC. They appear quite pleased to be freed from the rigidity of mainframe access. No student in the experimental class gave any indication of feeling disadvantaged in having to use this system. In fact, it would be difficult to imagine a more enthusiastic group.

In the semester following the study, students in a single section of the assembly language class were allowed to choose whether to use EAS or ASSIST, and were free to change to the other system at any time. Slightly over half of the students in this class chose to use EAS, and none of them switched to ASSIST. Students in classes taught by other instructors have also chosen to use EAS.

The user interface of EAS will continue to be improved based on the reactions of students who use it, and whatever other inspirations arise. Some instructions will be added to emulator, the halfword integer instructions, for example. Consideration will be given to whether macro capability should be included, however, this is not currently a high priority. It is the intention of the author to continue to support this system. Indeed, he has plans to use it in his courses for many years to come.

References

[1]   Bill E. Swafford. *A Comparison of Interactive and Batch Instruction for IBM 370 Assembly Language Programming.* In Preparation.

TEACHING THE SPIRIT
OF COMPUTATIONAL SCIENCE

Dean Sanders

Applied Computer Science

Illinois State University

Normal, IL 61761

bitnet: nsander@ecncdc

Abstract

The development of sophisticated visualization techniques, has led to increased interest in computational science. Students need direct experience with the relationship between computation, theory, and experimentation. Activities related to approximating the roots of a complex function are an excellent means of providing this experience.

1 Introduction

There are three modes of modern science: experimental, theoretical, and computational. When combined with visualization techniques for displaying the results, computational science is a powerful tool for scientific inquiry. The result of a computation can be used to suggest specific experiments or to pose questions for theoretical investigation. Conversely, experimentation and theory can be used to construct, correct, and improve computational models. It is important for computer science students to be introduced to the symbiotic relationships that exist among these modes of science. Students need to learn that computational models and spectacular pictures are not an end unto themselves; they are yet another means of gaining insight. Scientific progress comes from the interplay between computation, theory, and experimentation. The interplay is the true spirit of computational science. This paper describes how the author has used root approximation algorithms to introduce computer science students to the spirit of computational science.

2 A specific problem

A basic computational problem is to approximate the roots of a function $f(Z)$. The problem is more interesting if Z and $f(Z)$ are complex numbers. Newton's method is one of several techniques that can be used to solve this problem.

Newton's Method. If the function is differentiable, then Newton's method can be used to derive a sequence of approximations $Z_0, Z_1, ... , Z_N$. The first term of the sequence, Z_0, may be chosen somewhat arbitrarily. The remaining terms are computed by the formula $Z_{i+1} = Z_i - f(Z_i)/f'(Z_i)$. A test must be used to determine whether or not the sequence has converged. Two tests are used in the experiments described later in this paper.

Standard test. The most common test is based on the Euclidean norm. Convergence occurs whenever $| Z_N - Z_{N-1} |$ is less that some predetermined tolerance.

Alternate test. An alternate convergence test was described by Pickover [1]. With his test convergence occurs whenever the quantity $| | Z_N |^2 - | Z_{N-1} |^2 |$ is less than some predetermined tolerance.

Computational technique. There are three steps to the computational technique that was used for this problem. (1) Partition a region of the complex plane into a rectangular grid. (2) Use each grid point as the beginning point for Newton's (or other) method. (3) For each grid point, record both the number of steps required for convergence and the root to which the sequence converged. The sequence is judged to have diverged if the number of terms exceeds a predefined maximum or if the denominator of a quotient becomes too close to zero.

Visualization technique. There are two steps to the visualization technique. (1) Associate each grid point with a pixel on the screen. (2) Color that pixel based on the results of applying the approximation algorithm to the corresponding grid point. Three types of pictures, or maps, can be created: a root map in which pixels are colored according to the root to which the sequence converged, a rate map in which pixels are colored according to the number of steps required for the sequence to converge, and a dual map which is colored according to both the rate of convergence and the root to which the sequence converged. The best way to prepare a dual map is to use shades of a single color for each root.

3 The programming model

The recommended technique for constructing the software is to partition the work into two sets of programs, a modelling set and a graphing set. Each program in the modelling set should be based on a single algorithm, such as Newton's method, and should create a data file for use by any of the graphing programs. Each graphing program should produce a picture from any of the data files. In some environments, it would be reasonable to use a menu driven system to select the desired program from each set.

There are several advantages to separating the modelling programs from those that produce the graphs. First, the modelling process is very time consuming, but can be scheduled as an overnight batch job if the graphing activities have been placed in another program. Second, the division of work between modelling and graphing makes it easy to execute the programs on separate, perhaps specialized, computers. Third, this partitioning of the work is a subtle reminder to the students that modelling and graphing are completely separate activities. Finally, the design of the overall software offers an excellent opportunity to discuss the importance of standards for creating data files, a topic often unappreciated by students.

4 Specific experiments and symbiosis

This section contains descriptions of specific experiments that have been used to introduce students to the interactions between computation, theory, and experimentation. The function $f(Z) = Z^3 - 1$ was used for each of these experiments because the roots are known and there are not so many roots as to overtax the color capability of commonly available microcomputers.

Experiment 1 (Compare convergence tests). Apply Newton's method with the Standard test to a rectangular region, and apply Newton's method with the Alternate test to the same region. Produce root maps and rate maps from each data file. The rectangle which has its lower left corner at (-2.0, -2.0) and its upper right corner at (2.0, 2.0) is a good region for this activity. This experiment is a good way to introduce both the value and the limitations of visualization.

Each map contains three intriguing strips that appear to be centered on rays that are midway between the roots. Within the strips, there are intricately interwoven regions for which complex, almost chaotic, patterns of behavior are readily apparent. These strips can be used to introduce the concept of "sensitivity to initial conditions" which means that a very small change to the input to an algorithm can lead to significant changes in the results.

The rate map for the Standard test contains regions with smooth boundaries, but the corresponding regions on the rate map for the Alternate test have long tentacle-like projections. These tentacles are quite unexpected. A close examination of the graph shows that the tentacles narrow and appear to degenerate into disconnected points near their tips, yet intuition suggests that the tentacles should be continuous. This conflict between intuition and the graph is an excellent opportunity to discuss the limitations of approximating a continuous process with a discrete algorithm. The apparent discontinuities near the ends of the tentacles can be explained as an artifact that is due to the relationship between the width of the tentacle and the resolution of the grid that was used for the modelling process.

If the rate map for the Alternate test is appropriately colored, the students can be asked to search for a relationship between the number of tentacles and the number of iterations needed for convergence. Most students will be able to hypothesize that each region for which the algorithm converges in N steps has 2^N tentacles. By forming this hypothesis, students have an opportunity to see how computational science can be used to suggest a question for theoretical research. Is the hypothesis true for all regions?

Experiment 2 (Closer views). Apply Newton's method to interesting subsets of the region that was used in experiment 1. Interesting subsets exist inside each of the chaotic rays, around the origin, and around the roots. One close-up view leads to additional insight.

Apply Newton's method with the Alternate test to a region around the real root (1,0) then prepare a rate map that highlights the set of points for which the algorithm converges in one step. If the resolution of the modelling grid is sufficiently fine, the picture should contain a region with two long narrow tentacles. The length of the tentacles is somewhat disturbing. Is it possible to start that far from a root and converge in a single step?

This question should lead to an experiment. Identify a point that is not too close to the root but for which the algorithm converged in a single step; an appropriate point can be determined by examining the data file. Once a starting point has been selected, compute the first term of the approximation sequence and determine the distance from that term to the root. If all goes well, this little bit of experimental science will indicate that there is a weakness in the computational model. The appropriate remedy is to modify both the Standard test and the Alternate test by adding the condition that $f(Z_N)$ be close to zero before determining that the sequence has converged.

By completing this activity, the students learn that experimentation can be used to detect weaknesses in a computational technique. This experiment also emphasizes the danger in blindly accepting the results of spectacular visualizations.

Experiment 3 (A subtle error). Change the method that is used to avoid division by zero. Rather than declare that a sequence diverges whenever $f(Z_i)$ is too small, add a small "fudge factor" to Z_i and continue.

If the "fudge factor" is properly chosen, the corresponding graphs appear to be identical to those produced by earlier experiments. After a more critical examination, perhaps through close-up views, it becomes apparent that these graphs lack the symmetry that is present in the earlier pictures. This observation leads to a question for theoretical investigation. Should the root maps and rate maps have some sort of symmetry? It is a straightforward exercise to prove that the maps should contain three symmetrical regions, each of which is a wedge with its vertex at the origin. It is clear from this proof that using the "fudge factor" produces incorrect results. This exercise has more impact if the students are simply shown the graphs but are not told, until later, how they were produced.

Experiment 4 (Find the better test). Try to determine which test normally leads to the fastest determination of convergence? Theoretical techniques are not very

AUTHOR INDEX

Aboelaze, M. A. 139
Ahmed, K. U. 147
Alijnai, G. S. 336
Ancona, M. 307
Bagga, K. S. 8, 307
Beaven, M. 364
Bhatia, S. K. 91
Bruzzone, E. 307
Buchheit, P. 84
Burnstein, I. 98
Campbell, G. 234
Carino, R. 293
Carlson, R. 350
Chao, M.-C. 242
Chapin, S. J. 371
Chen, J. 399
Cleave, N. V. 329
Coleman, W. P. 406
Dawes, R. W. 161
Deogun, J.S. 91, 307
deDoncker, E. 293
El-Ruby, M. 350
Elrod, D. W. 392
Esfahanian, A.-H. 357
Evens,M. 70,77,98,264,378
Ewerbring, L. M. 286
Floriani, L. D. 307
Fotouhi, F. 249
Gaetano, A. D. 406
Galarce, C. E. 249
Geisler, F. 406
Genz, A. 279
Georgakis, D. C. 70
Ginn, M. E. 98
Gold, G. 65
Gordon, G. L. 111
Grier, J. B. 234
Gunawardena, K. L. D. 213
Haskell, R. E. 118
Houstis, C. E. 139
Hu, G. 419
Johns, G. L. 29
Kaur, H. 234
Keller, R. F. 125
Kenevan, J. 350
Khalil, K. 350
Kountanis, D. 15
Kubicka, E. 15
Kubicki, G. 15

Lee, T.-C. 29
Lee, Y. H. 77
Lewis, F. D. 329
Lewis, T. 155
Lin, S.-J. 22
Luk, F. T. 286
Lyness, J. N. 271
Ma, H.-N. N. 378
Maggiora, G. M. 392
Magliveras, S. S. 199
Makowski, G. 105
Manning, J. 1
McAlpin, J. 179
Mehta, A. 170
Memon, N. D. 199
Meyer, R. M. 125
Michael, J. A. 77
Mo, Z. 34
Naeymi-Rad, F. 70, 378
Newman, W. 271
Nikolopoulos, C. 179
Noui-Mehidi, A. 118
Ongwisesphaiboon, V. 98
Owens, F. W. 8
Parks, D. 322
Perl, Y. 170
Pin-Ngern, S. 264
Pinkowski, B. 51
Prabhu, G. M. 154, 413
Puri, A. 98
Raghavan, V. V. 91
Raja, P. V. R. 206
Ramakrishnan, S. 343
Rao, V. 313
Richards, P. G. 242
Rizki, M. M. 385, 399
Robinson, I. 293
Rover, D. T. 154, 412
Rovick, A. A. 77
Rubin, S. H. 41
Saab, Y. 313
Sager, T. J. 22
Saiedian, H. 256
Samal, A. 132
Sanders, D. 433
Sanford, D. P. 406
Seevers, T. L. 125
Sprague, T. 300
Stansifer, R. 364, 371

Strutz, R. 264
Swafford, B. E. 426
Tamburino, L. A. 385
Trace, D. A. 70, 378
Trenary, R. G. 392
Tzeng, C.-H. 58
Vishnubhotla,S.R. 220,227
Vogel, G. 412
Wainer, M. S. 185
Wedde, H. F. 336
Wetklow, D. 364
Williams, K. 34
Wright, C. T. 154, 413
Yeh, D.-Y. 147
Yim, R. 419
Zheng, S.-Q. 192
Zimmerman, G. W. 357
Zmuda, M. A. 385

useful in this case. Fortunately, a well designed visualization can be used to give a useful rule of thumb.

Apply Newton's method with both the Standard test and the Alternate test to the same region. Create a graph with three colors. Use one color for the regions where the Standard test yields faster convergence; use a second color for the regions where the Alternate test yields faster convergence; and use a third color for the regions where the tests yield convergence in the same number of iterations. It should be clear from the distribution of colors that one test is much better than the other at producing a rapid determination of convergence.

5 Summary

The process of approximating the roots of a complex valued function has been used to construct a set of activities that give students a good overview of the relationships between the three modes of modern science. The computational model and corresponding visualization techniques are straightforward. The results generally conform to the students' intuition but there are a few surprises. After studying the pictures, the students can form hypotheses for theoretical study and can suggest interesting experiments. Theoretical arguments and appropriate experiments can be used to examine apparent errors in a model. Alternate techniques can be compared, and some limitations of the computational models can be studied. These are worthwhile classroom activities.

References

[1] Pickover, C. A Note on Chaos and Halley's Method.
Communications of the ACM 31, 11 (Nov. 1988), 1326-1328.

Lecture Notes in Computer Science

For information about Vols. 1–420

please contact your bookseller or Springer-Verlag

Vol. 421: T. Onodera, S. Kawai, A Formal Model of Visualization in Computer Graphics Systems. X, 100 pages. 1990.

Vol. 422: B. Nebel, Reasoning and Revision in Hybrid Representation Systems. XII, 270 pages. 1990 (Subseries LNAI).

Vol. 423: L.E. Deimel (Ed.), Software Engineering Education. Proceedings, 1990. VI, 164 pages. 1990.

Vol. 424: G. Rozenberg (Ed.), Advances in Petri Nets 1989. VI, 524 pages. 1990.

Vol. 425: C.H. Bergman, R.D. Maddux, D.L. Pigozzi (Eds.), Algebraic Logic and Universal Algebra in Computer Science. Proceedings, 1988. XI, 292 pages. 1990.

Vol. 426: N. Houbak, SIL – a Simulation Language. VII, 192 pages. 1990.

Vol. 427: O. Faugeras (Ed.), Computer Vision – ECCV 90. Proceedings, 1990. XII, 619 pages. 1990.

Vol. 428: D. Bjørner, C.A.R. Hoare, H. Langmaack (Eds.), VDM '90. VDM and Z – Formal Methods in Software Development. Proceedings, 1990. XVII, 580 pages. 1990.

Vol. 429: A. Miola (Ed.), Design and Implementation of Symbolic Computation Systems. Proceedings, 1990. XII, 284 pages. 1990.

Vol. 430: J.W. de Bakker, W.-P. de Roever, G. Rozenberg (Eds.), Stepwise Refinement of Distributed Systems. Models, Formalisms, Correctness. Proceedings, 1989. X, 808 pages. 1990.

Vol. 431: A. Arnold (Ed.), CAAP '90. Proceedings, 1990. VI, 285 pages. 1990.

Vol. 432: N. Jones (Ed.), ESOP '90. Proceedings, 1990. IX, 436 pages. 1990.

Vol. 433: W. Schröder-Preikschat, W. Zimmer (Eds.), Progress in Distributed Operating Systems and Distributed Systems Management. Proceedings, 1989. V, 206 pages. 1990.

Vol. 434: J.-J. Quisquater, J. Vandewalle (Eds.), Advances in Cryptology – EUROCRYPT '89. Proceedings, 1989. X, 710 pages. 1990.

Vol. 435: G. Brassard (Ed.), Advances in Cryptology – CRYPTO '89. Proceedings, 1989. XIII, 634 pages. 1990.

Vol. 436: B. Steinholtz, A. Sølvberg, L. Bergman (Eds.), Advanced Information Systems Engineering. Proceedings, 1990. X, 392 pages. 1990.

Vol. 437: D. Kumar (Ed.), Current Trends in SNePS – Semantic Network Processing System. Proceedings, 1989. VII, 162 pages. 1990. (Subseries LNAI).

Vol. 438: D.H. Norrie, H.W. Six (Eds.), Computer Assisted Learning – ICCAL '90. Proceedings, 1990. VII, 467 pages. 1990.

Vol. 439: P. Gorny, M. Tauber (Eds.), Visualization in Human-Computer Interaction. Proceedings, 1988. VI, 274 pages. 1990.

Vol. 440: E. Börger, H. Kleine Büning, M.M. Richter (Eds.), CSL '89. Proceedings, 1989. VI, 437 pages. 1990.

Vol. 441: T. Ito, R.H. Halstead, Jr. (Eds.), Parallel Lisp: Languages and Systems. Proceedings, 1989. XII, 364 pages. 1990.

Vol. 442: M. Main, A. Melton, M. Mislove, D. Schmidt (Eds.), Mathematical Foundations of Programming Semantics. Proceedings, 1989. VI, 439 pages. 1990.

Vol. 443: M.S. Paterson (Ed.), Automata, Languages and Programming. Proceedings, 1990. IX, 781 pages. 1990.

Vol. 444: S. Ramani, R. Chandrasekar, K.S.R. Anjaneyulu (Eds.), Knowledge Based Computer Systems. Proceedings, 1989. X, 546 pages. 1990. (Subseries LNAI).

Vol. 445: A.J.M. van Gasteren, On the Shape of Mathematical Arguments. VIII, 181 pages. 1990.

Vol. 446: L. Plümer, Termination Proofs for Logic Programs. VIII, 142 pages. 1990. (Subseries LNAI).

Vol. 447: J.R. Gilbert, R. Karlsson (Eds.), SWAT '90. 2nd Scandinavian Workshop on Algorithm Theory. Proceedings, 1990. VI, 417 pages. 1990.

Vol. 448: B. Simons, A. Spector (Eds.), Fault Tolerant Distributed Computing. VI, 298 pages. 1990.

Vol. 449: M.E. Stickel (Ed.), 10th International Conference on Automated Deduction. Proceedings, 1990. XVI, 688 pages. 1990. (Subseries LNAI).

Vol. 450: T. Asano, T. Ibaraki, H. Imai, T. Nishizeki (Eds.), Algorithms. Proceedings, 1990. VIII, 479 pages. 1990.

Vol. 451: V. Marík, O. Stepánková, Z. Zdráhal (Eds.), Artificial Intelligence in Higher Education. Proceedings, 1989. IX, 247 pages. 1990. (Subseries LNAI).

Vol. 452: B. Rovan (Ed.), Mathematical Foundations of Computer Science 1990. Proceedings, 1990. VIII, 544 pages. 1990.

Vol. 453: J. Seberry, J. Pieprzyk (Eds.), Advances in Cryptology – AUSCRYPT '90 Proceedings, 1990. IX. 462 pages. 1990.

Vol. 454: V. Diekert, Combinatorics on Traces. XII, 165 pages. 1990.

Vol. 455: C.A. Floudas, P.M. Pardalos, A Collection of Test Problems for Constrained Global Optimization Algorithms. XIV, 180 pages. 1990.

Vol. 456: P. Deransart, J. Maluszyn´ski (Eds.), Programming Language Implementation and Logic Programming. Proceedings, 1990. VIII, 401 pages. 1990.

Vol. 457: H. Burkhart (Ed.), CONPAR '90 – VAPP IV. Proceedings, 1990. XIV, 900 pages. 1990.

Vol. 458: J.C.M. Baeten, J.W. Klop (Eds.), CONCUR '90. Proceedings, 1990. VII, 537 pages. 1990.

Vol. 459: R. Studer (Ed.), Natural Language and Logic. Proceedings, 1989. VII, 252 pages. 1990. (Subseries LNAI).

Vol. 460: J. Uhl, H.A. Schmid, A Systematic Catalogue of Reusable Abstract Data Types. XII, 344 pages. 1990.

Vol. 461: P. Deransart, M. Jourdan (Eds.), Attribute Grammars and their Applications. Proceedings, 1990. VIII, 358 pages. 1990.

Vol. 462: G. Gottlob, W. Nejdl (Eds.), Expert Systems in Engineering. Proceedings, 1990. IX, 260 pages. 1990. (Subseries LNAI).

Vol. 463: H. Kirchner, W. Wechler (Eds.), Algebraic and Logic Programming. Proceedings, 1990. VII, 386 pages. 1990.

Vol. 464: J. Dassow, J. Kelemen (Eds.), Aspects and Prospects of Theoretical Computer Science. Proceedings, 1990. VI, 298 pages. 1990.

Vol. 465: A. Fuhrmann, M. Morreau (Eds.), The Logic of Theory Change. Proceedings, 1989. X, 334 pages. 1991. (Subseries LNAI).

Vol. 466: A. Blaser (Ed.), Database Systems of the 90s. Proceedings, 1990. VIII, 334 pages. 1990.

Vol. 467: F. Long (Ed.), Software Engineering Environments. Proceedings, 1969. VI, 313 pages. 1990.

Vol. 468: S.G. Akl, F. Fiala, W.W. Koczkodaj (Eds.), Advances in Computing and Information – ICCI '90. Proceedings, 1990. VII, 529 pages. 1990.

Vol. 469: I. Guessarian (Ed.), Semantics of Systeme of Concurrent Processes. Proceedings, 1990. V, 456 pages. 1990.

Vol. 470: S. Abiteboul, P.C. Kanellakis (Eds.), ICDT '90. Proceedings, 1990. VII, 528 pages. 1990.

Vol. 471: B.C. Ooi, Efficient Query Processing in Geographic Information Systems. VIII, 208 pages. 1990.

Vol. 472: K.V. Nori, C.E. Veni Madhavan (Eds.), Foundations of Software Technology and Theoretical Computer Science. Proceedings, 1990. X, 420 pages. 1990.

Vol. 473: I.B. Damgård (Ed.), Advances in Cryptology – EUROCRYPT '90. Proceedings, 1990. VIII, 500 pages. 1991.

Vol. 474: D. Karagiannis (Ed.), Information Syetems and Artificial Intelligence: Integration Aspects. Proceedings, 1990. X, 293 pages. 1991. (Subseries LNAI).

Vol. 475: P. Schroeder-Heister (Ed.), Extensions of Logic Programming. Proceedings, 1989. VIII, 364 pages. 1991. (Subseries LNAI).

Vol. 476: M. Filgueiras, L. Damas, N. Moreira, A.P. Tomás (Eds.), Natural Language Processing. Proceedings, 1990. VII, 253 pages. 1991. (Subseries LNAI).

Vol. 477: D. Hammer (Ed.), Compiler Compilers. Proceedings, 1990. VI, 227 pages. 1991.

Vol. 478: J. van Eijck (Ed.), Logics in AI. Proceedings, 1990. IX, 562 pages. 1991. (Subseries in LNAI).

Vol. 480: C. Choffrut, M. Jantzen (Eds.), STACS 91. Proceedings, 1991. X, 549 pages. 1991.

Vol. 481: E. Lang, K.-U. Carstensen, G. Simmons, Modelling Spatial Knowledge on a Linguistic Basis. IX, 138 pages. 1991. (Subseries LNAI).

Vol. 482: Y. Kodratoff (Ed.), Machine Learning – EWSL-91. Proceedings, 1991. XI, 537 pages. 1991. (Subseries LNAI).

Vol. 483: G. Rozenberg (Ed.), Advances In Petri Nets 1990. VI, 515 pages. 1991.

Vol. 484: R. H. Möhring (Ed.), Graph-Theoretic Concepts In Computer Science. Proceedings, 1990. IX, 360 pages. 1991.

Vol. 485: K. Furukawa, H. Tanaka, T. Fullsaki (Eds.), Logic Programming '89. Proceedings, 1989. IX, 183 pages. 1991. (Subseries LNAI).

Vol. 486: J. van Leeuwen, N. Santoro (Eds.), Distributed Algorithms. Proceedings, 1990. VI, 433 pages. 1991.

Vol. 487: A. Bode (Ed.), Distributed Memory Computing. Proceedings, 1991. XI, 506 pages. 1991.

Vol. 488: R. V. Book (Ed.), Rewriting Techniques and Applications. Proceedings, 1991. VII, 458 pages. 1991.

Vol. 489: J. W. de Bakker, W. P. de Roever, G. Rozenberg (Eds.), Foundations of Object-Oriented Languages. Proceedings, 1990. VIII, 442 pages. 1991.

Vol. 490: J. A. Bergstra, L. M. G. Feljs (Eds.), Algebraic Methods 11: Theory, Tools and Applications. VI, 434 pages. 1991.

Vol. 491: A. Yonezawa, T. Ito (Eds.), Concurrency: Theory, Language, and Architecture. Proceedings, 1989. VIII, 339 pages. 1991.

Vol. 492: D. Sriram, R. Logcher, S. Fukuda (Eds.), Computer-Aided Cooperative Product Development. Proceedings, 1989 VII, 630 pages. 1991.

Vol. 493: S. Abramsky, T. S. E. Maibaum (Eds.), TAPSOFT '91. Volume 1. Proceedings, 1991. VIII, 455 pages. 1991.

Vol. 494: S. Abramsky, T. S. E. Maibaum (Eds.), TAPSOFT '91. Volume 2. Proceedings, 1991. VIII, 482 pages. 1991.

Vol. 495: 9. Thalheim, J. Demetrovics, H.-D. Gerhardt (Eds.), MFDBS '91. Proceedings, 1991. VI, 395 pages. 1991.

Vol. 496: H.-P. Schwefel, R. Männer (Eds.), Parallel Problem Solving from Nature. Proceedings, 1991. XI, 485 pages. 1991.

Vol. 497: F. Dehne, F. Fiala. W.W. Koczkodaj (Eds.), Advances in Computing and Intormation - ICCI '91 Proceedings, 1991. VIII, 745 pages. 1991.

Vol. 498: R. Andersen, J. A. Bubenko jr., A. Sølvberg (Eds.), Advanced Information Systems Engineering. Proceedings, 1991. VI, 579 pages. 1991.

Vol. 499: D. Christodoulakis (Ed.), Ada: The Choice for '92. Proceedings, 1991. VI, 411 pages. 1991.

Vol. 500: M. Held, On the Computational Geometry of Pocket Machining. XII, 179 pages. 1991.

Vol. 501: M. Bidoit, H.-J. Kreowski, P. Lescanne, F. Orejas, D. Sannella (Eds.), Algebraic System Specification and Development. VIII, 98 pages. 1991.

Vol. 502: J. Bārzdiňš, D. Bjørner (Eds.), Baltic Computer Science. X, 619 pages. 1991.

Vol. 503: P. America (Ed.), Parallel Database Systems. Proceedings, 1990. VIII, 433 pages. 1991.

Vol. 504: J. W. Schmidt, A. A. Stogny (Eds.), Next Generation Information System Technology. Proceedings, 1990. IX, 450 pages. 1991.

Vol. 505: E. H. L. Aarts, J. van Leeuwen, M. Rem (Eds.), PARLE '91. Parallel Architectures and Languages Europe, Volume I. Proceedings, 1991. XV, 423 pages. 1991.

Vol. 506: E. H. L. Aarts, J. van Leeuwen, M. Rem (Eds.), PARLE '91. Parallel Architectures and Languages Europe, Volume II. Proceedings, 1991. XV, 489 pages. 1991.

Vol. 507: N. A. Sherwani, E. de Doncker, J. A. Kapenga (Eds.), Computing in the 90's. Proceedings, 1989. XIII, 441 pages. 1991.